FUNDAMENTALS OF JAVA

AP* Computer Science Essentials for the A Exam

Lambert and Osborne

THOMSON
COURSE TECHNOLOGY

Australia • Canada • Mexico • Singapore • Spain • United Kingdom • United States

**Fundamentals of Java: AP* Computer Science Essentials
for the A Exam, Third Edition**

by Kenneth Lambert, Martin Osborne

Sr. Acquistions Editor:
Jane Mazares

Sr. Marketing Manager:
Kim Ryttel

Product Manager:
David Rivera

Developmental Editors
Rose Marie Kuebbing,
Rita Rebholz
Custom Editorial Productions, Inc.

Editorial Assistant:
Jeannine Lawless

Associate Production Manager:
Jennifer Goguen

Production Editor
GEX Publishing Services

Sr. Manufacturing Coordinator:
Justin Palmeiro

**Manuscript Quality Assurance
Lead:**
Burt LaFountain

Cover Design:
Deborah Van Rooyen

Cover Image:
Paul Vismara

Compositor
GEX Publishing Services

Printer:
TransContinental Interglobe
Printing

Any additional questions about permissions can be submitted by email to thomsonrights@thomson.com

Disclaimer
Thomson Course Technology reserves the right to revise this publication and make changes from time to time in its content without notice.

ISBN 0-619-24378-3

Thomson Course Technology is proud to release *AP* Computer Science Review Companion for Fundamentals of Java*

Our new Java textbooks wouldn't be complete without a proper review companion. We know that studying isn't easy. This review companion can make studying for programming a snap.

Chapter Summary and Outline—helpful synopsis reviews the order of the chapter and highlights.

Vocabulary—a list of key terms and their definitions are conveniently listed in each appropriate lesson for quick review.

Relevance to the AP* Exam—more than a mapping of each key requirement for the A and AB exams, this section makes concrete connections between key requirements and the textbook's tables, figures, and specific paragraphs.

CHAPTER 3   SYNTAX, ERRORS, AND DEBUGGING

CHAPTER SUMMARY

Programming languages, like natural languages such as English, have vocabulary, syntax, and semantics. In order to write Java programs, you must be familiar with the rules of the language. The rules for a programming language are generally more strict and rigid than the rules for a natural language, but the vocabulary is much smaller. This chapter discusses the syntax and semantics of several Java language elements, including the following:

- **Data Types:** There are two categories of data types – primitive and reference. Primitive data types include numeric data types, boolean data types, and character data types. Reference types are defined by classes. Every class is a distinct data type.
- **Literals:** Values that do not change in a program.

OUTLINE

   3.1 Language Elements
   3.2 Basic Java Syntax and Semantics
   3.3 Terminal I/O for Different Data Types
   3.4 Comments
        Case Study 1: Income Tax Calculator

VOCABULARY

Arithmetic expression: A statement involving numerical operands and arithmetic operators that evaluates to a specific numerical result.
Comments: Explanatory sentences inserted into a program in such a manner that the compiler ignores them. Single line comments begin with the characters //. Multi-line comments are contained within the characters /* and */.

RELEVANCE TO AP EXAM – COMPUTER SCIENCE A AND AB

The following sections describe the relevance of the contents of this chapter to specific goals of the Computer Science AP Exam. Unless otherwise noted, the AP goals listed apply to both the Computer Science A and the Computer Science AB exams.

AP Goal: Object-Oriented Program Design > Program Design > Read and understand a problem description, purpose, and goals: The two cases studied in this chapter illustrate the processes involved in analyzing and designing a program based on a problem description. In case study 2, a thorough analysis of a complicated problem is examined. This case study illustrates the types of questions that must be posed when attempting to understand the problem.

AP Goal: Object-Oriented Program Design > Class Design > Choose appropriate data representation and algorithms: Section 3.2 introduces most of the primitive data types. When analyzing, designing, and implementing a program you must be aware of the constraints placed on various data types and when each data type should be used. For instance, it is inappropriate for a variable that stores a monetary amount to be typed as an int.

FILL IN THE BLANK

Complete the following sentences by writing the correct word or words in the blanks provided.

1. The Java programming language has a total of _____ numeric data types.

2. An item in a program whose value can change during program execution is called a(n) _____.

TRUE/FALSE

Circle T if the statement is true or F if the statement is false.

T F 1. Java's syntax consists of the rules for combining words and symbols into a program statement.

T F 2. When defining a variable in Java, you must always declare the variable's data type.

MULTIPLE CHOICE

Select the best response for the following statements.

1. What is the maximum positive value that can be stored in a Java variable of type int?
    a. 32,755   **b.** 1,073,741,824
    c. 2,147,483,647   **d.** 4,294,967,294

2. Which of the following statements shows the correct syntax for declaring a variable named alpha, of data type double?
    a. `alpha = double;`   **b.** `alpha(double);`
    c. `double(alpha);`   **d.** `double alpha;`

WRITTEN QUESTIONS

Write a brief answer to each of the following questions.

1. What are the two categories of data types in the Java programming language? Give an example of a data type in each of the two categories.

CASE PROJECT

Now you will gain some experience writing and using methods. Assume that the requirements for the problem now state that there will be three types of debt to process. **For each debt amount, only the minimum payment will be made**. The final balance, interest paid, and principle paid will be displayed for each debt amount. In addition, once all of the payments have been calculated, the program should display how much of the disposable income was left over. You will be writing a `main` method and one additional method – `processDebt`. The `processDebt` method should take the disposable income as a parameter, gather the information for a single debt amount, calculate the amount to be applied to the debt, and return the disposable income minus the amount applied to the debt. Use the following program shell to get you started. The comments indicate the tasks that you must complete. All variables declarations are provided. Copy this "shell" into your text editor, save it as a *.java* file, and fill in the appropriate program statements to yield the correct program behavior.

So make studying programming a snap!

AP* Computer Essentials Review Companion for Fundamentals of Java by Adelman and Nagin and 1-4239-0381-1 Softcover, reviews all requirements for the AP* Computer Science for the A & AB Exams

PREFACE

This text is intended for a complete course in programming and problem solving. The book covers the material of typical Computer Science 1 courses at the undergraduate level, but it is intended for the high school audience. The book is Advanced Placement (AP)-compliant for the A level, covering all of the required subset of Java™ for that level.

We present six major aspects of computing, some in standalone chapters and others spread across several chapters:

1. **Programming Basics.** This deals with the basic ideas of problem solving with computers, including primitive data types, control structures, methods, algorithm development, and complexity analysis.

2. **Object-Oriented Programming.** OOP is today's dominant programming paradigm. All the essentials of this subject are covered.

3. **Data and Information Processing.** Fundamental data structures are discussed. These include strings, arrays, files, and lists. The general concept of abstract data type is introduced, and complexity analysis is used to evaluate the running times of different implementations of algorithms.

4. **Software Development Life Cycle.** Rather than isolate software development techniques in one or two chapters, the book deals with them throughout in the context of numerous case studies.

5. **Graphical User Interfaces and Event-Driven Programming.** Many books at this level restrict themselves to character-based terminal I/O. The reason is simple. Graphical user interfaces and event-driven programming usually are considered too complex for beginning students. In this book, we circumvent the complexity barrier and show how to develop programs with graphical user interfaces with almost the same ease as their terminal-based counterparts.

6. **Web Basics.** The programming of Web pages with HTML and applets is introduced.

Focus on Fundamental Computer Science Topics

There seem to be two types of introductory Java textbooks. The first emphasizes basic problem-solving and programming techniques, and the second emphasizes language features. This book takes the former approach and introduces Java features as they are needed to support programming concepts. In this way, all the AP-required syntax is covered without allowing the book to be syntax driven. Some additional and more advanced Java features, not part of the AP requirement, are covered in end-of-chapter sections and in the appendices.

Methods and Objects, Early or Late?

Occasionally, people argue about whether methods and objects should be introduced early or late in the first course. In Java, even the simplest program involves both, so the problem really becomes one of how to introduce these concepts in a clear and meaningful manner from the outset. Starting with the first program, we show how to instantiate and send messages to objects. The book's early chapters (2 through 4) focus on the use of objects, arithmetic expressions, control constructs, and algorithms in the context of short, simple programs. As programs become more complex, it becomes advantageous to decompose them into cooperating components. With this end in mind, Chapter 5 shows how to develop systems of cooperating classes and methods. Thus, we take a pragmatic rather than an ideological approach to the question of when to introduce methods and objects with complete confidence that students will master both by the end of the course.

Revisiting Control Structures, Classes, and Arrays

Years of teaching experience have demonstrated that beginning programming students have the most difficulty with control structures, classes, and arrays. In this text, we have sought to soften the blow by introducing these ideas in two steps. First, a chapter gives an initial overview of a topic using the most basic features in simple but realistic applications. A follow-up chapter then revisits the topic to fill in and refine the details.

New in This Edition

The Advanced Placement test now requires an understanding of certain new features available in Java 5.0. From the AP perspective, the most important new feature in Java 5.0 is the generic collection. A generic collection requires the programmer to specify the collection's element type. AP A level students must know how to use the generic array list collection. They must also know how to use an enhanced `for` loop with arrays and array lists. The material on arrays, array lists and `for` loops has been updated to reflect these changes in requirements.

As in previous years, the AP test requires an understanding of simple standard terminal output but no input. A realistic first course will need some form of input, if only from the keyboard. Java 5.0 includes a delightful new Scanner class for input from the keyboard and from text files. Also included are methods for formatting data for output. The new edition of the book now uses these new features instead of an open source toolkit for text I/O.

In response to the suggestions of some instructors, we have moved the material on graphics and GUIs, which is not required for the AP test, to end-of-chapter sections. The introduction of this extra material is gradual enough that we have been able to dispense with the use of an open source toolkit and rely on the standard Java toolkits in the new edition. Instructors are now free to view graphics and GUIs as extra material to challenge students, and will not have to install or teach non-standard toolkits to accomplish this.

However, one non-standard toolkit, a TurtleGraphics package, has proven to be so popular with instructors and students that we have retained it in a late chapter to illustrate some advanced concepts. As usual, this toolkit is available on the instructor resource CD and from the Web site *http://www.wlu.edu/~lambertk/hsjava/*. The Web site is the preferred source because it contains the latest release of TurtleGraphics together with online documentation and other related materials. An online tutorial that introduces the use of TurtleGraphics is also available from the Web site.

Because of these changes, there is now no need to retain the extra unit of chapters on material such as graphics, file processing, the Web, and GUIs from the previous edition. The chapter on the Web and applets has been moved up so it can be examined earlier in the course; the material on file processing has been moved to an appendix.

Case Studies, the Software Life Cycle, and Comments

The book contains numerous case studies. These are complete Java programs ranging from the simple to the substantial. To emphasize the importance and usefulness of the software development life cycle, case studies are presented in the framework of a user request followed by analysis, design, and implementation, with well-defined tasks performed at each stage. Some case studies are carried through several chapters or extended in end-of-chapter programming projects.

Programming consists of more than just writing code, so we encourage students to submit an analysis and design as part of major programming assignments. We also believe that code should be properly commented, and for purposes of illustration, we include comments in selected examples of the code in the book.

Exercises

The book contains several different types of exercises. Most sections end with exercise questions that reinforce the reading by asking basic questions about the material in the section. Each chapter ends with a set of review exercises. All chapters except the first one include programming projects of varying degrees of difficulty. Finally, each chapter has a critical thinking activity that allows the student to reflect on a major topic covered in the chapter.

Special Features

Scattered throughout the book are short essays called Notes of Interest. These present historical and social aspects of computing, including computer ethics and security.

We Appreciate Your Feedback

We have greatly appreciated all of the helpful suggestions and comments from the many instructors who have used the previous edition of this book. As always, we have tried to produce a high-quality text, but should you encounter any errors, please report them to *klambert@wlu.edu*. A listing of errata, should they exist, and other information about the book will be posted on the Web site *http://www.wlu.edu/~lambertk/hsjava/*.

Acknowledgments

We would like to thank several people whose work made this book possible:

Rose Marie Kuebbing
Developmental Editor
Custom Editorial Productions Inc.

Rita Rebholz
Developmental Editor
Custom Editorial Productions Inc.

Kelly Murphy
Production Editor
GEX Publishing Services

Jane Mazares
Senior Acquisitions Editor
Thomson Course Technology

David Rivera
Product Manager
Thomson Course Technology

Kim Ryttel
Senior Marketing Manager
Thomson Course Technology

Jennifer Goguen
Associate Product Manager
Thomson Course Technology

Burt LaFountain
Manuscript Quality Assurance Lead
Thomson Course Technology

Justin Palmeiro
Senior Manufacturing Coordinator
Thomson Course Technology

Deborah Van Rooyen
Design Director
Thomson Course Technology

In addition, several individuals contributed material to the Instructor Resource Kit:

Jeannine Lawless
Editorial Assistant
Thomson Course Technology

Jan Clavey
Assistant Product Manager
Custom Editorial Production, Inc.

Dedication

To Carolyn and Smokey

Kenneth A. Lambert
Lexington, Virginia

Martin Osborne
Bellingham, Washington

TABLE OF CONTENTS

UNIT 1 GETTING STARTED WITH JAVA

UNit 2   THE NEXT STEP WITH JAVA

UNIT 3   ARRAYS, RECURSION, AND COMPLEXITY

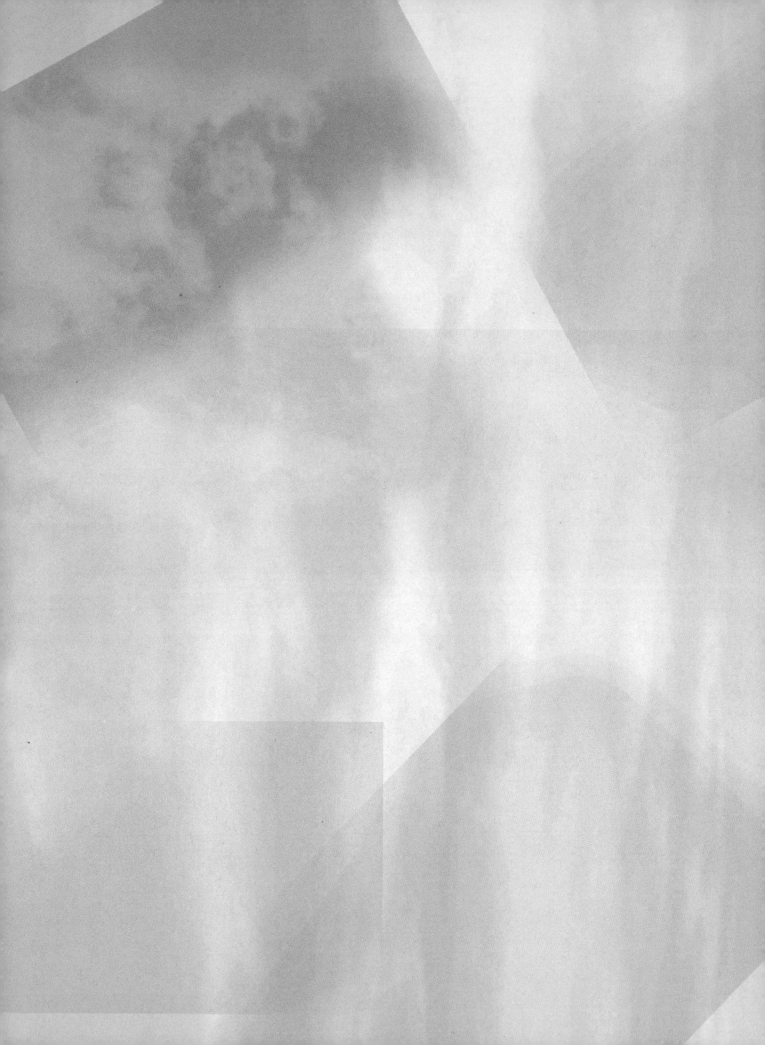

GETTING STARTED WITH JAVA

Unit 1

 Estimated Time for Unit: 13 hours

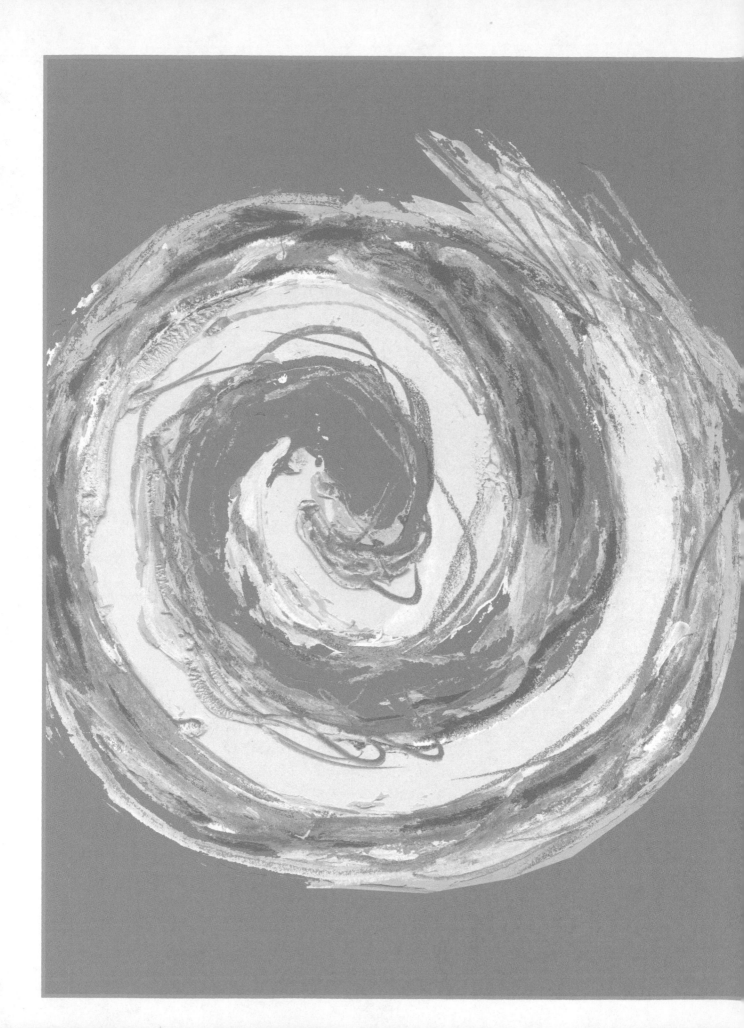

BACKGROUND

This is the only chapter in the book that is not about the details of writing Java programs. This chapter discusses computing in general, hardware and software, the representation of information in binary (i.e., as 0s and 1s), and general concepts of object-oriented programming. All this material will give you a broad understanding of computing and a foundation for your study of programming.

1.1 History of Computers

ENIAC, or Electronic Numerical Integrator and Computer, built in the late 1940s, was one of the world's first digital electronic computers. It was a large standalone machine that filled a room and used more electricity than all the houses on an average city block. ENIAC contained hundreds of miles of wire and thousands of heat-producing vacuum tubes. The mean time between failures was less than an hour, yet because of its fantastic speed when compared to hand-operated electromechanical calculators, it was immensely useful.

In the early 1950s, IBM sold its first business computer. At the time, it was estimated that the world would never need more than 10 such machines. By comparison, however, its awesome computational power was a mere 1/2000 of the typical 2-gigahertz Pentium personal computer purchased for about $1000 in 2006. Today, there are hundreds of millions of computers in the world, most of which are PCs. There are also billions of computers embedded in everyday products such as handheld calculators, microwave ovens, cell phones, cars, refrigerators, and clothing.

The first computers could perform only a single task at a time, and input and output were handled by such primitive means as punch cards and paper tape.

In the 1960s, time-sharing computers, costing hundreds of thousands and even millions of dollars, became popular at organizations large enough to afford them. These computers were powerful enough for 30 people to work on them simultaneously—and each felt as if he or she were the sole user. Each person sat at a teletype connected by wire to the computer. By making a connection through the telephone system, teletypes could even be placed at a great distance from the computer. The teletype was a primitive device by today's standards. It looked like an electric typewriter with a large roll of paper attached. Keystrokes entered at the keyboard were transmitted to the computer, which then echoed them back on the roll of paper. In addition, output from the computer's programs was printed on this roll.

In the 1970s, people began to see the advantage of connecting computers in networks, and the wonders of e-mail and file transfers were born.

In the 1980s, PCs appeared in great numbers, and soon after, local area networks of interconnected PCs became popular. These networks allowed a local group of PCs to communicate and share such resources as disk drives and printers with each other and with large centralized multiuser computers.

The 1990s saw an explosion in computer use. Hundreds of millions of computers appeared on many desktops and in many homes. Most of them are connected through the Internet (Figure 1-1).

FIGURE 1-1
An interconnected world of computers

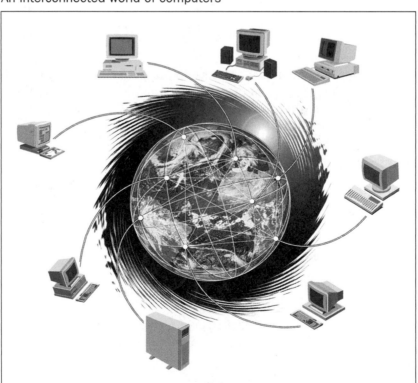

During the first decade of the 21st century, computing has become *ubiquitous* (meaning anywhere and everywhere). Tiny computer chips play the role of brains in cell phones, digital cameras, portable music players, and PDAs (portable digital assistants). Many of these devices now connect to the Internet via wireless technology, giving users unprecedented mobility.

And the common language of many of these computers is Java.

1.2 Computer Hardware and Software

Computers can be viewed as machines that process information. They consist of two primary components: hardware and software. *Hardware* consists of the physical devices that you see on your desktop, and *software* consists of the programs that give the hardware useful functionality. The main business of this book, which is programming, concerns software. But before diving into programming, let us take a moment to consider some of the major hardware and software components of a typical PC.

Bits and Bytes

It is difficult to discuss computers without referring to bits and bytes. A *bit*, or *binary digit*, is the smallest unit of information processed by a computer and consists of a single 0 or 1. A *byte* consists of eight adjacent bits. The capacity of computer memory and storage devices is usually expressed in bytes. Some commonly used quantities of bytes are shown in Table 1-1.

TABLE 1-1
Some commonly used quantities of information storage

UNIT OF BYTES	NUMBER OF BYTES	TYPE OF STORAGE
Kilobyte	1000 bytes	A single file
Megabyte	1 million bytes	Large files, RAM, flash memory, CDs
Gigabyte	1 billion bytes	RAM, hard disk drives, DVDs
Terabyte	1000 gigabytes	File server disks

Computer Hardware

As illustrated in Figure 1-2, a PC consists of six major subsystems.

FIGURE 1-2
A PC's six major subsystems

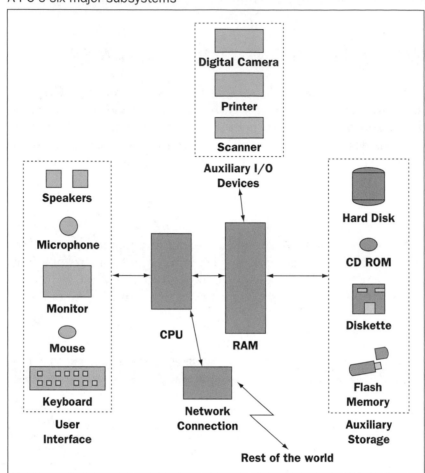

Listed in order from outside and most visible to inside and most hidden, the six major subsystems are as follows:

- The user interface, which supports moment-to-moment communication between a user and the computer

- Auxiliary input/output (I/O) devices such as printers and scanners

- Auxiliary storage devices for long-term storage of data and programs

- A network connection for connecting to the Internet and thus the rest of the world

- Internal memory, or RAM, for momentary storage of data and programs

- The all important CPU, or central processing unit

  Now we explore each of these subsystems in greater detail.

User Interface

The user interface consists of several devices familiar to everyone who has used a PC. In this book, we assume that our readers have already acquired basic computer literacy and have performed common tasks such as using a word processor or surfing the Internet. The keyboard and mouse are a computer's most frequently used input devices, and the monitor or screen is the principal output device. Also useful, and almost as common, are a microphone for input and speakers for output.

Auxiliary I/O Devices

Computers have not yet produced a paper-free world, so we frequently rely on the output from printers. Scanners are most commonly used to enter images, but in conjunction with appropriate software they can also be used to enter text. Digital cameras can record static images and video for transfer to a computer. Numerous other I/O devices are available for special applications, such as joysticks for games.

Auxiliary Storage Devices

The computer's operating system, the applications we buy, and the documents we write are all stored on devices collectively referred to as auxiliary storage or *secondary memory*. The current capacity of these devices is incredibly large and continues to increase rapidly. In 2006, as these words are being written, *hard disks* typically store tens of billions of bytes of information, or gigabytes (GB) as they are commonly called. In addition to hard disks, which are permanently encased within computers, there are several *portable storage media*. Most computer software is now purchased on *CD-ROMs*. CD stands for compact disk and ROM stands for read-only memory. The term *ROM* is becoming somewhat misleading in this context as PCs are increasingly being equipped with CD devices that can read and write. Most CDs have a capacity of about 700 million bytes (megabytes or MB), enough for a little over an hour of music or a small PC software package. Currently, CDs are being supplanted by *DVD*s, which have about 10 times a CD's capacity. *Flash memory* sticks with a capacity of 100MB to 2GB are the most convenient portable storage devices. They support input and output and are used primarily for transporting data between computers that are not interconnected and for making backup copies of crucial computer files.

Network Connection

A network connection is now an essential part of every PC, connecting it to all the resources of the Internet. For home computer users, a modem has long been the most widely used connection device. *Modem* stands for modulator–demodulator and refers to the fact that the device converts the digital information (0s and 1s) of the computer to an analog form suitable for transmission on phone lines and vice versa. Of course, as phone technology becomes increasingly digital, the term *modem* is fast becoming a misnomer. Other devices for connecting to the Internet include cable modems, which use a TV cable or a satellite dish rather than a phone connection; Ethernet cards, which attach directly to local area networks and from there to the Internet; and wireless cards, which transmit digital information through the air and many other objects.

Internal Memory

Although auxiliary storage devices have great capacity, access to their information is relatively slow in comparison to the speed of a computer's central processing unit. For this reason, computers include high-speed internal memory, also called *random access memory (RAM)* or *primary memory*. The contents of RAM are lost every time the computer is turned off, but when the computer is running, RAM is loaded from auxiliary storage with needed programs and data.

Because a byte of RAM costs about 100 times as much as a byte of hard disk storage, PCs usually contain only about 512MB to 1GB of RAM. Consequently, RAM is often unable to simultaneously hold all the programs and data a person might be using during a computer session. To deal with this situation, the computer swaps programs and data backward and forward between RAM and the hard disk as necessary. Swapping takes time and slows down the apparent speed of the computer from the user's perspective. Often the cheapest way to improve a computer's performance is to install more RAM.

Another smaller piece of internal memory is called *ROM*—short for *read-only memory*. This memory is usually reserved for critical system programs that are used when the computer starts up and that are retained when the computer is shut down.

Finally, most computers have 64MB or 128MB of specialized *video RAM* for storing images for graphics and video applications.

Central Processing Unit

The *central processing unit (CPU)* does the work of the computer. Given the amazing range of complex tasks performed by computers, one might imagine that the CPU is intrinsically very complex, but such is not the case. In fact, the basic functions performed by the CPU consist of the everyday arithmetic operations of addition, subtraction, multiplication, and division together with some comparison and I/O operations. The complexity lies in the programs that direct the CPU's operations rather than in the CPU itself, and it is the programmer's job to determine how to translate a complex task into an enormous series of simple operations, which the computer then executes at blinding speed. One of the authors of this book uses a computer that operates at 1 billion cycles per second (1 GHz), and during each cycle, the CPU executes all or part of a basic operation.

Perhaps we have gone too far in downplaying the complexity of the CPU. To be fair, it too is highly complex—not in terms of the basic operations it performs, but rather in terms of how it achieves its incredible speed. This speed is achieved by packing several million transistors onto a silicon chip roughly the size of a postage stamp. Since 1955, when transistors were first used in computers, hardware engineers have been doubling the speed of computers about every 18 months, principally by increasing the number of transistors on computer chips. This phenomenon is commonly known as *Moore's Law*. However, basic laws of physics guarantee that the process of miniaturization that allows ever greater numbers of transistors to be packed onto a single chip will soon end. How soon this will be, no one knows.

The *transistor*, the basic building block of the CPU and RAM, is a simple device that can be in one of two states—ON, conducting electricity, or OFF, not conducting electricity. All the information in a computer—programs and data—is expressed in terms of these ONs and OFFs, or 1s and 0s, as they are more conveniently called. From this perspective, RAM is merely a large array of 1s and 0s, and the CPU is merely a device for transforming patterns of 1s and 0s into other patterns of 1s and 0s.

To complete our discussion of the CPU, we describe a typical sequence of events that occurs when a program is executed, or run:

1. The program and data are loaded from disk into separate regions of RAM.

2. The CPU copies the program's first instruction from RAM into a decoding unit.

3. The CPU decodes the instruction and sends it to the Arithmetic and Logic Unit (ALU) for execution; for instance, it may add a number at one location in RAM to one at another location and store the result at a third location.

4. The CPU determines the location of the next instruction and repeats the process of copy, decode, and execute until the end of the program is reached.

5. After the program has finished executing, the data portion of RAM contains the results of the computation performed by the program.

Needless to say, this description has been greatly simplified. We have, for instance, ignored the use of separate processors for graphics and all issues related to input and output; however, the description provides a view of the computational process that will help you understand what follows.

Computer Software

Computer hardware processes complex patterns of electronic states or 0s and 1s. Computer software transforms these patterns, allowing them to be viewed as text, images, and so forth. Software is generally divided into two broad categories—*system software* and *application software*.

System Software

System software supports the basic operations of a computer and allows human users to transfer information to and from the computer. This software includes

■ The operating system, especially the file system for transferring information to and from disk and schedulers for running multiple programs concurrently

■ Communications software for connecting to other computers and the Internet

■ Compilers for translating user programs into executable form

■ The user interface subsystem, which manages the look and feel of the computer, including the operation of the keyboard, the mouse, and a screen full of overlapping windows

Application Software

Application software allows human users to accomplish specialized tasks. Examples of types of application software include

■ Word processors

■ Spreadsheets

■ Database systems

■ Multimedia software for digital music, photography, and video

■ Other programs we write

*E*XERCISE 1.2

1. What is the difference between a bit and a byte?

2. Name two input devices and two output devices.

3. What is the purpose of auxiliary storage devices?

4. What is RAM and how is it used?

5. Discuss the differences between hardware and software.

1.3 Binary Representation of Information and Computer Memory

As we saw in the previous section, computer memory stores patterns of electronic signals, which the CPU manipulates and transforms into other patterns. These patterns in turn can be viewed as strings of binary digits or bits. Programs and data are both stored in memory, and there is no discernible difference between program instructions and data; they are both just sequences of 0s and 1s. To determine what a sequence of bits represents, we must know the context. We now examine how different types of information are represented in binary notation.

Integers

We normally represent numbers in decimal (base 10) notation, whereas the computer uses binary (base 2) notation. Our addiction to base 10 is a physiological accident (10 fingers rather than 8, 12, or some other number). The computer's dependence on base 2 is due to the on/off nature of electric current.

To understand base 2, we begin by taking a closer look at the more familiar base 10. What do we really mean when we write a number such as 5403? We are saying that the number consists of 5 thousands, 4 hundreds, 0 tens, and 3 ones, or expressed differently:

$$(5 * 10^3) + (4 * 10^2) + (0 * 10^1) + (3 * 10^0)$$

In this expression, each term consists of a power of 10 times a coefficient between 0 and 9. In a similar manner, we can write expressions involving powers of 2 and coefficients between 0 and 1. For instance, let us analyze the meaning of 10011_2, where the subscript 2 indicates that we are using a base of 2:

$$10011_2 = (1 * 2^4) + (0 * 2^3) + (0 * 2^2) + (1 * 2^1) + (1 * 2^0)$$
$$= 16 + 0 + 0 + 2 + 1 = 19$$
$$= (1 * 10^1) + (9 * 10^0)$$

The inclusion of the base as a subscript at the end of a number helps us avoid possible confusion. Here are four numbers that contain the same digits but have different bases and thus different values:

$$1101101_{16}$$
$$1101101_{10}$$
$$1101101_8$$
$$1101101_2$$

Computer scientists use bases 2 (*binary*), 8 (*octal*), and 16 (*hexadecimal*) extensively. Base 16 presents the dilemma of how to represent digits beyond 9. The accepted convention is to use the letters A through F, corresponding to 10 through 15. For example:

$$3BC4_{16} = (3 * 16^3) + (11 * 16^2) + (12 * 16^1) + (4 * 16^0)$$
$$= (3 * 4096) + (11 * 256) + (12 * 16) + 4$$
$$= 15300_{10}$$

As you can see from these examples, the next time you are negotiating your salary with an employer, you might allow the employer to choose the digits as long as she allows you to pick the base. Table 1-2 shows some base 10 numbers and their equivalents in base 2. An important fact of the base 2 system is that 2^N distinct values can be represented using N bits. For example, four bits represent 2^4 or 16 values 0000, 0001, 0010, ..., 1110, 1111. A more extended discussion of number systems appears in Appendix E of this book.

TABLE 1-2
Some base 10 numbers and their base 2 equivalents

BASE 10	BASE 2
0	0
1	1
2	10
3	11
4	100
5	101
6	110
7	111
43	101011

Floating-Point Numbers

Numbers with a fractional part, such as 354.98, are called *floating-point numbers*. They are a bit trickier to represent in binary than integers. One way is to use the *mantissa/exponent notation* in which the number is rewritten as a value between 0 and 1, inclusive ($0 \leq x < 1$), times a power of 10. For example:

$$354.98_{10} = 0.35498_{10} * 10^3$$

where the mantissa is 35498, and the exponent is 3, or the number of places the decimal has moved. Similarly, in base 2

$$10001.001_2 = 0.10001001_2 * 2^5$$

with a mantissa of 10001001 and exponent of $5_{10} = 101_2$. In this way we can represent any floating-point number by two separate sequences of bits, with one sequence for the mantissa and the other for the exponent.

Many computers follow the slightly different IEEE standard in which the mantissa contains one digit before the decimal or binary point. In binary, the mantissa's leading 1 is then suppressed. Originally, this was a 7-bit code, but it has been extended in various ways to 8 bits.

Characters and Strings

To process text, computers must represent characters such as letters, digits, and other symbols on a keyboard. There are many encoding schemes for characters. One popular scheme is called *ASCII* (*American Standard Code for Information Interchange*). In this scheme, each character is represented as a pattern of 8 bits or a byte.

In binary notation, byte values can range from 0000 0000 to 1111 1111, allowing for 256 possibilities. These are more than enough for the characters

- A...Z

- a...z

- 0...9

- +, -, *, /, etc.

- And various unprintable characters such as carriage return, line feed, a ringing bell, and command characters

Table 1-3 shows some characters and their corresponding ASCII bit patterns.

TABLE 1-3
Some characters and their corresponding ASCII bit patterns

CHARACTER	BIT PATTERN	CHARACTER	BIT PATTERN	CHARACTER	BIT PATTERN
A	0100 0001	a	0110 0001	0	0011 0000
B	0100 0010	b	0110 0010	1	0011 0001
. . .	. . .	. . .	. . .	. . .	. .
Z	0101 1010	z	0111 1010	9	0011 1001

Java, however, uses a scheme called *Unicode* rather than ASCII. In this scheme, each character is represented by a pattern of 16 bits, ranging from 0000 0000 0000 0000 to 1111 1111 1111 1111. Unicode allows for 65,536 possibilities and can represent many alphabets simultaneously. Within Unicode, the patterns 0000 0000 0000 0000 to 0000 0000 1111 1111 duplicate the ASCII encoding scheme.

Strings are another type of data used in text processing. Strings are sequences of characters, such as "The cat sat on the mat." The computer encodes each character in ASCII or Unicode and strings them together.

Sound

The information contained in sound is *analog*. Unlike integers and text, which on a computer have a finite range of discrete values, analog information has a continuous range of infinitely many values. The analog information in sound can be plotted as a periodic waveform such as the one shown in Figure 1-3. The amplitude or height of a waveform measures the volume of the sound. The time that a waveform takes to make one complete cycle is called its period. The frequency or number of cycles per second of a sound's waveform measures its pitch. Thus, the higher a wave is, the louder the sound's volume, and the closer together the cycles are, the higher the sound's pitch.

FIGURE 1-3
A sound waveform

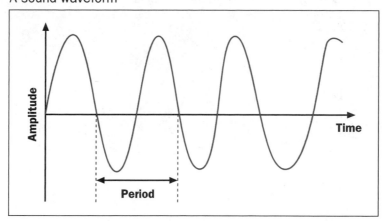

An input device for sound must translate this continuous analog information into discrete, digital values. A technique known as sampling takes a reading of the amplitude values on a waveform at regular intervals, as shown in Figure 1-4a. If the intervals are short enough, the digital information can be used to reconstruct a waveform that approximates a sound that most human beings cannot distinguish from the original. Figure 1-4b shows the waveform generated for output from the waveform sampled in Figure 1-4a. The original waveform is shown as a dotted line, whereas the regenerated waveform is shown as a solid line. As you can see, if the sampling rate is too low, some of the measured amplitudes (the heights and depths of the peaks and valleys in the waves) will be inaccurate. The sampling rate must also be high enough to capture the range of frequencies (the waves and valleys themselves), from the lowest to the highest, that most humans can hear. Psychologists and audiophiles agree that this range is from 20 to 22,000 Hertz (cycles per second). Because a sample must capture both the peak and the valley of a cycle, the sampling rate must be double the frequency. Therefore, a standard rate of 44,000 samples per second has been established for sound input. Amplitude is usually measured on a scale from 0 to 65,535.

FIGURE 1-4a
Sampling a waveform

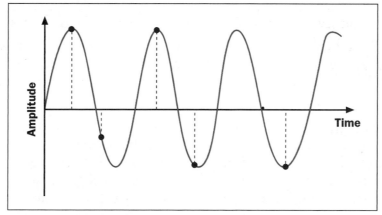

FIGURE 1-4b
Regenerating the sound from the samples

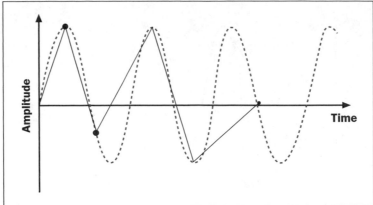

Because of the high sampling rate, the memory requirements for storing sound are much greater than those of text. For example, to digitize an hour of stereo music, the computer must perform the following steps:

■ For each stereo channel, every 1/44,000 of a second, measure the amplitude of the sound on a scale of 0 to 65,535.

■ Convert this number to binary using 16 bits.

Thus, 1 hour of stereo music requires

$$2 \text{ channels} * \frac{1 \text{ hour}}{\text{channel}} * \frac{60 \text{ minutes}}{\text{hour}} * \frac{60 \text{ seconds}}{\text{minute}} * \frac{44{,}000 \text{ samples}}{\text{second}} * \frac{16 \text{ bits}}{\text{sample}}$$

= 5,068,800,000 bits
= 633,600,000 bytes

which is the capacity of a standard CD.

The sampling rate of 44,000 times a second is not arbitrary, but corresponds to the number of samples required to reproduce accurate sounds with a frequency of up to 22,000 cycles per second. Sounds above that frequency are of more interest to dogs, bats, and dolphins than to people.

Many popular sound-encoding schemes, such as MP3, use data compression techniques to reduce the size of a digitized sound file while minimizing the loss of fidelity.

Images

Representing photographic images on a computer poses similar problems to those encountered with sound. Once again, analog information is involved, but in this case we have an infinite set of color and intensity values spread across a two-dimensional space. And once again, the solution involves the sampling of enough of these values so that the digital information can reproduce an image that is more or less indistinguishable from the original.

Sampling devices for images are flatbed scanners and digital cameras. These devices measure discrete values at distinct points or *pixels* in a two-dimensional grid. In theory, the more pixels that are taken, the more continuous and realistic the resulting image will appear. In practice, however, the human eye cannot discern objects that are closer together than 0.1 mm, so a sampling rate of 10 pixels per linear millimeter (250 pixels per inch and 62,500 pixels per square inch) would be plenty accurate. Thus, a 3-by-5-inch image would need

```
3 * 5 * 62,500 pixels/inch² = 937,500 pixels
```

For most purposes, however, we can settle for a much lower sampling rate and thus fewer pixels per square inch.

The values sampled are of course color values, and there are an infinite number of these on the spectrum. If we want a straight black-and-white image, we need only two possible values, or one bit of information, per pixel. For grayscale images, 3 bits allow for 8 shades of gray, while 8 bits allow for 256 shades of gray. A true-color scheme called RGB is based on the fact that the human retina is sensitive to red, green, and blue components. This scheme uses 8 bits for each of the three color components, for a total of 24 bits or 16,777,216 (the number of possible sequences of 24 bits) color values per pixel. No matter which color scheme is used, the sampling device selects a discrete value that is closest to the color and intensity of the image at a given point in space.

The file size of a true-color digitized image can be quite large. For example, the 3-by-5-inch image discussed earlier would need 937,500 pixels * 24 bits/pixel or about 2.5MB of storage. As with sound files, image files can be saved in a compressed format, such as GIF or JPEG, without much loss of realism.

Video

Video consists of a soundtrack and a set of images called *frames*. The sound for a soundtrack is recorded, digitized, and processed in the manner discussed earlier. The frames are snapshots or images recorded in sequence during a given time interval. If the time intervals between frames are short enough, the human eye will perceive motion in the images when they are replayed. The rate of display required for realistic motion is between 16 and 24 frames per second.

The primary challenge in digitizing video is achieving a suitable data compression scheme. Let's assume that you want to display each frame on a 15-inch laptop monitor. Each frame will then cover about 120 square inches, so even with a conservative memory allocation of 10 kilobytes (KB) of storage per square inch of image, we're looking at 1.2MB/frame * 16 frames/second = 19MB/second of storage. A 2-hour feature film would need 432,000 seconds * 19MB/second = 8,208,000MB without the soundtrack! A typical DVD has space for several gigabytes of data, so our uncompressed video would obviously not fit on a DVD. Needless to say, very sophisticated data compression schemes, such as MPEG, have been developed that allow 3-hour films to be placed on a DVD and shorter, smaller-framed video clips to be downloaded and played from the Internet.

Program Instructions

Program instructions are represented as a sequence of bits in RAM. For instance, on some hypothetical computer, the instruction to add two numbers already located in RAM and store their sum at some third location in RAM might be represented as follows:

```
0000 1001 / 0100 0000 / 0100 0010 / 0100 0100
```

where

- The first group of 8 bits represents the ADD command and is called the *operation code*, or *opcode* for short

- The second group of 8 bits represents the location (64_{10}) in memory of the first operand

- The third group of 8 bits represents the location (66_{10}) in memory of the second operand

- The fourth group of 8 bits represents the location (68_{10}) at which to store the sum

In other words, add the number at location 64 to the number at location 66 and store the sum at location 68.

Computer Memory

We can envision a computer's memory as a gigantic sequence of bytes. A byte's location in memory is called its *address*. Addresses are numbered from 0 to 1 less than the number of bytes of memory installed on that computer, say, $32M - 1$, where M stands for *megabyte*.

A group of contiguous bytes can represent a number, a string, a picture, a chunk of sound, a program instruction, or whatever, as determined by context. For example, let us consider the meaning of the two bytes starting at location 3 in Figure 1-5.

FIGURE 1-5
A 32MB RAM

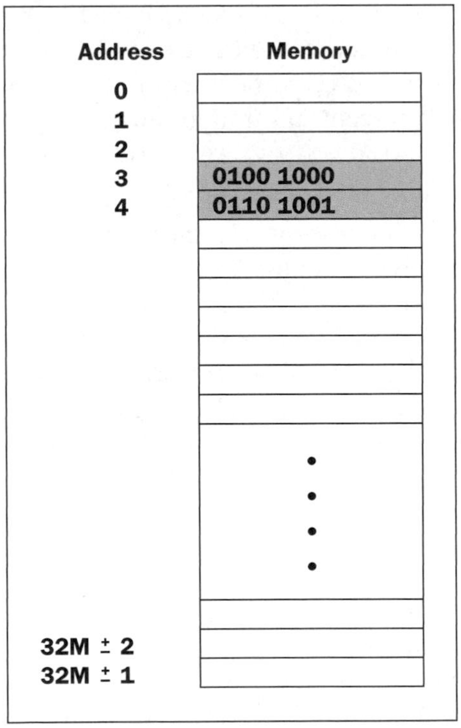

Address	Memory
0	
1	
2	
3	0100 1000
4	0110 1001
	•
	•
	•
	•
32M − 2	
32M − 1	

The several possible meanings include these:

- If it is a string, then the meaning is "Hi".

- If it is a binary encoded integer, then the meaning is 18537_{10}.

- If it is a program instruction, then it might mean ADD, depending on the type of computer.

EXERCISE 1.3

1. Translate 11100011_2 to a base 10 number. *227*

2. Translate $45B_{16}$ to a base 10 number. *1115*

3. What is the difference between Unicode and ASCII?

ASCII 256
UNICODE 65,536

4. Assume that 4 bits are used to represent the intensities of red, green, and blue. How many total colors are possible in this scheme?

5. An old-fashioned computer has just 16 bits available to represent an address of a memory location. How many total memory locations can be addressed in this machine? *(65536 - 1)*

4   4   4
RED   BLUE   GREEN

1111
16 · 16 · 16
256 · 16 = 4096

2^{16}	2^{15}	2^{14}	2^{13}	2^{12}	2^{11}	2^{10}	2^{9}	2^{8}	2^{7}	2^{6}	2^{5}	2^{4}	2^{3}	2^{2}	2^{1}	2^{0}
65536	16384		4096	1024	512	256	128	64	32	16	8	4	2	1		

32568   8192   2048

Computer Ethics

THE ACM CODE OF ETHICS

The Association for Computing Machinery (ACM) is the flagship organization for computing professionals. The ACM supports publications of research results and new trends in computer science, sponsors conferences and professional meetings, and provides standards for computer scientists as professionals. The standards concerning the conduct and professional responsibility of computer scientists have been published in the ACM Code of Ethics. The code is intended as a basis for ethical decision making and for judging the merits of complaints about violations of professional ethical standards.

The code lists several general moral imperatives for computer professionals:

- Contribute to society and human well-being.

- Avoid harm to others.

- Be honest and trustworthy.

- Be fair and take action not to discriminate.

- Honor property rights including copyrights and patents.

- Give proper credit for intellectual property.

- Respect the privacy of others.

- Honor confidentiality.

The code also lists several more specific professional responsibilities:

- Strive to achieve the highest quality, effectiveness, and dignity in both the process and products of professional work.

- Acquire and maintain professional competence.

- Know and respect existing laws pertaining to professional work.

- Accept and provide appropriate professional review.

- Give comprehensive and thorough evaluations of computer systems and their impacts, including analysis of possible risks.

- Honor contracts, agreements, and assigned responsibilities.

- Improve public understanding of computing and its consequences.

- Access computing and communication resources only when authorized to do so.

In addition to these principles, the code offers a set of guidelines to provide professionals with explanations of various issues contained in the principles. The complete text of the ACM Code of Ethics is available at the ACM's Web site, http://www.acm.org.

1.4 Programming Languages

Question: "If a program is just some very long pattern of electronic states in a computer's memory, then what is the best way to write a program?" The history of computing provides several answers to this question in the form of generations of programming languages.

Generation 1 (Late 1940s to Early 1950s)—Machine Languages

Early on, when computers were new, they were very expensive, and programs were very short. Programmers toggled switches on the front of the computer to enter programs and data directly into RAM in the form of 0s and 1s. Later, devices were developed to read the 0s and 1s into memory from punched cards and paper tape. There were several problems with this machine language-coding technique:

- Coding was error prone (entering just a single 0 or 1 incorrectly was enough to make a program run improperly or not at all).

- Coding was tedious and slow.

- It was extremely difficult to modify programs.

- It was nearly impossible for one person to decipher another's program.

- A program was not portable to a different type of computer because each type had its own unique machine language.

Needless to say, this technique is no longer used!

Generation 2 (Early 1950s to Present)—Assembly Languages

Instead of the binary notation of machine language, assembly language uses mnemonic symbols to represent instructions and data. For instance, here is a machine language instruction followed by its assembly language equivalent:

```
0011 1001 / 1111 0110 / 1111 1000 / 1111 1010
ADD         A,          B,          C
```

meaning

1. Add the number at memory location 246, which we refer to as A

2. To the number at memory location 248, which we refer to as B

3. And store the result at memory location 250, which we refer to as C

Each *assembly language* instruction corresponds exactly to one machine language instruction. The standard procedure for using assembly language consists of several steps:

1. Write the program in assembly language.

2. Translate the program into a machine language program—this is done by a computer program called an *assembler*.

3. Load and run the machine language program—this is done by another program called a *loader*.

When compared to machine language, assembly language is

■ More programmer friendly

■ Still unacceptably (by today's standards) tedious to use, difficult to modify, and so forth

■ No more portable because each type of computer still has its own unique assembly language

Assembly language is used as little as possible by programmers today, although sometimes it is used when memory or processing speed are at a premium. Thus, every student of computer science probably learns at least one assembly language.

Generation 3 (Mid-1950s to Present)—High-Level Languages

Early examples of *high-level languages* are FORTRAN and COBOL, which are still in widespread use. Later examples are BASIC, C, and Pascal. Recent examples include Smalltalk, C++, and Java. All these languages are designed to be human friendly—easy to write, easy to read, and easy to understand—at least when compared to assembly language. For example, all high-level languages support the use of algebraic notation, such as the expression $x + (y * z)$.

Each instruction in a high-level language corresponds to many instructions in machine language. Translation to machine language is done by a program called a *compiler*. Generally, a program written in a high-level language is portable, but it must be recompiled for each different type of computer on which it is going to run. Java is a notable exception because it is a high-level language that does not need to be recompiled for each type of computer. We learn more about this in Chapter 2. The vast majority of software written today is written in high-level languages.

E XERCISE 1.4

1. State two of the difficulties of programming with machine language.

2. State two features of assembly language.

3. What is a loader, and what is it used for?

4. State one difference between a high-level language and assembly language.

1.5 The Software Development Process

H igh-level programming languages help programmers write high-quality software in much the same sense as good tools help carpenters build high-quality houses, but there is much more to programming than writing lines of code, just as there is more to building houses than pounding nails. The "more" consists of organization and planning and various diagrammatic conventions for expressing those plans. To this end, computer scientists have developed a view of the software development process known as the **software development life cycle (SDLC)**. We now present a particular version of this life cycle called the **waterfall model**.

The waterfall model consists of several phases:

1. *Customer request*—In this phase, the programmers receive a broad statement of a problem that is potentially amenable to a computerized solution. This step is also called the *user requirements phase.*

2. *Analysis*—The programmers determine what the program will do. This is sometimes viewed as a process of clarifying the specifications for the problem.

3. *Design*—The programmers determine how the program will do its task.

4. *Implementation*—The programmers write the program. This step is also called the *coding phase.*

5. *Integration*—Large programs have many parts. In the integration phase, these parts are brought together into a smoothly functioning whole, usually not an easy task.

6. *Maintenance*—Programs usually have a long life; a life span of 5 to 15 years is common for software. During this time, requirements change and minor or major modifications must be made.

The interaction between the phases is shown in Figure 1-6. Note that the figure resembles a waterfall, in which the results of each phase flow down to the next. A mistake detected in one phase often requires the developer to back up and redo some of the work in the previous phase. Modifications made during maintenance also require backing up to earlier phases.

FIGURE 1-6
The waterfall model of the software development life cycle

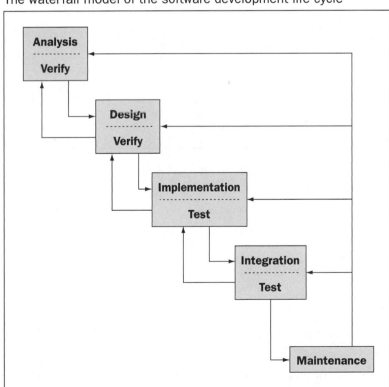

Programs rarely work as hoped the first time they are run; hence, they should be subjected to extensive and careful testing. Many people think that testing is an activity that applies only to the implementation and integration phases; however, the outputs of each phase should be scrutinized carefully. In fact mistakes found early are much less expensive to correct than those found late. Figure 1-7 illustrates some relative costs of repairing mistakes when found in different phases.

FIGURE 1-7
Relative costs of repairing mistakes when found in different phases

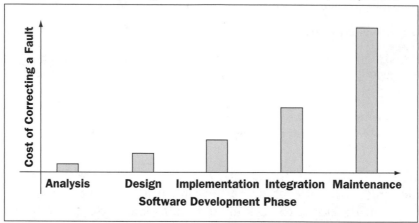

Finally, the cost of developing software is not spread equally over the phases. The percentages shown in Figure 1-8 are typical.

FIGURE 1-8
Percentage of total cost incurred in each phase of the development process

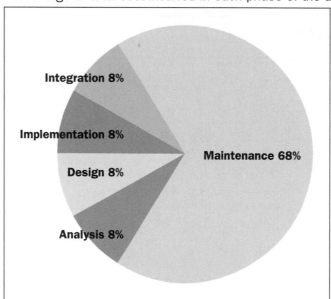

Most people probably think that implementation takes the most time and therefore costs the most. However, maintenance is, in fact, the most expensive aspect of software development. The cost of maintenance can be reduced by careful analysis, design, and implementation.

As you read this book and begin to sharpen your programming skills, you should remember two points:

1. There is more to software development than hacking out code.

2. If you want to reduce the overall cost of software development, write programs that are easy to maintain. This requires thorough analysis, careful design, and good coding style. We have more to say about coding style throughout the book.

*E*XERCISE 1.5

1. What happens during the analysis and design phases of the software development process?

2. Which phase of the software development process incurs the highest cost to developers?

3. How does the waterfall model of software development work?

4. In which phase of the software development process is the detection and correction of errors the least expensive?

For a thorough discussion of the software development process and software engineering in general, see Stephen R. Schach, *Software Engineering with Java* (Chicago: Irwin, 1997).

1.6 Basic Concepts of Object-Oriented Programming

The high-level programming languages mentioned earlier fall into two major groups, and these two groups utilize two different approaches to programming. The first group, consisting of the older languages (COBOL, FORTRAN, BASIC, C, and Pascal), uses what is called a *procedural approach*. Inadequacies in the procedural approach led to the development of the *object-oriented approach* and to several newer languages (Smalltalk, C++, and Java). There is little point in trying to explain the differences between these approaches in an introductory programming text, but suffice it to say that everyone considers the object-oriented approach to be the superior of the two. There are also several other approaches to programming, but that too is a topic for a more advanced text.

Most programs in the real world contain hundreds of thousands of lines of code. Writing such programs is a highly complex task that can only be accomplished by breaking the code into communicating components. This is an application of the well-known principle of "divide and conquer" that has been applied successfully to many human endeavors. There are various strategies for subdividing a program, and these depend on the type of programming language used. We now give an overview of the process in the context of *object-oriented programming* (OOP)—that is, programming with objects. Along the way, we introduce fundamental OOP concepts, such as class, inheritance, and polymorphism. Each of these concepts is also discussed in greater detail later in the book. For best results, reread this section as you encounter each concept for a second time.

We proceed by way of an extended analogy in an attempt to associate something already familiar with something new. Like all analogies, this one is imperfect but ideally useful. Imagine that it is your task to plan an expedition in search of the lost treasure of Balbor. How familiar can this be, you ask? Well, that depends on your taste in books, movies, and video games. Your overall approach might consist of the following steps:

1. *Planning*—You determine the different types of team members needed, including leaders, pathfinders, porters, and trail engineers. You then define the responsibilities of each member in terms of

   ■ A list of the resources used—these include the materials and knowledge needed by each member

   ■ The rules of behavior followed—these define how the team member behaves and responds in various situations

   Finally, you decide how many of each type will be needed.

2. *Execution*—You recruit the team members and assemble them at the starting point, send the team on its way, and sit back and wait for the outcome. (There is no sense in endangering your own life, too.)

3. *Outcome*—If the planning was done well, you will be rich; otherwise, prepare for disappointment.

How does this analogy relate to OOP? We give the answer in Table 1-4. On the left side of the table we describe various aspects of the expedition, and on the right side are listed corresponding aspects of OOP. Do not expect to understand all the new terms now. We explore them with many other examples in the rest of this book.

TABLE 1-4
Expedition analogy to OOP

THE WORLD OF THE EXPEDITION	THE WORLD OF OOP
The trip must be planned.	Computer software is created in a process called ***programming***.
The team is composed of different types of team members, and each type is characterized by its list of resources and rules of behavior.	A program is comprised of different types of software components called ***classes***. A class defines or describes a list of data resources called *instance variables* and rules of behavior called ***methods***. Combining the description of resources and behaviors into a single software entity is called ***encapsulation***.
First the trip must be planned. Then it must be set in motion.	First a program must be written. Then it must be run, or executed.
When the expedition is in progress, the team is composed of individual members and not types. Each member is, of course, an instance of a particular type.	An executing program is composed of interacting objects, and each object's resources (instance variables) and rules of behavior (methods) are described in a particular class. An object is said to be an instance of the class that describes its resources and behavior.
At the beginning of the expedition, team members must be recruited.	While a program is executing, it creates, or instantiates, objects as needed.

TABLE 1-4 Continued
Expedition analogy to OOP

THE WORLD OF THE EXPEDITION	THE WORLD OF OOP
Team members working together accomplish the mission of the expedition. They do this by asking each other for services.	Objects working together accomplish the mission of the program. They do this by asking each other for services or, in the language of OOP, by sending messages to each other.
When a team member receives a request for service, she follows the instructions in a corresponding rule of behavior.	When an object receives a message, it refers to its class to find a corresponding rule or method to execute.
If someone who is not a pathfinder wants to know where north is, she does not need to know anything about compasses. She merely asks one of the pathfinders, who are well-known providers of this service. Even if she did ask a pathfinder for his compass, he would refuse. Thus, team members tell others about the services they provide but never anything about the resources they use to provide these services.	If an object A needs a service that it cannot provide for itself, then A requests the service from some well-known provider B. However, A knows nothing of B's data resources and never asks for access to them. This principle of providing access to services but not to data resources is called *information hiding*.
The expedition includes general-purpose trail engineers plus two specialized subtypes. All trail engineers share common skills, but some specialize in bridge building and others in clearing landslides. Thus, there is a hierarchy of engineers.	Classes are organized into a hierarchy also. The class at the root, or base, of the hierarchy defines methods and instance variables that are shared by its subclasses, those below it in the hierarchy. Each subclass then defines additional methods and instance variables. This process of sharing is called *inheritance*.
Trail Engineer → Bridge Expert, Landslide Expert	Base Class → Subclass One, Subclass Two
At the end of the day, the leader tells each member to set up camp. All members understand this request, but their responses depend on their types. Each type responds in a manner consistent with its specific responsibilities.	Different types of objects can understand the same message. This is referred to as *polymorphism*. However, an object's response depends on the class to which it belongs.

TABLE 1-4 Continued
Expedition analogy to OOP

THE WORLD OF THE EXPEDITION	THE WORLD OF OOP
During the trip, everyone is careful not to ask an individual to do something for which he is not trained—that is, for which he does not have a rule of behavior.	When writing a program, we never send a message to an object unless its class has a corresponding method.
One can rely on team members to improvise and resolve ambiguities and contradictions in rules.	In contrast, a computer does exactly what the program specifies—neither more nor less. Thus, programming errors and oversights, no matter how small, are usually disastrous. Therefore, programmers need to be excruciatingly thorough and exact when writing programs.

EXERCISE 1.6

1. In what way is programming like planning?

2. An object-oriented program is a set of objects that interact by sending messages to each other. Explain.

3. What is a class, and how does it relate to objects in an object-oriented program?

4. Explain the concept of inheritance with an example.

5. Explain the concept of information hiding with an example.

Computer Ethics

COPYRIGHT, INTELLECTUAL PROPERTY, AND DIGITAL INFORMATION

For hundreds of years, copyright law has existed to regulate the use of intellectual property. At stake are the rights of authors and publishers to a return on their investment in works of the intellect, which include printed matter (books, articles, etc.), recorded music, film, and video. More recently, copyright law has been extended to include software and other forms of digital information. For example, copyright law protects the software used with this book. This prohibits the purchaser from reproducing the software for sale or free distribution to others. If the software is stolen or "pirated" in this way, the perpetrator can be prosecuted and punished by law. However, copyright law also allows for "fair use"—the purchaser may make backup copies of the software for personal use. When the purchaser sells the software to another user, the seller thereby relinquishes the right to use it, and the new purchaser acquires this right.

When governments design copyright legislation, governments try to balance the rights of authors and publishers to a return on their work against the rights of the public to fair use. In the case of printed matter and other works that have a physical embodiment, the meaning of fair use is usually clear. Without fair use, borrowing a book from a library or playing a CD at a high school dance would be unlawful.

With the rapid rise of digital information and its easy transmission on networks, different interest groups—authors, publishers, users, and computer professionals—are beginning to question the traditional balance of ownership rights and fair use. For example, is browsing a copyrighted manuscript on a network service an instance of fair use? Or does it involve a reproduction of the manuscript that violates the rights of the author or publisher? Is the manuscript a physical piece of intellectual property when browsed or just a temporary pattern of bits in a computer's memory? When you listen to an audio clip on a network are you violating copyright, or only when you download the clip to your hard drive? Users and technical experts tend to favor free access to any information placed on a network. Publishers and to a lesser extent authors tend to worry that their work, when placed on a network, will be resold for profit.

Legislators struggling with the adjustment of copyright law to a digital environment face many of these questions and concerns. Providers and users of digital information should also be aware of the issues. For more information about these topics, visit the Creative Commons Web site at http://creativecommons.org/.

SUMMARY

In this chapter, you learned:

- The modern computer age began in the late 1940s with the development of ENIAC. Business computing became practical in the 1950s, and time-sharing computers advanced computing in large organizations in the 1960s and 1970s. The 1980s saw the development and first widespread sales of personal computers, and the 1990s saw personal computers connected in networks.

- Modern computers consist of two primary components: hardware and software. Computer hardware is the physical component of the system. Computer software consists of programs that enable us to use the hardware.

- All information used by a computer is represented in binary form. This information includes numbers, text, images, sound, and program instructions.

- Programming languages have been developed in the course of three generations: generation 1 is machine language, generation 2 is assembly language, and generation 3 is high-level language.

- The software development process consists of several standard phases: customer request, analysis, design, implementation, integration, and maintenance.

- Object-oriented programming is a style of programming that can lead to better quality software. Breaking code into easily handled components simplifies the job of writing a large program.

VOCABULARY *Review*

Define the following terms:

Application software	Information hiding	Software development life
Bit	Object-oriented programming	cycle (SDLC)
Byte	Primary memory	System software
Central processing unit (CPU)	Secondary memory	Ubiquitous computing
Hardware	Software	Waterfall model

REVIEW *Questions*

WRITTEN QUESTIONS

Write a brief answer to each of the following questions.

1. What are the three major hardware components of a computer?

2. Name three input devices.

3. Name two output devices.

4. What is the difference between application software and system software?

5. Name a first-generation programming language, a second-generation programming language, and a third-generation programming language.

FILL IN THE BLANK

Complete the following sentences by writing the correct word or words in the blanks provided.

1. All information used by a computer is represented using _____ notation.

2. The _____ phase of the software life cycle is also called the *coding phase*.

3. More than half of the cost of developing software goes to the _____ phase of the software life cycle.

4. ACM stands for _____.

5. Copyright law is designed to give fair use to the public and to protect the rights of _____ and _____.

PROJECTS

PROJECT 1-1

Take some time to become familiar with the architecture of the computer you will use for this course. Describe your hardware and software using the following guidelines:

- What hardware components make up your system?

- How much memory does your system have?

- What are the specifications of your CPU? (Do you know its speed and what kind of microprocessor it has?)

- What operating system are you using? What version of that operating system is your computer currently running?

- What major software applications are loaded on your system?

CRITICAL *Thinking*

You have just written some software that you would like to sell. Your friend suggests that you copyright your software. Discuss why this might be a good idea.

FIRST JAVA PROGRAMS

VOCABULARY

Applet

Assignment operator

Byte code

DOS development environment

Graphical user interface (GUI)

Hacking

Integrated development environment (IDE)

Java virtual machine (JVM)

Just-in-time compilation (JIT)

Parameter

Source code

Statement

Terminal I/O user interface

Variable

Programs are written in programming languages, and the language used in this book is Java. This chapter gets you up and running with a couple of simple Java programs. We show how to write these first programs, compile them, and run them. In the process, you will become acquainted with a Java programming environment, the structure of a simple Java program, and the basic ideas of variables, input and output (I/O) statements, and sending messages to objects.

2.1 Why Java?

Java is the fastest growing programming language in the world. Companies such as IBM and Sun have adopted Java as their major application development language. There are several reasons for this.

First, Java is a modern object-oriented programming language. The designers of Java spent much time studying the features of classical object-oriented languages such as Smalltalk and C++ and made a successful effort to incorporate the good features of these languages and omit the less desirable ones.

Second, Java is secure, robust, and portable. That is, the Java language

- Enables the construction of virus-free, tamper-free systems (secure)

- Supports the development of programs that do not overwrite memory (robust)

- Yields programs that can be run on different types of computers without change (portable)

These features make Java ideally suited to develop distributed, network-based applications, which is an area of ever-increasing importance.

Third, Java supports the use of advanced programming concepts such as threads. A *thread* is a process that can run concurrently with other processes. For example, a single Java application might consist of two threads. One thread transfers an image from one machine to another across a network, while the other thread simultaneously interacts with the user.

Fourth and finally, Java bears a superficial resemblance to C++, which is currently the world's most popular industrial-strength programming language. Thus, it is easy for a C++ programmer to learn Java and for a Java programmer to learn C++. Compared to C++, however, Java is easier to use and learn, less error prone, more portable, and better suited to the Internet.

On the negative side, Java runs more slowly than most modern programming languages because it is interpreted. To understand this last point we must now turn our attention to the Java virtual machine and byte code.

*E*XERCISE 2.1

1. What is a portable program?

2. Describe two features of Java that make it a better language than C++.

3. What is a thread? Describe how threads might be used in a program.

2.2 *The Java Virtual Machine and Byte Code*

Compilers usually translate a higher-level language into the machine language of a particular type of computer. However, the Java compiler translates Java not into machine language, but into a pseudomachine language called Java **byte code**. Byte code is the machine language for an imaginary Java computer. To run Java byte code on a particular computer, you must install a **Java virtual machine** (JVM) on that computer, unless you use a computer such as Apple's Macintosh, in which the JVM comes with the operating system.

A JVM is a program that behaves like a computer. Such a program is called an *interpreter*. An interpreter has several advantages as well as some disadvantages. The main disadvantage of an interpreter is that a program pretending to be a computer runs programs more slowly than an actual computer. JVMs are getting faster every day, however. For instance, some JVMs translate byte code instructions into machine language when they are first encountered—called *just-in-time compilation* (JIT)—so that the next time the instruction is encountered it is executed as fast machine code rather than being interpreted as slow byte code. Also, new computer chips are being developed that implement a JVM directly in hardware, thus avoiding the performance penalty.

The main advantage of an interpreter is that any computer can run it. Thus, Java byte code is highly portable. For instance, many of the pages you download on the Web contain small Java programs already translated into byte code. These are called *applets*, and they are run in a JVM that is incorporated into your Web browser. These applets range from the decorative (displaying a comical animated character on a Web page) to the practical (displaying a continuous stream of stock market quotes).

Because Java programs run inside a virtual machine, it is possible to limit their capabilities. Thus, ideally, you never have to worry about a Java applet infecting your computer with a virus, erasing the files on your hard drive, or stealing sensitive information and sending it across the Internet to a competitor. In practice, however, computer hackers have successfully penetrated Java's security mechanisms in the past and may succeed again in the future. But all things considered, Java applets really are very secure, and security weaknesses are repaired as soon as they become known.

EXERCISE 2.2

1. What does JVM stand for?

2. What is byte code? Describe how the JVM uses byte code.

3. What is an applet? Describe how applets are used.

2.3 Choosing a User Interface Style

Before writing our first program, we must make a difficult decision. What type of user interface do we want to use? There are two choices: the *graphical user interface* (GUI), familiar to all PC users, and the less common *terminal I/O user interface*. Figure 2-1 illustrates both in the context of a program that converts degrees Fahrenheit to degrees Celsius. The graphical user interface on the left is familiar and comfortable. The user enters a number in the first box, clicks the command button, and the program displays the answer in the second box. The terminal-based interface on the right begins by displaying the prompt "Enter degrees Fahrenheit: ". The user then enters a number and presses the Enter key. The program responds by displaying the answer.

FIGURE 2-1
Two user interfaces for a temperature conversion program

 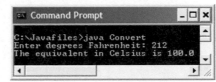

We use terminal I/O user interface in most of the program examples in this book. Beginning with this chapter, an optional end-of-chapter section introduces various aspects of graphics and GUI programming. In the long run, you will discover that this book's core material is independent of interface issues. There are three reasons for using terminal I/O. First, in Java and many other languages, a terminal user interface is easier to implement than a GUI, although in other languages, such as Visual BASIC, the opposite is true. Second, there are programming situations that require terminal I/O rather than a GUI, so familiarity with the techniques of terminal-oriented programming is important. Third, terminal-oriented programs are similar in structure to programs that process files of sequentially organized data, and what we learn here will be transferable to that setting.

2.4 Hello World

In conformance with a long and honorable tradition dating back to the early days of the language C, a textbook's first program often does nothing more than display the words "Hello World" in a terminal window. Actually, as you can see in Figure 2-2, we could not resist adding a few embellishments. In case you have not guessed, the imagery is the words "Hello World" rising like steam from the cup of hot Java.

FIGURE 2-2
Hello World

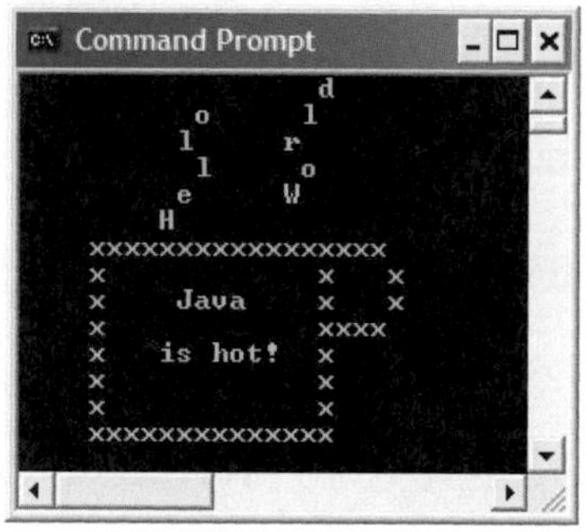

The Source Code

Just as a recipe is a sequence of instructions for a chef, a program is a sequence of instructions for a computer. And just as a recipe does nothing until executed by a chef, so a program does nothing until executed by a computer. With that in mind, the following is the bulk of the instructions, or *source code*, for our HelloWorld program:

```
System.out.println("                  d        ");
System.out.println("             o       l       ");
System.out.println("          l       r          ");
System.out.println("           l      o           ");
System.out.println("          e       W          ");
System.out.println("          H                  ");
System.out.println("      xxxxxxxxxxxxxxxx        ");
System.out.println("      x              x   x    ");
System.out.println("      x    Java      x   x    ");
System.out.println("      x            xxxx       ");
System.out.println("      x   is hot!  x          ");
System.out.println("      x            x          ");
System.out.println("      x            x          ");
System.out.println("      xxxxxxxxxxxxx           ");
```

The Explanation

In this code

■ `System.out` is the name of an object that knows how to display or print characters in a terminal window.

■ `println` is the name of the message being sent to the `System.out` object.

■ The strings enclosed in quotation marks contain the characters to be printed.

■ Semicolons (;) mark the end of each *statement* or sentence in the program.

As mentioned at the end of Chapter 1, an object-oriented program accomplishes its tasks by sending messages to objects. In this program, a `System.out` object responds to a `println` message by printing a string of characters in the terminal window. The string of characters that appears between the parentheses following the message is called a *parameter*. Some messages require several parameters, separated from each other by commas, whereas other messages have no parameters. The "ln" in the message `println` stands for "line" and indicates that the `System.out` object should advance to the beginning of the next line after printing a string.

Sending messages to objects always takes the form

```
<name of object>.<name of message>(<parameters>)
```

The period (.) between the object's name and the message's name is called a *method selector operator*. The period between the words `System` and `out` is not a method selector operator. For now you can just think of it as part of the object's name.

The Larger Framework

The program as presented so far is not complete. It must be embedded in a larger framework defined by several additional lines of code. No attempt will be made to explain this code until a later chapter, but, fortunately, it can be reused with little change from one program to the next. Following then is the complete program with the new lines shown in color:

```
// Example 2.1: Our first program

public class HelloWorld{

    public static void main(String [] args) {
        System.out.println("                    d            ");
        System.out.println("              o        l         ");
        System.out.println("            l       r            ");
        System.out.println("            l          o         ");
        System.out.println("              e       W          ");
        System.out.println("           H                     ");
        System.out.println("       xxxxxxxxxxxxxxxx           ");
        System.out.println("     x              x    x        ");
        System.out.println("     x     Java     x    x        ");
        System.out.println("     x                 xxxx       ");
        System.out.println("     x    is hot!   x             ");
        System.out.println("     x              x             ");
        System.out.println("     x              x             ");
        System.out.println("       xxxxxxxxxxxxx              ");
    }
}
```

To reuse the framework, replace `HelloWorld` with the name of another program:

```
public class <name of program> {
    public static void main(String [] args) {
        . . . put the source code here . . .
    }
}
```

In this text, we write program comments in green, reserved words in blue, and the rest of the program code in black. Program comments and reserved words will be explained in Chapter 3.

*E*XERCISE 2.4

1. Give a short definition of "program."

2. What is the effect of the message `println`?

3. Describe how to use the `System.out` object.

4. Write a sequence of statements to display your name, address, and phone number in the terminal window.

2.5 Edit, Compile, and Execute

In the preceding section, we presented the source code for our first program. Now we discuss how to enter it into a computer and run it. There are three steps:

1. *Edit*. In the first step, the programmer uses a word processor or editor to enter the source code into the computer and save it in a text file. The name of the text file must match the name of the program with the extension `.java` added, as in `HelloWorld.java`.

2. *Compile*. In the second step, the programmer invokes the Java language compiler to translate the source code into Java byte code. In this example, the compiler translates source code in the file `HelloWorld.java` to byte code in the file `HelloWorld.class`. The extension for a byte code file is always `.class`.

3. *Execute*. In the third step, the programmer instructs the JVM to load the byte code into memory and execute it. At this point the user and the program can interact, with the user entering data and the program displaying instructions and results.

Figure 2-3 illustrates the steps. The ovals represent the processes edit, compile, and execute. The names of the files `HelloWorld.java` and `HelloWorld.class` are shown between parallel lines.

FIGURE 2-3
Editing, compiling, and running a program

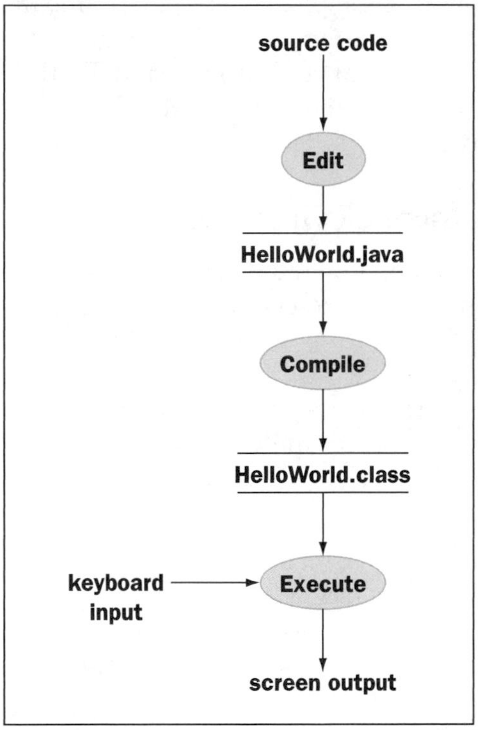

Development Environments

The details involved in editing, compiling, and running a program vary with the development environment being used. Some common development environments available to Java programmers include the following:

- UNIX or Linux using a standard text editor with command-line activation of the compiler and the JVM. UNIX is available on any Macintosh computer that runs MacOS X.

- Various versions of Microsoft Windows using Notepad for the editor with command-line activation of the compiler and the JVM from inside a command or DOS window. We call this the *DOS development environment.*

- Windows or MacOS using an *integrated development environment* (IDE) such as Metrowerks' Code Warrior, Microsoft's Visual J++, Borland's Jbuilder, or free educational-use-only IDEs such as BlueJ and JGrasp.

The first two options are free and may require you to download and install the Java software development kit (SDK) as described in Appendix A. The third option, an integrated development environment, may cost money, but it has the advantage of combining an editor, a Java compiler, a debugger, and a JVM in a manner intended to increase programmer productivity. IDEs take time to master, however, and they can obscure fundamental details of the edit, compile, and run sequence.

Because we cannot possibly discuss all of these environments simultaneously, we give our instructions in terms of the DOS development environment that has the most widespread use. Macintosh users can use the UNIX command prompt and TextEdit. The installation and use of some of the major alternatives are presented in our supplemental materials on the book's Web site (the URL is in Appendix A).

Preparing Your Development Environment

Before writing your first program, you must install a Java development environment on your computer. Guidelines for doing this are presented in Appendix A.

Step-by-Step Instructions

We are now ready to present step-by-step instructions for editing, compiling, and running the `HelloWorld` program. These instructions apply to users of the Windows XP system. After reading what follows, read the supplemental material for an explanation that matches the development environment on your computer.

Step 1. Use Windows Explorer to create the directory in which you intend to work (for instance, C:\Javafiles). Open a terminal window by selecting **Command Prompt** (or something similar) on the **Start/All Programs/Accessories** menu. In the terminal window, use the **cd** command to move to the working directory as illustrated in Figure 2-4.

FIGURE 2-4
Using the **cd** command to move to the working directory

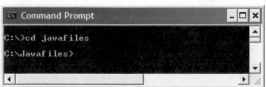

Step 2. Open the Notepad editor and create the file `HelloWorld.java` by typing the text as shown in Figure 2-5.

FIGURE 2-5
Activating Notepad to edit the program

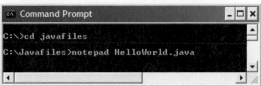

Once Notepad opens, type in the lines of code for the program. Figure 2-6 shows the Notepad window after the program has been entered.

FIGURE 2-6
The program as typed into Notepad

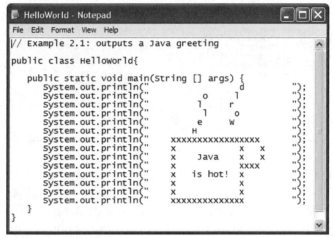

Step 3. Save the file and switch back to the terminal window. Compile the program by typing `javac HelloWorld.java`. The DOS prompt returns when the compilation is complete.

Step 4. Run the program by typing `java HelloWorld`. Figure 2-7 illustrates this step as well as the previous step.

FIGURE 2-7
Compiling and running the program

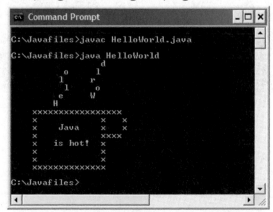

Compile-Time Errors

It is inevitable that we will make typographical errors when we edit programs, and the compiler will nearly always detect them. Mistakes detected by the compiler are called *syntax errors* or *compile-time errors*. To illustrate these, we modify the program so that it includes a syntax error. After reading this subsection, read the supplemental material that matches your development environment.

On line 6 of the program we misspell `println` as `prinrln`. Figure 2-8 shows the program with the error as it appears in Notepad.

FIGURE 2-8
The program with a compile-time error on line 6

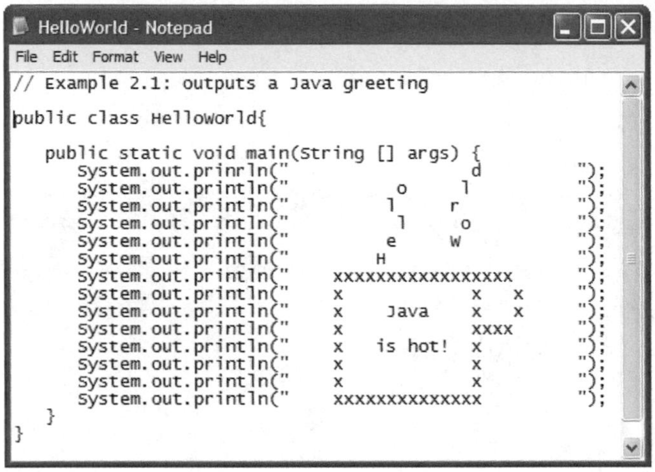

When the program is compiled, the compiler prints a list of errors in the terminal window as shown in Figure 2-9. The error message is not difficult to understand. It refers to line 6 of the source program and says that a symbol cannot be found. More specifically, the symbol for method `prinrln` within the class `java.io.PrintStream` cannot be found. In fact, the object `System.out` is a member of this class, and the program has attempted to send a message that the class does not recognize. A caret symbol (^) points to the location of the error in the code. Unfortunately, some error messages may be difficult to decipher, but at least they indicate where the compiler encountered text it could not translate into byte code.

FIGURE 2-9
The compiler's error message

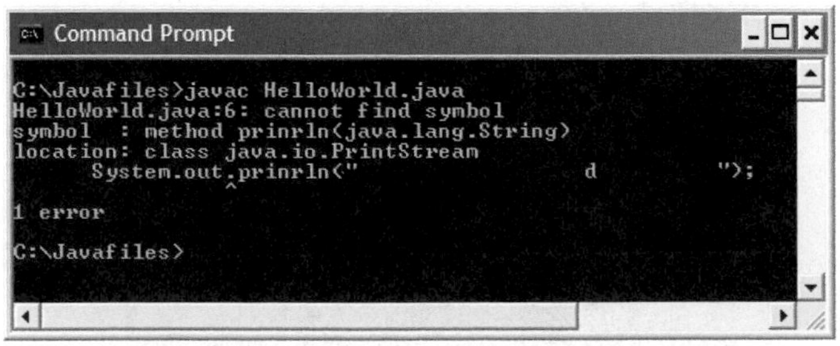

Readability

Programs typically have a long life and are usually maintained by many people other than their original authors. For this reason, if for no other, it is extremely important to write programs that are highly readable. The main factor affecting a program's readability is its layout. Indentation, the inclusion of blank lines and spaces, and other typographical considerations make the difference between an intelligible program and an incomprehensible mess. Interestingly, the compiler completely ignores a program's format, provided that there are no line breaks in the middle of words or quoted strings. Throughout the book, we attempt to format our programs in a pleasing and consistent manner, and you should strive to do the same. For your enjoyment the following example is a very unreadable but completely functional rendering of the `HelloWorld` program:

```
public class
      HelloWorld
{public static void main (String [] args) {System.out.println(
"                   d              ");System.out.println
        ("           o     l              ");
System.out.println("           l     r              ");
 System.   out
.println("           l        o             ")
; System.out.println("           e     W              ");System.out
.println("         H                      ");System.out.println
("     xxxxxxxxxxxxxxxx         ");System.out.println(
"    x           x   x       ")
;System.out.println("     x     Java    x     x       ");
      System.out.println("     x                  xxxx          ");
            System.out.println("     x    is hot!   x            ");
System.out.println("     x                 x             ");
      System.out.println("     x              x            ");
            System.out.println("       xxxxxxxxxxxxx                  "); } }
```

 Computer Ethics

INTRUSIVE HACKING

Hacking is a term whose use goes back to the early days of computing. In its original sense, a "hack" is a programmer who exhibits rare problem-solving ability and commands the respect of other programmers. The culture of hackers began in the late 1950s at the MIT computer science labs. These programmers, many of them students and later professionals and teachers in the field, regarded hacking as an accomplishment along the lines of Olympic gymnastics. These programmers even advocated a "hacker ethic," which stated, among other things, that hackers should respect the privacy of others and distribute their software for free. For a narrative of the early tradition of hacking, see Steven Levy, *Hackers: Heroes of the Computer Revolution* (Garden City, New York: Anchor Press/Doubleday, 1984).

Unfortunately, the practice of hacking has changed over the years, and the term has acquired darker connotations. Programmers who break into computer systems in an unauthorized way are called hackers, whether their intent is just to impress their peers or to cause actual harm. Students and professionals who lack a disciplined approach to programming are also called hackers. An excellent account of the most famous case of intrusive hacking can be found in Clifford Stoll, *The Cuckoo's Egg: Tracking Through the Maze of Computer Espionage* (New York: Doubleday, 1989).

EXERCISE 2.5

1. Name the three steps in writing and running a program.   *EDIT, COMPILE, EXECUTE*

2. What are compile-time errors?   *SYNTAX OR MISTAKES*

3. Find the compile-time errors in the following statements:
   a. System.out.println("Here is an error);   *2ND QUOTE*
   b. System.out.println("Here is another error";   *2ND PAREN*

4. Why is readability a desirable characteristic of a program?   *MAINTANENCE*

2.6 Temperature Conversion

We now present code for the temperature conversion program illustrated earlier in the chapter. To refresh your memory, we show the user interface again in Figure 2-10. This program is fundamentally more interesting than the `HelloWorld` program because it reads user inputs and performs computations. Despite its brevity and simplicity, the program demonstrates several important concepts.

FIGURE 2-10
The user interface for the temperature conversion program

The Source Code

The program's source code is

```java
// Example 2.2: inputs degrees Fahrenheit
// from the keyboard and outputs degrees Celsius

import java.util.Scanner;

public class Convert{

   public static void main(String [] args){
      Scanner reader = new Scanner(System.in);
      double fahrenheit;
      double celsius;

      System.out.print("Enter degrees Fahrenheit: ");
      fahrenheit = reader.nextDouble();

      celsius = (fahrenheit - 32.0) * 5.0 / 9.0;
```

```
        System.out.print("The equivalent in Celsius is ");
        System.out.println(celsius);
    }
}
```

The Explanation

Following is a line-by-line explanation of the most significant portions of the program.

```
import java.util.Scanner;
```

The program's first line of code is an *import statement*. The program must read inputs entered at the keyboard, and this functionality is provided by something called a scanner object. Such objects are instances of the class `Scanner`. In this line of code, we are telling the compiler where to find complete specifications for the class. The periods that appear in this statement are NOT method selectors.

```
Scanner reader = new Scanner(System.in);
```

In this statement, we instantiate or create a `Scanner` object. We have arbitrarily decided to call the object `reader`. The name suggests what the object does, so it is a good choice. As mentioned in Chapter 1, an object is always an instance of a class and must be created, or instantiated, before being used. In general, instantiation is done like this:

```
SomeClass someObject = new SomeClass(some parameters);
```

The code `System.in` names a variable in the `System` class that refers to the keyboard. This object is passed as a parameter to the code that instantiates the `Scanner` object in order to connect the two objects. Parameters are used to share information between objects.

```
double fahrenheit;
double celsius;
```

In these statements, we declare that the program will use two numeric variables called `fahrenheit` and `celsius`. A numeric *variable* names a location in RAM in which a number can be stored. The number is usually referred to as the variable's *value*. During the course of a program, a variable's value can change, but its name remains constant. The variables in this program are of type `double`, which means they will contain only floating-point numbers. It is customary, though not required, to begin variable names with a lowercase letter, thus `fahrenheit` rather than `Fahrenheit`. We are allowed to declare as many variables as we want in a program, and we can name them pretty much as we please. Restrictions are explained in Chapter 3.

```
System.out.print("Enter degrees Fahrenheit: ");
```

This statement is similar to those we saw in the `HelloWorld` program, but there is a minor difference. The message here is `print` rather than `println`. A `print` message positions the cursor immediately after the last character printed rather than moving it to the beginning of the next line.

```
fahrenheit = reader.nextDouble();
```

In this statement, the `reader` object responds to the message `nextDouble` by waiting for the user to type a number and then press Enter, at which point the `reader` object returns the number to the program. The number is then assigned to the variable `fahrenheit` by means of the *assignment operator* (=). The number entered by the user is now stored in the variable. Note that although the `nextDouble` message has no parameters, the parentheses are still required. As the user types at the keyboard, the characters are automatically echoed in the terminal window, but not until the user presses Enter does this input become available to the program.

```
celsius = (fahrenheit - 32.0) * 5.0 / 9.0;
```

In this statement, the expression to the right of the assignment operator (=) is evaluated, and then the resulting value is stored in memory at location `celsius`. Statements utilizing an assignment operator are called *assignment statements*. When the computer evaluates the expression, it uses the value stored in the variable `fahrenheit`. Notice that all the numbers (32.0, 5.0, and 9.0) contain a decimal point. In Java, some unexpected rules govern what happens when integers and floating-point numbers are mixed in an expression, so until we discuss the rules in Chapter 3, we will not mix integers and floating-point numbers. In the expression, as in algebra, the following symbols are used:

*   indicates the multiplication operator

/   indicates the division operator

-     indicates the subtraction operator

Of course, there is another common operator, namely + for *addition*. Notice the use of parentheses in the previous expression. In Java, as in algebra, multiplication and division are done before addition and subtraction unless parentheses are used to change the order of the computations; in other words, multiplication and division have higher precedence than addition and subtraction.

```
System.out.print("The equivalent in Celsius is ");
```

Here the `System.out` object prints the string "The equivalent in Celsius is ". The cursor is positioned after the last character in preparation for the next line of code.

```
System.out.println(celsius);
```

Here the `System.out` object prints the value of the variable `celsius`. The parameter for a `print` or `println` message can be a string in quotation marks, a variable, or even an expression. When a variable is used, the variable's value is printed, not its name. When an expression is used, the expression is evaluated before its value is printed.

Variables and Objects

Figure 2-11 depicts four of the variables and objects used in the program. All of these exist in the computer's memory while the program is running. The variables `fahrenheit` and `celsius` each hold a single floating-point number. At any given instant, the value stored in a variable depends on the effect of the preceding lines of code. The variables `reader` and `System.out` are very different from the variables `fahrenheit` and `celsius`. Instead of holding numbers, they hold references to objects. The arrows in the figure are intended to suggest this fact. During the course of the program, we think of the `reader` variable as being the name of an object. As the figure indicates, we know nothing about what lies inside the `reader` object (information hiding), but we do know that it responds to the message `nextDouble`. `System.out` also names an object, but one that is never declared in our programs. How this can be so is explained in a later chapter. The `System.out` object responds to the messages `print` and `println`. One of the really significant facts about object-oriented programming is that we can use objects without having the least idea of their internal workings. Likewise, we can design objects for others to use without telling them anything about the implementation details.

FIGURE 2-11
Variables and objects used in the conversion program

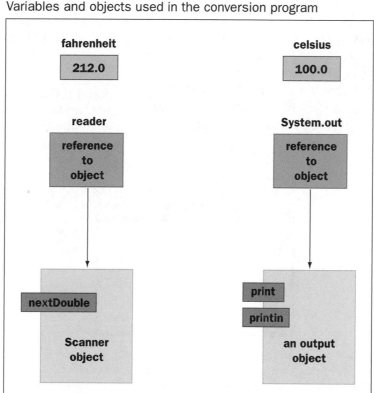

EXERCISE 2.6

1. What is a variable in a program and how is it used? *NAME OF A MEMORY LOCATION (RAM) WHERE*

2. Describe the role of the assignment (=) operator in a program. *TO STORE VALUES IN VARS*

3. What is a `Scanner` object? *JAVA OBJECT THAT READS FROM KEYBOARD*

4. Explain the difference between a variable of type `double` and a variable of type `Scanner`.

5. Describe the difference between `print` and `println`, and give an appropriate example of the use of each.

2.7 Graphics and GUIs: Windows and Panels

Java comes with a large array of classes that support graphics and GUI programming. In this section, we examine how to set up and manipulate an application window, explore the use of colors, and lay out regions within the window.

A Simple Application Window

Graphics and GUI programs in Java can run either as standalone applications or as applets. We discuss applets, which run in a Web browser, in Chapter 8. A standalone GUI application runs in a window. The window for our first GUI application is shown in Figure 2-12. The visual appearance or "look and feel" of a window might vary from computer to computer, but several features are constant.

Extra Challenge

This is our first end-of-chapter section on graphics and GUIs. In these sections, we give you an opportunity to explore the concepts and programming techniques required to develop modern graphics applications and GUIs. None of this material is required for the other chapters of the book. But if you elect to go through it, you will learn how to write programs that display colors and geometric shapes, allow the user to interact by manipulating a mouse, animate shapes and images, and employ various "widgets" such as command buttons, text fields, sliders, and drop-down menus to accomplish useful tasks.

FIGURE 2-12
A GUI program with an empty window

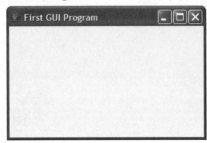

The window has a title bar that displays the message "First GUI Program." The user can drag the window to another position on the desktop by moving the mouse cursor to the title bar and then clicking and dragging.

The title bar contains some controls that allow the user to minimize the window (moving it to the desktop tray or dock), zoom it to full screen size, or close it (which usually quits the application).

The window has an initial width and height that the user can modify by selecting its lower-right corner and dragging appropriately.

Other than exhibiting the basic features and common behavior of all GUI applications, our first GUI application displays no other GUI components and does nothing. Here is the code for the application, followed by an explanation.

```java
// Example 2.3: an empty frame

import javax.swing.*;        // Access JFrame

public class GUIWindow{

    public static void main(String[] args){
        JFrame theGUI = new JFrame();
        theGUI.setTitle("First GUI Program");
        theGUI.setSize(300, 200);
        theGUI.setDefaultCloseOperation(JFrame.EXIT_ON_CLOSE);
        theGUI.setVisible(true);
    }
}
```

The code for application windows in Java is located in the class `JFrame`, which is imported from the package `javax.swing`. The `main` method simply creates an instance of `JFrame` and sends it messages to set up and display the window. Unlike a terminal I/O application, the program does not quit when the end of the `main` method is reached but stays alive until the user selects the window's close box.

A `JFrame` object responds to many messages, among them messages to set its title to a given string, set its initial size to a width and height in pixels, set the operation that will be performed when it closes (exits the application), and set its visibility (true/visible or false/invisible). A set of commonly used `JFrame` methods is listed in Table 2-1.

TABLE 2-1
Some commonly used `JFrame` methods

JFRAME METHOD	WHAT IT DOES
`Container getContentPane()`	Returns the frame's container to which components can be added
`void setResizable(boolean b)`	If b is `false`, the user cannot resize the window; if b is `true`, the user can resize the window. The default is that the window is resizable.
`void setDefaultCloseIndicator(int i)`	Sets the operation to be performed when the user closes the frame
`void setSize(int width, int height)`	Sets the size of the frame to the width and height in pixels
`void setTitle(String title)`	Displays the title in the frame's title bar
`void setVisible(boolean b)`	Displays the frame if b is `true` or hides it if b is `false`

Panels and Colors

An application window is really just an empty container that we can fill with other objects. One such object is called a *panel*. A panel is a flat, rectangular area suitable for displaying other objects such as geometric shapes and images. Windows are often organized into multiple panels or *panes*, each of which contains related objects such as images and widgets. Panels themselves have fairly simple features, including a width, height, and background color. The class `JPanel`, also in `javax.swing`, represents panels in Java.

As we mentioned in Chapter 1, colors in most computer systems use the RGB scheme, which encodes 16,777,216 distinct colors. The `Color` class, which appears in the package `java.awt`, can be used to create any of these color values, as follows:

```
Color aColor = new Color(redValue, greenValue, blueValue)
```

where the red, green, and blue values are integers ranging from 0 to 255. Recall that 255 indicates the maximum intensity of a color component, whereas 0 indicates the absence of that component. Thus, the code `new Color(0, 0, 0)` would create an object representing the color black. For convenience, the `Color` class also includes constants for several commonly used colors, which are listed with their RGB values in Table 2-2.

TABLE 2-2
Some `Color` constants

COLOR CONSTANT	RGB VALUE
Color.red	new Color(255, 0, 0)
Color.green	new Color(0, 255, 0)
Color.blue	new Color(0, 0, 255)
Color.yellow	new Color(255, 255, 0)
Color.cyan	new Color(0, 255, 255)
Color.magenta	new Color(255, 0, 255)
Color.orange	new Color(255, 200, 0)
Color.pink	new Color(255, 175, 175)
Color.black	new Color(0, 0, 0)
Color.white	new Color(255, 255, 255)
Color.gray	new Color(128, 128, 128)
Color.lightGray	new Color(192, 192, 192)
Color.darkGray	new Color(64, 64, 64)

Our next example program creates a panel, sets its background color to pink, and adds the panel to the application window.

```
// Example 2.4: a frame with an empty, pink panel

import javax.swing.*;      // For JFrame and JPanel
import java.awt.*;         // For Color and Container

public class GUIWindow{

    public static void main(String[] args){
        JFrame theGUI = new JFrame();
        theGUI.setTitle("Second GUI Program");
        theGUI.setSize(300, 200);
        theGUI.setDefaultCloseOperation(JFrame.EXIT_ON_CLOSE);
        JPanel panel = new JPanel();
        panel.setBackground(Color.pink);
        Container pane = theGUI.getContentPane();
        pane.add(panel);
        theGUI.setVisible(true);
    }
}
```

When this program is run, its window looks just like that of the first program, except that the area below the title bar is pink. Note the procedure for adding the panel to the window. We must first obtain the window's container object by running the method `getContentPane()`. We then add the panel to this container.

Layout Managers and Multiple Panels

The previous example displayed a single panel in an application window. When we have more than one panel or other objects to display in a window, we have to be concerned about how they are organized or laid out. In Java, each container object, such as a frame or a panel, uses an object called a *layout manager* to accomplish this. Thus, when a program adds an object to a container, the container's layout manager actually influences its placement. Each type of container has a default layout manager, which we can reset to a different type of layout manager if the default does not suit our needs.

The default layout manager for frames is an instance of the class `BorderLayout`. A border layout allows us to arrange up to five objects in positions that correspond to the directions north (top), east (right), south (bottom), west (left), and center. If we add fewer than five objects, the layout manager stretches some of them to fill the unoccupied areas. To see what these areas look like when they are all occupied, we modify our second program to add five colored panels to the window. The north and south panels are red, the east and west panels are blue, and the center panel is white. The result is displayed in Figure 2-13.

```java
// Example 2.5: a frame with 5 colored panels
// that show the border layout

import javax.swing.*;      // For JFrame and JPanel
import java.awt.*;         // For Color and Container

public class GUIWindow{

    public static void main(String[] args){
        JFrame theGUI = new JFrame();
        theGUI.setTitle("Third GUI Program");
        theGUI.setSize(300, 200);
        theGUI.setDefaultCloseOperation(JFrame.EXIT_ON_CLOSE);
        JPanel northPanel = new JPanel();
        northPanel.setBackground(Color.red);
        JPanel eastPanel = new JPanel();
        eastPanel.setBackground(Color.blue);
        JPanel southPanel = new JPanel();
        southPanel.setBackground(Color.red);
        JPanel westPanel = new JPanel();
        westPanel.setBackground(Color.blue);
        JPanel centerPanel = new JPanel();
        centerPanel.setBackground(Color.white);
        Container pane = theGUI.getContentPane();
        pane.add(northPanel, BorderLayout.NORTH);
        pane.add(eastPanel, BorderLayout.EAST);
        pane.add(southPanel, BorderLayout.SOUTH);
        pane.add(westPanel, BorderLayout.WEST);
        pane.add(centerPanel, BorderLayout.CENTER);
        theGUI.setVisible(true);
    }
}
```

FIGURE 2-13
A border layout with five panels

Note the use of the BorderLayout constants to specify the area of the container to which an object is added. When the constant is omitted, as it was in our previous program, a border layout places the object in the center area.

Suppose we want to organize the colored areas in a grid to make a checkerboard. A border layout will not do. Fortunately, the package `java.awt` includes the class `GridLayout` for this purpose. When it's created, a grid layout is given a number of rows and columns. The areas of the cells in the resulting grid are the same size. The objects are placed in cells from left to right, starting with the first row and moving down. Our final program example resets the container's layout to a 2-by-2 grid layout and then places four panels colored white, black, gray, and white in it. The result is shown in Figure 2-14.

```java
// Example 2.6: a frame with a 2 by 2 grid of colored panels

import javax.swing.*;      // For JFrame and JPanel
import java.awt.*;         // For Color, Container, and GridLayout

public class GUIWindow{

    public static void main(String[] args){
        JFrame theGUI = new JFrame();
        theGUI.setTitle("Fourth GUI Program");
        theGUI.setSize(300, 200);
        theGUI.setDefaultCloseOperation(JFrame.EXIT_ON_CLOSE);
        JPanel panel1 = new JPanel();
        panel1.setBackground(Color.white);
        JPanel panel2 = new JPanel();
        panel2.setBackground(Color.black);
        JPanel panel3 = new JPanel();
        panel3.setBackground(Color.gray);
        JPanel panel4 = new JPanel();
        panel4.setBackground(Color.white);
        Container pane = theGUI.getContentPane();
        pane.setLayout(new GridLayout(2, 2));
        pane.add(panel1);
        pane.add(panel2);
        pane.add(panel3);
        pane.add(panel4);
        theGUI.setVisible(true);
    }
}
```

FIGURE 2-14

A 2-by-2 grid layout with four panels

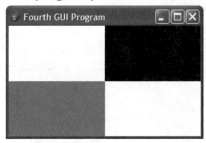

EXERCISE 2.7

1. Write the integer values of red, green, and blue for the following RGB colors:
   a. white
   b. black
   c. highest intensity blue
   d. medium gray

2. Describe the roles and responsibilities of a frame, a panel, and a layout manager in a GUI application.

3. Where are panels displayed when a border layout is used to control their placement in a window?

4. Write a code segment that would be used to set the layout for adding panels to a 5-by-5 grid in a window. You may assume that the panel's content pane is named pane.

SUMMARY

In this chapter, you learned:

■ Java is the fastest growing programming language in the world. It is secure, robust, and portable. It is also similar to C++, the world's most popular programming language.

■ The Java compiler translates Java into a pseudomachine language called Java byte code. Byte code can be run on any computer that has a Java virtual machine installed. The Java virtual machine (JVM) is a program that behaves like a computer—an interpreter.

■ Java programs include variables, arithmetic expressions, statements, objects, messages, and methods.

■ Three basic steps in the coding process are editing, compiling, and running a program using a Java development environment. Programmers should pay attention to a program's format to ensure readability.

■ Java programs accomplish many tasks by sending messages to objects. Examples are sending text to the terminal window for output and receiving input data from the keyboard.

■ There are several user interface styles, among them terminal based and graphical based.

VOCABULARY *Review*

Define the following terms:

Applet	Hacking	Parameter
Assignment operator	Integrated development	Source code
Byte code	environment (IDE)	Statement
DOS development	Java virtual machine (JVM)	Terminal I/O interface
environment	Just-in-time compilation (JIT)	Variable
Graphical user interface (GUI)		

REVIEW *Questions*

WRITTEN QUESTIONS

Write a brief answer to each of the following questions.

1. List three reasons why Java is an important programming language.

2. What is byte code?

3. What is the JVM?

4. List two objects that are used for terminal input and output in Java programs.

5. Give examples of two compile-time errors.

6. What steps must be followed to run a Java program?

7. What is the purpose of an import statement in a Java program?

FILL IN THE BLANK

Complete the following sentences by writing the correct word or words in the blanks provided.

1. Two user interface styles are _____ and _____.

2. The message _____ is used to output data to the terminal window.

3. The message _____ is used to input a number from the keyboard.

4. A(n) _____ names a place where data can be stored in a Java program.

5. A(n) _____ stores the value of the expression in the variable.

6. Programs manipulate objects by sending them _____.

PROJECTS

Beginning with this chapter, we conclude each chapter with a set of programming problems and activities. We want to emphasize that programming is not just coding. Thus, a complete solution to each exercise in this section would include not just a set of .java and .class files for the program but also a report that covers the analysis, design, and results of testing the program. Ideally, you would do analysis and design before coding, and perhaps turn in this work for review before coding proceeds. How this is done depends on the size of the class and the time available to the instructor. In any case, when you see the words "write a program that . . .", you should at least pause to reflect on the nature of the problem before coding the solution. For example, your analysis might consist of a description of how the program would be used.

PROJECT 2-1

Write a program that displays your name, address, and telephone number.

PROJECT 2-2

A yield sign encloses the word YIELD within a triangle. Write a program that displays a yield sign. (Use stars to represent the sides of the triangle.)

PROJECT 2-3

Write a program that takes as input a number of kilometers and prints the corresponding number of nautical miles. You may rely on the following items of information:

■ A kilometer represents 1/10,000 of the distance between the North Pole and the equator.

■ There are 90 degrees, containing 60 minutes of arc each, between the North Pole and the equator.

■ A nautical mile is 1 minute of an arc.

PROJECT 2-4

Write a program that calculates and prints the number of minutes in a year.

PROJECT 2-5

An object's momentum is its mass multiplied by its velocity. Write a program that expects an object's mass (in kilograms) and velocity (in meters per second) as inputs and prints its momentum.

PROJECT 2-6

National flags are displayed on various Web sites, such as http://flagspot.net/flags/. The flags of France, Mauritius, and Bulgaria consist of flat, colored areas. Write separate programs that display these flags.

PROJECT 2-7

Write a program that displays a 3-by-3 grid of black and white rectangles. The rectangles should be positioned so that no two rectangles of the same color are adjacent to each other.

CRITICAL *Thinking*

You have an idea for a program that will help the local pizza shop handle takeout orders. Your friend suggests an interview with the shop's owner to discuss her user requirements before you get started on the program. Explain why this is a good suggestion, and list the questions you would ask the owner to help you determine the user requirements.

Syntax, Errors, and Debugging

OBJECTIVES

Upon completion of this chapter, you should be able to:

- Construct and use numeric and string literals.

- Name and use variables and constants.

- Create arithmetic expressions.

- Understand the precedence of different arithmetic operators.

- Concatenate two strings or a number and a string.

- Know how and when to use comments in a program.

- Tell the difference between syntax errors, run-time errors, and logic errors.

- Insert output statements to debug a program.

- Understand the difference between Cartesian coordinates and screen coordinates.

- Work with color and text properties.

Estimated Time: 4.0 hours

VOCABULARY

Arithmetic expression

Comments

Coordinate system

Exception

Graphics context

Literal

Logic error

Origin

Package

Pseudocode

Reserved words

Run-time error

Screen coordinate system

Semantics

Syntax

Virus

To use a programming language, one must become familiar with its vocabulary and the rules for forming grammatically correct statements. You must also know how to construct meaningful statements and statements that express the programmer's intent. Errors of form, meaning, and intent are possible, so finally one must know how to detect these errors and correct them. This chapter discusses the basic elements of the Java language in detail and explores how to find and correct errors in programs.

3.1 Language Elements

Before writing code in any programming language, we need to be aware of some basic language elements. Every natural language, such as English, Japanese, and German, has its own vocabulary, syntax, and semantics. Programming languages also have these three elements.

Vocabulary is the set of all of the words and symbols in the language. Table 3-1 illustrates some examples taken from Java.

TABLE 3-1
Some Java vocabulary

TYPE OF ELEMENT	EXAMPLES
arithmetic operators	`+` `–` `*` `/`
assignment operator	`=`
numeric literals	`5.73` `9`
programmer defined variable names	`fahrenheit celsius`

Syntax consists of the rules for combining words into sentences, or *statements*, as they are more usually called in programming languages. Following are two typical syntax rules in Java:

1. In an expression, the arithmetic operators for multiply and divide must not be adjacent. Thus,

    `(f - 32) * / 9`

    is invalid.

2. In an expression, left and right parentheses must occur in matching pairs. Thus,

    `)f - 32( * 5 / 9`

    and

    `f - 32) * 5 / 9`

    are both invalid.

    Semantics define the rules for interpreting the meaning of statements. For example, the expression

    `(f - 32.0) * 5.0 / 9.0`

means "go into the parentheses first, subtract `32.0` from the variable quantity indicated by `f`, then multiply the result by `5.0`, and finally divide the whole thing by `9.0`."

Programming versus Natural Languages

Despite their similarities, programming languages and natural languages differ in three important ways: size, rigidity, and literalness.

Size

Programming languages have small vocabularies and simple syntax and semantics compared to natural languages. Thus, their basic elements are not hard to learn.

Rigidity

In a programming language one must get the syntax absolutely correct, whereas a grammatically incorrect English sentence is usually comprehensible. This strict requirement of correctness often makes writing programs difficult for beginners, though no more difficult than writing grammatically correct sentences in English or any other natural language.

Literalness

When we give a friend instructions in English, we can be a little vague, relying on the friend to fill in the details. In a programming language, we must be exhaustively thorough. Computers follow instructions in a very literal manner. They do exactly what they are told—no more and no less. When people blame problems on computer errors, they should more accurately blame sloppy programming. This last difference is the one that makes programming difficult even for experienced programmers.

Although programming languages are simpler than human languages, the task of writing programs is challenging. It is difficult to express complex ideas using the limited syntax and semantics of a programming language.

EXERCISE 3.1

1. What is the vocabulary of a language? Give an example of an item in the vocabulary of Java.

2. Give an example of a syntax rule in Java.

3. What does the expression (x + y) * z mean?

4. Describe two differences between programming languages and natural languages.

3.2 Basic Java Syntax and Semantics

Having seen several Java programs in Chapter 2, we are ready for a more formal presentation of the language's basic elements. Some points have already been touched on in Chapter 2, but others are new.

Data Types

In Chapter 1, we showed that many types of information can be represented in computer memory as patterns of 0s and 1s, and as far as we know, so can information of every type. In this book, however, we are less ambitious and restrict our attention to just a few types of data. These fall into two main categories. The first category consists of what Java calls *primitive data types* and includes numbers (both integer and floating-point), characters (such as *A*, *B*, and *C*), and Booleans (restricted to the logical values `true` and `false`). The second category consists of objects, for instance, scanners. Strings are also in this second category.

Syntax

Java's syntax for manipulating primitive data types differs distinctly from the syntax for manipulating objects. Primitive data types are combined in expressions involving operators, such as addition and multiplication. Objects, on the other hand, are sent messages. In addition, objects must be instantiated before use, and there is no comparable requirement for primitive data types. For more information about data types, see Appendix B.

Actually, this concise picture is confused slightly by strings, which on the one hand are objects and are sent messages, but on the other hand do not need to be instantiated and can be combined using something called the *concatenation operator*.

Numbers

We close this subsection with a few details concerning the primitive data types for representing numbers, or *numeric data types*, as they are called for short. Java includes six numeric data types, but we restrict ourselves to just two. These are int (for integer) and double (for floating-point numbers—numbers with decimals). The range of values available with these two data types is shown in Table 3-2.

TABLE 3-2
Some Java numeric data types

TYPE	STORAGE REQUIREMENTS	RANGE
int	4 bytes	–2,147,483,648 to 2,147,483,647
double	8 bytes	–1.79769313486231570E+308 to 1.79769313486231570E+308

The other numeric data types are *short* (2 bytes for small integers), *long* (4 bytes for large integers), *byte*, and *float* (4 bytes for smaller, less precise floating-point numbers). The data types for Booleans and characters will be discussed in Chapters 6 and 7, respectively. A complete table of the storage requirements and range of each type appears in Appendix B.

Numeric calculations are a central part of most, though not all, programs, so we will become very familiar with the numeric data types. Programs that manipulate numeric data types often share a common format: input numeric data, perform calculations, output numeric results. The temperature conversion program in Chapter 2 adhered to this format.

EXERCISE 3.2

1. What is the difference between double and int data types?

2. How does the syntax for manipulating numeric data types and objects differ?

Literals

Literals are items in a program whose values do not change. They are restricted to the primitive data types and strings. Examples from the temperature conversion program in Chapter 2 included the numbers 5.0 and 9.0 and the string "Enter degrees Fahrenheit: ". Table 3-3 gives other examples of numeric literals (note that numeric literals never contain commas).

TABLE 3-3
Examples of numeric literals

EXAMPLE	DATA TYPE
51	an integer
–31444843	a negative integer
3.14	a floating-point number (double)
5.301E5	a floating-point number equivalent to $5.301 * 10^5$, or 530,100
5.301E–5	a floating-point number equivalent to $5.301 * 10^{-5}$, or 0.00005301 (double)

The last two examples in Table 3-3 are written in what is called *exponential* or *scientific notation* and are expressed as a decimal number followed by a power of 10. The letter *E* can be written in upper- or lowercase.

EXERCISE 3.2 Continued

3. Convert the following floating-point numbers to exponential notation:

  a. 23.5

  b. 0.046

4. Convert the following numbers from exponential notation to floating-point notation:

  a. 32.21E4

  b. 55.6E–3

5. Give two examples of string literals.

Variables and Their Declarations

A variable is an item whose value can change during the execution of a program. A variable can be thought of as a named location or cell in the computer's memory. Changing the value of a variable is equivalent to replacing the value that was in the cell with another value (Figure 3-1). For instance, at one point in a program we might set the value of the variable `fahrenheit` to 78.5. Later in the program, we could set the variable to another value such as –23.7. When we do this, the new value replaces the old one.

FIGURE 3-1
Changing the value of a variable

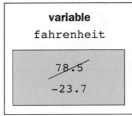

Although the value of a variable can change, the type of data it contains cannot; in other words, during the course of a program a specific variable can hold only one type of data. For instance, if it initially holds an integer, then it can never hold a floating-point number, and if it initially holds a reference to a pen, it can never hold a reference to a scanner.

Declarations

Before using a variable for the first time, the program must declare its type. This is done in a *variable declaration statement*, as illustrated in the following code:

```
int age;
double celsius;
String name;
Scanner reader;
```

The type appears on the left and the variable's name on the right. Frequently, we will speak of a *variable's type*, meaning the type indicator that appears on the left. Thus, we will say that celsius is a double.

It is permitted to declare several variables in a single declaration and simultaneously to assign them initial values. For instance, the following code segment initializes the variables z, q, pi, name, and reader:

```
int x, y, z = 7;
double p, q = 1.41, pi = 3.14, t;
String name = "Bill Jones";
Scanner reader = new Scanner(System.in);
```

The last statement declares the object variable reader, instantiates or creates a Scanner object that is attached to the keyboard input stream, System.in, and finally assigns the object to the variable. Instantiation takes the form

```
new <name of class>(<zero or more parameters>)
```

Object instantiation will be explained in detail in Chapter 5.

Constants

When initializing a variable, we occasionally want to specify that its value cannot change thereafter. This seems somewhat contradictory but is useful, as we shall see later. The next example illustrates how to do this:

```
final double SALES_TAX_RATE = .0785;
```

The keyword here is final, and a variable declared in this way is called a *constant*. It is customary to write the names of constants in uppercase. Any attempt to change the value of a constant after it is initialized is flagged by the compiler as an error.

EXERCISE 3.2 Continued

6. Why is a variable called a variable?

7. Return to the programs in Chapter 2 and find an example of each of the different types of variables. Which of the types listed in this subsection are not included?

EXERCISE 3.2 Continued

8. Declare a floating-point variable called `payRate` and simultaneously initialize it to $35.67.

9. Declare three integer variables (a, b, c) in a single declaration and simultaneously initialize b to 4.

10. Give two examples of data that cannot be stored in a variable of type `int`.

11. There are approximately 2.2 pounds in a kilogram. Name and declare a constant to represent this value.

Assignment Statements

An assignment statement has the following form:

```
<variable> = <expression>;
```

where the value of the expression on the right is assigned to the variable on the left. For instance,

```
double celsius, fahrenheit;
String name;
Scanner reader;
. . .
fahrenheit = reader.nextDouble();
celsius = (fahrenheit - 32.0) * 5.0 / 9.0;
name = "Bill Smith";
reader = new Scanner(System.in);
```

Arithmetic Expressions

An *arithmetic expression* consists of operands and operators combined in a manner familiar from algebra. The usual rules apply:

- Multiplication and division are evaluated before addition and subtraction; that is, multiplication and division have higher precedence than addition and subtraction.

- Operators of equal precedence are evaluated from left to right.

- Parentheses can be used to change the order of evaluation.

Unlike in algebra, multiplication must be indicated explicitly: thus, a * b cannot be written as ab. Binary operators are placed between their operands (a * b, for example), whereas unary operators are placed before their operands (-a, for example). Table 3-4 shows several operands from the conversion program in Chapter 2, and Table 3-5 shows some common operators and their precedence.

TABLE 3-4
Examples of operands

TYPE	EXAMPLE
Literals	32.0 5.0 9.0
Variables	fahrenheit celsius
Parenthesized expressions	(fahrenheit - 32.0)

TABLE 3-5
Common operators and their precedence

OPERATOR	SYMBOL	PRECEDENCE (FROM HIGHEST TO LOWEST)	ASSOCIATION
Grouping	( )	1	Not applicable
Method selector	.	2	Left to right
Unary plus	+	3	Not applicable
Unary minus	−	3	Not applicable
Instantiation	new	3	Right to left
Cast	(double) (int)	3	Right to left
Multiplication	*	4	Left to right
Division	/	4	Left to right
Remainder or modulus	%	4	Left to right
Addition	+	5	Left to right
Subtraction	−	5	Left to right
Assignment	=	10	Right to left

Division

Several points concerning operators need explanation. The semantics of division are different for integer and floating-point operands. Thus,

```
5.0 / 2.0   yields   2.5
5 / 2 yields 2 (a quotient in which the fractional portion of the answer is
   simply dropped)
```

Modulus

The operator % yields the remainder obtained when one number is divided by another. Thus,

```
9 % 5 yields 4
9.3 % 5.1 yields 4.2
```

Precedence

When evaluating an expression, Java applies operators of higher precedence before those of lower precedence, unless overridden by parentheses. The highest precedence is 1.

```
3 + 5 * 3   yields 18
-3 + 5 * 3   yields 12
```

```
+3 + 5 * 3   yields 18 (use of unary + is uncommon)
3 + 5 * -3`  yields -12
3 + 5 * +3   yields 18 (use of unary + is uncommon)
(3 + 5) * 3  yields 24
3 + 5 % 3    yields 5
(3 + 5) % 3  yields 2
```

Association

The column labeled "Association" in Table 3-5 indicates the order in which to perform operations of equal precedence. Thus,

```
18 - 3 - 4   yields 11
18 / 3 * 4   yields 24
18 % 3 * 4   yields 0
a = b = 7;   assigns 7 to b and then b to a
```

More Examples

Some more examples of expressions and their values are shown in Table 3-6. In this table, we see the application of two fairly obvious rules governing the use of parentheses:

1. Parentheses must occur in matching pairs.

2. Parenthetical expressions may be nested but must not overlap.

TABLE 3-6
Examples of expressions and their values

EXPRESSION	SAME AS	VALUE
3 + 4 − 5	7 − 5	2
3 + (4 − 5)	3 + (−1)	2
3 + 4 * 5	3 + 20	23
(3 + 4) * 5	7 * 5	35
8 / 2 + 6	4 + 6	10
8 / (2 + 6)	8 / 8	1
10 − 3 − 4 − 1	7 − 4 − 1	2
10 − (3 − 4 − 1)	10 − (−2)	12
(15 + 9) / (3 + 1)	24 / 4	6
15 + 9 / 3 + 1	15 + 3 + 1	19
(15 + 9) / ((3 + 1) * 2)	24 / (4 * 2) 24 / 8	3
(15 + 9) / (3 + 1) * 2	24 / 4 * 2 6 * 2	12

EXERCISE 3.2 Continued

12. Assume that the integer variable x is 5 and the integer variable y is 10. Give the values of the following expressions:

    a. x + y * 2

    b. x – y + 2

    c. (x + y) * 2

    d. y % x

13. Find the syntax errors in the following expressions:

    a. a – * b + c

    b. – (a + b) * c)

    c. ()

Maximum, Minimum, and Arithmetic Overflow

Numeric data types in any programming language support a finite range of values. For example, values of type `int` in Java range from a minimum of –2,147,483,648 to a maximum of 2,147,483,647. Instead of having to remember these numbers, the programmer can refer to them with the constants `Integer.MIN_VALUE` and `Integer.MAX_VALUE`, respectively. The same constants are included in the `Double` class for the bounds of double values.

It is natural to ask what would happen if a program tried to add 1 to the maximum integer value. This would result in a condition known as arithmetic overflow. Subtracting 1 from the minimum value would produce the same error. Programs written in some languages would halt with a run-time error, whereas others would continue after ruining part of the computer's operating system. The JVM simply inverts the sign of the number and allows the program to continue. Thus, adding 1 to `Integer.MAX_VALUE` would produce `Integer.MIN_VALUE`. So, if you see large negative integers in your program's output, you might have this type of error.

Mixed-Mode Arithmetic

When working with a handheld calculator, we do not give much thought to the fact that we intermix integers and floating-point numbers. This is called *mixed-mode arithmetic.* For instance, if a circle has radius 3, we compute the area as follows:

```
3.14 * 3 * 3
```

In Java, when there is a binary operation on operands of different numeric types, the less inclusive type (`int`) is temporarily and automatically converted to the more inclusive type (`double`) before the operation is performed. Thus, in

```
double d;
d = 5.0 / 2;
```

the value of d is computed as `5.0/2.0`, yielding `2.5`. However, problems can arise when using mixed-mode arithmetic. For instance

```
3 / 2 * 5.0 yields   1 * 5.0   yields   5.0
```

whereas

```
3 / 2.0 * 5 yields   1.5 * 5   yields   7.5
```

Mixed-mode assignments are also allowed, provided the variable on the left is of a more inclusive type than the expression on the right. Otherwise, a syntax error occurs, as shown in the following code segment:

```
double d;
int i;
i = 45;   ← OK, because we assign an int to an int.
d = i;    ← OK, because d is more inclusive than i. The value 45.0 is stored in d.
i = d;    ← Syntax error because i is less inclusive than d.
```

EXERCISE 3.2 Continued

14. Assume that x is 4.5 and y is 2. Write the values of the following expressions:

   a. x / y

   b. y / x

   c. x % y

15. Assume that x and y are of type `double` and z is of type `int`. For each of the following assignment statements, state which are valid and which produce syntax errors:

   a. x = z

   b. x = y * z

   c. z = x + y

Casting to `int` and `double`

The difficulties associated with mixed-mode arithmetic can be circumvented using a technique called *casting*, which allows one data type to be explicitly converted to another. For instance, consider the following example:

```
int i;
double d;

i = (int)3.14;        ← i equals 3, truncation toward 0
d = (double)5 / 4;    ← d equals 1.25
```

The cast operator, either `(int)` or `(double)`, appears immediately before the expression it is supposed to convert. The `(int)` cast simply throws away the digits after the decimal point, which has the effect of truncation toward 0.

Precedence

The cast operator has high precedence (see Table 3-5) and must be used with care, as illustrated in the following code:

```
double x, y;

x = (double)5 / 4;      ← x equals 5.0 / 4 equals 1.25
y = (double)(5 / 4);    ← y equals (double)(1) equals 1.0
```

Rounding

The cast operator is useful for rounding floating-point numbers to the nearest integer:

```
int m, n;
double x, y;

x = . . . ;              ← some positive value is assigned to x
m = (int)(x + 0.5);

y = - . . .;             ← some negative value is assigned to y
n = (int)(x - 0.5);
```

Other numeric casts such as (`char`) and (`float`) are discussed in Appendix B.

EXERCISE 3.2 Continued

16. Assume that x is of type `double` and y is of type `int`. Also assume that x is 4.5 and y is 2. Write the values of the following expressions:

a. (int) x * y

b. (int) (x * y)

17. Assume that x is of type `double` and y is of type `int`. Write a statement that assigns the value contained in x to y after rounding this value to the nearest whole number.

String Expressions and Methods

Strings are used in programs in a variety of ways. As already seen, they can be used as literals or assigned to variables. Now we see that they can be combined in expressions using the concatenation operator, and they also can be sent messages.

Simple Concatenation

The concatenation operator uses the plus symbol (+). The following is an example:

```
String firstName,                                  // declare four string
      lastName,                                     // variables
      fullName,
      lastThenFirst;

firstName = "Bill";                                // initialize firstName
lastName = "Smith";                                // initialize lastName

fullName = firstName + " " + lastName;             // yields "Bill Smith"
lastThenFirst = lastName + ", " + firstName        // yields "Smith, Bill"
```

Concatenating Strings and Numbers

Strings also can be concatenated to numbers. When this occurs, the number is automatically converted to a string before the concatenation operator is applied:

```
String message;
int x = 20, y = 35;
```

```
message = "Bill sold " + x + " and Sylvia sold " + y + " subscriptions.";
// yields "Bill sold 20 and Sylvia sold 35 subscriptions."
```

Precedence of Concatenation

The concatenation operator has the same precedence as addition, which can lead to unexpected results:

```
"number " + 3 + 4        → "number 3" + 4     → "number 34"
"number " + (3 + 4)      → "number " + 7      → "number 7"
"number " + 3 * 4        → "number " + 12     → "number 12"
3 + 4 + "number"         → 7 + "number"       → "7 number"
```

Escape Character

String literals are delimited by quotation marks ("..."), which presents a dilemma when quotation marks are supposed to appear inside a string. Placing a special character before the quotation mark, indicating the quotation mark is to be taken literally and not as a delimiter, solves the problem. This special character, also called the *escape character*, is a back slash (\).

```
message = "As the train left the station, " +
          "the conductor yelled, \"All aboard.\"";
```

Other Uses for the Escape Character

The escape character also is used when including other special characters in string literals. The sequence backslash-t (\t) indicates a tab character, and backslash-n (\n) indicates a newline character. These special sequences involving the backslash character are called *escape sequences*. The following code gives an example of the use of escape sequences followed by the output generated by the code:

Code

```
System.out.print ("The room was full of animals: \n" +
                  "\tdogs,\n\tcats, and\n\tchimpanzees.\n";
```

Output

```
The room was full of animals:
        dogs,
        cats, and
        chimpanzees.
```

Escaping the Escape Character

In solving one problem, we have introduced another. The backslash is the designated escape character, but sometimes a string must contain a backslash. This is accomplished by placing two backslashes in sequence:

```
path = "C:\\Java\\Ch3.doc";        ◆ yields the string C:\Java\Ch3.doc
```

There are several other escape sequences, but we omit them from this discussion (see Appendix B for further details).

The `length` Method

Strings are objects and implement several methods. In this chapter, we consider only the `length` method and defer discussions of others until Chapters 6 and 11 (for users of the Introductory and Comprehensive texts). A string returns its length in response to a `length` message:

```
String theString;
int theLength;

theString = "The cat sat on the mat.";
theLength = theString.length();          ← yields 23
```

EXERCISE 3.2 Continued

18. Assume that x refers to the string "`Wizard`" and y refers to the string "`Java`". Write the values of the following expressions:

a. y + x

b. y + y.length() + x

c. y + "\n" + x + "\n"

19. Declare a variable of type `String` called `myInfo` and initialize it to your name, address, and telephone number. Each item of information in this string should be followed by a newline character.

Methods, Messages, and Signatures

Classes implement methods, and objects are instances of classes. An object can respond to a message only if its class implements a corresponding method. To correspond, the method must have the same name as the message. Thus a pen object responds to the `move` message because the `StandardPen` class defines a `move` method.

Messages are sometimes accompanied by parameters and sometimes not:

```
double x = reader .nextDouble();   // No parameters expected
System.out.println(50.5);          // One parameter expected
```

The parameters included when a message is sent must match exactly in number and type the parameters expected by the method. For instance, the `Math.sqrt` method expects a single parameter of type `double`.

```
double d = 24.6;

Math.sqrt(d)            // Perfect! A parameter of type double is expected.
Math.sqrt(2.0 * d)      // Perfect! The expression yields a double.
Math.sqrt(4)            // Fine! Integers can stand in for doubles.
Math.sqrt();            // Error! A parameter is needed.
Math.sqrt(6.7, 3.4);    // Error! One parameter only please.
Math.sqrt("far");       // Error! A string parameter is NOT acceptable.
```

Some methods return a value and others do not. The `println` method does not return a value; however, the method `nextDouble` in class `Scanner` does:

```
Scanner reader = new Scanner();
double x;

x = reader.nextDouble();          // Returns the number entered by the user.
```

To use a method successfully we must know

- What type of value it returns

- Its name

- The number and type of the parameters it expects

A method's name and the types and number of its parameters are called the method's *signature*. From now on, when we introduce a new class, we will make a point of listing method signatures together with brief descriptions of what the methods do. Following are two examples, the first from the `Scanner` class and the second from the `PrintStream` class:

```
double nextDouble()       Returns a double entered by the user at the
                          keyboard.
void  println (double n)  Writes n to the print stream.
```

The word `void` indicates that the method does not return a value.

EXERCISE 3.2 Continued

20. What is the difference between a message and a method?

21. Describe the purpose of each item of information that appears in a method's signature.

User-Defined Symbols

Variable and program names are examples of user-defined symbols. You will see other examples later in the book. We now explain the rules for forming or naming user-defined symbols. These names must consist of a letter followed by a sequence of letters and/or digits. Letters are defined to be

- A ... Z

- a ... z

- _ and $

- Symbols that denote letters in several languages other than English

Digits are the characters 0 ... 9. Names are case-sensitive; thus, `celsius` and `Celsius` are different names.

Some words cannot be employed as user-defined symbols. These words are called *keywords* or *reserved words* because they have special meaning in Java. Table 3-7 shows a list of Java's reserved words. You will encounter most of them by the end of the book. They appear in blue in program code examples. These words are case-sensitive also, thus "import" is a reserved word but "Import" and "IMPORT" are not.

TABLE 3-7
Java's reserved words

abstract	double	int	static
assert	false	strictfp	true
boolean	else	interface	super
break	extends	long	switch
byte	final	native	synchronized
case	finally	new	this
catch	float	null	throw
char	for	package	throws
class	goto	private	transient
const	if	protected	try
continue	implements	public	void
default	import	return	volatile
do	instanceof	short	while

Here are examples of valid and invalid variable names:

Valid Names   surfaceArea3   _$_$$$

Invalid Names   3rdPayment   pay.rate   abstract

The first invalid name begins with a digit. The second invalid name contains a period. The third invalid name is a reserved word.

Well-chosen variable names greatly increase a program's readability and maintainability; consequently, it is considered good programming practice to use meaningful names such as

    radius   rather than   r

    taxableIncome   rather than   ti

When forming a compound variable name, programmers usually capitalize the first letter of each word except the first. For instance,

    taxableIncome   rather than

    taxableincome   or

    TAXABLEINCOME   or

    TaxableIncome

On the other hand, all the words in a program's name typically begin with a capital letter, for instance, ComputeEmployeePayroll. Finally, constant names usually are all uppercase. The goal of these rules and of all stylistic conventions is to produce programs that are easier to understand and maintain.

EXERCISE 3.2 Continued

22. State whether each of the following are valid or invalid user-defined symbols in Java:
   a. pricePerSquareInch
   b. student2
   c. 2GuysFromLexington
   d. PI
   e. allDone?

23. Write names for the following items that follow good programming practice:
   a. A variable that represents the diameter of a circle
   b. A constant that represents the standard deduction for an income tax return
   c. A method that draws a rectangle

Packages and the `import` statement

Programmers seldom write programs from scratch. Instead, they rely heavily on code written by many other programmers, most of whom they will never meet. Fortunately, Java provides a mechanism called a *package* that makes it easy for programmers to share code. Having written a class or group of classes that provide some generally useful service, a programmer can collect the classes together in a package. Other programmers who want to use the service can then import classes from the package. The programs in Chapter 2 illustrated the use of a package called `java.util`. The Java programming environment typically includes a large number of standard packages, some of which we use in subsequent chapters. These packages are standard because we expect to find them in every Java programming environment. Some packages are nonstandard and are created by their authors to support various applications.

When using a package, a programmer imports the desired class or classes. The general form of an `import` statement is

```
import x.y.z;
```

where

- `x` is the overall name of the package.
- `y` is the name of a subsection within the package.
- `z` is the name of a particular class in the subsection.

It is possible to import all the classes within a subsection at once; however, we do not usually do so. The statement to import all the classes with a subsection looks like this:

```
import x.y.*;
```

In general, a package can have any number of subsections, including zero, which is the case for several packages used in this book, and each subsection can in turn have any number of subsubsections, and so on. When used, an asterisk (*) can appear only at the lowest level. The asterisk is used to make available all of the classes in a package.

EXERCISE 3.2 Continued

24. Describe the role of the items x, y, and z in the statement import x.y.z;.

25. What happens when the computer executes the statement import x.y.*;?

3.3 *Terminal I/O for Different Data Types*

Objects support terminal input and output (I/O). An instance of the class Scanner supports input and the object System.out supports output. The latter object is an instance of the class PrintStream. This class, together with a number of others, is available to Java programmers without specifying their names in import statements. Although System.out is an instance of the class PrintStream, do not try to instantiate this class until you become familiar with working in Java files.

Table 3-8 summarizes some of the methods in the class Scanner. The object System.out understands two messages, print and println. Both messages expect a single parameter, which can be of any type, including an object; however, we postpone using an object as a parameter until Chapter 5.

TABLE 3-8
Methods in class Scanner

METHOD	DESCRIPTION
double nextDouble()	Returns the first double in the input line. Leading and trailing spaces are ignored.
int nextInt()	Returns the first integer in the input line. Leading and trailing spaces are ignored.
String nextLine()	Returns the input line, including leading and trailing spaces. *Warning*: A leading newline is returned as an empty string.

The following program illustrates the major features of terminal I/O:

```
// Example 3.1: tests 3 types of input data

import java.util.Scanner;

public class TestTerminalIO {

    public static void main (String [] args) {
        Scanner reader = new Scanner(System.in);

        String name;
        int age;
        double weight;
```

```
         System.out.print ("Enter your name (a string): ");
         name = reader.nextLine();

         System.out.print ("Enter your age (an integer): ");
         age = reader.nextInt();

         System.out.print ("Enter your weight (a double): ");
         weight = reader.nextDouble();

         System.out.println ("Greetings " + name +
                             ". You are " + age +
                             " years old and you weigh " + weight +
                             " pounds.");

      }
   }
```

When the program encounters an input statement—for instance, `reader.nextInt();`—it pauses and waits for the user to press Enter, at which point the `reader` object processes the user's input. The interaction with the user looks something like this, where the user's input is shown in boldface and the use of the Enter key is shown in italics:

```
Enter your name (a string): Carole JonesEnter
Enter your age (an integer): 45Enter
Enter your weight (a double): 130.6Enter
Greetings Carole Jones. You are 45 years old and you weigh 130.6 pounds.
```

The example program in this section reads a line of text followed by two numbers. Let's consider a code segment that reads numbers followed by a line of text, as follows:

```
System.out.print("Enter your age (an integer): ");
age = reader.nextInt();

System.out.print("Enter your weight (a double): ");
weight = reader.nextDouble();

System.out.print("Enter your name (a string): ");
name = reader.nextLine();
```

The program will receive the numbers as entered, but unfortunately the string input on the last line of code will be empty (""). The reason for this is that the method `nextDouble`, which input the last number two steps earlier, ignored but did not consume the newline that the user entered following the number. Therefore, this newline character was waiting to be consumed by the next call of `nextLine`, which was expecting more data! To avoid this problem, you should either input all the lines of text before the numbers or, when that is not feasible, run an extra call of `nextLine` after numeric input to eliminate the trailing newline character. Here is code that uses the second alternative:

```
System.out.print("Enter your age (an integer): ");
age = reader.nextInt();

System.out.print("Enter your weight (a double): ");
weight = reader.nextDouble();
```

```
reader.nextLine();    // Consume the newline character

System.out.print("Enter your name (a string): ");
name = reader.nextLine();
```

EXERCISE 3.3

1. Write code segments that perform the following tasks:

    a. Prompt the user for an hourly wage and read the wage into a `double` variable `wage`.

    b. Prompt the user for a Social Security number and read this value into the `String` variable `ssn`.

2. What is the purpose of the method `nextInt()`?

3. Explain what happens when a program reads a number from the keyboard and then attempts to read a line of text from the keyboard.

 Programming Skills

THE JAVA API AND javadoc

Most programming languages are defined in language reference manuals. These manuals show the syntax, the semantics, and how to use the basic features of the language. For Java, this documentation can be found in the Java Application Programming Interface (API). You can browse the Java API online at Sun's Web site or download the API for your particular version of Java to browse locally on your own computer.

You can browse for a given class's information by selecting the name of the class from a master list of classes or by selecting its package from a master list of packages. You can quickly drill down from there to a list of the class's methods and finally to the information for an individual method. The screen shots in Figure 3-2 show part of the method list in the `Scanner` class and the detailed information for the method `hasNext()`, respectively. The API for Java is enormous, with dozens of packages, hundreds of classes, and thousands of methods. However, the browser allows you to locate most information on a given item with a few mouse clicks, and links provide helpful cross-references to related items.

In addition to the `javac` and `java` commands for compiling and running programs, Sun provides a `javadoc` command that allows you to create browsable documentation for your own code. We explore how to create this documentation when we examine interfaces for user-defined classes in Chapter 10.

FIGURE 3-2
A portion of Sun's documentation for the Java API

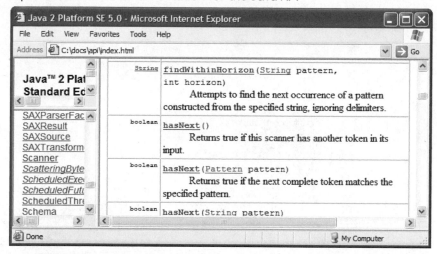

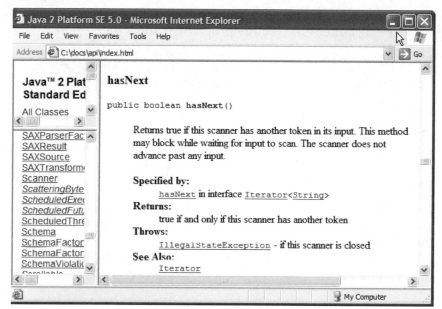

3.4 Comments

When we first write a program, we are completely familiar with all its nuances; however, six months later, when we or someone else has to modify it, the code that was once so clear often seems confusing and mysterious. There is, however, a technique for dealing with this situation. The remedy is to include comments in the code. **Comments** are explanatory sentences inserted in a program in such a manner that the compiler ignores them. There are two styles for indicating comments:

- End of line comments: these include all of the text following a double slash (//) on any given line; in other words, this style is best for just one line of comment.

- Multiline comments: these include all of the text between an opening /* and a closing */.

Comments appear in green in this book. The following code segment illustrates the use of both kinds of comments:

```
/* This code segment illustrates the
use of assignment statements and comments */

a = 3;              // assign 3 to variable a
b = 4;              // assign 4 to variable b
c = a + b;          // add the number in variable a
                    //    to the number in variable b
                    //    and assign the result, 7, to variable c
c = c * 3;          // multiply the number in variable c by 3
                    //    and assign the result, 21, to variable c
```

Although this code segment illustrates the mechanics of how to include comments in a program, it gives a misleading idea of when to use them. The main purpose of comments is to make a program more readable and thus easier to maintain. With this end in mind, we usually

- Begin a program with a statement of its purpose and other information that would help orient a programmer called on to modify the program at some future date.

- Accompany a variable declaration with a comment that explains the variable's purpose.

- Precede major segments of code with brief comments that explain their purpose.

- Include comments to explain the workings of complex or tricky sections of code.

The case study in the next section follows these guidelines and illustrates a reasonable and helpful level of comments. Because the programs in this book usually are accompanied by an extensive discussion of what they do, we sometimes include few or no comments; however, the programs you write should always be well commented.

Too many comments are as harmful as too few because, over time, the burden of maintaining the comments becomes excessive. No matter how many comments are included in a program, future programmers must still read and understand the region of code they intend to modify. Common sense usually leads to a reasonable balance. We should always avoid comments that do nothing more than restate the obvious. For instance, the next comment is completely pointless:

```
a = 3;      // assign 3 to variable a. Duh!
```

The best-written programs are self-documenting; that is, the reader can understand the code from the symbols used and from the structure and overall organization of the program.

EXERCISE 3.4

1. Describe the difference between an end-of-line comment and a multiline comment.

2. State two rules of thumb for writing appropriate comments in a program.

Case Study 1: Income Tax Calculator

It is now time to write a program that illustrates some of the concepts we have been presenting. We do this in the context of a case study that adheres to the software development life cycle discussed in Chapter 1. This life cycle approach may seem overly elaborate for small programs, but it scales up well when programs become larger.

Each year nearly everyone with an income faces the unpleasant task of computing his or her income tax return. If only it could be done as easily as suggested in this case study.

Request

Write a program that computes a person's income tax.

Analysis

Here is the relevant tax law (mythical in nature):

- There is a flat tax rate of 20 percent.

- There is a $10,000 standard deduction.

- There is a $2000 additional deduction for each dependent.

- Gross income must be entered to the nearest penny.

- The income tax is expressed as a decimal number.

The user inputs are the gross income and number of dependents. The program calculates the income tax based on the inputs and the tax law and then displays the income tax. Figure 3-3 shows the proposed terminal user interface. Characters in boldface indicate user inputs. The program prints the rest. The inclusion of a user interface at this point is a good idea because it allows the customer and the programmer to discuss the intended program's behavior in a context understandable to both.

FIGURE 3-3
The user Interface for the income tax calculator

```
Enter the gross income: 50000.50
Enter the number of dependents: 4
The income tax is $6400.1
```

Design

During analysis, we specify what a program is going to do, and during design we describe how it is going to do it. This involves writing the algorithm used by the program. *Webster's New Collegiate Dictionary* defines an *algorithm* as "a step-by-step procedure for solving a problem or accomplishing some end." A recipe in a cookbook is a good example of an algorithm. Program algorithms are often written in a somewhat stylized version of English called ***pseudocode***. The following is the pseudocode for our income tax program:

```
read grossIncome
read numDependents
compute taxableIncome = grossIncome - 10000 - 2000 * numDependents
compute incomeTax = taxableIncome * 0.20
print incomeTax
```

Although there are no precise rules governing the syntax of pseudocode, you should strive to describe the essential elements of the program in a clear and concise manner. Over time, you will develop a style that suits you.

Implementation

Given the preceding pseudocode, an experienced programmer now would find it easy to write the corresponding Java program. For a beginner, on the other hand, writing the code is the most difficult part of the process. The following is the program:

```
/*Case study 3.1: an income tax calculator
Compute a person's income tax
1. Significant constants
        tax rate
        standard deduction
        deduction per dependent
2. The inputs are
        gross income
        number of dependents
3. Computations:
        net income = gross income - the standard deduction -
                        a deduction for each dependent
        income tax = is a fixed percentage of the net income
4. The outputs are
        the income tax
*/

import java.util.Scanner;

public class IncomeTaxCalculator{

    public static void main(String [] args){

        // Constants
        final double TAX_RATE = 0.20;
        final double STANDARD_DEDUCTION = 10000.0;
        final double DEPENDENT_DEDUCTION = 2000.0;

        Scanner reader = new Scanner(System.in);

        double grossIncome;         // the gross income (input)
        int  numDependents;         // the number of dependents (input)
        double taxableIncome;       // the taxable income (calculated)
        double incomeTax;           // the income tax (calculated and
                                    // output)

        // Request the inputs
        System.out.print("Enter the gross income: ");
        grossIncome = reader.nextDouble();
        System.out.print("Enter the number of dependents: ");
        numDependents = reader.nextInt();
```

```
    // Compute the income tax
    taxableIncome = grossIncome - STANDARD_DEDUCTION -
                    DEPENDENT_DEDUCTION * numDependents;
    incomeTax = taxableIncome * TAX_RATE;

    // Display the income tax
    System.out.println("The income tax is $" + incomeTax);
  }
}
```

Notice that we have used mixed-mode arithmetic, but in a manner that does not produce any undesired effects.

 Computer Ethics

COMPUTER VIRUSES

A **virus** is a computer program that can replicate itself and move from computer to computer. Some programmers of viruses intend no harm; they just want to demonstrate their prowess by creating viruses that go undetected. Other programmers of viruses intend harm by causing system crashes, corruption of data, or hardware failures.

Viruses migrate by attaching themselves to normal programs, and then become active again when these programs are launched. Early viruses were easily detected if one had detection software. This software examined portions of each program on the suspect computer and could repair infected programs.

Viruses and virus detectors have coevolved through the years, however, and both kinds of software have become very sophisticated. Viruses now hide themselves better than they used to; virus detectors can no longer just examine pieces of data stored in memory to reveal the presence or absence of a virus. Researchers have recently developed a method of running a program that might contain a virus to see whether or not the virus becomes active. The suspect program runs in a "safe" environment that protects the computer from any potential harm. As you can imagine, this process takes time and costs money. For an overview of the history of viruses and the new detection technology, see Carey Nactenberg, "Computer Virus-Antivirus Coevolution," *Communications of the ACM*, Volume 40, No. 1 (January 1997): 46–51.

3.5 Programming Errors

According to an old saying, we learn from our mistakes, which is fortunate because most people find it almost impossible to write even simple programs without making numerous mistakes. These mistakes, or errors, are of three types: syntax errors, run-time errors, and logic errors.

The Three Types of Errors

Syntax errors, as we learned in Chapter 2, occur when we violate a syntax rule, no matter how minor. These errors are detected at compile time. For instance, if a semicolon is missing at the end of a statement or if a variable is used before it is declared, the compiler is unable to translate the program into byte code. The good news is that when the Java compiler finds a syntax error, it prints an error message, and we can make the needed correction. The bad news, as we saw previously, is that the error messages are often quite cryptic. Knowing that there is a syntax error at a particular point in a program, however, is usually a sufficient clue for finding the error.

Run-time errors occur when we ask the computer to do something that it considers illegal, such as dividing by 0. For example, suppose that the symbols x and y are variables. Then the expression x/y is syntactically correct, so the compiler does not complain. However, when the expression is evaluated during execution of the program, the meaning of the expression depends on the values contained in the variables. If the variable y has the value 0, then the expression cannot be evaluated. The good news is that the Java runtime environment will print a message telling us the nature of the error and where it was encountered. Once again, the bad news is that the error message might be hard to understand.

Logic errors (also called *design errors* or *bugs*) occur when we fail to express ourselves accurately. For instance, in everyday life, we might give someone the instruction to turn left when what we really meant to say is to turn right. In this example,

- The instruction is phrased properly, and thus the syntax is correct.

- The instruction is meaningful, and thus the semantics are valid.

- But the instruction does not do what we intended, and thus is logically incorrect.

The bad news is that programming environments do not detect logic errors automatically. The good news is that this text offers useful tips on how to prevent logic errors and how to detect them when they occur.

Now let's look at examples of each of these types of errors.

Illustration of Syntax Errors

We have already seen examples of syntax errors in Chapter 2; however, seeing a few more will be helpful. The following is a listing of the income tax calculator program with the addition of two syntax errors. See if you can spot them. The line numbers are not part of the program but are intended to facilitate the discussion that follows the listing.

```
1    import java.util.Scanner;
2
3    public class IncomeTaxCalculator{
4      public static void main(String [] args){
5
6         final double TAX_RATE = 0.20;
7         final double STANDARD_DEDUCTION = 10000.0;
```

```
8           final double DEPENDENT_DEDUCTION = 2000.0;
9
10          Scanner reader = new Scanner(System.in);
11
12          double grossIncome;
13          int numDependents;
14          double taxableIncome;
15          double incomeTax;
16
17          System.out.print("Enter the gross income: ");
18          grossIncome = reader.readDouble();
19          System.out.print("Enter the number of dependents: ");
20          numDependents = reader.nextInt();
21
22          taxableIncome = grossincome - STANDARD_DEDUCTION -
23                          DEPENDENT_DEDUCTION * numDependents;
24          incomeTax = taxableIncome * TAX_RATE
25
26          System.out.println("The income tax is $" + incomeTax);

27     }
28 }
```

Just in case you could not spot them, the errors in the code are

■ In line 22, where `grossIncome` has been misspelled as `grossincome` (remember Java is case-sensitive)

■ In line 24, where the semicolon is missing at the end of the line

When the program is compiled, the terminal window contains the following error message (we could show a snapshot of the window, but we think the following plain text is more readable):

```
IncomeTaxCalculator.java:25: ';' expected
^
1 error-
```

Although the compiler says that the error occurs on line 25, the semicolon is actually missing on the previous line. The corrective action is to go back into the editor, fix this error, save the file, and compile again. Then you will see a message to the effect that the symbol `grossincome` cannot be found. You may need to repeat this process a number of times until the compiler stops finding syntax errors.

Turn to the supplemental materials and read any additional instructions that apply to your development environment.

Illustration of Run-time Errors

There are a variety of run-time errors. We now present several of the most basic. We encounter others later in the book.

Division by Integer Zero

For our first run-time error, we write a small program that attempts to perform division by 0. As is well known, division by 0 is not a well-defined operation and should be avoided. Nonetheless, we must ask what happens if we accidentally write a program that tries it. The following is a trivial program that illustrates the situation:

```java
// Example 3.2: attempt to divide an int by zero

public class DivideByIntegerZero{
   public static void main(String [] args){
      int i, j = 0;
      i = 3 / j;
      System.out.println("The value of i is " + i);
   }
}
```

When we attempt to run this program, execution stops prematurely, and the following error message is displayed:

```
Exception in thread "main" java.lang.ArithmeticException: / by zero
        at DivideByIntegerZero.main(DivideByIntegerZero.java:4)
```

In this circumstance, we say that the JVM has thrown an *exception*. The message indicates the nature of the problem, "ArithmeticException: / by zero," and its location, in line 4 of method main.

Division by Floating-Point Zero

Interestingly, the JVM responds rather differently when the division involves a floating-point rather than an integer 0. Consider the following nearly identical program:

```java
// Example 3.3: attempt to divide a double by zero

public class DivideByFloatingPointZero {
   public static void main(String [] args) {
      double i, j = 0.0;
      i = 3.0 / j;
      System.out.println ("The value of i is " + i);
      System.out.println ("10 / i equals " + 10 / i);
   }
}
```

The program now runs to completion, and the output is

```
The value of i is Infinity
10 / i equals 0.0
```

In other words, the value of the variable i is considered to be Infinity, which is to say it falls outside the range of a double, and if we now divide another number by i, we obtain 0.

Null Pointer Exception

Not all run-time errors involve arithmetic. Variables frequently represent objects. Sending a message to such a variable before the corresponding object has been instantiated causes a null pointer exception. Fortunately, many compilers detect the possibility of this error before it arises; however, later in this book the problem occurs in situations that the compiler cannot detect. The following is an example program with the accompanying compiler error message:

The Program

```
import java.util.Scanner;

public class Test{
    public static void main(String [] args){
        Scanner reader;
        int age;
        age = reader.nextInt();
    }
}
```

The Compiler Error Message

```
C:\Test.java:7: Variable reader may not have been initialized.
        age = reader.nextInt();
                  ^

1 error
```

In this code, the compiler says that the variable `reader` may not have been initialized. If that's true (and in this case, it is), the attempt to send a message to it at runtime will cause an error. The reason the variable is not initialized is that no value has been assigned to it with an assignment statement.

No Such Method Error

The following is a final, and rather puzzling, example of a run-time error. You might not notice it, even after you examine the program and the error message.

The Program

```
// Example 3.4: a puzzling run-time error

public class PuzzlingRuntimeError{
    public static void Main(String [] args){
        System.out.println ("Hello World!");
    }
}
```

The Run-time Error Message

```
Exception in thread "main" java.lang.NoSuchMethodError: main
```

Have you spotted the problem? The word `main` has been misspelled as `Main`. Remember that Java is case-sensitive, and computers are exasperatingly literal minded. They never try to guess what you meant to say, so every mistake, no matter how small, is significant.

Illustration of Logic Errors

Incorrect output is the most obvious indication that there is a logic error in a program. For instance, suppose our temperature conversion program converts 212.0 degrees Fahrenheit to 100.06 instead of 100.0 degrees Celsius. The error is small, but we notice it. And if we do not, our customers, for whom we have written the program, surely will. We caused the problem by incorrectly using 31.9 instead of 32 in the following statement:

```
celsius = (fahrenheit - 31.9) * 5.0 / 9.0;
```

Test Data

Errors of this sort are usually found by running a program with test data for which we already know the correct output. We then compare the program's output with the expected results. If there is a difference, we reexamine the program's logic to determine why the program is not behaving as expected.

But how many tests must we perform on a program before we can feel confident that it contains no more logic errors? Sometimes the fundamental nature of a program provides an answer. Perhaps your mathematical skills are sufficiently fresh to recognize that the statement

```
celsius = (fahrenheit  - 32.0) * 5.0 / 9.0;
```

is actually the equation of a line. Because two points determine a line, if the program works correctly for two temperatures, it should work correctly for all. In general, however, it is difficult to determine how many tests are enough. But we often can break down the data into categories and test one number in each, the assumption being that if the program works correctly for one number in a category, it will work correctly for all the other numbers in the same category. Careful choice of categories then becomes crucial.

Desk Checking

We can also reduce the number of logic errors in a program by rereading the code carefully after we have written it. This is called *desk checking* and is best done when the mind is fresh. It is even possible to use mathematical techniques to prove that a program or segment of a program is free of logic errors. Because programming requires exhausting and excruciating attention to detail, avoid programming for long stretches of time or when tired, a rule you will break frequently unless you manage your time well.

Usually, we never can be certain that a program is error free, and after making a reasonable but large number of tests, we release the program for distribution and wait anxiously for the complaints. If we release too soon, the number of errors will be so high that we will lose credibility and customers, but if we wait too long, the competition will beat us to the market.

*E*XERCISE 3.5

1. At what point in the program development process are syntax errors, run-time errors, and logic errors detected?

2. Give an example of a run-time error and explain why the computer cannot catch it earlier in the program development process.

EXERCISE 3.5 Continued

3. State the type of error (compile-time, run-time, or logic) that occurs in each of the following pieces of code:

a. x = y / 0

b. x + y = z

c. area = length + width

3.6 Debugging

After we have established that a program contains a logic error, or *bug* as it is more affectionately called, we still have the problem of finding it. Sometimes the nature of a bug suggests its general location in a program. We then can reread this section of the program carefully with the hope of spotting the error. Unfortunately, the bug often is not located where we expect to find it, and even if it is, we probably miss it. After all, we thought we were writing the program correctly in the first place, so when we reread it, we tend to see what we were trying to say rather than what we actually said.

Programmers, as a consequence, are frequently forced to resort to a rather tedious, but powerful, technique for finding bugs. We add to the program extra lines of code that print the values of selected variables in the terminal window. Of course, we add these lines where we anticipate they will do the most good—that is, preceding and perhaps following the places in the program where we think the bug is most likely located. We then run the program again, and from the extra output, we can determine if any of the variables deviate from their expected values. If one of them does, then we know the bug is close by, but if none do, we must try again at a different point in the program. A variable's value is printed in the terminal window as follows:

```
System.out.println ("<some message>" + <variable name>);
```

Now let us try to find a bug that has been secretly inserted into the temperature conversion program. Suppose the program behaves as shown in Figure 3-4. Something is seriously wrong. The program claims that 212 degrees Fahrenheit converts to 41.1 degrees Celsius instead of the expected 100.

FIGURE 3-4
Incorrect output from the temperature conversion program

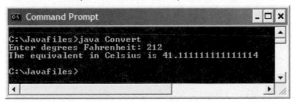

Perhaps we can find the problem by checking the value of fahrenheit just before celsius is calculated. The needed code looks like this:

```
System.out.println ("fahrenheit = " + fahrenheit);    ← This is the
                                                         debugging code
celsius = (fahrenheit - 32.0) * 5.0 / 9.0;
```

When we run the program again with the debugging code included, we get the following output:

```
Enter degrees Fahrenheit: 212
Fahrenheit = 106.0
The equivalent in Celsius is 41.111111111111114
```

We entered 212, but for some reason, the program says the value of `fahrenheit` is 106. Perhaps we should look at the surrounding code and see if we can spot the error. Here is the relevant code:

```
. . .
System.out.print ("Enter degrees Fahrenheit: ");
fahrenheit = reader.nextDouble() / 2.0;
System.out.println ("fahrenheit = " + fahrenheit);
celsius = (fahrenheit - 32.0) * 5.0 / 9.0;
. . .
```

Ah, there is the error. It looks as if the value entered by the user is divided by 2 just before it is assigned to the variable `fahrenheit`. Devious, but we cannot be deceived for long.

EXERCISE 3.6

1. Describe how one can modify code so that the cause of a logic error can be discovered.

2. The following program contains a logic error. Describe where to insert the appropriate debugging statements to help locate the error:

```
import java.util.Scanner;

public class AreaTriangle{

    public static void main(String [] args){

        double base, height, area;
        Scanner reader = new Scanner(System.in);

        System.out.print("Enter the base of the triangle: ");
        base = reader.nextDouble();
        System.out.print("Enter the height of the triangle: ");
        height = reader.nextDouble();
        area = base + height / 2;
        System.out.println("The area is " + area);

    }
}
```

Case Study 2: Count the Angels

Computers have been applied to many complex problems, from predicting the weather, to controlling nuclear power plants, to playing the best chess in the world. Now this case study extends computing into the realm of metaphysics. Although this case study is fanciful and humorous, it illustrates important issues regarding analysis and design. During analysis and design we deliberately introduce several subtle errors, which during implementation we incorporate into the program, yet the program runs perfectly and gives no hint that there are underlying problems. As you read the case study, see if you can spot the errors. At the end we will point out what they are and make some general comments about the software development process.

Request

Write a program that determines how many angels can dance on the head of a pin.

Analysis

To solve this problem, we first consulted several prominent theologians. We learned that the pertinent factors are the size of the pinhead, the space occupied by a single angel, and the overlap between adjacent angels. Although angels are incorporeal beings, there are limits to the amount of overlap they can tolerate. Also, no region of space is ever occupied by three angels simultaneously. This seems somewhat confusing. On further questioning, the experts explained that angels have what one might call an overlap factor. If, for instance, this factor is 30 percent, then

- An angel can share at most 30 percent of its space with other angels.

- 70 percent of its space cannot be shared.

- Within any shared region, only two angels can overlap.

  The inputs to the program are now fairly obvious: the radius of the pinhead, the space occupied by an angel, and the overlap factor. Based on these inputs, the program will calculate

- The area of pinhead = πr^2.

- Nonoverlapping space required by an angel = space occupied by an angel * (1 - overlap factor).

- Number of angels on pinhead = area of pinhead / nonoverlapping space required by an angel.

  The proposed user interface is shown in Figure 3-5.

FIGURE 3-5
Proposed interface for the count angels program

```
Enter the radius in millimeters: 10
Enter the space occupied by an angel in square micrometers: 0.0001
Enter the overlap factor: 0.75
The number of angels = 1.256E7
```

Design

Our rather crude estimate for π is 3.14. Obviously, more accurate estimates yield more accurate calculations of the area. Later we see how Java itself can provide an excellent estimate. Following is the pseudocode for the count angels program:

```
read radius
read angelSpace
read overlapFactor
area = 3.14 * radius * radius
nonOverlapSpace = angelSpace * (1.0 - overlapFactor)
numberAngels = area / nonOverlapSpace
print numberAngels
```

Implementation

The following code is a straightforward translation of the pseudocode into Java. Comments are included.

```java
/*Case study 2: count the angels
Count the number of angels that can dance on the head of a pin.
1. The user inputs are
        The radius of the pinhead
        The space occupied by an angel
        The allowed overlap between angels subject to the restriction
        that no space can simultaneously be occupied by more than two
2. The program computes
        The area of the pinhead based on its radius
        The amount of nonoverlapping space required by an angel
        The number of angels based on the preceding two values
3. The program ends by printing the number of angels.
*/

import java.util.Scanner;

public class CountAngels {
    public static void main(String [] args){

        Scanner reader = new Scanner(System.in);

        double radius;              //Radius of the pinhead in millimeters

        double angelSpace;          //Space occupied by an angel
                                    //in square micrometers
        double overlapFactor;       //Allowed overlap between angels from 0 to 1
        double area;                //Area of the pinhead in square millimeters
        double nonOverlapSpace;     //Nonoverlapping space required by an angel
        double numberAngels;        //Number of angels that can dance on the
                                    //pinhead

        //Get user inputs
        System.out.print ("Enter the radius in millimeters: ");
        radius = reader.nextDouble();
        System.out.print
```

```
        ("Enter the space occupied by an angel in square micrometers: ");
      angelSpace = reader.nextDouble();
      System.out.print ("Enter the overlap factor: ");
      overlapFactor = reader.nextDouble();

      //Perform calculations
      area = 3.14 * radius * radius;
      nonOverlapSpace = angelSpace * (1.0 - overlapFactor);
      numberAngels = area / nonOverlapSpace;

      //Print results
      System.out.print ("The number of angels = " + numberAngels);
    }
  }
```

Discussion

So what were the mysterious errors we mentioned and what is their general significance? There were three errors, two during analysis and one during design.

First Analysis Error

During analysis we did not consider the shape of the region occupied by an angel, overlapping or otherwise. To appreciate the significance of our oversight, consider the problem of placing as many pennies as possible on a plate without overlap. Because there are gaps between the pennies, the answer is not obtained by dividing the area of the plate by the area of a penny. Even if two pennies are allowed to overlap by some amount, there are still gaps. Thus our solution is correct only if angels can mold their shapes to eliminate all empty spaces. Unfortunately, we did not think of asking the theologians about this.

Second Analysis Error

Let us now simplify the problem and suppose that angels pack onto the pinhead without leaving empty spaces. Now the space occupied by two overlapping angels equals the space each would occupy alone minus the amount by which they overlap or

```
space for two overlapping angels
     = 2 * space occupied by an angel -
        space occupied by an angel * overlap factor
     = 2 * space occupied by an angel * (1.0 - overlap factor / 2)
```

Thus,

```
     space for one angel with overlap = space occupied by an angel *
        (1.0 - overlap factor / 2)
```

and

```
     number of angels on pinhead = area of pinhead / space for one
        angel with overlap
```

Well, we certainly got that wrong the first time.

Design Error

The radius of the pin is given in millimeters and the space requirements of an angel are given in square micrometers. Our calculations need to take this difference in units into account. We leave the actual correction as an exercise.

Conclusions

There are three lessons to draw from all this. First, the people who write programs usually are not the ones most familiar with the problem domain. Consequently, many programs fail to solve problems correctly either because they completely ignore important factors or because they treat factors incorrectly. Second, careful analysis and design are essential and demand careful thought. As you can see, the errors had nothing to do with programming per se, and they would have occurred even if we were solving the problem with paper and pencil. And by the way, before writing a program to solve a problem, we definitely need to know how to do it correctly by hand. We are not going to make a practice of making analysis and design errors, and we did so just this once in order to make a point. Third, just because computers perform complex calculations at lightning speed does not mean we should have unquestioning confidence in their outputs.

3.7 Graphics and GUIs: Drawing Shapes and Text

The GUI programs in Section 2.7 displayed one or more flat-colored rectangular areas. Now it is time to learn how to fill these areas with other objects, such as geometric shapes and text.

Defining a Specialized Panel Class

An application window in GUI programs has a clearly defined set of responsibilities. A window establishes its initial size, decides what it will do when the user resizes or closes it, and creates and lays out the panels that appear within it. Before we create and display other objects within a panel, we have to ask which will be responsible for them, the application window or the panel in which they appear? Because there might be many panels and many objects in each panel, it would be a good idea to assign at least some of the responsibilities for managing these objects to the panels themselves. We use two principles of any good organization: Divide the labor and Delegate responsibility.

>
> **Extra Challenge**
>
> This Graphics and GUIs section gives you the opportunity to explore concepts and programming techniques required to develop modern graphics applications and graphical user interfaces. This material is not required in order to proceed with the other chapters of the book.

A window does just what it did before: create a panel with a given background color. But a panel now has the additional responsibility of setting its own background color and displaying geometric shapes and text. To provide a panel with these additional capabilities, we define a new type of panel by extending the `JPanel` class. Our new class, called `ColorPanel`, has all of the behavior of a `JPanel`. But a `ColorPanel` also knows how to draw specific shapes and instantiate itself with a given background color. For example, instead of the code

```
JPanel panel = new JPanel();
panel.setBackround(Color.white);
```

an application window now uses the code

```
ColorPanel panel = new ColorPanel(Color.white);
```

to create a panel with a given background color. The following program sets up an application window for all of the examples discussed in this section.

```java
// Main application window for Chapter 3 graphics examples

import javax.swing.*;
import java.awt.*;

public class GUIWindow {

    public static void main(String[] args){
        JFrame theGUI = new JFrame();
        theGUI.setTitle("GUI Program");
        theGUI.setSize(300, 200);
        theGUI.setDefaultCloseOperation(JFrame.EXIT_ON_CLOSE);
        ColorPanel panel = new ColorPanel(Color.white);
        Container pane = theGUI.getContentPane();
        pane.add(panel);
        theGUI.setVisible(true);
    }
}
```

The class `ColorPanel` in each example extends `JPanel` and includes a constructor that expects a `Color` parameter. The constructor runs when the panel is instantiated and sets its background color. Here is the code for this minimal behavior:

```java
// Example 3.5: an empty colored panel

import javax.swing.*;
import java.awt.*;

public class ColorPanel extends JPanel{

    public ColorPanel(Color backColor){
        setBackground(backColor);
    }
}
```

All we have done thus far is substitute a new class, `ColorPanel`, for the `JPanel` class used in the examples of Section 2.7. Those example programs would have the same behavior if they used the new class. The only difference is that the code for the application windows would be slightly simplified.

When you're working with more than one programmer-defined class, the source code for the classes is usually maintained in separate files and edited and compiled separately. An easy way to compile all of the classes in your current working directory is to use the command `javac *.java` at the command line prompt. The `java` command to run a program is used as before, with the byte code file that contains the `main` method.

Coordinate Systems

Underlying every graphics application is a ***coordinate system***. Positions in this system are specified in terms of points. Points in a two-dimensional system have x and y coordinates. For example, the point (10, 30) has an x coordinate of 10 and a y coordinate of 30.

The x and y coordinates of a point express its position relative to the system's ***origin*** at (0, 0). Figure 3-6 presents some examples of points in the familiar Cartesian coordinate system. In this system, two perpendicular lines define an x axis and a y axis. The point of intersection is labeled (0, 0). Increasing values of x are to the right and increasing values of y are upward.

FIGURE 3-6
A Cartesian coordinate system

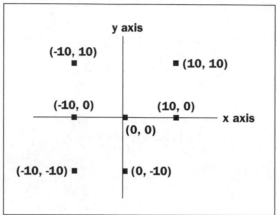

In Java and most other programming languages, the coordinate system is oriented as shown in Figure 3-7. Note that the only quadrant shown is the one that defines the coordinates of the computer's screen. In the positive direction, it extends downward and to the right from the point (0, 0) in the upper-left corner. The other three quadrants exist, but the points in them never appear on the screen. This is called a ***screen coordinate system***.

FIGURE 3-7
Orientation of Java's coordinate system

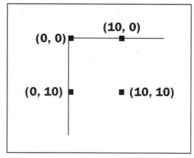

In a window-based application, each window has a coordinate system whose origin is located at the upper-left outside corner of the window. Each integer point in this coordinate system, extending from the origin to the window's lower-right corner, locates the position of a pixel, or picture element, in the window. By an integer point, we mean a point both of whose coordinates are integers. Each panel also has its own coordinate system that is similar in form to the window's coordinate system. In the discussion that follows, we assume that we are drawing geometric shapes and text in panels.

The Graphics Class

The package `java.awt` provides a `Graphics` class for drawing in a panel. A panel maintains an instance of this class, called a *graphics context*, so that the program can access and modify the panel's bitmap. The program sends messages to the graphics context to perform all graphics operations. Hereafter, we refer to the graphics context using the variable name g. Some commonly used `Graphics` drawing methods are listed in Table 3-9. The table also shows the results of running these methods in a window that has a single panel.

TABLE 3-9
Common methods in the `Graphics` class

GRAPHICS METHOD	EXAMPLE CALL AND OUTPUT	WHAT IT DOES

`drawLine(`
`  int x1,`
`  int y1,`
`  int x2,`
`  int y2)`
	`g.drawLine(10, 25, 40, 55)`	Draws a line from point (x1, y1) to (x2, y2).

`drawRect(`
`  int x,`
`  int y,`
`  int width,`
`  int height)`
	`g.drawRect(10, 25, 40, 30)`	Draws a rectangle whose upper-left corner is (x, y) and whose dimensions are the specified width and height.

`drawOval(`
`  int x,`
`  int y,`
`  int width,`
`  int height)`
	`g.drawOval(10, 25, 50, 25)`	Draws an oval that fits within a rectangle whose origin (upper-left corner) is (x, y) and whose dimensions are the specified width and height. To draw a circle, make the width and height equal.

TABLE 3-9 Continued
Common methods in the `Graphics` class

GRAPHICS METHOD	EXAMPLE CALL AND OUTPUT	WHAT IT DOES

`drawArc(`
 	
   `int x,`
   `int y,`
   `int width,`
   `int height,`
   `int startAngle,`
   `int arcAngle)`
	`g.drawArc(10, 25, 50, 50, 0, 90)`	Draws an arc that fits within a rectangle whose upper-left corner is (x, y) and whose dimensions are the specified width and height. The arc is drawn from `startAngle` to `startAngle + arcAngle`. The angles are expressed in degrees. A start angle of 0 indicates the 3 o'clock position. A positive arc indicates a counterclockwise rotation, and a negative arc indicates a clockwise rotation from 3 o'clock.

`drawRoundRect(`
   `int x,`
   `int y,`
   `int width,`
   `int height,`
   `int arcWidth,`
   `int arcHeight)`
	`g.drawRoundRect(10, 25, 40, 30, 20, 20)`	Draws a rounded rectangle.

`drawString(`
   `String str,`
   `int x,`
   `int y)`
	`g.drawString("Java rules!", 10, 50)`	Draws a string. The point (x, y) indicates the position of the base line of the first character.

In addition, there are the methods `fillArc`, `fillRect`, and `fillOval`, which draw filled shapes.

Each shape is drawn in a graphics context with a foreground color, which by default is black. This color can be changed using the method `setColor(aColor)`, which affects the color of all images drawn subsequently but not earlier. In general, if you want to draw a shape in a given color, it's a good idea to set the color of the graphics object immediately before drawing the shape. The following code draws a filled red circle in the graphics context g:

```
g.setColor(Color.red);
g.fillOval(100, 100, 50, 50);
```

You can erase a shape by setting the foreground color to the same color as the panel's background color and redrawing the shape. The methods getColor() and getBackground() return the colors of a graphics context and a panel's background, respectively.

Drawing Shapes with the Method paintComponent

The responsibilities of a panel class are to draw images in response to messages from an application and also to redraw images whenever the window is refreshed. We discuss the refresh process in this section and examine how a panel receives messages from an application in later chapters.

When a window opens, the JVM sends the message paintComponent to each object contained in the window. If an object has any images to draw, its paintComponent method accomplishes this. Thus, for example, when a window containing a button opens at program startup, the button's paintComponent method draws the image of the button on the screen. This process also occurs whenever the window is refreshed—for instance, after it is minimized and restored. The important point here is that the application never calls paintComponent directly; it is triggered automatically by the JVM in response to certain events. paintComponent receives the panel's graphics context as a parameter, so this object is accessible for drawing. The method also is implemented in a superclass of the class ColorPanel, so the programmer can override it to draw the appropriate images.

Our next program example uses a modified version of the code for the ColorPanel class. We have added a paintComponent method that draws a blue rectangle containing a red text message when the window opens and whenever it is refreshed. The resulting window is shown in Figure 3-8.

```
// Example 3.6: A colored panel containing a red text
// message in a blue rectangle

import javax.swing.*;
import java.awt.*;

public class ColorPanel extends JPanel{

    public ColorPanel(Color backColor){
        setBackground(backColor);
    }

    public void paintComponent(Graphics g){
        super.paintComponent(g);
        g.setColor(Color.blue);
        g.drawRect(10, 5, 120, 20);
        g.setColor(Color.red);
        g.drawString("Hello world!", 20, 20);
    }
}
```

FIGURE 3-8
Displaying a shape and text in a panel

Note that the `paintComponent` method first calls the same method in the superclass, using the reserved word `super`. The reason is that the method in the superclass paints the background of the panel. This effectively clears any images in the panel before they are redrawn.

Finding the Width and Height of a Panel

Occasionally, it is useful to know the width and height of a panel. For instance, one might want to center an image in a panel and keep the image centered when the user resizes the window. The methods `getWidth()` and `getHeight()` return the current width and height of a panel, respectively. If these methods are called before the window is opened, they return a default value of 0. Our next `ColorPanel` example maintains the shapes of the previous example near the center of the panel:

```
// Example 3.7: A colored panel containing a red text
// message in a blue rectangle, centered in the panel

import javax.swing.*;
import java.awt.*;

public class ColorPanel extends JPanel{

    public ColorPanel(Color backColor){
        setBackground(backColor);
    }

    public void paintComponent(Graphics g){
        super.paintComponent(g);
        int x = getWidth() / 2 - 60;
        int y = getHeight() / 2;
        g.setColor(Color.blue);
        g.drawRect(x, y, 120, 20);
        g.setColor(Color.red);
        g.drawString("Hello world!", x + 10, y + 15);
    }
}
```

Text Properties and the Font Class

In the context of a bitmapped display, text is drawn like any other image. A text image has several properties, as shown in Table 3-10. These are set by adjusting the color and font properties of the graphics context in which the text is drawn.

TABLE 3-10
Text properties

TEXT PROPERTY	EXAMPLE
Color	Red, green, blue, white, black, etc.
Font style	Plain, **bold**, *italic*
Font size	10 point, 12 point, etc.
Font name	Courier, Times New Roman, etc.

An object of class Font has three basic properties: a name, a style, and a size. The following code creates one Font object with the properties **Courier bold 12** and another with the properties *Arial bold italic 10*:

```
Font courierBold12    = new Font("Courier", Font.BOLD, 12);

Font arialBoldItalic10 = new Font("Arial", Font.BOLD + Font.ITALIC, 10);
```

The Font constants PLAIN, BOLD, and ITALIC define the font styles. The font size is an integer representing the number of points, where one point equals 1/72 of an inch. The available font names depend on your particular computer platform.

Our final program example modifies the previous one so that the text message is displayed in Courier bold 14 font.

```
// Example 3.8: A colored panel containing a red text
// message in a blue rectangle
// Text font is Courier bold 14

import javax.swing.*;
import java.awt.*;

public class ColorPanel extends JPanel{

   public ColorPanel(Color backColor){
      setBackground(backColor);
   }

   public void paintComponent(Graphics g){
      super.paintComponent(g);
      int x = getWidth() / 2 - 60;
      int y = getHeight() / 2;
      g.setColor(Color.blue);
      g.drawRect(x, y, 120, 20);
      g.setColor(Color.red);
      Font font = new Font("Courier", Font.BOLD, 14);
      g.setFont(font);
      g.drawString("Hello world!", x + 10, y + 15);
   }
}
```

EXERCISE 3.7

1. Write the code segments that would draw the following objects in the graphics context `g`:
   a. A filled rectangle with corner point (45, 20) and size 100 by 50
   b. A line segment with end points (20, 20) and (100, 100)
   c. A circle with center point (100, 100) and radius 50
   d. A triangle with vertices (100, 100), (50, 50), and (200, 200)

2. Describe the design of a program that displays a filled blue rectangle on a red background.

3. How does one compute the center point of a panel?

4. List the three properties of a text font.

SUMMARY

In this chapter, you learned:

- Java programs use the `int` data type for whole numbers (integers) and `double` for floating-point numbers (numbers with decimals).

- Java variable and method names consist of a letter followed by additional letters or digits. Java keywords cannot be used as names.

- Final variables behave as constants; their values cannot change after they are declared.

- Arithmetic expressions are evaluated according to precedence. Some expressions yield different results for integer and floating-point operands.

- Strings may be concatenated to form a new string.

- The compiler catches syntax errors. The JVM catches run-time errors. Logic errors, if they are caught, are detected by the programmer or user of the program at runtime.

- A useful way to find and remove logic errors is to insert debugging output statements to view the values of variables.

- Java uses a screen coordinate system to locate the positions of pixels in a window or panel. The origin of this system is in the upper-left corner or the drawing area, and the x and y axes increase to the right and downward, respectively.

- The programmer can modify the color with which images are drawn and the properties of text fonts for a given graphics object.

VOCABULARY *Review*

Define the following terms:		
Arithmetic expression	Logic error	Screen coordinate system
Comments	Origin	Semantics
Coordinate system	Package	Syntax
Exception	Pseudocode	Virus
Graphics context	Reserved words	
Literal	Run-time error	

REVIEW *Questions*

WRITTEN QUESTIONS

Write a brief answer to the following questions.

1. Write a pseudocode algorithm that determines the batting average of a baseball player. *Hint*: To compute a batting average, divide number of hits by number of at-bats. Batting averages have three decimal places.

2. Give examples of an integer literal, a floating-point literal, and a string literal.

3. Declare variables to represent a person's name, age, and hourly wage.

4. Why must care be taken to order the operators in an arithmetic expression?

5. Is it possible to assign a value of type `int` to a variable of type `double`? Why or why not?

6. State which of the following are valid Java identifiers. For those that are not valid, explain why.
   A. length

   B. import

   C. 6months

   D. hello-and-goodbye

   E. HERE_AND_THERE

FILL IN THE BLANK

Complete the following sentences by writing the correct word or words in the blanks provided.

1. In mixed-mode arithmetic with operand types `int` and `double`, the result type is always _____ .

2. A method's name, parameters, and return type are also known as its _____ .

3. The operation that joins two strings together is called _____ .

4. End-of-line comments begin with the symbol _____ .

5. A quotient results when the _____ operator is used with two operands of type _____ .

PROJECTS

PROJECT 3-1

The surface area of a cube can be known if we know the length of an edge. Write a program that takes the length of an edge (an integer) as input and prints the cube's surface area as output. (*Remember*: analyze, design, implement, and test.)

PROJECT 3-2

Write a program that takes the radius of a sphere (a double) as input and outputs the sphere's diameter, circumference, surface area, and volume.

PROJECT 3-3

The kinetic energy of a moving object is given by the formula $KE=(1/2)mv^2$, where m is the object's mass and v is its velocity. Modify the program of Chapter 2, Project 2-5, so that it prints the object's kinetic energy as well as its momentum.

PROJECT 3-4

An employee's total weekly pay equals the hourly wage multiplied by the total number of regular hours plus any overtime pay. Overtime pay equals the total overtime hours multiplied by 1.5 times the hourly wage. Write a program that takes as inputs the hourly wage, total regular hours, and total overtime hours and displays an employee's total weekly pay.

PROJECT 3-5

Modify the program of Project 3-4 so that it prompts the user for the regular and overtime hours of each of five working days.

PROJECT 3-6

The Müller-Lyer illusion is caused by an image that consists of two parallel line segments. One line segment looks like an arrow with two heads, and the other line segment looks like an arrow with two tails. Although the line segments are of exactly the same length, they appear to be unequal (see Figure 3-9). Write a graphics program that illustrates this illusion.

FIGURE 3-9
The Müller-Lyer Illusion

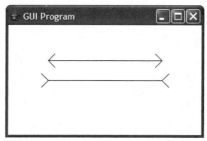

PROJECT 3-7

Write a graphics program that displays the coordinates of the center point of a panel in the form (x, y). This information should be displayed at the panel's center point and be automatically updated when the panel is resized.

CRITICAL *Thinking*

During the summer before the academic year, the registrar's office must enter new data for incoming freshmen. Design and implement a program that prompts the user for the following inputs:

Last name

First name

Class year (an integer)

Campus phone

After all the inputs are taken, the program should echo them as output.

CHAPTER 4

INTRODUCTION TO CONTROL STATEMENTS

OBJECTIVES

Upon completion of this chapter, you should be able to:

- Use the increment and decrement operators.
- Use standard math methods.
- Use `if` and `if-else` statements to make choices.
- Use `while` and `for` loops to repeat a process.
- Construct appropriate conditions for control statements using relational operators.
- Detect and correct common errors involving loops.

Estimated Time: 3.5 hours

VOCABULARY

Control statements

Counter

Count-controlled loop

Entry-controlled loop

Flowchart

Infinite loop

Iteration

Off-by-one error

Overloading

Sentinel

Task-controlled loop

All the programs to this point have consisted of short sequences of instructions that are executed one after the other. Such a scheme, even if we allowed the sequence of instructions to become extremely long, would not be very useful. In computer programs, as in real life, instructions must express repetition and selection. Expressing these notions in Java is the major topic of this chapter, but before doing so we present a couple of topics that we use throughout the rest of the chapter.

4.1 Additional Operators

Strange to say, the operators presented in this section are completely unnecessary, and we could easily manage without them; however, Java programmers use them frequently, and we cannot ignore them. Fortunately, they are convenient and easy to use.

Extended Assignment Operators

The assignment operator can be combined with the arithmetic and concatenation operators to provide extended assignment operators. Following are several examples:

```
int a = 17;
String s = "hi";

a += 3;              // Equivalent to a = a + 3;
a -= 3;              // Equivalent to a = a - 3;
a *= 3;              // Equivalent to a = a * 3;
a /= 3;              // Equivalent to a = a / 3;
a %= 3;              // Equivalent to a = a % 3;
s += " there";       // Equivalent to s = s + " there";
```

All of these examples have the format

```
variable op= expression;
```

which is equivalent to

```
variable = variable op expression;
```

Note that there is no space between op and =. The extended assignment operators and the standard assignment operator have the same precedence. For more information about these additional operators, see Appendix C.

Increment and Decrement

Java includes increment (++) and decrement (--) operators that increase or decrease a variable's value by one:

```
int m = 7;
double x = 6.4;

m++;        // Equivalent to m = m + 1;
x--;        // Equivalent to x = x - 1.0;
```

Here and throughout the book we use these operators only in the manner just illustrated; however, they can also appear in the middle of expressions. The rules for doing so are tricky and involve complexities that lead to programming errors and confusion. We encourage you to restrict yourself to the simplest uses of these operators. The precedence of the increment and decrement operators is the same as unary plus, unary minus, and cast.

*E*XERCISE 4.1

1. Translate the following statements to equivalent statements that use extended assignment operators:
   a. x = x * 2;
   b. y = y % 2;

EXERCISE 4.1 Continued

2. Translate the following statements to equivalent statements that do not use the extended assignment operators:

a. `x += 5;`

b. `x *= x;`

4.2 Standard Classes and Methods

The standard Java library includes two classes that are frequently useful. These are the `Math` and the `Random` classes. The `Math` class provides a range of common mathematical methods, whereas the `Random` class supports programs that incorporate random numbers.

The `Math` Class

The `Math` class is quite extensive; however, we limit our attention to the methods listed in Table 4-1. Notice that two methods in the table are called `abs`. They are distinguished from each other by the fact that one takes an integer and the other takes a double parameter. Using the same name for two different methods is called *overloading*.

TABLE 4-1
Seven methods in the Math class

METHOD	WHAT IT DOES
`static int abs(int x)`	Returns the absolute value of an integer x
`static double abs(double x)`	Returns the absolute value of a double x
`static double pow(double base,` `    double exponent)`	Returns the base raised to the exponent
`static long round(double x)`	Returns x rounded to the nearest whole number (Note: Returned value must be cast to an `int` before assignment to an `int` variable.)
`static int max(int a, int b)`	Returns the greater of a and b
`static int min(int a, int b)`	Returns the lesser of a and b
`static double sqrt(double x)`	Returns the square root of x

The `sqrt` Method

The next code segment illustrates the use of the `sqrt` method:

```
// Given the area of a circle, compute its radius.
// Use the formula a = pr², where a is the area and r is the radius.

double area = 10.0, radius;
radius = Math.sqrt(area / Math.PI);
```

To understand this code we must consider two points. First, messages are usually sent to objects; however, if a method's signature is labeled `static`, the message is sent to the method's class. Thus, to invoke the `sqrt` method, we send the `sqrt` message to the `Math` class. Second, in addition to methods, the `Math` class includes good approximations to several important constants. Here we use `Math.PI`, which is an approximation for π accurate to about 17 decimal places.

The Remaining Methods

The remaining methods described in Table 4-1 are illustrated in the following program code:

```
int m;
double x;

m = Math.abs(-7);           // m equals 7
x = Math.abs(-7.5);         // x equals 7.5

x = Math.pow(3.0, 2.0);     // x equals 3.0^2.0 equals 9.0
x = Math.pow(16.0, 0.25);   // x equals 16.0^0.25 equals 2.0

m = Math.max(20, 40);       // m equals 40
m = Math.min(20, 40);       // m equals 20
m = (int) Math.round(3.14); // m equals 3
m = (int) Math.round(3.5);  // m equals 4
```

The methods `pow` and `sqrt` both expect parameters of type `double`. If an `int` is used instead, it is automatically converted to a double before the message is sent. The methods `max` and `min` also have versions that work with doubles. Other useful methods, including trigonometric methods, are described in Appendix B.

The Random Class

Programs are often used to simulate random events such as the flip of a coin, the arrival times of customers at a bank, the moment-to-moment fluctuations of the stock market, and so forth. At the heart of all such programs is a mechanism called a *random number generator* that returns numbers chosen at random from a predesignated interval. Java's random number generator is implemented in the `Random` class and utilizes the methods `nextInt`, and `nextDouble`, as described in Table 4-2.

TABLE 4-2
Methods in the Random class

METHOD	WHAT IT DOES
`int nextInt(int n)`	Returns an integer chosen at random from among 0, 1, 2, ..., $n - 1$
`double nextDouble()`	Returns a double chosen at random between 0.0, inclusive, and 1.0, exclusive

A program that uses the `Random` class first must import `java.util.Random`. Following is a segment of code that illustrates the importing of `java.util.Random` and the use of the `nextInt` method:

```
import java.util.Random;
. . .

// Generate an integer chosen at random from among 0, 1, 2

Random generator = new Random();
System.out.print(generator.nextInt(3));
```

The output from this segment of code is different every time it is executed. Following are the results from three executions:

```
2
0
1
```

The method `nextDouble` behaves in a similar fashion but returns a `double` greater than or equal to 0.0 and less than 1.0.

*E*XERCISE 4.2

1. Assume that x has the value 3.6 and y has the value 4. State the value of the variable z after the following statements:
   a. `z = Math.sqrt(y);`
   b. `z = Math.round(x);`
   c. `z = Math.pow(y, 3);`
   d. `z = Math.round(Math.sqrt(x));`

2. Write code segments to print the following values in a terminal window:
   a. A random integer between 1 and 20, inclusive
   b. A random double between 1 and 10, inclusive

4.3 A Visit to the Farm

To introduce the main topic of this chapter, control statements, we begin with a "real world" example. Once upon a time in a faraway land, Jack visited his cousin Jill in the country and offered to milk the cow. Jill gave him a list of instructions:

```
fetch the cow from the field;
tie her in the stall;
milk her into the bucket;
pour the milk into the bottles;
drive her back into the field;
clean the bucket;
```

Although Jack was a little taken aback by Jill's liberal use of semicolons, he had no trouble following the instructions. A year later, Jack visited again. In the meantime, Jill had acquired a herd of cows, some red and some black. This time, when Jack offered to help, Jill gave him a more complex list of instructions:

```
herd the cows from the field into the west paddock;
while (there are any cows left in the west paddock){
   fetch a cow from the west paddock;
   tie her in the stall;
   if (she is red){
      milk her into the red bucket;
      pour the milk into red bottles;
   }else{
      milk her into the black bucket;
      pour the milk into black bottles;
   }
   put her into the east paddock;
}
herd the cows from the east paddock back into the field;
clean the buckets;
```

These instructions threw Jack for a loop (pun intended) until Jill explained that

```
while (some condition){
   do stuff;
}
```

means "do the stuff repeatedly as long as the condition holds true," and

```
if (some condition){
   do stuff 1;
}else{
   do stuff 2;
}
```

means "if some condition is true, do stuff 1, and if it is false, do stuff 2."

"And what about all the semicolons and braces?" asked Jack.

"Those," said Jill, "are just a habit I picked up from programming in Java, where `while` and `if-else` are called *control statements*."

EXERCISE 4.3

1. Why does Jill use a `while` statement in her instructions to Jack?

2. Why does Jill use an `if-else` statement in her instructions to Jack? Write pseudocode control statements that are similar in style to the farm example for the following situations:

   a. If a checker piece is red, then put it on a red square; otherwise, put it on a black square.

   b. If your shoes are muddy, then take them off and leave them outside the door.

   c. Pick up all the marbles on the floor and put them into a bag.

EXERCISE 4.3 Continued

3. Describe in English what the following code segments do:

a.

```
if (x is larger than y){
   temp = x;
   x = y;
   y = temp;
}else{
   temp = y;
   y = x;
   x = temp;
}
```

b.

```
sum = 0;
count = 1;
read an integer into total;
while (count is less than or equal to total){
   read an integer into x;
   sum = sum + Math.abs(x);
   count++;
}
if (total is greater than 0)
   print (sum / total)
```

4.4 The if and if-else Statements

We now explore in greater detail the if-else statement and the slightly simpler but related if statement. The meanings of if and else in Java sensibly adhere to our everyday usage of these words. Java and other third-generation programming languages achieve their programmer–friendly qualities by combining bits and pieces of English phrasing with some of the notational conventions of elementary algebra.

Principal Forms

To repeat, in Java, the if and if-else statements allow for the conditional execution of statements. For instance,

```
if (condition){
   statement;        //Execute these statements if the
   statement;        //condition is true.
}

if (condition){
   statement;        //Execute these statements if the
   statement;        //condition is true.
}else{
   statement;        //Execute these statements if the
   statement;        //condition is false.
}
```

The indicated semicolons and braces are required; however, the exact format of the text depends on the aesthetic sensibilities of the programmer, who should be guided by a desire to make the program as readable as possible. Notice that braces always occur in pairs and that no semicolon immediately follows a closing brace.

Additional Forms

The braces can be dropped if only a single statement follows the word `if` or `else`; for instance,

```
if (condition)
    statement;

if (condition)
    statement;
else
    statement;

if (condition){
    statement;
        ...
    statement;
}else
    statement;

if (condition)
    statement;
else{
    statement;
        ...
    statement;
}
```

Braces

In general, it is better to overuse braces than to under use them. Likewise, in expressions it is better to overuse parentheses. The extra braces or parentheses can never do any harm, and their presence helps to eliminate logic errors.

Boolean Expressions

The condition in an `if` statement must be a *Boolean expression*. This type of expression returns the value `true` or `false`.

Flowchart

Figure 4-1 shows a diagram called a *flowchart* that illustrates the behavior of `if` and `if-else` statements. When the statements are executed, either the left or the right branch is executed depending on whether the condition is `true` or `false`.

FIGURE 4-1
Flowcharts for the `if` and `if-else` statements

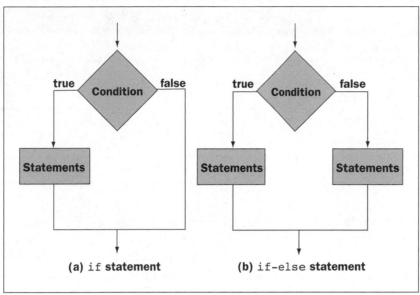

(a) `if` **statement**   (b) `if-else` **statement**

Examples

Following are some examples of `if` statements:

```
// Increase a salesman's commission by 10% if his sales are over $5000
if (sales > 5000)
    commission *= 1.1;

// Pay a worker $14.5 per hour plus time and a half for overtime
pay = hoursWorked * 14.5;
if (hoursWorked > 40){
    overtime = hoursWorked - 40;
    pay += overtime * 21.75;
}

// Let c equal the larger of a and b
if (a > b)
    c = a;
else
    c = b;
```

Relational Operators

The previous examples all use the relational operator for greater than (>); however, there are five other relational operators. Table 4-3 shows the complete list of relational operators available for use in Java.

TABLE 4-3
Relational operators

OPERATOR	WHAT IT MEANS
>	greater than
>=	greater than or equal to
<	less than
<=	less than or equal to
==	equal to
!=	not equal to

The notation for the last two relational operators is rather peculiar at first glance, but it is necessary. The double equal signs (==) distinguish the equal-to operator from the assignment operator (=). In the not-equal-to operator, the exclamation mark (!) is read as *not*. When these expressions are evaluated, their values will be either true or false, depending on the values of the operands involved. For example, suppose

```
a = 3          c = 10
b = 7          d = -20
```

then

```
a < b          is true
a <= b         is true
a == b         is false
a != b         is true
a - b > c + d  is true (the precedence of > is lower than + and -)
a < b < c      is invalid (syntactically incorrect)
a == b == c    is invalid
```

Checking Input for Validity

if-else statements are commonly used to check user inputs before processing them. For example, consider an admittedly trivial program that inputs the radius of a circle and outputs its area. If the user enters a negative number, the program should not go ahead and use it to compute an area that would be meaningless. Instead, the program should detect this problem and output an error message. Our next program example does this.

```
// Example 4.1: Computes the area of a circle if the
// radius >= 0, or displays an error message otherwise

import java.util.Scanner;

public class CircleArea{

    public static void main(String[] args){
        Scanner reader = new Scanner(System.in);
        System.out.print("Enter the radius: ");
        double radius = reader.nextDouble();
        if (radius < 0)
            System.out.println("Error: Radius must be >= 0");
        else{
            double area = Math.PI * Math.pow(radius, 2);
            System.out.println("The area is " + area);
        }
    }
}
```

EXERCISE 4.4

1. What type of expression must the condition of an `if` statement contain?

2. Describe the role of the curly braces (`{}`) in an `if` statement.

3. What is the difference between an `if` statement and an `if-else` statement?

4. Assume that x is 5 and y is 10. Write the values of the following expressions:
   a. `x <= 10`
   b. `x - 2 != 0`
   c. `x > y`

5. Given the following mini-specifications, write expressions involving relational operators:
   a. Determine if an input value x is greater than 0.
   b. Determine if a given number of seconds equals a minute.
   c. If a, b, and c are the lengths of the sides of a triangle and c is the largest side, determine if the triangle is a right triangle. (*Hint:* Use the Pythagorean equation and round the operand before comparing.)

6. Write the outputs of the following code segments:
   a.

```
int x = 20, y = 15, z;

if (x < y)
    z = 10;
else
    z = 5;
System.out.println(z);
```

EXERCISE 4.4 Continued

b.

```
int x = 2;

if (Math.round(Math.sqrt(x)) == 1)
    System.out.println("Equal");
else
    System.out.println("Not equal");
```

7. Given the following mini-specifications, write expressions involving `if-else` statements and output statements:

a. Print the larger of two numbers.

b. Prompt the user for two whole numbers and input them. Then print the numbers in numeric order.

4.5 *The* `while` *Statement*

The `while` statement provides a looping mechanism that executes statements repeatedly for as long as some condition remains true. Following is the `while` statement's format:

```
while (condition)      // loop test
    statement;             // one statement inside the loop body


while (condition){     // loop test
    statement;             // many statements
    statement;             // inside the
    ...                    // loop body
}
```

If the condition is false from the outset, the statement or statements inside the loop never execute. Figure 4-2 uses a flowchart to illustrate the behavior of a `while` statement.

FIGURE 4-2
Flowchart for a `while` statement

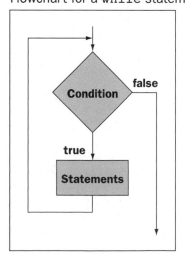

To help you become familiar with `while` statements, several short examples follow.

Compute 1 + 2 + ... + 100

The first example computes and displays the sum of the integers between 1 and 100, inclusive:

```
// Compute 1 + 2 + ... + 100

int sum = 0, cntr = 1;
while (cntr <= 100){
    sum += cntr;    // point p (we refer to this location in Table 4-4)
    cntr++;         // point q (we refer to this location in Table 4-4)
}
System.out.println (sum);
```

The behavior of this portion of code is clear. The variable `cntr` acts as a counter that controls how many times the loop executes. The counter starts at 1. Each time around the loop, it is compared to 100 and incremented by 1. Clearly the code inside the loop is executed exactly 100 times, and each time through the loop, `sum` is incremented by increasing values of `cntr`.

Count-Controlled Loops

This is an example of what is called a *count-controlled loop*. The variable `cntr` is called the *counter*.

Tracing the Variables

To fully understand the loop, we must analyze the way in which the variables change on each pass or *iteration* through the loop. Table 4-4 helps in this endeavor. On the 100th iteration, `cntr` is increased to 101, so there is never a 101st iteration, and we are confident that the `sum` is computed correctly.

TABLE 4-4
Trace of how variables change on each iteration through a loop

ITERATION NUMBER	VALUE OF CNTR AT POINT P	VALUE OF SUM AT POINT P	VALUE OF CNTR AT POINT Q
1	1	1	2
2	2	1 + 2	3
...	...	...	...
100	100	1 + 2 +...+ 100	101

Adding Flexibility

In the next example, we again add a sequence of integers, but vary the counter's starting value, ending value, and increment:

```java
// Display the sum of the integers between a startingValue
// and an endingValue, using a designated increment.

int cntr, sum, startingValue, endingValue, increment;

startingValue = 10;
endingValue = 100;
increment = 7;

sum = 0;
cntr = startingValue;
while (cntr <= endingValue){
   sum += cntr;
   cntr += increment;
}
System.out.println (sum);
```

This portion of code computes the value of 10 + 17 + 24 + ... + 94. For greater flexibility the code could be modified to ask the user for the starting value, the ending value, and the increment.

Counting Backward

We can also run the counter backward as in the next example, which displays the square roots of the numbers 25, 20, 15, and 10. Here the counter variable is called number:

```java
// Display the square roots of 25, 20, 15, and 10

int number = 25;
while (number >= 10){
   System.out.println ("The square root of " + number +
                       " is " + Math.sqrt (number));
   number -= 5;
}
```

The output is

```
The square root of 25 is 5.0
The square root of 20 is 4.47213595499958
The square root of 15 is 3.872983346207417
The square root of 10 is 3.1622776601683795
```

Task-Controlled Loop

Sometimes loops are structured so that they continue to execute until some task is accomplished. These are called *task-controlled loops*. To illustrate, we write code that finds the first integer for which the sum 1 + 2 + ... + n is over 1 million:

```java
// Display the first value n for which 1 + 2 + . . . + n
// is greater than 1 million

int sum = 0;
int number = 0;
while (sum <= 1000000){
   number++;
   sum += number;            // point p
}

System.out.println (number);
```

To verify that the code works as intended, we can reason as follows:

- The first time we reach point p, number = 1, sum = 1, and sum <= 1,000,000.

- The second time we reach point p, number = 2, sum = 1 + 2, and sum <= 1,000,000.

- Etc. ...

- The last time we reach point p, number = n, sum = 1 + 2 + ... + n, and sum > 1,000,000.

- After that we will not enter the loop again, and number contains the first value to force the sum over a million.

Common Structure

All the preceding examples share a common structure:

```
initialize variables                           // initialize
while (condition){                             // test
    perform calculations and                   // loop body
    change variables involved in the condition
}
```

For the loop to terminate, each iteration through the loop must move the variables involved in the condition significantly closer to satisfying the condition.

Computing Factorial

The factorial of a given number n is the product of the numbers between 1 and n, inclusive (1 * 2 * 3 * ... * n). The following program prompts the user for n and displays its factorial:

```java
// Example 4.2: Compute and display the factorial of n

import java.util.Scanner;

public class Factorial{

    public static void main(String[] args){
        Scanner reader = new Scanner(System.in);
        System.out.print("Enter a number greater than 0: ");
        int number = reader.nextInt();
        int product = 1;
        int count = 1;
        while (count <= number){
            product = product * count;
            System.out.println(product);
            count++;
        }
        System.out.println("The factorial of " + number +
                        " is " + product);
    }
}
```

EXERCISE 4.5

1. When does a `while` loop terminate execution?

2. List the three components of a `while` loop.   *when condition false*

3. What happens if the condition of a `while` loop is false from the outset?

4. Describe in English what the following code segments do:

   a.

   ```java
   int expo = 1, limit = 10;

   while (expo <= limit){
       System.out.println(expo + " " + Math.pow(2, expo));
   expo++;
       }
   ```

   b.

   ```java
   Scanner reader = new Scanner(System.in);
   int product = 1;
   System.out.print("Enter a positive number or -999 to halt");
   int x = reader.nextInt();

   while (x != -999){
       product *= x;
       System.out.print("Enter a positive number or -999 to halt");
       x = reader.nextInt();
   }
   ```

5. Write code segments to perform the following tasks:
   a. Print the squares and cubes of the first 10 positive integers.
   b. Print 10 random integers between 1 and 10 inclusive.
   c. Input names and ages of people until a person's age is 100.

4.6 The for Statement

Count-controlled loops are used so frequently that many programming languages (including Java) include a special statement to make them easy to write. It is called *the for statement*, and it combines counter initialization, condition test, and update into a single expression. Following is its form:

```java
for (initialize counter; test counter; update counter)
    statement;     // one statement inside the loop body

for (initialize counter; test counter; update counter){
    statement;     // many statements
    statement;     // inside the
    . . .;         // loop body
}
```

When the statement is executed[hidden] [hidden] test yields
true, the statements in the loop b[hidden] [hidden] is essential to
understand that the counter is upd[hidden] [hidden]ts in the body
have been executed. Even though [hidden] [hidden]executed at the
bottom.

To demonstrate how the fo[hidden] [hidden]-controlled loops
presented in the previous secti[hidden]

```
// Compute 1 + 2 + …[hidden]

int sum = 0, cntr;
for (cntr = 1; cntr <= 100; cn[hidden]
    sum += cntr;
System.out.println (sum);
```

```
// Display the sum of the integers between a startingValue
// and an endingValue, using a designated increment.

int cntr, sum, startingValue, endingValue, increment;

startingValue = 10;
endingValue = 100;
increment = 7;

sum = 0;
for (cntr = startingValue; cntr <= endingValue; cntr += increment)
    sum += cntr;
System.out.println (sum);
```

```
// Display the square roots of 25, 20, 15, and 10

int number;
for (number = 25; number >= 10; number -= 5)
    System.out.println ("The square root of " + number +
                        " is " + Math.sqrt (number));
```

Count-Controlled Input

Programs often need to read and process repeating inputs. For instance, consider a program that computes the average of a list of numbers. Here the repeating input is a single number. As each number is read into the program, it is added to a sum. When all the numbers have been read, the program computes and prints the average. For maximum flexibility the program must process a list of any length, but this requirement seemingly creates a dilemma. When we write the program, we have no way of knowing how many numbers will be in the list. So how can we write the program? There are two approaches. We illustrate one method in this section and the other in Section 4.8.

Read Pg 105 - 116
Do EX 4.1 - 4.4
25 pts

In the first method, we begin by asking the user for the length of the list and then we read exactly that many additional values:

```java
Scanner reader = new Scanner(System.in);
double number, sum = 0;
int i, count;

System.out.print("How long is the list? ");
count = reader.nextInt();
for (i = 1; i <= count; i++){
   System.out.print("Enter a positive number: ");
   number = reader.nextDouble();
   sum += number;
}

if (count == 0)
   System.out.println ("You entered no numbers.");
else
   System.out.println ("The average is " + sum / count);
```

Following is a sample run:

```
How long is the list? 3
Enter a positive number: 1.1
Enter a positive number: 2.2
Enter a positive number: 3.3
The average is 2.1999999999999997
```

Declaring the Loop Control Variable in a `for` Loop

The loop control variables in the examples shown thus far have been declared outside of and above the loop structure. However, the `for` loop allows the programmer to declare the loop control variable inside of the loop header. Following are equivalent loops that show these two alternatives:

```java
int i;                               // Declare control variable above loop

for (i = 1; i <= 10; i++)
   System.out.println(i);



for (int i = 1; i <= 10; i++)     // Declare control variable in loop header
   System.out.println(i);
```

Although both loops are equivalent in function, the second alternative is considered preferable on most occasions for two reasons:

1. The loop control variable is visible only within the body of the loop where it is intended to be used.

2. The same name can be declared again in other `for` loops in the same program.

    We discuss this important property of variable names, called *scope*, in more detail in Chapter 5.

Choosing a while Loop or a for Loop

Because while loops and for loops are quite similar, the following question arises: Which type of loop is more appropriate in a given situation? Both for loops and while loops are *entry-controlled loops*. This means that a continuation condition is tested at the top of the loop on each pass, before the loop's body of code is executed. If this condition is true, the loop continues. If it is false, the loop terminates. This also means that the loop's body of code might not execute at all (when its continuation condition is initially false). Thus, both types of loops can be used in exactly the same situations.

The choice between a while loop and a for loop is often a matter of programmer style or taste. However, some programmers argue that there are two minor advantages in using a for loop:

1. All of the loop control information, including the initial setting of the loop control variable, its update, and the test of the continuation condition, appears within the for loop's header. By contrast, only the test appears in the header of a while loop. Some programmers argue that you are more likely to forget the update in a while loop, which can cause a logic error.

2. The loop control variable of a for loop can be declared in its header. This restricts the variable's visibility to the body of the loop, where it is relevant. Although there are exceptions to this practice, restricting the visibility of variables in a program can make it more likely to be free of logic errors. We discuss this idea in more detail in Chapter 5.

*E*XERCISE 4.6

1. Describe in English what the following code segments do:

   a.
   ```
   for (int expo = 1; expo <= limit; expo++)
                System.out.println(expo + " " + Math.pow(2, expo));
   ```

   b.
   ```
           int base = 2;

           for (int count = expo; count > 1; count-)
       base = base * base;
   ```

2. Write code segments that use for loops to perform the following tasks:
   a. Print the squares and cubes of the first 10 positive integers.
   b. Build a string consisting of the first 10 positive digits in descending order.

3. Translate the following for loops to equivalent while loops:
   a.
   ```
       Scanner reader new Scanner(System.in);

       for (int i = 1; i <= 5; i++){
          System.out.print("Enter an integer: ");
          int number = reader.nextInt();
          System.out.println(Math.pow(number, 2));
       }
   ```

EXERCISE 4.6 Continued

b.

```
int base = 2;

for (int count = expo; count > 1; count-)
   base = base * base;
```

4.7 Nested Control Statements and the break Statement

Control statements can be nested inside each other in any combination that proves useful. We now present several illustrative examples and also demonstrate a mechanism for breaking out of a loop early, that is, before the loop condition is false. All the examples use for loops, but similar examples can be constructed using while loops.

Print the Divisors

As a first example, we write a code segment that asks the user for a positive integer n, and then prints all its proper divisors, that is, all divisors except 1 and the number itself. For instance, the proper divisors of 12 are 2, 3, 4, and 6. A positive integer d is a divisor of n if d is less than n and n % d is zero. Thus, to find n's proper divisors, we must try all values of d between 2 and n / 2. Here is the code:

```
// Display the proper divisors of a number

System.out.print("Enter a positive integer: ");
int n = reader.nextInt();

int limit = n / 2;

for (int d = 2; d <= limit; d++){
   if (n % d == 0)
      System.out.print (d + " ");
}
```

Is a Number Prime?

A number is prime if it has no proper divisors. We can modify the previous code segment to determine if a number is prime simply by counting its proper divisors. If there are none, the number is prime. Following is code that implements this plan:

```
// Determine if a number is prime

System.out.print(("Enter an integer greater than 2: ");
int n = reader.nextInt();

int count = 0;
int limit = n/2;
```

```
for (int d = 2; d <= limit; d++){
   if (n % d == 0)

      count++;
}

if (count != 0)
   System.out.println ("Not prime.");
else
   System.out.println ("Prime.");
```

The break Statement

Most programmers, including the authors of this text, enjoy the challenge of trying to write efficient programs. You can do two things to improve the efficiency of the previous segment of code. First, the limit does not need to be as large as n / 2. If a*b equals n, then either a or b must be less than or equal to the square root of n. Second, as soon as we find the first divisor of n, we know n is not prime, so there is no point in going around the loop again. To get out of a loop prematurely, that is, before the loop condition is false, we can use a break statement. A loop, either for or while, terminates immediately when a break statement is executed.

In the following segment of code, we check d after the for loop terminates. If n has a divisor, the break statement executes, the loop terminates early, and d is less than or equal to the limit. Following is the code:

```
// Determine if a number is prime

System.out.print("Enter an integer greater than 2: ");
int n = reader.nextInt();

int limit = (int)Math.sqrt (n);

int d;                                    // Declare control variable here

for (d = 2; d <= limit; d++){
   if (n % d == 0)
      break;
}

if (d <= limit)                           // So it's visible here
   System.out.println ("Not prime.");
else
   System.out.println ("Prime.");
```

Note that the loop control variable d must now be declared above the loop so that it will be visible below it.

Sentinel-Controlled Input

In addition to the count-controlled input mentioned in the previous section, there is a second method for handling repeating user inputs. We again use the example of finding the average of a list of numbers. Now we read numbers repeatedly until we encounter a special value called a *sentinel* that marks the end of the list. For instance, if all the numbers in the list are positive, then the sentinel could be −1, as shown in the following code:

```
Scanner reader = new Scanner(System.in);
double number, sum = 0;
int count = 0;

while (true){
    System.out.print("Enter a positive number or -1 to quit: ");
    number = reader.nextDouble();
    if (number == -1) break;
    sum += number;
    count++;
}

if (count == 0)
    System.out.println ("The list is empty.");
else
    System.out.println ("The average is " + sum / count);
```

Following is a sample run:

```
Enter a positive number or -1 to quit: 1.1
Enter a positive number or -1 to quit: 2.2
Enter a positive number or -1 to quit: 3.3
Enter a positive number or -1 to quit: -1
The average is 2.1999999999999997
```

Like any other high-level language, Java is rich in control statements. For example, the switch statement, the do-while statement, and the continue statement allow the programmer to express selection and repetition in a different manner than the control statements in this chapter. For details on these statements, see Appendix B.

EXERCISE 4.7

1. Describe in English what the following code segments do:
   a.

   ```
   for (int i = 1; i <= limit; i++)
       if (i % 2 == 0)
           System.out.println(i);
   ```
   b.

   ```
   Random gen = new Random();
   int myNumber = gen.nextInt(10);
   int x = 0;
   int yourNumber;

   while (x == 0){
       System.out.println("I'm guessing a number between 1 and 10.");
       System.out.print("Which number is it? ");
       yourNumber = reader.nextInt();
   ```

EXERCISE 4.7 Continued

```
        if (myNumber == yourNumber){
           System.out.println("That's it!");
           break;
        }else System.out.println("Sorry, try again");
   }
```

2. Write code segments that use loops to perform the following tasks:

    a. Print the squares and cubes of the first 10 positive, odd integers.

    b. Build a string consisting of the first 10 positive, even digits in descending order.

4.8 Using Loops with Text Files

Thus far in this book, we have seen examples of programs that have taken input data from human users at the keyboard. Most of these programs can receive their input data from text files as well. A text file is a software object that stores data on a permanent medium such as a disk, CD, or flash memory. When compared to keyboard input from a human user, the main advantages of taking input data from a file are as follows:

■ The data set can be much larger.

■ The data can be input much more quickly and with less chance of error.

■ The data can be used repeatedly with the same program or with different programs.

Text Files and Their Format

The data in a text file can be created, saved, and viewed with a text editor, such as Notepad. Alternatively, a program can output the data to a file, a procedure that we discuss shortly. The data in a text file can be viewed as characters, words, numbers, or lines of text, depending on the text file's format and on the purposes for which the data is used. When the data are treated as numbers (either integers or floating-points), they must be separated by whitespace characters. These are the space, tab, and newline characters. For example, a text file containing six floating-point numbers might look like

```
34.6 22.33 66.75
77.12 21.44 99.01
```

when examined with a text editor.

Any text file, including the special case of an empty file, must contain at least one special character that marks the end of the file. This character can serve as a sentinel for a program loop that reads each datum until the end-of-file condition is encountered. When a program opens a file, an input pointer is set to the first character in it. Assuming that the end-of-file condition has not yet been reached, when each datum is read, the pointer moves to the next datum.

The Scanner and File Classes

Fortunately, we can use the same `Scanner` class for text file input that we use for keyboard input. The first step is to create a scanner object by opening it on a file object rather than the keyboard object. File objects are instances of the class `File`, which appears in the package `java.io`. We obtain a file object by running the code `new File(aFileName)`, where `afileName` is a pathname or the name of a file in the current working directory. For example, let's assume that we have a text file of floating-point numbers named `"numbers.txt"`. The following code opens a scanner on this file:

```
Scanner reader = new Scanner(new File("numbers.txt"));
```

A sentinel-controlled loop can then be used to read all of the data from the file. Before each datum is read, we must check to see if the end of the file condition has been reached. The `Scanner` method `hasNext()` returns `true` if the end of file is not yet present. Now let's assume that we want to compute the average of the numbers in the file. A slight modification of the sentinel-controlled loop from section 4.7 accomplishes this:

```
Scanner reader = new Scanner(new File("numbers.txt"));
double number, sum = 0;
int count = 0;

while (reader.hasNext()){
    number = reader.nextDouble();
    sum += number;
    count++;
}
```

Note that we test for the sentinel before reading the data and we omit the output of the prompt to the user.

Files and Exceptions

When a Java program encounters an operation that it cannot perform at runtime, the JVM throws an exception. We have seen examples of exceptions thrown in earlier chapters when a program commits run-time errors, such as an attempt to divide an integer by zero. When working with files, a program may encounter errors that it cannot handle. For example, the file could be missing when the program tries to open it, or the file's data may be corrupted on the storage medium. In these cases, an I/O exception is thrown. I/O exceptions are generally so serious that they belong to a category called *checked exceptions*. This means that a program must at least acknowledge they might be thrown, if not do something to recover from them. We see how to recover from an exception in Chapter 10. For now, to meet the minimal requirement, we can place the simple phrase `throws IOException` after the header of the `main` method of any program that does text file input. If the program encounters an `IOException`, the JVM will halt execution with an error message.

The following program uses our sentinel-controlled loop to compute and display the average of the numbers in a text file:

```
// Example 4.3: Computes and displays the average of
// a file of floating-point numbers

import java.io.*;              // For File and IOException
import java.util.Scanner;
```

```
public class ComputeAverage{
   public static void main(String[] args) throws IOException {
      Scanner reader = new Scanner(new File("numbers.txt"));
      double number, sum = 0;
      int count = 0;

      while (reader.hasNext()){
         number = reader.nextDouble();
         sum += number;
         count++;
      }
      if (count == 0)
         System.out.println("The file had no numbers");
      else
         System.out.println("The average of " + count + " numbers is " +
                             sum / count);
   }
}
```

Output to Text Files

Data can be output to a text file using the class `PrintWriter`. This class includes the methods `print` and `println` that you have already used for terminal output, so there is not much new to be learned. A `PrintWriter` is opened like scanner, using the form

```
PrintWriter writer = new PrintWriter(new File(aFileName));
```

After the outputs have been completed, you must close the `PrintWriter` with the statement

```
writer.close();
```

Failure to close the output file may result in no data being saved to it. Because an `IOException` might be thrown during these operations, the `main` method must use a `throws IOException` clause to keep the compiler happy.

Our next example program filters a set of integers by removing all of the zeroes and retaining the other values. The inputs are in a text file named `numbers.txt`, whereas the outputs go to a file named `newnumbers.txt`. Here is the code:

```
// Example 4.4: Inputs a text file of integers and writes these
// to an output file without the zeroes

import java.io.*;              // For File, IOException, and PrintWriter
import java.util.Scanner;

public class FilterZeroes{

   public static void main(String[] args) throws IOException {

      // Open the scanner and print writer
      Scanner reader = new Scanner(new File("numbers.txt"));
      PrintWriter writer = new PrintWriter(new File("newnumbers.txt"));
```

```
    // Read the numbers and write all but the zeroes
    while (reader.hasNext()){
        int number = reader.nextInt();
        if (number != 0)
            writer.println(number);
    }

    // Remember to close the output file
    writer.close();
  }
}
```

Note that this program also runs correctly with an empty input file or one that contains no zeroes.

EXERCISE 4.8

1. Describe in English what the following code segment does:

```
Scanner reader = new Scanner(new File("myfile.txt"));
```

2. Write code segments that use loops to perform the following tasks:
- **a.** Read integers from a file and display them in the terminal window.
- **b.** Assume that there are an even number of integers in a file. Read them in pairs from the file and display the larger value of each pair in the terminal window.

Case Study: The Folly of Gambling

It is said, with some justification, that only the mathematically challenged gamble. Lotteries, slot machines, and gambling games in general are designed to take in more money than they pay out. Even if gamblers get lucky and win a few times, in the long run they lose. For this case study we have invented a game of chance called Lucky Sevens that seems like an attractive proposition, but which is, as usual, a sure loser for the gambler. The rules of the game are simple:

- Roll a pair of dice.

- If the sum of the spots equals 7, the player wins $4; else the player loses $1.

To entice the gullible, the casino tells players that there are lots of ways to win: (1, 6), (2, 5), etc. A little mathematical analysis reveals that there are not enough ways to win to make the game worthwhile; however, many people's eyes glaze over at the first mention of mathematics, so the challenge is to write a program that demonstrates the futility of playing the game.

Request

Write a program that demonstrates the futility of playing Lucky Sevens.

Analysis

We use the random number generator to write a program that simulates the game. The program asks the user how many dollars he has, plays the game repeatedly until the money is gone, and displays the number of rolls taken. The program also displays the maximum amount of money held by the player, thus demonstrating that getting ahead at some point does not avoid the inevitable outcome. Figure 4-3 shows the proposed interface.

FIGURE 4-3

Interface for the lucky sevens simulator

```
How many dollars do you have? 100
You are broke after 543 rolls.
You should have quit after 47 rolls when you had $113
```

Design

The design is captured in the following pseudocode:

```
read the initial amount the gambler has to wager
initialize to zero a counter representing the number of rolls

the maximum amount equals the initial amount
the count at the maximum equals zero

while (there is any money left){
   increment the rolls counter
   roll the dice

   if (the dice add to seven)
      add $4 to the gambler's amount
   else
      subtract $1 from the gambler's amount

   if (the amount is now greater than ever before){
      remember this maximum amount
      remember the current value of the rolls counter
   }
}
display the rolls counter
display the maximum amount
display the count at the maximum amount
```

Implementation

Following is a program based on the pseudocode:

```
/*LuckySevens.java
Simulate the game of lucky sevens until all funds are depleted.
1) Rules:
        roll two dice
        if the sum equals 7, win $4, else lose $1
2) The inputs are:
        the amount of money the user is prepared to lose
3) Computations:
        use the random number generator to simulate rolling the dice
        loop until the funds are depleted
        count the number of rolls
        keep track of the maximum amount
4) The outputs are:
        the number of rolls it takes to deplete the funds
        the maximum amount
*/

import java.util.Scanner;
import java.util.Random;

public class LuckySevens {
   public static void main (String [] args) {

      Scanner reader = new Scanner(System.in);
      Random generator = new Random();

      int die1, die2,        // two dice
          dollars,           // initial number of dollars (input)
          count,             // number of rolls to reach depletion
          maxDollars,        // maximum amount held by the gambler
          countAtMax;        // count when the maximum is achieved

      // Request the input
      System.out.print("How many dollars do you have? ");
      dollars = reader.nextInt();

      // Initialize variables
      maxDollars = dollars;
      countAtMax = 0;
      count = 0;

      // Loop until the money is gone
      while (dollars > 0){
         count++;

         // Roll the dice.
         die1 = generator.nextInt (6) + 1; // 1-6
         die2 = generator.nextInt (6) + 1; // 1-6
```

```
        // Calculate the winnings or losses
        if (die1 + die2 == 7)
           dollars += 4;
        else
           dollars -= 1;

        // If this is a new maximum, remember it
        if (dollars > maxDollars){
           maxDollars = dollars;
           countAtMax = count;
        }
      }

      // Display the results
      System.out.println
         ("You are broke after " + count + " rolls.\n" +
          "You should have quit after " + countAtMax +
          " rolls when you had $" + maxDollars + ".");
   }
}
```

Output

Running this program is just about as exciting (in our opinion) as going to Las Vegas, and it's a lot cheaper. (Perhaps we should translate it into a Java applet as shown in Chapter 8 of this book, make it part of a Web page, and charge people 10 cents each to run it.) Following are the results from several trial runs:

```
How many dollars do you have? 100
You are broke after 255 rolls.
You should have quit after 35 rolls when you had $110.

How many dollars do you have? 100
You are broke after 500 rolls.
You should have quit after 179 rolls when you had $136.

How many dollars do you have? 1000000
You are broke after 6029535 rolls.
You should have quit after 97 rolls when you had $1000008.
```

These results show that there is very little money to be gained in this game of chance—regardless of how much you have available to gamble.

4.9 Errors in Loops

We can easily make logic errors when coding loops, but we can avoid many of these errors if we have a proper understanding of a loop's typical structure. A loop usually has four component parts:

1. *Initializing statements.* These statements initialize variables used within the loop.
2. *Terminating condition.* This condition is tested before each pass through the loop to determine if another iteration is needed.
3. *Body statements.* These statements execute with each iteration and implement the calculation in question.

4. *Update statements.* These statements, which usually are executed at the bottom of the loop, change the values of the variables tested in the terminating condition.

A careless programmer can introduce logic errors into any one of these components. To demonstrate, we first present a simple but correct `while` loop and then show several revised versions, each with a different logic error. The correct version is

```
//Compute the product of the odd integers from 1 to 100
//Outcome - product will equal 3*5*...*99
int product = 1;
int i = 3;
while (i <= 100){
    product = product * i;
    i = i + 2;
}
System.out.println (product);
```

Initialization Error

We first introduce an error into the initializing statements. Because we forget to initialize the variable `product`, it retains its default value of zero.

```
//Error - failure to initialize the variable product
//Outcome - zero is printed
int product;
int i = 3;
while (i <= 100){
    product = product * i;
    i = i + 2;
}
System.out.println (product);
```

Off-by-One Error

The next error involves the terminating condition:

```
//Error - use of "< 99" rather than "<= 100" in the
//    terminating condition
//Outcome - product will equal 3*5...*97
int product = 1;
int i = 3;
while (i < 99){
    product = product * i;
    i = i + 2;
}
System.out.println (product);
```

This is called an *off-by-one error*, and it occurs whenever a loop goes around one too many or one too few times. This is one of the most common types of looping errors and is often difficult to detect. Do not be fooled by the fact that, in this example, the error is glaringly obvious.

Infinite Loop

Following is another error in the terminating condition:

```
//Error - use of "!= 100" rather than "<= 100" in the terminating condition
//Outcome - the program will never stop
int product = 1;
int i = 3;

while (i != 100){
   product = product * i;
   i = i + 2;
}
System.out.println (product);
```

The variable i takes on the values 3, 5, ..., 99, 101, ... and never equals 100. This is called an *infinite loop*. Anytime a program responds more slowly than expected, it is reasonable to assume that it is stuck in an infinite loop. Do not pull the plug. Instead, on a PC, select the terminal window and press Ctrl+C; that is, press the Control and "C" keys simultaneously. This will stop the program.

Error in Loop Body

Following is an error in the body of the loop. Again, the error is comically obvious because we are pointing it out, but these kinds of errors often can be difficult to detect—particularly for the person who wrote the program.

```
//Error - use of + rather than * when computing product
//Outcome - product will equal 3+5+...+99
int product = 1;
int i = 3;
while (i <= 100){
   product = product + i;
   i = i + 2;
}
System.out.println (product);
```

Update Error

If the update statement is in the wrong place, the calculations can be thrown off even if the loop iterates the correct number of times:

```
//Error - placement of the update statement in the wrong place
//Outcome - product will equal 5*7*...*99*101
int product = 1;
int i = 3;
while (i <= 100){
   i = i + 2;             //this update statement should follow the calculation
   product = product * i;
}
System.out.println (product);
```

Effects of Limited Floating-Point Precision

Numbers that are declared as `double` have about 18 decimal digits of precision. This is very good, but it is not perfect and can lead to unexpected errors. Consider the following lines of code, which seem to be free of logic errors, yet produce an infinite loop:

```
double x;
for (x = 0.0; x != 1.0; x += 0.1)
   System.out.print (x + " ");
```

When this code runs, the expected output is

```
 0.0   0.1   0.2   0.3   0.4   0.5   0.6   0.7   0.8   0.9   1.0
```

However, the actual output is

```
0.0   0.1   0.2   0.30000000000000004   0.4   0.5   0.6   0.7   0.7999999999999999
0.8999999999999999   0.9999999999999999   1.0999999999999999   1.2   1.3
1.4000000000000001   1.5000000000000002   ... etc ...
```

To understand what went wrong, consider the decimal representation of ⅓. It is 0.33333... The 3s go on forever, and consequently no finite representation is exact. The same sort of thing happens when 1/5 is represented in binary as a `double`. Consequently, in the previous code, x never exactly equals 1.0 and the loop never terminates. To fix the code, we rewrite it as

```
double x, delta;
delta = 0.01;
for (x = 0.0; x <= 1.0 + delta; x += 0.1)
   System.out.print (x + " ");
```

The code now works correctly, provided `delta` is less than the increment 0.1. The new output is

```
0.0   0.1   0.2   0.30000000000000004   0.4   0.5   0.6   0.7   0.7999999999999999
0.8999999999999999   0.9999999999999999
```

Debugging Loops

If you suspect that you have written a loop that contains a logic error, inspect the code and make sure the following items are true:

- Variables are initialized correctly before entering the loop.

- The terminating condition stops the iterations when the test variables have reached the intended limit.

- The statements in the body are correct.

- The update statements are positioned correctly and modify the test variables in such a manner that they eventually pass the limits tested in the terminating condition.

In addition, when writing terminating conditions, it is usually safer to use one of the operators

```
<       <=       >       >=
```

than either of the operators

```
==      !=
```

as demonstrated earlier.

Also, if you cannot find an error by inspection, then use `System.out.println` statements to "dump" key variables to the terminal window. Good places for these statements are

- Immediately after the initialization statements
- Inside the loop at the top
- Inside the loop at the bottom

You will then discover that some of the variables have values different than expected, and this will provide clues that reveal the exact nature and location of the logic error.

EXERCISE 4.9

1. Describe the logic errors in the following loops:

a.

```
// Print the odd numbers between 1 and limit, inclusive
for (int i = 1; i < limit; i++)
   if (i % 2 == 1)
      System.out.println(i);
```

b.

```
// Print the first ten positive odd numbers
int number = 1;
while (number != 10)
   System.out.println(number);
   number += 2;
}
```

4.10 Graphics and GUIs: I/O Dialog Boxes and Loops

Our graphics and GUI programs in earlier chapters displayed images but were not interactive, in that they did not accept user input. In this section we explore the use of dialog boxes for I/O. We also examine the use of loops and selection statements in graphics and GUI-based programs.

Extra Challenge

This Graphics and GUIs section gives you the opportunity to explore concepts and programming techniques required to develop modern graphics applications and graphical user interfaces. This material is not required in order to proceed with the other chapters of the book.

I/O Dialogs

A very convenient way to accept input from a user is to pop up an *input dialog box*. A typical input dialog box is a small window that contains a message asking for information, a text field for entering it, and command buttons labeled OK and Cancel. The text field can either be empty or contain a default data value, such as a number, when the dialog box pops up. The user places her mouse cursor in the text field and edits the data. She then clicks **OK** to accept the data or **Cancel** to back out of the interaction.

The class `JOptionPane` in the package `javax.swing` includes several versions of the method `showInputDialog` for input dialog boxes. One such version expects two strings as parameters. The first string is the message to be displayed in the dialog box. The second string is the default data value to be displayed in the input text field. If you want the field to be empty, you can pass the empty string ("") in this position. The following code segment pops up the input dialog box shown in Figure 4-4, which asks for the user's age:

```
String inputStr = JOptionPane.showInputDialog("Enter your age", "");
```

FIGURE 4-4
An input dialog

If the user clicks **OK**, the dialog box closes and returns the string that happens to be in the text input field. In our example, the code assigns this string to the variable `inputStr`. If the user clicks **Cancel** to back out, the dialog box closes and returns the value `null`, which our code also assigns to `inputStr`. Clearly, the program code must then check for `null` before passing the input datum on to the next step. The simplest way to handle the `null` value is shown in the next code segment:

```
if (inputStr == null)
   return;
```

The `return` statement in this code quits the method if the input string is `null`.

If the expected input is a number, one other thing must be done before it can be processed. The dialog box returns a string of digits, which must be converted to an `int` or a `double`. The methods `Integer.parseInt(aString)` and `Double.parseDouble(aString)` accomplish this for integers and floating-point numbers, respectively.

To output a message, we can use a *message dialog box*. The method `JOptionPane.showMessageDialog(anObserver, aString)` pops up a small window that displays the second parameter and waits for the user to click the OK button. For now, the first parameter is `null`.

The next program example incorporates dialog box I/O into the `CircleArea` program of Section 4.4. Shots of the dialog boxes from an interaction are shown in Figure 45.

```
// Example 4.5: CircleARea with dialog I/O

import javax.swing.JOptionPane;

public class CircleArea{

    public static void main(String[] args){
        String inputStr = JOptionPane.showInputDialog("Enter the radius", "0");
        if (inputStr == null)
           return;
        double radius = Double.parseDouble(inputStr);
        if (radius < 0)
           JOptionPane.showMessageDialog(null, "Error: Radius must be >= 0");
        else{
           double area = Math.PI * Math.pow(radius, 2);
           JOptionPane.showMessageDialog(null, "The area is " + area);
        }
    }
}
```

FIGURE 4-5
Dialog I/O user interface for the circle area program

Unlike the graphics and GUI programs shown earlier, this one runs in the terminal window and does not pop up a main program window. Note also that if the user cancels the input dialog box, the program simply quits by returning from the main method.

Setting Up Lots of Panels

Some of our early graphics programs used multiple panels. Occasionally, many panels are called for. For example, a program might display a regular pattern such as those seen on quilts. In these situations, a loop can be used to initialize and install the panels. Consider the following fanciful program, which prompts the user for the dimensions of a grid of randomly colored panels and then displays them:

```
// Example 4.6: Display random colors in a grid
// whose dimensions are input by the user

import javax.swing.*;
import java.awt.*;
import java.util.Random;

public class GUIWindow{

    public static void main(String[] args){
        JFrame theGUI = new JFrame();
        theGUI.setTitle("GUI Example");
        String inputStr = JOptionPane.showInputDialog("Number of rows", "5");
```

```
        if (inputStr == null) return;
        int rows = Integer.parseInt(inputStr);
        inputStr = JOptionPane.showInputDialog("Number of columns", "5");
        if (inputStr == null) return;
        int cols = Integer.parseInt(inputStr);
        theGUI.setSize(cols  * 50, rows * 50);
        theGUI.setDefaultCloseOperation(JFrame.EXIT_ON_CLOSE);
        Container pane = theGUI.getContentPane();
        pane.setLayout(new GridLayout(rows, cols));
        Random gen = new Random();
        for (int i = 1; i <= rows * cols; i++){
            int red = gen.nextInt(256);
            int green = gen.nextInt(256);
            int blue = gen.nextInt(256);
            Color backColor = new Color(red, green, blue);
            ColorPanel panel = new ColorPanel(backColor);
            pane.add(panel);
        }
        theGUI.setVisible(true);
    }
}
```

The user's inputs not only determine the number of rows and columns in the grid, but also the initial size of the application window. The loop works correctly, whether these values are the defaults (5 by 5), or 1 by 1, or 50 by 50 (a pretty big window).

Setting the Preferred Size of a Panel

In the graphics program we have seen thus far, the main window class sets its dimensions at program startup. The dimensions of any panels that appear within the main window are then adjusted to fit within the window when it is displayed. Another way to arrange things is to give each panel a preferred size and ask the window to shrink-wrap its dimensions to accommodate all of the panels. This alternative is useful when we want to fix the exact size of each panel before it is displayed. For instance, if we want the size of each panel to be exactly 50 by 50, the code in the previous example will not do because the window's title bar and borders occupy some of its "real estate."

To solve this problem, we drop the call of the method `setSize` from the main window class and add a call of the method `pack()`. This method asks the window to wrap itself around the minimal area necessary to display all of its components (panels or other widgets) at their preferred sizes. Here is the code for the `main` method of that program with the needed changes:

```
public static void main(String[] args){
    JFrame theGUI = new JFrame();
    theGUI.setTitle("GUI Example");
    String inputStr = JOptionPane.showInputDialog("Number of rows", "5");
    if (inputStr == null) return;
    int rows = Integer.parseInt(inputStr);
    inputStr = JOptionPane.showInputDialog("Number of columns", "5");
    if (inputStr == null) return;
    int cols = Integer.parseInt(inputStr);
    //theGUI.setSize(cols  * 50, rows * 50);   Dropped!!!
    theGUI.setDefaultCloseOperation(JFrame.EXIT_ON_CLOSE);
    Container pane = theGUI.getContentPane();
```

```
        pane.setLayout(new GridLayout(rows, cols));
        Random gen = new Random();
        for (int i = 1; i <= rows * cols; i++){
            int red = gen.nextInt(256);
            int green = gen.nextInt(256);
            int blue = gen.nextInt(256);
            Color backColor = new Color(red, green, blue);
            //Use new constructor to specify the preferred size of the panel
            ColorPanel panel = new ColorPanel(backColor, 50, 50);
            pane.add(panel);
        }
        theGUI.pack();                              //Added!!
        theGUI.setVisible(true);
    }
```

If a panel does not set its own preferred size, its default size is 0 by 0. We add a second constructor to the `ColorPanel` class that receives a preferred width and height from the client. This constructor calls the method `setPreferredSize`, which expects an object of class `Dimension` as a parameter. This object, in turn, is created with the width and height received from the client. Here is the modified code for the `ColorPanel` class:

```
// Example 4.7: A color panel whose background is
// a color provided by the client
// A client-specified preferred size is optional

import javax.swing.*;
import java.awt.*;

public class ColorPanel extends JPanel{

    // Client provides color and preferred width and height
    public ColorPanel(Color backColor, int width, int height){
        setBackground(backColor);
        setPreferredSize(new Dimension(width, height));
    }

    // Client provides color
    // Preferred width and height are 0, 0 by default
    public ColorPanel(Color backColor){
        setBackground(backColor);
    }
}
```

Drawing Multiple Shapes

Consider the problem of displaying a bull's-eye, as shown in Figure 4-6. This particular bull's-eye is a pattern of five concentric filled ovals, whose colors alternate. Each oval is centered in the panel. The outermost oval's width and height are the width and height of the panel minus 1. Each oval's radius is a constant amount (called the thickness) larger than the next smaller oval's radius. One can create this pattern by drawing the largest oval first and then drawing the other ovals on top, layering them in descending order of size. The algorithm starts with a thickness of the panel's width divided by 10, an initial corner point of (0, 0), a size of the panel's width − 1 and height − 1, and the color red. The algorithm then runs a loop that performs the following steps five times:

1. Draw the oval with the current color, corner point, and size.

2. Adjust the corner point by subtracting the thickness from each coordinate.

3. Adjust the size by subtracting twice the thickness from each dimension.

4. Adjust the color (to white if red, or to red otherwise).

FIGURE 4-6
A bull's eye

This algorithm is implemented in the `paintComponent` method of the following `ColorPanel` class:

```
// Example 4.8: A color panel containing
// a red and white bull's eye

import javax.swing.*;
import java.awt.*;

public class ColorPanel extends JPanel{

    // Client provides color and preferred width and height
    public ColorPanel(Color backColor, int width, int height){
        setBackground(backColor);
        setPreferredSize(new Dimension(width, height));
    }

    // Client provides color
    // Preferred width and height are 0, 0 by default
    public ColorPanel(Color backColor){
        setBackground(backColor);
    }

    public void paintComponent(Graphics g){
        super.paintComponent(g);

        //Set the attributes of the outermost oval
        int thickness = getWidth() / 10;
        int x = 0;
        int y = 0;
        int width = getWidth() - 1;
        int height = getHeight() - 1;
        Color ringColor = Color.red;
```

```
for (int count = 1; count <= 5; count++){
    g.setColor(ringColor);
    g.fillOval(x, y, width, height);

    //Adjust corner point for next oval
    x = x + thickness;
    y = y + thickness;

    //Adjust width and height for next oval
    width = width - thickness * 2;
    height = height - thickness * 2;

    //Change the color for the next oval
    if (ringColor == Color.red)
        ringColor = Color.white;
    else
        ringColor = Color.red;
}
}
}
```

As you can see, it would be easy to modify the appearance of the bull's-eye by changing the number of ovals drawn, their thickness, and the colors.

*E*XERCISE 4.10

1. Write a code segment that uses an I/O dialog box to prompt the user for her name.

2. Write a code segment that displays your name and address in a message box. Your name and address should be formatted on separate lines by using the "\n" character.

3. Explain why we need to use the methods `Integer.parseInt` and `Double.parseDouble` when receiving numeric input from an I/O dialog box.

4. Give an example of a situation where you would want a panel to set its preferred size, rather than allow the size of the main window to determine that.

Design, Testing, and Debugging Hints

- Most errors involving selection statements and loops are not syntax errors caught at compile time. Thus, you will detect these errors only after running the program, and perhaps then only with extensive testing.

- The presence or absence of the {} symbols can seriously affect the logic of a selection statement or loop. For example, the following selection statements have a similar look but a very different logic:

```
if (x > 0){
    y = x;
    z = 1 / x;
}
```

```
if (x > 0)
   y = x;
   z = 1 / x;
```

The first selection statement guards against division by 0; the second statement only guards against assigning x to y. The next pair of code segments shows a similar problem with a loop:

```
while (x > 0){
   y = x;
   x = x - 1;
}

while (x > 0)
   y = x;
   x = x - 1;
```

The first loop terminates because the value of x decreases within the body of the loop; the second loop is infinite because the value of x decreases below the body of the loop.

- When testing programs that use `if` or `if-else` statements, be sure to use test data that forces the program to exercise all of the logical branches.

- Use an `if-else` statement rather than two `if` statements when the alternative courses of action are mutually exclusive.

- When testing a loop, be sure to use limit values as well as typical values. For example, if a loop should terminate when the control variable equals 0, run it with the values 0, –1, and 1.

- Be sure to check entry conditions and exit conditions for each loop.

- For a loop with errors, use debugging output statements to verify the values of the control variable on each pass through the loop. Check this value before the loop is initially entered, after each update, and after the loop is exited.

- Text files are convenient to use when the data set is large, when the same data set must be used repeatedly with different programs, and when these data must be saved permanently.

SUMMARY

In this chapter, you learned:

- Java has some useful operators for extended assignment, such as +=, and for increment and decrement.

- The `Math` class provides several useful methods, such as `sqrt` and `abs`.

- The `Random` class allows you to generate random integers and floating-point numbers.

- `if` and `if-else` statements are used to make one-way and two-way decisions.

- The comparison operators, such as ==, <=, and >=, return Boolean values that serve as conditions of control statements.

- The `while` loop allows the program to run a set of statements repeatedly until a condition becomes false.

- The `for` loop is a more concise version of the `while` loop.

- Other control statements, such as an `if` statement, can be nested within loops. A `break` statement can be used in conjunction with an `if` statement to terminate a loop early.

- There are many kinds of logic errors that can occur in loops. Examples are the off-by-one error and the infinite loop.

VOCABULARY *Review*

Define the following terms:

Control statements	Flowchart	Overloading
Counter	Infinite loop	Sentinel
Count-controlled loop	Iteration	Task-controlled loop
Entry-controlled loop	Off-by-one error	

REVIEW *Questions*

WRITTEN QUESTIONS

Write a brief answer to the following questions.

1. Assume that the variables `x` and `y` contain the values 19 and 2, respectively. Indicate if the Boolean expressions below are true, false, or syntactically incorrect.
   A. `x <= y`
   B. `x * 2 > y`
   C. `x - 1 == y * 9`
   D. `x < y < 25`
   E. `x * 2 != y`

2. For each of the following items, write a valid Java statement.
   A. Display "greater" if the value of variable `x` is greater than the value of variable `y`. Otherwise, display "less" if the value of variable `x` is less than the value of variable `y`. Otherwise, display "equal."
   B. Add 10 to the value of `x` and display this value if the variable `y` is negative.
   C. Display the string A if `x` is greater than 90, B if `x` is greater than 80 and less than or equal to 90, or C otherwise.

3. Indicate whether or not each of the following loop headings is syntactically correct. If incorrect, explain why.
   A. `while (x > 0)`
   B. `while (y = 10)`
   C. `while x != 0`

4. Write a valid Java statement for each of the following items.
   A. Output the positive numbers from `x` up to `y`.
   B. Output the product of the squares of the numbers from `x` up to `y`.
   C. Output the numbers from `y` down to 0.

5. Assume that the variables `x` and `y` contain integers. Write code to perform the following tasks.
   A. Output the largest value, using an `if` statement.
   B. Output the largest value, using the method `Math.max`.

PROJECTS

PROJECT 4-1

When you first learned to divide, you expressed answers using a quotient and a remainder rather than a fraction or decimal quotient. For example, if you divided 9 by 2, you gave the answer as 4r. 1. Write a program that takes two integers as inputs and displays their quotient and remainder as outputs. Do not assume that the integers are entered in any order, but be sure to divide the larger integer by the smaller integer.

PROJECT 4-2

Write a program that takes the lengths of three sides of a triangle as inputs. The program should display whether or not the triangle is a right triangle.

PROJECT 4-3

A 2-minute telephone call to Lexington, Virginia, costs $1.15. Each additional minute costs $0.50. Write a program that takes the total length of a call in minutes as input and calculates and displays the cost.

PROJECT 4-4

Run the `Factorial` program of Section 4.5 with inputs of 5, 10, and 20. Notice that the number for the last output is large but negative. Place an output statement in the loop so that you can view the value of `count` and `number` on each pass. Can you explain what the problem is? Now change the type of `product` from `int` to `long`, recompile the program, and run it again with the same inputs. Explain what happens. How large does the input have to be before you encounter the same problem again?

PROJECT 4-5

The German mathematician Gottfried Leibniz developed the following method to approximate the value of π:

$\pi/4 = 1 - 1/3 + 1/5 - 1/7 + \ldots$

Write a program that allows the user to specify the number of iterations used in this approximation and displays the resulting value.

PROJECT 4-6

A local biologist needs a program to predict population growth. The inputs would be the initial number of organisms, the rate of growth (a real number greater than 0), the number of hours it takes to achieve this rate, and a number of hours during which the population grows. For example, one might start with a population of 500 organisms, a growth rate of 2, and a growth period to achieve this rate of 6 hours. Assuming that none of the organisms die, this would imply that this population would double in size every 6 hours. Thus, after allowing 6 hours for growth, we would have 1000 organisms, and after 12 hours, we would have 2000 organisms. Write a program that takes these inputs and displays a prediction of the total population.

PROJECT 4-7

Computers use the binary system, which is based on powers of 2. Write a program that displays the positive powers of 2. When the user enters the exponent at a prompt, the program displays 2 to that power. The program halts when the user enters –1.

PROJECT 4-8

Modify the program of Project 4-7 so that the user can specify the base (2 or higher) as well. The first line of the output should display which base was entered.

PROJECT 4-9

Modify the program of Project 4-8 so that it processes a file of inputs. Each line of the file contains a base and an exponent. The program should read the data from each line, compute the result, and display each set of inputs and their result on an output line in the terminal window.

PROJECT 4-10

Teachers in most school districts are paid on a schedule that provides a salary based on their number of years of teaching experience. For example, a beginning teacher in the Bellingham School District might be paid $20,000 the first year. For each year of experience after this up to 10 years, a 2 percent increase over the preceding value is received. Write a program that displays a salary schedule for teachers in a school district. The inputs are the starting salary, the percentage increase, and the number of years in the schedule. Each row in the schedule should contain the year number and the salary for that year.

PROJECT 4-11

A checkerboard consists of an 8-by-8 grid of black and red squares in which no two squares of the same color are adjacent. Write a graphics program that displays a checkerboard.

PROJECT 4-12

Modify the program of Project 4-11 so that it prompts the user for the number of rows and columns of the board before displaying them. Use I/O dialog boxes to accept the inputs.

PROJECT 4-13

An interesting optical illusion is caused by a phenomenon known as *induced contrast*. This illusion occurs when two images of the same shade are placed on backgrounds of sharply contrasting shades, as shown in Figure 4-7. One image appears darker than the other, even though they are exactly the same shade. Write a graphics program that generates such an illusion. (*Hint*: Use two panels that draw the same shape.)

FIGURE 4-7
The phenomenon of induced contrast

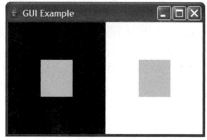

CRITICAL *Thinking*

Do the mathematical analysis needed to show that the Lucky Sevens game is not so lucky for the gambler. (*Hint*: The answer involves comparing the number of possible combinations of all totals and the number of possible combinations of 7.)

GETTING STARTED WITH JAVA

REVIEW *Questions*

TRUE/FALSE

Circle T if the statement is true or F if it is false.

T F 1. The first generation of programming language is assembly language.

T F 2. Java is an example of a high-level language.

T F 3. Mistakes found early in the coding process are much more expensive to fix than mistakes found later in the process.

T F 4. Byte code is a program that behaves like a computer.

T F 5. An arithmetic expression consists of operands and binary operators combined, as in algebra.

T F 6. Programs manipulate objects by sending them methods.

T F 7. An integer is a positive or negative whole number.

T F 8. Strings are objects, not primitive data types.

T F 9. A relational operator is used to compare data items.

T F 10. Most, but not all, information in a computer is represented in binary form.

FILL IN THE BLANK

Complete the following sentences by writing the correct word or words in the blanks provided.

1. OOP stands for _____.

2. The software responsible for translating a program in a high-level language to machine code is called a(n) _____.

3. JVM stands for _____.

4. When an object receives a message, the object responds by running a block of code called a(n) _____.

5. Numbers with a fractional part are called _____.

6. When evaluating an expression, Java performs operations of higher _____ first unless overridden by _____.

7. Use the _____ operator to create a new string out of existing strings.

8. The `while` statement implements a(n) _____.

9. A(n) _____ error occurs when a loop goes around one too many or one too few times.

10. A(n) _____ error occurs when a loop never stops.

WRITTEN QUESTIONS

Write a brief answer to each of the following questions or problems.

1. What is the purpose of a variable in a program?

2. What are the three types of programming errors? Give a brief example of each.

3. Describe the differences between the data types `double` and `int`.

4. Assume that the variables `x` and `y` contain the values 8 and 4, respectively. What are the values of the expressions listed below?
   A. `x + y * 2`
   B. `(x + y) / 3`
   C. `x - y * 3`
   D. `x + y * 1.5`

5. Write a valid Java statement that adds 5 to the value of variable `x` if the value of variable `y` is greater than 10.

6. A program has the following loop heading: while (3 < x < 10). Is the heading syntactically correct? If incorrect, explain why.

7. Write a loop that outputs the first 10 positive powers of 2.

PROJECTS

PROJECT 1

The surface area of a cube is the sum of the areas of its faces. Write a program that expects the length of a cube's edge as input and displays its surface area.

PROJECT 2

Write a program that expects the length and width of a rectangle as inputs. The program should calculate and display the rectangle's area and perimeter.

PROJECT 3

Top-pick videos rent for $3.00 per night, whereas oldies rent for $2.00. Write a program that prompts the user for the number of each type of video to rent and outputs the total cost for that night.

PROJECT 4

The local bookstore has a markup of 10 percent on each book sold. Write a program that takes the sales price of a book as input and displays the following outputs:

■ The markup amount of the book just sold

■ The wholesale amount (to go to the publisher) of the book just sold

■ The total sales prices of all of the books sold thus far

■ The total markup amount of all of the books sold thus far

CRITICAL *Thinking*

Modify the program of Project 4 so that it continues to prompt the user for the price of books. The prompts should end when the user enters a negative number for the price. The program should then display the total sales price and total markup of the books sold.

THE NEXT STEP WITH JAVA

Unit 2

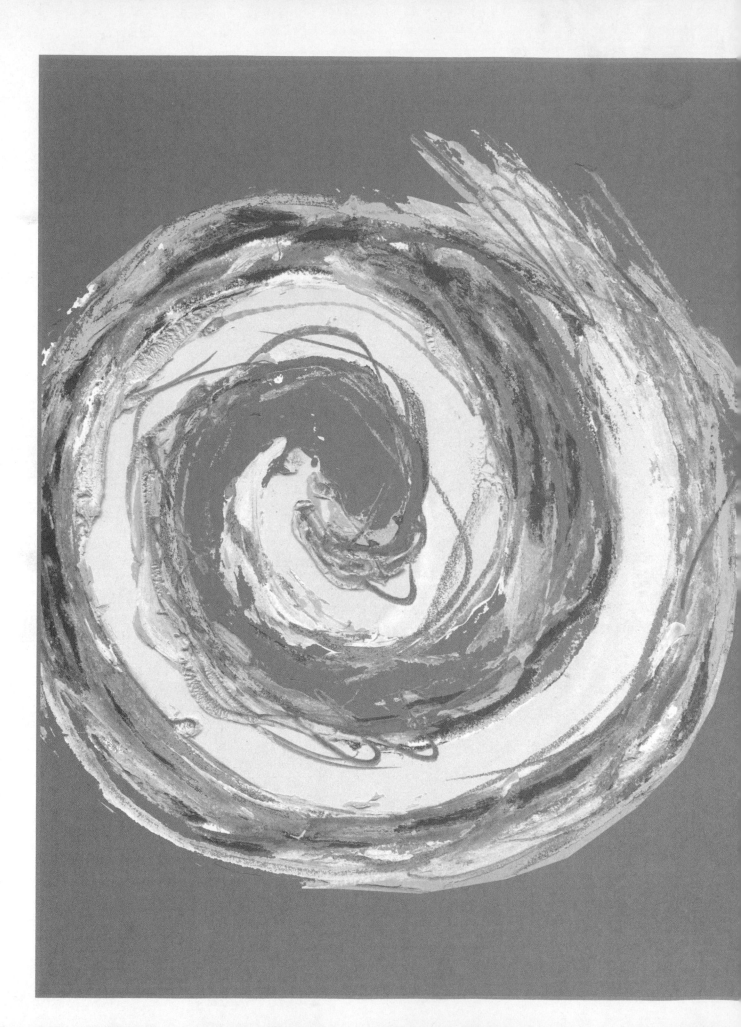

CHAPTER 5

INTRODUCTION TO DEFINING CLASSES

OBJECTIVES

Upon completion of this chapter, you should be able to:

- Design and implement a simple class from user requirements.
- Organize a program in terms of a view class and a model class.
- Use visibility modifiers to make methods visible to clients and restrict access to data within a class.
- Write appropriate mutator methods, accessor methods, and constructors for a class.
- Understand how parameters transmit data to methods.
- Use instance variables, local variables, and parameters appropriately.
- Organize a complex task in terms of helper methods.

Estimated Time: 3.5 hours

VOCABULARY

Accessor

Actual parameter

Behavior

Constructor

Encapsulation

Formal parameter

Helper method

Identity

Instantiation

Lifetime

Mutator

Scope

State

Visibility modifier

We introduced basic object-oriented terminology in Chapter 1 and have used it repeatedly since then. Until now, we have focused on choosing among predefined classes to solve problems. We have shown how to declare variables of different classes, assign objects to these variables, and send them messages. In this chapter, we explore the internal workings of objects. We introduce the basic structure of class definitions so that you will be able to read and modify classes and create classes of your own. We restrict our focus to a few simple concepts and add more detail in later chapters.

5.1 The Internal Structure of Classes and Objects

As we stated in Chapter 1, an object is a runtime entity that contains data and responds to messages. A class is a software package or template that describes the characteristics of similar objects. These characteristics are of two sorts: variable declarations that define an object's data requirements (instance variables) and methods that define its behavior in response to messages.

The combining of data and behavior into a single software package is called *encapsulation*. An object is an instance of its class, and the process of creating a new object is called *instantiation*.

Classes, Objects, and Computer Memory

We begin our discussion of classes and objects by considering how the Java virtual machine (JVM) handles them. When a Java program is executing, the computer's memory must hold

- All class templates in their compiled form
- Variables that refer to objects
- Objects as needed

Each method's compiled byte code is stored in memory as part of its class's template. Memory for data, on the other hand, is allocated within objects. Although all class templates are in memory at all times, individual objects come and go. An object first appears and occupies memory when it is instantiated, and it disappears automatically when no longer needed. The JVM knows if an object is in use by keeping track of whether or not there are any variables referencing it. Because unreferenced objects cannot be used, Java assumes that it is okay to delete them from memory. Java does this during a process called *garbage collection*. In contrast, C++ programmers have the onerous responsibility of deleting objects explicitly. Forgetting to delete unneeded objects wastes scarce memory resources, and accidentally deleting an object too soon or more than once can cause programs to crash. In large programs, these mistakes are easy to make and difficult to find. Fortunately, Java programmers do not have to worry about this problem.

Three Characteristics of an Object

Three characteristics of objects must be emphasized. First, an object has *behavior* as defined by the methods of its class. Second, an object has *state*, which is another way of saying that at any particular moment its instance variables have particular values. Typically, the state changes over time in response to messages sent to the object. Third, an object has its own unique *identity*, which distinguishes it from all other objects in the computer's memory, even those that might momentarily have the same state. An object's identity is handled behind the scenes by the JVM and should not be confused with the variables that might refer to the object. Of the variables, there can be none, one, or several. When there are none, the garbage collector purges the object from memory. Shortly, we will see an example in which two variables refer to the same object.

Clients, Servers, and Interfaces

When messages are sent, two objects are involved—the sender and the receiver, also called the *client* and the *server*, respectively. A client's interactions with a server are limited to sending it messages, so consequently a client needs to know nothing about the internal workings of a server. A client needs to know only a server's *interface*, that is, the list of the methods supported by the server. The server's data requirements and the implementation of its methods are hidden from the client, an approach we referred to as *information hiding* in Chapter 1. Only the person who writes a class needs to understand its internal workings. In fact, a class's implementation details can be changed radically without affecting any of its clients, provided its interface remains the same.

EXERCISE 5.1

1. What is the difference between a class and an object?

2. What happens to an object's memory storage when it is no longer referenced by a variable?

3. List the three important characteristics of an object.

4. Describe the client–server relationship.

5. What is the interface of a class?

5.2 A Student Class

The first class we develop in this chapter is called Student. We begin by considering the class from a client's perspective. Later we show its implementation. From a client's perspective, it is enough to know that a Student object stores a name and three test scores and responds to the messages shown in Table 5-1.

TABLE 5-1
The interface for the Student class

METHODS	DESCRIPTIONS
void setName(aString)	Example: stu.setName ("Bill"); sets the name of stu to Bill
String getName()	Example: str = stu.getName(); returns the name of stu
void setScore (whichTest, testScore)	Example: stu.setScore (3, 95); sets the score on test 3 to 95 if whichTest is not 1, 2, or 3, then 3 is substituted automatically
int getScore(whichTest)	Example: score = stu.getScore (3); returns the score on test 3 if whichTest is not 1, 2, or 3, then 3 is substituted automatically
int getAverage()	Example : average = stu.getAverage(); returns the average of the test scores
int getHighScore()	Example: highScore = stu.getHighScore(); returns the highest test score
String toString()	Example: str = stu.toString(); returns a string containing the student's name and test scores

Using Student Objects

Some portions of code illustrate how a client instantiates and manipulates Student objects. First, we declare several variables, including two variables of type Student.

```
Student s1, s2;        // Declare the variables
String str;
int i;
```

As usual, we do not use variables until we have assigned them initial values. We assign a new Student object to s1 using the operator new:

```
s1 = new Student();    // Instantiate a student and associate it with the
                       // variable s1
```

It is important to emphasize that the variable s1 is a reference to a Student object and is *not* a student object itself.

A Student object keeps track of the name and test scores of an actual student. Thus, for a brand new Student object, what are the values of these data attributes? That depends on the class's internal implementation details, but we can find out easily by sending messages to the Student object via its associated variable s1:

```
str = s1.getName();
System.out.println (str);    // yields ""

i = s1.getHighScore();
System.out.println (i);      // yields 0
```

Apparently, the name was initialized to an empty string and the test scores to zero. Now we set the object's data attributes by sending it some messages:

```
s1.setName ("Bill");   // Set the student's name to "Bill"
s1.setScore (1,84);    // Set the score on test 1 to 84
s1.setScore (2,86);    //              on test 2 to 86
s1.setScore (3,88);    //              on test 3 to 88
```

Messages that change an object's state are called *mutators*. To see if the mutators worked correctly, we use other messages to access the object's state (called *accessors*):

```
str = s1.getName();    // str equals "Bill"
i = s1.getScore (1);   // i equals 84
i = s1.getHighScore(); // i equals 88
i = s1.getAverage();   // i equals 86
```

The object's string representation is obtained by sending the toString message to the object:

```
str = s1.toString();
  // str  now equals
  // "Name:    Bill\nTest 1:  84\nTest2:  86\nTest3:  88\nAverage: 86"
```

When displayed in a terminal window (Figure 5-1), the string is broken into several lines as determined by the placement of the newline characters ('\n'). In addition to the explicit use of the toString method, there are other situations in which the method is called automatically. For instance, toString is called implicitly when a Student object is concatenated with a string or is an argument to the method println:

```
str = "The best student is: \n" + s1;
  // Equivalent to: str = "The best student is: \n" + s1.toString();
System.out.println (s1);
  // Equivalent to: System.out.println (s1.toString());
```

FIGURE 5-1
Implicit use of toString when a Student object is sent to a terminal window

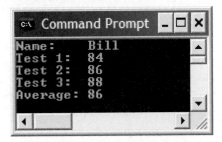

Because of these valuable implicit uses of the toString method, we frequently include this method in the classes we write. If we forget, however, Java provides a very simple version of the method through the mechanism of inheritance (mentioned in Chapter 1). The simplified version does little more than return the name of the class to which the object belongs.

Objects, Assignment, and Aliasing

We close this demonstration by associating a Student object with the variable s2. Rather than instantiating a new student, we assign s1 to s2:

```
s2 = s1;               // s1 and s2 now refer to the same student
```

The variables s1 and s2 now refer to the *same* Student object. This might come as a surprise because we might reasonably expect the assignment statement to create a second Student object equal to the first, but that is not how Java works. To demonstrate that s1 and s2 now refer to the same object, we change the student's name using s2 and retrieve the same name using s1:

```
s2.setName ("Ann");    // Set the name
str = s1.getName();    // str equals "Ann". Therefore, s1 and s2 refer
                       // to the same object.
```

Table 5-2 shows code and diagrams that clarify the manner in which variables are affected by assignment statements. At any time, it is possible to break the connection between a variable and the object it references. Simply assign the value null to the variable:

```
Student s1;
s1 = new Student();    // s1 references the newly instantiated student
...                    // Do stuff with the student
s1 = null;             // s1 no longer references anything
```

TABLE 5-2
How variables are affected by assignment statements

CODE	DIAGRAM	COMMENTS
`int i, j;`	i ??? j ???	i and j are memory locations that have not yet been initialized, but which will hold integers.
`i = 3;` `j = i;`	i 3 j 3	i holds the integer 3. j holds the integer 3.
`Student s, t;`	s ??? t ???	s and t are memory locations that have not yet been initialized, but which will hold references to Student objects.
`s = new Student();` `t = s;`	s t → student object	s holds a reference to a Student object. t holds a reference to the same Student object.

Table 5-2 demonstrates that assignment to variables of numeric types such as `int` produces genuine copies, whereas assignment to variables of object types does not.

Primitive Types, Reference Types, and the `null` Value

We mentioned earlier that two or more variables can refer to the same object. To better understand why this is possible we need to consider how Java classifies types. In Java, all types fall into two fundamental categories:

1. *Primitive types*: `int`, `double`, `boolean`, `char`, and the shorter and longer versions of these

2. *Reference types*: all classes, for instance, `String`, `Student`, `Scanner`, and so on

As we first pointed out in Chapter 2, variables in these two categories are represented differently in memory. A variable of a primitive type is best viewed as a box that contains a value of that primitive type. In contrast, a variable of a reference type is thought of as a box that contains a pointer to an object. Thus, the state of memory after the following code is executed is shown in Figure 5-2.

```
int number = 45;
String word = "Hi";
```

FIGURE 5-2
The difference between primitive and reference variables

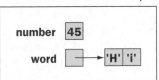

As previously mentioned, reference variables can be assigned the value null. If a reference variable previously pointed to an object, and no other variable currently points to that object, the computer reclaims the object's memory during garbage collection. This situation is illustrated in the following code segment and in Figure 5-3:

```
Student student = new Student("Mary", 70, 80, 90);
student = null;
```

FIGURE 5-3
The Student variable before and after it has been assigned the value null

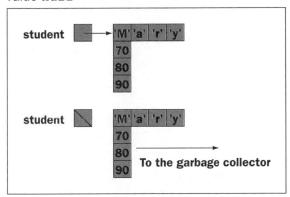

A reference variable can be compared to the null value, as follows:

```
if (student == null)
    …                 // Don't try to run a method with that student!
else
    …                 // Process the student

while (student != null){
    …                 // Process the student
                      // Obtain the next student from whatever source
}
```

As we already know from Chapter 3, when a program attempts to run a method with an object that is null, Java throws a *null pointer exception*, as in the following example:

```
String str = null;

System.out.println (str.length());   // OOPS! str is null, so Java throws a
                                     // null pointer exception
```

The Structure of a Class Template

Having explored the Student class from a client's perspective, we now address the question of how to implement it. All classes have a similar structure consisting of four parts:

1. The class's name and some modifying phrases

2. A description of the instance variables

3. One or more methods that indicate how to initialize a new object (called *constructor* methods)

4. One or more methods that specify how an object responds to messages

The order of these parts can be varied arbitrarily provided part 1 (the class's name) comes first; however, for the sake of consistency, we will usually adhere to the order listed, which yields the following class template:

```
public class <name of class> extends <some other class>{

    // Declaration of instance variables
    private <type> <name>;
    ...

    // Code for the constructor methods
    public <name of class>() {
    // Initialize the instance variables
       ...
    }
    ...

    // Code for the other methods
    public <return type> <name of method> (<parameter list>){
       ...
    }
    ...
}
```

Some of the phrases used in the template need to be explained:

```
public class
```

Class definitions usually begin with the keyword public, indicating that the class is accessible to all potential clients. There are some alternatives to public that we ignore for now.

```
<name of class>
```

Class names are user-defined symbols, and thus they must adhere to the rules for naming variables and methods. It is common to start class names with a capital letter and variable and method names with a lowercase letter. There is one exception. Names of final variables are usually completely capitalized.

```
extends <some other class>
```

Java organizes its classes in a hierarchy (see Chapter 1). At the root, or base, of this hierarchy is a class called `Object`. In the hierarchy, if class A is immediately above another class B, we say that A is the *superclass* or *parent* of B and B is a *subclass* or *child* of A (Figure 5-4). Each class, except `Object`, has exactly one parent and can have any number of children.

FIGURE 5-4
Relationship between superclass and subclass

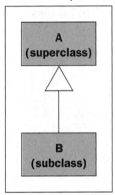

When a new class is created, it is incorporated into the hierarchy by extending an existing class. The new class's exact placement in the hierarchy is important because a new class inherits the characteristics of its superclass through a process called *inheritance* (Chapter 1). The new class then adds to and modifies these inherited characteristics, or in other words, the new class *extends* the superclass. If the clause `extends <some other class>` is omitted from the new class's definition, then by default the new class is assumed to be a subclass of `Object`.

```
private <type> <name>
```

Instance variables are nearly always declared to be `private`. This prevents clients from referring to the instance variables directly. Making instance variables `private` is an important aspect of information hiding.

```
public <return type> <name of method>
```

Methods are usually declared to be `public`, which allows clients to refer to them.

`private` and `public` are *visibility modifiers*. If both `private` and `public` are omitted, the consequences vary with the circumstances. Without explaining why, suffice it to say that in most situations, omitting the visibility modifier is equivalent to using `public`. In most situations, we use `private` for instance variables unless there is some compelling reason to declare them `public`.

To illustrate the difference between `private` and `public`, suppose the class `Student` has a private instance variable `name` and a public method `setName`. Then

```
Student s;
s = new Student();
s.name = "Bill";      // Rejected by compiler because name is private
s.setName ("Bill")    // Accepted by compiler because setName is public
```

As a final note concerning our class template, notice that the constructor does not have a return type, that is, the name of the type of the value that it returns. All other methods do.

Implementation of the `Student` Class

Adhering to the format of our class template, we now implement the `Student` class. It is important to realize that other implementations are acceptable provided they adhere to the interface standards already established for student classes. Following is the code:

```java
/* Student.java
Manage a student's name and three test scores.
*/
public class Student {

  // Instance variables
  // Each student object has a name and three test scores
  private String name;         // Student name
  private int test1;           // Score on test 1
  private int test2;           // Score on test 2
  private int test3;           // Score on test 3

  // Constructor method

  public Student(){
  // Initialize a new student's name to the empty string and the test
  // scores to zero.
     name = "";
     test1 = 0;
     test2 = 0;
     test3 = 0;
  }

  // Other methods

  public void setName (String nm){
  // Set a student's name
     name = nm;
  }
  public String getName (){
  // Get a student's name
     return name;
  }

  public void setScore (int i, int score){
  // Set test i to score
```

```
    if      (i == 1) test1 = score;
    else if (i == 2) test2 = score;
    else             test3 = score;
}

public int getScore (int i){
// Retrieve score i
    if      (i == 1) return test1;
    else if (i == 2) return test2;
    else             return test3;
}

public int getAverage(){
// Compute and return the average
    int average;
    average = (int) Math.round((test1 + test2 + test3) / 3.0);
    return average;
}

public int getHighScore(){
// Determine and return the highest score
    int highScore;
    highScore = test1;
    if (test2 > highScore) highScore = test2;
    if (test3 > highScore) highScore = test3;
    return highScore;
}

public String toString(){
// Construct and return a string representation of the student
    String str;
    str = "Name:     " + name  + "\n" +    // "\n" denotes a newline
          "Test 1:  " + test1 + "\n" +
          "Test 2:  " + test2 + "\n" +
          "Test 3:  " + test3 + "\n" +
          "Average: " + getAverage();
    return str;
}
}
```

We explore the structure and behavior of methods in more detail later in this chapter. For now, the meaning of the code is fairly obvious. All the methods, except the constructor method, have a return type, although the return type may be void, indicating that the method in fact returns nothing. To summarize: When an object receives a message, the object activates the corresponding method. The method then manipulates the object's data as represented by the instance variables.

Constructors

The principal purpose of a constructor is to initialize the instance variables of a newly instantiated object. Constructors are activated when the keyword new is used and at no other time. A constructor is never used to reset instance variables of an existing object.

A class template can include more than one constructor, provided each has a unique parameter list; however, all the constructors must have the same name—that is, the name of the class. The constructors we have seen so far have had empty parameter lists and are called *default constructors*.

If a class template contains no constructors, the JVM provides a primitive default constructor behind the scenes. This constructor initializes numeric variables to zero and object variables to null, thus indicating that the object variables currently reference no objects. If a class contains even one constructor, however, the JVM no longer provides a default constructor automatically.

To illustrate these ideas, we add several constructors to the Student class. The following code lists the original default constructor and two additional ones:

```
// Default constructor -- initialize name to the empty string and
// the test scores to zero.
public Student(){
   name = "";
   test1 = 0;
   test2 = 0;
   test3 = 0;
}


// Additional constructor -- initialize the name and test scores
// to the values provided.
public Student(String nm, int t1, int t2, int t3){
   name = nm;
   test1 = t1;
   test2 = t2;
   test3 = t3;
}


// Additional constructor -- initialize the name and test scores
// to match those in the parameter s.
public Student(Student s){
   name = s.name;
   test1 = s.test1;
   test2 = s.test2;
   test3 = s.test3;
}
```

A class is easier to use when it has a variety of constructors. Following is some code that shows how to use the different Student constructors. In a program, we would use the constructor that best suited our immediate purpose:

```
Student s1, s2, s3;
s1 = new Student();                    // First student object has
                                       // name "" and scores 0,0,0

s2 = new Student ("Bill",70,80,90);    // Second student object has
                                       // name "Bill" and scores 70,80,90

s3 = new Student (s2);                 // Third student object also has
                                       // name "Bill" and scores 70,80,90
```

```
s3.setName ("Ann");              // Third student object now has
s3.setScore (1,75);              // name "Ann" and scores 75,80,90
```

There are now three completely separate student objects. For a moment, two of them had the same state—that is, the same values for their instance variables—but that changed in the last two lines of code.

Chaining Constructors

When a class includes several constructors, the code for them can be simplified by *chaining* them. For example, the three constructors in the Student class each do the same thing—initialize the instance variables. We can simplify the code for the first and third constructors by calling the second constructor. To call one constructor from another constructor, we use the notation

```
this(<parameters>);
```

Thus, the code for the constructors shown earlier becomes

```
// Default constructor -- initialize name to the empty string and
// the test scores to zero.
public Student(){
   this("", 0, 0, 0);
}

// Additional constructor -- initialize the name and test scores
// to the values provided.
public Student(String nm, int t1, int t2, int t3){
   name = nm;
   test1 = t1;
   test2 = t2;
   test3 = t3;
}

// Additional constructor -- initialize the name and test scores
// to match those in the parameter s.
public Student(Student s){
   this(s.name, s.test1, s.test2, s.test3);
}
```

*E*XERCISE 5.2

1. What are mutators and accessors? Give examples.

2. List two visibility modifiers and describe when they are used.

3. What is a constructor?

4. Why do we include a toString method with a new user-defined class?

5. How can two variables refer to the same object? Give an example.

EXERCISE 5.2 Continued

6. Explain the difference between a primitive type and a reference type, and give an example of each.

7. What is the `null` value?

8. What is a null pointer exception? Give an example.

9. How does a default constructor differ from other constructors?

10. How does Java handle the initialization of instance variables if no constructors are provided?

11. What is the purpose of a constructor that expects another object of the same class?

5.3 Editing, Compiling, and Testing the Student Class

To use the `Student` class, we must save it in a file called `Student.java` and compile it by typing

```
javac Student.java
```

in a terminal window. If there are no compile-time errors, the compiler creates the byte code file `Student.class`. Once the `Student` class is compiled, applications can declare and manipulate `Student` objects provided that one of the following is true:

- The code for the application and `Student.class` are in the same directory.

- The `Student.class` is part of a package (see Appendix G).

Following is a small program that uses and tests the `Student` class. Figure 5-5 shows the results of running such a program.

```java
// Example 5.1: Tester program for Student class

public class TestStudent{

    public static void main (String[] args){
        Student s1, s2;

        s1 = new Student();     // Instantiate a student object
        s1.setName("Bill");     // Set the student's name to "Bill"
        s1.setScore(1,84);      // Set the score on test 1 to 84
        s1.setScore(2,86);      //              on test 2 to 86
        s1.setScore(3,88);      //              on test 3 to 88
        System.out.println("\nHere is student s1\n" + s1);

            s2 = s1;            // s1 and s2 now refer to the same object
        s2.setName("Ann");      // Set the name through s2
        System.out.println("\nName of s1 is now: " + s1.getName());
    }
}
```

FIGURE 5-5
Output from the `TestStudent` program

Command Prompt
Here is student s1
Name: Bill
Test 1:   84
Test 2:   86
Test 3:   88
Average: 86
Name of s1 is now: Ann

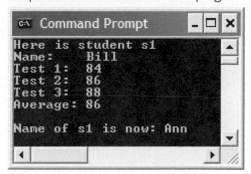

Finding the Location of Run-time Errors

Finding run-time errors in programs is no more difficult when there are several classes instead of just one. To illustrate, we introduce a run-time error into the `Student` class and then run the `TestStudent` program again. Following is a listing of the modified and erroneous lines of code. Figure 5-6 shows the error messages generated when the program runs.

```
public int getAverage(){
    int average = 0;
    average = (int) Math.round((test1 + test2 + test3) / average);
    return average;
}
```

FIGURE 5-6
Divide by zero run-time error message

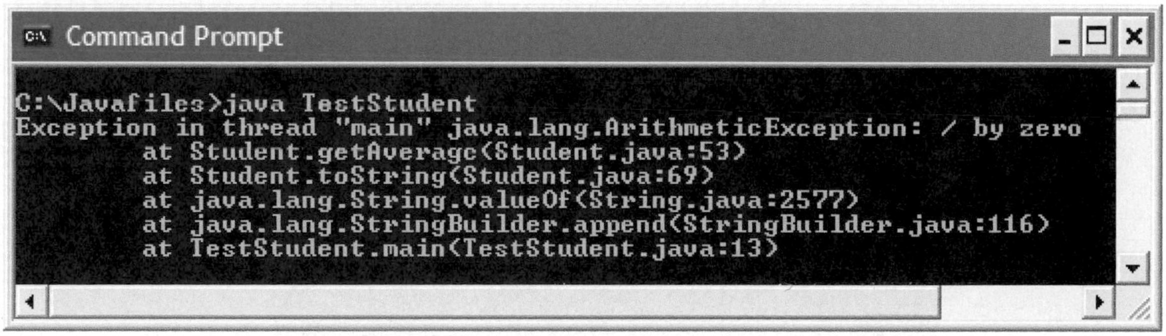

Command Prompt
C:\Javafiles>java TestStudent
Exception in thread "main" java.lang.ArithmeticException: / by zero
at Student.getAverage(Student.java:53)
at Student.toString(Student.java:69)
at java.lang.String.valueOf(String.java:2577)
at java.lang.StringBuilder.append(StringBuilder.java:116)
at TestStudent.main(TestStudent.java:13)

The messages indicate that

- An attempt was made to divide by zero in the `Student` class's `getAverage` method (line 53),
- Which had been called from the `Student` class's `toString` method (line 69),
- Which had been called by some methods we did not write,
- Which, finally, had been called from the `TestStudent` class's `main` method (line 13).

Following are the lines of code mentioned:

```
Student getAverage line 53 :
        average = (int) Math.round ((test1 + test2 + test3) / average);
Student toString line 69   :
        "Average: " + getAverage();
TestStudent main line 13        :
        System.out.println ("\nHere is student s1\n" + s1);
```

We can now unravel the error

- In line 13 of main, the concatenation (+) of s1 makes an implicit call s1.toString().

- In line 69 of toString, the getAverage method is called.

- In line 53 of getAverage, a division by zero occurs.

Case Study 1: Student Test Scores

Request

Write a program that allows the user to compare test scores of two students. Each student has three scores.

Analysis

A user's interaction with the program is shown in Figure 5-7.

FIGURE 5-7
The user interface for the student test scores program

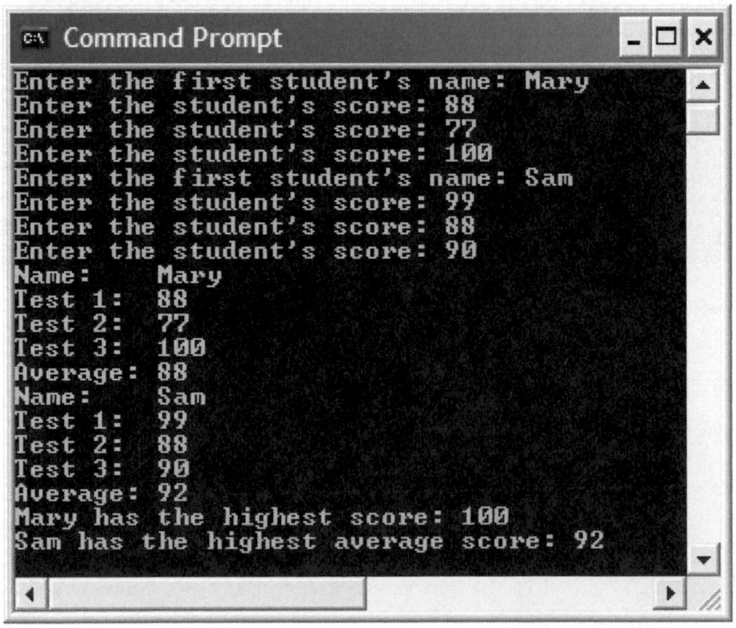

As you can see, the program

1. Prompts the user for the data for the two students

2. Displays the information for each student, followed by the names of the students with the highest score and the highest average score

As a standard part of analysis, we determine which classes are needed to support the application, and we delineate each class's overall responsibilities. The nature of the current problem suggests the use of two classes:

1. `Student`: Not surprisingly, the `Student` class presented earlier exactly fits the needs of this program.

2. `StudentApp`: This class supports the user interface and declares and manipulates two `Student` objects.

In general, it is a good idea to divide the code for most interactive applications into at least two sets of classes. One set of classes, which we call the *view*, handles the interactions with the human users, such as input and output operations. The other set of classes, called the *model*, represents the data used by the application. One of the benefits of this separation of responsibilities is that one can write different views for the same data model, such as a terminal-based view and a graphical-based view, without changing a line of code in the data model. Alternatively, one can write different representations of the data model without altering a line of code in the views. In most of the case studies that follow, we apply this framework, called the *model/view pattern*, to structure the code.

Design

During analysis, we decided to base the implementation on two classes: `Student` and `StudentApp`. Now, during design, we specify the characteristics of these classes in detail. This involves determining the data requirements of each class and the methods that will be needed by the clients of the classes. This process is usually straightforward. To illustrate, let us pretend for the moment that we have not already written the `Student` class.

Designing the `Student` Class

We know from the work completed during analysis that a `Student` object must keep track of a name and three test scores. The high score and the average can be calculated when needed. Thus, the data requirements are clear. The `Student` class must declare four instance variables:

```
private String name;
private int test1;
private int test2;
private int test3;
```

To determine the `Student` class's methods, we look at the class from the perspective of the clients who will be sending messages to `Student` objects. In this application, the user interface is the only client. There are some clues that help us pick the appropriate methods:

The user interface needs to instantiate two `Student` objects. This indicates the need for a constructor method, which we always include anyway.

When the user enters input data, the view needs to tell each `Student` object its name and three test scores. This can be handled by two mutator methods: `setName(theName)` and `setScore(whichTest, testScore)`.

The view needs to ask the `Student` objects for their complete information, the highest score, and the average score. This suggests four accessor methods: `toString()`, `getScore(whichTest)`, `getHighScore()`, and `getAverage()`.

We summarize our findings in a *class summary* box:

```
Class:
  Student
Private Instance Variables:
  String name
  int test1
  int test2
  int test3
Public Methods:
  constructors
  void setName (theName)
  String getName()
  void setScore (whichTest, testScore)
  int getScore (whichTest)
  int getAverage()
  int getHighScore()
    String toString()
```

Normally, we would complete a class's design by writing pseudocode for methods whose implementation is not obvious, so we skip this step here.

Designing the `StudentApp` Class

The following is the class summary box for the `StudentApp` class:

```
Class:
  StudentApp
Public Methods:
  static void main (args)
```

Implementation

The code for the `Student` class has already been presented. Code for the `StudentApp` class follows:

```java
import java.util.Scanner;

public class StudentApp{

    public static void main (String[] args){
        // Instantiate the students and the keyboard object
        Student student1 = new Student();
```

```
        Student student2 = new Student();
        Scanner reader = new Scanner(System.in);

        String name;
        int score;

        // Input the first student's data
        System.out.print("Enter the first student's name: ");
        name = reader.nextLine();
        student1.setName(name);
        for (int i = 1; i <= 3; i++){
            System.out.print("Enter the student's score: ");
            score = reader.nextInt();
            student1.setScore(i, score);
        }
        // Consume the trailing newline character
        reader.nextLine();

        // Input the second student's data
        System.out.print("Enter the second student's name: ");
        name = reader.nextLine();
        student2.setName(name);
        for (int i = 1; i <= 3; i++){
            System.out.print("Enter the student's score: ");
            score = reader.nextInt();
            student2.setScore(i, score);
        }

        // Output the two students' information
        System.out.println(student1);
        System.out.println(student2);

        // Output the student with the highest score
        if (student1.getHighScore() > student2.getHighScore()){
            name = student1.getName();

            score = student1.getHighScore();
        }else{
            name = student2.getName();
            score = student2.getHighScore();
        }
        System.out.println(name + " has the highest score: " + score);

        // Output the student with the highest average score
        if (student1.getAverage() > student2.getAverage()){
            name = student1.getName();
            score = student1.getAverage();
        }else{
            name = student2.getName();
            score = student2.getAverage();
        }
        System.out.println(name + " has the highest average score: " +
                        score);
    }
}
```

5.4 The Structure and Behavior of Methods

As mentioned in earlier chapters, a method is a description of a task that is performed in response to a message. The purpose of this section is to examine more closely some related concepts such as parameters, return types, and local variables.

The Structure of a Method Definition

Methods generally have the following form:

```
<visibility modifier> <return type> <method name> (<parameter list>){

    <implementing code>
}
```

Note the following points:

- The visibility modifier `public` is used when the method should be available to clients of the defining class. The visibility modifier `private` should be used when the method is merely a "helper" used by other methods within the class. We say more about helper methods shortly.

- The return type should be `void` when the method returns no value. A `void` method often is a mutator, that is, a method that modifies an object's variables. If not `void`, the return type can be any primitive or reference type. Methods that return a value often are accessors, that is, methods that allow clients to examine the values of instance variables.

- Method names have the same syntax as other Java identifiers. The programmer should be careful to use names that describe the tasks that the methods perform, however; the names of verbs or verb phrases, such as `getName`, are usually appropriate for methods.

- As mentioned earlier in this book, parentheses are required whether or not parameters are present. The parameter list, if present, consists of one or more pairs of type names and parameter names, separated by commas.

A method's implementing code can be omitted. In that case, the method is called a *stub*. Stubs are used to set up skeletal, incomplete, but running programs during program development. For example, here is a class that contains only variable declarations and method stubs:

```java
public class SomeClass{

    private int someVariable1, someVariable2;

    public void mutator1(int valueIn){}

    public void mutator2(int valueIn){}

    public int accessor1(){
        return 0;
    }
}
```

Return Statements

If a method has a return type, its implementing code must have at least one `return` statement that returns a value of that type. There can be more than one `return` statement in a method; however, the first one executed ends the method. Following is an example of a method that has two `return` statements but executes just one of them:

```
boolean odd(int i){
   if (i % 2 == 0)
      return false;
   else
      return true;
}
```

A `return` statement in a `void` method quits the method and returns nothing

Formal and Actual Parameters

Parameters listed in a method's definition are called *formal parameters*. Values passed to a method when it is invoked are called *arguments* or *actual parameters*. As an example, consider the following two code segments:

```
// Client code

Student s = new Student();
Scanner reader = new Scanner(System.in);
System.out.print("Enter a test score:");
int testScore = reader.nextInt();
s.setScore(1, testScore);
```

```
// Server code

public void setScore (int i, int score){
   if       (i == 1) test1 = score;
   else if (i == 2) test2 = score;
   else              test3 = score;
}
```

In our example, the literal 1 and the variable `testScore` are the actual parameters and the names `i` and `score` are the formal parameters. When a method is called, the value of the actual parameter is automatically transferred to the corresponding formal parameter immediately before the method is activated. Thus, the number 1 and value of `testScore` are transferred to `i` and `score` immediately before `setScore` is activated (see Figure 5-8). It is important to understand that the variable `testScore` and the parameter `score` are otherwise completely independent of each other. For instance, changing the value of `score` would have no effect on the value of `testScore`.

FIGURE 5-8
Parameter passing

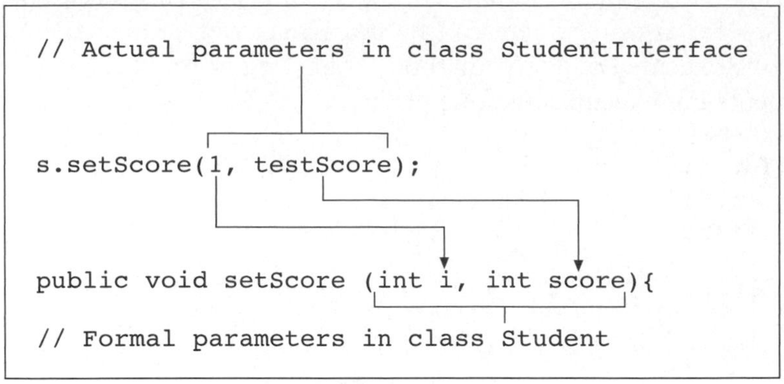

```
// Actual parameters in class StudentInterface




s.setScore(1, testScore);



public void setScore (int i, int score){

// Formal parameters in class Student
```

As mentioned in Chapter 3, when a method has multiple parameters, the caller must provide the right number and types of values. That is, the actual parameters must match the formal parameters in position and type. The rules for matching the types of a formal and an actual parameter are similar to those for assignment statements. The actual parameter's type must be either the same as or less inclusive than the type of the corresponding formal parameter. For example, the method Math.sqrt, which has a single formal parameter of type double, can receive either a double or an int as an actual parameter from the caller.

Parameters and Instance Variables

The purpose of a parameter is to pass information to a method. The purpose of an instance variable is to maintain information in an object. These roles are clearly shown in the method setScore. This method receives the score in the formal parameter score. This value is then transferred to one of the instance variables test1, test2, or test3.

Local Variables

Occasionally, it is convenient to have temporary working storage for data in a method. The programmer can declare *local variables* for this purpose. A good example occurs in the method getAverage. This method declares a variable average, assigns it the result of computing the average of the integer instance variables, and returns its value:

```
public int getAverage(){
   int average;
   average = (int) Math.round((test1 + test2 + test3) / 3.0);
   return average;
}
```

Note that there is no need for the method to receive data from the client, so we do not use a parameter. Likewise, there is no need for the object to remember the average, so we do not use an instance variable for that.

Helper Methods

Occasionally, a task performed by a method becomes so complex that it helps to break it into subtasks to be solved by several other methods. To accomplish this, a class can define one or more methods to serve as *helper methods*. These methods are usually private because only methods already defined within the class need to use them. For example, it is helpful to define a `debug` method when testing a class. This method expects a string and a double as parameters and displays these values in the terminal window. Following is the code:

```
private void debug(String message, double value){
   System.out.println(message + " " + value);
}
```

This method can be called from any other method in the class to display information about the state of an integer or double variable. For example, the `Student` method `getAverage` might use this method as follows:

```
public int getAverage(){
   int average;
   average = (int) Math.round((test1 + test2 + test3) / 3.0);
   debug("Average:", average);
   return average;
}
```

The advantage to this approach is that debugging statements throughout the class can be turned on or off by commenting out a single line of code:

```
private void debug(String message, double value){
   // System.out.println(message + " " + value);
}
```

We see other examples of helper methods in later chapters.

*E*XERCISE 5.4

1. Explain the difference between formal parameters and actual parameters.

2. How does Java transmit data by means of parameters?

3. Define a method `sum`. This method expects two integers as parameters and returns the sum of the numbers ranging from the first integer to the second one.

4. What is the purpose of local variables?

5.5 Scope and Lifetime of Variables

As we have seen repeatedly, a class definition consists of two principal parts: a list of instance variables and a list of methods. When an object is instantiated, it receives its own complete copy of the instance variables, and when it is sent a message, it activates the corresponding method in its class. Thus, it is the role of objects to contain data and to respond to messages, and it is the role of classes to provide a template for creating objects and to store the code for methods. When a method is executing, it does so on behalf of a particular object, and the method has complete access to the object's instance variables. From the perspective of the methods, the instance variables form a common pool of variables accessible to all of the class's methods. For this reason, we sometimes refer to them as *global variables*, in contrast to the variables declared within a method, which we call *local variables*.

Scope of Variables

The *scope* of a variable is that region of the program within which it can validly appear in lines of code. The scope of a parameter or a local variable is restricted to the body of the method that declares it, whereas the scope of a global or instance variable is all the methods in the defining class. Fortunately, the compiler flags as an error any attempt to use variables outside of their scope. Following is an example that illustrates the difference between local and global scope:

```java
public class ScopeDemo {

    private int iAmGlobal;

    public void clientMethod (int parm){

        int iAmLocal;
        ...
    }

    private int helperMethod (int parm1, int parm2){

        int iAmLocalToo;
        ...
    }
    ...
}
```

Table 5-3 shows where each of the variables and parameters can be used (i.e., its scope):

TABLE 5-3
Variables and their scope

VARIABLE	helperMethod	clientMethod
iAmGlobal	Yes	Yes
parm	No	Yes
iAmLocal	No	Yes
parm1 and parm2	Yes	No
iAmLocalToo	Yes	No

Notice that formal parameters are also local in scope; that is, their visibility is limited to the body of the method in which they are declared.

Block Scope

Within the code of a method, there can also be nested scopes. Variables declared within any compound statement enclosed in braces are said to have *block scope*. They are visible only within the code enclosed by braces. For example, consider the following `for` loop to sum 10 input numbers. The accumulator variable `sum` is declared above the loop so the program can access it after the loop terminates. The loop declares its control variable `i` within its header and a local variable `number` to accept input within its body. The variables `i` and `number` thus have block scope, which is appropriate because they are needed only within the loop, and not outside it:

```
int sum = 0;
Scanner reader = new Scanner(System.in);
for (int i = 1; i <= 10; i++){
   System.out.print("Enter a number: ");
   int number = reader.nextInt();
   sum += number;
}
System.out.println("The sum is " + sum);
```

Lifetime of Variables

The *lifetime* of a variable is the period during which it can be used. Local variables and formal parameters exist during a single execution of a method. Each time a method is called, it gets a fresh set of formal parameters and local variables, and once the method stops executing, the formal parameters and local variables are no longer accessible. Instance variables, on the other hand, last for the lifetime of an object. When an object is instantiated, it gets a complete set of fresh instance variables. These variables are available every time a message is sent to the object, and they, in some sense, serve as the object's memory. When the object stops existing, the instance variables disappear as well.

Duplicating Variable Names

Because the scope of a formal parameter or local variable is restricted to a single method, the same name can be used within several different methods without causing a conflict. Whether or not we use the same name in several different methods is merely a matter of taste. When the programmer reuses the same local name in different methods, the name refers to a different area of storage in each method. In the next example, the names `iAmLocal` and `parm1` are used in two methods in this way:

```
public class ScopeDemo {

   private int iAmGlobal;

   public void clientMethod (int parm1){

      int iAmLocal;
      ...
   }

   private int helperMethod (int parm1, int parm2){

      int iAmLocal;
      ...
   }
   ...
}
```

A local name and a global variable name can also be the same, as shown in the following code segment:

```java
public class ScopeDemo {

    private int iAmAVariable;

    public void someMethod (int parm){

        int iAmAVariable;
        ...
        iAmAVariable = 3;              // Refers to the local variable
        this.iAmAVariable = 4;         // Refers to the global variable
        ...
    }

    public void someOtherMethod(int iAmAVariable){
        ...
        this.iAmAVariable = iAmAVariable;     // Assign the value of the
// parameter
        ...
// to the global variable
        }
        ...
    }
```

In this example, the local variable `iAmAVariable` is said to *shadow* the global variable with the same name. Shadowing is considered a dangerous programming practice because it greatly increases the likelihood of making a coding error. When the variable name is used in the method, it refers to the local variable, and the global variable can be referenced only by prefixing `this.` to the name. The programmer uses the symbol `this` to refer to the current instance of a class within that class's definition.

When to Use Instance Variables, Parameters, and Local Variables

The only reason to use an instance variable is to remember information within an object. The only reason to use a parameter is to transmit information to a method. The only reason to use a local variable is for temporary working storage within a method. A very common mistake is to misuse one kind of variable for another. Following are the most common examples of these types of mistakes.

MISTAKE 1: GLOBAL VARIABLE USED FOR TEMPORARY WORKING STORAGE

This is perhaps the most common mistake programmers make with variables. As we have seen, a global variable is in fact not temporary, but survives the execution of the method. No harm may be done. If more than one method (or the same method on different calls) uses the same variable for its temporary storage, however, these methods might share information in ways that cause subtle bugs. For instance, suppose we decide to include an instance variable `sum` to compute the average score in the Student class. We also decide to compute the sum with a loop that uses the method getScore as follows:

```
private int sum;
...

public int getAverage(){
   for (int i = 1; i <= 3; i++)
      sum += getScore(i);
   return (int) Math.round(sum / 3.0);
}
```

The method is quite elegant but contains an awful bug. It runs correctly only the first time. The next time the method is called, it adds scores to the sum of the previous call, thus producing a much higher average than expected.

MISTAKE 2: LOCAL VARIABLE USED TO REMEMBER INFORMATION IN AN OBJECT

As we have seen, this intent cannot be realized because a local variable disappears from memory after its method has executed. This mistake can lead to errors in cases in which the programmer uses the same name for a local variable and a global variable and believes that the reference to the local variable is really a reference to the global variable (see our earlier discussion of shadowing). All that is required to cause this error is the use of a type name before the first assignment to the variable when it is used in a method. Following is an example from the Student class:

```
public void setName (String nm){
// Set a student's name
   String name = nm;      // Whoops! we have just declared name local.
}
```

In this case, the variable name has been accidentally "localized" by prefixing it with a type name. Thus, the value of the parameter nm is transferred to the local variable instead of the instance variable, and the student object does not remember this change.

MISTAKE 3: METHOD ACCESSES DATA BY DIRECTLY REFERENCING GLOBAL VARIABLE WHEN IT COULD USE PARAMETER INSTEAD

Methods can communicate by sharing a common pool of variables or by the more explicit means of parameters and return values. Years of software development experience have convinced computer scientists that the second approach is better even though it seems to require more programming effort. There are three reasons to prefer the use of parameters:

1. Suppose that several methods share a pool of variables and that one method misuses a variable. Then other methods can be affected, and the resulting error can be difficult to find. For example, as the following code segment shows, if method m1 mistakenly sets the variable x to 0 and if method m2 uses x as a divisor, then when the program is run, the computer will signal an error in m2, even though the source of the error is in m1.

```
// Server class

public class ServerClass{

  private int x;

  public void m1(){

     ...
     x = 0;              // The real source of the error
  }

  public void m2(){
     int y = 10 / x;   // Exact spot of run-time error
  }

  ...
}
// Client class


public class ClientClass{
   private s = new ServerClass();
   public void m3(){
      s.m1();            // Misuse of x occurs, but is hidden from client
      s.m2();            // Run-time error occurs
   }
   ...
}
```

2. It is easier to understand methods and the relationships between them when communications are explicitly defined in terms of parameters and return values.

3. Methods that access a pool of shared variables can be used only in their original context, whereas methods that are passed parameters can be reused in many different situations. Reuse of code boosts productivity, so programmers try to create software components (in this case, methods) that are as reusable as possible. The method `Math.sqrt` is a good example of a context-independent method.

To summarize, it is a good idea to keep the use of global variables to a minimum, using them only when necessary to track the state of objects, and to use local variables and parameters wherever possible.

EXERCISE 5.5

1. What are the lifetimes of an instance variable, a local variable, and a parameter?

2. What is shadowing? Give an example and describe the bad things that shadowing might cause in a program.

EXERCISE 5.5 Continued

3. Consider the following code segment:

```
public class SomeClass{

    private int a, b;

    public void aMutator(int x, y){
        int c, d;
        <lots of code goes here>
    }
}
```

a. List the instance variables, parameters, and local variables in this code.

b. Describe the scope of each variable or parameter.

c. Describe the lifetime of each variable or parameter.

5.6 Graphics and GUIs: Images, a `Circle` Class, and Mouse Events

Realistic graphics applications display many kinds of images, including those that are created under program control and those that are simply loaded from existing image files. As the program-constructed images grow in number and complexity, it becomes useful to delegate responsibility for managing some of their attributes and behavior to the images themselves. This section discusses how to use image files, how to define classes that represent geometric shapes, and how to make graphics programs respond to a user's mouse manipulations.

> **Extra Challenge**
>
> This Graphics and GUIs section gives you the opportunity to explore concepts and programming techniques required to develop modern graphics applications and graphical user interfaces. This material is not required in order to proceed with the other chapters of the book.

Loading Images from Files and Displaying Them

Images are commonly stored in files in JPEG, GIF, or PNG format. You can obtain them from a variety of sources including a digital camera, a flatbed scanner, a screen capture program, or a Web site (but be careful of copyright laws, as discussed in Chapter 1). Once an image file is available, a Java application can load the image into RAM for program use by running the following code:

```
ImageIcon image = new ImageIcon(fileName);
```

where `fileName` is the name of an image file or its pathname. This code creates an `ImageIcon` object with a bitmap for the data in the image. Any images that come from files are typically loaded at program startup and passed to panels when they are instantiated. The panels are then responsible for displaying the images.

Our first example program has a main application class that loads an image of a cat named "Smokey" and passes the image to a new `ColorPanel`. The main window is shown in Figure 5-9. Here is the code for the application class:

```
// Example 5.2: Loading an image from a file

import javax.swing.*;
import java.awt.*;

public class GUIWindow{

    public static void main(String[] args){
        JFrame theGUI = new JFrame();
        theGUI.setTitle("GUI Program");
        theGUI.setSize(300, 300);
        theGUI.setDefaultCloseOperation(JFrame.EXIT_ON_CLOSE);
        ImageIcon image = new ImageIcon("smokey.jpg");
        ColorPanel panel = new ColorPanel(Color.black, image);
        Container pane = theGUI.getContentPane();
        pane.add(panel);
        theGUI.setVisible(true);
    }
}
```

FIGURE 5-9
Displaying an image

The `ColorPanel` receives the image icon at instantiation and saves a reference to it in an instance variable. When the panel paints itself, it paints the image icon. The code for painting the image appears in the panel's `paintComponent` method and has the following form:

```
anImageIcon.paintIcon(this, g, x, y)
```

where `this` refers to the panel itself, `g` is the panel's graphics context, and `x` and `y` are the panel coordinates of the image's upper-left corner.

The methods `getIconWidth()` and `getIconHeight()` return the width and height, respectively, of an image in pixels. These methods can be used with the `getWidth()` and `getHeight()`

methods of the panel class to compute the position of the image relative to the center of the panel. Here is the code for a `ColorPanel` class that displays a centered image:

```
// Displays an image centered in the panel

import javax.swing.*;
import java.awt.*;

public class ColorPanel extends JPanel{

    private ImageIcon image;

    public ColorPanel(Color backColor, ImageIcon i){
        setBackground(backColor);
        image = i;
    }

    public void paintComponent(Graphics g){
        super.paintComponent(g);
        int x = (getWidth() - image.getIconWidth()) / 2;
        int y = (getHeight() - image.getIconHeight()) / 2;
        image.paintIcon(this, g, x, y);
    }
}
```

This `ColorPanel` is different from panels discussed in earlier chapters in that it maintains another object, an image, as part of its state. Another difference is that this panel displays the image by asking an object to paint itself. We see this pattern repeated in the examples that follow.

Geometric Shapes

Graphics examples in earlier chapters displayed geometric shapes such as rectangles and ovals by running the corresponding drawing or filling methods of the `Graphics` class. There are several reasons why it will now be useful to view each shape as a distinct object with its own methods:

1. A shape has its own attributes, such as a color, a position, and a size. Defining a class for a shape allows a user to manipulate it by changing its color, position, or size.

2. Defining shape classes allows us to program with more specific shapes than those implied by the drawing methods of the `Graphics` class. For example, a circle is a specific type of oval, but we usually think of a circle in terms of its center point and radius rather than a corner point, width, and height. This also holds true for triangles and other more complex shapes.

3. If a shape already knows about its own attributes, it just needs a graphics context in order to display itself. Users can then more easily display shapes by asking them to display themselves, using a single `draw(aGraphicsObject)` or `fill(aGraphicsObject)` method.

4. Programs that use multiple shapes in complex arrangements can more easily compose these and manipulate them by using instances of shape classes.

Defining a `Circle` Class

Circles have a color, a center point, and a radius. In addition to modifying any of these attributes, a user can ask a circle to draw itself (just the circumference) or fill itself (like a solid disk) in its current color. Finally, a user can determine whether or not a circle contains a given point (x,y). The methods of our `circle` class are listed in Table 5-4.

TABLE 5-4
Methods in class `Circle`

METHOD	WHAT IT DOES
`Circle(int x, int y, int r, Color c)`	Constructor; creates a circle with center point (x, y), radius r, and color c
`int getX()`	Returns the x coordinate of the center
`int getY()`	Returns the y coordinate of the center
`int getRadius()`	Returns the radius
`Color getColor()`	Returns the color
`void setX(int x)`	Modifies the x coordinate of the center
`void setY(int y)`	Modifies the y coordinate of the center
`void setRadius(int r)`	Modifies the radius
`Color setColor(Color c)`	Modifies the color
`void draw(Graphics g)`	Draws an outline of the circle in the graphics context
`void fill(Graphics g)`	Draws a filled circle in the graphics context
`boolean containsPoint(int x, int y)`	Returns true if the point (x, y) lies in the circle or false otherwise
`void move(int xAmount, int yAmount)`	Moves the circle by xAmount horizontally to the right and yAmount vertically downward; Negative amounts move to the left and up.

Implementation of the `Circle` Class

For the most part, the implementation of the `circle` class is trivial. The constructor receives the coordinates of the center point, the radius, and the color from the user and assigns these values to instance variables. We focus on just two methods: `draw` and `containsPoint`. The `draw` method uses `drawOval` to draw the circle. The `drawOval` method expects the position and extent of the circle's bounding rectangle, which can be derived from the circle's center and radius as shown in the following code:

```
public void draw (Graphics g){
    // Save the current color of the graphics context
    // and set color to the circle's color.
    Color oldColor = g.getColor();
    g.setColor(color);
```

```
    // Translate the circle's position and radius
    // to the bounding rectangle's top left corner, width, and height.
    g.drawOval(centerX - radius, centerY - radius, radius * 2, radius * 2);

    // Restore the color of the graphics context.
    g.setColor(oldColor);
}
```

To determine if a point is in a circle, we consider the familiar equation for all points on the circumference of a circle:

$$(x - xc)^2 + (y - yc)^2 = r^2 \qquad \text{(Eq. 1)}$$

or

$$(x - xc)^2 + (y - yc)^2 - r^2 = 0 \qquad \text{(Eq. 2)}$$

where (xc, yc) is the circle's center and r is its radius. A point (x, y) is then in the circle if the left side of Equation 2 is less than or equal to 0. For example, given a circle of radius 2 and center $(0, 0)$, the point $(1, 1)$ produces the result

$$1^2 + 1^2 - 2^2 = -2$$

implying that the point is in the circle.

The following method results from this design:

```
public boolean containsPoint (int x, int y){
    int xSquared = (x - centerX) * (x - centerX);
    int ySquared = (y - centerY) * (y - centerY);
    int radiusSquared = radius * radius;
    return xSquared + ySquared - radiusSquared <= 0;
}
```

Here is a partial listing of the Circle class:

```
// Circle.java: Represents a circle

import java.awt.*;

public class Circle{

    private int centerX, centerY, radius;
    private Color color;

    public Circle(int x, int y, int r, Color c){
        centerX = x;
        centerY = y;
        radius = r;
        color = c;
    }
```

```java
public void draw(Graphics g){
   Color oldColor = g.getColor();
   g.setColor(color);
   // Translates circle's center to rectangle's origin for drawing.
   g.drawOval(centerX - radius, centerY - radius,
              radius * 2, radius * 2);
   g.setColor(oldColor);
}

public void fill(Graphics g){
   Color oldColor = g.getColor();
   g.setColor(color);
   // Translates circle's center to rectangle's origin for drawing.
   g.fillOval(centerX - radius, centerY - radius,
              radius * 2, radius * 2);
   g.setColor(oldColor);
}

public boolean containsPoint(int x, int y){
   int xSquared = (x - centerX) * (x - centerX);
   int ySquared = (y - centerY) * (y - centerY);
   int radiusSquared = radius * radius;
   return xSquared + ySquared - radiusSquared <= 0;
}

public void move(int xAmount, int yAmount){
   centerX = centerX + xAmount;
   centerY = centerY + yAmount;
}
}
```

Using the `Circle` Class

Our next example program creates and displays two `Circle` objects (see Figure 5-10). The main window class just creates a `ColorPanel` with a background color and adds it to the window. The `ColorPanel`'s constructor sets two instance variables to different `Circle` objects. When the window is refreshed, the `ColorPanel`'s `paintComponent` method draws one circle and fills the other. Here is the code for `ColorPanel`:

```java
// Example 5.3: Displays a circle and a filled circle

import javax.swing.*;
import java.awt.*;

public class ColorPanel extends JPanel{

   private Circle c1, c2;

   public ColorPanel(Color backColor){
      setBackground(backColor);
      c1 = new Circle(200, 100, 25, Color.red);
      c2 = new Circle(100, 100, 50, Color.blue);
   }
```

```
    public void paintComponent(Graphics g){
       super.paintComponent(g);
       c1.fill(g);
       c2.draw(g);
    }
  }
```

FIGURE 5-10
Displaying two `Circle` objects

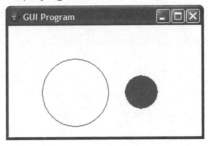

The Method `repaint`

Suppose we want to move a shape or image to a new position in a panel in response to a mouse click. Let's assume we have the coordinates of the new position (we see how to get these in the next subsection). There are then just two steps remaining:

1. Set the shape's position to the new position.

2. Refresh the panel, which has the effect of clearing the panel and redrawing the shape at its new position.

The method `repaint` is used to force a refresh of any GUI component, such as a panel. The method essentially invokes that object's `paintComponent` method. Thus, there are two kinds of situations in which `paintComponent` is called:

1. Automatically, by the JVM, at startup; or whenever the main window is altered

2. Under program control, by a call of `repaint`, when the program has made a change to the objects to be displayed

The code that calls `repaint` typically appears in a panel method that has modified one or more shapes in the panel. This method might have the following form:

```
    public void modifySomeShapes(someParameters){
       // modify the attributes of one or more shapes
       repaint();
    }
```

Responses to Mouse Events

Until now, we have limited our use of the mouse to clicking on command buttons and editing data in I/O dialog boxes. Everyone who has used a drawing program knows that much more can be done with the mouse. Drawing applications usually detect and respond to the following mouse events: button presses and releases, mouse movement, and dragging the mouse (i.e., moving the mouse while a button is depressed). In addition, a program can respond to the mouse's entry into and exit from a given region.

A program can detect and respond to mouse events by attaching *listener objects* to a panel. When a particular type of mouse event occurs in a panel, its listeners are informed. If a listener has a method whose parameter matches that type of event, the JVM automatically runs this method and passes the event object to it as a parameter. The event object contains the mouse's current panel coordinates. The code in the method carries out the program's response to that mouse event.

For example, let's say that a panel should display the coordinates of the mouse whenever its button is pressed in a panel. The panel's constructor sets some instance variables to default coordinates, say, (100,100), and attaches a new listener object to the panel. The class for this listener object, also defined within the panel class, implements the method `mousePressed`, which will be triggered whenever a mouse-pressed event occurs in that panel. This method receives an event object as a parameter from the JVM. The method resets the coordinates to the ones contained in the event object and calls `repaint` to refresh the panel. The panel's `paintComponent` method simply draws the coordinates.

Our next example program shows a `ColorPanel` class that responds to mouse presses by displaying the mouse's coordinates. The class includes a nested listener class, `PanelListener`, which we explain following the listing.

```
// Example 5.4: Tracks mouse presses by displaying
// the current mouse position

import javax.swing.*;
import java.awt.*;
import java.awt.event.*;      //For the mouse events

public class ColorPanel extends JPanel{

    int x, y;    // Used to track mouse coordinates

    public ColorPanel(Color backColor){
       setBackground(backColor);
       // Establish the default coordinates
       x = 100;
       y = 100;
       // Instantiate and attach the panel's listener
       addMouseListener(new PanelListener());
    }

    public void paintComponent(Graphics g){
       super.paintComponent(g);
       // Draw the current coordinates
       g.drawString("(" + x + ", " + y + ")", x, y);
    }

    private class PanelListener extends MouseAdapter{

       public void mousePressed(MouseEvent e){
       // Obtain the current mouse coordinates and refresh
```

```
            x = e.getX();
            y = e.getY();
            repaint();
        }
    }
}
```

The `ColorPanel` class imports the package `java.awt.event`, which includes the classes `MouseEvent` and `MouseAdapter`. The panel's constructor uses the method `addMouseListener` to attach a `PanelListener`. This class is defined internally within the `ColorPanel` class, so its methods will have access to all of the panel's instance variables and methods.

The `PanelListener` class extends the class `MouseAdapter`. `MouseAdapter` includes several methods that respond to mouse events by doing nothing (very simple default behavior). One of these methods is `mousePressed`. `PanelListener` overrides the default definition of `mousePressed` by redefining it. The method extracts the coordinates of the mouse from the `MouseEvent` parameter using the methods `getX()` and `getY()`. It resets the panel's instance variables `x` and `y` to these values and then repaints the panel. Note that the visibility modifier of the `PanelListener` class is `private` because the enclosing panel class is its only user.

When you want the panel to respond to other types of mouse events, you just include code for the corresponding method in your listener class. At runtime, the JVM takes care of feeding the event object to the appropriate method.

The `MouseAdapter` class includes methods for all but two mouse events, mouse motion and mouse dragging. The methods for these two events are included in the `MouseMotionAdapter` class. Thus, you will have to define a separate class that extends `MouseMotionAdapter` and include either or both of its methods if you want your program to respond to mouse motion events. The method `addMouseMotionListener` is used to add listeners of this type to a panel. Table 5-5 lists the methods and the corresponding mouse events in the `MouseAdapter` and `MouseMotionAdapter` classes.

TABLE 5-5
Methods for responding to mouse events

CLASS	METHOD	TYPE OF EVENT
MouseAdapter	public void mouseEntered(MouseEvent e) public void mouseExited(MouseEvent e) public void mousePressed(MouseEvent e) public void mouseReleased(MouseEvent e) public void mouseClicked(MouseEvent e)	Enter Exit Press Release Click
MouseMotionAdapter	public void mouseMoved(MouseEvent e) public void mouseDragged(MouseEvent e)	Move Drag

Dragging Circles

Our final program example puts together our ideas about shape objects and mouse events to create a simple program for dragging circles around in a window. The user selects a circle by pressing the mouse within it and then moves it by dragging it to a desired position.

The ColorPanel class has the same two instance variables for circles as in the previous version (see Example 5.2). To these we add instance variables for saving the mouse coordinates and for saving a reference to the selected circle. This last variable is null at startup and after a circle has been deselected.

Here are the types of mouse events and the associated responses of the program:

1. *Mouse press.* Save the current coordinates of the mouse. If one of the shapes contains those coordinates, save a reference to that shape (thereby selecting it).

2. *Mouse release.* Deselect the selected shape, if there is one, by setting the saved reference to null.

3. *Mouse drag.* Compute the *x* and *y* distances by using the current mouse coordinates and the saved mouse coordinates. If a shape is currently selected, move it using the distances and repaint. Finally, set the saved coordinates to the current mouse coordinates.

Here is a complete listing of the ColorPanel class for dragging shapes:

```java
// Example 5.5: Displays a circle and a filled circle
// Allows the user to drag a circle to another position

import javax.swing.*;
import java.awt.*;
import java.awt.event.*;              //For the mouse events

public class ColorPanel extends JPanel{

   private Circle c1, c2;
   private Circle selectedCircle;     // Used to track selected shape
   private int x, y;                  // Used to track mouse coordinates

   public ColorPanel(Color backColor){
      setBackground(backColor);
      c1 = new Circle(200, 100, 25, Color.red);
      c2 = new Circle(100, 100, 50, Color.blue);
      selectedCircle = null;
      addMouseListener(new PanelListener());
      addMouseMotionListener(new PanelMotionListener());
   }

   public void paintComponent(Graphics g){
      super.paintComponent(g);
      c1.fill(g);
      c2.draw(g);
   }

   private class PanelListener extends MouseAdapter{
```

```
   public void mousePressed(MouseEvent e){
      // Select a circle if it contains the mouse coordinates
      x = e.getX();
      y = e.getY();
      if (c1.containsPoint(x, y))
         selectedCircle = c1;
      else if (c2.containsPoint(x, y))
         selectedCircle = c2;
   }

   public void mouseReleased(MouseEvent e){
      // Deselect the selected circle
      x = e.getX();
      y = e.getY();
      selectedCircle = null;
   }
}

private class PanelMotionListener extends MouseMotionAdapter{

   public void mouseDragged(MouseEvent e){
      // Compute the distance and move the selected circle
      int newX = e.getX();
      int newY = e.getY();
      int dx = newX - x;
      int dy = newY - y;
      if (selectedCircle != null)
         selectedCircle.move(dx, dy);
      x = newX;
      y = newY;
      repaint();
   }
}
}
```

In later chapters, we explore how to write programs that manipulate an arbitrary number of graphical objects.

EXERCISE 5.6

1. The program example that displayed an image in this section has a problem. If the image size is larger than that of the window, the user must resize the window to view the entire image. Describe how to fix the program so that the window size exactly fits the image size at startup.

2. Geometric shapes can be scaled up or down in size. For example, scaling by a factor of 3 triples the size of a shape, whereas scaling by a factor of 0.5 reduces the size of a shape by one-half. Write a method scale that expects a parameter of type `double` and scales a circle by that factor.

3. Explain how a program can detect and respond to the user's pressing of a mouse button.

SUMMARY

In this chapter, you learned:

■ Java class definitions consist of instance variables, constructors, and methods.

■ Constructors initialize an object's instance variables when the object is created. A default constructor expects no parameters and sets the variables to reasonable default values. Other constructors expect parameters that allow clients to set up objects with specified data.

■ Mutator methods modify an object's instance variables, whereas accessor methods merely allow clients to observe the values of these variables.

■ The visibility modifier `public` is used to make methods visible to clients, whereas the visibility modifier `private` is used to encapsulate or restrict access to variables and methods.

■ Helper methods are methods that are called from other methods in a class definition. They are usually declared to be private.

■ Variables within a class definition can be instance variables, local variables, or parameters. Instance variables are used to track the state of an object. Local variables are used for temporary working storage within a method. Parameters are used to transmit data to a method.

■ A formal parameter appears in a method's signature and is referenced in its code. An actual parameter is a value passed to a method when it is called. A method's actual parameters must match its formal parameters in number, position, and type.

■ The scope of a variable is the area of program text within which it is visible. The scope of an instance variable is the entire class within which it is declared. The scope of a local variable or a parameter is the body of the method within which it is declared.

■ The lifetime of a variable is the period of program execution during which its storage can be accessed. The lifetime of an instance variable is the same as the lifetime of a particular object. The lifetime of a local variable and a parameter is the time during which a particular call of a method is active.

VOCABULARY *Review*

Define the following terms:

Accessor	Formal parameter	Mutator
Actual parameter	Helper method	Scope
Behavior	Identity	State
Constructor	Instantiation	Visibility modifier
Encapsulation	Lifetime	

REVIEW *Questions*

WRITTEN QUESTIONS

Write a brief answer to the following questions.

1. Explain the difference between a class and an instance of a class.

2. Explain the difference between the visibility modifiers `public` and `private`.

3. What are accessor and mutator methods?

4. Develop a design for a new class called `BaseballPlayer`. The variables of this class are

   name (a `String`)

   team (a `String`)

   home runs (an `int`)

   batting average (a `double`)

   Express your design in terms of a class summary box. The class should have a constructor and methods for accessing and modifying all of the variables.

5. Explain how a parameter transmits data to a method.

6. What are local variables and how should they be used in a program?

PROJECTS

PROJECT 5-1

Add the extra constructors to the `Student` class of this chapter's first case study (Student Test Scores), and test these methods thoroughly with a `Tester` program.

PROJECT 5-2

A `Student` object should validate its own data. The client runs this method, called `validateData()`, with a `Student` object, as follows:

```
String result = student.validateData();
if (result == null)
    <use the student>
else
    System.out.println(result);
```

If the student's data are valid, the method returns the value `null`; otherwise, the method returns a string representing an error message that describes the error in the data. The client can then examine this result and take the appropriate action.

A student's name is invalid if it is an empty string. A student's test score is invalid if it lies outside the range from 0 to 100. Thus, sample error messages might be

```
"SORRY: name required"
```

and

```
"SORRY: must have 0 <= test score <= 100".
```

Implement and test this method.

PROJECT 5-3

Develop a new class for representing fractions. The numerator and denominator of a fraction are integers. The constructor expects these values as parameters. Define accessor methods to obtain the numerator and the denominator. Use the rules of fraction arithmetic to define methods to add, subtract, multiply, and divide fractions. Each of these methods expects a fraction object as a parameter. This object is considered to be the right operand of the operation. The left operand is the receiver object, that is, the one containing the instance variables for the numerator and denominator. Each arithmetic method builds a new instance of the fraction class with the results of its calculation and returns it as the method's value. Finally, include a `toString()`

method that returns a string of the form <numerator>/<denominator>. Write a tester program that exercises all of the methods. Here are the rules for fraction arithmetic:

$$\frac{n_1}{d_1} + \frac{n_2}{d_2} = \frac{n_1 d_2 + n_2 d_1}{d_1 d_2}$$

$$\frac{n_1}{d_1} - \frac{n_2}{d_2} = \frac{n_1 d_2 - n_2 d_1}{d_1 d_2}$$

$$\frac{n_1}{d_1} \times \frac{n_2}{d_2} = \frac{n_1 n_2}{d_1 d_2}$$

$$\frac{n_1/d_1}{n_2/d_2} = \frac{n_1 d_2}{d_1 n_2}$$

PROJECT 5-4

Redo the Lucky Sevens dice-playing program from Chapter 4 so that it uses dice objects. That is, design and implement a Dice class. Each instance of this class should contain the die's current side. There should be an accessor method for a die's current value. The method roll is the only mutator method. Be sure to test the Dice class in a simple tester program before incorporating it into the application.

PROJECT 5-5

Develop a new class called BankAccount. A bank account has an owner's name and a balance. Be sure to include a constructor that allows a client to supply the owner's name and an initial balance. A bank account needs accessors for the name and balance, mutators for making deposits and withdrawals, and a toString method. Test-drive your new class with a program similar to the one used to test the Student class in Section 5.3.

PROJECT 5-6

Patrons of a library can borrow up to three books. A patron, therefore, has a name and up to three books. A book has an author and a title. Design and implement two classes, Patron and Book, to represent these objects and the following behavior:

- The client can instantiate a book with a title and author.
- The client can examine but not modify a book's title or author.
- The client can ask a patron whether it has borrowed a given book (identified by title).
- The client can tell a patron to return a given book (identified by title).
- The client can tell a patron to borrow a given book.

The Patron class should use a separate instance variable for each book (a total of three). Each of these variables is initially null. When a book is borrowed, the patron looks for a variable that is not null. If no such variable is found, the method returns false. If a null variable is found, it is reset to the new book and the method returns true. Similar considerations apply to the other methods. Use the method aString.equals(aString) to compare two strings for equality. Be sure to include appropriate toString methods for your classes and test them with a tester program.

PROJECT 5-7

Write a program that allows the user to display 1, 2, or 4 images in a grid of panels. At program startup, the user is prompted for the number of images. If the input number is not 1, 2, or 4, the program quits with an error message. Otherwise, the program prompts the user for the name of each image file, loads the image, installs it in a ColorPanel, and adds the panel to a grid.

PROJECT 5-8

Define a Rectangle class to represent rectangles. Modify the program of Section 5.6 so that it uses two rectangles instead of two circles.

PROJECT 5-9

Write a program that displays an 8-by-8 grid of panels, all of which are initially colored white. When the user presses the mouse within a panel, its color should change to a randomly generated color.

CRITICAL *Thinking*

Explain how you could modify the fraction class created in Project 5-3 to display a fraction in a form that is reduced to lowest terms.

CONTROL STATEMENTS CONTINUED

OBJECTIVES

Upon completion of this chapter, you should be able to:

- Construct complex Boolean expressions using the logical operators && (AND), || (OR), and ! (NOT).

- Construct truth tables for Boolean expressions.

- Understand the logic of nested if statements and extended if statements.

- Test if statements in a comprehensive manner.

- Construct nested loops.

- Create appropriate test cases for `if` statements and loops.

- Understand the purpose of assertions, invariants, and loop verification.

Estimated Time: 5 hours

VOCABULARY

Arithmetic overflow

Boundary condition

Combinatorial explosion

Complete code coverage

Equivalence class

Extended if statement

Extreme condition

Input assertion

Logical operator

Loop invariant

Loop variant

Nested if statement

Nested loop

Output assertion

Quality assurance

Robust

Truth table

This chapter explores more advanced aspects of the control statements introduced in Chapter 4. Topics include logical operators, nested `if` statements, and nested loops. The chapter also describes strategies for testing programs that contain control statements. Programmers try to write programs that are free of logic errors, but they seldom succeed. Consequently, they must test their programs thoroughly before releasing them—and even so, errors will still slip through. Notice that we say "will" instead of "might." Software is so incredibly complex that no significant software product has ever been released free of errors; however, the situation would be much worse if we stopped emphasizing the importance of testing.

6.1 Logical Operators

Java includes three logical operators equivalent in meaning to the English words AND, OR, and NOT. These operators are used in the Boolean expressions that control the behavior of `if`, while, and for statements. Before we examine how these operators are used in Java, we review their usage in English. For instance, consider the following sentences:

1. If the sun is shining AND it is 8 a.m. then let's go for a walk else let's stay home.

2. If the sun is shining OR it is 8 a.m. then let's go for a walk else let's stay home.

3. If NOT the sun is shining then let's go for a walk else let's stay home.

The structure of all three sentences is similar, but their meanings are very different. For clarity we have emphasized key words. In these sentences, the phrases "the sun is shining" and "it is 8 a.m." are operands and the words AND, OR, and NOT are operators. At any particular moment, the value of a condition (true or false) depends on the values of the operands (also true or false) and the operator's meaning. For instance,

■ In the first sentence, the operator is AND. Consequently, if both operands are true, the condition as a whole is true. If either or both are false, the condition is false.

■ In the second sentence, which uses OR, the condition is false only if both operands are false; otherwise, it is true.

■ In the third sentence, the operator NOT has been placed before the operand, as it would be in Java. This looks a little strange in English but is still understandable. If the operand is true, then the NOT operator makes the condition as a whole false.

We summarize these observations in the three parts of Table 6-1. Each part is called a truth table, and it shows how the value of the overall condition depends on the values of the operands. All combinations of values are considered. When there is one operand, there are two possibilities. For two operands, there are four; and for three operands, there are eight possibilities. In general there are 2^n combinations of true and false for n operands.

TABLE 6-1
Truth tables for three example sentences

THE SUN IS SHINING	IT IS 8 A.M.	THE SUN IS SHINING AND IT IS 8 A.M.	ACTION TAKEN
true	true	true	go for a walk
true	false	false	stay at home
false	true	false	stay at home
false	false	false	stay at home
THE SUN IS SHINING	**IT IS 8 A.M.**	**THE SUN IS SHINING OR IT IS 8 A.M.**	**ACTION TAKEN**
true	true	true	go for a walk
true	false	true	go for a walk
false	true	true	go for a walk
false	false	false	stay at home
THE SUN IS SHINING	**NOT THE SUN IS SHINING**	**ACTION TAKEN**	
true	false	stay at home	
false	true	go for a walk	

Dropping the column labeled "action taken," we can combine the information in the three truth tables in Table 6-1 into one table of general rules, as illustrated in Table 6-2. The letters P and Q represent the operands.

TABLE 6-2
General rules for AND, OR, and NOT

P	Q	P AND Q	P OR Q	NOT P
true	true	true	true	false
true	false	false	true	
false	true	false	true	true
false	false	false	false	

Three Operators at Once

Now that we know the rules, it is easy to construct and understand more complex conditions. Consider the following sentences:

A. If (the sun is shining AND it is 8 a.m.) OR (NOT your brother is visiting) then let's go for a walk else let's stay at home.

We have added parentheses to remove ambiguity. As usual, expressions inside parentheses are evaluated before those that are not. So now when do we go for a walk? The answer is at 8 a.m. on sunny days or when your brother does not visit; however, rearranging the parentheses changes the meaning of the sentence:

B. If the sun is shining AND (it is 8 a.m. OR (NOT your brother is visiting)) then let's go for a walk else let's stay at home.

Now before we go for a walk, the sun must be shining. In addition, one of two things must be true. Either it is 8 a.m. or your brother is not visiting. It does get a little confusing. Making truth tables for these sentences would make their meanings completely clear.

Java's Logical Operators and Their Precedence

In Java the operators AND, OR, and NOT are represented by &&, ||, and !, respectively. Before writing code that uses these operators, we must consider their precedence as shown in Table 6-3. Observe that NOT (!) has the same high precedence as other unary operators, whereas AND (&&) and OR (||) have low precedence, with OR below AND.

TABLE 6-3
Positions of the logical and relational operators in the precedence scheme

OPERATION	SYMBOL	PRECEDENCE (FROM HIGHEST TO LOWEST)	ASSOCIATION
Grouping	( )	1	Not applicable
Method selector	.	2	Left to right
Unary plus	+	3	Not applicable
Unary minus	–	3	Not applicable
Not	!	3	Not applicable
Multiplication	*	4	Left to right
Division	/	4	Left to right
Remainder or modulus	%	4	Left to right
Addition	+	5	Left to right
Subtraction	–	5	Left to right
Relational operators	< <= > >= == !=	6	Not applicable
And	&&	8	Left to right
Or	||	9	Left to right
Assignment operators	= *= /= %= += –=	10	Right to left

A complete table of operator precedence can be found in Appendix C.

Examples Using Logical Operators

Following are some illustrative examples based on the employment practices at ABC Company. The company screens all new employees by making them take two written tests. A program then analyzes the scores and prints a list of jobs for which the applicant is qualified. Following is the relevant code:

```
Scanner reader = new Scanner(System.in);
int score1, score2;
System.out.print("Enter the first test score: ");
score1 = reader.nextInt();
System.out.print("Enter the second test score: ");
score2 = reader.nextInt();
```

```
// Managers must score well (90 or above) on both tests.
if (score1 >= 90 && score2 >= 90)
   System.out.println("Qualified to be a manager");

// Supervisors must score well (90 or above) on just one test
if (score1 >= 90 || score2 >= 90)
   System.out.println("Qualified to be a supervisor");

// Clerical workers must score moderately well on one test

// (70 or above), but not badly (below 50) on either.
if ((score1 >= 70 || score2 >= 70) &&
    !(score1 < 50 || score2 < 50))
   System.out.println("Qualified to be a clerk");
```

Boolean Variables

The complex Boolean expressions in the preceding examples can be simplified by using Boolean variables. A Boolean variable can be true or false and is declared to be of type `boolean`. Now we rewrite the previous examples using Boolean variables:

```
Scanner reader = new Scanner(System.in);
int score1, score2;
boolean bothHigh, atLeastOneHigh, atLeastOneModerate, noLow;
System.out.print("Enter the first test score: ");
score1 = reader.nextInt();
System.out.print("Enter the second test score: ");
score2 = reader.nextInt();

bothHigh           =  (score1 >= 90 && score2 >= 90); // parentheses
atLeastOneHigh     =  (score1 >= 90 || score2 >= 90); // optional
atLeastOneModerate =  (score1 >= 70 || score2 >= 70); // here
noLow              = !(score1 <  50 || score2 <  50);
if (bothHigh)
   System.out.println("Qualified to be a manager");
if (atLeastOneHigh)
   System.out.println("Qualified to be a supervisor");
if (atLeastOneModerate && noLow)
   System.out.println("Qualified to be a clerk");
```

Rewriting Complex Boolean Expressions

A complex `if` statement is sometimes so confusing that it is better rewritten as a series of simpler ones. Here is an example in a mixture of English and Java that we call Javish:

```
if (the sun shines && (you have the time || it is Sunday))
   let's go for a walk;
else
   let's stay home;
```

To rewrite the previous code, we first create a truth table for the complex if statement, as shown in Table 6-4.

TABLE 6-4
Truth table for complex if statement

P: THE SUN SHINES	Q: YOU HAVE TIME	R: IT IS SUNDAY	P && (Q || R)	ACTION TAKEN
true	true	true	true	walk
true	true	false	true	walk
true	false	true	true	walk
true	false	false	false	stay home
false	true	true	false	stay home
false	true	false	false	stay home
false	false	true	false	stay home
false	false	false	false	stay home

Then implement each line of the truth table with a separate `if` statement involving only `&&` (AND) and `!` (NOT). Applying the technique here yields

```
if ( the sun shines &&  you have time &&  it is Sunday) walk;
if ( the sun shines &&  you have time && !it is Sunday) walk;
if ( the sun shines && !you have time &&  it is Sunday) walk;
if ( the sun shines && !you have time && !it is Sunday) stay home;
if (!the sun shines &&  you have time &&  it is Sunday) stay home;
if (!the sun shines &&  you have time && !it is Sunday) stay home;
if (!the sun shines && !you have time &&  it is Sunday) stay home;
if (!the sun shines && !you have time && !it is Sunday) stay home;
```

In this particular example, the verbosity can be reduced without reintroducing complexity by noticing that the first two `if` statements are equivalent to

```
if ( the sun shines &&  you have time) walk;
```

and the last four are equivalent to

```
if (!the sun shines) stay home;
```

Putting all this together yields

```
if ( the sun shines &&  you have time) walk;
if ( the sun shines && !you have time &&  it is Sunday) walk;
if (the sun shines && !you have time  && !it is Sunday) stay home
if (!the sun shines) stay home;
```

Of course, it is also possible to go in the other direction: that is, combine several `if` statements into a single more complex one, but no matter how we choose to represent complex conditions, truth tables are an essential tool for verifying the accuracy of the result. We can use them anytime we are uncertain about the meaning of the `if` statements we write.

Some Useful Boolean Equivalences

There is often more than one way to write a Boolean expression. For instance, the following pairs of Boolean expressions are equivalent, as truth tables readily confirm:

!(p ‖ q)	equivalent to	!p && !q
!(p && q)	equivalent to	!p ‖ !q
p ‖ (q && r)	equivalent to	(p ‖ q) && (p ‖ r)
p && (q ‖ r)	equivalent to	(p && q) ‖ (p && r)

Using these equivalences sometimes enables us to rewrite a condition in a more easily understood form. Following is an example in which we display the word "reject" if x is not in the interval [3, 5], or alternatively, if x is less than 3 or greater than 5:

```
if (!(3 <= x && x <= 5))   System.out.println("reject");
if (!(3 <= x) || !(x <= 5)) System.out.println("reject");
if (x < 3 || x > 5)        System.out.println("reject");
```

Short-circuit Evaluation

The Java virtual machine sometimes knows the value of a Boolean expression before it has evaluated all of its parts. For instance, in the expression (`p && q`), if `p` is false, then so is the expression, and there is no need to evaluate q. Likewise, in the expression (`p || q`), if `p` is true, then so is the expression, and again there is no need to evaluate q. This approach, in which evaluation stops as soon as possible, is called short-circuit evaluation. In contrast, some programming languages use complete evaluation, in which all parts of a Boolean expression are always evaluated. These two methods nearly always produce the same results; however, there are times when short-circuit evaluation is advantageous. Consider the following example:

```
Scanner reader = new Scanner(System.in);
int count, sum;
System.out.print("Enter the count: ");
count = reader.nextInt;
System.out.print("Enter the sum: ");
sum = reader.nextInt();

if (count > 0 && sum / count > 10)
    System.out.println("average > 10");
else
    System.out.println("count = 0 or average <= 10");
```

If the user enters 0 for the count, the condition (`count > 0 && sum / count > 10`) contains a potential division by zero; however, because of short-circuit evaluation the division by zero is avoided.

EXERCISE 6.1

1. Fill in the truth values in the following truth table:

P	Q	! ((P || Q) && (P && Q))

2. Assume that A is true and B is false. Write the values of the following expressions:

   a. A \|\| B

   b. A && B

   c. A && ! B

   d. ! (A \|\| B)

3. Construct truth tables for the expressions listed under the heading "Some Useful Boolean Equivalences" in this section to show that they are equivalent.

4. List the logical operators in the order in which each one would be evaluated at run time.

5. Construct a Boolean expression that tests whether the value of variable x is within the range specified by the variables min (the smallest) and max (the largest).

Case Study 1: Compute Weekly Pay

We illustrate the use of logical operators by writing a program to compute weekly pay.

Request

Write a program to compute the weekly pay of hourly employees.

Analysis

Employees are paid at a base rate for the first 40 hours they work each week. Hours over 40 are paid at an overtime rate equal to twice the base rate. An exception is made for part-time employees, who are always paid at the regular rate, no matter how many hours they work. The hourly rate is in the range $6.75 to $30.50 and hours worked in the range 1 to 60. We use a type attribute to distinguish between full-time (type 1) and part-time (type 2) employees. Figure 6-1 shows the user interface.

We would also like the program to be *robust*, that is, to handle invalid inputs without crashing or producing meaningless results. The easiest and best way to achieve this end is to check data values as soon as they are entered and reject those that are invalid. The user is then given another opportunity to enter a correct value, as shown in Figure 6-2.

FIGURE 6-1
Interface for the compute weekly pay program

```
Enter employee data
  Name (or blank to quit): Susan Jones
  Type (1 or 2): 1
  Hourly rate (between 6.75 and 30.50, inclusive): 10.50
  Hours worked (between 1 and 60, inclusive): 50
  The weekly pay for Susan Jones is $630.0
Enter employee data
  Name (or blank to quit): Bill Smith
  Type (1 or 2): 2
  Hourly rate (between 6.75 and 30.50, inclusive): 15.00
  Hours worked (between 1 and 60, inclusive): 60
  The weekly pay for Bill Smith is $900.0
Enter employee data
  Name (or blank to quit):
```

FIGURE 6-2
How the program responds to invalid inputs

```
Enter employee data
  Name (or blank to quit): Patricia Nelson
  Type (1 or 2): 3
  Type (1 or 2): 0
  Type (1 or 2): 1
  Hourly rate (between 6.75 and 30.50, inclusive): 99.00
  Hourly rate (between 6.75 and 30.50, inclusive): 3.75
  Hourly rate (between 6.75 and 30.50, inclusive): 20.89
  Hours worked (between 1 and 60, inclusive): 100
  Hours worked (between 1 and 60, inclusive): 25
  The weekly pay for Patricia Nelson is $522.25
```

Following the approach introduced in Chapter 5, we divide the work of the application into two classes: a user interface class (PayrollSystemApp) and an employee class (Employee). The Employee class has four instance variables:

■ Name

■ Type

■ Rate

■ Hours

and three responsibilities:

■ Provide information about data validation rules (getNameRules, getTypeRules, etc).

■ Set instance variables provided the values are valid (return true if valid and false otherwise).

■ Get the name and weekly pay.

Figure 6-3 summarizes these points. The user interface class has the usual structure and has the single method main, so we omit a class summary.

FIGURE 6-3
Summary of the Employee class

```
Class:
      Employee
Private Instance Variables:
   String name
   int type
   double rate
   int hours
Public Methods:
   constructor
   String getNameRules()
   String getTypeRules()
   String getRateRules()
   String getHoursRules()
   boolean setName(String nm)
   boolean setType(int tp)
   boolean setRate(double rt)
   boolean setHours(int hrs)
   String getName()
   double getPay()
```

Design

Following is the pseudocode for the user interface:

```
while (true){
    read name, break if blank else set the employee name
    read type until valid and set the employee type
    read rate until valid and set the employee rate
    read hours until valid and set the employee hours
    ask the employee for name and pay and print these
}
```

An employee object computes pay as follows:

```
if (hours <= 40 || type == 2)
    pay = rate * hours;
else
    pay = rate * 40 +  rate * 2 * (hours - 40);
```

Implementation

The implementation uses two new string methods, trim and equals. When a trim() message is sent to a string, a new string that contains no leading or trailing spaces is returned:

```
String inputName, trimmedName;
System.out.print("Enter the name: ")
inputName = reader.nextLine;
trimmedName = inputName.trim();
```

The `equals` method is used to determine if two string objects contain equal strings. This is in contrast to the `==` operator, which determines if two string variables refer to the same object. Following is an illustration:

```
String a, b;
a = "cat";
System.out.print("What do you call a small domestic feline? ");
b = reader.nextLine;

if (a == b)
   System.out.println("a and b reference the same object.");
else
   System.out.println("a and b reference different objects.");

if (a.equals(b))
   System.out.println
   ("a and b reference objects that contain equal strings.");
else
   System.out.println
   ("a and b reference objects that contain unequal strings");
```

If the user enters "cat" when this code is run, the output is

```
a and b reference different objects.
a and b reference objects that contain equal strings.
```

We now return to the case study program and present the implementation, which is complicated by all the error checking we have decided to do. The user interface class restricts itself to interacting with the user, and the `Employee` class controls data validation and computation of pay:

```
/* Case Study 6.1: PayrollSystemApp.java
1. Request employee name, type, pay rate, and hours.
2. Print employee name and pay.
3. Repeat until the name is blank.*/

import java.util.Scanner;

public class PayrollSystemApp{

    public static void main (String [] args) {
        Scanner reader = new Scanner(System.in);
        Employee emp;      // employee
        String name;       //   name
        int     type;      //   type
        double rate;       //   hourly pay rate
        int     hours;     //   hours worked
        String prompt;     // user prompt;

        while (true){

            // Get the name and break if blank
            System.out.println("Enter employee data");
            System.out.print("  Name (or blank to quit): ");
            name = reader.nextLine();
```

```java
            name = name.trim(); // Trim off leading and trailing spaces
            if (name.length() == 0) break;
            emp = new Employee();
            emp.setName(name);

            // Get the type until valid
            while (true){
                prompt = "  Type (" + emp.getTypeRules() + "): ";
                System.out.print(prompt);
                type = reader.nextInt();
                if (emp.setType(type)) break;
            }

            // Get the hourly pay rate until valid
            while (true){
                prompt = "  Hourly rate (" + emp.getRateRules() + "): ";
                System.out.print(prompt);
                rate = reader.nextDouble();
                if (emp.setRate(rate)) break;
            }

            // Get the hours worked until valid
            //   To illustrate the possibilities we compress
            //   into a hard-to-read set of statements.
            System.out.print("Hours worked (" +
                            emp.getHoursRules() + "): ");
            while (!emp.setHours(reader.nextInt()))
                    System.out.print("Hours worked (" +
                                    emp.getHoursRules() + "): ");

            // Consume the trailing newline
            reader.nextLine();

            // Print the name and pay
            System.out.println("  The weekly pay for " + emp.getName() +
                            " is $" + emp.getPay());
        }
    }
}




/*  Employee.java
1. Instance variables: name, type, rate, hours
2. Methods to
   get data validation rules
   set instance variables if data are valid
   get name and pay */

public class Employee{

    // Private Instance Variables:
    private String name;
```

```
private int type;
private double rate;
private int hours;

// Public Methods:
public Employee(){
    name = "";
    type = 0;
    rate = 0;
    hours = 0;
}

  public String getNameRules(){
    return "nonblank";
}

  public String getTypeRules(){
    return "1 or 2";
}

  public String getRateRules(){
    return "between 6.75 and 30.50, inclusive";
}

public String getHoursRules(){
    return "between 1 and 60, inclusive";
}

  public boolean setName(String nm){
    if (nm.equals(""))
       return false;
    else{
       name = nm;
       return true;
    }
}

public boolean setType(int tp){
    if (tp != 1 && tp != 2)
       return false;
    else{
       type = tp;
       return true;
    }
}

public boolean setRate(double rt){
    if (!(6.75 <= rt && rt <= 30.50))
       return false;
    else{
       rate = rt;
       return true;
    }
}
```

```java
public boolean setHours(int hrs){
   if (!(1 <= hrs && hrs <= 60))
      return false;
   else{
      hours = hrs;
      return true;
   }
}

public String getName(){
   return name;
}

public double getPay(){
   double pay;
   if (hours <= 40 || type == 2)
      pay = rate * hours;
   else
      pay = rate * 40 +  rate * 2 * (hours - 40);
   return pay;
}
}
```

6.2 Testing `if` Statements

Q*uality assurance* is the ongoing process of making sure that a software product is developed to the highest standards possible subject to the ever-present constraints of time and money. As we learned in Chapter 1, faults are fixed most inexpensively early in the development life cycle; however, no matter how much care is taken at every stage during a program's development, eventually the program must be run against well-designed test data. Such data should exercise a program as thoroughly as possible. At a minimum, the test data should try to achieve *complete code coverage*, which means that every line in a program is executed at least once. Unfortunately, this is not the same thing as testing all possible logical paths through a program, which would provide a more thorough test, but also might require considerably more test data.

We now design test data for the preceding case study. Because the program is so simple, the test data will provide complete code coverage and test all possible logical paths through the program. Varying the hourly rate has no particular significance in this problem, so we use an hourly rate of $10 for all the tests.

First, we test with an employee type of 1 and hours worked equal to 30 and 50 hours. Because we must compare the program's output with the expected results, we have chosen numbers for which it is easy to perform the calculations by hand. Having tested the program for the input 30 hours, we feel no need to test it for 29 or 31 hours because we realize that exactly the same code is executed in all three cases. Likewise, we do not feel compelled to test the program for 49 and 51 hours. All the sets of test data that exercise a program in the same manner are said to belong to the same *equivalence class*, which means they are equivalent from the perspective of testing the same paths through the program. When the employee type is 1, test data for the payroll program fall into just two equivalence classes: hours between 0 and 40 and hours greater than 40.

The test data should also include cases that assess a program's behavior under *boundary conditions*—that is, on or near the boundaries between equivalence classes. It is common for programs to fail at these points. For the payroll program, this requirement means testing with hours equal to 39, 40, and 41.

We should test under *extreme conditions*—that is, with data at the limits of validity. For this we choose hours worked equal to 0 and 168 hours.

Testing with an employee type of 2 is much simpler because the number of hours does not matter, but just to be on the safe side, we test with the hours equal to 30 and 50.

Finally, we must test the data validation rules. We need to enter values that are valid and invalid, and we must test the boundary values between the two. This suggests that we test using

- Type equal to 0, 1, 2, and 3

- Hourly rate equal to 6.74, 6.75, 10, 30.50, and 30.51

- Hours worked equal to 0, 1, 30, 60, and 61

Table 6-5 summarizes our planned tests. If from this discussion you draw the conclusion that testing is a lot of work, you are correct. Many software companies spend as much money on testing as they do on analysis, design, and implementation combined. The programs in this book, however, are fairly short and simple, and testing takes only a moderate amount of time.

For a discussion of an approach that puts testing at the center of software development, see Kent Beck, Extreme Programming Explained: Embrace Change (Boston: Addison-Wesley, 2000).

TABLE 6-5
Test data for the payroll program

TYPE OF TEST	DATA USED
Code coverage	employee type: 1 hourly rate: 10 hours worked: 30 and 50
Boundary conditions	employee type: 1 hourly rate: 10 hours worked: 39, 40, and 41
Extreme conditions	employee type: 1 hourly rate: 10 hours worked: 0 and 168
Tests when the employee type is 2	employee type: 2 hourly rate: 10 hours worked: 30 and 50
Data validation rules	type: 0, 1, 2, and 3 hourly rate: 6.74, 6.75, 10, 30.50, and 30.51 hours worked: 0, 1, 30, 60, and 61

EXERCISE 6.2

1. Describe appropriate test data for the following code segments:

   a.

   ```
   if (number > 0)
       <action 1>
   else
       <action 2>
   ```

   b.

   ```
    if (0 < number && 100 > number)
       <action 1>
   else
       <action 2>
   ```

2. What happens when we provide complete code coverage of a program?

3. What is an equivalence class? Give an example.

4. What are boundary conditions? Give an example.

5. What are extreme conditions? Give an example.

6. Suppose a teacher uses grades from 0 to 100 and wants to discount all grades below 60 in her records. Discuss the equivalence classes, boundary conditions, and extreme conditions used to test a program that processes this information.

6.3 Nested if Statements

A program's logic is often complex. Logical operators (&&, ||, and !) provide one mechanism for dealing with this complexity. Nested if statements offer an alternative. Following is an everyday example of nested ifs written in Javish:

```
if (the time is after 7 PM){
    if (you have a book)
        read the book;
    else
        watch TV;
}else
    go for a walk;
```

Technology Careers

ARTIFICIAL INTELLIGENCE, ROBOTS, AND SOFTBOTS

You have seen in this chapter that a computer not only calculates results but also responds to conditions in its environment and takes the appropriate actions. This additional capability forms the basis of a branch of computer science known as artificial intelligence, or AI. AI programmers attempt to construct computational models of intelligent human behavior. These tasks involve, among many others, interacting in English or other natural languages, recognizing objects in the environment, reasoning, creating and carrying out plans of action, and pruning irrelevant information from a sea of detail.

There are many ways to construct AI models. One way is to view intelligent behavior as patterns of production rules. Each rule contains a set of conditions and a set of actions. In this model, an intelligent agent, either a computer or a human being, compares conditions in its environment to the conditions of all of its rules. Those rules with matching conditions are scheduled to fire—meaning that their actions are triggered—according to a higher-level scheme of rules. The set of rules is either hand-coded by the AI programmer or "learned" by using a special program known as a neural net.

Among other things, AI systems have been used to control *robots*. Although not quite up to the performance of Data in the TV series *Star Trek: The Next Generation*, these robots do perform mundane tasks such as assembling cars.

AI systems also are embedded in software agents known as *softbots*. For example, softbots exist to filter information from electronic mail systems, to schedule appointments, and to search the World Wide Web for information.

For a detailed discussion of robots and softbots, see Rodney Brooks, "Intelligence Without Representation," in *Mind Design II*, ed. John Haugeland (Cambridge, MA: MIT Press, 1997), and Patti Maes, "Agents That Reduce Work and Information Overload," *Communications of the ACM*, Volume 37, No. 7 (July 1994): 30–40.

Although this code is not complicated, it is a little difficult to determine exactly what it means without the aid of the truth table illustrated in Table 6-6.

TABLE 6-6
Truth table for reading a book, watching TV, or going for a walk

AFTER 7 P.M.	HAVE A BOOK	ACTION TAKEN
true	true	read book
true	false	watch TV
false	true	walk
false	false	walk

Having made the table, we are certain that we understand the code correctly. Of course, it is better to make the table first and then write code to match. As a substitute for a truth table, we can draw a flowchart as shown in Figure 6-4. Again, it is better to draw the flowchart before writing the code. Truth tables and flowcharts are useful design tools whenever we must deal with complex logic.

FIGURE 6-4
Flowchart for reading a book, watching TV, or going for a walk

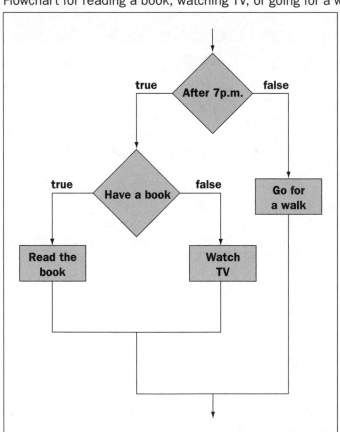

Determine a Student's Grade

Following is a second example of nested `if` statements. The code determines a student's grade based on his test average:

```java
System.out.print("Enter the test average: ");
testAverage = reader.nextInt();
if (testAverage >= 90)
   System.out.println("grade is A");
else{
   if (testAverage >= 80)
      System.out.println("grade is B");
   else{
      if (testAverage >= 70)
         System.out.println("grade is C");
      else{
         if (testAverage >= 60)
            System.out.println("grade is D");
         else{
            System.out.println("grade is F");
         }
      }
   }
}
```

Because in the absence of braces an else is associated with the immediately preceding `if`, we can drop the braces and rewrite the code as follows:

```java
System.out.print("Enter the test average: ");
testAverage = reader.nextInt();
if (testAverage >= 90)
   System.out.println("grade is A");
else
   if (testAverage >= 80)
      System.out.println("grade is B");
   else
      if (testAverage >= 70)
         System.out.println("grade is C");
      else
         if (testAverage >= 60)
            System.out.println("grade is D");
         else
            System.out.println("grade is F");
```

or after changing the indentation slightly as follows:

```java
System.out.print("Enter the test average: ");
testAverage = reader.nextInt();
if (testAverage >= 90)
   System.out.println("grade is A");
else if (testAverage >= 80)
   System.out.println("grade is B");
else if (testAverage >= 70)
```

```
    System.out.println("grade is C");
else if (testAverage >= 60)
    System.out.println("grade is D");
else
    System.out.println("grade is F");
```

This last format is very common and is used whenever a variable is compared to a sequence of threshold values. This form of the `if` statement is sometimes called an extended `if` statement or a multiway `if` statement, as compared to the two-way and one-way `if` statements we have seen earlier.

In Java, the `switch` statement provides an alternative to the extended if statement. See Appendix B for details.

EXERCISE 6.3

1. Construct a truth table that shows all the possible paths through the following nested if statement:

```
if (the time is before noon)
    if (the day is Monday)
        take the computer science quiz
    else
        go to gym class
else
    throw a Frisbee in the quad
```

2. What is the difference between a nested if statement and a multiway if statement?

6.4 Logical Errors in Nested `if` statements

It is easy to make logical errors when writing nested `if` statements. In this section we illustrate several fairly typical mistakes.

Misplaced Braces

One of the most common mistakes involves misplaced braces. Consider how repositioning a brace affects the following code:

```
// Version 1
if (the weather is wet){
    if (you have an umbrella)
        walk;
    else
        run;
}

// Version 2
if (the weather is wet){
    if (you have an umbrella)
        walk;
}else
    run;
```

To demonstrate the differences between the two versions, we construct a truth table—as shown in Table 6-7.

TABLE 6-7
Truth table for version 1 and version 2

THE WEATHER IS WET	YOU HAVE AN UMBRELLA	VERSION 1 OUTCOME	VERSION 2 OUTCOME
true	true	walk	walk
true	false	run	none
false	true	none	run
false	false	none	run

The truth table shows exactly how different the two versions are.

Removing the Braces

This example raises an interesting question. What happens if the braces are removed? In such situations, Java pairs the else with the closest preceding if. Thus

```
if (the weather is wet)
   if (you have an umbrella)
      walk;
   else
      run;
```

Remember that indentation is just a stylistic convention intended to improve the readability of code and means nothing to the computer. Consequently, reformatting the above code as follows does not change its meaning but will almost certainly mislead the unwary programmer.

```
if (the weather is wet)
   if (you have an umbrella)
      walk;
else
   run;
```

Introducing a Syntax Error

Now we consider a final variation:

```
if (the weather is wet)
   if (you have an umbrella)
      open umbrella;
      walk;
   else
      run;
```

Oops, this contains a compile-time error. Can you spot it? The second `if` is followed by more than one statement, so braces are required:

```
if (the weather is wet)
    if (you have an umbrella){
       open umbrella;
       walk;
    }else
       run;
```

Remembering that it is better to overuse than to underuse braces, we could rewrite the code as follows:

```
if (the weather is wet){
    if (you have an umbrella){
       open umbrella;
       walk;
    }else{
       run;
    }
}
```

Computation of Sales Commissions

We now attempt to compute a salesperson's commission and introduce a logical error in the process. Commissions are supposed to be computed as follows:

- 10% if sales are greater than or equal to $5000

- 20% if sales are greater than or equal to $10,000

  Following is our first attempt at writing the corresponding code:

```
if (sales >= 5000)
    commission = sales * 0.1;     // line a
else if (sales >= 10000)
    commission = sales * 0.2;     // line b
```

To determine if the code works correctly, we check it against representative values for the sales, namely, sales that are less than $5000, equal to $5000, between $5000 and $10,000, equal to $10,000, and greater than $10,000. As we can see from Table 6-8, the code is not working correctly.

TABLE 6-8
Calculation of commissions for various sales levels

VALUE OF SALES	LINES EXECUTED	VALIDITY
1,000	neither line a nor line b	correct
5,000	line a	correct
7,000	line a	correct
10,000	line a	incorrect
12,000	line a	incorrect

Corrected Computation of Sales Commissions

After a little reflection, we realize that the conditions are in the wrong order. Here is the corrected code:

```
if (sales >= 10000)
    commission = sales * 0.2;        // line b
else if (sales >= 5000)
    commission = sales * 0.1;        // line a
```

Table 6-9 confirms that the code now works correctly.

TABLE 6-9
Corrected calculation of commissions for various sales levels

VALUE OF SALES	LINES EXECUTED	VALIDITY
1,000	neither line a nor line b	correct
5,000	line a	correct
7,000	line a	correct
10,000	line b	correct
12,000	line b	correct

Avoiding Nested `if` statements

Sometimes getting rid of nested `if`s is the best way to avoid logical errors. This is easily done by rewriting nested `if`s as a sequence of independent `if` statements. For example, consider the following code for computing sales commissions:

```
if (5000 <= sales && sales < 10000)
    commission = sales * 0.1;
if (10000 <= sales)
    commission = sales * 0.2;
```

And here is another example involving the calculation of student grades:

```
if (90 <= average                  ) grade is A;
if (80 <= average && average < 90) grade is B;
if (70 <= average && average < 80) grade is C;
if (60 <= average && average < 70) grade is D;
if (               average < 60) grade is F;
```

The first question people usually ask when confronted with these alternatives is, "Which is faster?", by which they mean, "Which will execute most rapidly?" In nearly all situations the difference in speed is negligible, so a much better question is, "Which is easier to write and maintain correctly?" There is no hard-and-fast answer to this question, but you should always consider it when writing complex code.

EXERCISE 6.4

1. A tax table provides rates for computing tax based on incomes up to and including a given amount. For example, income above $20,000 up to and including $50,000 is taxed at 18%. Find the logic errors in the following code that determines the tax rate for a given income:

```
if (income > 10000)
    rate = 0.10;
else if (income > 20000)
    rate = 0.18;
else if (income > 50000)
    rate = 0.40;
else
    rate = 0.0;
```

2. Write a correct code segment for the problem in Question 1.

6.5 Nested Loops

There are many programming situations in which a loop is placed within another loop—this is called a *nested loop*. The first case study in this chapter provided an example of this. We now consider another. In Chapter 4, we showed how to determine if a number is prime. The code involved a for loop, and by nesting this for loop inside another, we can compute all the primes between two limits. The outside loop feeds a sequence of numbers to the inside loop. Following is the code:

```
System.out.print("Enter the lower limit: ");
lower = reader.nextInt();
System.out.print("Enter the upper limit: ");
upper = reader.nextInt();
for (n = lower; n <= upper; n++){
   innerLimit = (int)Math.sqrt (n);
   for (d = 2; d <= innerLimit; d++){
      if (n % d == 0)
         break;
   }
   if (d > innerLimit)
      System.out.println (n + " is prime");
}
```

Following is the output when the user enters 55 and 75:

```
59 is prime
61 is prime
67 is prime
71 is prime
73 is prime
```

If the user wants to enter repeated pairs of limits, we enclose the code in yet another loop:

```
System.out.print("Enter the lower limit or -1 to quit: ");
lower = reader.nextInt();
```

```
while (lower != -1){
   System.out.print("Enter the upper limit: ");
   upper = reader.nextInt();
   for (n = lower; n <= upper; n++){
      innerLimit = (int)Math.sqrt (n);
      for (d = 2; d <= innerLimit; d++){
         if (n % d == 0)
            break;
      }
      if (d > innerLimit)
         System.out.println (n + " is prime");
   }
   System.out.print("Enter the lower limit or -1 to quit: ");
   lower = reader.nextInt();
}
```

 Note of Interest

RELIABILITY OF COMPUTER SYSTEMS

The next time you step onto an airliner or lie down beneath an x-ray machine, you might ask yourself about the quality of the software system that helps to run them. There are several measures of software quality, such as readability, maintainability, correctness, and robustness. But perhaps the most important measure is *reliability*. Reliability should not be confused with correctness. Software is correct if its design and implementation are consistent with its specifications. That means that the software actually does what it is supposed to do, as described in what we have called analysis. However, software can be correct in this sense yet still be unreliable.

During the analysis phase of software development, we construct a model of what the user wants the software to do, and from this model we build a model of what the software will do. Our design and implementation may reflect this second model correctly, but the software may still be unreliable. It is unreliable if we have built the wrong models during analysis—that is, if we have misunderstood the user's request (have the wrong model of the user) or we have built a model of the software that does not do what we correctly have understood the user to require.

For example, several decades ago, the Navy contracted with a software firm to build a software system to detect the movements of missiles. The software worked just fine in detecting missiles but was thrown off by the presence of the moon in certain cases.

There have been many reports of software unreliability in commercial software installations as well. One of the more tragic cases is that of the x-ray machine Therac-25, which killed several patients a few years ago.

A classic discussion of software reliability in military applications can be found in Alan Borning, "Computer System Reliability and Nuclear War," *Communications of the ACM*, Volume 30, Number 2 (February 1987):112–131. Almost every textbook on computer ethics has case studies on computer reliability in commercial applications. A good place to start is Sara Baase, *A Gift of Fire, Second Edition* (Upper Saddle River, NJ: Prentice Hall, 2002), Chapter 4.

EXERCISE 6.5

1. Write the outputs of the following code segments:

a.

```
for (int i = 1; i <= 3; i++)
   for (int j = 1; j <= 3; j++)
      System.out.print(j + " ");
```

b.

```
for (int i = 1; i <= 3; i++){
   for (int j = 1; j <= 3; j++)
      System.out.print(j + " ");
   System.out.println("");
}
```

2. Write code segments that solve the following problems:

a. Output the numbers 1 to 25 in consecutive order, using five rows of five numbers each.

b. Output five rows of five numbers. Each number is the sum of its row position and column position. The position of the first number is (1, 1).

6.6 *Testing Loops*

The presence of looping statements in a program increases the challenge of designing good test data. Frequently, loops do not iterate some fixed number of times, but instead iterate zero, one, or more than one time depending on a program's inputs. When designing test data, we want to cover all three possibilities. To illustrate, we develop test data for the print divisors program presented in Chapter 4. First, let's look at the code again:

```
// Display the proper divisors of a number
System.out.print("Enter a positive integer: ");
int n = reader.nextInt();
int limit = n / 2;
for (int d = 2; d <= limit; d++){
   if (n % d == 0)
      System.out.print (d + " ");
}
```

By analyzing the code, we conclude that if n equals 0, 1, 2, or 3, the limit is less than 2, and the loop is never entered. If n equals 4 or 5, the loop is entered once. If n is greater than 5, the loop is entered multiple times. All this suggests the test data shown in Table 6-10. After testing the program with this data, we feel reasonably confident that it works correctly.

TABLE 6-10
Test data for the count divisors program

TYPE OF TEST	DATA USED
No iterations	0, 1, 2, and 3
One iteration	4 and 5
Multiple iterations for a number with divisors	24
Multiple iterations for a number without divisors	29

Combinatorial Explosion

The surprisingly large amount of testing needed to validate even a small program suggests an interesting question. Suppose a program is composed of three parts and that it takes five tests to verify each part independently. Then how many tests does it take to verify the program as a whole? In the unlikely event that the three parts are independent of each other and utilize the same five sets of test data, then five tests suffice. However, it is far more likely that the behavior of each part affects the other two and also that the parts have differing test requirements. Then all possible combinations of tests should be tried, that is 5*5*5 or 125. We call this multiplicative growth in test cases a combinatorial explosion, and it pretty much guarantees the impossibility of exhaustively testing large complex programs; however, programmers still must do their best to test their programs intelligently and well.

Robust Programs

So far, we have focused on showing that a program that uses loops produces correct results when provided with valid inputs, but, surprisingly, that is not good enough. As we learned when we were testing programs with if statements earlier in this chapter, we also should consider how a program behaves when confronted with invalid data. After all, users frequently make mistakes or do not fully understand a program's data entry requirements. As we have learned, a program that tolerates errors in user inputs and recovers gracefully is robust. The best and easiest way to write robust programs is to check user inputs immediately on entry and reject those that are invalid. We illustrate this technique in the next case study. At this stage, there are limits to how thoroughly we can check inputs, so in the case study, we merely make sure that inputs fall in the range specified by the prompt.

EXERCISE 6.6

1. Describe appropriate test data for the following code segments:

   a.
```
while (number > 0)
   <action>
```

   b.
```
while (0 < number && 100 > number)
   <action>
```

EXERCISE 6.6 Continued

2. Design test data for Project 4-6 (in Chapter 4).

3. What would be reasonable test data for a loop that does not execute a fixed number of times?

4. What is a robust program? Give an example.

Case Study 2: Fibonacci Numbers

There is a famous sequence of numbers that occurs frequently in nature. In 1202, the Italian mathematician Leonardo Fibonacci presented the following problem concerning the breeding of rabbits. He assumed somewhat unrealistically that

1. Each pair of rabbits in a population produces a new pair of rabbits each month.

2. Rabbits become fertile one month after birth.

3. Rabbits do not die.

He then considered how rapidly the rabbit population would grow on a monthly basis when starting with a single pair of newborn rabbits.

To answer the question, we proceed one month at a time:

■ At the beginning of month 1, there is one pair of rabbits (total = 1 pair).

■ At the beginning of month 2, our initial pair of rabbits, A, will have just reached sexual maturity, so there will be no offspring (total = 1 pair).

■ At the beginning of month 3, pair A will have given birth to pair B (total = 2 pair).

■ At the beginning of month 4, pair A will have given birth to pair C and pair B will be sexually mature (total = 3 pair).

■ At the beginning of month 5, pairs A and B will have given birth to pairs D and E, while pair C will have reached sexual maturity (total = 5 pair).

■ And so on.

If we continue in this way, we obtain the following sequence of numbers
1 1 2 3 5 8 13 21 34 55 89 144 233 …

called the *Fibonacci numbers*. Notice that each number, after the first two, is the sum of its two predecessors. Referring back to the rabbits, see if you can demonstrate why this should be the case. Although the sequence of numbers is easy to construct, there is no known formula for calculating the nth Fibonacci number, which gives rise to the following program request.

Request

Write a program that can compute the nth Fibonacci number on demand, where n is a positive integer.

Analysis, Design, and Implementation

The user input should be a positive integer or -1 to quit. Other integer inputs are rejected. The proposed user interface is shown in Figure 6-5.

FIGURE 6-5
Interface for the Fibonacci program

```
Enter a positive integer or -1 to quit: 8
Fibonacci of 8 is 21
```

Here is the code:

```java
// Case Study 6.2: Display the nth Fibonacci number

import java.util.Scanner;

public class Fibonacci {

    public static void main (String [] args) {
        Scanner reader = new Scanner(System.in);
        int n;            // The number entered by the user
        int fib;          // The nth Fibonacci number
        int a,b,count;    // Variables that facilitate the computation

        while (true){

            // Ask the user for the next input
            System.out.print("Enter a positive integer or -1 to quit: ");
            n = reader.nextInt();
            if (n == -1) break;
            else if (n >= 1){

                // Calculate the nth Fibonacci number
                fib = 1;                // Takes care of case n = 1 or 2
                a = 1;
                b = 1;
                count = 3;
                while (count <= n){  // Takes care of case n >= 3
                    fib = a + b;      // Point p. Referred to later.
                    a = b;
                    b = fib;
                    count = count + 1;
                }

                // Print the nth Fibonacci number
                System.out.println ("Fibonacci of " + n + " is " + fib);
            } // end else
        }     // end while
    }         // end main
}
```

Loop Analysis

The loop in the Fibonacci program is not obvious at first glance, so to clarify what is happening, we construct Table 6-11. This table traces the changes to key variables on each pass through the loop.

TABLE 6-11
Changes to Key Variables on Each Pass Through the Loop

COUNT AT POINT P	A AT POINT P	B AT POINT P	FIBONACCI NUMBER AT POINT P
3	1	1	2
4	1	2	3
5	2	3	5
6	3	5	8
...	...	...	...
n	$(n-2)$th Fibonacci number	$(n-1)$th Fibonacci number	nth Fibonacci number

Test Data

We complete the case study by developing suitable test data:

- To make sure the program is robust, we try the following sequence of inputs for n: -3, 0, 1, 2, –1.

- To make sure the computation is correct when the second inner loop is not entered, we try n equal to 1 and 2.

- To make sure the computation is correct when the second inner loop is entered one or more times, we let n equal 3 and 6.

Because all these tests were successful, we can hardly be blamed for thinking that our program works perfectly; however, it contains a completely unexpected problem. When n equals 80, the program returns the value –285,007,387. The problem is due to **arithmetic overflow**. In Java and most programming languages, integers have a limited range (see Chapter 3) and exceeding that range leads to strange results. Adding one to the most positive integer in the range yields the most negative integer, whereas subtracting one from the most negative yields the most positive. Welcome to the strange world of computer arithmetic, where bizarre behavior is always lurking to trip the unwary. To detect the problem automatically, we could include extra lines of code that test for an unexpected switch to a negative value. A somewhat similar problem cost the French space program half a billion dollars and a great deal of embarrassment when a computer guided rocket and its payload exploded shortly after takeoff.

6.7 Loop Verification

Loop verification is the process of guaranteeing that a loop performs its intended task, independently of testing. Some work has been done on constructing formal proofs to determine if loops are "correct." We now examine a modified version of loop verification; a complete treatment of the issue will be the topic of subsequent course work.

The `assert` Statement

Java includes an `assert` statement that allows the programmer to evaluate a Boolean expression and halt the program with an error message if the expression's value is false. If its value is true, the program continues execution. Here are some examples of `assert` statements:

```
assert x != 0;              // Halt if x is 0
assert x >= 0 && x <= MAX;  // Halt if x is not in this range
assert x % 2 == 0;          // Halt if x is not even
```

The general form is `assert <Boolean expression>`. Note that parentheses are omitted. At run time, if the Boolean expression evaluates to false, the JVM will halt with an error message. To enable this mechanism when running the program, use the command line

```
java -enableassertions AJavaProgram
```

Figure 6-6 shows the output of the following short program that includes an `assert` statement:

```java
// Example 6.1: Assert that x != 0

public class TestAssert{

    public static void main(String[] args){
        int x = 0;
        assert x != 0;
    }
}
```

FIGURE 6-6
The failure of an `assert` statement

Running a program with `assert` enabled will slow it down, but we do this only during development and testing.

Assertions with Loops

Input assertions state what can be expected to be true before a loop is entered. *Output assertions* state what can be expected to be true when the loop is exited.

To illustrate input and output assertions, we consider the mathematical problem of summing the proper divisors of a positive integer. For example, suppose we have the integers shown in Table 6-12.

TABLE 6-12
The sums of the proper divisors of some integers

INTEGER	PROPER DIVISORS	SUM
6	1, 2, 3	6
9	1, 3	4
12	1, 2, 3, 4, 6	16

The following loop performs this task:

```
divisorSum = 0;
for (trialDivisor = 1; trialDivisor <= num / 2; ++trialDivisor)
   if (num % trialDivisor == 0)
      divisorSum = divisorSum + trialDivisor;
```

Input assertions for this loop are

> 1. num is a positive integer.
> 2. divisorSum == 0.

An output assertion is

```
divisorSum is the sum of all proper divisors of num.
```

When these are placed with the previous code, we have

```
divisorSum = 0;
assert num > 0 && divisorSum == 0;
for (trialDivisor = 1; trialDivisor <= num / 2; ++trialDivisor)
   if (num % trialDivisor == 0)
      divisorSum = divisorSum + trialDivisor;
// Output assertion: divisorSum is the sum of all proper divisors of num.
```

Note that we pass the Boolean expression to the `assert` mechanism of Java so that the JVM actually establishes the truth of that assertion. However, we cannot do this with the output assertion because the sum of all the proper divisors of a number is just what we are computing in the loop!

Invariant and Variant Assertions

A *loop invariant* is an assertion that expresses a relationship between variables that remains constant throughout all iterations of the loop. In other words, it is a statement that is true both before the loop is entered and after each pass through the loop. An invariant assertion for the preceding code segment could be

```
divisorSum is the sum of proper divisors of num that are less than or equal
   to trialDivisor.
```

A *loop variant* is an assertion whose truth changes between the first and final execution of the loop. The loop variant expression should be stated in such a way that it guarantees the loop is exited. Thus, it contains some statement about the loop variable being incremented (or decremented) during execution of the loop. In the preceding code, we could have

```
trialDivisor is incremented by 1 each time through the loop.
It eventually exceeds the value num / 2, at which point the loop is exited.
```

Variant and invariant assertions usually occur in pairs.

We now use four kinds of assertions—input, output, variant, and invariant—to produce the formally verified loop that follows:

```
divisorSum = 0;

// 1. num is a positive integer.                       (input assertion)
// 2. divisorSum == 0.

assert num > 0 && divisorsum == 0;

for (trialDivisor = 1; trialDivisor <= num / 2; ++trialDivisor)

// trialDivisor is incremented by 1 each time          (variant assertion)
// through the loop. It eventually exceeds the
// value (num / 2), at which point the loop is exited.

    if (num % trialDivisor == 0)
        divisorsum = divisorSum + trialDivisor;

// divisorSum is the sum of proper divisors of          (invariant assertion)
// num that are less than or equal to trialDivisor.

// divisorSum is the sum of                             (output assertion)
// all proper divisors of num.
```

In general, code that is presented in this text does not include formal verification of the loops. This issue is similar to that of robustness. In an introductory course, a decision must be made on the trade-off between learning new concepts and writing robust programs with formal verification of loops. We encourage the practice, but space and time considerations make it inconvenient to include such documentation at this level. We close this discussion with another example illustrating loop verification.

Consider the problem of finding the greatest common divisor (gcd) of two positive integers. Table 6-13 shows some sample inputs and outputs for this problem.

TABLE 6-13
Several examples of the greatest common divisor (GCD) of two numbers

NUM1	NUM2	GCD(NUM 1, NUM2)
8	12	4
20	10	10
15	32	1
70	40	10

A segment of code to produce the gcd of two positive integers after they have been ordered as small, large is

```
int trialGcd = small;
boolean gcdFound = false;
while (! gcdFound)
   if ((large % trialGcd == 0) && (small % trialGcd == 0)){
      gcd = trialGcd;
      gcdFound = true;
   }
   else
      trialGcd = trialGcd - 1;
```

Using assertions as previously indicated, this code would appear as

```
int trialGcd = small;
boolean gcdFound = false;

//      1. small <= large
//      2. trialGcd (small) is the first candidate for gcd
//      3. gcdFound is false

assert small <= large && small == trialGcd && ! gcdFound;

while (! gcdFound)

// trialGcd assumes integer values ranging from small
// to 1. It is decremented by 1 each time through the
// loop. When trialGcd divides both small and large,
// the loop is exited. Exit is guaranteed since 1
// divides both small and large.
```

```
    if ((large % trialGcd == 0) && (small % trialGcd == 0)){

// When trialGcd divides both large and small,
// then gcd is assigned that value.

        assert large % trialGcd == 0 && small % trialGcd == 0;

        gcd = trialGcd;
        gcdFound = true;
    }
    else
        trialGcd = trialGcd - 1;

// Output assertion: gcd is the greatest common divisor of small and large.
```

EXERCISE 6.7

1. Write appropriate input assertions and output assertions for each of the following loops.

a.
```
score = reader.nextInt();
while (score != -999){
    numScores = numScores + 1;
    sum = sum + score;
    System.out.print("Enter a score; -999 to quit: ");
    score = reader.nextInt();
}
```
b.
```
count = 0;
power2 = 1;
while (power2 < 100){
    System.out.println(power2);
    power2 = power2 * 2;
    count = count + 1;
}
```

2. Write appropriate loop invariant and loop variant assertions for each of the loops in Question 1 above.

EXERCISE 6.7 Continued

3. Consider the following loop. The user enters a number, guess, and the computer then displays a message indicating whether the guess is correct, too high, or too low. Add appropriate input assertions, output assertions, loop invariant assertions, and loop variant assertions to the following code.

```java
correct = false;
count = 0;
while ((count < MAX_TRIES) && (! correct)){
    count = count + 1;
    System.out.print("Enter choice number " + count + ": ");
    guess = reader.nextInt();
    if (guess == choice)
    {
        correct = true;
        System.out.println("Congratulations!");
    }
    else if (guess < choice)
        System.out.println("Your guess is too low");
    else
        System.out.println("Your guess is too high");
}
```

6.8 Graphics and GUIs: Timers and Animations

The shapes, text, and images that we have displayed in graphics applications thus far have been more or less passive objects. The user can move them around a window with a mouse, but none of them know how to move on their own. Now it is time to make these graphics objects active. In this section, we explore the use of timers to construct simple animations.

The Basic Principles of Animation

As described in Chapter 1, our perception of movement in a motion picture is based on a rapid display of successive frames. In each frame, an object is shown at a different position, but if we are shown 24 frames per second, these changes of position appear as the continuous motion of the object itself.

> **Extra Challenge**
>
> This Graphics and GUIs section gives you the opportunity to explore concepts and programming techniques required to develop modern graphics applications and graphical user interfaces. This material is not required in order to proceed with the other chapters of the book.

We already know how to change the position of a graphical object and repaint a panel, so the basic tools for displaying the same object in multiple frames are already available. The speed with which an object appears to change its position depends on the distance it travels between frames and on the number of frames displayed per unit of time. Faster objects can travel a greater distance between frames than slower ones. The realistic depiction of motion also involves many other factors, such as rates of acceleration, the resistance of friction, and some qualities of the objects themselves, such as the "bounciness" of a ball. In addition, computer video artists must worry about such phenomena as the "flicker" caused by the speed of the display medium when painting large, complex images that must appear to move rapidly. In the examples that follow, we ignore most of these details and focus on the simple display of constant motion in two dimensions.

Direction and Velocity of Moving Objects

A moving object has a velocity, which is the distance (in pixels) traveled in a given unit of time, and a direction. An object's direction can be fixed as the angle of its path relative to a base direction. Let's assume that the base direction is due east (to the right of the panel), at 0 degrees. Moving clockwise, south (to the bottom) is 90 degrees, west (to the left) is 180 degrees, north (to the top) is 270 degrees, and 360 degrees returns the direction to due east, as shown in Figure 6-7.

FIGURE 6-7
Representing directions in two dimensions

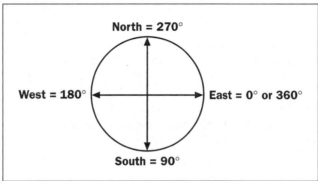

At any given time, we should be able to change a graphical object's velocity and direction. Using good object-oriented style, we ask a graphical object, where possible, to track its own velocity and direction. For example, we can add some instance variables and methods to the circle class of Chapter 5 to give it this functionality. Circles have an initial velocity of 0 and an initial direction of 0 degrees (due east). Table 6-14 lists these new methods.

TABLE 6-14
New methods for the circle class

NEW CIRCLE METHOD	WHAT IT DOES
void move()	Changes the position of the circle using its current velocity and direction.
void setDirection(int degrees)	Sets the direction of the circle to the given direction in degrees (the default is 0 degrees for due east).
void setVelocity(int v)	Sets the velocity of the circle to the given velocity (the default is 0 pixels).
void turn(int degrees)	Adds the given amount of degrees to the circle's current direction. If degrees is positive, the direction rotates clockwise. If degrees is negative, the direction rotates counterclockwise.

The critical new method for movable objects is `move()`. This method moves an object a given distance in a given direction. To implement this method, we must calculate the distances to move in the x and y directions based on the object's current position, its velocity, and its direction. According to basic trigonometry, the x distance is equal to the velocity multiplied by the cosine of the direction angle in radians. The y distance is equal to the velocity multiplied by the sine of the direction angle in radians. We use the methods `Math.radians`, `Math.cos`, and `Math.sin` to compute these values and then cast the results to integers. Here is the code for the new methods:

```java
public void setVelocity(int v){
    velocity = v;
}

public void setDirection(int degrees){
    direction = degrees % 360;
}

public void turn(int degrees){
    direction = (direction + degrees) % 360;
}

public void move(){
    move((int)(velocity * Math.cos(Math.toRadians(direction))),
        (int)(velocity * Math.sin(Math.toRadians(direction))));
}
```

Note that the methods `setDirection` and `turn` use the `%` operator to wrap the direction around if it's greater than 360 degrees (for example, `365 % 360` is the same direction as `5`).

Moving a Circle with the Mouse

Our next example program illustrates the use of our new Circle methods. The program displays a filled circle at the center of the panel. When the user presses the mouse, the circle moves 50 pixels in its current direction and then turns 45 degrees. Repeated mouse presses (or "clicks") cause the circle to move in a circular pattern and return to its original position. Here is the code for the panel class:

```java
// Example 6.2: Moves the circle 50 pixels and
// turns it 45 degrees in response to a mouse press

import javax.swing.*;
import java.awt.*;
import java.awt.event.*;

public class ColorPanel extends JPanel{

    private Circle circle;
```

```java
public ColorPanel(Color backColor, int width, int height){
   setBackground(backColor);
   setPreferredSize(new Dimension(width, height));
   // Circle centered in the panel with radius 25
   circle = new Circle(width / 2, height / 2, 25, Color.red);
   circle.setFilled(true);
   // Move 50 pixels per mouse press
   circle.setVelocity(50);
   addMouseListener(new MoveListener());
}

public void paintComponent(Graphics g){
   super.paintComponent(g);
   circle.draw(g);
}

private class MoveListener extends MouseAdapter{

   public void mousePressed(MouseEvent e){
      circle.move();
      circle.turn(45);    // Turn 45 degrees
      repaint();
   }
}
}
```

Timers

A basic algorithm for animating a graphical object can be expressed as follows:

```
Set the initial position of the shape
At regular intervals
   Move the object
   Repaint the panel
```

The first step of the algorithm is accomplished when the panel is instantiated. When the window is displayed, the object is painted in its initial position. The last two steps are accomplished by sending the standard messages to move the object and repaint the panel. But how can this be done automatically at regular intervals? A simple loop will not work. Because execution speeds vary from computer to computer, a simple loop might move the same object faster on one computer than on another.

Java provides a special type of object called a timer to schedule events at regular intervals. When a timer is instantiated, it is given an interval in milliseconds and a listener object similar to those discussed in Chapter 5. When the timer is sent the start message, its clock starts ticking. When each interval of time passes, the listener's actionPerformed method is triggered. In the case of our animation, this method runs the operations to move the object and repaint the panel. Because the timer uses the computer's clock to measure the intervals, they will not vary with the execution speed of the computer.

The timer for animations is an instance of the class `Timer`, which is included in the package `javax.swing`. Assuming that we have the listener class `MoveListener` at our disposal, we can declare, instantiate, and start a timer as follows:

```
javax.swing.Timer projectortimer;
timer  = new javax.swing.Timer(5, new MoveListener());
timer.start();
```

Note that we prefix the `Timer` class with its package name, so as to distinguish this `Timer` from a different class with the same name in the package `java.util`. This practice will allow us eventually to use resources from `java.util` without name conflicts. Our timer is started with an interval of 5 milliseconds. The timer ticks for 5 milliseconds and then fires an event. The `MoveListener` detects this event and runs its `actionPerformed` method. The timer automatically repeats this process until it is stopped or the program quits.

The definition of the class `MoveListener`, like the listener classes for mouse events in Chapter 5, is nested in the panel class. This placement allows the listener's `actionPerformed` method to access the data within the panel. Unlike the earlier listener classes, however, `MoveListener` does not extend an adapter class, but instead implements the `ActionListener` interface. For now, we won't worry about this difference, but just assume that our class includes an `actionPerformed` method. Here is a template for this class:

```
private class MoveListener implements ActionListener{

    public void actionPerformed(ActionEvent e){
       // Code for moving objects goes here
       repaint();
    }
}
```

Like the code for other listener classes, this code requires you to import the package `javax.awt.event`.

Moving a Circle with a Timer

Our next example program automates the movement of the circle in the previous program by using a timer. The `ColorPanel` class still has the same basic structure, but the `MoveListener` class now implements the `ActionListener` interface and packages the code to move the circle in an `actionPerformed` method. After the circle is instantiated, we create a timer with an interval of 125 milliseconds (1/8 of a second). The timer is also passed a new `MoveListener` and then started up. The rest, as they say, is automatic. Here is the code for the modified `ColorPanel` class:

```
// Example 6.3: Moves the circle 50 pixels and
// turns it 45 degrees in response to timer events

import javax.swing.*;
import java.awt.*;
import java.awt.event.*;

public class ColorPanel extends JPanel{
```

```java
   private Circle circle;
   private javax.swing.Timer timer;

   public ColorPanel(Color backColor, int width, int height){
      setBackground(backColor);
      setPreferredSize(new Dimension(width, height));
      // Circle centered in the panel with radius 25
      circle = new Circle(width / 2, height / 2, 25, Color.red);
      circle.setFilled(true);:
      // Move 50 pixels per timer event
      circle.setVelocity(50);
      // Fire timer events every 1/8 second
      timer = new javax.swing.Timer(125, new MoveListener());
      timer.start();
   }

   public void paintComponent(Graphics g){
      super.paintComponent(g);
      circle.draw(g);
   }

   private class MoveListener implements ActionListener{

      public void actionPerformed(ActionEvent e){
         circle.move();
         circle.turn(45);    // Turn 45 degrees
         repaint();
      }
   }
}
```

A Final Example: A Bouncing Circle

Let's incorporate the ideas examined thus far into a program that bounces a circle back and forth horizontally in its panel. At program startup, the circle's left side is flush with the left border of the panel. It moves continuously to the right, until its right side is flush with the panel's right border. At that point, the circle reverses direction and returns to the left border, where it reverses direction again, and so on, indefinitely.

Clearly, the action to move the circle must check to see if the circle has hit a panel boundary and then change the circle's direction if necessary. The circle's default direction is due east (0 degrees). Because the circle is already near the left boundary of the panel at startup, we set its initial direction to due west (180 degrees) so that it hits the left boundary first. Here is the code for the ColorPanel class:

```java
// Example 6.4: A filled circle moves back and forth
// across the panel, appearing to bounce off its edges

import javax.swing.*;
import java.awt.*;
import java.awt.event.*;

public class ColorPanel extends JPanel{
```

```java
private Circle circle;
private javax.swing.Timer timer;

public ColorPanel(Color backColor, int width, int height){
   setBackground(backColor);
   setPreferredSize(new Dimension(width, height));
   // Circle with center point (25, height / 2) and radius 25
   circle = new Circle(25, height / 2, 25, Color.red);
   circle.setFilled(true);:
   // Aim due west to hit left boundary first
   circle.setDirection(180);
   // Move 5 pixels per unit of time
   circle.setVelocity(5);
   // Move every 5 milliseconds
   timer = new javax.swing.Timer(5, new MoveListener());
   timer.start();
}

public void paintComponent(Graphics g){
   super.paintComponent(g);
   circle.draw(g);
}

private class MoveListener implements ActionListener{

   public void actionPerformed(ActionEvent e){
      int x = circle.getX();
      int radius = circle.getRadius();
      int width = getWidth();
      // Check for boundaries and reverse direction
      // if necessary
      if (x - radius <= 0 || x + radius >= width)
         circle.turn(180);
      circle.move();
      repaint();
   }
}
}
```

Other Timer Methods

Once it is started, a timer fires events until it is stopped or the program quits. The Timer class includes methods for stopping a timer, restarting it, changing its time interval, and so forth. Some of the more commonly used methods are listed in Table 6-15.

TABLE 6-15
Some commonly used timer methods

TIMER METHOD	WHAT IT DOES
`boolean isRunning()`	Returns true if the timer is firing events or false otherwise
`void restart()`	Restarts a timer, causing it to fire the first event after its initial delay
`void setDelay(int delay)`	Sets the timer's delay to the number of milliseconds between events
`void setInitialDelay(int delay)`	Sets the timer's initial delay, which by default is its between-event delay
`void stop()`	Stops the timer, causing it to cease firing events

*E*XERCISE 6.8

1. Describe how to set up a timer and explain what it does.

2. Describe the factors that affect our perception of the movement of a graphical object.

3. What causes flicker? How can flicker be eliminated?

4. How do the direction and velocity of an object determine where it will be placed after a given unit of time?

Design, Testing, and Debugging Hints

■ Most errors involving selection statements and loops are not syntax errors caught at compile time. Thus, you will detect these errors only after running the program, and perhaps then only with extensive testing.

■ The presence or absence of braces can seriously affect the logic of a selection statement or loop. For example, the following selection statements have a similar look but a very different logic:

```
if (x > 0){
   y = x;
   z = 1 / x;
}
```

```
if (x > 0)
    y = x;
    z = 1 / x;
```

- The first selection statement above guards against division by 0; the second statement only guards against assigning x to y. The following pair of code segments shows a similar problem with a loop:

```
while (x > 0){
    y = x;
    x = x - 1;
}
```

```
while (x > 0)
    y = x;
    x = x - 1;
```

- The first loop above terminates because the value of x decreases within the body of the loop; the second loop is infinite because the value of x decreases below the body of the loop.

- When testing programs that use `if` or `if-else` statements, be sure to use test data that force the program to exercise all of the logical branches.

- When testing a program that uses `if` statements, it helps to formulate equivalence classes, boundary conditions, and extreme conditions.

- Use an `if-else` statement rather than two `if` statements when the alternative courses of action are mutually exclusive.

- When testing a loop, be sure to use limit values as well as typical values. For example, if a loop should terminate when the control variable equals 0, run it with the values 0, –1, and 1.

- Be sure to check entry conditions and exit conditions for each loop.

- For a loop with errors, use debugging output statements to verify the values of the control variable on each pass through the loop. Check this value before the loop is initially entered, after each update, and after the loop is exited.

SUMMARY

In this chapter, you learned:

- A complex Boolean expression contains one or more Boolean expressions and the logical operators && (AND), || (OR), and ! (NOT).

- A truth table can determine the value of any complex Boolean expression.

- Java uses short-circuit evaluation of complex Boolean expressions. The evaluation of the operands of || stops at the first true value, whereas the evaluation of the operands of && stops at the first false value.

- Nested `if` statements are another way of expressing complex conditions. A nested `if` statement can be translated to an equivalent `if` statement that uses logical operators.

- An extended or multiway `if` statement expresses a choice among several mutually exclusive alternatives.

- Loops can be nested in other loops.

- Equivalence classes, boundary conditions, and extreme conditions are important features used in tests of control structures involving complex conditions.

- Loops can be verified to be correct by using assertions, loop variants, and loop invariants.

VOCABULARY*Review*

Define the following terms:

Arithmetic overflow	Extreme condition	Nested loop
Boundary condition	Input assertion	Output assertion
Combinatorial explosion	Logical operator	Quality assurance
Complete code coverage	Loop invariant	Robust
Equivalence class	Loop variant	Truth table
Extended if statement	Nested if statement	

REVIEW*Questions*

WRITTEN QUESTIONS

Write a brief answer to each of the following questions.

1. List the three logical operators.

2. Construct a truth table for the expression P OR NOT Q.

3. Suppose P is true and Q is false. What is the value of the expression P AND NOT Q?

4. Write an `if` statement that displays whether or not a given number is between a lower bound `min` and an upper bound `max`, inclusive. Use a logical operator in the condition.

5. Rewrite the `if` statement in Question 4 to use a nested `if` statement.

6. Write a nested loop that displays a 10-by-10 square of asterisks.

7. Give an example of an assertion and show how it can be checked with Java's assert statement.

8. Explain the role that variant and invariant assertions play in showing that a loop is correct.

PROJECTS

In keeping with the spirit of this chapter, each program should be robust and should validate the input data. You should try also to formulate the appropriate equivalence classes, boundary conditions, and extreme conditions and use them in testing the programs.

PROJECT 6-1

In a game of guessing numbers, one person says, "I'm thinking of a number between 1 and 100." The other person guesses "50." The first person replies, "No, the number is less." The second person then guesses "25," and so on, until she guesses correctly. Write a program that plays this game. The computer knows the number (a random number between 1 and 100) and the user is the guesser. At the end of the game, the computer displays the number of guesses required by the user to guess the number correctly.

PROJECT 6-2

Rewrite the program of Project 6-1 so that the user knows the number and the computer must guess it.

PROJECT 6-3

Write a program that expects a numeric grade as input and outputs the corresponding letter grade. The program uses the following grading scale:

NUMERIC RANGE	LETTER GRADE
96–100	A+
92–95	A
90–91	A–
86–89	B+
82–85	B
80–81	B–
76–79	C+
72–75	C
70–71	C–
66–69	D+
62–65	D
60–61	D–
0–59	F

PROJECT 6-4

Write a Java method getLetterGrade that is based on the grading scale of Project 6-3. This method expects the numeric grade as a parameter and returns a string representing the letter grade. The method header should have the prefix static so it can be called from main. Use this method in a program that inputs a list of grades (ending with –1) and outputs the class average, the class minimum, and the class maximum as letter grades.

PROJECT 6-5

The Euclidean algorithm can be used to find the greatest common divisor (gcd) of two positive integers (n1, n2). You can use this algorithm in the following manner:
A. Compute the remainder of dividing the larger number by the smaller number.
B. Replace the larger number with the smaller number and the smaller number with the remainder.
C. Repeat this process until the smaller number is zero:

The larger number at this point is the gcd of n1 and n2.

Write a program that lets the user enter two integers and then prints each step in the process of using the Euclidean algorithm to find their gcd.

PROJECT 6-6

Review the case study in Chapter 4 in which the Lucky Sevens gambling game program was created. Remove the code that deals with the maximum amount held. Then modify the program so that it runs the simulation 100 times and prints the average number of rolls. (Hint: Put the while loop inside a for statement that loops 100 times. Accumulate the total count and at the end divide by 100.)

PROJECT 6-7

Write a program to print the perimeter and area of rectangles using all combinations of heights and widths running from 1 foot to 10 feet in increments of 1 foot. Print the output in headed, formatted columns.

PROJECT 6-8

Modify the example program of Section 6.8 so that the circle stops moving when the user clicks the mouse. When the user clicks the mouse again, the circle should resume moving. (*Hint:* Define a mouse listener class as shown in Chapter 5.)

PROJECT 6-9

Add another circle to the program of Project 6-8. The second circle should be placed at the right margin of the panel at program startup, exactly opposite the first circle. Both circles should reverse direction when they hit a boundary.

PROJECT 6-10

Use your knowledge of physics to make an interesting change to the program of Project 6-9. Set the initial directions of the two circles to angles other than horizontal (say, 120 degrees for one and 30 degrees for the other). When a circle hits a boundary, it should rebound at the appropriate angle. (Hint: The angle of reflection should equal the angle of incidence.)

CRITICAL *Thinking*

Read the sections of the ACM Code of Ethics that deal with designing and testing reliable computer systems. Prepare a written report to present to your class on the way in which the ACM Code deals with this issue.

IMPROVING THE USER INTERFACE

CHAPTER 7

OBJECTIVES

Upon completion of this chapter, you should be able to:

- Construct a query-driven terminal interface.

- Construct a menu-driven terminal interface.

- Construct a graphical user interface.

- Format text, including numbers, for output.

- Handle number format exceptions during input.

Estimated Time: 3.5 hours

VOCABULARY

Menu-driven program

Query-controlled input

We do not judge a book by its cover because we are interested in its contents, not its appearance. However, we do judge a software product by its user interface because we have no other way to access its functionality. In this chapter, we explore several ways to improve a program's user interface. First, we present some standard techniques for enhancing terminal-based interfaces, including query-driven input/output (I/O) and menu-driven I/O. This chapter then shows how to format numerical data and examines the output of columns of strings and numbers. The handling of errors in the format of input data is also discussed. Finally, we include a discussion of procedural decomposition and top-down development as methods of organizing a complex task.

7.1 A Thermometer Class

Several examples in this chapter involve converting temperatures between Fahrenheit and Celsius. To support these conversions we first introduce a `Thermometer` class. This class stores the temperature internally in Celsius; however, the temperature can be set and retrieved in either Fahrenheit or Celsius. Here is the code:

```java
public class Thermometer {

    private double degreesCelsius;

    public void setCelsius(double degrees){
        degreesCelsius = degrees;
    }

    public void setFahrenheit(double degrees){
```

```java
public void setFahrenheit(double degrees){
    degreesCelsius = (degrees - 32.0) * 5.0 / 9.0;
}

public double getCelsius(){
    return degreesCelsius;
}

public double getFahrenheit(){
    return degreesCelsius * 9.0 / 5.0 + 32.0;
}
}
```

7.2 *Repeating Sets of Inputs*

In Chapter 4, we introduced two techniques for handling repeating sets of inputs. We called these count-controlled and sentinel-controlled input. We now present a third technique that we call *query-controlled input*. Before each set of inputs after the first, the program asks the user if there are more inputs. Figure 7-1 shows an example of query-controlled input.

FIGURE 7-1
Interface for a query controlled temperature conversion program

```
Enter degrees Fahrenheit: 32
The equivalent in Celsius is 0.0

Do it again (y/n)? y

Enter degrees Fahrenheit: 212
The equivalent in Celsius is 100.0

Do it again (y/n)?
```

The program is implemented by means of two classes—a class to handle the user interface and the `Thermometer` class. Following is pseudocode for the interface class:

```
instantiate a thermometer
String doItAgain = "y"
while (doItAgain equals "y" or "Y"){
    read degrees Fahrenheit and set the thermometer
    ask the thermometer for the degrees in Celsius and display
    read doItAgain                    //The user responds with y or n
}
```

The key to this pseudocode is the `String` variable `doItAgain`. This variable controls how many times the loop repeats. Initially, the variable equals `"y"`. As soon as the user enters a string other than `"y"` or `"Y"`, the program terminates. Following is a complete listing of the user interface class:

```
/* Example 7.1: ConvertWithQuery.java
Repeatedly convert from Fahrenheit to Celsius until the user
signals the end.
*/

import java.util.Scanner;

public class ConvertWithQuery {

    public static void main(String [] args){
        Scanner reader = new Scanner(System.in);
        Thermometer thermo = new Thermometer();
        String doItAgain = "y";

        while (doItAgain.equals("y") || doItAgain.equals("Y")){
            System.out.print("\nEnter degrees Fahrenheit: ");
            thermo.setFahrenheit(reader.nextDouble());
            // Consume the trailing newline
            reader.nextLine();
            System.out.println("The equivalent in Celsius is " +
                                thermo.getCelsius());
            System.out.print("\nDo it again (y/n)? ");
            doItAgain = reader.nextLine();
        }
    }
}
```

Note that "Y" and "y" are not equal. Note also that the input of a `double` leaves behind a newline character in the input stream that must be consumed before the next query is read.

EXERCISE 7.2

1. Describe the structure of a query-controlled loop that processes repeated sets of inputs.

2. Browse into the String class in Sun's Java API documentation. Explain how the method toLowerCase() could be used to simplify the loop control condition of the query-driven loop in the example program.

7.3 A Menu-Driven Conversion Program

Menu-driven programs begin by displaying a list of options from which the user selects one. The program then prompts for additional inputs related to that option and performs the needed computations, after which it displays the menu again. Figure 7-2 shows how this idea can be used to extend the temperature conversion program.

FIGURE 7-2

Interface for a menu-driven version of the temperature conversion program

```
1) Convert from Fahrenheit to Celsius
2) Convert from Celsius to Fahrenheit
3) Quit
Enter your option: 1

Enter degrees Fahrenheit: 212
The equivalent in Celsius is 100

1) Convert from Fahrenheit to Celsius
2) Convert from Celsius to Fahrenheit
3) Quit
Enter your option: 2

Enter degrees Celsius: 0
The equivalent in Fahrenheit is 32

1) Convert from Fahrenheit to Celsius
2) Convert from Celsius to Fahrenheit
3) Quit
Enter your option: 3

Goodbye!
```

Here is a pseudocode design, followed by the program:

```
instantiate a thermometer
menuOption = 4
while (menuOption != 3){
 print menu
 read menuOption
 if (menuOption == 1){
    read fahrenheit and set the thermometer
    ask the thermometer to convert and print the results
 }
 else if (menuOption == 2){
    read celsius and set the thermometer
    ask the thermometer to convert and print the results
 }
 else if (menuOption == 3)
    print "Goodbye!"
 else
    print "Invalid option"
}

/* Example 7.2: ConvertWithMenu.java
A menu-driven temperature conversion program that converts from
Fahrenheit to Celsius and vice versa.
*/

import java.util.Scanner;
```

```java
public class ConvertWithMenu {
    public static void main (String [] args) {
        Scanner reader = new Scanner(System.in);
        Thermometer thermo = new Thermometer();
        String menu;            //The multiline menu
        int menuOption;         //The user's menu selection

        //Build the menu string
        menu = "\n1) Convert from Fahrenheit to Celsius"
             + "\n2) Convert from Celsius to Fahrenheit"
             + "\n3) Quit"
             + "\nEnter your option: ";

        //Set up the menu loop
        menuOption = 4;
        while (menuOption != 3){

            //Display the menu and get the user's option
            System.out.print(menu);
            menuOption = reader.nextInt();
            System.out.println("");

            //Determine which menu option has been selected

            if (menuOption == 1){

                //Convert from Fahrenheit to Celsius
                System.out.print("Enter degrees Fahrenheit: ");
                thermo.setFahrenheit(reader.nextDouble());
                System.out.println("The equivalent in Celsius is " +
                                 thermo.getCelsius());

            }else if (menuOption == 2){

                //Convert from Celsius to Fahrenheit
                System.out.print("Enter degrees Celsius: ");
                thermo.setCelsius(reader.nextDouble());
                System.out.println("The equivalent in Fahrenheit is " +
                                 thermo.getFahrenheit());

            }else if (menuOption == 3)

                //User quits, sign off
                System.out.println("Goodbye!");

            else

                //Invalid option
                System.out.println("Invalid option");
        }
    }
}
```

EXERCISE 7.3

1. What role does a menu play in a program?

2. Describe the structure of a menu-driven command loop.

3. Write the code for a menu that gives the user options to specify the size of a pizza, various toppings (mushrooms, peppers, sausage, etc.), place the order, or return to the main menu.

7.4 Formatted Output with `printf` and `format`

The example programs thus far in this book have used the methods `print` and `println` to output data to the terminal. These methods are easy to use and work well in many applications. However, occasionally a program must format data, especially numbers, more carefully. In this section, we examine a couple of methods to accomplish that.

Using printf to Format Numbers

The precision of a floating-point number is the number of digits to the right of the decimal point supported by the programming language. Java supports the type `double` for numbers with many digits of precision. The methods `print` and `println` do not generally display all of these digits, but only enough to convey the necessary information about the number. Sometimes we get too many digits, and other times we get too few. For example, a whole number would be displayed with a single zero to the right of the decimal point, but in financial applications we would want to see dollars and cents displayed with two zeroes. For example, consider the following code segment and its output:

```
double dollars = 25;
double tax = dollars * 0.125;
System.out.println("Income: $" + dollars);
System.out.println("Tax owed: $" + tax);
```

Output:

```
Income: $25.0
Tax owed: $3.125
```

The amount of money on the first line has too few digits to the right of the decimal point, whereas the amount on the second line has too many.

Fortunately, Java 5.0 includes the method `printf` for formatting output. The following code segment modifies the previous one to show these capabilities for floating-point numbers:

```
double dollars = 25;
double tax = dollars * 0.125;
System.out.printf("Income: $%.2f%n", dollars);
System.out.printf("Tax owed: $%.2f%n", tax);
```

The output produced by this code segment is

```
Income: $25.00
Tax owed: $3.13
```

The parameters of the method `printf` consist of a *format string* and one or more data values, according to the following general form:

```
printf(<format string>, <expression-1>, …, <expression-n>)
```

The format string is a combination of literal string information and formatting information. The formatting information consists of one or more *format specifiers*. These codes begin with a '%' character and end with a letter that indicates the format type. In our example code segment, the format specifier `%.2f` says display a number in fixed-point format with exactly two digits to the right of the decimal point. The format specifier `%n` says display an end-of-line character. Table 7-1 lists some commonly used format types.

TABLE 7-1
Commonly used format types

CODE	FORMAT TYPE	EXAMPLE VALUE
d	Decimal integer	34
x	Hexadecimal integer	A6
o	Octal integer	47
f	Fixed floating-point	3.14
e	Exponential floating-point	1.67e+2
g	General floating-point (large numbers in exponential and small numbers in fixed-point)	3.14
s	String	Income:
n	Platform-independent end of line	

The symbol `%n` can be used to embed an end-of-line character in a format string. The symbol `%%` (consecutive percent symbols) produces the literal '%' character. Otherwise, when the compiler encounters a format specifier in a format string, it attempts to match that specifier to an expression following the string. The two must match in type and position. For example, the code

```
int idNum = 758;
double wage = 10.5;
printf("The wage for employee %d is $%.2f per hour.", idNum, wage);
```

matches the code `%d` to the value of the variable `idNum` and the code `&.2f` to the value of the variable `wage` to produce the output

```
The wage for employee 758 is $10.50 per hour.
```

Text Justification and Multiple Columns

Data-processing applications frequently display tables that contain columns of words and numbers. Unless these tables are formatted carefully, they are unreadable. To illustrate, Figure 7-3 shows a table of names, sales, and commissions, with and without formatting. Although both tables contain exactly the same data, only the formatted one is readable. The key feature of a formatted table is that each column has a designated width, and all the values in a column are justified in the same manner—either to the left, right, or center of the column. In the sales table, the names in the first column are left-justified, and the numbers in the other two columns are right-justified.

FIGURE 7-3
A table of sales figures shown with and without formatting

```
            NAME SALES COMMISSION
            Catherine 23415 2341.5
            Ken 321.5 32.15
            Martin 4384.75 438.48
            Tess 3595.74 359.57
```

Version 1: Unreadable without formatting

```
    NAME                  SALES      COMMISSION
    Catherine          23415.00         2341.50
    Ken                  321.50           32.15
    Martin              4384.75          438.48
    Tess                3595.74          359.57
```

Version 2: Readable with formatting

The columns of text in Version 2 are produced by displaying pieces of text that are justified within fields. A field consists of a fixed number of columns within which the characters of a data value can be placed. A data value is left-justified when its display begins in the leftmost column of its field. The value is right-justified when its display ends in the rightmost column of its field. In either case, trailing or leading spaces are used to occupy columns that are not filled by the value. The column of names in Version 2 is left-justified, whereas the two columns of numbers are both right-justified.

The method `printf` includes several *format flags* that support the justification of text as well as other format styles. Some commonly used format flags are listed in Table 7-2

TABLE 7-2
Some commonly used format flags

FLAG	WHAT IT DOES	EXAMPLE VALUE
-	Left justification	34
,	Show decimal separators	20,345,000
0	Show leading zeroes	002.67
^	Convert letters to uppercase	1.56E+3

To output data in formatted columns, we establish the width of each field and then choose the appropriate format flags and format specifiers to use with `printf`. The width of a field that contains a `double` appears before the decimal point in the format specifier `f`. For example, the format specifer `%6.2f` says to use a precision of 2 digits and a field of 6 columns when displaying the floating-point number. One column is reserved for the decimal point and the number is right-justified by default. Thus, the number 4.5 is displayed with three leading spaces. The number 45000.5, on the other hand, exceeds the size of the field and is not right-justified. In general, when the width of the field is less than or equal to the string representation of the number, the string is left-justified. The same rule holds when the field is omitted before the decimal point. You should take care to ensure that the field width for your data is large enough to accommodate them.

The format specifier `%10s` says to use a field of 10 columns to display a string with right justification. However, for the leftmost column of a table, we would like the strings to be left-justified. This is accomplished by using the format flag '–' in the format specifier. Thus, `%-10s` says to use left justification when filling the columns for the string. Table 7-3 shows some examples of format strings and the output results.

TABLE 7-3
Some example format strings and their outputs

VALUES	FORMAT STRING	OUTPUT
34, 56.7	"%d%7.2f"	34 56.70
34, 56.7	"%4d%7.2f"	34 56.70
34, 56.7	"%-4d$%7.2f"	34 $ 56.70
34, 56.7	"%-4d$%.2f"	34 $56.70

Our next program example puts these ideas together to display a formatted table of data contained in two text files. The first file contains the last names of employees. The second file contains their salaries. The program assumes that each file contains the same number of data values and that the position of an employee's name in one file corresponds to the position of her salary in the other file. We also know that no name exceeds 15 letters and no salary exceeds 6 figures. To illustrate the required format for the output, we are given the following example:

```
NAME                        SALARY
Barker                    4,000.00
Lambert                  36,000.00
Osborne                 150,000.00
```

Note that the numbers contain commas in the standard places. Using this information, we present the following design of the program in pseudocode:

```
Open the file of names
Open the file of salaries
Output the formatted header of the table
While there are more names in the file of names
    Read a name from the file of names
    Read a salary from the file of salaries
    Output a formatted line containing the name and salary
```

To format the column of names, we left-justify the header and each name within 16 columns. To format the column of salaries, we right-justify the header within 12 columns and each salary is given 12 columns of width and two columns of precision. In addition, we use a format flag to place commas in the numbers. Here is the code for the program:

```java
// Example 7.3: Display a table of names and salaries

import java.io.*;
import java.util.Scanner;

public class DisplayTable{

    public static void main(String[] args) throws IOException{
        Scanner names = new Scanner(new File("names.txt"));
        Scanner salaries = new Scanner(new File("salaries.txt"));
        System.out.printf("%-16s%12s%n", "NAME", "SALARY");
        while (names.hasNext()){
            String name = names.nextLine();
            double salary = salaries.nextDouble();
            System.out.printf("%-16s%,12.2f%n", name, salary);
        }
    }
}
```

Formatting with String.format

The `String` method `format` can be used to build a formatted string. This method expects the same parameters as `printf` and returns a formatted string. For example, the call `String.format("Income: %,.2f", 2500000)` returns the string `"Income: 2,500,000.00"`.

EXERCISE 7.4

1. Write code segments to output the following formatted strings:

   a. " One space"

   b. " Two spaces"

   c. "Three spaces   "

   d. The value of int variable i, right-justified in a field of six columns

   e. The value of double variable d, right-justified in a field of 10 columns with a precision of 2

2. Write the values returned by the following expressions (include spaces within the strings where relevant):

   a. String.format("%-10s%,10.2f", "Price", 10000.50)

   b. String.format("%6d%7d", 45, 632)

   c. String.format("%5.2f", 34.543)

7.5 Handling Number Format Exceptions during Input

In Sections 4.4 and 6.1, we discussed the idea of programs that respond to errors, particularly when input data are invalid. If data are found to be invalid after input, the program can display an error message and prompt for the data again. Typical errors are input numbers that do not lie within a certain range. However, what happens if the user enters a number in an invalid format? For example, the user might type in the characters "12r8" when she really intends "1258". The datum in that case is not even a number, let alone an invalid one.

Clearly, the implementer of the input methods must detect and do something about number format errors. The `Scanner` methods `nextInt` and `nextDouble` do just that. When format errors are detected, these methods throw an exception that results in halting the program. The bad format is detected, but before the client code can react to the error. It's too late; the program is halted. This behavior may be acceptable during testing and debugging. However, crashing with an arcane error message is the last thing we would want the final release of a program to do.

Fortunately, there is a way to detect and respond to an exception under program control so that the exception does not halt the program. The programmer embeds the call to an input method in a `try-catch` statement. As its name implies, this statement consists of two parts, as shown in the following simplified form:

```
try{
   <statements that might throw exceptions>
}catch(Exception e){
   <code to recover from an exception if it's thrown>
}
```

The statements within the `try` clause are executed until one of them throws an exception. If that happens, an exception object is created and sent immediately to the `catch` clause. The code within the `catch` clause is then executed. Alternatively, if no statement throws an exception within the `try` clause, the `catch` clause is skipped. There are actually many specific types of exceptions that could be thrown; our example `try-catch` statement catches all of them. A more detailed discussion of Java exceptions appears in Appendix F.

The next program modifies the query-driven example of Section 7.2 to illustrate the recovery from number format errors. We add a nested input loop that cycles around a `try-catch` statement. The display of the prompt, the input statement, and a `break` statement occur within the `try` clause. If no exception occurs during input, the thermometer is set with the input number and the input loop is broken. Otherwise, when an exception occurs, the `catch` clause immediately displays an error message and consumes the trailing end of line, and the input loop continues. Here is the code:

```
/* Example 7.4: ConvertWithQuery.java
Repeatedly convert from Fahrenheit to Celsius until the user
signals the end. Recovers from a number format error with an
error message.
*/

import java.util.Scanner;
```

```java
public class ConvertWithQuery {
    public static void main(String [] args) {
        Scanner reader = new Scanner(System.in);
        Thermometer thermo = new Thermometer();
        String doItAgain = "y";

        while (doItAgain.equals("y") || doItAgain.equals("Y")){
            // Nested loop until input number is well-formed
            while (true)
                try{
                    // Attempt statements that might throw exceptions
                    System.out.print("\nEnter degrees Fahrenheit: ");
                    thermo.setFahrenheit(reader.nextDouble());
                    break;
                }catch(Exception e){
                    // Code for error recovery
                    System.out.println("Error in number format!");
                    // Consume the trailing newline due to bad input
                    reader.nextLine();
                }
            System.out.println("The equivalent in Celsius is " +
                thermo.getCelsius());
            System.out.print("\nDo it again (y/n)? ");
            // Consume the trailing end of line
            reader.nextLine();
            doItAgain = reader.nextLine();
        }
    }
}
```

As you can see, this version of the program is robust for number format errors. The input loop continues until a properly formatted number is entered.

EXERCISE 7.5

1. Assume that a program is trying to read a double value from the keyboard. The user enters the characters "$12.55". Explain what happens next.

2. Explain how a try-catch statement works.

3. Write a code segment that loops until the user has entered a well-formed double value at the keyboard.

7.6 *Graphics and GUIs*

Because developing GUIs in Java is usually quite complicated, many introductory textbooks either restrict themselves to terminal-based I/O or present a rather limited and distorted version of GUIs. Thus far in this book, we have gradually introduced two limited types of GUIs: those that display and allow the user to interact with graphical images (Chapters 2–6), and those that use

> **Extra Challenge**
>
> This Graphics and GUIs section gives you the opportunity to explore concepts and programming techniques required to develop modern graphics applications and graphical user interfaces. This material is not required in order to proceed with the other chapters of the book.

dialog boxes for numeric and text I/O (Chapter 4). Although dialog box I/O suffices for some simple applications, it really does not reflect the true power of a GUI. A program that uses dialog box I/O forces the user to respond to a rigid sequence of pop-up prompts for data. If more than a single data value must be entered, this process can become quite tedious for the user. Moreover, the user might want to refer back to a datum already entered in the sequence before entering the next value, but the earlier dialog box has already disappeared. This problem only gets worse as the number of data values increases. In contrast, a more realistic and powerful GUI presents the user with entry fields for many of the data values simultaneously. Many different command options are also available, via command buttons or drop-down menus. The user can edit any of the fields until she's satisfied that the right combination of the data is present and then select the appropriate command. The results of the computation can then be displayed in the same window.

In this section, we present several realistic but still fairly simple GUIs of this type. In the process, we show how realistic GUIs also allow a programmer to better organize code to solve problems.

The Model/View/Controller Pattern

We start with a very simple application: the temperature conversion program discussed in Section 7.1. Figure 7-4 shows the user interface for a GUI-based version of this program. To use the program, we enter a temperature in the field labeled **Degrees Fahrenheit** and click the **Convert >>>** button below it. The converted temperature is then displayed in the field labeled **Degrees Celsius**. We can repeat the process as many times as desired and click the window's close icon when finished.

FIGURE 7-4
Interface for the GUI-based temperature conversion program

As you might expect, the GUI version can use the same `Thermometer` class used by all of the other versions of the program in this chapter. We call this class the *data model*, or *model* for short. Its responsibilities are to initialize and manage the data used by the program. A second set of classes is called the *view*. The view consists of a window, buttons, data fields, and labels visible to the user. The view is responsible for displaying a view of the data model and providing the user with visible controls for interaction. A third set of classes is called the *controller*. These controller classes are listeners such as those introduced in Chapters 4 through 6. They are responsible for handling user interaction with the program, usually by responding to events that occur in the view. For example, a listener attached to a button is informed that the user has clicked it. The listener responds by sending a message to the data model and then updates the view with the results.

These three sets of classes make up the *model/view/controller pattern*, which we use to structure all of the GUIs in this section. Last but not least, we use a separate class that sets up these other elements in a `main` method, so as to provide an entry point for running a Java program. We call this type of class, for lack of a better term, the *application*.

Putting Together the Temperature Conversion Program

Our program consists of four programmer-defined classes: ConvertWithGUI, GUIWindow, FahrenheitListener, and Thermometer. ConvertWithGUI is the application class. It defines a main method that instantiates the application's main window, sets some of its attributes, and makes it visible. The code for this class is quite straightforward:

```
/* ConvertWithGUI.java
Application class for a GUI-based temperature conversion
program that coverts from Fahrenheit to Celsius.
*/

import javax.swing.*;

public class ConvertWithGUI{

   // Execution begins in the method main as usual.
   public static void main(String[] args){
      GUIWindow theGUI = new GUIWindow();
      theGUI.setTitle("F to C Converter");
      theGUI.setDefaultCloseOperation(JFrame.EXIT_ON_CLOSE);
      theGUI.pack();
      theGUI.setVisible(true); //Make the window visible
   }
}
```

The main thing to note about this code is that we instantiate a GUIWindow instead of a JFrame for the main window. We then send to the GUIWindow the usual JFrame messages to set its attributes. The reason we can do this is that class GUIWindow extends JFrame (just like ColorPanel extends JPanel as discussed in previous chapters). Therefore, a GUIWindow is just a JFrame with some extra behavior.

GUIWindow is the main view class. It has the following responsibilities:

1. Instantiate and maintain a reference to the data model, a Thermometer.

2. Instantiate and maintain references to the data fields and the command button.

3. Add these widgets to the window's container, under the influence of the appropriate layout.

4. Instantiate and attach a FarhenheitListener to the command button.

The class FahrenheitListener is a private class defined within GUIWindow. This follows the practice established in earlier chapters, in which the code for a listener has access to the data variables of the enclosing view class. Our listener in this case must take input from one data field, use it to reset the thermometer's Fahrenheit value, and reset the other data field with the thermometer's Celsius value. Here is the code for the two new classes, heavily commented to mark the model, view, and controller:

```
/* Example 7.5 GUIWindow.java
The main view for a GUI-based temperature conversion
program that coverts from Fahrenheit to Celsius.
*/
```

```java
import javax.swing.*;
import java.awt.*;
import java.awt.event.*;

public class GUIWindow extends JFrame{

    // >>>>>>> The model <<<<<<<<

    // Declare and instantiate the thermometer
    private Thermometer thermo = new Thermometer();

    // >>>>>>> The view <<<<<<<<

    // Declare and instantiate the widgets.
    private JLabel fahrLabel          = new JLabel("Degrees Fahrenheit");
    private JLabel celsiusLabel       = new JLabel("Degrees Celsius");
    private JTextField fahrField      = new JTextField("32.0");
    private JTextField celsiusField   = new JTextField("0.0");
    private JButton fahrButton        = new JButton("Convert >>>");

    // Constructor
    public GUIWindow(){
        // Set up panels to organize widgets and
        // add them to the window
        JPanel dataPanel = new JPanel(new GridLayout(2, 2, 12, 6));
        dataPanel.add(fahrLabel);
        dataPanel.add(celsiusLabel);
        dataPanel.add(fahrField);
        dataPanel.add(celsiusField);
        JPanel buttonPanel = new JPanel();
        buttonPanel.add(fahrButton);
        Container container = getContentPane();
        container.add(dataPanel, BorderLayout.CENTER);
        container.add(buttonPanel, BorderLayout.SOUTH);
        // Attach a listener to the convert button
        fahrButton.addActionListener(new FahrenheitListener());
    }

    // >>>>>>> The controller <<<<<<<<

    private class FahrenheitListener implements ActionListener{
        public void actionPerformed(ActionEvent e){
            String input = fahrField.getText();            // Obtain input
            double fahr = Double.parseDouble(input);       // Convert to a double
            thermo.setFahrenheit(fahr);                    // Reset thermometer
            double celsius = thermo.getCelsius();          // Obtain Celsius
            celsiusField.setText("" + celsius);            // Output result
        }
    }
}
```

The creation of the model and the widgets needs no further comment (although you should browse the Java API for JButton, JTextField, and JLabel if you are curious about setting their attributes, such as the color, text font, and so forth). However, the code in the constructor and the listener call for more detailed explanation.

Although this is a fairly simple GUI with only five widgets, we have to take some care in planning their layout. We decide that a reasonable layout would place the two labels and the two data fields in parallel rows. The single command button would then occupy the third row by itself. Recall that the default layout of a `JFrame` is a `BorderLayout`, but its five regions do not reflect the desired positions of the five widgets. Alternatively, a 2-by-2 `GridLayout` would nicely organize the rows of labels and fields, but what about the button? If we could just get all the data widgets with their grid layout into the center region of the border layout, we could put the button into its south region. The solution is to create a separate panel with a grid layout, add the data widgets to this panel, and then add the panel to the frame's center pane. We also create a new panel for the button because adding it directly to a border layout's region would stretch the button to fill that region. This panel's flow layout causes the button to be centered with its preferred size in the panel. Note finally that the grid layout is created with two extra parameters, which specify the amounts of horizontal and vertical padding around the widgets in pixels.

The code for the `FahrenheitListener` class represents this application's controller. When the **Convert >>>** button is clicked, the listener's `actionPerformed` method is automatically triggered. The first line of code uses the method `getText()` to fetch the string currently in the input field. The method `Double.parseDouble(aString)` then converts this string to a number of type `double`. The number is fed to the thermometer as a Fahrenheit value, and the equivalent Celsius value is then extracted, as in the previous examples. Finally, the method `setText(aString)` is used to output the result to the output field. Note that the number must be converted back to a string before output. Table 7-4 lists some commonly used `JTextField` methods.

TABLE 7-4
Some JtextField methods

JTEXTFIELD METHOD	WHAT IT DOES
`String getText()`	Returns the string currently occupying the field
`void setEditable(boolean b)`	The field is read-only by the user if b is `false`. The user can edit the field if b is `true`. The default is `true`.
`void setText(String s)`	Displays the string s in the field

Our first GUI program is simple as far as GUI programs go, but there was quite a lot to learn! However, the basic pattern of model/view/controller helps to organize our code and will be used in most of the GUI examples that remain in this book.

On the other hand, we now have a user interface that's both prettier and easier to use than the corresponding query-driven interface. And we didn't even have to write a loop like we did in the terminal-based version of Section 7.1. This illustrates an important point about GUI-based programs: unlike programs based on terminal I/O or even dialog box I/O, real GUI programs are *event-driven*. This means that when a GUI program opens, it just sits there and waits for events (the user clicking the mouse, typing characters into a field, etc.). You can imagine the JVM running a loop behind the scenes, which halts only when the user clicks the window's close icon. When any other event occurs within this loop, control shifts to the GUI program's method for handling that event, if there is one. When that method finishes, control returns to the JVM's loop. If there are no methods for handling events, they are ignored.

Making Temperature Conversion Go Both Ways

The menu-driven version of the temperature conversion program in Section 7.2 allows the user to convert a Fahrenheit value to a Celsius value or a Celsius value to a Fahrenheit value. This change involved a major restructuring of the query-driven program of Section 7.1, as well as a major change in the user interface. Let's examine the changes in the GUI version to make the conversion go both ways.

The only change to the user interface is the addition of a second button, as shown in Figure 7-5. When the user clicks the **Convert >>>** button, the program uses the Fahrenheit field for input and the Celsius field for output, as before. When the user clicks the new button, **<<< Convert**, the program uses the Celsius field for input and the Fahrenheit field for output.

FIGURE 7-5
A temperature converter that goes both ways

There are only minor changes to the code as well. The GUIWindow class

- Declares and instantiates the second button:
    ```
    private JButton celsiusButton  = new JButton("<<< Convert");
    ```
- Adds this button to the button panel:
    ```
    buttonPanel.add(celsiusButton);
    ```
- Creates a listener object and attaches it to the button:
    ```
    celsiusButton.addActionListener(new CelsiusListener());
    ```
- Defines a separate listener class that converts from Celsius to Fahrenheit:

    ```
    // Example 7.6: Listener to convert Celsius to Fahrenheit
    private class CelsiusListener implements ActionListener{
       public void actionPerformed(ActionEvent e){
          String input = celsiusField.getText();        // Obtain input
          double celsius = Double.parseDouble(input);    // Convert to a double
          thermo.setCelsius(celsius);                    // Reset thermometer
          double fahr = thermo.getFahrenheit();          // Obtain Fahrenheit
          fahrField.setText("" + fahr);                  // Output result
       }
    }
    ```

In short, we simply add a new command button and the corresponding controller to take action when the user clicks this button. No matter how many new widgets are added to the GUI, if we maintain the correspondence between a widget and its controller, the basic structure of the program will never change. And still no loop!

Making Temperature Conversion Robust

Section 7.5 discussed a strategy for recovering from format errors in numeric input. A similar technique can be applied to catch input errors with text fields in GUI programs. The methods `Double.parseDouble(aString)` and `Integer.parseInt(aString)` are used to convert strings to numbers of type `double` and `int`, respectively. If either of these methods encounters a number format error, it throws an exception. Let's modify the code that converts from Fahrenheit to Celsius to catch a number format exception and recover from it. The code for `actionPerformed` is now enclosed in a `try-catch` statement. If an exception is thrown, control is shifted to the `catch` clause, which pops up a message dialog box to inform the user. Here is the code for the modified listener:

```java
// Example 7.7: A robust listener for number format errors
private class FahrenheitListener implements ActionListener{
   public void actionPerformed(ActionEvent e){
      try{
         String input = fahrField.getText();        // Obtain input
         double fahr = Double.parseDouble(input);    // Convert to a double
         thermo.setFahrenheit(fahr);                 // Reset thermometer
         double celsius = thermo.getCelsius();       // Obtain Celsius
         celsiusField.setText("" + celsius);         // Output result
      }catch(Exception ex){
         JOptionPane.showMessageDialog(GUIWindow.this,
                              "Bad number format",
                              "Temperature Converter",
                              JOptionPane.ERROR_MESSAGE);

      }
   }
}
```

The code for the normal processing of this command is nested in the try clause. If an exception is thrown in the call of `parseDouble`, control is transferred immediately to the `catch` clause, which pops up an error message dialog box.

Note that the first parameter of the method `showMessageDialog` is the expression `GUIWindow.this`, which in this context refers to the current instance of the `GUIWindow` class. This parameter allows the JVM to track the "parent" of the dialog box, that is, the main window from which it was opened. In the examples of earlier chapters, the first parameter had been `null` because no parent window was involved. If we had simply used the parameter `this` instead, the compiler would think that we meant the current instance of `FahrenheitListener`, which is not a GUI component.

Finally, `showMessageDialog` includes two other parameters for the dialog box's title and its type, which displays an error icon, as shown in Figure 7-6.

FIGURE 7-6
Responding to a number format error

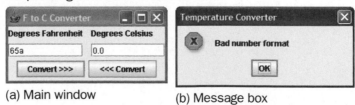

(a) Main window

(b) Message box

EXERCISE 7.6

1. Write a code segment that obtains an input from a text field called inputField, converts the input to an integer, and outputs the square root of the integer to a text field called outputField.

2. Assume that an action listener has been added to a button. Which method runs when the user clicks the button?

3. Describe the roles and responsibilities of the model, view, and controller classes in a GUI program.

SUMMARY

In this chapter, you learned:

- A terminal input/output (I/O) interface can be extended to handle repeated sets of inputs, by using either a query-based pattern or a menu-driven pattern.

- A graphical user interface (GUI) allows the user to interact with a program by displaying window objects and handling mouse events.

- In a terminal-based program, the program controls most of the interaction with the user, whereas GUI-based programs are driven by user events.

- The two primary tasks of a GUI-based program are to arrange the window objects in a window and handle interactions with the user.

VOCABULARY *Review*

Define the following terms:
Menu-driven progam   Query-controlled input

REVIEW *Questions*

FILL IN THE BLANK

Complete each of the following statements by writing your answer in the blank provided.

1. In contrast to terminal I/O programs, GUI programs are _____ driven.

2. A button allows the user to select a(n) _____.

3. Two types of window objects that support numeric I/O are a(n) _____ and a(n) _____.

4. A window object that supports the I/O of a single line of text is a(n) _____.

5. A separate window that pops up with information is a(n) _____.

PROJECTS

PROJECT 7-1

Newton's method for computing the square root of a number consists of approximating the actual square root by means of a set of transformations. Each transformation starts with a guess at the square root. A better approximation is then (guess + number / guess) / 2. This result becomes the guess for the next approximation. The initial guess is 1. Write a query-driven program that allows the user to enter a number and the number of approximations to compute its square root.

PROJECT 7-2

Modify the program of Project 7-1 so that the user can view the successive approximations. (Hint: Build a formatted string of the approximations during the computation.)

PROJECT 7-3

John has $500 to invest. Sue knows of a mutual fund plan that pays 10 percent interest, compounded quarterly (that is, every 3 months, the principal is multiplied by the 2.5 percent and the result is added to the principal; more generally, the amount of gain each quarter is equal to current balance * (1 + interest rate / 400)). Write a program that will tell John how much money will be in the fund after 20 years. Make the program general; that is, it should take as inputs the interest rate, the initial principal, and the number of years to stay in the fund. The output should be a table whose columns are the year number, the principal at the beginning of the year, the interest earned, and the principal at the end of the year.

PROJECT 7-4

The TidBit Computer Store has a credit plan for computer purchases. There is a 10-percent down payment and an annual interest rate of 12 percent. Monthly payments are 5 percent of the listed purchase price minus the down payment. Write a program that takes the purchase price as input. The program should display a table of the payment schedule for the lifetime of the loan. Use appropriate headers. Each row of the table should contain the following items:

■ Month number (beginning with 1)

■ Current total balance owed

■ Interest owed for that month

■ Amount of principal owed for that month

■ Payment for that month

■ Balance remaining after payment

The amount of interest for a month is equal to balance * rate / 12. The amount of principal for a month is equal to the monthly payment minus the interest owed.

PROJECT 7-5

Modify the final temperature conversion program of Section 7.6 so that it displays the results of each conversion rounded to the nearest hundredth of a degree.

PROJECT 7-6

Write a GUI program that takes a radius as input. The outputs, displayed in separate fields, are the area of a circle, the surface area of a sphere, and the volume of a sphere of this radius.

CRITICAL *Thinking*

A company approaches you about the need for a program and wonders whether to ask for a terminal-based user interface or a graphical user interface. Discuss the issues involved in choosing between these two interfaces from a client's perspective.

CHAPTER 8

INTRODUCTION TO HTML AND APPLETS

OBJECTIVES

Upon completion of this chapter, you should be able to:

- ■ Understand the basic features of hypertext, hypermedia, and the World Wide Web.

- ■ Use basic HTML markup tags to format text for a Web page.

- ■ Construct an HTML list and an HTML table to represent a linear sequence of items and a two-dimensional grid of items, respectively.

- ■ Use the appropriate markup tags to include images in Web pages.

- ■ Create links to other Web pages using absolute or relative path names.

- ■ Convert a Java application to an applet and embed the applet in a Web page.

- ■ Understand the constraints on applets that distinguish them from Java applications.

Estimated Time: 3.5 hours

VOCABULARY

Absolute path name

Associative link

Definition list

External image

Hyperlinks

Hypermedia

Hypertext

Hypertext markup language (HTML)

Inline image

Markup tag

Memex

Relative path name

Uniform resource locator (URL)

8.1 Hypertext, Hypermedia, and the World Wide Web

In 1945, Vannevar Bush, a scientist at MIT, published a prophetic essay, "As We May Think," in the *Atlantic Monthly*. According to Bush, although computers were already wonderful for number crunching, they would soon be used for data storage, data manipulation, and logical reasoning. These predictions came to pass in the 1950s and 1960s, with the advent of such branches of computer science as database management and artificial intelligence.

Bush also raised and attempted to answer the following question: How could we improve the way in which we consult our information sources during research? The traditional researcher used indexing schemes, such as card catalogs, but this method restricts the user to a linear or binary search. By contrast, the human mind uses association to search its own memory bank. For example, when I hear the word "wife," I instantly think of a particular person, namely, my own wife. My mind does not go through a complex search process to retrieve the associated information. Somehow, it just gets it.

Bush proposed to use computer technology to link chunks of information associatively. A *table* or *keyed list* is a data structure that allows a computer to look up an item or entry associated with a given key. An online phone book is an example of such a table, where the keys are owner's names and the entries are their addresses and phone numbers. Now imagine that the entries in such a table also contain embedded keys or links to other entries in other tables. Bush called his imaginary machine a *memex*. Each individual would have a desktop memex, as a virtual extension of his or her memory. The memex would receive chunks of information from a photocopy machine, a keyboard, or a stylus. The information would be stored on microfilm. The user would establish links between chunks of information by means of a few simple keystrokes.

The computer would maintain these *associative links* and also traces of the user's explorations of them. The user could come back to that trail or give it to another user to link into a more general trail. Research would involve following the trails blazed by the masters, not just the examination of their end products.

Hypertext and Hypermedia

By the late 1960s, the technology for realizing Bush's dream became available. In 1967, Theodor Holm Nelson coined the term *hypertext* to refer to Bush's machine. A hypertext is a structure consisting of nodes and the links between them. Each node is a document or chunk of text. Normally, links to other nodes are displayed to the user as embedded, highlighted terms within a given chunk of text. The user moves to a node by using an arrow key or mouse to select an associated term.

Early hypertext systems were

- Douglas Englebart's NLS/Augment (1968)
- Cognetics Corporation's Hyperties (mid-1980s)

In 1987, Apple Computer released Hypercard, one of the first hypermedia platforms. *Hypermedia* is like hypertext, but adds

- GUIs
- Images
- Sound
- Animation
- Applications

For example, a link might appear as an icon or image rather than as highlighted text. The targeted chunk of information might be a full-screen image, a movie, a musical recording, or a computer application such as a database program.

Networks and the World Wide Web

All of the early hypertext systems ran on separate standalone machines, which maintained data storage for the individual user. With the development of the Internet, people began to think of sharing hypertext across a network of communicating machines. Chunks of information, or pages as they are now called, could be stored on many different physical machines around the world. Each page would be linked in a gigantic hypermedia system, the World Wide Web. The Web is now a reality, taken for granted by millions of users.

The Web consists of two kinds of machines:

- Servers, on which pages of information reside

- Clients, which run browsers to access information on the servers

  In some cases the client and server reside on the same machine.

  When you open a browser, you are presented with an initial page of information. Embedded in this page are links to other nodes. When you select a link, the following sequence occurs:

- The browser sends a message to the node's machine, requesting a transfer of its information.

- If the request is successful, the information at the node is downloaded to the user's browser.

  Because there are different types of computers, a networked hypermedia system requires a uniform means of:

- Representing information using a machine-independent hypertext markup language

- Assigning node addresses using machine-independent uniform resource locators (URLs)

- Transmitting information from site to site using machine-independent network transmission protocols

- Displaying information with browsers from different vendors, subject to the restriction that all the browsers behave in a similar manner

*E*XERCISE 8.1

1. Describe the basic ideas underlying hypertext.

2. What is the difference between hypertext and hypermedia?

3. What is a URL?

8.2 Overview of the Hypertext Markup Language

The *hypertext markup language* (HTML) was developed as a machine-independent way of representing information in a networked-based hypermedia system. Early word-processing systems such as WordStar bracketed text with codes that specified print formats. For example, the code ^I (control I) indicated italics and ^B indicated bold. To illustrate, the text

```
Bush, Vannevar, ^BAs We May Think^B, ^IAtlantic Monthly^I, July, 1945.
```

would have been printed as

```
Bush, Vannevar, As We May Think, Atlantic Monthly, July, 1945.
```

HTML uses a similar scheme. Codes, called *markup tags*, can indicate the format of textual elements or links to other nodes. Browsers interpret these codes as commands and display the text in the desired format. Figure 8-1 shows the relationship between authors and users of HTML documents.

FIGURE 8-1
The Internet

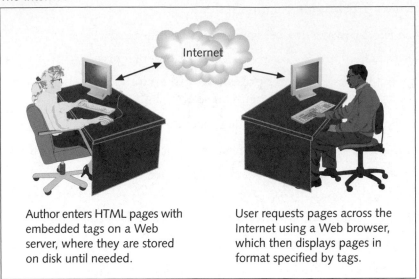

Author enters HTML pages with embedded tags on a Web server, where they are stored on disk until needed.

User requests pages across the Internet using a Web browser, which then displays pages in format specified by tags.

A Short Example

As a first example of using HTML, we show you how to create the Web page shown in Figure 8-2.

FIGURE 8-2
A simple Web page

The page includes markup tags for

- A title
- A heading
- Two paragraphs of text

The author of the page had to write an HTML document that looks like this:

```
<HTML>
<HEAD>
<TITLE>A Short HTML Document</TITLE>
```

```
</HEAD>
<BODY>
<H1>This is a first heading</H1>
<P>You probably thought that Java applications were fun. Wait until
you get going with HTML and applets!</P>
<P>You will learn to write simple Web pages as platforms
for launching Java programs.</P>
</BODY>
</HTML>
```

When a browser displays the document, the title appears at the top of the browser's window.

There is a blank line between the heading and the first paragraph and between the two paragraphs. The browser uses word wrap to fit the text within the window's boundaries. A typical HTML document consists of multiple HTML pages.

The document must be stored in a file having the extension ".html" on a UNIX system and ".htm" on a Windows system. Pages can be any size, from a few lines to many hundreds of lines. We now turn to a discussion of the tags that define the HTML protocol.

Markup Tags

A markup tag in HTML begins with a left angle bracket (<) and ends with a right angle bracket (>), for example, <title>. Tags are not case sensitive. For instance, the tags <title>, <TITLE>, and< TiTlE> are equivalent, though not equally readable. In this chapter, we use uppercase only to allow you to pick out the tags easily.

Tags usually occur in pairs, for example, <TITLE> and </TITLE>. The opening tag tells the browser where to begin the format, and the closing tag, which includes a slash (/), tells the browser where to end the format.

Tags can include attributes. For example, the tag <P ALIGN=CENTER> tells the browser to align the next paragraph in the center of the window. In this example, ALIGN is the attribute's name and CENTER is the attribute's value. Some commonly used markup tags are listed in Table 8-1.

TABLE 8-1
Basic HTML markup tags

MARKUP TAG	WHAT IT DOES
HTML	Designates an HTML document
HEAD	Designates the head of the document
BODY	Designates the contents of the document
TITLE	Designates the title that appears in the browser's window
P	Designates a paragraph of text
H1, H2, etc.	Designates a heading; there are six levels of headings.
PRE	Designates text to be formatted literally
BR	Indicates a line break
UL	Designates a bulleted (ordered) list
OL	Designates a numbered (ordered) list
LI	Indicates an item within a list

Minimal Document Structure

Every HTML document should have the following minimal structure:

```
<HTML>
<HEAD>
<TITLE> the title goes here </TITLE>
</HEAD>
<BODY>
the text for the document goes here
</BODY>
</HTML>
```

Note the following points:

- The HTML tag informs the browser that it is dealing with an HTML document.

- The HEAD tag identifies the first part of the document.

- The TITLE tag identifies the document's title. The title is displayed at the top of the browser's window and is used during searches for the document. The title is also displayed in bookmark lists (a list of the user's favorite links). We recommend short, descriptive titles.

- The BODY tags enclose the information provided by the HTML document.

- The browser ignores extra white space, such as blank lines and tab characters.

Commenting an HTML Document

Authors often add comments to HTML documents. The browser does not interpret comments or show them to the reader. The form of a comment is

```
<!-- text of comment -->
```

In the following example, we have modified the first example by inserting blank lines and comments to make it more readable. However, a browser will display this page exactly as before.

```
<HTML>
<!-- Authors: Kenneth A. Lambert and Martin Osborne
     Last update: November 30, 2005                -->
<HEAD>
<TITLE>A Short HTML Document</TITLE>
</HEAD>

<BODY>
<H1>This is a first heading</H1>

<P>You probably thought that Java applications were fun. Wait until
you get going with HTML and applets!</P>

<P>You will learn to write simple Web pages as platforms
for launching Java programs.</P>

</BODY>
</HTML>
```

EXERCISE 8.2

1. What does HTML stand for?

2. What is the purpose of HTML tags?

3. Write an HTML code segment that shows the minimal HTML document structure for a Web page.

4. What is an HTML comment? Give an example.

8.3 Simple Text Elements

There are several basic elements for formatting text in a Web page.

Headings

HTML provides six levels of document headings, numbered H1 through H6. The form of a heading is

```
<Hnumber>Text of heading</Hnumber>
```

Headings are displayed in a different font size and style from normal text. The browser inserts a blank line after each heading.

Paragraphs

The end tag </P> may be omitted. The browser then ends the paragraph at the beginning of the next paragraph or heading tag. The browser uses word wrap to fit a paragraph within the borders of the browser's window. Most browsers insert a blank line after the end of each paragraph; however, they ignore blank lines within a paragraph.

The browser recognizes the following alignment attributes:

- LEFT (the default)
- RIGHT
- CENTER

This next example uses headings of several sizes and paragraphs with different alignments:

```
<H1>The first level heading</H1>
<P ALIGN=RIGHT>The first paragraph.</P>
<H2>The second level heading</H2>
<P ALIGN=CENTER>The second paragraph.</P>
<H3>The third level heading</H3>
<P>The third paragraph.</P>
```

The results of this example are shown in Figure 8-3.

FIGURE 8-3
Headings and paragraphs coded with HTML

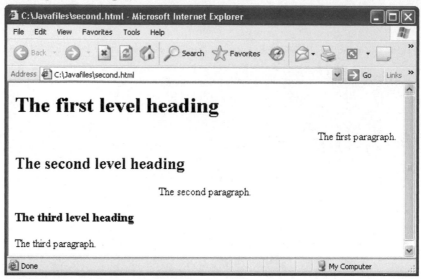

Forced Line Breaks

Occasionally, a Web page author or designer wants to display several lines of text without word wrap. The line break tag, <BR>, is used for this purpose. For example, the following HTML segment would display an address:

```
Department of Computer Science<BR>
Washington and Lee University<BR>
Lexington, VA 24450<BR>
```

Because a line break tag tells the browser where to break a line, no other end tag is required.

Preformatted Text

Suppose you want the browser to display text "as is," with line breaks, extra spaces, and tabs. The <PRE> tag accomplishes this. For example, the following HTML segment displays some Java program code with the indicated indentation and line breaks:

```
<PRE>
     public static void main (String[] args){
     // Lots of code goes here
     }
</PRE>
```

In general, you should not use other markup tags within a chunk of preformatted text.

*E*XERCISE 8.3

1. When does the HTML programmer need to use forced line breaks?

2. When do we use preformatted text in an HTML document?

3. Write an HTML code segment that shows a level 1 heading and a level 2 heading.

8.4 Character-Level Formatting

In addition to the format of headings and paragraphs, HTML provides some control over the format of characters. Table 8-2 lists some of the commonly used tags and their effects:

TABLE 8-2
Some character format tags

MARKUP TAG	WHAT IT DOES	EXAMPLE HTML	DISPLAYED TEXT
EM	Emphasis, usually italics	<EM>Italics</EM>, for emphasis	*Italics*, for emphasis
STRONG	Strong emphasis, usually bold	<STRONG>Bold</STRONG>, for more emphasis	**Bold**, for more emphasis
CITE	Used for titles of books, etc., usually italics	Plato's <CITE>Republic</CITE>	Plato's *Republic*
B	Bold text	<B>Bold</B> text	**Bold** text
I	Italic text	<I>Italic</I> text	*Italic* text
TT	Typewriter text, a fixed-width font	<TT>Typewriter</TT> text	`Typewriter` text

Escape Sequences

HTML treats <, >, and & as special characters. For example, the characters < and > are treated as the delimiters of an HTML tag. If you want the browser to display these characters rather than interpret them, you must use the escape sequences listed in Table 8-3.

TABLE 8-3
Some escape sequences

CHARACTER	ESCAPE SEQUENCE	EXAMPLE HTML	DISPLAYED TEXT
<	&lt;	The character < begins an HTML markup tag.	The character < begins an HTML markup tag.
>	&gt;	The character > ends an HTML markup tag.	The character > ends an HTML markup tag
&	&amp;	& is an ampersand.	& is an ampersand.

The escape sequences for < and > are easy to remember if you remember that "lt" stands for "less than" and "gt" stands for "greater than."

EXERCISE 8.4

1. What happens if you forget to close the markup tag for italics on a piece of text?

2. What is the purpose of the escape sequences in HTML? Give an example.

8.5 Lists

There are three kinds of lists that can be displayed in a Web page:

- Unordered (bulleted) lists—tag <UL>
- Numbered (ordered) lists—tag <OL>
- Definition (association) lists—tag <DL>

For bulleted and numbered lists, you perform the following steps:

1. Start with the desired list tag (<UL> or <OL>).

2. For each item, enter the <LI> (list item) tag followed by the text of the item. No closing tags are needed for the items.

3. End with the desired list tag.

The markup tags for lists can easily be remembered if you note that "UL" stands for "unordered list," "OL" stands for "ordered list" (i.e., 1, 2, 3, etc.), "DL" stands for "definition list," and "LI" stands for "list item."

An Unordered List Example

The next HTML segment displays a bulleted list of courses that one of the authors taught last year.

```
<UL>
<LI>Fundamentals of Data Structures
<LI>Programming Language Design
<LI>Operating Systems
<LI>Artificial Intelligence
</UL>
```

Figure 8-4 shows the page resulting from this HTML segment.

FIGURE 8-4
An unordered (bulleted) list

A Definition List Example

A *definition list* displays terms and their associated definitions. Several tags are used with these lists:

- The tag <DL> begins the definition list and ends it.

- The tag <DT> precedes each term in a definition list.

- The tag <DD> precedes each definition in a definition list.

The following example uses a definition list to add course numbers to the course list.

```
<DL>

<DT>CSCI111
<DD>Fundamentals of Data Structures

<DT>CSCI312
<DD>Programming Language Design
```

```
<DT>CSCI330
<DD>Operating Systems

<DT>CSCI315
<DD>Artificial Intelligence

</DL>
```

Figure 8-5 shows the page resulting from this HTML segment.

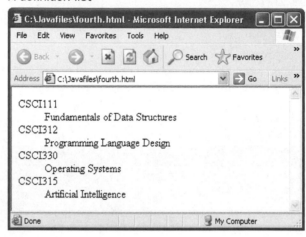

FIGURE 8-5
A definition list

A Nested List Example

Lists can be nested within other lists to any depth, but more than three levels deep can be difficult to read. The following HTML segment nests a numbered list within an unordered one:

```
<UL>
<LI>Fundamentals of Data Structures

<!--The nested, numbered list begins here. -->
<OL>
<LI>Analysis of algorithms
<LI>Collections
<LI>Linked lists
<LI>Stacks
<LI>Queues
<LI>Recursion
<LI>Binary search trees
</OL>
<!--The nested list ends here. -->

<LI>Programming Language Design
<LI>Operating Systems
<LI>Artificial Intelligence
</UL>
```

Figure 8-6 shows the page resulting from this HTML segment.

FIGURE 8-6
A nested list

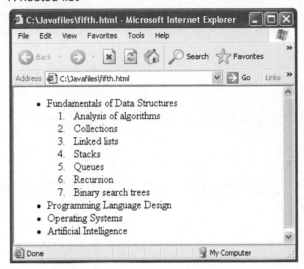

*E*XERCISE 8.5

1. List three types of HTML lists and describe their characteristics.

2. Write an HTML code segment that uses a list to display the names of your grandparents and your parents. The list should be organized to show the relationships clearly.

8.6 *Linking to Other Documents*

Links, also called *hyperlinks* or hypertext references, allow readers to move to other pages in the Web. The markup tag for a link is <A>, which stands for anchor. Placing a link in an HTML document involves the following steps:

1. Identify the target document that will be at the other end of the link. This identifier should be a path name or a URL (see the discussion in the following subsections).

2. Determine the text that labels the link in the browser.

3. Place this information within an anchor, using the following format:

```
<A HREF="target document identifier">text of link</A>
```

For example, the next HTML anchor sets up a link to the file **courses.html** and labels the link "courses last year":

```
<A HREF="courses.html">courses last year</A>
```

Links or anchors can appear within any HTML element. They are often embedded as items in a list or as terms in a paragraph. For example, the following segment displays a link to the file **courses.html** in a sentence that mentions the author's courses:

```
<P>
My <A HREF="courses.html">courses last year</A> were Fundamentals of Data
    Structures, Programming Language Design, Operating Systems, and
    Artificial Intelligence.
</P>
```

When the user browses this page, the link is highlighted in some fashion (i.e., a different color text) and usually underlined, as in Figure 8-7.

FIGURE 8-7
A link to another page

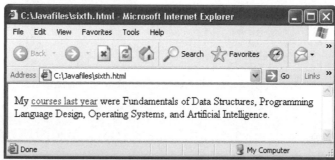

When the user clicks on the link, the browser retrieves and displays the target document, provided that the document has been placed at the appropriate location.

Path Names

Note the path name in the **Address** field in the header portion of Figure 8-7. The path name specifies the path to the file sixth.html on the author's computer. This file contains the page currently being displayed. The path name is said to be an *absolute path name* because it specifies the exact or absolute position of the file in the computer's directory structure.

In HTML anchors, we can use absolute or *relative path names* to specify the location of a target document. A relative path name specifies a document's position relative to that of the currently displayed document. Table 8-4 shows some examples of the relative path name to `MyPage.html`.

TABLE 8-4
Relative path names to MyPage.html

POSITION OF MYPAGE.HTML RELATIVE TO CURRENT PAGE	RELATIVE PATH NAME
In the same directory	`MyPage.html`
Below, in a subdirectory called **Sub1**	`/Sub1/MyPage.html`
In the directory immediately above	`../MyPage.html`
In the directory two levels above	`../../MyPage.html`
In a directory Twin1, which is up one and then down one from the current directory	`../Twin1/MyPage.html`

In general, relative path names are easier to use than absolute path names because

- They are shorter and require less figuring out and typing.

- They need not be changed when a group of documents is moved, even to another computer, provided the documents retain their relative positions.

URLs

When a target document resides on another server in the network, a path name no longer suffices to locate the document. Instead, we use a *uniform resource locator* (URL) to locate the document on another machine. A URL to another Web site (called a host) has the following format:

```
http://server name/document path name
```

For instance, the URL for author Ken Lambert's home page is

```
<A HREF="http://www.wlu.edu/~lambertk">Ken Lambert</A>
```

Please feel free to visit.

*E*XERCISE 8.6

1. Write the form of the markup tag for links.

2. What is an absolute path name? Give an example.

3. What is a relative path name? Give an example.

4. Write the format of a URL to another Web site.

8.7 Multimedia

As a true hypermedia language, HTML supports the presentation of a range of nontextual information such as images, sounds, and movies.

Inline Images

Inline images are graphical images that are displayed when the user opens a page. The form of the markup tag for an inline image is

```
<IMG SRC="ImageLocation">
```

where *ImageLocation* is a URL or path name. Images can be encoded in the GIF or JPEG format and are stored in files with extensions of .gif, .jpg, or .jpeg.

Several parameters can be used with the markup tag of an inline image:

- Size attributes: These specify the height and width of the image in pixels. For example,

```
<IMG SRC="mypicture.gif" HEIGHT=100 WIDTH=100>
```

- Alignment attribute: This specifies the position of text relative to the image. By default, text that follows an image starts at the image's lower-right corner. The text moves to the upper right or to the center right of the image when TOP or CENTER are specified. For example,

```
<IMG SRC="mypicture.gif" ALIGN=CENTER>
```

To detach an image from surrounding text, place the image in a separate paragraph. For instance,

```
<P ALIGN=CENTER>

<IMG SRC="mypicture.gif">
</P>
```

External Images

Inline images increase a document's size and slow its transfer across the Internet. For that reason, documents sometimes provide links to *external images*, which are not displayed until the user clicks on a link. The following HTML segment shows two ways of linking to an external image. The first link is a string of text. The second link is a smaller version of the image (sometimes called a thumbnail):

```
<A HREF="mypicture.gif">Sample picture</A>

<A HREF="mypicture.gif"><IMG SRC="mythumbnail.gif"></A>
```

This strategy is also used with other media, such as sound recordings and movies.

Colors and Backgrounds

Browsers normally display black text on a white background with links highlighted in blue. However, an HTML author can easily change the colors of these elements. Background, text, and link colors are controlled by the BGCOLOR, TEXT, and LINK attributes of the <BODY> tag. For example, the following tag sets the background to black, text to white, and links to red:

```
<BODY BGCOLOR="#000000" TEXT="#FFFFFF" LINK="#FF0000">
```

A string of three two-digit hexadecimal numbers specifies a color by indicating the RGB (red, green, blue) components of the color. The first two digits represent the red component, the second the green, and the third the blue. Thus, a total of 224 colors are possible. The string "#000000" indicates black, a total absence of any color, whereas "#FFFFFF" represents white, a total saturation of all colors. Bright red is "#FF0000" and bright green is "#00FF00". There are many useful Web sites that show how to use colors. One good example is http://www.pagetutor. com/pagetutor/makapage/picker/.

Another way to customize a background is to display an image on it. The following tag shows how to use an image as a background:

```
<BODY BACKGROUND="mybackground.jpg">
```

If the image is small, the browser fills the window with the image by a process called *tiling*, which repeatedly displays the image across and down the screen, thus creating a wallpaper-like effect.

Other Media

Table 8-5 shows filename extensions for some typical media used in HTML documents.

TABLE 8-5
Some hypermedia filename extensions

FILE NAME EXTENSION	TYPE OF MEDIUM
.au	AU sound file
.wav	WAV sound file
.mov	QuickTime movie
.mpeg or .mpg	MPEG movie

EXERCISE 8.7

1. What is the difference between an inline image and an external image?

2. Write the simplest version of the format of the markup tag for an inline image.

3. Write a markup tag that loads an inline image of the file image.gif, centers the image, and scales its size to 200 pixels × 200 pixels.

4. What are two ways of tagging an external image? Give an example of each.

8.8 Tables

It is often useful to organize information in tables. The page in Figure 8-8 uses a table to display the first two weeks of topics in a data structures course.

FIGURE 8-8
A table

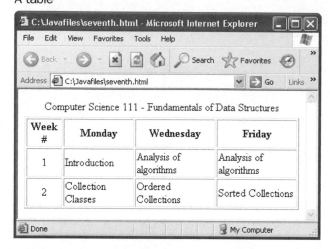

As you have seen in earlier chapters, tables provide a highly structured way of accessing information. This is true of tables in user interfaces as well.

Tables usually contain the following elements:

■ A caption or title, normally at the top of the table.

■ A first row containing column headers; each header describes the kind of data contained in the column beneath it.

■ Several rows of data; the cells in a row can contain any HTML elements (text, images, links, etc.).

Table 8-6 provides a list of the HTML markup tags used with tables.

TABLE 8-6
Table format tags

TABLE MARKUP TAG	WHAT IT DOES
<TABLE>	Defines a table
<CAPTION>	Defines the title of the table (The default position of the title is at the top of the table, but ALIGN=BOTTOM can also be used.)
<TR>	Defines a row within a table
<TH>	Defines a table header cell
<TD>	Defines a table data cell

The table markup tags accept the attributes shown in Table 8-7.

TABLE 8-7
Table attributes

ATTRIBUTE	TAG	WHAT IT DOES
BORDER	<TABLE>	Display a border
ALIGN (LEFT, CENTER RIGHT)	All	Horizontal alignment of elements in cells
VALIGN (TOP, MIDDLE, BOTTOM)	All except <CAPTION>	Vertical alignment of cells
ROWSPAN=n	<TD>	The number of rows that a cell spans
COLSPAN=n	<TD>	The number of columns that a cell spans
NOWRAP	All except <CAPTION>	Turn off word wrap within a cell

Cell attributes override row attributes, and row attributes override table attributes.

Typical Table Format

The format of a typical table follows. The blank lines between rows increase readability but do not affect the manner in which the table is displayed:

```
<TABLE>
<CAPTION> title of the table </CAPTION>

<TR>
<TH> header of first column </TH>
.
.
<TH> header of last column </TH>
</TR>

<TR>
<TD> contents of first data cell in first row </TD>
.
.
<TD> contents of last data cell in first row </TD>
</TR>
.
.
<TR>
<TD> contents of first data cell in last row </TD>
.
<TD> contents of last data cell in last row </TD>
</TR>
</TABLE>
```

A Simple Example

The table shown in Figure 8-8 at the beginning of this section was created using the following HTML code:

```
<TABLE BORDER>

<CAPTION ALIGN=CENTER>
Computer Science 111 - Fundamentals of Data Structures
</CAPTION>

<TR>
<TH>Week #</TH>
<TH>Monday</TH>
<TH>Wednesday</TH>
<TH>Friday</TH>
</TR>

<TR>
<TD ALIGN=CENTER>1</TD> <TD>Introduction</TD>
<TD>Analysis of algorithms</TD> <TD>Analysis of algorithms</TD>
</TR>

<TR>
<TD ALIGN=CENTER>2</TD> <TD>Collection Classes</TD>
<TD>Ordered Collections</TD> <TD>Sorted Collections</TD>
</TR>

</TABLE>
```

EXERCISE 8.8

1. Describe how you create a table using the HTML table tags.

2. Write an HTML code segment that displays a 3 × 3 table with cells that are numbered as follows:
1 2 3
4 5 6
7 8 9

8.9 Applets

An *applet* is a Java application that runs in a Web page. Two components are needed to run an applet:

1. An HTML document that contains an applet markup tag

2. A byte code file for the applet—that is, a compiled Java applet in a `.class` file

An applet markup tag has the following form:

```
<APPLET CODE="byte code file name" WIDTH=width HEIGHT=height></APPLET>
```

The width and height are the width and height, respectively, of the applet's screen area in pixels.

Applets present a graphical user interface. The examples used in this section are revised versions of GUI applications presented in earlier end-of-chapter sections on graphics and GUIs. You might want to review those sections, particularly in Chapters 6 and 7, before continuing.

Example 1: The Temperature Converter

Let us assume that the Fahrenheit/Celsius temperature converter from Chapter 7 has already been rewritten as a Java applet. It might appear in a Web page as shown in Figure 8-9.

FIGURE 8-9
An applet within a Web page

The applet retains just two classes from the earlier version: GUIWindow (the view) and Thermometer (the model). Here is the HTML code for the example:

```
<HTML>
<HEAD>
<TITLE>Temperature Converter</TITLE>
</HEAD>

<BODY>
<H1>Temperature Converter</H1>
<UL>
<LI>Enter degrees Fahrenheit or degrees Celsius.
<LI>Click the <STRONG>Convert >>></STRONG> button and the
Celsius equivalent will be displayed.
<LI>Click the <STRONG><<< Convert</STRONG> button and the
Fahrenheit equivalent will be displayed.
</UL>

<APPLET CODE="GUIWindow.class" WIDTH=250 HEIGHT=100>
</APPLET>
```

```
<P>
Applets greatly increase the power of the Web.

</BODY>
</HTML>
```

Note that the Web page loads the byte code for the view class into a rectangular area large enough to accommodate the GUI components. The Web page also displays a title for the applet. Thus, you can think of the Web page as playing the role of the application class, ConvertWithGUI, in the earlier version of the program.

Converting an Application to an Applet

For applications that use a specialized view class for the main window, the conversion to an applet is surprisingly simple. In Section 7.6, the class GUIWindow played this role. We just do two things to this class:

1. Replace the name JFrame with the name JApplet at the beginning of the class definition (extends JApplet).

2. Replace the class's constructor by the method init:

```
public void init(){
    ...
}
```

The following listing comments these changes in just two lines of code in the GUIWindow class:

```
/* GUIWindow.java
The main view for a GUI-based temperature conversion
program that coverts from Fahrenheit to Celsius and back again.
*/

import javax.swing.*;
import java.awt.*;
import java.awt.event.*;

public class GUIWindow extends JApplet{      // First change here!!!

    // >>>>>>> The model <<<<<<<<

    // Declare and intantiate the thermometer
    private Thermometer thermo = new Thermometer();

    // >>>>>>> The view <<<<<<<<

    // Declare and instantiate the window objects.
    private JLabel fahrLabel          = new JLabel("Degrees Fahrenheit");
    private JLabel celsiusLabel       = new JLabel("Degrees Celsius");
    private JTextField fahrField      = new JTextField("32.0");
    private JTextField celsiusField   = new JTextField("0.0");
    private JButton fahrButton        = new JButton("Convert >>>");
    private JButton celsiusButton     = new JButton("<<< Convert");
```

```
    // Constructor
    public void init(){                          // Second change here!!!
        // Set up panels to organize widgets and
        // add them to the window
        JPanel dataPanel = new JPanel(new GridLayout(2, 2, 12, 6));
        dataPanel.add(fahrLabel);
        dataPanel.add(celsiusLabel);
        dataPanel.add(fahrField);
        dataPanel.add(celsiusField);
        JPanel buttonPanel = new JPanel();
        buttonPanel.add(fahrButton);
        buttonPanel.add(celsiusButton);
        Container container = getContentPane();
        container.add(dataPanel, BorderLayout.CENTER);
        container.add(buttonPanel, BorderLayout.SOUTH);
        // Attach a listener to the convert button
        fahrButton.addActionListener(new FahrenheitListener());
        celsiusButton.addActionListener(new CelsiusListener());
    }

    // >>>>>>> The controller <<<<<<<<

    private class FahrenheitListener implements ActionListener{
        public void actionPerformed(ActionEvent e){
            try{
                String input = fahrField.getText();      // Obtain input
                double fahr = Double.parseDouble(input);  // Convert to double
                thermo.setFahrenheit(fahr);               // Reset thermometer
                double celsius = thermo.getCelsius();     // Obtain Celsius
                celsiusField.setText("" + celsius);       // Output result
            }catch(Exception ex){
                JOptionPane.showMessageDialog(null,       // Now null, because we're in an applet
                                    "Bad number format",
                                    "Temperature Converter",
                                    JOptionPane.ERROR_MESSAGE);
            }
        }
    }

    private class CelsiusListener implements ActionListener{
        public void actionPerformed(ActionEvent e){
            String input = celsiusField.getText();       // Obtain input
            double celsius = Double.parseDouble(input);   // Convert to double
            thermo.setCelsius(celsius);                   // Reset thermometer
            double fahr = thermo.getFahrenheit();         // Obtain Fahrenheit
            fahrField.setText("" + fahr);                 // Output result
        }
    }
}
```

Note that the first parameter of the method showMessageDialog is now null. No other changes are necessary. With a few exceptions to be discussed shortly, applets can use all of the view and controller features of standalone applications.

Example 2: Graphics Programs

The structure of the graphics programs introduced in Chapters 2 through 6 is slightly different than that of the temperature conversion program of Chapter 7. The earlier programs consist of a main window class called GUIWindow and one or more specialized panel classes for drawing shapes. In these cases, GUIWindow includes a main method that creates a simple JFrame, to which the panels are added. The main method also sets the frame's attributes and displays it. Here is the code for a typical version of this class, which does not vary much from application to application:

```java
// A frame with a specialized panel

import javax.swing.*;
import java.awt.*;

public class GUIWindow{

    public static void main(String[] args){
        JFrame theGUI = new JFrame();
        theGUI.setTitle("GUI Program");
        theGUI.setSize(300, 200);
        theGUI.setDefaultCloseOperation(JFrame.EXIT_ON_CLOSE);
        ColorPanel panel = new ColorPanel(Color.white);
        Container pane = theGUI.getContentPane();
        pane.add(panel);
        theGUI.setVisible(true);
    }
}
```

To convert programs with this structure to applets, we must do several things:

1. GUIWindow now extends JApplet.

2. Replace public static void main(String[] args) with public void init().

3. Do not create a JFrame. The operations to set its title, size, close operation, and visibility go away.

We simply create the panel, get the applet's content pane, and add the panel to it. Here is the code for the modified GUIWindow class:

```java
// Example 8.2: An applet with a specialized panel
import javax.swing.*;
import java.awt.*;

public class GUIWindow extends JApplet{

    public void init(){
        ColorPanel panel = new ColorPanel(Color.white);
        Container pane = theGUI.getContentPane();
        pane.add(panel);
    }
}
```

As we said earlier, slight variations of this example will convert to applets any of the graphics programs discussed in Chapters 2 through 6.

Using the Applet Viewer

Sun's JDK comes with a tool called an *applet viewer*. This tool allows the programmer to run an applet and view just its GUI, without the surrounding Web page. To use the applet viewer, you must

1. Compile the Java source program as usual.

2. Create an HTML file with at least the minimal applet tag for the applet.

3. At the command line prompt, run the following command:

```
appletviewer <html file name>
```

Figure 8-10 shows the converter applet running within the applet viewer.

FIGURE 8-10
An applet within the applet viewer

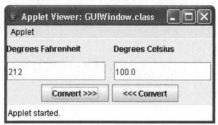

Constraints on Applets

There are several major differences between applets and applications:

- To ensure security on the user's machine, applets cannot access files on that machine. Imagine how dangerous it would be to download applets across the Web if the applets could read or trash the files on your computer.

- Applets and the HTML documents that use them should be placed in the same directory. This rule can be violated, but doing so is beyond the scope of this book. Java programs, whether they are standalone applications or applets, frequently utilize classes in addition to those in the standard Java libraries. These classes should usually be in the same directory as the applet.

- The programs in this book use Java 5.0, so only Web browsers that support Java 5.0 can run the applets in this chapter. One such browser is available from www.sun.com.

- The technique for using dialog boxes in applications, as described in Chapter 4, applies to applets, with three qualifications:

  - The parent parameter of the dialog box's constructor should not be the applet, but `null` instead.

  - You might see a warning message at the bottom of the dialog box.

  - The dialog box does not prevent you from returning to the Web page. Once there, you cannot interact with the applet, but you can browse to other pages, quit the browser, and perhaps hang up (or lock up) the computer.

Loading Images into Applets

It is possible to load images into applets. These images must reside on the Web server from which the applet's byte code was sent. The JApplet method getDocumentBase() locates and returns the URL of the applet's Web server. The JApplet method getImage expects this URL and the filename of an image as parameters. The method downloads the image from the Web server and returns an object of the class Image. This object can be converted to an ImageIcon object for further processing by using the ImageIcon(anImage) constructor.

To illustrate, here is the code for the main window class that loaded an image of Smokey the cat in Chapter 5, followed by the corresponding applet:

```java
// Example 5.2: Loading an image from a file (standalone application)

import javax.swing.*;
import java.awt.*;

public class GUIWindow{

    public static void main(String[] args){
        JFrame theGUI = new JFrame();
        theGUI.setTitle("GUI Program");
        theGUI.setSize(300, 300);
        theGUI.setDefaultCloseOperation(JFrame.EXIT_ON_CLOSE);
        ImageIcon image = new ImageIcon("smokey.jpg");
        ColorPanel panel = new ColorPanel(Color.black, image);
        Container pane = theGUI.getContentPane();
        pane.add(panel);
        theGUI.setVisible(true);
    }
}


// Example 8.3: Loading an image from a file (applet)

import javax.swing.*;
import java.awt.*;

public class GUIWindow extends JApplet{

    public void init(){
        // Locate this applet's Web server and load the image
        Image image = getImage(getDocumentBase(), "smokey.jpg");
        // Convert to an image icon for further processing
        ImageIcon imageIcon = new ImageIcon(image);
        ColorPanel panel = new ColorPanel(Color.black, imageIcon);
        Container pane = getContentPane();
        pane.add(panel);
    }
}
```

Passing Parameters to Applets

It is possible to send information from an HTML page to an applet. The information is passed in HTML parameter tags and is retrieved in the applet's code. In the following example, a parameter tag binds the string "5" to the name `"numberOfCourses"`. The parameter tag must appear between the opening and closing applet tag:

```
<APPLET CODE="Courses.class" WIDTH=150 HEIGHT=100>
<PARAM NAME=numberOfCourses VALUE="5">
</APPLET>
```

At any point within the applet, the method `getParameter` can retrieve the parameter's value, but always as a string:

```
String str = getParameter ("numberOfCourses");
int num = Integer.pasreInt(str);
```

A common location for such code is in the `init` method.

If there are several parameters, each requires its own tag.

For a fairly complete reference on HTML and Web page design, enter the following URL in your Web browser:

```
http://www.mcli.dist.maricopa.edu/tut/lessons.html
```

*E*XERCISE 8.9

1. Describe the simplest format of an HTML applet tag. Give an example.

2. How is an application converted to an applet?

3. What can an application do that an applet cannot do?

4. Describe the steps required to load an image into an applet.

SUMMARY

In this chapter, you learned:

- The World Wide Web is a hypermedia system that allows users to navigate among and use various resources in a nonlinear manner.

- HTML tags can be used to format text for Web pages. Other markup tags can be used to organize information in lists and tables in a Web page.

- Links to other pages using absolute or relative path names also can be included in HTML elements.

- Web pages also can contain applets or Java applications that are downloaded from a Web server and run in the user's Web browser.

- There are a few simple steps to convert a Java application to an applet. Applets have most of the functionality of applications, including the GUI, but they lack file access to the user's disks.

VOCABULARY *Review*

Define the following terms:

Absolute path name	Hypermedia	Markup tag
Associative link	Hypertext	Memex
Definition list	Hypertext markup language	Relative path name
External image	(HTML)	Uniform resource locator
Hyperlinks	Inline image	(URL)

REVIEW *Questions*

FILL IN THE BLANK

Complete the following sentences by writing the correct word or words in the blanks provided.

1. _____ generalizes hypertext to include images, sound, video, and embedded applications.

2. HTML stands for _____.

3. The three markup tags that any HTML document usually contains are _____, _____, and _____.

4. The _____ markup tag is used to display text in its original format.

5. A(n) _____ markup tag is used to lay out elements in a two-dimensional grid.

6. The _____ method serves a similar role to a constructor for applets.

7. Two program features that are not allowed in applets are _____ and _____.

8. The JDK's _____ allows the programmer to run an applet without a Web browser.

9. URL stands for _____.

10. A(n) _____ path name is used to obtain a resource from a remote server.

PROJECTS

PROJECT 8-1

If you have not done so already, create a home page on your local Web server. Include a title, a brief paragraph that states who you are, and a picture of your favorite pastime.

PROJECT 8-2

Add a list of courses you are currently taking to the home page created for Project 8-1.

PROJECT 8-3

Make each item in the list from Project 8-2 a link to a page that describes that item. Create these pages and test your hypertext thoroughly.

PROJECT 8-4

Add links to each of the pages created in Project 8-3 that return the user to your home page.

PROJECT 8-5

Write an applet that plays the game of guess the number with the user. The applet contains four labeled data fields. One is for the user's input, two are for the lower and upper bounds of the range of numbers to guess, and the fourth is for the program's messages to the user. At startup, the program displays two numbers chosen at random in its two number fields. The program also selects a number at random between these two numbers but keeps it hidden from the user. The user guesses this number by entering a number in the input field and clicking a Guess button. If the user guesses correctly, the program displays a message to that effect and resets its fields to new random numbers for another game. Otherwise, the program displays the message "Too low" or "Too high" and waits for further input.

CRITICAL *Thinking*

Write a short essay that compares the advantages and disadvantages of using Java applications and applets.

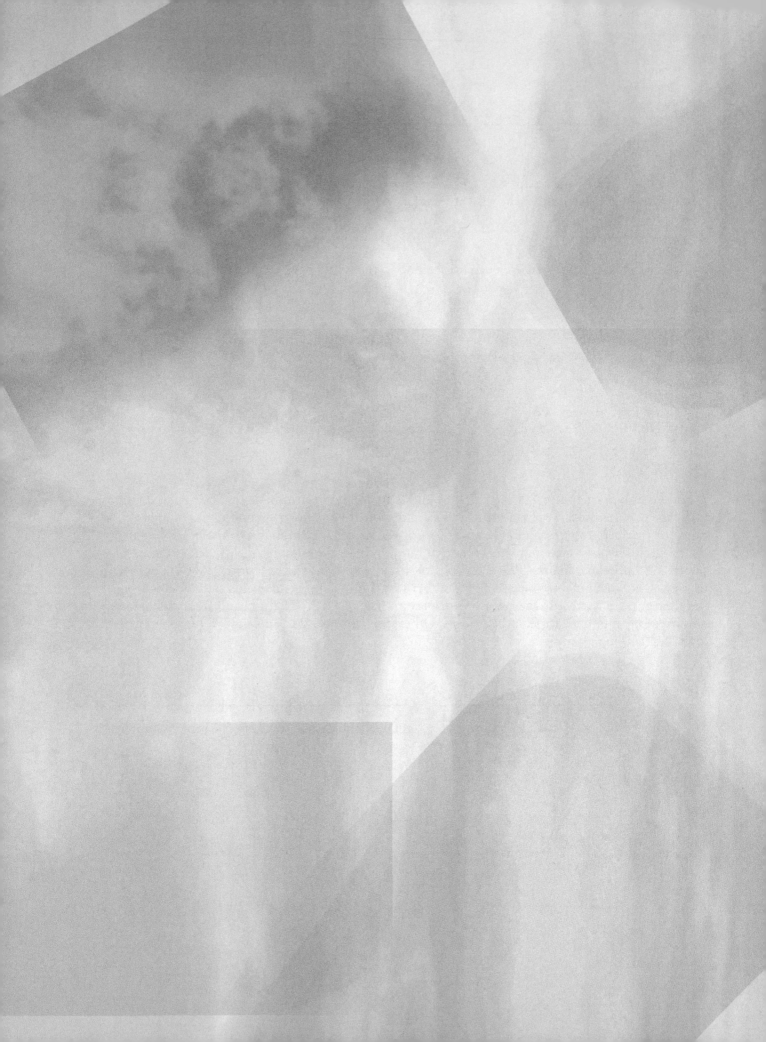

THE NEXT STEP WITH JAVA

REVIEW *Questions*

TRUE/FALSE

Circle T if the statement is true or F if it is false.

T F 1. A mutator method is used to ask an object for the values of its data attributes.

T F 2. The purpose of a constructor is to change the data type of an object.

T F 3. Two variables can refer to the same object.

T F 4. `private` variables are visible within their class and to all clients of that class.

T F 5. Each method can declare its own private variables, called local variables.

T F 6. The lifetime of a variable is the region on the program within which it can be used.

T F 7. An extended `if` statement allows a program to choose among mutually exclusive alternatives.

T F 8. The logical operator OR is indicated by !.

T F 9. A `boolean` variable is used to manipulate characters and strings.

T F 10. It is possible to test all programs to show that they are completely correct.

FILL IN THE BLANK

Complete the following sentences by writing the correct word or words in the blanks provided.

1. The process of creating a new object is called _____.

2. The process of deleting unreferenced objects from memory is called _____.

3. If a variable is declared outside all methods, it is said to be _____.

4. The access modifier that makes methods visible to all clients is _____.

5. Two methods in a program that have the same name but not the same number and types of parameters are said to be _____.

6. When a variable of a reference type is declared but not given a value, its default value is _____.

7. The easiest way to increase numbers by one in a program is to use the _____ operator.

8. The logical operators are _____, _____, and _____.

9. The _____ statement provides a simple way to get out of a loop before all of the statements in the loop process.

10. To determine all the possible values of a Boolean expression, one can use a(n) _____ table.

WRITTEN QUESTIONS

Write your answers to the following questions or problems.

1. Explain the difference between a global variable and a local variable and give an example of each.

2. Assume that x, y, and z are boolean variables. Draw truth tables for the following expressions.
   A. x && y || z

   B. !(x || y || z)

   C. x && (y || z)

3. Define a class called counter. A counter contains an integer that initially is 0 but that can be incremented, decremented, or reset to 0. Counter objects should respond to the mutators increment(), decrement(), and reset(), and to the accessor getValue().

4. What is data encapsulation? Why is it important?

5. Describe what a class constructor does.

PROJECTS

PROJECT 1

Write a program that takes as inputs the lengths of three sides of a triangle and displays in a message box whether the triangle is scalene, isosceles, or equilateral. Following are some useful facts:

- In a triangle, the longest side must be less than the sum of the other two sides.
- A scalene triangle has all sides unequal.
- An isosceles triangle has two sides equal.
- An equilateral triangle has all sides equal.

PROJECT 2

In the game of craps, a player provides an initial bankroll and bets from this amount on each roll of the dice. On each roll, the sum of the faces is taken. The outcomes are as follow:

- If 7 or 11 is rolled, the player wins.
- If 2, 3, or 12 is rolled, the player loses.
- Otherwise, the number rolled becomes the player's point. The player rolls the dice repeatedly until the player wins by making point (getting the same number as on the first roll) or loses by crapping out (getting a 7).

Design and implement a craps machine that allows the user to play craps. This machine should be defined as a new class. The interface accepts an amount of money representing an initial bankroll. Before each roll of the dice, the user must make a bet. At the end of the game, the program should display the amount of the user's current bankroll (after adding the gains and deducting the losses).

PROJECT 3

A perfect number is a positive integer such that the sum of the divisors equals the number. Thus, 28 = 1 + 2 + 4 + 7 + 14 is a perfect number. If the sum of the divisors is less than the number, it is deficient. If the sum exceeds the number, it is abundant. Write a program that takes a positive integer as input and displays whether the number entered is perfect, deficient, or abundant. Your program should define the following two methods:

```
boolean isDivisor (int number, int divisor)

int divisorSum (int number)
```

The method `isDivisor` returns `true` if the `divisor` parameter is a divisor of the `number` parameter and `false` otherwise. The `divisorSum` method uses `isDivisor` to accumulate and return the sum of the proper divisors of the `number` parameter. Be sure to design and test the program incrementally; that is, verify that `isDivisor` works correctly before using it in `divisorSum`.

PROJECT 4

A standard physics experiment is to drop a ball to see how high it bounces. Once the "bounciness" of the ball is determined, the ratio gives a bounciness index. For example, if a ball dropped from a height of 10 feet bounces 6 feet high, the index is 0.6 and the total distance traveled by the ball is 16 feet after one bounce. If the ball continues bouncing, the distance after two bounces would be $(10 + 6) + (6 + 3.6) = 25.6$ feet. Note that the distance traveled for each bounce is the distance to the floor plus 0.6 of that distance as the ball comes back up.

Write a program that takes as inputs the initial height of the ball (in feet), the index of the ball's bounciness, and the number of times the ball is allowed to continue bouncing. The program should output the total distance traveled by the ball. At some point in the process, the distance traveled by the ball after a bounce might become negligible, for example, less than 0.00001 inches. If that stage is reached, terminate the process and output the total distance.

CRITICAL *Thinking*

A number is prime if it has no divisors (other than 1) that are less than or equal to its square root. The number 1 is not prime. Design and implement a method, `isPrime`, that returns `true` if its parameter is a prime number and `false` otherwise. You should use the `isDivisor` method developed in Project U2-3 in the implementation of `isPrime`. Then use these methods in a program that takes as input a number N and displays as output a list of the first N prime numbers.

ARRAYS, RECURSION, AND COMPLEXITY

Unit 3

 Estimated Time for Unit: 19.5 hours

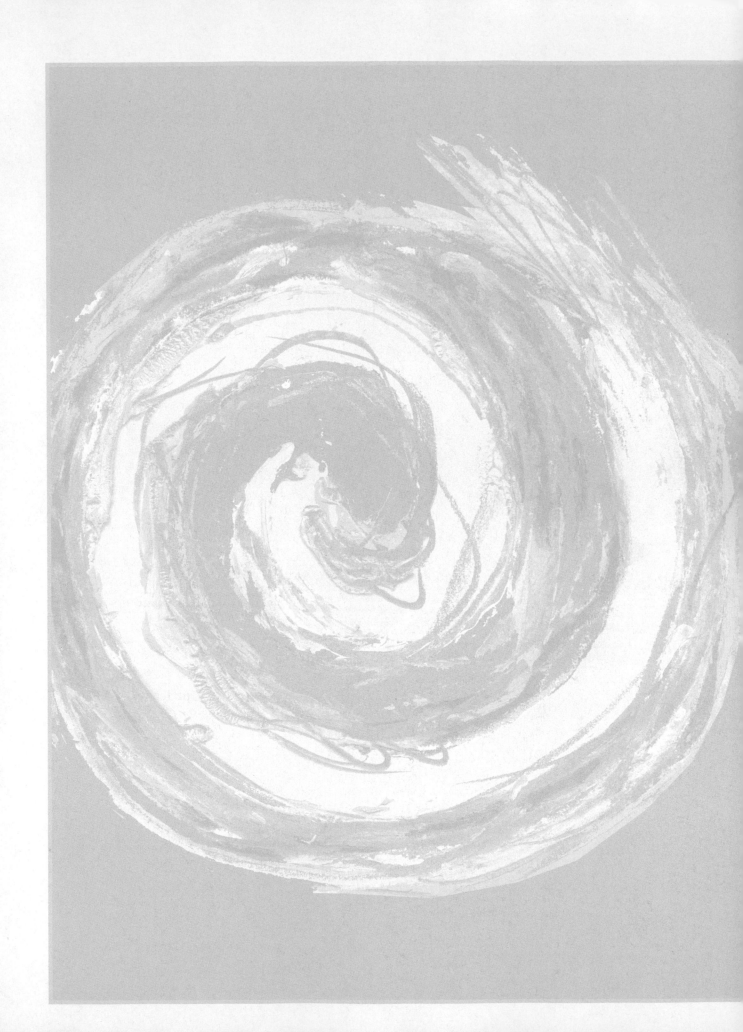

INTRODUCTION TO ARRAYS

CHAPTER 9

OBJECTIVES

Upon completion of this chapter, you should be able to:

- Write programs that handle collections of similar items.

- Declare array variables and instantiate array objects.

- Manipulate arrays with loops, including the enhanced `for` loop.

- Write methods to manipulate arrays.

- Create parallel arrays and two-dimensional arrays.

Estimated Time: 5 hours

VOCABULARY

Array

Element

Enhanced `for` loop

Index

Initializer list

Logical size

Multidimensional array

One-dimensional array

Parallel arrays

Physical size

Procedural decomposition

Ragged array

Range-bound error

Structure chart

Subscript

Two-dimensional array

There are situations in which programs need to manipulate many similar items, a task that would be extremely awkward using the language features encountered so far. Earlier we developed a Student class with a name and three test scores. Each test score required a separate instance variable. Imagine how tedious and lengthy the code would have become if a student had 20 scores. Fortunately, there is a way to handle this dilemma. Most programming languages, including Java, provide a data structure called an *array*, which consists of an ordered collection of similar items. An array, as a whole, has a single name, and the items in an array are referred to in terms of their position within the array. This chapter explains the mechanics of declaring arrays and several basic algorithms for manipulating them. Using an array, it is as easy to manipulate a million test scores as it is three.

9.1 Conceptual Overview

To demonstrate the need for arrays, let us consider the data for a `Student` class if there are no arrays, but there are 20 rather than 3 test scores. The declarations for the instance variables look like this:

```
private String name;
private int test1,  test2,  test3,  test4,  test5,
            test6,  test7,  test8,  test9,  test10,
            test11, test12, test13, test14, test15,
            test16, test17, test18, test19, test20;
```

and the computation of the average score looks like this:

```
// Compute and return a student's average
public int getAverage(){
    int average;
    average = (test1 + test2  + test3  + test4  + test5 +
              test6  + test7  + test8  + test9  + test10 +
              test11 + test12 + test13 + test14 + test15 +
              test16 + test17 + test18 + test19 + test20) / 20;
    return average;
}
```

Other methods are affected in a similar manner; however, arrays restore sanity to the situation. The items in an array are called *elements*, and for any particular array, all of the elements must be of the same type. The type can be any primitive or reference type. For instance, we can have an array of test scores, an array of names, or even an array of student objects. Figure 9-1 illustrates these ideas. In the figure, each array contains five elements, or has a *length* of five. The first element in the array `test` is referred to as `test[0]`, the second as `test[1]`, and so on. Here we encounter Java's convention of numbering starting with 0 rather than 1, a convention that is guaranteed to cause us grief whenever we accidentally revert to our lifelong habit of counting from 1. Thus, the elements in an array of length 100 are numbered from 0 to 99. An item's position within an array is called its *index* or *subscript*. In Figure 9-1, the array indexes appear within square brackets (`[ ]`).

FIGURE 9-1

Three arrays, each containing five elements

	Array of five integers called **test**		Array of five strings called **name**		Array of five characters called **grade**	
1st	85	test[0]	"Bill"	name[0]	'B'	grade[0]
2nd	100	test[1]	"Sue"	name[1]	'C'	grade[1]
3rd	75	test[2]	"Grace"	name[2]	'B'	grade[2]
4th	87	test[3]	"Tom"	name[3]	'A'	grade[3]
5th	68	test[4]	"John"	name[4]	'C'	grade[4]

EXERCISE 9.1

1. A program needs many variables to store and process data. How does an array solve this problem?
   same name diff index

2. How does the programmer access an item in an array? *through index*

3. Mary is using an array of doubles to store an employee's wage amounts for each day of the week (Monday through Friday). Draw a picture of this array with sample items and references to each one.

days (or days) 2   3

$6	$3	$8	$3.	$3.

9.2 Simple Array Manipulations

The mechanics of manipulating arrays are fairly straightforward, as illustrated in the following segments of code. First, we declare and instantiate an array of 500 integer values. (Section 9.4 discusses array declarations in greater detail.) By default, all of the values are initialized to 0:

```
int[] abc = new int[500];
```

Next, we declare some other variables:

```
int i = 3;
int temp;
double avFirstFive;
```

The basic syntax for referring to an array element has the form

```
<array name>[<index>]
```

where `<index>` must be between 0 and the array's length less 1. The subscript operator (`[ ]`) has the same precedence as the method selector (`.`). To illustrate, we assign values to the first five elements:

```
abc[0] = 78;                      // 1st element 78
abc[1] = 66;                      // 2nd element 66
abc[2] = (abc[0] + abc[1]) / 2;   // 3rd element average of first two
abc[i] = 82;                      // 4th element 82 because i is 3
abc[i + 1] = 94;                  // 5th element 94 because i + 1 is 4
```

When assigning a value to the 500th element, we must remember that its index is 499, not 500:

```
abc[499] = 76;                    // 500th element 76
```

Fortunately, the JVM checks the values of subscripts before using them and throws an `ArrayIndexOutOfBoundsException` if they are out of bounds (less than 0 or greater than the array length less 1). The detection of a ***range-bound error*** is similar to the JVM's behavior when a program attempts to divide by 0.

In our present example, subscripts must be between 0 and 499. Later in the chapter, we show how to work with arrays of any size and how to write loops that are not tied to a literal value (in this case, 500).

```
abc[-1] = 74;              // NO! NO! NO! Out of bounds
abc[500] = 88;             // NO! NO! NO! Out of bounds
```

To compute the average of the first five elements, we could write

```
avFirstFive = (abc[0] + abc[1] + abc[2] + abc[3] + abc[4])/5;
```

It often happens that we need to interchange elements in an array. To demonstrate, following is code that interchanges any two adjacent elements:

```
// Initializations
. . .
abc[3] = 82;
abc[4] = 95;
i = 3;
. . .

// Interchange adjacent elements
temp = abc[i];                    // temp      now equals 82
abc[i] = abc[i + 1];              // abc[i]    now equals 95
abc[i + 1] = temp;               // abc[i + 1] now equals 82
```

We frequently need to know an array's length, but we do not have to remember it. The array itself makes this information available by means of a public instance variable called length:

```
System.out.println ("The size of abc is: " + abc.length);
```

EXERCISE 9.2

1. Assume that the array a contains the five integers 34, 23, 67, 89, and 12. Write the values of the following expressions:

   a. a[1] = 23

   b. a[a.length – 1] = 12

   c. a[2] + a[3] 67 + 89 = 156

2. What happens when a program attempts to access an item at an index that is less than 0 or greater than or equal to the array's length?

   OUT OF BOUNDS ERROR

9.3 Looping Through Arrays

There are many situations in which it is necessary to write a loop that iterates through an array one element at a time. Following are some examples based on the array abc of 500 integers. Later in this section, we show how to work with arrays of any size and how to write loops that are not tied to a literal value (in this case, 500).

Sum the Elements

The following is code that sums the numbers in the array abc. Each time through the loop we add a different element to the sum. On the first iteration we add abc[0] and on the last abc[499].

```
int sum;
sum = 0;
for (int i = 0; i < 500; i++)
   sum += abc[i];
```

Count the Occurrences

We can determine how many times a number x occurs in the array by comparing x to each element and incrementing count every time there is a match:

```
int x;
int count;
x = ...;                          // Assign some value to x
count = 0;
for (int i = 0; i < 500; i++){
   if (abc[i] == x)
      count++;                    // Found another element equal to x
}
```

Determine Presence or Absence

To determine if a particular number is present in the array, we could count the occurrences, but, alternatively, we could save time by breaking out of the loop as soon as the first match is found. The following is code based on this idea. The Boolean variable found indicates the outcome of the search:

```
int x;
boolean found;
x = ...;
found = false;              // Initially assume x is not present
for (int i = 0; i < 500; i++){
   if (abc[i] == x){
      found = true;
      break;                // No point in continuing once x is found
   }                        // so break out of the loop
}
if (found)
```

```
      System.out.println("Found");
else
      System.out.println("Not Found");
```

Determine First Location

As a variation on the preceding example, we now show how to find the first location of x in the array. The variable loc initially equals –1, meaning that we have not found x yet. We then iterate through the array, comparing each element to x. As soon as we find a match, we set loc to the location and break out of the loop. If x is not found, loc remains equal to –1.

```
int x;
int loc;
x = ...;
loc = -1;
for (int i = 0; i < 500; i++){
   if (abc[i] == x){
      loc = i;
      break;
   }
}
if (loc == -1)
   System.out.println("Not Found");
else
   System.out.println("Found at index " + loc);
```

Working with Arrays of Any Size

The examples in this section have assumed that the array contains 500 elements. It is possible and also desirable to write similar code that works with arrays of any size, however. We simply replace the literal 500 with a reference to the array's instance variable length in each of the loops. For example, this code would sum the integers in an array of any size:

```
int sum;
sum = 0;
for (int i = 0; i < abc.length; i++)
   sum += abc[i];
```

EXERCISE 9.3

1. Write a loop that prints all of the items in an array a to the terminal screen.

for (x=0, x< length ;x++)
System.out.println (x)

2. Repeat Question 1 but print the items in reverse order.

3. Write a loop that locates the first occurrence of a negative integer in an array a. When the loop is finished, the variable index should contain the index of the negative number or the length of the array if there were no negative numbers in the array.

for (x = array.length -1; x<=0; x--)
System.out.println (x)

EXERCISE 9.3 Continued

4. Describe what the following code segments do:

a.
```
for (int i = 0; i < a.length; i++)
   a[i] = Math.abs(a[i]);
```
gives the pos value of array elements

b.
```
String str = "";
for (int i = 0; i < a.length; i++)
   str += a[i];
```
makes a null string

5. What is the advantage of using the instance variable `length` in a loop with an array?

If you don't know length – will never get OOT OF Bounds error!

9.4 Declaring Arrays

Earlier, we declared an array of 500 integers as follows:

```
int[] abc = new int[500];
```

In doing so, we combined two separate statements:

```
int[] abc;            // Declare abc to be a variable that can
                      // reference an array of integers.
abc = new int[500];   // Instantiate an array of 500 integers for abc to
                      // reference.
```

Arrays are objects and must be instantiated before being used. Several array variables can be declared in a single statement like this:

```
int[] abc, xyz;
abc = new int[500];
xyz = new int[10];
```

or like this:

```
int[] abc = new int[500], xyz = new int[10];
```

Array variables are `null` before they are assigned array objects. Failure to assign an array object can result in a null pointer exception, as shown in the next code segment:

```
int[] abc;
abc[1] = 10;   // run-time error: null pointer exception
```

Because arrays are objects, two variables can refer to the same array, as indicated in Figure 9-2 and the next segment of code:

```
int[] abc, xyz;
abc = new int[5];                       // Instantiate an array of five
                                        // integers
xyz = abc;                              // xyz and abc refer to the same array
xyz[3] = 100;                           // Changing xyz changes abc as well.
System.out.println (abc[3]);            // 100 is displayed.
```

FIGURE 9-2
Two variables can refer to the same array object

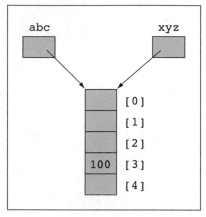

If we want abc and xyz to refer to two separate arrays that happen to contain the same values, we could copy all of the elements from one array to the other, as follows:

```
int[] abc, xyz;              // Declare two array variables
int i;
abc = new int[10];           // Instantiate an array of size 10
for (i = 0; i < 10; i++)     // Initialize the array
    abc[i] = i*i;            // a[0]=0 and a[1]=1 and a[2]=4, etc.

xyz = new int[10];           // Instantiate another array of size 10
for (i = 0; i < 10; i++)     // Initialize the second array
    xyz[i] = abc[i];
```

Also, because arrays are objects, Java's garbage collector sweeps them away when they are no longer referenced:

```
int[] abc, xyz;
abc = new int[10];    // Instantiate an array of 10 integers.
xyz = new int[5];     // Instantiate an array of 5 integers.
xyz = null;           // The array of 5 integers is no longer referenced
                      // so the garbage collector will sweep it away.
```

Arrays can be declared, instantiated, and initialized in one step. The list of numbers between the braces is called an *initializer list*.

```
int[] abc = {1,2,3,4,5}; // abc now references an array of five integers.
```

As mentioned at the outset, arrays can be formed from any collection of similar items. Following then are arrays of doubles, characters, Booleans, strings, and students:

```
double[]   ddd = new double[10];
char[]     ccc = new char[10];
boolean[]  bbb = new boolean[10];
String[]   ggg = new String[10];
Student[]  sss = new Student[10];
String     str;

ddd[5] = 3.14;
ccc[5] = 'Z';
bbb[5] = true;
ggg[5] = "The cat sat on the mat.";
sss[5] = new Student();

sss[5].setName ("Bill");
str = sss[5].getName() + ggg[5].substring(7);
   // str now equals "Bill sat on the mat."
```

There is one more way to declare array variables, but its use can be confusing. Here it is:

```
int aaa[];             // aaa is an array variable.
```

That does not look confusing, but what about this?

```
int aaa[], bbb, ccc[]; // aaa and ccc are array variables.
                       // bbb is not. This fact might go unnoticed.
```

Instead, it might be better to write:

```
int[] aaa, ccc;        // aaa and ccc are array variables
int bbb;               // bbb is not. This fact is obvious.
```

Once an array is instantiated, its size cannot be changed, so make sure the array is large enough from the outset.

EXERCISE 9.4

1. Declare and instantiate array variables for the following data:
   a. An array of 15 doubles
   b. An array of 20 strings

double y = new double [15]
string y = new String [20] "

2. What is an initializer list?

brackets with each ele of array sep by commas!

EXERCISE 9.4 Continued

3. Use an initializer list to create the following arrays:
   a. five test scores of 100, 90, 75, 60, and 88
   b. three interest rates of 0.12, 0.05, and 0.15
   c. two strings, your first name and last name

4. Why is it better to use the form `<type>[] <variable>` instead of `<type> <variable>[]` when declaring an array variable?

9.5 Working with Arrays That Are Not Full

When an array is instantiated, the computer automatically fills its cells with default values. For example, each cell in an array of `int` initially contains the value 0. The application then replaces these values with new ones as needed. An application might not use all the cells available in an array, however. For example, one might create an array of 20 ints but receive only 5 ints from interactive input. This array has a *physical size* of 20 cells but a *logical size* of 5 cells currently used by the application. From the application's perspective, the remaining 15 cells contain garbage. Clearly, the application should only access the first five cells when asked to display the data, so using the array's physical size as an upper bound on a loop will not do. We solve this problem by tracking the array's logical size with a separate integer variable. The following code segment shows the initial state of an array and its logical size:

```
int[] abc = new int[50];
int size = 0;
```

Note that `abc.length` (the physical size) is 50, whereas `size` (the logical size) is 0.

Processing Elements in an Array That Is Not Full

In Section 9.3, we showed how to generalize a loop to process all the data in an array of any size. The loop accesses each cell from position 0 to position `length - 1`, where `length` is the array's instance variable. When the array is not full, one must replace the array's physical length with its logical size in the loop. Following is the code for computing the sum of the integers currently available in the array `abc`:

```
int[] abc = new int[50];
int size = 0;

... code that puts values into some initial portion of the array and sets
    the value of size ...

int sum = 0;
for (int i = 0; i < size; i++)
   sum += abc[i];
```

Adding Elements to an Array

The simplest way to add a data element to an array is to place it after the last available item. One must first check to see if there is a cell available and then remember to increment the array's logical size. The following code shows how to add an integer to the end of array `abc`:

```
if (size < abc.length){
   abc[size] = anInt;
   size++;
}
```

When `size` equals `abc.length`, the array is full. The `if` statement prevents a range error from occurring. Remember that Java arrays are of fixed size when they are instantiated, so eventually they become full. We examine a way of skirting this limitation of arrays in Chapter 11.

We can also insert an element at an earlier position in the array. This process requires a shifting of other elements and is also presented in Chapter 11.

Removing Elements from an Array

Removing a data element from the end of an array requires no change to the array itself. We simply decrement the logical size, thus preventing the application from accessing the garbage elements beyond that point. (Removing a data element from an arbitrary position is discussed in Chapter 11.)

Arrays and Text Files

We conclude this section with two short programs that use arrays in conjunction with text files. The first program prompts the user for integers and inserts them at the logical end of an array. This process stops when the user enters –1 as input or when the array becomes full. The program then outputs the contents of the array to a text file. Here is the code:

```java
// Example 9.1: Input numbers from the keyboard into an array and
// output the array's numbers to a text file

import java.io.*;
import java.util.Scanner;

public class ArrayToFile{

    public static void main(String[] args) throws IOException {
        // Set up scanner and array
        Scanner reader = new Scanner(System.in);
        int[] array = new int[10];
        int count = 0;

        // Input numbers until full or user enters -1
        while (count < array.length){
            System.out.print("Enter a number (-1 to quit): ");
            int number = reader.nextInt();
            if (number == -1)
                break;
            array[count] = number;
            count++;
        }
```

```
      // Output the numbers to a text file
      PrintWriter writer = new PrintWriter(new File("numbers.txt"));
      for (int i = 0; i < count; i++)
         writer.println(array[i]);
      writer.close();
   }
}
```

The critical variable in this first example is count. This variable tracks the number of numbers input as well as the logical size of the array. The output loop also uses count to test for the logical end of the array.

Our second example program reads numbers from a text file, inserts them into an array, and then displays them in the terminal window. If there is not enough room in the array, an error message is also displayed.

```
// Example 9.2: Input numbers from a file into an array and
// output the array's numbers to the terminal window

import java.io.*;
import java.util.Scanner;

public class FileToArray{

   public static void main(String[] args) throws IOException {
      // Set up scanner and array
      Scanner reader = new Scanner(new File("numbers.txt"));
      int[] array = new int[10];
      int count = 0;

      // Input numbers until full or end of file is reached
      while (count < array.length  && reader.hasNext()){
         int number = reader.nextInt();
         array[count] = number;
         count++;
      }

      // Output the numbers to the terminal window
      for (int i = 0; i < count; i++)
         System.out.println(array[i]);

      // Display error message if not all data are read from file
      if (reader.hasNext())
         System.out.println("Some data lost during input");
   }
}
```

Once again, the critical variable is count, which tracks the number of integers input from the file and the number of integers stored in the array. Arrays that receive data from input are often only partially filled. In extreme cases, an array might not be large enough to hold the number of inputs offered. We examine techniques for dealing with this problem in Chapter 11.

EXERCISE 9.5

1. What happens when the programmer tries to access an array cell whose index is greater than or equal to its logical size?   *array out of bounds error*

2. Describe an application that uses an array that might not be full.   *class enrollment?*

9.6 Parallel Arrays

There are situations in which it is convenient to declare what are called *parallel arrays*. Suppose we want to keep a list of people's names and ages. This can be achieved by using two arrays in which corresponding elements are related. For instance

```
String[] name = {"Bill", "Sue", "Shawn", "Mary", "Ann"};
int[]    age  = {20    , 21   , 19     , 24    , 20};
```

Thus, Bill's age is 20 and Mary's is 24. Note that related items have the same index. There are many other uses for parallel arrays, but continuing on with our present example, the following is a segment of code that finds the age of a particular person:

```
String searchName;
int correspondingAge = -1;

searchName = ...;                              // Set this to the desired name
for (int i = 0; i < name.length; i++){ // name.length is the array's size
   if (searchName.equals (name[i])){
      correspondingAge = age[i];
      break;
   }
}

if (correspondingAge == -1)
   System.out.println(searchName + " not found.");
else
   System.out.println("The age is " + correspondingAge);
```

In this example, the parallel arrays are both full and the loops use the instance variable `length`. When the arrays are not full, the code will need an extra variable to track their logical sizes, as discussed earlier.

EXERCISE 9.6

1. What are parallel arrays?   *2 arrays with related corresponding elements*

2. Describe an application in which parallel arrays might be used.   *name/age   name/addr*

3. Declare and instantiate the variables for parallel arrays to track the names, ages, and social security numbers of 50 employees.

String name = new String [50]
int ages = new int [50]
int ssn = new int [50]

for (int N=0; 4 < 50; X++)
System.out.println (name[x] + " " + number[x]);

EXERCISE 9.6 Continued

4. Assume that the array `names` contains the names of people in a phone book and the parallel array `numbers` contains their phone numbers. Write a code segment that displays each name and number in formatted columns (using the method `printf` introduced in Chapter 7). Names should be left-justified in a width of 20 columns. You may assume that each number is the same length.

5. Write a code segment that creates parallel arrays containing the first 10 nonnegative powers of 2. One array should contain the exponent and the other array should contain 2 raised to that power.

int exp = new int [10]
int power = new int [10]

9.7 Two-Dimensional Arrays

for (x=0; x < exp.length; x++)
exp[x] = x;
power[x] = pow(2,x);

The arrays we have been studying so far can represent only simple lists of items and are called *one-dimensional arrays*. For many applications, *multidimensional arrays* are more useful. A table of numbers, for instance, can be implemented as a *two-dimensional array*. Figure 9-3 shows a two-dimensional array with four rows and five columns.

FIGURE 9-3
A two-dimensional array with four rows and five columns

	col 0	col 1	col 2	col 3	col 4
row 0	00	01	02	03	04
row 1	10	11	12	13	14
row 2	20	21	22	23	24
row 3	30	31	32	33	34

Suppose we call the array `table`; then to indicate an element in `table`, we specify its row and column position, remembering that indexes start at 0:

```
x = table[2][3];   // Set x to 23, the value in (row 2, column 3)
```

Sum the Elements

The techniques for manipulating one-dimensional arrays are easily extended to two-dimensional arrays. For instance, the following is code that sums all the numbers in `table`. The outer loop iterates four times and moves down the rows. Each time through the outer loop, the inner loop iterates five times and moves across a different row.

```
int sum = 0;
for (int i = 0; i < 4; i++){     // There are four rows: i = 0,1,2,3
   for (int j = 0; j < 5; j++){ // There are five columns: j = 0,1,2,3,4
      sum += table[i][j];
   }
}
```

This segment of code can be rewritten without using the numbers 4 and 5. The value `table.length` equals the number of rows, and `table[i].length` is the number of columns in row i.

```
int sum = 0;
for (int i = 0; i < table.length; i++){
   for (int j = 0; j < table[i].length; j++){
      sum += table[i][j];
   }
}
```

Sum the Rows

Rather than accumulate all the numbers into a single sum, we now compute the sum of each row separately and place the results in a one-dimensional array called rowSum. This array has four elements, one for each row of the table. The elements in rowSum are initialized to 0 automatically by virtue of the declaration.

```
int[] rowSum = new int[4];
for (int i = 0; i < table.length; i++){
   for (int j = 0; j < table[i].length; j++){
      rowSum[i] += table[i][j];
   }
}
```

Declare and Instantiate

Declaring and instantiating two-dimensional arrays is accomplished by extending the processes used for one-dimensional arrays:

```
int[][] table;              // The variable table can reference a
                            // two-dimensional array of integers.
table = new int[4][5];      // Instantiate table as an array of size 4,
                            // each of whose elements will reference an array
                            // of 5 integers.
```

Figure 9-4 shows another diagram of `table` that illustrates the perspective revealed in the previous piece of code. The variable `table` references an array of four elements. Each of these elements in turn references an array of five integers. Although the diagram is complex, specifying an element in the resulting two-dimensional array is the same as before, for instance, `table[2][3]`.

FIGURE 9-4
Another way of visualizing a two-dimensional array

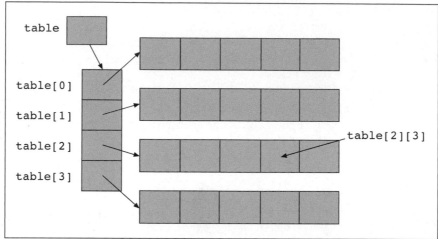

Initializer lists can be used with two-dimensional arrays. This requires a list of lists. The number of inner lists determines the number of rows, and the size of each inner list determines the size of the corresponding row. The rows do not have to be the same size, but they are in this example:

```
int[][] table = {{ 0, 1, 2, 3, 4},      // row 0
                 {10,11,12,13,14},      // row 1
                 {20,21,22,23,24},      // row 2
                 {30,31,32,33,34}};     // row 3
```

Variable Length Rows

Occasionally, the rows of a two-dimensional array are not all the same length. We call these *ragged arrays*, and we just mention them in passing. Consider the following improbable declaration:

```
int[][] table;
table    = new int[4][];   // table has 4 rows
table[0] = new int[6];     // row 0 has 6   elements
table[1] = new int[10];    // row 1 has 10  elements
table[2] = new int[100];   // row 2 has 100 elements
table[3] = new int[1];     // row 3 has 1   element
```

Finally, remember that all the elements of a two-dimensional array must be of the same type, whether they are integers, doubles, strings, or whatever.

EXERCISE 9.7

1. What are two-dimensional arrays? *an array of arrays*

2. Describe an application in which a two-dimensional array might be used. *spreadsheets*

3. Write a code segment that searches a two-dimensional array for a negative integer. The loop should terminate at the first instance of a negative integer in the array, and the variables `row` and `col` should be set to its position. Otherwise, the variables `row` and `col` should equal the number of rows and columns in the array (we assume that each row has the same number of columns). *2 for loops with row & col*

4. Describe the contents of the array after the following code segment is run:

```
int [][] matrix = new int[5][5];

for (int row = 0; row < matrix.length; row++)
    for (int col = 0; col < matrix[row].length; col++)
        matrix[row][col] = row * col;
```

Handwritten table:

	0	1	2	3	4
0	0	0	0	0	0
1	0	1	2	3	4
2	0	2	4	6	8
3	0	3	6	9	12
4	0	4	8	12	16

9.8 Using the Enhanced for Loop

Most of the loops used with arrays follow common patterns, such as visiting every element from the first position to the last one, or visiting elements until a particular element is found. These loops require the use of an index variable, which is initialized to the first position. They must then test the index for less than the last position to continue. Finally, they must increment the index on each pass. Java 5.0 provides an *enhanced* `for` *loop* that frees the programmer from managing these details. This type of loop visits each element in an array from the first position to the last position. On each pass through the loop, the element at the current position is automatically assigned to a temporary variable. No other loop control information is required.

The syntax of the enhanced `for` loop is much simpler than that of the standard `for` loop:

```
for (<temporary variable declaration> : <array object>)
    <statement>
```

The type of the temporary variable must be compatible with the element type of the array.

To see how the enhanced `for` loop can simplify code, let's modify two earlier examples where we computed the sum of an array of integers and the sum of a two-dimensional array of integers. We place the revised code segments in a short tester program, which should display the results 9 and 27 for the two arrays:

```
// Example 9.3: Testing the enhanced for loop

public class TestForLoop{

    public static void main(String[] args){

        // Sum the elements in a one-dimensional array
        int[] abc = {2, 3, 4};
        int sum = 0;
```

```
      for (int element : abc)
         sum += element;
      System.out.println("First sum: " + sum);

      // Sum the elements in a two-dimensional array
      int[][] table = {{2, 3, 4}, {2, 3, 4}, {2, 3, 4}};
      sum = 0;
      for (int[]row : table)
         for (int element : row)
            sum += element;
      System.out.println("Second sum: " + sum);
   }
}
```

On each pass through the first loop, the integer at the current position in the array abc is automatically assigned to the temporary variable element. On each pass through the second loop, the two-dimensional array's current row is assigned to the temporary variable row. The nested loop then iterates through this array, assigning each integer at the current column position to another temporary variable element.

A break statement can also be used when we want to terminate an enhanced for loop early. For example, we can revise our earlier example of a search loop as follows:

```
int x = ...;
boolean found = false;        // Initially assume x is not present
for (int element : abc){
   if (element == x){
      found = true;
      break;                  // No point in continuing once x is found
   }                          // so break out of the loop
}
if (found)
   System.out.println("Found");
else
   System.out.println("Not Found");
```

An enhanced for loop is clearly simpler to write than a standard for loop with an index. The enhanced for loop is also less error-prone because Java automates the setup and processing of the loop control information. However, this type of loop *cannot* be used to

- Move through an array in reverse, from the last position to the first position

- Assign elements to positions in an array

- Track the index position of the current element in an array

- Access any element other than the current element on each pass

All of these options require a loop with an index. In general, it's also not a good idea to use an enhanced for loop on an array that's not filled. Therefore, if you choose an enhanced for loop, be sure that the array is filled, that you're going to visit each element from the first to the last, and that you do not need to assign a value to an element at a given position.

EXERCISE 9.8

1. Assume that array `abc` is filled with strings. Convert the following loops to simpler versions using the enhanced `for` loop:

a.

```
for (int i = 0; i < abc.length; i++)
    System.out.println(abc[i]);
```

b.

```
String target = …;
    boolean found = false;
    for (int i = 0; i < abc.length; i++)
      if (target.equals(abc[i])){
        found = true;
        break;
      }
```

2. List two different problems for which an enhanced `for` loop would not be appropriate.

9.9 Arrays and Methods

When any object is used as a parameter to a method, what actually gets passed is a reference to the object and not the object itself, as illustrated in Figure 9-5. In other words, the actual and formal parameters refer to the same object, and changes the method makes to the object's state are still in effect after the method terminates. In the figure, the method changes the student's name to Bill, and after the method finishes executing the name is still Bill.

FIGURE 9-5
Passing a reference to an object as a parameter

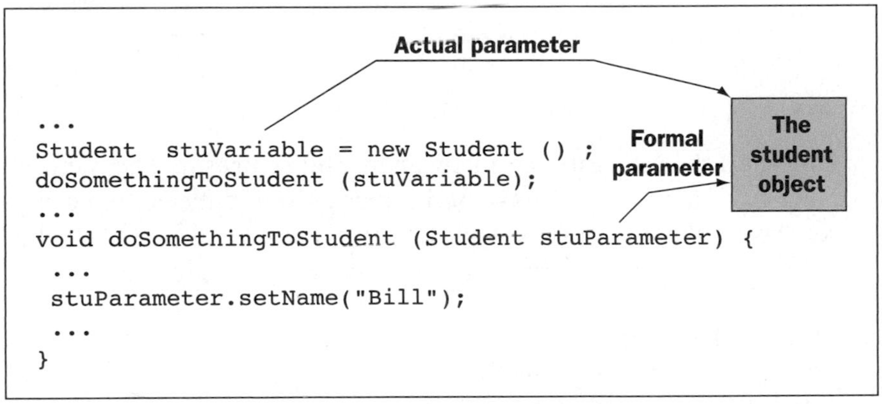

Arrays are objects, so the same rules apply. When an array is passed as a parameter to a method, the method manipulates the array itself and not a copy. Changes made to the array in the method are still in effect after the method has completed its execution. Consequently, passing an array to a method leads to trouble if the method accidentally mishandles the array. A method can also instantiate a new object or a new array and return it using the `return` statement. Following are some illustrations based on examples presented earlier.

Sum the Elements

First, we look at a method that computes the sum of the numbers in an integer array. When the method is written, there is no need to know the array's size. The method works equally well with integer arrays of all sizes, as long as those arrays are full; however, the method cannot be used with arrays of other types, for instance, doubles. Notice that the method makes no changes to the array and therefore is "safe."

```
int sum (int[] a){
   int result = 0;
   for (int element : a)
      result += element;
   return result;
}
```

Using the method is straightforward:

```
int[] array1 = {10, 24, 16, 78, -55, 89, 65};
int[] array2 = {4334, 22928, 33291};
...
if (sum(array1) > sum(array2)) ...
```

Search for a Value

The code to search an array for a value is used so frequently in programs that it is worth placing in a method. Following is a method to search an array of integers. The method returns the location of the first array element equal to the search value or –1 if the value is absent:

```
int search (int[] a, int searchValue){
   for (int i = 0; i < a.length; i++)
      if (a[i] == searchValue)
         return i;
   return -1;
}
```

Sum the Rows

Following is a method that instantiates a new array and returns it. The method computes the sum of each row in a two-dimensional array and returns a one-dimensional array of row sums. The method works even if the rows are not all the same size. We also rely on the fact that Java provides a default value of 0 at each position in the new array.

```
int[] sumRows (int[][] a){
   int[] rowSum = new int[a.length];
   for (int i = 0; i < a.length; i++){
      for (int j = 0; j < a[i].length; j++){
         rowSum[i] += a[i][j];
      }
   }
   return rowSum;
}
```

Following is code that uses the method. Notice that we do not have to instantiate the array oneD because that task is done in the method sumRows.

```
int[][] twoD = {{1,2,3,4}, {5,6}, {7,8,9}};
int[] oneD;

oneD = sumRows (twoD); // oneD now references the array created and
                       // returned by the method sumRows.
                       // It equals {10, 11, 24}
```

Copy an Array

Earlier, we saw that copying an array must be done with care. Assigning one array variable to another does not do the job. It merely yields two variables referencing the same array. We now examine a method that attempts to solve the problem. The first parameter represents the original array, and the second is the copy. The original is instantiated before the method is called, and the copy is instantiated in the method.

```
void copyOne(int[] original, int[] copy){
   copy = new int[original.length];
   for (int i = 0; i < original.length; i++){
      copy[i] = original[i];
   }
}
```

We now run this method in the following code segment:

```
int[] orig = {1,2,3,4,5};
int[] cp;
...
copyOne (orig, cp);
```

When copyOne terminates, we would like the variable cp to refer to copy. However, that does not happen. Even though the method creates a copy of the original array and assigns it to the array parameter (copy = new int[original.length];), the original variable cp is not changed and does not refer to the array created in the method. We can achieve our goal more successfully by writing a method that returns a copy. We then call the method and assign the returned copy to cp. Following is the code:

```
// First the method
int[] copyTwo (int[] original){
   int[] copy = new int[original.length];
   for (int i = 0; i < original.length; i++){
      copy[i] = original[i];
   }
   return copy;
}

// And here is how we call it.
int[] orig = {1,2,3,4,5};
int[] cp = copyTwo (orig);
```

EXERCISE 9.9

1. What happens when one uses the assignment operator (=) with two array variables?

2. Discuss the issues involved with copying an array.

3. Write a method that returns the average of the numbers in an array of `double`.

4. Write a method `subArray` that expects an array of `int` and two `ints` as parameters. The integers represent the starting position and the ending position of a subarray within the parameter array. The method should return a new array that contains the elements from the starting position to the ending position.

5. Write a method that searches a two-dimensional array for a given integer. This method should return an object of class `Point`, which contains a row and a column. The constructor for `Point` is `Point(anInteger, anInteger)`.

9.10 Arrays of Objects

We examined the use of an array of strings earlier in this chapter. Arrays can hold objects of any type, or more accurately, references to objects. For example, one can declare, instantiate, and fill an array of students (see Chapter 5) as follows:

```
// Declare and reserve 10 cells for student objects
Student[] studentArray = new Student[10];

// Fill array with students
for (int i = 0; i < studentArray.length; i++)
    studentArray[i] = new Student("Student " + i, 70+i, 80+i, 90+i);
```

When an array of objects is instantiated, each cell is `null` by default until reset to a new object. The next code segment prints the average of all students in the `studentArray`. Pay special attention to the technique used to send a message to each object in the array:

```
// Print the average of all students in the array.
int sum = 0;
for (Student s : studentArray)
    sum += s.getAverage();              // Send message to object in array
System.out.println("The class average is " + sum / studentArray.length);
```

EXERCISE 9.10

1. Write a method `getHighStudent` that expects an array of students as a parameter. The method returns the `Student` object that contains the highest score. You may assume that the `Student` class has a method `getHighScore()`. (*Hint*: The method should declare a local variable of type `Student` to track the student with the highest score. The initial value of this variable should be `null`.)

EXERCISE 9.10 Continued

2. What happens when the following code segment is executed?

```
// Declare and reserve 10 cells for student objects
Student[] studentArray = new Student[10];

// Add 5 students to the array
for (int i = 0; i < 5; i++)
    studentArray[i] = new Student("Student " + i, 70+i, 80+i, 90+i);

// Print the names of the students
for (int i = 0; i < studentArray.length; i++)
    System.out.println(studentArray[i].getName());
```

CASE STUDY: Student Test Scores Again

In Chapter 5 we developed a program for keeping track of student test scores. We now build on that program in two ways:

1. We extend the program so that it allows the user to maintain information on many students.

2. We modify the student class so that the grades are stored in an array rather than in separate instance variables.

Both changes illustrate the use of arrays to maintain lists of data.

Request

Modify the student test scores program from Chapter 5 so that it allows the user to maintain information on many students.

Analysis

The user interface for this program should allow the user to enter information for a new student, edit existing information, and navigate through the database of students to access each student's information. The student records are arranged in a linear sequence in the database, so the interface allows the user to navigate through this sequence. In addition, the interface should display the overall class average and the student with the highest score on demand. A menu-driven interface will work well. Here are the menu options:

1. Display the current student

2. Display the class average

3. Display the student with the highest grade

4. Display all of the students

5. Edit the current student

6. Add a new student

7. Move to the first student

8. Move to the last student

9. Move to the next student

10. Move to the previous student

11. Quit the program

Each option runs a command, displays the results, and waits for the user to press the Enter key before returning to the menu. When the menu is displayed, the program also displays the number of students currently in the database and the index position of the current student.

Because the user interface and the data are complex, we use the model/view pattern introduced in Chapter 5 to structure our code. The view class, called `TestScoresView`, is responsible for displaying the menu and handling interactions with the user. The model classes, called `Student` and `TestScoresModel`, are responsible for managing the students' data. A simple "application" class, called `TestScoresApp`, starts the application in a `main` method by instantiating the view and the model.

Our system is in fact complex enough that it would help to diagram the relationships among its classes. Figure 9-6 shows a *UML diagram* that depicts these relationships. UML, which stands for Unified Modeling Language, is a graphical notation developed by software professionals to design and document object-oriented systems. As you can see, the name of each class appears in a box. Various types of connecting lines designate the relationships between the classes. A dashed line ending in a solid arrow indicates that one class simply depends on another. Thus, `TestScoresApp` depends on both `TestScoresView` and `TestScoresModel`. A solid line ending in a diamond indicates that the class nearest the diamond contains and is in part composed of the class at the other end. The numbers that label these lines show the number of instances of the contained class. These numbers can be simple, indicating a fixed number, or a range from one simple number to another, or a star (*), which means zero or more. Thus, `TestScoresView` contains exactly one `TestScoresModel` object, whereas `TestScoresModel` contains any of 0 through 10 `Student` objects.

FIGURE 9-6
A UML diagram of the classes in the student test scores program

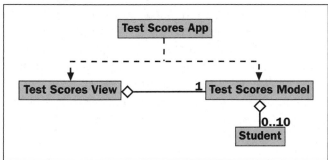

Design of the Data Model

We break the design into two parts, one for each set of classes used in the program.

For this program we make two major changes to the `Student` class described in Chapter 5:

1. The three test scores are stored in an array. This provides more flexibility than did the use of a separate instance variable for each test score and allows clients to use the class to deal with a larger number of scores.

2. The `Student` class provides a `validateData` method. Now any application that needs to validate student data can do so easily. For variety, the approach taken to data validation is somewhat different than that used in the `Employee` class of Chapter 6. If the validation code is placed in the user interface class, it would need to be repeated in every user interface that works with student objects, an approach that is wasteful, tedious, and difficult to maintain.

The `TestScoresModel` class represents the database of students. Viewed as a black box, it provides an interface or set of public methods listed in Table 9.1.

TABLE 9-1
Public methods of `TestScoresModel`

METHOD	WHAT IT DOES
`int size()`	Returns the number of students in the database
`int currentPosition()`	Returns the index position of the current student
`Student currentStudent()`	If the database is empty, returns `null`, otherwise returns the current student
`String toString()`	Returns a string containing the string representations of all of the students
`int getClassAverage()`	Returns the average of all of the scores in the database
`Student getHighScore()`	If the database is empty, returns `null`; otherwise, returns the first student with the highest score in the database
`String add(Student s)`	If there is not room for the new student, returns an error message; otherwise, adds `s` to the end of the database, makes the last position current, and returns `null`
`String replace(Student s)`	If the database is empty, returns an error message; otherwise, replaces the student at the current position with `s` and returns `null`
`Student first()`	If the database is empty, returns `null`; otherwise, moves to the first student and returns that student
`Student last()`	If the database is empty, returns `null`; otherwise, moves to the last student and returns that student
`Student next()`	If the database is empty, returns `null`; otherwise, if the current student is the last one, returns that student; otherwise, moves to the next student and returns that student
`Student previous()`	If the database is empty, returns `null`; otherwise, if the current student is the first one, returns that student; otherwise, moves to the previous student and returns that student

Note that we have set up the class's interface to make the management of data as easy as possible for its users (easier, at any rate, than it would be to directly manipulate an array). The following short tester program shows how the database of students might be used:

```
// Case Study 9.1: A tester program for TestScoresModel

public class TestModel{

    public static void main (String[] args){
```

```
// Create and display an empty model
TestScoresModel model = new TestScoresModel();
System.out.println(model);

// Display the size, current position, and current student
System.out.println(model.size());
System.out.println(model.currentPosition());
System.out.println(model.currentStudent());

// Add and display 3 students
for (int i = 1; i <= 3; i++){
   Student s = new Student("S" + i);
   model.add(s);
}
System.out.println(model);

// Move to the first student and display it
System.out.println(model.first());

// Move to the next and previous and display them
System.out.println(model.next());
System.out.println(model.previous());

// Move to the last and next and display them
System.out.println(model.last());
System.out.println(model.next());

// Display size, current position, and current student
System.out.println(model.size());
System.out.println(model.currentPosition());
System.out.println(model.currentStudent());

// Replace the current student and display the model
int[] grades = {99, 88, 77};
Student newStudent = new Student("Beth", grades);
model.replace(newStudent);
System.out.println(model);

// Add more students and display results
for (int i = 6; i <= 13; i++){
   Student s = new Student("S" + i);
   System.out.println(model.add(s));
}
   }
}
```

The `TestScoresModel` class maintains its data in three instance variables:

- An array of `Student` objects
- The selected index (an `int`)
- The current number of students (an `int`).

The use of a separate class to represent the database of students will allow us to choose among several different data structures for holding the students, without disturbing the view classes. We examine some other options for representing collections of objects in later chapters.

Design of the View and Application Classes

At program startup, the `main` method in the `TestScoresApp` class instantiates a `TestScoresModel` and passes it as a parameter to a new instance of `TestScoresView`. The constructor for `TestScoresView` then starts the main command loop. Here is the code for `TestScoresApp`:

```
// Case Study 9.1: The main application class

public class TestScoresApp{
   public static void main(String[] args){
      TestScoresModel model = new TestScoresModel();
      new TestScoresView(model);
   }
}
```

The `TestScoresView` class maintains a single instance variable for the database, of type `TestScoresModel`. The top-level method of `TestScoresModel` is called `run()`. This method runs the main command loop. Here is the pseudocode for method `run()`:

```
while (true)
   display the count and current index
   display the menu
   prompt for and input a command
   if the command is to quit then
      break
   run the command
   wait for the user to press Enter
```

Because some of these tasks, such as displaying the menu, getting a valid command number from the user, and running a command, are themselves complex, we can decompose them into separate, private helper methods. A refinement of the pseudocode shows how `run()` calls these methods:

```
while (true)
   display the count and current position
   displayMenu()
   command = getCommand("Enter a number [1-11]: ", 1, 11)
   if command == 11
      break
   runCommand(command)
```

`displayMenu()` simply displays the menu options in the terminal window.

`getCommand(aString, anInt, anInt)` expects the prompt and the smallest and largest command numbers as parameters. The method displays the prompt for input and attempts to read a number from the keyboard. If the input is a well-formed number and is within the range of valid command numbers, the method returns this number. Otherwise, the method displays an error message and repeats this process.

runCommand(anInt) expects a command number as a parameter. The method performs the appropriate task and waits for the user to press the Enter key. Some of the tasks are simple and require only one line of code, but others, such as adding a new student or editing an existing student, are complex enough to warrant further procedural decomposition.

Figure 9-7 shows a **structure chart** that depicts the relationships among the cooperating methods in the class TestScoresView. Needless to say, the single data model object is visible to all of these methods.

FIGURE 9-7
A structure chart for the methods of class TestScoresView

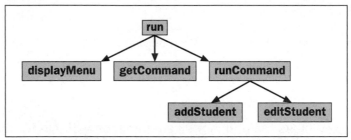

Procedural decomposition is a powerful design tool in situations where a problem calls for one or more complex tasks that operate on the same set of data.

Implementation of the Model

Following is the code for the classes Student and TestScoresModel. To save space we have kept comments to a minimum; however, we have used descriptive names for variables and methods and hope you will find the code fairly self-documenting. Pay special attention to the constructors in the Student class. Note the different options that they give the client for creating a student object and the manner in which chaining them simplifies their code.

```
// Case Study 9.1: Student class

public class Student {

    private String name;
    private int[] tests;

    // Default: name is "" and 3 scores are 0
    public Student(){
       this("");
    }

    // Default: name is nm and 3 scores are 0
    public Student(String nm){
       this(nm, 3);
    }

    // Name is nm and n scores are 0
    public Student(String nm, int n){
```

```java
      name = nm;
      tests = new int[n];
      for (int i = 0; i < tests.length; i++)
         tests[i] = 0;
   }

   // Name is nm and scores are int
   public Student(String nm, int[] t){
      name = nm;
      tests = new int[t.length];
      for (int i = 0; i < tests.length; i++)
         tests[i] = t[i];
   }

   // Builds a copy of s
   public Student(Student s){
      this(s.name, s.tests);
   }

   public void setName (String nm){
      name = nm;
   }

   public String getName (){
      return name;
   }

   public void setScore (int i, int score){
      tests[i - 1] = score;
   }

   public int getScore (int i){
      return tests[i - 1];
   }

   public int getAverage(){
      int sum = 0;
      for (int score : tests)
         sum += score;
      return sum / tests.length;
   }

   public int getHighScore(){
      int highScore = 0;
      for (int score : tests)
         highScore = Math.max (highScore, score);
      return highScore;
   }

   public String toString(){
      String str = "Name:     " + name  + "\n";
      for (int i = 0; i < tests.length; i++)
         str += "test " + i + ":   " + tests[i] + "\n";
      str += "Average: " + getAverage();
```

```java
         return str;
   }


   // Returns null if there are no errors else returns
   // an appropriate error message.
   public String validateData(){
      if (name.equals ("")) return "SORRY: name required";
      for (int score : tests){
         if (score < 0 || score > 100){
            String str = "SORRY: must have "+ 0
                          + " <= test score <= " + 100;
            return str;
         }
      }
      return null;
   }
}


// Case Study 9.1: TestScoresModel class

public class TestScoresModel{

   private Student[] students;          // Array of students
   private int indexSelectedStudent;    // Position of current student
   private int studentCount;            // Current number of students

   public TestScoresModel(){

      // Initialize the data
      indexSelectedStudent = -1;
      studentCount = 0;
      students = new Student[10];
   }


   // Mutator methods for adding and replacing students

   public String add(Student s){
      if (studentCount == students.length)
         return "SORRY: student list is full";
      else{
         students[studentCount] = s;
         indexSelectedStudent = studentCount;
         studentCount++;
         return null;
      }
   }

   public String replace(Student s){
      if (indexSelectedStudent == -1)
         return "Must add a student first";
      else{
         students[indexSelectedStudent] = s;
         return null;
```

```java
      }
}

// Navigation methods

public Student first(){
   Student s = null;
   if (studentCount == 0)
      indexSelectedStudent = -1;
   else{
      indexSelectedStudent = 0;
      s = students[indexSelectedStudent];
   }
   return s;
}

 public Student previous(){
   Student s = null;
   if (studentCount == 0)
      indexSelectedStudent = -1;
   else{
      indexSelectedStudent
          = Math.max (0, indexSelectedStudent - 1);
      s = students[indexSelectedStudent];
   }
   return s;
}

public Student next(){
   Student s = null;
   if (studentCount == 0)
      indexSelectedStudent = -1;
   else{
      indexSelectedStudent
          = Math.min (studentCount - 1, indexSelectedStudent + 1);
      s = students[indexSelectedStudent];
   }
   return s;
}

public Student last(){
   Student s = null;
   if (studentCount == 0)
      indexSelectedStudent = -1;
   else{
      indexSelectedStudent = studentCount - 1;
      s = students[indexSelectedStudent];
   }
   return s;
}

// Accessors to observe data
```

```java
    public Student currentStudent(){
        if (indexSelectedStudent == -1)
            return null;
        else
            return students[indexSelectedStudent];
    }

    public int size(){
        return studentCount;
    }

    public int currentPosition(){
        return indexSelectedStudent;
    }

    public int getClassAverage(){
        if (studentCount == 0)
            return 0;
        int sum = 0;
        for (int i = 0; i < studentCount; i++)
            sum += students[i].getAverage();
        return sum / studentCount;
    }

    public Student getHighScore(){
        if (studentCount == 0)
            return null;
        else{
            Student s = students[0];
            for (int i = 1; i < studentCount; i++)
                if (s.getHighScore() < students[i].getHighScore())
                    s = students[i];
            return s;
        }
    }

    public String toString(){
        String result = "";
        for (int i = 0; i < studentCount; i++)
            result = result + students[i] + "\n";
        return result;
    }
}
```

Implementation of the View

We include a skeletal listing of the class TestScoresView and leave the completion of its methods as an exercise. Even so, the entire program now compiles and allows the user to enter command numbers at run time. Here is the code:

```java
// Case Study 9.1: TestScoresView class

import java.util.Scanner;
```

```java
public class TestScoresView{

    private TestScoresModel model;

    public TestScoresView(TestScoresModel m){
        model = m;
        run();
    }

    // Menu-driven command loop
    private void run(){
        while (true){
            System.out.println("Number of students: " + model.size());
            System.out.println("Index of current student: " +
                               model.currentPosition());
            displayMenu();
            int command = getCommand("Enter a number [1-11]: ", 1, 11);
            if (command == 11)
                break;
            runCommand(command);
        }
    }

    private void displayMenu(){
    // Exercise: List the menu options
    }

    // Prompts the user for a command number and runs until
    // the user enters a valid command number
    // Parameters: prompt is the string to display
    //             low is the smallest command number
    //             high is the largest command number
    // Returns: a valid command number (>= low && <= high)
    private int getCommand(String prompt, int low, int high){
      // Exercise: recover from all input errors
        Scanner reader = new Scanner(System.in);
        System.out.print(prompt);
        return reader.nextInt();
    }

    // Selects a command to run based on a command number,
    // runs the command, and asks the user to continue by
    // pressing the Enter key
    private void runCommand(int command){
        // Exercise
    }
}
```

9.11 Graphics and GUIs: Changing the View of Student Test Scores

In the preceding case study, we organized the code in two sets of classes called the *model* and the *view*. This strategy split the code fairly equally between managing the interface (getting data from the user and displaying results and error messages) and manipulating a database (including worrying about whether or not an array is full and updating the student count and the index of the selected student). In addition to simplifying the code, this separation of concerns allows us to change the style of the user interface without changing the code for managing the database. To illustrate this point, we now show how to attach a GUI to the same data model.

Extra Challenge

This Graphics and GUIs section gives you the opportunity to explore concepts and programming techniques required to develop modern graphics applications and graphical user interfaces. This material is not required in order to proceed with the other chapters of the book.

Analysis

Figure 9-8 shows a GUI that allows us to view the current student in the database of students. The interface has buttons that support navigation through this database by moving to the first (<<), last (>>), next (>), or previous (<) student. The interface also has buttons that allow the user to add a new student to the end of the database or modify an existing student. The interface displays the index of the current student (**Current Index**) and the current size of the database (**Count**). Table 9-2 explains each of these features in more detail.

FIGURE 9-8
GUI for the student test scores program

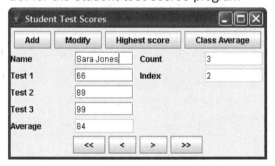

TABLE 9-2
Description of buttons

BUTTON	WHAT IT DOES
Add	Creates a new student object with the data displayed and inserts it at the end of the array; the new student becomes the current student. Error-checking makes sure that the array of students is not yet full and that the student data is valid.
Modify	Replaces the current student's data with the data displayed, provided it is valid
<<	Moves to the first student in the database and displays its data
<	Moves to the previous student in the database and displays its data
>	Moves to the next student in the database and displays its data
>>	Moves to the last student in the database and displays its data

Design

The structure of the GUI version of the `TestScoresView` class is similar to that of the `GUIWindow` class for the temperature conversion program discussed in Section 7.6. Here are the main changes to `TestScoresView` from the terminal-based version:

- In addition to the instance variable for the data model, the view class must now contain instance variables for the various widgets, such as labels, text fields, and command buttons.

- The constructor now sets up several panels using the appropriate layouts, adds the widgets to the panels, and instantiates and adds listeners to the command buttons. The constructor can also set the title of the window, set its closing action, and show it (no changes are then necessary in the `main` method of the `TestScoresApp` class).

- The code to handle the individual commands now goes in the listener classes. The best way to do this is to define a separate listener class for each command button. Each listener class then has a fairly simple task, which may involve taking data from text fields, sending messages to the model, and updating the text fields with the results. As usual, the listener classes are defined as private inner classes within the view class.

- In addition to the constructor and listener classes, `TestScoresView` defines two private helper methods to perform the tasks of displaying the model's data in the text fields and creating a new `Student` object from the data in the text fields.

Implementation

The listing that follows is a skeletal version but will compile and display a partially functioning GUI. Its completion is left as an exercise.

```java
// Example 9.4: TestScoresView class (GUI version)

import javax.swing.*;
import java.awt.*;
import java.awt.event.*;

public class TestScoresView extends JFrame{

    // >>>>>>> The model <<<<<<<<

    // Declare the model
    private TestScoresModel model;

    // >>>>>>> The view <<<<<<<<

    // Declare and instantiate the window objects.
    private JButton    addButton       = new JButton("Add");
    private JButton    modifyButton    = new JButton("Modify");
    private JButton    firstButton     = new JButton("<<");
    private JButton    previousButton  = new JButton("<");
    private JButton    nextButton      = new JButton(">");
    private JButton    lastButton      = new JButton(">>");
    private JButton    highScoreButton = new JButton("Highest score");
    private JButton    aveScoreButton  = new JButton("Class Average");
```

```java
private JLabel      nameLabel     = new JLabel("Name");
private JLabel      test1Label    = new JLabel("Test 1");
private JLabel      test2Label    = new JLabel("Test 2");
private JLabel      test3Label    = new JLabel("Test 3");
private JLabel      averageLabel  = new JLabel("Average");
private JLabel      countLabel    = new JLabel("Count");
private JLabel      indexLabel    = new JLabel("Index");
private JTextField nameField      = new JTextField("");
private JTextField test1Field     = new JTextField("0");
private JTextField test2Field     = new JTextField("0");
private JTextField test3Field     = new JTextField("0");
private JTextField averageField   = new JTextField("0");
private JTextField countField     = new JTextField("0");
private JTextField indexField     = new JTextField("-1");

// Constructor
public TestScoresView(TestScoresModel m){
   model = m;
   // Set attributes of fields
   averageField.setEditable(false);
   countField.setEditable(false);
   indexField.setEditable(false);
   averageField.setBackground(Color.white);
   countField.setBackground(Color.white);
   indexField.setBackground(Color.white);
   // Set up panels to organize widgets and
   // add them to the window
   JPanel northPanel = new JPanel();
   JPanel centerPanel = new JPanel(new GridLayout(5, 4, 10, 5));
   JPanel southPanel = new JPanel();
   Container container = getContentPane();
   container.add(northPanel, BorderLayout.NORTH);
   container.add(centerPanel, BorderLayout.CENTER);
   container.add(southPanel, BorderLayout.SOUTH);
   // Data access buttons
   northPanel.add(addButton);
   northPanel.add(modifyButton);
   northPanel.add(highScoreButton);
   northPanel.add(aveScoreButton);
   // Row 1
   centerPanel.add(nameLabel);
   centerPanel.add(nameField);
   centerPanel.add(countLabel);
   centerPanel.add(countField);
   // Row 2
   centerPanel.add(test1Label);
   centerPanel.add(test1Field);
   centerPanel.add(indexLabel);
   centerPanel.add(indexField);
   // Row 3
   centerPanel.add(test2Label);
   centerPanel.add(test2Field);
   centerPanel.add(new JLabel(""));  // For empty cell in grid
```

```java
        centerPanel.add(new JLabel(""));
        // Row 4
        centerPanel.add(test3Label);
        centerPanel.add(test3Field);
        centerPanel.add(new JLabel(""));
        centerPanel.add(new JLabel(""));
        // Row 5
        centerPanel.add(averageLabel);
        centerPanel.add(averageField);
        centerPanel.add(new JLabel(""));
        centerPanel.add(new JLabel(""));
        // Navigation buttons
        southPanel.add(firstButton);
        southPanel.add(previousButton);
        southPanel.add(nextButton);
        southPanel.add(lastButton);
        // Attach listeners to buttons
        addButton.addActionListener(new AddListener());
        previousButton.addActionListener(new PreviousListener());
        // Other attachments will go here (exercise)
        // Set window attributes
        setTitle("Student Test Scores");
        setDefaultCloseOperation(JFrame.EXIT_ON_CLOSE);
        pack();
        setVisible(true);
    }

    // Updates fields with info from the model
    private void displayInfo(){
        Student s = model.currentStudent();
        if (s == null){   // No current student, so clear fields
            nameField.setText("");
            test1Field.setText("0");
            test2Field.setText("0");
            test3Field.setText("0");
            averageField.setText("0");
            countField.setText("0");
            indexField.setText("-1");
        } else{            // Refresh with student's data
            nameField.setText(s.getName());
            test1Field.setText("" + s.getScore(1));
            test2Field.setText("" + s.getScore(2));
            test3Field.setText("" + s.getScore(3));
            averageField.setText("" + s.getAverage());
            countField.setText("" + model.size());
            indexField.setText("" + model.currentPosition());
        }
    }

    // Creates and returns new Student from field info
    private Student getInfoFromScreen(){
        Student s = new Student(nameField.getText());
        s.setScore(1, Integer.parseInt(test1Field.getText()));
```

```
        s.setScore(2, Integer.parseInt(test2Field.getText()));
        s.setScore(3, Integer.parseInt(test3Field.getText()));
        return s;
    }

    // >>>>>>> The controller <<<<<<<<

    // Responds to a click on the Add button
    private class AddListener implements ActionListener{
        public void actionPerformed(ActionEvent e){
            // Get inputs, validate, and display error and quit if invalid
            Student s = getInfoFromScreen();
            String message = s.validateData();
            if (message != null){
                JOptionPane.showMessageDialog(TestScoresView.this, message);
                return;
            }
            // Attempt to add student and display error or update fields
            message = model.add(s);
            if (message != null)
                JOptionPane.showMessageDialog(TestScoresView.this, message);
            else
                displayInfo();
        }
    }

    // Responds to a click on the < button
    private class PreviousListener implements ActionListener{
        public void actionPerformed(ActionEvent e){
            model.previous();
            displayInfo();
        }
    }

    // Other listeners for modify, highest score, class average, and
    // navigation go here (exercise)
}
```

E XERCISE 9.11

1. Write the code for the listener class that displays the class average in the GUI version of the student test scores program.

2. An alternative way to define listeners for command buttons is to define a single listener class and attach a single instance of this class to all of the buttons. The code for the `actionPerformed` method compares each button to the source of the event and takes the appropriate action. The source of the event is obtained by running the method `getSource()` with the `ActionEvent` parameter. Discuss the advantages and disadvantages of this strategy for implementing listeners.

Design, Testing, and Debugging Hints

- Three things should be done to set up an array:
  1. Declare an array variable.
  2. Instantiate an array object and assign it to the array variable.
  3. Initialize the cells in the array with data, as appropriate.

- When creating a new array object, try to come up with an accurate estimate of the number of cells for the data. If you underestimate, some data will be lost; if you overestimate, some memory will be wasted.

- Remember that array variables are `null` until they are assigned array objects.

- To avoid index out-of-bounds errors, remember that the index of an array cell ranges from 0 (the first position) to the length of the array minus 1.

- To access the last cell in an array, use the expression `<array>.length - 1`.

- As a rule of thumb, it is best to avoid having more than one array variable refer to the same array object. When you want to copy the contents of one array to another, do not use the assignment `A = B`; instead, write a copy method and use the assignment `A = arrayCopy(B)`.

- When an array is not full, take care to track the current number of elements and do not attempt to access a cell that is beyond the last element.

SUMMARY

In this chapter, you learned:

- Arrays are collections of similar items or elements. The items in arrays are ordered by position. Arrays are useful when a program needs to manipulate many similar items, such as a group of students or a number of test scores.

- Arrays are objects. Thus, they must be instantiated and they can be referred to by more than one variable.

- An array can be passed to a method as a parameter and returned as a value.

- Parallel arrays are useful for organizing information with corresponding elements.

- Two-dimensional arrays store values in a row-and-column arrangement similar to a table.

- The enhanced `for` loop is a simplified version of a loop for visiting each element of an array from the first position to the last position.

VOCABULARY *Review*

Define the following terms:

Array	Multidimensional array	Ragged array
Element	One-dimensional array	Range-bound error
Enhanced `for` loop	Parallel arrays	Structure chart
Index	Physical size	Subscript
Initializer list	Procedural decomposition	Two-dimensional array
Logical size		

REVIEW *Questions*

WRITTEN QUESTIONS

Write a brief answer to the following questions.

1. Assume the following declarations are made and indicate which items below are valid subscripted variables.

    ```
    int a[] = new int[10];
    char b[] = new char[6];
    int x = 7, y = 2;
    double z = 0.0;
    ```

    A. `a[0]`

    B. `b[0]`

    C. `c[1.0]`

    D. `b['a']`

    E. `b[a]`

    F. `a[x + y]`

    G. `a[x % y]`

    H. `a[10]`

    I. `c[-1]`

    J. `a[a[4]]`

2. Assume that the array a defined in Question 1 contains the following values.

    1   4   6   8   9   3   7   10   2   9

    Indicate if the following are valid subscripts of a and, if so, state the value of the subscript. If invalid, explain why.

    A. a[2]

    B. a[5]

    C. a[a[2]]

    D. a[4 + 7]

    E. a[a[5] + a[2]]

    F. a[Math.sqrt(2)]

3. List the errors in the following array declarations.

   A. `int intArray[] = new double[10];`

   B. `int intArray[] = new int[1.5];`

   C. `double[] doubleArray = new double[-10]`

   D. `int intMatrix[] [] = new int[10];`

4. Write a method `selectRandom` that expects an array of integers as a parameter. The method should return the value of an array element at a randomly selected position.

5. Write code to declare and instantiate a two-dimensional array of integers with five rows and four columns.

6. Write code to initialize the array of Question 5 with randomly generated integers between 1 and 20.

PROJECTS

In some of the following projects, you are asked to write helper methods to process arrays. If you are calling these methods from the main method, be sure to begin the helper method's header with the reserved word static.

PROJECT 9-1

Write a program that takes 10 integers as input. The program places the even integers into an array called evenList, the odd integers into an array called oddList, and the negative integers into an array called negativeList. The program displays the contents of the three arrays after all of the integers have been entered.

PROJECT 9-2

Write a program that takes 10 floating-point numbers as inputs. The program displays the average of the numbers followed by all of the numbers that are greater than the average. As part of your design, write a method that takes an array of doubles as a parameter and returns the average of the data in the array.

PROJECT 9-3

The mode of a list of numbers is the number listed most often. Write a program that takes 10 numbers as input and displays the mode of these numbers. Your program should use parallel arrays and a method that takes an array of numbers as a parameter and returns the value that appears most often in the array.

PROJECT 9-4

The median of a list of numbers is the value in the middle of the list if the list is arranged in order. Add to the program of Project 9-3 the capability of displaying the median of the list of numbers.

PROJECT 9-5

Modify the program of Project 9-4 so that it displays not only the median and mode of the list of numbers but also a table of the numbers and their associated frequencies.

PROJECT 9-6

Complete the student test scores application from this chapter's case study and test it thoroughly.

PROJECT 9-7

A magic square is a two-dimensional array of positive integers such that the sum of each row, column, and diagonal is the same constant. The following example is a magic square whose constant is 34:

16	3	2	13
5	10	11	8
9	6	7	12
4	15	14	1

Write a program that takes 16 integers as inputs. The program should determine whether or not the square is a magic square and display the result in a text area.

PROJECT 9-8

Pascal's triangle can be used to recognize coefficients of a quantity raised to a power. The rules for forming this triangle of integers are such that each row must start and end with a 1, and each entry in a row is the sum of the two values diagonally above the new entry. Thus, four rows of Pascal's triangle are

$$
\begin{array}{ccccccc}
 & & & 1 & & & \\
 & & 1 & & 1 & & \\
 & 1 & & 2 & & 1 & \\
1 & & 3 & & 3 & & 1
\end{array}
$$

This triangle can be used as a convenient way to get the coefficients of a quantity of two terms raised to a power (binomial coefficients). For example

$(a+b)^3=1{\times}a^3+3a^2b+3ab^2+1{\times}b^3$

where the coefficients 1, 3, 3, and 1 come from the fourth row of Pascal's triangle.

Write a program that takes the number of rows (up to, say, 10) as input and displays Pascal's triangle for those rows.

PROJECT 9-9

Complete the GUI version of the student test scores program.

PROJECT 9-10

In the game of Penny Pitch, a two-dimensional board of numbers is laid out as follows:

```
1  1  1  1  1

1  2  2  2  1

1  2  3  2  1

1  2  2  2  1

1  1  1  1  1
```

A player tosses five pennies on the board, aiming for the number with the highest value. At the end of the game, the sum total of the tosses is returned. Develop a program that plays this game. The program should display the board and then perform the following steps each time the user presses Enter:

■ Generate two random numbers for the row and column of the toss.

■ Add the number at this position to a running total.

■ Display the board, replacing the numbers with Ps where the pennies land.

(*Hint*: You should use a two-dimensional array of `Square` objects for this problem. Each square contains a number like those shown and a Boolean flag that indicates whether or not a penny has landed on that square.)

CRITICAL *Thinking*

You have been using a method to search for data in arrays like the one described in this chapter, when your friend tells you that it's a poor way to search. She says that you're examining every element in the array to discover that the target element is not there. According to her, a better way is to assume that the elements in the array are in alphabetical order. Start by examining the element at the middle position in the array. If that element matches the target element, you're done. Otherwise, if that element is less than the target element, continue the same kind of search in just the portion of the array to the left of the element just examined. Otherwise, continue the same kind of search in just the portion of the array to the right of the element just examined.

Write an algorithm for this search process, and explain why it is better than the search algorithm discussed in this chapter.

CHAPTER 10

CLASSES CONTINUED

OBJECTIVES

Upon completion of this chapter, you should be able to:

- Know when it is appropriate to include class (`static`) variables and methods in a class.

- Understand the role of Java interfaces in a software system and define an interface for a set of implementing classes.

- Understand the use of inheritance by extending a class.

- Understand the use of polymorphism and know how to override methods in a superclass.

- Place the common features (variables and methods) of a set of classes in an abstract class.

- Understand the implications of reference types for equality, copying, and mixed-mode operations.

- Know how to define and use methods that have preconditions, postconditions, and throw exceptions

Estimated Time: 5 hours

VOCABULARY

Abstract class

Abstract method

Aggregation

Class (`static`) method

Class (`static`) variable

Concrete class

Dependency

Final method

Inheritance

Interface

Overriding

Postcondition

Precondition

Chapter 5 presented an overview of classes that allowed you to learn to read, modify, and define them. The examples of classes discussed there are simplified versions of what real programmers would see, however. Defining classes is only one aspect of object-oriented programming. The real power of object-oriented programming comes from its capacity to reduce code and to distribute responsibilities for such things as error handling in a software system. This capability can be exploited only when you have an understanding of some related concepts. Following is a brief summary of some of these concepts, which we explore in detail in this chapter:

Static Variables and Methods. When information needs to be shared among all instances of a class, that information can be represented in terms of static variables and it can be accessed by means of static methods.

Interfaces. A Java interface specifies the set of methods available to clients of a class. An interface provides a way of requiring a class to implement a set of methods and a way of informing clients about services regardless of implementation detail. Interfaces thus provide the glue that holds a set of cooperating classes together.

Inheritance. Java organizes classes in a hierarchy. Classes inherit the instance variables and methods of the classes above them in the hierarchy. A class can extend its inherited characteristics by adding instance variables and methods and by overriding inherited methods. Thus, *inheritance* provides a mechanism for reusing code and can greatly reduce the effort required to implement a new class.

Abstract Classes. Some classes in a hierarchy must never be instantiated. They are called *abstract classes*. Their sole purpose is to define features and behavior common to their subclasses.

Polymorphism. Methods in different classes with a similar function are usually given the same name. This is called *polymorphism*. Polymorphism makes classes easier to use because programmers need to memorize fewer method names. In a well-designed class hierarchy, polymorphism is employed as much as possible. A good example of a polymorphic message is toString. Every object, no matter which class it belongs to, understands the toString message and responds by returning a string that describes the object.

Preconditions and Postconditions. Clients need to know how to use a method correctly and what results to expect if it is so used. Preconditions specify the correct use of a method and postconditions describe what will result if the preconditions are satisfied.

Exceptions for Error Handling. When a method's preconditions are violated, a foolproof way to catch the errors is to throw exceptions, thereby halting program execution at the point of the errors.

Reference Types. The identity of an object and the fact that there can be multiple references to the same object are issues that arise when comparing two objects for equality and when copying an object. There are also subtle rules to master when manipulating objects of different but related types in a hierarchy.

Unfortunately, there is a lot to digest here. But we take you through it one step at a time, and by the end of the chapter you will become a connoisseur of this flavor of programming.

10.1 Class (static) Variables and Methods

The variables and methods discussed thus far in the book have been instance variables and methods. An instance variable belongs to an object and is allocated storage when the object is created. Each object has its own set of instance variables. An instance method is activated when a message is sent to the object. Java also supports the use of class variables and methods. A *class variable* belongs to a class. Its storage is allocated at program startup and is independent of the number of instances created. A *class method* is activated when a message is sent to the class rather than to an object. The modifier static is used to designate class variables and methods. To illustrate, we make some modifications to the Student class introduced in Chapter 9.

Counting the Number of Students Instantiated

Suppose we want to count all the student objects instantiated during the execution of an application. To do so, we introduce a variable, which we call studentCount. This variable is incremented in the constructor every time a student object is instantiated. Because the variable is independent of any particular student object, it must be a class variable. In addition, we need one method to access the studentCount variable. This method, called getStudentCount, returns the variable's value on demand. Because getStudentCount does not manipulate any particular student object, it must be a class method.

Modifying the Student Class

Following are the modifications needed to add the class variable and the the class method in the Student class. We are adding the class variable and method to the end of the class template. There is no rule that says they must be placed there, but it is as good a location as any other and is the one usually used in this book.

```java
public class Student {

    private String name;
    ... rest of the instance variables go here ...

    public Student(){
        this("");
     }

    public Student(String nm){
        studentCount++;      // Increment the count when a student is
                             // instantiated
        name = nm;
        tests = new int[3];
        for (int i = 0; i < tests.length; i++)
            tests[i] = 0;
    }

    public Student(String nm, int[] t){
        studentCount++;      // Increment the count when a student is
                             // instantiated
        name = nm;
        tests = new int[t.length];
        for (int i = 0; i < tests.length; i++)
            tests[i] = t[i];
    }

    public Student(Student s){
        this(s.name, s.tests);
    }
    ... rest of the methods without change go here ...

    //--------------- class variables and methods ----------------

    static private int studentCount = 0;

    static public void setStudentCount(int count){
        studentCount = count;
    }

    static public int getStudentCount(){
        return studentCount;
    }
}
```

Following is a code segment that illustrates the new capabilities of the Student class:

```
...
s1 = new Student();                             // Instantiate a student object
...
s2 = new Student();                             // Instantiate a student object
...
s3 = new Student();                             // Instantiate a student object
System.out.println(Student.getStudentCount());      // Displays 3
```

Notice that class messages are sent to a class and not to an object. Also, notice that we do not attempt to manipulate the studentCount variable directly because, in accordance with the good programming practice of information hiding, we declared the variable to be private.

In general, we use a static variable in any situation in which all instances share a common data value. We then use static methods to provide public access to these data.

Class Constants

By using the modifier final in conjunction with static, we create a *class constant*. The value of a class constant is assigned when the variable is declared, and it cannot be changed later. To illustrate the use of class constants, we modify the Student class again by adding two class constants: MIN_SCORE and MAX_SCORE. We use these constants in the method setScore to hold the score between MIN_SCORE and MAX_SCORE. It is customary to capitalize the names of class constants. Following are the relevant modifications to the Student class:

```
public class Student {

   private String name;

 ... rest of the instance variables go here ...

 ... no changes in the methods up to this point ...

   public void setScore (int i, int score){
      // Limit the score to the interval [MIN_SCORE, MAX_SCORE]
      score = Math.max (MIN_SCORE, score);
      score = Math.min (MAX_SCORE, score);

      tests[i - 1] = score;
   }
   ... no changes in the methods here ...

//--------------- static variables and methods ---------------

   static final public int MIN_SCORE = 0;
   static final public int MAX_SCORE = 100;
   ... no changes in the rest of the static stuff ...

}
```

The method `max` in class `Math` returns the maximum of its two parameters and `min` returns their minimum. We declare the two class constants as public because clients might like to access them. Following is a segment of code that illustrates the `Student` class's new features:

```
s = new Student();
s.setScore(1, -20);          // Too small, will be set to MIN_SCORE
s.setScore(2, 150);          // Too large, will be set to MAX_SCORE
s.setScore(3, 55);           // Value is acceptable
System.out.println (s);      // Displays scores of 0, 100, and 55
System.out.println (Student.MIN_SCORE);      // Displays 0
System.out.println (Student.MAX_SCORE);      // Displays 100
```

Rules for Using `static` Variables

There are two simple rules to remember when using `static` variables:

1. Class methods can reference only the `static` variables and never the instance variables.

2. Instance methods can reference `static` and instance variables.

The `Math` Class Revisited

By now you may have guessed that all the methods and variables in the `Math` class are static. `Math.PI` refers to a static constant, whereas `Math.max(MIN_SCORE, score)` activates a static method.

The `Static` Method `Main`

All the application classes presented so far have included the `static` method `main`. Now we can understand more about how `main` works. Consider the following example:

```
import ...;
import ...;

public class MyApp ...{
   ...

   public static void main (String[] args){
      ...
   }
}
```

When the user runs this program by typing

```
java MyApp
```

the Java interpreter sends the message `main` to the class `MyApp`.

EXERCISE 10.1

1. Define a static constant for the default number of test scores in the `student` class.

2. Describe the manner in which Java allocates memory for instance variables and `static` variables.

3. List two possible situations in which `static` methods might be included in classes.

4. What error occurs in the following code?

```
public class SomeClass{
    private int instVar = 0;
    static public void someMethod(int x){
        classVar = instVar + classVar + x;
    }
    static private int classVar = 0;
    …
}
```

5. Why is it a good idea to define all constants as `public` and `static`?

10.2 *Turtle Graphics*

Java comes with a large array of classes that support graphics operations, many of which are discussed in the optional sections at the end of each chapter of this book. In the next few sections we use `TurtleGraphics`, a nonstandard, open-source Java package, to illustrate various features of object-oriented programming. The implementation of `TurtleGraphics` is discussed in Appendix I.

Turtle graphics were originally developed as part of the children's programming language Logo created by Seymour Papert and his colleagues at MIT in the late 1960s. The name suggests the way in which we can think about the drawing process. Imagine a turtle crawling on a piece of paper with a pen tied to its tail. Commands direct the turtle as it moves across the paper and tell it to lift or lower its tail, turn some number of degrees left or right, and move a specified distance. Whenever the tail is down, the pen drags along the paper leaving a trail. In this manner it is possible to "program" the turtle to draw pictures ranging from the simple to the complex.

Turtle Graphics Messages

In Java, we dispense with the turtle and focus on the pen, which is an instance of the class `StandardPen` (later we will encounter some other not-so-standard pens). Drawing is done in a window. We command a pen by sending it messages such as those shown in Table 10-1.

TABLE 10-1
Pen messages

PEN MESSAGE	WHAT IT DOES
home()	The pen jumps to the center of the graphics window without drawing and points north.
setDirection(degrees)	The pen points in the indicated direction. Due east corresponds to 0 degrees, north to 90 degrees, west to 180 degrees, and south to 270 degrees. Because there are 360 degrees in a circle, setting the direction to 400 degrees would be equivalent to 400 – 360 or 40 degrees and setting it to –30 degrees would be equivalent to 360 – 30 or 330 degrees.
turn(degrees)	The pen adds the indicated degrees to its current direction. Positive degrees correspond to turning counterclockwise. The degrees can be an integer or floating-point number.
down()	The pen lowers itself to the drawing surface.
up()	The pen raises itself from the drawing surface.
move(distance)	The pen moves the specified distance in the current direction. The distance can be an integer or floating-point number and is measured in pixels (picture elements). The size of a pixel depends on the monitor's resolution. For instance, when we say that a monitor's resolution is 800 by 600, we mean that the monitor is 800 pixels wide and 600 pixels high.
setColor(aColor)	Sets the pen's color to aColor.

Initially, a pen is

- In the center of a graphics window (at position [0,0] of a Cartesian coordinate system)
- In the down position
- Pointing north

Drawing a Square with a Pen

The following example is a program that draws a square, 50 pixels per side, in the center of a graphics window:

```
// Example 10.1: Draw a square using Turtle Graphics

import TurtleGraphics.StandardPen;

public class DrawSquare {

    public static void main(String [] args) {

        // Instantiate a pen object
        StandardPen pen = new StandardPen();
```

```
        // Lift the pen, move it to the square's upper-left corner,
        // and lower it again
        pen.up();
        pen.move(25);
        pen.turn(90); pen.move(25);
        pen.down();

        // Draw the square
        pen.turn(90); pen.move(50);
        pen.turn(90); pen.move(50);

        pen.turn(90); pen.move(50);
        pen.turn(90); pen.move(50);
    }
}
```

Figure 10-1 shows the graphics window after the program has completed execution. If the window is resized, the square is automatically redrawn in the center of the window without rerunning the program. The window can be closed in the usual manner.

FIGURE 10-1
A square drawn at the center of a graphics window

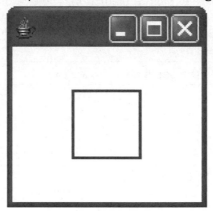

Installing Turtle Graphics

Before you can compile and run a program that uses the `TurtleGraphics` package, you must install that package on your hard drive. You can obtain the package at the authors' Web site (see Appendix I for details) or from your instructor. If you're using the command prompt to compile and run Java programs, by far the easiest way to install the package is to copy the `TurtleGraphics` directory that contains the byte codes into your current working directory. When this has been done, your current working directory should contain your `.java` file that imports `TurtleGraphics` and also the `TurtleGraphics` directory. The Java compiler and the JVM should then be able to locate the `TurtleGraphics` package.

If you move to another directory to compile and run a Java program that uses `TurtleGraphics`, you must move the `TurtleGraphics` directory as well. To avoid this annoying maintenance, you can install the file `TurtleGraphics.jar` in the appropriate Java system directories on your hard drive, where it will be accessible no matter where you run the compiler or JVM. This is also the preferred installation alternative when you're running a development environment like BlueJ. See Appendix I for further details on this type of installation.

10.3 Java Interfaces—The Client Perspective

The term *interface* is used in two different ways. On the one hand, an interface is the part of a software system that interacts with human users. On the other, it is a list of a class's public methods. Throughout this chapter we use the term in its latter sense. A class's interface provides the information needed to use a class without revealing anything about its implementation.

When related classes have the same interface, they can be used interchangeably in a program. House painting provides an everyday example. Small delicate brushes are used to paint around windows and doors and large coarse brushes to paint expanses of wall. Yet the different types of brushes are used in the same manner. They are all dipped in paint and wiggled backward and forward on the painting surface. They have, in other words, the same interface. Instructions for how to use one apply to all. Likewise, in a program, code for manipulating a class applies equally to all classes that share the same interface.

We can illustrate these ideas in Java using turtle graphics. The StandardPen used earlier is just one of five classes that conform to the same interface. Two others are WigglePen and RainbowPen. A WigglePen draws wiggly lines, and a RainbowPen draws randomly colored lines. We can think of these as special effects pens; but as pens, they all have the same general behavior and respond to the same messages.

The Pen Interface

Earlier we described the interface for a standard pen by listing its methods in Table 10-1; however, Java provides a more formal mechanism called, not surprisingly, an interface. Following is the code for the Pen interface:

```
// Pen.java: The behavior common to all types of pens

import java.awt.Color;

public interface Pen{
    public void    down();
    public void    drawString(String text);
    public void    home();
    public void    move(double distance);
    public void    move(double x, double y);
    public void    setColor(Color color);
    public void    setDirection(double direction);
    public void    setWidth(int width);
    public String  toString();
    public void    turn(double degrees);
    public void    up();
}
```

Note that this code is quite simple. It consists of the signatures of the methods followed by semicolons. The interface provides programmers with the information needed to use pens of any type correctly. It is important to realize that an interface is not a class; however, when a class is defined, there is a mechanism, which we see shortly, to specify that the class conforms to the interface.

The Color class, which is defined in the java.awt package, represents colors in Java. The class includes several constants, such as Color.white, Color.black, and Color.blue (the default color of many of the pens), to represent commonly used individual colors.

Drawing with Different Types of Pens

As a short example, we write code to draw a square with three different types of pens:

```
// Example 10.2: Draw squares with three types of pens

import TurtleGraphics.*;

public class TestPens{

    public static void main(String[] args){
        // Declare three variables of the interface type called Pen.
        Pen p1, p2, p3;

        // Instantiate three different types of pens and
        // associate them with the Pen variables.
        p1 = new StandardPen();
        p2 = new WigglePen();
        p3 = new RainbowPen();

        // Draw a square with the standard pen.
        for (int i = 1; i <= 4; i++){
            p1.move(50);
            p1.turn(90);
        }

        // Draw a square with the wiggle pen.
        for (int i = 1; i <= 4; i++){
            p2.move(50);
            p2.turn(90);
        }

        // Draw a square with the rainbow pen.
        for (int i = 1; i <= 4; i++){
            p3.move(50);
            p3.turn(90);
        }
    }
}
```

The three pen variables (p1, p2, and p3) are given the type Pen, which is the name of the interface. Then the variables are associated with specialized types of pen objects. Each object responds to exactly the same messages, those listed in the Pen interface, but with slightly different behaviors. This is an example of polymorphism, which was first mentioned in Chapter 1.

The output from the program is shown in Figure 10-2. Because this book is not printed in full color, some of the detail may be lost. The first square is in blue and has straight sides. The second square, also in blue, has wiggly sides. The third square has straight sides, and each side is in a different randomly chosen color. Note that when the program executes, the windows may appear stacked on top of each other and may have to be separated by dragging them with the mouse.

FIGURE 10-2
A square drawn with three types of pens

Static Helper Methods

The code for drawing squares in the last example suffers from redundancy: it repeats the same for loop with three different types of pens. We can factor this common pattern of code into a method where it's written just once. The new method, named drawSquare, is then called with each pen as a parameter from the main method, as follows:

```
drawSquare(p1);
drawSquare(p2);
drawSquare(p3);
```

Because drawSquare is called from the static method main, it must also be defined as a static method. The single parameter of the method is of type Pen (the interface), so it can accept an actual parameter of any class that implements Pen. Here is the code for the method:

```
static private void drawSquare(Pen p){
    // Draw a square with any pen.
    for (int i = 1; i <= 4; i++){
        p.move(50);
        p.turn(90);
    }
}
```

Using Interface Names

In general, when you declare a variable, a formal parameter of a method, or a method's return type, it's a good idea to use an interface name for the type name wherever possible. Thus, code in the last example used Pen for the variables' type, instead of StandardPen or any of the other pen class names. Using an interface name has two benefits:

1. Methods that use interface types are more general, in that they work with any classes that implement the interface. If we had used StandardPen for the parameter of drawSquare, that method would only work with one type of pen.

2. It's easier to maintain a program that uses interface types. If you want to modify the program to use a different type of pen, for example, you only have to change the code that instantiates the pen. The code that manipulates the pen does not have to change at all.

EXERCISE 10.3

1. State the purpose of a Java interface and explain how it differs from a class.

2. Modify the method `drawSquare` so that it expects parameters for the pen, the coordinates of the square's upper-left corner point, and the length of its side. The method should draw the appropriate square with the pen.

10.4 Java Interfaces—The Implementation Perspective

We now show the role interfaces play in the implementation of classes. The implementation of the pen classes in the `TurtleGraphics` package is rather complicated, so a discussion of it is deferred to Appendix I. However, a simpler example is available. Suppose we need to perform some basic manipulations on circles and rectangles. The manipulations include positioning, moving, and stretching these basic geometric shapes. In addition, we want shapes to implement methods that compute their area, draw themselves with a pen, and return descriptions of themselves. Without any concern for implementation details, we can now describe this behavior in an interface called `Shape`, which is shared by circles and rectangles, as shown in the following code:

```
// Shape.java: Behavior common to all shapes

import TurtleGraphics.Pen;

public interface Shape{
   public double area();
   public void    draw(Pen p);
   public double getXPos();
   public double getYPos();
   public void    move(double xLoc, double yLoc);
   public void    stretchBy(double factor);
   public String toString();
}
```

Classes `Circle` and `Rect`

We implement circles and rectangles in classes we call `Circle` and `Rect`, respectively. We do not use the more obvious name `Rectangle` because Java already includes a class with that name. Working with two classes that have the same name is not impossible, but it does involve complexities we are not ready to discuss. The outline for both implementations look like this:

```
public class Circle implements Shape{
   ...
}
public class Rect implements Shape{
   ...
}
```

The key feature is the phrase `implements Shape`. The presence of this phrase implies that

- Both classes implement all the methods listed in the `Shape` interface.
- A variable declared as a `Shape` can be associated with an object of either class.

Following is a complete implementation of both classes:

```java
// Circle.java: Implementation of circles

import TurtleGraphics.Pen;

public class Circle implements Shape{

   private double xPos, yPos;
   private double radius;

   public Circle(){
      xPos = 0;
      yPos = 0;
      radius = 1;
   }

   public Circle(double xLoc, double yLoc, double r){
      xPos = xLoc;
      yPos = yLoc;
      radius = r;
   }

   public double area(){
      return Math.PI * radius * radius;
   }

   public void draw(Pen p){
      double side = 2.0 * Math.PI * radius / 120.0;
      p.up();
      p.move (xPos + radius, yPos - side / 2.0);
      p.setDirection (90);
      p.down();
      for (int i = 0; i < 120; i++){
         p.move (side);
         p.turn (3);
      }
   }

   public double getXPos(){
      return xPos;
   }

   public double getYPos(){
      return yPos;
   }
```

```java
    public void move(double xLoc, double yLoc) {
        xPos = xLoc;
        yPos = yLoc;
    }

    public void stretchBy(double factor) {
        radius *= factor;
    }

    public String toString(){
        String str = "CIRCLE\n"
                    + "Radius: " + radius + "\n"
                    + "(X,Y) Position: (" + xPos + "," + yPos + ")\n"
                    + "Area: " + area();
        return str;
    }
}

// Rect.java: Implementation of rectangles

import TurtleGraphics.Pen;

public class Rect implements Shape{

    private double xPos, yPos;
    private double height, width;

    public Rect(){
        xPos = 0;
        yPos = 0;
        height = 1;
        width = 1;
    }

    public Rect(double xLoc, double yLoc, double w, double h){
        xPos = xLoc;
        yPos = yLoc;
        height = h;
        width = w;
    }

    public double area(){
        return height * width;
    }

    public void draw(Pen p){
        p.up();
        p.move (xPos, yPos);
        p.down();
        p.setDirection (0); p.move (width);
        p.turn(-90); p.move(height);
        p.turn(-90); p.move(width);
        p.turn(-90); p.move(height);
    }
```

```
    public double getXPos(){
        return xPos;
    }

    public double getYPos(){
        return yPos;
    }

    public void move(double xLoc, double yLoc){
        xPos = xLoc;
        yPos = yLoc;
    }

    public void stretchBy(double factor){
        height *= factor;
        width *= factor;
    }

    public String toString(){
        String str = "RECTANGLE\n"
                    + "Width & Height: " + width + " & " + height +"\n"
                    + "(X,Y) Position: (" + xPos + "," + yPos + ")\n"
                    + "Area: " + area();
        return str;
    }
}
```

Testing the Classes

The code for both classes is easy to understand, so we now write a small test program that instantiates a circle and a rectangle and subjects them to a few basic manipulations. Embedded comments explain what is happening, and Figure 10-3 shows the output:

```
// Example 10.3: Try out some shapes

import TurtleGraphics.*;
import java.awt.Color;
import java.util.Scanner;

public class TestShapes{

    public static void main(String[] args){

        // Declare and instantiate a pen, a circle and a rectangle
        Pen p = new StandardPen();
        Shape s1 = new Circle(20, 20, 20);
        Shape s2 = new Rect(-20, -20, 20, 10);

        // Draw the circle and rectangle
        s1.draw (p);
        s2.draw (p);
```

```
        // Display a description of the circle and rectangle
        System.out.println(s1);   // toString method called implicitly
        System.out.println(s2);   // toString method called implicitly

        // Pause until the user is ready to continue
        System.out.print("Press <Enter> to continue: ");
        Scanner reader = new Scanner(System.in);
        reader.nextLine();

        // Erase the circle and rectangle and set the pen's color to red
        p.setColor(Color.white);
        s1.draw(p);
        s2.draw(p);
        p.setColor(Color.red);

        // Move the circle and rectangle, change their size, and redraw
        s1.move(30, 30);         s2.move(-30, -30);
        s1.stretchBy(2);         s2.stretchBy(2);
        s1.draw(p);              s2.draw(p);
    }
}
```

FIGURE 10-3
Output from the `TestShapes` program

Initial Configuration   Command Window   Final Configuration

Final Observations

Before closing this section, we must mention several points:

■ An interface contains only methods, never variables.

■ The methods in an interface are usually public.

■ If more than one class implements an interface, its methods are polymorphic.

■ A class can implement methods in addition to those listed in the interface, as we illustrate soon.

■ A class can implement more than one interface.

■ Interfaces can be organized in an inheritance hierarchy.

EXERCISE 10.4

1. Write an interface named `Account` for bank accounts. Clients should be able to make deposits and withdrawals and check their balances.

2. When the programmer uses the expression `implements <an interface>` in a class definition, what does the compiler expect to see in that definition?

10.5 Code Reuse Through Inheritance

In Java, all classes are part of an immense hierarchy, with the class `Object` at the root. Each class inherits the characteristics (variables and methods) of the classes above it in the hierarchy. A class can add new variables to these inherited characteristics as needed. It also can add new methods and/or modifies inherited methods.

Review of Terminology

To make it easier to talk about inheritance, we begin by reviewing the needed terminology. Figure 10-4 shows part of a class hierarchy, with `Object` as always at the `root` (the top position in an upside-down tree). Below `Object` are its subclasses, but we show only one, which we call `AAA`. Because `AAA` is immediately below `Object`, we say that it extends `Object`. Similarly, `BBB` and `CCC` extend `AAA`. The class immediately above another is called its superclass, so `AAA` is the superclass of `BBB` and `CCC`. A class can have many subclasses, and all classes, except `Object`, have exactly one superclass. The `descendants` of a class consist of its subclasses, plus their subclasses, and so on.

FIGURE 10-4
Part of a class hierarchy

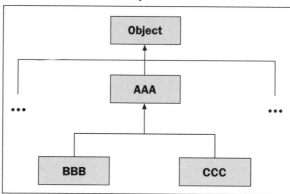

`Wheel` as a Subclass of `Circle`

As our first illustration of inheritance, we implement the class `Wheel` as a subclass of `Circle`. A wheel is just a circle with spokes, so much of the code needed to implement `Wheel` is already in `Circle`. We first present the code and a brief test. Comments in the code should make it fairly self-explanatory, but a more detailed explanation follows:

```
import TurtleGraphics.Pen;

public class Wheel extends Circle{
```

```java
        private int spokes;        // The number of spokes in the wheel
                                   // xPos, yPos, and radius are inherited
                                   // from Circle

        public Wheel() {
            super();               // Activate the constructor Circle() to
                                   // initialize xPos, yPos, and radius.
            spokes = 0;            // Now initialize spokes.
        }

        public Wheel(double xLoc, double yLoc, double r, int s){
            super(xLoc, yLoc, r);  // Activate the constructor
                                   // Circle(double xLoc, double yLoc, double r)
                                   // to initialize xPos, yPos, and radius.
            spokes = s;            // Now initialize spokes.
        }

        public void draw(Pen p){
            // Draw the wheel's rim by calling the draw method in the superclass.
            super.draw(p);

            // Draw the spokes
            for (int i = 1; i <= spokes; i++){
                p.up();
                p.move(xPos, yPos);
                p.setDirection(i * 360.0 / spokes);
                p.down();
                p.move(radius);
            }
        }

        public void setSpokes (int s){
            spokes = s;
        }

        public String toString(){
            String str = "WHEEL\n"
                        + "Radius: " + radius + "\n"
                        + "Spokes: " + spokes + "\n"
                        + "(X,Y) Position: (" + xPos + "," + yPos + ")\n"
                        + "Area: " + area();
            return str;
        }
    }
```

Testing the Wheel Class

Following is a test program that draws a circle and a wheel:

```java
// Example 10.4: Draw a circle and a wheel

import TurtleGraphics.*;

public class TestShapes {
```

```
    public static void main (String[] args) {
       // Declare and instantiate a pen, a circle and a wheel
       Pen p = new StandardPen();
       Shape s1 = new Circle(20, 20, 20);
       Shape s2 = new Wheel(-20, -20, 20, 6);

       // Draw the circle and wheel
       s1.draw(p);
       s2.draw(p);
    }
}
```

Figure 10-5 shows the results of this program.

FIGURE 10-5
A circle and a wheel with the same radius but different positions

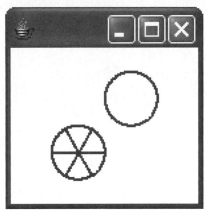

Detailed Explanation

We now explain the implementation of Wheel in detail.

Class Header

In the class header, we see that Wheel extends Circle, thereby indicating that it is a subclass of Circle and inherits all of Circle's variables and methods. The clause "implements Shape" is omitted from the header because Wheel inherits this property from Circle automatically.

Variables

The variable spokes, indicating the number of spokes in a wheel, is the only variable declared in the class. The other variables (xPos, yPos, and radius) are inherited from Circle; however, to reference these variables in Wheel methods, Circle must be modified slightly. In Circle, these variables must be declared protected instead of private. This designation indicates that Circle's descendants can access the variables while still hiding them from all other classes. The change in Circle looks like this:

```
protected double xPos, yPos;
protected double radius;
```

Protected Methods

Methods can be designated as protected also; however, we will not have any reason to use protected methods in this chapter. As with protected variables, a protected method is accessible to a class's descendants, but not to any other classes in the hierarchy.

Constructors and super

Constructors in class Wheel explicitly initialize the variable spokes; however, constructors in the superclass Circle initialize the remaining variables (xPos, yPos, and radius). The keyword super is used to activate the desired constructor in Circle, and the parameter list used with super determines which constructor in Circle is called. When used in this way, super must be the first statement in Wheel's constructors.

Other Methods and super

The keyword super also can be used in methods other than constructors, but in a slightly different way. First, it can appear in any place within a method. Second, it takes the form

```
super.<method name> (<parameter list>);
```

Such code activates the named method in the superclass (note that the two methods are polymorphic). In comparison, the code

```
this.<method name> (<parameter list>);     // Long form
                                           //    or
<method name> (<parameter list>);          // Short form
```

activates the named method in the current class. We see an example in the Wheel class's draw method:

```
// Draw the wheel's rim
super.draw (p);
```

Why Some Methods Are Missing

Not all the Shape methods are implemented in Wheel. Instead they are inherited unchanged from Circle. For instance, if the move message is sent to a wheel object, the move method in Circle is activated.

Why Some Methods Are Modified

Whenever a wheel object must respond differently to a message than a circle object, the corresponding method must be redefined in class Wheel. The methods draw and toString are examples. When convenient, the redefined method can use super to activate a method in the superclass.

Why There Are Extra Methods

A subclass often has methods that do not appear in its superclass. The method setSpokes is an example. This method provides a more specific piece of behavior than you would find in circles.

What Messages Can Be Sent to a Wheel

Because Wheel is a subclass of Circle, it automatically implements Shape. Therefore, a variable of type Shape can be instantiated as a new Wheel and can receive all Shape messages:

```
Shape someShape = new Wheel();
someShape.<any Shape message>;
```

The variable someShape cannot be sent the message setSpokes, however, even though it is actually a wheel. From the compiler's perspective, someShape is limited to receiving messages in the Shape interface. There are two ways to circumvent this limitation. The variable someShape is either declared as type Wheel in the first place, or it is cast to class Wheel when it is sent a message unique to class Wheel. Following is an example:

```
Wheel v1 = new Wheel();
Shape v2 = new Wheel();

v1.setSpokes (6);          // v1 can be sent all Wheel messages
((Wheel)v2).setSpokes (6); // v2 must first be cast to class Wheel before
                           // being sent this message
```

Of course, it is a mistake to cast a variable to a type that conflicts with its true identity. Doing so results in a run-time error. For instance:

```
Shape s = new Circle();    // s is a circle

((Wheel)s).setSpokes (6);  // s cannot be cast to class Wheel
```

We cover more examples of casting objects in Chapter 11.

EXERCISE 10.5

1. What is a class hierarchy? Give an example.

2. What syntax is used to get one class to inherit data and behavior from another class?

3. How does the keyword super work with constructors?

4. How does the keyword super work with methods other than constructors?

5. What is the role of the visibility modifier protected in a class hierarchy?

6. Find the error in the following code and suggest a remedy for the problem:
   ```
   Shape s = new Wheel();
   s.setSpokes (5);
   ```

10.6 Inheritance and Abstract Classes

When we examine the `Circle` and `Rect` classes, we see duplication of code. Inheritance provides a mechanism for reducing this duplication. To illustrate, we define a new class that is a superclass of `Circle` and `Rect` and contains all the variables and methods common to both. We will never have any reason to instantiate this class, so we will make it an *abstract class*, that is, a class that cannot be instantiated. The classes that extend this class and that are instantiated are called *concrete classes*.

It would be nice to call the new class `Shape`; however, `Shape` is already the name of our interface. Instead we will call the class `AbstractShape`. It is convenient, though not necessary, to have this new class implement the `Shape` interface. Then, the subclasses `Circle` and `Rect` no longer need to implement `Shape` explicitly.

Because `AbstractShape` is going to implement `Shape`, it must include all the `Shape` methods, even those such as `area` that are completely different in the subclasses and share no code. Methods in `AbstractShape` such as `area` for which we cannot write any code are called *abstract methods*, and we indicate that fact by including the word `abstract` in their headers.

Our extended hierarchy of classes is shown in Figure 10-6.

FIGURE 10-6
The shapes hierarchy

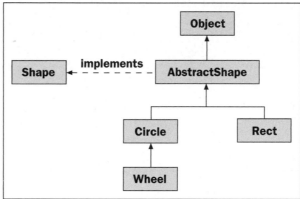

It takes rather a lot of code to implement all these classes; however, the code is straightforward, and the embedded comments explain the tricky parts. Pay particular attention to the attribute `final`, which is used for the first time in a method definition in class `AbstractShape`. A *final method* is a method that cannot be overridden by a subclass.

```
// AbstractShape.java: The abstract class for all shapes

import TurtleGraphics.Pen;

// Notice the use of the word "abstract" in the class header.
// This class implements the Shape interface.
// We don't need to say that the class extends Object as that is the
// default.

abstract public class AbstractShape implements Shape{

    // Here we declare variables common to all subclasses.
```

```
   protected double xPos;
   protected double yPos;

   // Even though this class is never instantiated, it needs constructors
   // to initialize its variables.

   public AbstractShape(){
      xPos = 0;
      yPos = 0;
   }

   public AbstractShape(double xLoc, double yLoc){
      xPos = xLoc;
      yPos = yLoc;
   }

   // There is no code for the next two methods; therefore,
   // they are abstract and terminate with a semicolon.
   // All subclasses must define these methods.

   abstract public double area();

   abstract public void draw(Pen p);

   // These next three methods will never be changed in a subclass;
   // therefore, they are declared final, meaning they
   // cannot be overridden.

   public final double getXPos(){
      return xPos;
   }

   public final double getYPos(){
      return yPos;
   }

   public final void move (double xLoc, double yLoc){
      xPos = xLoc;
      yPos = yLoc;
   }

   // Another abstract method to be defined in subclasses.

   abstract public void stretchBy (double factor);

   // Subclasses will override this method.
   // Notice that the method calls area(). More will be said about
   // this later.

   public String toString(){
      String str = "(X,Y) Position: (" + xPos + "," + yPos + ")\n"
                 + "Area: " + area();
      return str;
   }
}
```

```java
// Circle.java: The class for circles

import TurtleGraphics.Pen;

// This class extends AbstractShape and in the process implements
// the Shape interface.

public class Circle extends AbstractShape{

    protected double radius;

    public Circle(){
        super();                // Activate a constructor in AbstractShape.
        radius = 1;             // Then initialize radius.
    }

    public Circle (double xLoc, double yLoc, double r){
        super (xLoc, yLoc);     // Activate a constructor in AbstractShape.
        radius = r;             // Then initialize radius.
    }

    // The next three methods were abstract in the superclass.
    // Now we define them.

    public double area(){
        return Math.PI * radius * radius;
    }

    public void draw (Pen p){
        double side = 2.0 * Math.PI * radius / 120.0;
        p.up();
        p.move (xPos + radius, yPos - side / 2.0);
        p.setDirection (90);
        p.down();
        for (int i = 0; i < 120; i++){
            p.move (side);
            p.turn (3);
        }
    }

    public void stretchBy (double factor){
        radius *= factor;
    }

    // Notice that the toString method calls the corresponding method in the
    // superclass in order to accomplish its task.

    // In the superclass, the toString method calls area, which will
    // activate the area method in this class and not the area method in the
    // superclass.

    public String toString(){
        String str = "CIRCLE\n"
                    + "Radius: " + radius + "\n"
```

```
                            + super.toString();
            return str;
        }
    }

    // Wheel.java: The class for wheels

    // We have already explained most of the major points in this class.

    import TurtleGraphics.Pen;

    public class Wheel extends Circle{

        private int spokes;

        public Wheel(){
            super();
            spokes = 0;
        }

        public Wheel (double xLoc, double yLoc, double r, int s){
            super (xLoc, yLoc, r);
            spokes = s;
        }

        public void draw (Pen p){
            // Draw the wheel's rim
            super.draw (p);

            // Draw the spokes
            for (int i = 1; i <= spokes; i++){
                p.up();
                p.move (xPos, yPos);
                p.setDirection (i * 360.0 / spokes);
                p.down();
                p.movc (radius);
            }
        }

        public void setSpokes (int s){
            spokes = s;
        }

        // We could not call super.toString() in this toString method, because
        // doing so would have activated the method in Circle rather than the
        // method we wanted in AbstractShape.

        public String toString(){
            String str = "WHEEL\n"
                        + "Radius: " + radius + "\n"
                        + "Spokes: " + spokes + "\n"
                        + "(X,Y) Position: (" + xPos + "," + yPos + ")\n"
                        + "Area: " + area();
            return str;
```

```java
        }
    }

    // Rect.java: The class for rectangles

    // No additional comments are needed in this class. All the important
    // points have already been made.

    import TurtleGraphics.Pen;

    public class Rect extends AbstractShape {

        private double height, width;

        public Rect() {
            super();
            height = 1;
            width = 1;
        }

        public Rect (double xLoc, double yLoc, double w, double h) {
            super (xLoc, yLoc);
            height = h;
            width = w;
        }

        public double area() {
            return height * width;
        }

        public void draw (Pen p) {
            p.up();
            p.move (xPos, yPos);
            p.down();
            p.setDirection (0); p.move (width);
            p.turn (-90); p.move (height);
            p.turn (-90); p.move (width);
            p.turn (-90); p.move (height);
        }

        public void stretchBy (double factor) {
            height *= factor;
            width *= factor;
        }

        public String toString() {
            String str = "RECTANGLE\n"
                        + "Width & Height: " + width + " & " + height +"\n"
                        + super.toString();
            return str;
        }
    }
```

EXERCISE 10.6

1. What is an abstract class? Give an example.

2. Why do we declare abstract methods?

3. What is a final method? Give an example.

4. What is a protected variable? Give an example.

10.7 Some Observations about Interfaces, Inheritance, and Relationships among Classes

We now quickly review some major features of interfaces and inheritance and make a few additional observations.

- A Java interface has a name and consists of a list of method headers.

- One or more classes can implement the same interface.

- If a variable is declared to be of an interface type, then it can be associated with an object from any class that implements the interface.

- If a class implements an interface, then all its subclasses do so implicitly.

- A subclass inherits all the characteristics of its superclass. To this basis, the subclass can add new variables and methods or modify inherited methods.

- Characteristics common to several classes can be collected in a common abstract superclass that is never instantiated.

- An abstract class can contain headers for abstract methods that are implemented in the subclasses.

- A class's constructors and methods can utilize constructors and methods in the superclass.

- Inheritance reduces repetition and promotes the reuse of code.

- Interfaces and inheritance promote the use of polymorphism.

Now let us consider additional observations.

Finding the Right Method

When a message is sent to an object, Java looks for a matching method. The search starts in the object's class and if necessary continues up the class hierarchy.

- Consequently, in the preceding program, when the move message is sent to a circle or a rectangle, the move method in the AbstractShape class is activated. There is no move method in either the Circle or Rect classes.

- On the other hand, when the stretchBy message is sent to a circle, Java uses the corresponding method in the Circle class.

■ When the `toString` message is sent to a circle, execution begins in the `circle` class, temporarily transfers to the superclass, and finishes up in the `circle` class.

```
public String toString() {
   String str = "CIRCLE\n"
               + "Radius: " + radius + "\n"
               + super.toString();          // Transfer to superclass
   return str;
}
```

In the superclass `AbstractShape`, however, something tricky happens:

```
public String toString(){
   String str = "(X,Y) Position: (" + xPos + "," + yPos + ")\n"
               + "Area: " + area();          // Something tricky here
   return str;
}
```

Which `area` method is being called, the one in `AbstractShape` or the one in `Circle`? Actually, this question is not so hard to answer. We must stop to consider which object is involved in all of this. It is a circle object; therefore, the `area` method in the `Circle` class is activated. Nonetheless, it does seem strange that the `toString` method in the superclass activates the `area` method in the subclass.

To be fair, we (the authors) must admit that the last example was specially contrived to be tricky. You may work with Java for a year or more before encountering anything similar.

Implementation, Extension, Overriding, and Finality

You may have noticed that there are four ways in which methods in a subclass can be related to methods in a superclass:

1. *Implementation of an abstract method*: As we have seen, each subclass is forced to implement the abstract methods specified in its superclass. Abstract methods are thus a means of requiring certain behavior in all subclasses.

2. *Extension*: There are two kinds of extension:
   A. The subclass method does not exist in the superclass.
   B. The subclass method invokes the same method in the superclass and also extends the superclass's behavior with its own operations.

3. *Overriding*: In the case of **overriding**, the subclass method does not invoke the superclass method. Instead, the subclass method is intended as a complete replacement of the superclass method.

4. *Finality*: The method in the superclass is complete and cannot be modified by the subclasses. We declare such a method to be `final`.

Working Without Interfaces

Interfaces are a useful and powerful mechanism for organizing code; however, they are not necessary. Without the `Shape` interface, the implementation of `AbstractShape` remains the same except for the header:

```
abstract public class AbstractShape {
```

And defining a variable as `AbstractShape` allows the variable to associate with objects from any shape class:

```
AbstractShape s1, s2, s3;
s1 = new Circle();
s2 = new Rect();
s3 = new Wheel();

s2.<any message in AbstractShape>;
```

Because the `AbstractShape` class contains a list of all the shape methods, we can send any of the shape messages to the variables `s1`, `s2`, and `s3`. Of course, we still cannot send the `setSpokes` message to `s3` without first casting `s3` to the `Wheel` class.

So should you or shouldn't you use interfaces? This is not really a question of vital importance in an introductory programming class where all the programs are relatively short and simple; however, the prevailing wisdom suggests that we use hierarchies of interfaces to organize behavior and hierarchies of classes to maximize code reuse. Justifying this advice is beyond this book's scope.

Relationships among Classes

Thus far in this book, we have seen that classes can be related to each other in several ways:

1. An object of one class can send a message to an object of another class. For example, a `Circle` object sends a message to a `StandardPen` object to draw that shape. In this case, the sender object's class *depends on* the receiver object's class, and their relationship is called *dependency*.

2. An object of one class can contain objects of another class as structural components. For example, the `TestScoresModel` object described in the case study of Chapter 9 contains `Student` objects. The relationship between a container class and the classes of the objects it contains is called *aggregation* or the *has-a* relationship.

3. An object's class can be a subclass of a more general class. For example, the `Wheel` class is a subclass of `Circle`, which in turn is a subclass of `AbstractShape`. These classes are related by *inheritance*, or the *is-a* relationship.

These three types of relationships among classes are depicted in the UML diagrams in Figure 10-7. Note that the third diagram also shows the relationship between a class (Abstract-Shape) and the interface (Shape) that it implements.

FIGURE 10-7
Three types of relationships among classes

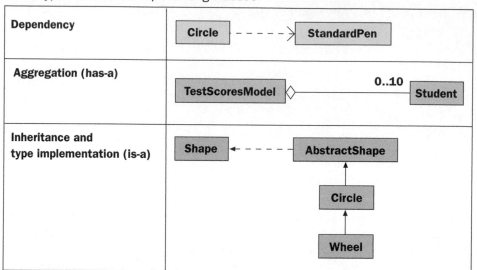

EXERCISE 10.7

1. Describe the process by which the Java Virtual Machine (JVM) locates the right method to execute at run time in the following example:

```
// In the server's code
private int myData;
public String someMethod(int x){
    return myData + super.someMethod(x);
}
// In the client's code
System.out.println(someObject.someMethod(10));
```

2. Give one example, other than those discussed in this chapter, of the relationships of dependency, aggregation, and inheritance among classes.

10.8 Acceptable Classes for Parameters and Return Values

The rules of Java, as enforced by the compiler, state that in any situation in which an object of class BBB is expected, it is always acceptable to substitute an object of a subclass but never of a superclass. The reason is simple. A subclass of BBB inherits all of BBB's methods, whereas no guarantees can be made about the methods in the superclass. The following code segment illustrates these points (the results would be the same if we substituted `Shape` for `AbstractShape` in the first line):

```
AbstractShape s;
Circle c;
Wheel w;

s = new Circle();    // Accepted by the compiler
c = new Circle();    // Accepted by the compiler
w = new Circle();    // Rejected by the compiler
c = new Wheel();     // Accepted by the compiler
```

In the rest of this section, we apply these principles to method parameters and return values. We already know that objects can be passed to and returned from methods. Actually, to speak more precisely, we should say references to objects can be passed to and returned from methods. It is obvious that an object must exist before it is passed to a method, but it is easy to forget that changes made to the object in the method persist after the method stops executing. On the other hand, an object returned by a method is usually created in the method, and it continues to exist after the method stops executing.

Rectangle In, Circle Out

For our first example we write a method that takes a rectangle as an input parameter and returns a circle. The circle has the same area and position as the rectangle. The method makes no changes to the rectangle, and it has to instantiate the circle:

```
static private Circle makeCircleFromRectangle (Rect rectangle){
   double area = rectangle.area();
   double radius = Math.sqrt (area / Math.PI);
   Circle circle = new Circle (rectangle.getXPos(),
                               rectangle.getYPos(),
                               radius);
   return circle;
}
```

Any Shape In, Circle Out

We now modify the previous method so that it accepts any shape as an input parameter—circle, rectangle, or wheel. The fact that all shapes understand the `area` method makes the task easy:

```
static private Circle makeCircleFromAnyShape (Shape shape){
   double area = shape.area();
   double radius = Math.sqrt (area / Math.PI);
   Circle circle = new Circle (shape.getXPos(),
                               shape.getYPos(),
                               radius);
   return circle;
}
```

Any Shape In, Any Shape Out

It is also possible for a method to return an arbitrary rather than a specific shape. The next method has two input parameters. The first parameter is a shape, and the second indicates the type of shape to return:

```
static private Shape makeOneShapeFromAnother (Shape inShape, String type){
   Shape outShape;                                    // declare outShape
   double area, radius, width, height;
   double x = inShape.getXPos();
   double y = inShape.getYPos();

   area = inShape.area();
   if (type.equals ("circle")){
      radius = Math.sqrt (area / Math.PI);
      outShape = new Circle (x, y, radius);           // assign a circle
   }
   else if (type.equals ("rectangle")){
      width = height = Math.sqrt (area);
      outShape = new Rect (x, y, width, height);      // assign a rectangle
   }
   else{ // it is a wheel
      radius = Math.sqrt (area / Math.PI);
      outShape = new Wheel (x, y, radius, 6);         // assign a wheel
   }
   return outShape;
}
```

The following code is a test of the previous method with the program's output shown in Figure 10-8.

```
// Example 10.5: Making one shape from another

public class TestShapes {

   public static void main (String[] args){
      Rect rect;
      Shape shape1, shape2, shape3;

      rect = new Rect (1,1,4,6);
      shape1 = makeOneShapeFromAnother (rect, "circle");
      shape2 = makeOneShapeFromAnother (rect, "rectangle");
      shape3 = makeOneShapeFromAnother (rect, "wheel");

      System.out.println ("\nRectangle Area: " + rect.area() +
                     "\nCircle    Area: " + shape1.area() +
                     "\nRectangle Area: " + shape2.area() +
                     "\nWheel     Area: " + shape3.area());
   }

   static private Shape makeOneShapeFromAnother (Shape inShape,
                                          String type){
```

```
... code as shown above ...
   }
}
```

FIGURE 10-8
Areas of various shapes made from a rectangle

```
Rectangle Area: 24.0
Circle    Area: 24.000000000000004
Rectangle Area: 23.999999999999996
Wheel     Area: 24.000000000000004
```

EXERCISE 10.8

1. State the rules for passing a parameter of one class to a method that expects a parameter of another class.

2. Class BB is a subclass of class AA. Method m expects a parameter of type BB. Which of the following method calls is syntactically incorrect?

a. m(new AA());

b. m(new BB());

10.9 Error Handling with Classes

In Chapter 6, we introduced a means of handling possible error conditions in a system that uses classes and objects. In this approach, a class's mutator method returns a boolean value to indicate whether the operation has been successful or an error has occurred and the operation has failed. In addition, the class provides a method that returns a string that states a rule describing the valid use of the mutator method. For example, following is the code for these two methods in an Employee object, followed by its use in some client code:

```
// In the Employee class
public String getHoursRules(){
   return "between 1 and 60, inclusive";
}

public boolean setHours(int hrs){
   if (!(1 <= hrs && hrs <= 60))
      return false;
   else{
      hours = hrs;
      return true;
   }
}
// In the client that uses an Employee object
// Input the hours worked until valid
System.out.print("Hours worked(" + emp.getHoursRules() + "): ");
while (!emp.setHours(reader.nextInt()));
```

Clearly, this kind of error checking improves the situation in Chapter 5, where our classes simply let errors go undetected. In this section, we introduce a more formal way of describing error conditions in code and another way of detecting and responding to errors.

Preconditions and Postconditions

Before we can implement code for error handling, we must determine what the error conditions for a class are. A systematic way to do this is to state these conditions in the class's interface as *preconditions* and *postconditions*. We can think of preconditions and postconditions as the subject of a conversation between the user and implementer of a method. Following is the general form of the conversation:

Implementer: "Here are the things that you must guarantee to be true before my method is invoked. They are its preconditions."

User: "Fine. And what do you guarantee will be the case if I do that?"

Implementer: "Here are the things that I guarantee to be true when my method finishes execution. They are its postconditions."

A method's preconditions describe what should be true before it is called, and its postconditions describe what will be true after it has finished executing. The preconditions describe the expected values of parameters and instance variables that the method is about to use. Postconditions describe the return value and any changes made to instance variables. Of course, if the caller does not meet the preconditions, then the method probably will not meet the postconditions.

In most programming languages, preconditions and postconditions are conveniently written as comments placed directly above a method's header. Let us add such documentation to a method header for the `Student` method `setScore` from Chapter 9. There are preconditions on each of the method's parameters:

1. The parameter `i`, which represents the position of the score, must be greater than or equal to 1 and less than or equal to the number of scores.

2. The parameter `score` must be greater than or equal to 0 and less than or equal to 100.

The method's postcondition states that the test score at position `i` has been set to `score`. We now return the `boolean` value `true` if the preconditions have been satisfied or `false` otherwise. Following is the code:

```
/*
 * Precondition: 1 <= i <= number of scores
 * Precondition: 0 <= score <= 100
 * Postcondition: test score at position i is set to score
 * Returns: true if the preconditions are satisfied or false otherwise
 */
public boolean setScore(int i, int score){
   if (i < 1 || i > tests.length || score < 0 || score > 100)
      return false;
   tests[i - 1] = score;
   return true;
}
```

Not all methods have pre- and postconditions. For example, the `Student` method `getName` simply returns the student's name, so its documentation mentions just the return value.

The writing of pre- and postconditions for each method might seem like a tedious task; however, that's how the developers of Java have done it, as an inspection of Sun's Java documentation reveals. And remember that, like the people at Sun, you are writing code primarily for other people to read.

EXERCISES 10.9

1. What do preconditions describe? Give an example.

2. What do postconditions describe? Give an example.

10.10 Exceptions

As you have seen in earlier chapters, Java throws an exception to signal a run-time error. There are occasions when you can throw your own exceptions in the classes you write. We now give an overview of how to do this.

Examples of Exceptions

Java provides a hierarchy of exception classes that represent the most commonly occurring exceptions. Following is a list of some of the commonly used exception classes in the package `java.lang`:

```
Exception
    RuntimeException
        ArithmeticException
        IllegalArgumentException
        IllegalStateException
        IndexOutOfBoundsException
            StringIndexOutOfBoundsException
            ArrayIndexOutOfBoundsException
        NullPointerException
        UnsupportedOperationException
```

Java throws an arithmetic exception when a program attempts to divide by 0 and a `null` pointer exception when a program attempts to send a message to a variable that does not reference an object. An array index out-of-bounds exception is thrown when the integer in an array subscript operator is less than 0 or greater than or equal to the array's length. Other types of exceptions, such as illegal state exceptions and illegal argument exceptions, can be used to enforce preconditions on methods. Other packages such as `java.util` define still more types of exceptions. In general, you determine which preconditions you want to enforce and then choose the appropriate type of exception to throw from Java's repertoire.

The syntax of the statement to throw an exception is

```
throw new <exception class>(<a string>);
```

where `<a string>` is the message to be displayed. When you are in doubt about which type of exception to throw, you can fall back on a `RuntimeException`. Following is an example:

```
if (number < 0)
    throw new RuntimeException("Number should be nonnegative");
```

How Exceptions Work

At run time, the computer keeps track of the dynamic context of a program. This context includes a chain of method calls, beginning with the method `main` in the main application class and ending with the currently executing method. When a piece of code in this method throws an exception, the computer examines the code immediately surrounding it for a `try-catch` statement (more on this statement later). If no such statement is found in this context, control returns immediately to the caller of the method. Once again, if no `try-catch` statement is found in that method, control moves up to its caller, and so on, until method `main` is reached. If no `try-catch` statement has been located at any point in this process, the computer halts the program with a trace of the method calls, the type of exception, and its error message, examples of which you have seen in earlier chapters.

Throwing Exceptions to Enforce Preconditions

A more hard-nosed approach to error handling is to have a class throw exceptions to enforce all of its methods' preconditions. Let's adopt that approach for the `Student` method `setScore` discussed earlier. We know the preconditions, so we begin by choosing the appropriate exception classes and describing these in the documentation. We will throw an `IllegalArgumentException` if either parameter violates the preconditions. Because the method either succeeds in setting a score or throws an exception, it returns `void` instead of a `boolean` value. The method header summarizes our error handling:

```
/*
 * Precondition: 1 <= i <= number of scores
 * Precondition: 0 <= score <= 100
 * Postcondition: test score at position i is set to score
 * throws IllegalArgumentException if i < 1 or i > number of scores
 * throws IllegalArgumentException if score < 0 or score > 100
 */
public void setScore (int i, int score){
    if (i < 1 || i > tests.length)
        throw new IllegalArgumentException(
                "i must be >= 1 and <= " + tests.length);
    if (score < MIN_SCORE || score > MAX_SCORE)
        throw new IllegalArgumentException(
                "score must be >= " +
                MIN_SCORE + " and <= " + MAX_SCORE);
    tests[i - 1] = score;
}
```

Catching an Exception

As you can see, the use of exceptions can make a server's code pretty foolproof. However, clients must still check the preconditions of such methods if they do not want these exceptions to halt their programs with run-time errors. There are two ways to do this:

1. Use a simple `if-else` statement to ask the right questions about the parameters before calling a method.

2. Embed the call to the method within a `try-catch` statement.

The `try-catch` statement allows a client to

■ Attempt the call of a method whose preconditions might be violated.

■ Catch any exceptions that the method might throw and respond to them gracefully.

For example, the following code displays the exception's error message in the terminal window instead of halting the program with the same message and a call trace:

```
int[] scores = {88, 99, 66};
Student s = new Student("Bill", scores);
try{
    s.setScore(4, 85);
}catch(IllegalArgumentException e){
    System.out.println(e);
}
```

When the `setScore` method throws the `IllegalArgumentException`, the computer passes it as a parameter to the `catch` clause, which assumes immediate control and continues execution.

This code catches and handles an exception only of the specified type. Suppose a method can throw two different types of exceptions, such as `IllegalArgumentException` and `IllegalStateException`. To catch either one of these, one can include two catch clauses:

```
try{
    someObject.someMethod(param1, param2);
}catch(IllegalStateException e){
    System.out.println(e);
}catch(IllegalArgumentException e){
    System.out.println(e);
}
```

The computer runs down the list of `catch` clauses until the exception's type matches that of a parameter or no match is found. If no match is found, the exception is passed up the call chain as described earlier.

To guarantee that any exception is caught, you can use the generic `Exception` class, which matches any exception type:

```
try{
    s.setScore(4, 200);
}catch(Exception e){
    System.out.println(e);
}
```

Creating Online Documentation With `javadoc`

As we mentioned in Chapter 5, Sun provides online, browsable documentation of all standard Java classes. This documentation is created with a tool called `javadoc`. You can create similar documentation for your own classes. To do so, you perform the following steps:

1. Edit the `.java` file to include special comment syntax to mark the information that will appear in the document pages. The items marked usually include a summary of the class's purpose, method parameters, method return values, and exceptions thrown by methods.

2. Run the `javadoc` command with the `.java` file to generate the online documentation. `javadoc` generates a set of HMTL files that can be loaded into a Web browser.

The next code listing shows the `Student` class from Chapter 9, updated with static constants and exceptions. We have also inserted comments for `javadoc`. Note the slight difference in syntax from the ordinary Java multiline comments. The symbol `/**` is used instead of `/*` to begin a comment. The comment that describes the purpose of the class should be placed between the class header and the `import` statements (if they exist). The lines that begin with the '`@`' character mark items that receive special formatting in the documentation.

```java
// Case Study 9.1: Student class

/**
Represents a student with a name and several test scores
*/

public class Student{

    /**
    The minimum score (0)
    */
    public static int MIN_SCORE = 0;

    /**
    The maximum score (100)
    */
    public static int MAX_SCORE = 100;

    private String name;
    private int[] tests;

    /**
    Default: name is "" and each of 3 scores is 0
    */
    public Student(){
        this("");
    }

    /**
    Name is nm and each of 3 scores is 0
    @param nm the name of the student
    */
    public Student(String nm){
        this(nm, 3);
    }
```

```java
/**
Name is nm and each of n scores is 0
@param nm the name of the student
@param n the number of scores
*/
public Student(String nm, int n){
   name = nm;
   tests = new int[n];
   for (int i = 0; i < tests.length; i++)
      tests[i] = 0;
}

/**
Name is nm and the scores are taken from array t
@param nm the name of the student
@param t an array of test scores
*/
public Student(String nm, int[] t){
   name = nm;
   tests = new int[t.length];
   for (int i = 0; i < tests.length; i++)
      tests[i] = t[i];
}

/**
Builds a copy of a student
@param s the student to be copied
*/
public Student(Student s){
   this(s.name, s.tests);
}

/**
Changes the student's name
@param nm the new name
*/
public void setName (String nm){
   name = nm;
}

/**
@return the student's name
*/
public String getName (){
   return name;
}

/**
@param i the ith
@param score the ith score
@throws IllegalArgumentException if i < 1 or i > number of scores
@throws IllegalArgumentException if score < MIN_SCORE or score >
MAX_SCORE
*/
public void setScore (int i, int score){
```

```java
        if (i < 1 || i > tests.length)
            throw new IllegalArgumentException(
                    "i must be >= 1 and <= " + tests.length);
        if (score < MIN_SCORE || score > MAX_SCORE)
            throw new IllegalArgumentException(
                    "score must be >= " +
                    MIN_SCORE + " and <= " + MAX_SCORE);
        tests[i - 1] = score;
    }

    /**
    @param i the ith
    @throws IllegalArgumentException if i < 1 or i > number of scores
    @return the student's ith score
    */
    public int getScore (int i){
        if (i < 1 || i >= tests.length)
            throw new IllegalArgumentException(
                    "i must be >= 1 and <= " + tests.length);
        return tests[i - 1];
    }

    /**
    @return the student's average score
    */
    public int getAverage(){
        int sum = 0;
        for (int i = 0; i < tests.length; i++)
            sum += tests[i];
        return sum / tests.length;
    }

    /**
    @return the student's highest score
    */
    public int getHighScore(){
        int highScore;
        highScore = tests[0];
        for (int i = 1; i < tests.length; i++)
            highScore = Math.max (highScore, tests[i]);
        return highScore;
    }

    /**
    @return the student's string representation
    */
    public String toString(){
        String str;
        str = "Name:     " + name  + "\n";
        for (int i = 0; i < tests.length; i++)
            str += "test " + i + ":   " + tests[i] + "\n";
        str += "Average: " + getAverage();
        return str;
    }
```

```
/**
@return null if there are no errors or an appropriate error message
*/
public String validateData(){
   if (name.equals ("")) return "SORRY: name required";
   for (int i = 0; i < tests.length; i++){
      if (tests[i] < 0 || tests[i] > 100){
         String str = "SORRY: must have "+ 0
                     + " <= test score <= " + 100;
         return str;
      }
   }
   return null;
}
}
```

@param, @return, and @throws are the standard tags recognized by javadoc. To process just the Student class, run javadoc as follows:

```
javadoc Student.java
```

Figure 10-9 shows screen shots of two portions of the resulting Web page.

FIGURE 10-9
javadoc Web pages for the Student class

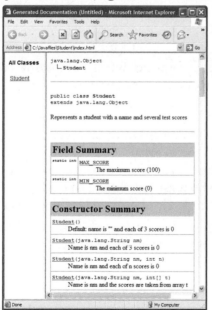

If you have several files to process, you can list them as command-line arguments to javadoc. For example, to process just Student and TestScoresModel from Chapter 9, you can run

```
javadoc Student.java TestScoresModel.java
```

To process all of the source files in the current directory, you can run

```
javadoc *.java
```

EXERCISES 10.10

1. When should a method throw an exception? Give an example.

2. Explain what happens at run time when a method throws an exception.

3. Explain how an exception can be handled under program control.

4. List the three standard tags used to create documentation with `javadoc` and describe their purposes.

10.11 Reference Types, Equality, and Object Identity

In Chapters 2, 5, and 6, we made a distinction between variables of primitive types—which contain numbers, characters, Booleans—and variables of reference types—which contain references or pointers to objects, but never the objects themselves. Thus, it is possible for more than one variable to point to the same object, a situation known as *aliasing*. This occurs when the programmer assigns one object variable to another. It is also possible, of course, for two object variables to refer to distinct objects of the same type.

Comparing Objects for Equality

The possibility of aliasing can lead to unintended results when comparing two object variables for equality. There are two ways to compare objects for equality:

1. Use the equality operator ==.

2. Use the instance method `equals`. This method is defined in the `Object` class and uses the == operator by default. This method is similar to the method `toString`, which was discussed earlier in this book and which, by default, returns the name of the object's class for any object that does not override it. All classes, which are subclasses of `Object`, inherit the method `equals` and use it when it is not overridden in the receiver object's class.

Consider the following code segment, which reads a string from the keyboard, uses both methods to compare this string to a string literal, and outputs the results:

```
String str = reader.nextLine();          // Read string from keyboard.

System.out.println (str == "Java");       // Displays false no matter what
                                          // string was entered.
System.out.println (str.equals ("Java")); // Displays true if the string
                                          // entered was "Java", and false
                                          // otherwise.
```

Following is the explanation:

- The objects referenced by the variable str and the literal "Java" are two different string objects in memory, even though the characters they contain might be the same. The first string object was created in the keyboard reader during user input; the second string object was created internally within the program.

- The operator == compares the references to the objects, not the contents of the objects. Thus, if the two references do not point to the same object in memory, == returns false. Because the two strings in our example are not the same object in memory, == returns false.

- The method equals returns true, even when two strings are not the same object in memory, if their characters happen to be the same. If at least one pair of characters fails to match, the method equals returns false.

- A corollary of these facts is that the operator != can return true for two strings, even though the method equals also returns true.

- To summarize, == tests for object identity, whereas equals tests for structural similarity as defined by the implementing class.

The operator == also can be used with other objects, such as buttons and menu items. In these cases, too, the operator tests for object identity: a reference to the same object in memory. With window objects, the use of == is appropriate because most of the time we want to compare references. For other objects, however, such as the student objects discussed in Chapter 9, the use of == should be avoided. To test two student objects for equality, we implement the method equals in the Student class. We will consider two students equal if

- They are identical, or

- They are instances of Student and their names are equal.

Following is the code for the method:

```
// Compare two students for equality
   public boolean equals (Object other){
      if (this == other)                    // Test for identity
         return true;
      if (! (other instanceof Student))    // Test for a Student
         return false;
      Student s = (Student)other;          // Cast to a Student
      return name.equals (s.getName());    // Compare the names
   }
```

Note that the method expects an Object as a parameter. This means that the user can pass an object of any class when the method is called. The method should first compare the receiver object (indicated by the word this) to the parameter object for identity using ==. If the two objects are not identical, the method examines their contents only if the parameter object is in fact an instance of the Student class. Therefore, the method must next do one of two things:

1. Return false if the parameter object is not an instance of Student. The operator instanceof is used to determine the class or interface of an object.

2. If the parameter object is an instance of class Student, cast its class down from Object to Student before accessing the data within it.

Copying Objects

As mentioned in Chapter 5, the attempt to copy an object with a simple assignment statement can cause a problem. The following code creates two references to one student object when the intent is to copy the contents of one student object to another:

```
Student s1, s2;
s1 = new Student("Mary");
s2 = s1;                              // s1 and s2 refer to the same
                                      // object
```

In Chapter 9, we added a constructor for students that expects another object of type Student as a parameter. This constructor copies the parameter's data into the instance variables of the new student:

```
Student s1, s2;
s1 = new Student("Mary");
s2 = new Student(s1);                 // s1 and s2 refer to
                                      // different objects
```

When clients of a class might copy objects, there is a more standard way of providing a method that does so. The class implements the Java interface Cloneable. This interface authorizes the method clone, which is defined in the Object class, to construct a field-wise copy of the object. We now can rewrite the foregoing code so that it creates a copy of a student object:

```
Student s1, s2;
s1 = new Student ("Mary");
s2 = s1.clone();                  // s1 and s2 refer to different objects
```

Note that == returns false and equals returns true for an object and its clone.

The implementation of the clone method returns a new instance of Student with the values of the instance variables from the receiver student. Following is the code for method clone:

```
// Clone a new student
public Object clone(){
   return new Student(name, tests);
}
```

Many of Java's standard classes, such as String, already implement the Cloneable interface, so they include a clone method. When instance variables of a class are themselves objects that are cloneable, it is a good idea to send them the clone message to obtain copies when implementing the clone method for that class. This process is called *deep copying* and can help minimize program errors.

Because tests for equality and cloning are fairly standard operations in all implementations, the methods equals and clone should be added to the Java interface for your classes, if there is one.

EXERCISES 10.11

1. Why should a programmer use the method `equals` instead of the operator `==` to compare two objects for equality?

2. What are the outputs when the following code segment is run?

```
Student s1 = new Student("Bill");
Student s2 = new Student("Bill");
String name = "Bill";

System.out.println(s1.equals(s2));
System.out.println(s1 == s2);
System.out.println(s1.equals(name));
```

3. What happens when an object is assigned to a variable?

4. How can you obtain a true copy of an object?

10.12 Graphics and GUIs: Drawing Multiple Shapes

The `TurtleGraphics` package used earlier in this chapter automatically refreshes the graphics window with any images that the pen has drawn. In this section, we examine the related problem of how to maintain multiple shapes in graphics programs such as those discussed in Chapters 3 through 6.

> **Extra Challenge**
>
> This Graphics and GUIs section gives you the opportunity to explore concepts and programming techniques required to develop modern graphics applications and graphical user interfaces. This material is not required in order to proceed with the other chapters of the book.

Java's Forgetful Bitmap

As we saw in previous chapters, images and shapes are painted in a GUI component by sending messages to that component's graphics context. This is normally done in the component's `paintComponent` method, which the JVM runs whenever the component's window needs to be refreshed. The method `repaint` also accomplishes a refresh under program control. For example, the programmer can call `repaint` after an image or shape has changed position. This method calls `paintComponent`, which paints the component's background color and redraws all of its shapes and images.

The bitmap of a Java graphics context does not retain the information about images and shapes after they are drawn to a window. This phenomenon is known as a *forgetful bitmap*. That's why the programmer must write a `paintComponent` method and use `repaint` for window refreshes. Actually, the forgetful bitmap is not much of a problem, as long as `paintComponent` knows where to go to find information about the images and shapes to paint. We now consider some simple solutions to this problem.

A Database of Circles

To guarantee that all images and shapes are painted on each refresh, a graphics application must maintain information about them in a database. In this section, we show how to set up and manage a simple database of circles.

In Chapter 5, we designed and implemented a class for representing circles. We then showed how to use this class in a sample application, which draws two circles in a panel. At startup, the panel instantiates the two circles and saves references to them in two instance variables. When the panel needs refreshing, the method `paintComponent` sends the appropriate messages to the two variables to paint the circles. (*A note of caution*: The `Circle` class discussed here is different from the one introduced in Section 10.4, which uses a turtle graphics pen to draw itself.)

When there are more than one or two circles to be accessed, we can store them in an array. The method `paintComponent` traverses the array to paint all of the circles. In addition, we can use the array to perform other functions, such as search for a circle that contains the current mouse coordinates.

Our first example program is a revised version of Example 5.5. This program displays two circles at startup and allows the user to move them around by dragging the mouse. In the new version of the program, an array of 10 circles replaces the two `Circle` instance variables in the `ColorPanel` class. The panel's constructor instantiates the array and fills it with circles of equal size and randomly generated color. `paintComponent` paints all of the circles. The method `mousePressed` in the class `PanelListener` searches the array for a circle that contains the mouse coordinates. If a circle is found, the variable `selectedCircle` is set to that circle. The classes `Circle` and `GUIWindow` remain as they were in Chapter 5. Here is the code for the revised `ColorPanel` class:

```
// Example 10.6: Displays 10 circles of random color
// Allows the user to drag a circle to another position

import javax.swing.*;
import java.awt.*;
import java.awt.event.*;            //For the mouse events
import java.util.Random;

public class ColorPanel extends JPanel{

   private Circle database[];          // The array of circles
   private Circle selectedCircle;      // Used to track selected shape
   private int x, y;                   // Used to track mouse coordinates

   public ColorPanel(Color backColor){
      setBackground(backColor);
      Random gen = new Random();
      // Create 10 circles of random color
      database = new Circle[10];
      for (int i = 0; i < database.length; i++){
         Color color = new Color(gen.nextInt(256), gen.nextInt(256),
                                 gen.nextInt(256));
         Circle c = new Circle(i * 40, 100, 25, color);
         c.setFilled(true);
         database[i] = c;
      }
      selectedCircle = null;
      addMouseListener(new PanelListener());
      addMouseMotionListener(new PanelMotionListener());
   }
```

```java
public void paintComponent(Graphics g){
   super.paintComponent(g);
   for (Circle c: database)      // Draw all the circles
      c.draw(g);
}

private class PanelListener extends MouseAdapter{

   public void mousePressed(MouseEvent e){
      //Select a circle if it contains the mouse coordinates
      x = e.getX();
      y = e.getY();
      // Search for a circle, starting with the last drawn
      for (int i = database.length  - 1; i >= 0; i--)
         if (database[i].containsPoint(x, y)){
            selectedCircle = database[i];
            break;
         }
   }

   public void mouseReleased(MouseEvent e){
      // Deselect the selected circle
      x = e.getX();
      y = e.getY();
      selectedCircle = null;
   }
}

private class PanelMotionListener extends MouseMotionAdapter{

   public void mouseDragged(MouseEvent e){
      // Compute the distance and move the selected circle
      int newX = e.getX();
      int newY = e.getY();
      int dx = newX - x;
      int dy = newY - y;
      if (selectedCircle != null)
         selectedCircle.move(dx, dy);
      x = newX;
      y = newY;
      repaint();
   }
}
}
```

Note that the method `containsPoint` searches the array of circles from right to left, whereas `paintComponent` draws them from left to right. More recently drawn circles will appear on top of other circles when overlap occurs. A search in reverse guarantees that the uppermost circle will be selected when the mouse is clicked in an area of overlap.

A Database of Shapes

The program in example 10.6 maintains a database of circles. More realistic graphics applications might use many other types of shapes as well, such as rectangles, triangles, and more specialized shapes such as houses. A complex shape such as a house might be composed of simpler shapes such as rectangles. If we organize all of these types of shapes in a hierarchy that implements a common interface, we can modify the program of Example 10.6 to draw any kind of shapes. Here is the code for the Shape interface:

```java
// Interface for shapes

import java.awt.*;

public interface Shape{

    public void draw(Graphics g);
    public boolean containsPoint(int x, int y);
    public void move(int xAmount, int yAmount);
    public void setFilled(boolean b);
}
```

Let's assume that we have just two types of shapes, called Circle and Rect (see Section 5.6), that implement Shape. The changes to the ColorPanel class of Example 10.5 are then quite straightforward. We replace each variable declaration of type Circle with a variable declaration of type Shape and alter the variable names for readability. For example, the array declaration is changed from

```java
private Circle[] database;
```

to

```java
private Shape[] database;
```

The array can now store any object whose class implements the Shape interface. Because any of the methods used with an object in the array, such as draw, containsPoint, and move, work with any shape, we don't have to change any other code. Here is a listing of a revised version of ColorPanel that displays several circles and rectangles:

```java
// Example 10.7: Displays 10 shapes of random color
// Allows the user to drag a shape to another position

import javax.swing.*;
import java.awt.*;
import java.awt.event.*;          //For the mouse events
import java.util.Random;

public class ColorPanel extends JPanel{

    private Shape database[];        // The array of shapes
    private Shape selectedShape;     // Used to track selected shape
    private int x, y;                // Used to track mouse coordinates
```

```java
public ColorPanel(Color backColor){
    setBackground(backColor);
    Random gen = new Random();
    // Create 10 shapes of random color
    database = new Shape[10];
    for (int i = 0; i < database.length; i++){
        Color color = new Color(gen.nextInt(256), gen.nextInt(256),
                                gen.nextInt(256));
        // Flip a coin to determine which type of shape to create
        Shape s;
        if (gen.nextInt(2) == 1)
            s = new Circle(i * 40, 50, 25, color);
        else
            s = new Rect(i * 40, 100, 50, 50, color);
        s.setFilled(true);
        database[i] = s;
    }
    selectedShape = null;
    addMouseListener(new PanelListener());
    addMouseMotionListener(new PanelMotionListener());
}

public void paintComponent(Graphics g){
    super.paintComponent(g);
    for (Shape s : database)      // Draw all the shapes
        s.draw(g);
}

private class PanelListener extends MouseAdapter{

    public void mousePressed(MouseEvent e){
        // Select a shape if it contains the mouse coordinates
        x = e.getX();
        y = e.getY();
        // Search for a shape, starting with the last one added
        for (int i = database.length  - 1; i >= 0; i--)
            if (database[i].containsPoint(x, y)){
                selectedShape = database[i];
                break;
            }
    }

    public void mouseReleased(MouseEvent e){
        // Deselect the selected shape
        x = e.getX();
        y = e.getY();
        selectedShape = null;
    }
}

private class PanelMotionListener extends MouseMotionAdapter{

    public void mouseDragged(MouseEvent e){
        //Compute the distance and move the selected shape
        int newX = e.getX();
```

```
                 int newY = e.getY();
                 int dx = newX - x;
                 int dy = newY - y;
                 if (selectedShape != null)
                    selectedShape.move(dx, dy);
                 x = newX;
                 y = newY;
                 repaint();
              }
           }
        }
```

The Model/View Pattern Revisited

We conclude this section with one more refinement of our shape manipulation program. The current version's color panel maintains an array of shapes. This design violates the division of responsibilities between model and view discussed in earlier chapters. The panel should be responsible for displaying shapes but should not have to manage an array of shapes. This problem will only get worse when we start to add and remove shapes based on user inputs.

We can solve the problem by placing all of the shapes in a distinct model object of type ShapeModel. This object is responsible for adding new shapes, selecting a shape, and drawing them. We now present a revised ColorPanel class that uses a ShapeModel with changes marked by comments. The model's implementation is similar to that of the TestScoresModel of Chapter 9 and is left as an exercise:

```java
// Example 10.8: Displays 10 shapes of random color
// Allows the user to drag a shape to another position

import javax.swing.*;
import java.awt.*;
import java.awt.event.*;             // For the mouse events
import java.util.Random;

public class ColorPanel extends JPanel{

   private ShapeModel database;      // Change: just a model
   private Shape selectedShape;      // Used to track selected shape
   private int x, y;                 // Used to track mouse coordinates

   public ColorPanel(Color backColor){
      setBackground(backColor);
      Random gen = new Random();
      // Change: create a model for 10 shapes
      database = new ShapeModel(10);
      for (int i = 0; i < 10; i++){
         Color color = new Color(gen.nextInt(256), gen.nextInt(256),
                                 gen.nextInt(256));
         // Flip a coin to determine which type of shape to create
         Shape s;
         if (gen.nextInt(2) == 1)
            s = new Circle(i * 40, 50, 25, color);
         else
```

```
            s = new Rect(i * 40, 100, 50, 50, color);
         s.setFilled(true);
         database.add(s);          // Change: no more array access
      }
      selectedShape = null;
      addMouseListener(new PanelListener());
      addMouseMotionListener(new PanelMotionListener());
   }

   public void paintComponent(Graphics g){
      super.paintComponent(g);
      // Change: draw all the shapes
      database.draw(g);           // Piece of cake!
   }

   private class PanelListener extends MouseAdapter{

      public void mousePressed(MouseEvent e){
         // Select a shape if it contains the mouse coordinates
         x = e.getX();
         y = e.getY();
         // Change: search returns the shape or null
         selectedShape = database.containsPoint(x, y);
      }

      public void mouseReleased(MouseEvent e){
         // Deselect the selected shape
         x = e.getX();
         y = e.getY();
         selectedShape = null;
      }
   }

   private class PanelMotionListener extends MouseMotionAdapter{

      public void mouseDragged(MouseEvent e){
         // Compute the distance and move the selected shape
         int newX = e.getX();
         int newY = e.getY();
         int dx = newX - x;
         int dy = newY - y;
         if (selectedShape != null)
            selectedShape.move(dx, dy);
         x = newX;
         y = newY;
         repaint();
      }
   }
}
```

Note that the model includes the methods `add`, `draw`, and `containsPoint`. These are the only methods needed for this application, but others could be added for more sophisticated applications, as we see in later chapters.

EXERCISE 10.12

1. This chapter presents two different class hierarchies for representing and drawing geometric shapes. One uses turtle graphics to draw the shapes and the other uses Java's standard graphics classes. Discuss the advantages and disadvantages of these two design strategies.

SUMMARY

In this chapter, you learned:

- Class (`static`) variables provide storage for data that all instances of a class can access but do not have to own separately. Class (`static`) methods are written primarily for class variables.

- An interface specifies a set of methods that implementing classes must include. An interface gives clients enough information to use a class.

- Polymorphism and inheritance provide a means of reducing the amount of code that must be written by servers and learned by clients in a system with a large number of cooperating classes. Classes that extend other classes inherit their data and methods. Methods in different classes that have the same name are polymorphic. Abstract classes, which are not instantiated, exist for the sole purpose of organizing related subclasses and containing their common data and methods.

- Error handling can be distributed among methods and classes by using preconditions, postconditions, and exceptions.

- Because of the possibility of aliasing, the programmer should provide an `equals` method for comparing two objects for equality and a `clone` method for creating a copy of an object.

VOCABULARY *Review*

Define the following terms:		
Abstract class	Concrete class	Interface
Abstract method	Dependency	Overriding
Aggregation	Final method	Postcondition
Class (`static`) method	Inheritance	Precondition
Class (`static`) variable		

REVIEW *Questions*

FILL IN THE BLANK

Complete the following sentences by writing the correct word or words in the blanks provided.

1. Methods and variables that belong to a class rather than an instance are called _____ or _____ variables and methods.

2. The keyword used to invoke a constructor or method in a superclass is called _____.

3. The visibility modifier _____ makes a method or variable visible to subclasses but not to other clients.

4. A(n) _____ class contains common behavior and data for a set of subclasses but is not instantiated.

5. A(n) _____ method consists of just a head and forces all subclasses to implement it.

6. _____ and _____ state the assumptions that are true before a method executes correctly and after it executes correctly.

7. The method _____ is the conventional Java method for comparing two objects for equality, whereas the method _____ is the conventional Java method for copying an object.

PROJECTS

PROJECT 10-1

Design a hierarchy of classes that models the classification of your favorite region of the animal kingdom. Your hierarchy should be at most three classes deep and should employ abstract classes on the first two levels.

PROJECT 10-2

Design a hierarchy of classes that represents the classification of artifacts, such as vehicles.

PROJECT 10-3

Add a method `perimeter` to the `Shape` hierarchy from this chapter. This method should return the circumference of a circle and a wheel and the perimeter of a rectangle.

PROJECT 10-4

Add a `Triangle` class to the `Shape` hierarchy from this chapter. Note the following points:

- A triangle is specified by three vertices or pairs of coordinates. The first pair is the position (xPos, yPos).

- The move method for a triangle, which adds the x and y distances to each of the vertices, must override the move method in the abstract class; therefore, the move method in the abstract class cannot be final.

- The distance between two points $(x1,y1)$ and $(x2,y2)$ is equal to the square root of $((x1 - x2) * (x1 - x2) + (y1 - y2) * (y1 - y2))$.

- The area of a triangle can be computed from its vertices using the formula ½ * the absolute value of $(x1 * y2 - x2 * y1 + x2 * y3 - x3 * y2 + x3 * y1 - x1 * y3)$.

- A triangle is stretched away from its position at $(xPos,yPos)$. Thus, the other two vertices are incremented by multiplying their distance from $(xPos,yPos)$ by the factors. For example, the new value of $x2$ is equal to $xPos + (x2 - xPos) * factor$.

PROJECT 10-5

Design a class hierarchy for bank accounts. The concrete types of accounts are checking accounts, savings accounts, and credit accounts. Common behavior includes deposits, withdrawals, and obtaining a balance. Credit and savings accounts have an interest rate. Credit accounts have a credit line or maximum amount that may be borrowed. Be sure your design includes the appropriate interface, abstract class, and concrete classes.

PROJECT 10-6

Browse Java's class hierarchy on Sun's Web site (see Appendix A). Write an essay that describes the design ideas underlying a class hierarchy that you find interesting among Java's classes.

PROJECT 10-7

Implement the ShapeModel class that maintains the shapes used in the drawing program of Section 10.12.

CRITICAL *Thinking*

Jack has written software that uses many similar classes and has written interfaces for them. However, he never writes abstract classes, which he considers too much work. Jill tells him that he needs to use abstract classes where they would be helpful. What can you say to support Jill's advice? Use an example from this chapter.

ARRAYS CONTINUED

OBJECTIVES	VOCABULARY
Upon completion of this chapter, you should be able to:	Array list
■ Use string methods appropriately.	Binary search
■ Write a method for searching an array.	Bubble sort
■ Understand why a sorted array can be searched more efficiently than an unsorted array.	Immutable object
■ Write a method to sort an array.	Insertion sort
■ Write methods to perform insertions and removals at given positions in an array.	Linear search
■ Understand the issues involved when working with arrays of objects.	Selection sort
■ Perform simple operations with Java's `ArrayList` class.	Substring
Estimated Time: 5 hours	Wrapper class

In Chapter 9, we examined how to declare array variables, instantiate array objects, and manipulate arrays using the subscript operator, loops, and methods. The current chapter covers more complex operations on arrays, such as searching, sorting, insertions, and removals. Along the way, we examine issues that arise in the use of arrays of objects and we introduce Java's `ArrayList` class. As a prelude to these topics, we begin with a look at some advanced string methods.

11.1 Advanced Operations on Strings

Thus far in this text, we have used strings without manipulating their contents very much. However, most text-processing applications spend time examining the characters in strings, taking them apart, and building new strings. For example, consider the problem of extracting words from a line of text. To obtain the first word, we could copy the string's characters to a new string until we reach the first space character in the string (assuming the delimiter between words is the space) or we reach the length of the string. Following is a code segment that uses this strategy:

```java
// Create a sample string
String str = "Hi there!";

// Variable to hold the first word, set to empty string
String word = "";

// Visit all the characters in the string
for (int i = 0; i < str.length(); i++){

   // Or stop when a space is found
   if (str.charAt(i) == ' ')
      break;

   // Add the non-space character to the word
   word += str.charAt(i);
}
```

As you can see, this code combines the tasks of finding the first space character and building a *substring* of the original string. The problem is solved much more easily by using two separate string methods that are designed for these tasks. The first method, `indexOf`, expects the target character as a parameter and returns the position of the first instance of that character or −1 if the character is not in the string. The second method, `substring`, expects two integer parameters indicating the starting and ending positions of the substring. This method returns the substring that runs from the starting position up to but not including the ending position. Here is a short program that uses these methods:

```java
// Example 11.1: Test the methods indexOf and substring

public class TestStringMethods{

   public static void main(String[] args){
      String str = "Hi there!";

      // Search for the position of the first space
      int endPosition = str.indexOf(' ');

      // If there is no space, use the whole string
      if (endPosition == -1)
         endPosition = str.length();

      // Extract the first word
      String word = str.substring(0, endPosition);

      // Output the results
      System.out.println(endPosition);    // Prints 2
      System.out.println(word);           // Prints "Hi"
   }
}
```

Table 11-1 describes some commonly used `string` methods.

TABLE 11-1
Some commonly used string methods

METHOD	DESCRIPTION
charAt (anIndex) returns char	Example: `chr = myStr.charAt(4);` Returns the character at the position `anIndex`. Remember that the first character is at position 0. An exception is thrown (i.e., an error is generated) if `anIndex` is out of range (i.e., does not indicate a valid position within `myStr`).
compareTo (aString) returns int	Example: `i = myStr.compareTo("abc");` Compares two strings alphabetically. Returns 0 if `myStr` equals `aString`, a value less than 0 if `myStr` string is alphabetically less than `aString`, and a value greater than 0 if `myStr` string is alphabetically greater than `aString`.
equals (aString) returns boolean	Example: `boolean = myStr.equals("abc");` Returns true if `myStr` equals `aString`; else returns false. Because of implementation peculiarities in Java, never test for equality like this: `myStr == aString`

equalsIgnoreCase
    (aString)
    returns boolean
	Similar to equals but ignores case during the comparison.

indexOf (aCharacter) returns int	Example: `i = myStr.indexOf('z')` Returns the index within `myStr` of the first occurrence of `aCharacter` or −1 if `aCharacter` is absent.

indexOf (aCharacter,
    beginIndex)
    returns int
	Example: `i = myStr.indexOf('z', 6);`
	Similar to the preceding method except the search starts at position `beginIndex` rather than at the beginning of `myStr`. An exception is thrown (i.e., an error is generated) if `beginIndex` is out of range (i.e., does not indicate a valid position within `myStr`).

indexOf (aSubstring) returns int	Example: `i = myStr.indexOf("abc")` Returns the index within `myStr` of the first occurrence of `aSubstring` or −1 if `aSubstring` is absent.

indexOf (aSubstring,
    beginIndex)
    returns int
	Example: `i = myStr.indexOf("abc", 6)`
	Similar to the preceding method except the search starts at position `beginIndex` rather than at the beginning of `myStr`. An exception is thrown (i.e., an error is generated) if `beginIndex` is out of range (i.e., does not indicate a valid position within `myStr`).

length() returns int	Example: `i = myStr.length();` Returns the length of `myStr`.

replace (oldChar,
    newChar)
    returns String
	Example: `str = myStr.replace('z', 'Z');`
	Returns a new string resulting from replacing all occurrences of `oldChar` in `myStr` with `newChar`. `myStr` is not changed.

TABLE 11-1 Continued
Some commonly used string methods

METHOD	DESCRIPTION
substring (beginIndex) returns String	Example: `str = myStr.substring(6);` Returns a new string that is a substring of `myStr`. The substring begins at location `beginIndex` and extends to the end of `myStr`. An exception is thrown (i.e., an error is generated) if `beginIndex` is out of range (i.e., does not indicate a valid position within `myStr`).
substring (beginIndex, endIndex) returns String	Example: `str = myStr.substring(4, 8);` Similar to the preceding method except the substring extends to location `endIndex - 1` rather than to the end of `myStr`.
toLowerCase() returns String	Example: `str = myStr.toLowerCase();` `str` is the same as `myStr` except that all letters have been converted to lowercase. `myStr` **is not changed.**
toUpperCase() returns String	Example: `str = myStr.toUpperCase();` `str` is the same as `myStr` except that all letters have been converted to uppercase. `myStr` **is not changed.**
trim() returns String	Example: `str = myStr.trim();` `str` is the same as `myStr` except that leading and trailing spaces, if any, are absent. `myStr` **is not changed.**

Note that there are no mutator methods for strings. The reason for this is that strings are *immutable objects*. Once a string is created, its length cannot change and one cannot modify any of its characters.

Counting the Words in a Sentence

Our next program illustrates the use of the string methods `length`, `indexOf`, and `substring` to solve a complex problem. The program accepts sentences as inputs from the keyboard. The program displays the number of words in each sentence and the average length of a word. The program assumes that words are separated by at least one blank. Punctuation marks are considered parts of words. The program halts when the user presses just the Enter key. Here is the code followed by a brief discussion:

```
// Example 11.2: Count the words and compute the average
// word length in a sentence

import java.util.Scanner;

public class SentenceStats{

    public static void main(String[] args){

        Scanner reader = new Scanner(System.in);

        // Keep taking inputs
        while (true){
            System.out.print("Enter a sentence: ");
            String input = reader.nextLine();
```

```java
            // Quit when the user just presses Enter
            if (input.equals(""))
                break;

            // Initialize the counters and indexes
            int wordCount = 0;
            int sentenceLength = 0;
            int beginPosition = 0;
            int endPosition = input.indexOf(' ');

            // Continue until a blank is not seen
            while (endPosition != -1){

                // If at least one nonblank character (a word) was seen
                if (endPosition > beginPosition){
                    wordCount++;
                    String word = input.substring(beginPosition, endPosition);
                    sentenceLength += word.length();
                }

                // Update the indexes to go to the next word
                beginPosition = endPosition + 1;
                endPosition = input.indexOf(' ', beginPosition);
            }

            // If at least one nonblank character was seen
            // at the end of the sentence, consider it a word
            if (beginPosition < input.length()){
                wordCount++;
                String word = input.substring(beginPosition, input.length());
                sentenceLength += word.length();
            }

            // Trap the case where there were no words
            if (wordCount > 0){
                System.out.println("Word count: " + wordCount);
                System.out.println("Sentence length: " + sentenceLength);
                System.out.println("Average word length: " +
                                   sentenceLength / wordCount);
            }
        }
    }
}
```

This program contains two loops. The outer loop accepts inputs from the user and runs the nested loop to process each input. The nested loop advances two indexes through an input string. On each pass through this loop, the indexes represent the beginning and ending positions of each word. Initially, the beginning position is 0 and the ending position is the result of running indexOf with a blank character. At this point, there are several cases to consider:

1. indexOf returns −1, meaning that a blank was not found. At this point, the nested loop has moved through the entire input string and there are no more blanks to be seen, or the loop is not entered at all. If the beginning position is less than the length of the input string at

this point (below the loop), the last word needs to be counted and extracted from the input string. The program uses the `substring` method with the length of the input string as the ending position in this case.

2. `indexOf` returns an ending position that is greater than the current beginning position. This means that at least one nonblank character (a word) has been seen before encountering a blank. In this case, the program continues in the nested loop. It increments the word count and extracts the word using `substring` with the current beginning and ending positions. The program then increments the sentence length by the length of the word.

3. `indexOf` returns an ending position that is equal to the current beginning position. This happens if there are any leading blanks in the sentence or there is more than one blank following a word. In this case, the program should not count a word or attempt to extract it from the input string, but just continue in the nested loop. This will have the effect of scanning over the extra blank and ignoring it.

4. In cases 2 and 3, the nested loop continues by updating the beginning and ending positions. The beginning position is incremented to 1 greater than the ending position. Then the ending position is reset to the result of running `indexOf` once more with a blank and the new beginning position. This has the effect of advancing the positions to the beginning and ending positions of the next word, if there is one.

As you can see, counting the words in a sentence using `String` methods is not a simple task. We see a much easier way to do this shortly.

Using a Scanner with a String

Until now, we have used a `Scanner` object to accept the input of integers, floating-point numbers, and lines of text from the keyboard or from text files. Interestingly, a scanner can also be used to read words from the keyboard, a text file, or a string. When used with a file, the `Scanner` method `next()` skips any leading blanks and reads and returns a string containing the next sequence of nonblank characters. The method `next()` has the same behavior when used with a scanner that has been opened on a string. The method `hasNext()` returns `true` if there are still more words in the string to be scanned. The following code segment opens a scanner on a string and uses it to scan and display the words in it:

```
String str = "The rain in Spain falls mainly on the plain.";
Scanner reader = new Scanner(str);
while (reader.hasNext())
   System.out.println(reader.next());
```

The scanner automatically handles the tedious details, such as skipping multiple spaces between words, which made the program of Example 11.2 so complicated. A project at the end of this chapter asks you to simplify this program by using a scanner.

*E*XERCISE 11.1

1. Indicate the outputs of the following code segments:

    a.
```
String str = "The rain in Spain falls mainly on the plain";
System.out.println(str.indexOf(' '));
```

EXERCISE 11.1 Continued

b.
```
String str = "The rain in Spain falls mainly on the plain";
System.out.println(str.indexOf(' ', 4));
```

c.
```
String str = "The rain in Spain falls mainly on the plain";
System.out.println(str.substring(4));
```

d.
```
String str = "The rain in Spain falls mainly on the plain";
System.out.println(str.substring(4, 8));
```

e.
```
String str = "The rain in Spain falls mainly on the plain";
int begin = 0;
while (begin < str.length()){
   int end = str.indexOf(' ', begin);
   if (end == -1)
      end = str.length();
   String word = str.substring(begin, end);
   System.out.println(word);
   begin = end + 1;
}
```

2. Write code segments that perform the following tasks:

   a. Replace every blank space character in the string `str` with a newline character (`'\n'`).

   b. Find the index of the first instance of the substring `"the"` in the string `str`.

   c. Find the index of the first instance of the substring `"the"` after the midpoint of the string `str`.

   d. Count the number of instances of the whole word `"the"` in the string `str`.

11.2 Searching

Searching collections of elements for a given target element is a very common operation in software systems. Some examples are the `indexOf` methods for strings discussed earlier. In this section, we examine two typical methods for searching an array of elements—a linear search and a binary search.

Linear Search

In Chapter 9, we developed the code for a method that searches an array of `int` for a given target value. The method returns the index of the first matching value or −1 if the value is not in the array. Following is the code:

```
int search (int[] a, int searchValue){
   for (int i = 0; i < a.length; i++)
      if (a[i] == searchValue)
         return i;
   return -1;
}
```

The method examines each element in sequence, starting with the first one, to determine if a target element is present. The loop breaks if the target is found. The method must examine every element to determine the absence of a target. This method of searching is usually called *linear search*.

Searching an Array of Objects

Suppose we have an array of names that we want to search for a given name. A name is a `String`. We cannot use the search method developed already. But we can use a similar loop in the code for a different search method that expects an array of `String` and a target `String` as parameters. The only change in the loop is that two string elements must be compared with the method `equals` instead of the operator `==`. Following is the code:

```
int search (String[] a, String searchValue){
   for (int i = 0; i < a.length; i++)
      if (a[i].equals(searchValue))
         return i;
   return -1;
}
```

This method can be generalized to work with any objects, not just strings. We simply substitute `Object` for `String` in the formal parameter list. The method still works for strings, and we can also use it to search an array of `Student` objects for a target student, assuming that the `Student` class includes an appropriate `equals` method. Following is a code segment that uses this single method to search arrays of two different types:

```
String[]  stringArray = {"Hi", "there", "Martin"};
Student[] studentArray = new Student[5];
Student   stu = new Student("Student 1");

for (int i = 0; i < studentArray.length; i++)
   studentArray[i] = new Student("Student " + (i + 1));

int stringPos = search(stringArray, "Martin");    // Returns 2
int studentPos = search(studentArray, stu);       // Returns 0
```

Binary Search

The method of linear search works well for arrays that are fairly small (a few hundred elements). As the array gets very large (thousands or millions of elements), however, the behavior of the search degrades (more on this in Chapter 12). When we have an array of elements that are in ascending order, such as a list of numbers or names, there is a much better way to proceed. For example, in ordinary life, we do not use a linear search to find a name in a phone book. If we are looking for "Lambert," we open the book at our estimate of the middle page. If we're not on the "La" page, we look before or after, depending on whether we have opened the book at the "M" page or the "K" page. For computation, we can formalize this kind of search technique in an algorithm known as *binary search*. This method is much faster than a linear search for very large arrays.

The basic idea of a binary search is to examine the element at the array's midpoint on each pass through the search loop. If the current element matches the target, we return its position. If the current element is less than the target, then we search the part of the array to the right of the midpoint (containing the positions of the greater items). Otherwise, we search the part of the array to the left of the midpoint (containing the positions of the lesser items). On each pass through the loop, the current leftmost position or the current rightmost position is adjusted to track the portion of the array being searched. Following is a Java method that performs a binary search on an array of integers:

```
int search (int[] a, int searchValue){
    int left = 0;                            // Establish the initial
    int right = a.length - 1;                // endpoints of the array
    while (left <= right){                    // Loop until the endpoints cross
        int midpoint = (left + right) / 2;   // Compute the current midpoint
        if (a[midpoint] == searchValue)      // Target found; return its index
            return midpoint;
        else if (a[midpoint] < searchValue)  // Target to right of midpoint
            left = midpoint + 1;
        else                                  // Target to left of midpoint
            right = midpoint - 1;
    }
    return -1;                                // Target not found
}
```

Figure 11-1 shows a trace of a binary search for the target value 5 in the array

1 3 5 7 9 11 13 15 17

Note that on each pass through the loop, the number of elements yet to be examined is reduced by half. As we see in Chapter 12, herein lies the advantage of binary search over linear search for very large arrays.

FIGURE 11-1

A trace of a binary search of an array

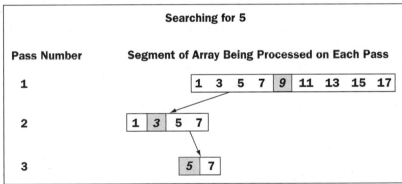

Comparing Objects and the Comparable Interface

When using binary search with an array of objects, we must compare two objects. But objects do not understand the < and > operators, and we have seen that == is not a wise choice for comparing two objects for equality. However, classes that implement the Comparable interface include the method compareTo, which performs the three different comparisons. Here is the signature of compareTo:

```
public int compareTo(Object other)
```

The behavior of `compareTo` is summarized in Table 11-2.

TABLE 11-2
The behavior of method `compareTo`

USAGE OF `compareTo`	VALUE RETURNED
`obj1.compareTo(obj2)`	0 if `obj1` is equal to `obj2`, using equals
`obj1.compareTo(obj2)`	A negative integer, if `obj1` is less than `obj2`
`obj1.compareTo(obj2)`	A positive integer, if `obj1` is greater than `obj2`

For example, the `String` class implements the `Comparable` interface; thus, the second output of the following code segment is 0:

```
String str = "Mary";
System.out.println(str.compareTo("Suzanne"));    // Outputs -6
System.out.println(str.compareTo("Mary"));       // Outputs 0
System.out.println(str.compareTo("Bob"));        // Outputs 11
```

The other output integers are system dependent, but the first should be negative, whereas the third should be positive (in the example given, they are –6 and 11, respectively).

Before sending the `compareTo` message to an arbitrary object, that object must be cast to `Comparable`, because `Object` does not implement the `Comparable` interface or include a `compareTo` method. Following is the code for the binary search of an array of objects:

```
int search (Object[] a, Object searchValue){
    int left = 0;
    int right = a.length - 1;
    while (left <= right){
        int midpoint = (left + right) / 2;
        int result = ((Comparable)a[midpoint]).compareTo(searchValue);
        if (result == 0)
            return midpoint;
        else if (result < 0)
            left = midpoint + 1;
        else
            right = midpoint - 1;
    }
    return -1;
}
```

Implementing the Method `compareTo`

As mentioned earlier, objects that are ordered by the relations less than, greater than, or equal to must understand the `compareTo` message. Their class must implement the `Comparable` interface and their interface, if there is one, should also include the method `compareTo`. Suppose, for example, that the `Student` class of Chapter 5, which has no interface, is modified to support comparisons of students' names. Following are the required changes to the code:

```
public class Student implements Comparable{

    <data declarations>
```

```
    public int compareTo(Object other){

        // The parameter must be an instance of Student
        if (! (other instanceof Student))
            throw new IllegalArgumentException("Parameter must be a Student");

        // Obtain the student's name after casting the parameter
        String otherName = ((Student)other).getName();

        // Return the result of comparing the two students' names
        return name.compareTo(otherName);
    }

    <other methods>
}
```

*E*XERCISE 11.2

1. Why is a linear search called "linear"?

2. Write a linear search method that searches an array of objects for a target object.

3. Which elements are examined during a binary search of the array 34 56 78 85 99 for the target element 100?

4. Jack advises Jill of a modification to linear search that improves its performance when the array is sorted: If the target element is less than the current element, the target cannot be in the array. Modify the linear search method for integers to accomplish this.

5. Describe what the following code segment does:

```
boolean inOrder = true;
for (int i = 0; i < a.length - 1; i++)
   if (a[i] > a[i + 1]){
      inOrder = false;
      break;
   }
```

11.3 Sorting

We have seen that if the elements in an array are in ascending order, we can write some efficient methods for searching the array. However, when the elements are in random order, we need to rearrange them before we can take advantage of any ordering. This process is called *sorting*.

Suppose we have an array a of five integers that we want to sort from smallest to largest. In Figure 11-2, the values currently in a are as depicted on the left; we want to end up with values as they appear on the right.

FIGURE 11-2
An array before and after sorting

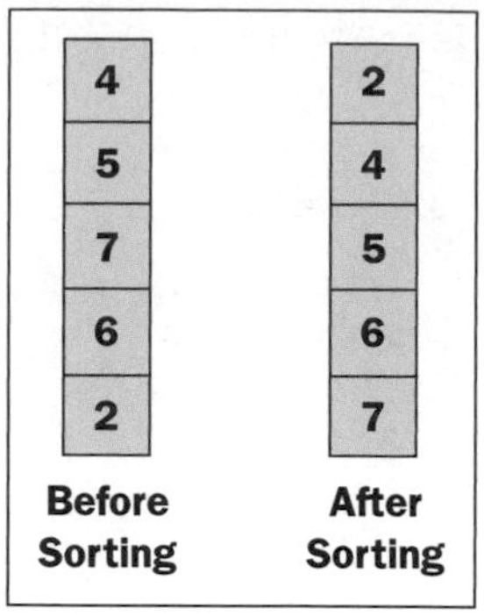

Before Sorting	After Sorting
4	2
5	4
7	5
6	6
2	7

Many sort algorithms have been developed, and in this section we cover a few that are easy to write but not very efficient to run. More sophisticated and more efficient sort algorithms are discussed in Chapter 12.

Selection Sort

The basic idea of a *selection sort* is

For each index position i
    Find the smallest data value in the array from positions i
      through length - 1, where length is the number of data values stored.
    Exchange the smallest value with the value at position i

Table 11-3 shows a trace of the elements of an array after each exchange of elements is made. The items just swapped are marked with asterisks, and the sorted portion is shaded. Notice that in the second and fourth passes, because the current smallest numbers are already in place, we need not exchange anything. Also, after the last exchange, the number at the end of the array is automatically in its proper place.

TABLE 11-3
A trace of the data during a selection sort

UNSORTED ARRAY	AFTER 1ST PASS	AFTER 2ND PASS	AFTER 3RD PASS	AFTER 4TH PASS
4	1*	1	1	1
2	2	2*	2	2
5	5	5	3*	3
1	4*	4	4	4*
3	3	3	5*	5

Before writing the algorithm for this sorting method, note the following:

- If the array is of length *n*, we need *n* – 1 steps.

- We must be able to find the smallest number.

- We need to exchange appropriate array items.

When the code is written for this sort, note that strict inequality (<) rather than weak inequality (<=) is used when looking for the smallest remaining value. The algorithm to sort by selection is

```
For each i from 0 to n - 1 do
   Find the smallest value among a[i], a[i + 1], . . . a[n - 1]
   and store the index of the smallest value in minIndex
   Exchange the values of a[i] and a[index], if necessary
```

In Chapter 9, we saw a segment of the code we need to find the smallest value of array a. With suitable changes, we will incorporate this segment of code in a method, findMinimum, for the selection sort. We also will use a method swap to exchange two elements in an array.

Using these two methods, the implementation of a selection sort method is

```
void selectionSort(int[] a){
   for (int i = 0; i < a.length - 1; i++){
      int minIndex = findMinimum(a, i);
      if (minIndex != i)
         swap(a, i, minIndex);
   }
}
```

The method for finding the minimum value in an array takes two parameters, the array and the position, to start the search. The method returns the index position of the minimum element in the array. Its implementation uses a for loop:

```
int findMinimum(int[] a, int first){
   int minIndex = first;

   for (int i = first + 1; i < a.length; i++)
      if (a[i] < a[minIndex])
         minIndex = i;

   return minIndex;
}
```

The swap method exchanges the values of two array cells:

```
void swap(int[] a, int x, int y){
   int temp = a[x];
   a[x] = a[y];
   a[y] = temp;
}
```

Bubble Sort

Given a list of items stored in an array, a *bubble sort* causes a pass through the array to compare adjacent pairs of items. Whenever two items are out of order with respect to each other, they are swapped. The effect of such a pass through an array of items is traced in Table 11-4. The items just swapped are marked with asterisks, and the sorted portion is shaded. Notice that after such a pass, we are assured that the array will have the item that comes last in order in the final array position. That is, the last item will "sink" to the bottom of the array, and preceding items will gradually "percolate" to the top.

TABLE 11-4
A trace of the data during one pass of a bubble sort

UNSORTED ARRAY	AFTER 1ST SWAP	AFTER 2ND SWAP	AFTER 3RD SWAP	AFTER 4TH SWAP
5	4*	4	4	4
4	5*	2*	2	2
2	2	5*	1*	1
1	1	1	5*	3*
3	3	3	3	5*

The bubble sort algorithm involves a nested loop structure. The outer loop controls the number of (successively smaller) passes through the array. The inner loop controls the pairs of adjacent items being compared. If we ever make a complete pass through the inner loop without having to make an interchange, we can declare the array sorted and avoid all future passes through the array. A pseudocode algorithm for bubble sort is

```
Initialize counter k to zero
Initialize boolean exchangeMade to true
While (k < n - 1) and exchangeMade
   Set exchangeMade to false
   Increment counter k
   For each j from 0 to n - k
      If item in jth position > item in (j + 1)st position
         Swap these items
         Set exchangeMade to true
```

A complete Java method to implement a bubble sort for an array of integers is shown in the following code:

```
void bubbleSort(int[] a){
   int k = 0;
   boolean exchangeMade = true;
```

```
// Make up to n - 1 passes through array, exit early if no exchanges
// are made on previous pass

while ((k < a.length - 1) && exchangeMade){
    exchangeMade = false;
    k++;
    for (int j = 0; j < a.length - k; j++)
        if (a[j] > a[j + 1]){
            swap(a, j, j + 1);
            exchangeMade = true;
        }
    }
}
```

Insertion Sort

Although it reduces the number of data interchanges, the selection sort apparently will not allow an effective—and automatic—loop exit if the array becomes ordered during an early pass. In this regard, bubble sort is more efficient than selection sort for an array that is nearly ordered from the beginning. Even with just one item out of order, however, bubble sort's early loop exit can fail to reduce the number of comparisons that are made.

The *insertion sort* attempts to take greater advantage of an array's partial ordering. The goal is that on the kth pass through, the kth item among

```
a[0], a[1], ..., a[k]
```

should be inserted into its rightful place among the first k items in the array. Thus, after the kth pass (k starting at 1), the first k items of the array should be in sorted order. This is analogous to the fashion in which many people pick up playing cards and order them in their hands. Holding the first $(k - 1)$ cards in order, a person will pick up the kth card and compare it with cards already held until its appropriate spot is found. The following steps will achieve this logic:

```
For each k from 1 to n - 1 (k is the index of array element to insert)
    Set itemToInsert to a[k]
    Set j to k - 1
    (j starts at k - 1 and is decremented until insertion position is found)
     While (insertion position not found) and (not beginning of array)
        If itemToInsert < a[j]
            Move a[j] to index position j + 1
            Decrement j by 1
        Else
            The insertion position has been found
            itemToInsert should be positioned at index j + 1
```

In effect, for each pass, the index j begins at the $(k - 1)$st item and moves that item to position $j + 1$ until we find the insertion point for what was originally the kth item.

An insertion sort for each value of k is traced in Table 11-5. In each column of this table, the data items are sorted in order relative to each other above the item with the asterisk; below this item, the data are not affected.

TABLE 11-5
A trace of the data during an insertion sort

UNSORTED ARRAY	AFTER 1ST PASS	AFTER 2ND PASS	AFTER 3RD PASS	AFTER 4TH PASS
2	2	1*	1	1
5 ←	5 (no insertion)	2	2	2
1	1 ←	5	4*	3*
4	4	4 ←	5	4
3	3	3	3 ←	5

To implement the insertion sort algorithm in Java, we use the following code:

```
void insertionSort(int[] a){
   int itemToInsert, j;
   boolean stillLooking;

   // On the kth pass, insert item k into its correct position among
   // the first k entries in array.

   for (int k = 1; k < a.length; k++){
      // Walk backwards through list, looking for slot to insert a[k]
      itemToInsert = a[k];
      j = k - 1;
      stillLooking = true;

      while ((j >= 0) && stillLooking )
         if (itemToInsert  < a[j]) {
            a[j + 1] = a[j];
            j--;
         }else
            stillLooking = false;
         // Upon leaving loop, j + 1 is the index
         // where itemToInsert  belongs
         a[j + 1] = itemToInsert;
   }
}
```

Sorting Arrays of Objects

Any of the sort methods can be modified to sort arrays of objects. We assume that the objects implement the `Comparable` interface and support the method `compareTo`. Then, we simply replace the type of all array parameters with `Object` and make the appropriate use of `compareTo` in which the comparison operators are used. For example, here is the relevant change for the selection sort in the method `findMinimum`:

```java
int findMinimum(Object[] a, int first){
   int minIndex = first;

   for (int i = first + 1; i < a.length(); i++)
      if (((Comparable)a[i]).compareTo(a[minIndex]) < 0)
         minIndex = i;

   return minIndex;
}
```

Testing Sort Algorithms

The sort algorithms developed thus far should be tested. The skeleton of a short tester program follows. The program loads an array with 20 random integers between 0 and 99, displays the array's contents, runs a sort method, and displays the array's contents again. Each sort method and their helper methods should be defined as `private static`.

```java
// Example 11.3: Test sort algorithms

import java.util.Random;

public class TestSortAlgorithms{

   public static void main(String[] args){
      Random gen = new Random();
      int[] a = new int[20];

      //Initialize the array to random numbers between 0 and 99
      for (int i = 0; i < a.length; i++)
         a[i] = gen.nextInt(100);

      printArray(a);
      selectionSort(a);               // Pick one of three to test
      //bubbleSort(a);
      //insertionSort(a);
      printArray(a);
   }

   private static void printArray(int[] a){
      for (int i : a)
         System.out.print(i  + " ");
      System.out.println("");
   }

   // private static sort methods and their helpers go here
}
```

You also should test the methods with an array that is already sorted.

EXERCISE 11.3

1. Draw a diagram that shows the contents of the array 8 7 6 5 4 after each number is moved in a selection sort.

2. Draw a diagram that shows the contents of the array 8 7 6 5 4 after each number is moved in a bubble sort, until the 8 arrives at the end of the array.

3. Describe the behavior of the selection sort, bubble sort, and insertion sort with an array that is already sorted. How many exchanges are made in each sort for an array of size *n*?

4. Modify the bubble sort method so that it sorts an array of objects.

11.4 *Insertions and Removals*

In Chapter 9, we discussed how to add or remove an element at the end of an array that is not full. In this section, we show how to perform these operations at arbitrary positions within an array. For simplicity, we make four assumptions:

1. Arrays are of fixed size; thus, when an array becomes full, insertions are not performed.

2. We are working with an array of objects, although we can modify the code to cover arrays of integers, employees, or whatever element type is desired.

3. For successful insertions, 0 <= target index <= logical size. The new element is inserted before the element currently at the target index, or after the last element if the target index equals the logical size.

4. For successful removals, 0 <= target index < logical size.

When an assumption is not satisfied, the operation is not performed and we return `false`; otherwise, the operation is performed and we return `true`.

In the code segments that follow, we use the following data declarations:

```
final int DEFAULT_CAPACITY = 5;
int logicalSize = 0;
Object[] array = new Object[DEFAULT_CAPACITY];
```

As you can see, the array has an initial logical size of 0 and a default physical capacity of 5. For each operation that uses this array, we provide a description of the implementation strategy and an annotated Java code segment. At the end of this section, we ask you to develop some static methods to perform these operations on arrays.

Inserting an Item into an Array at an Arbitrary Position

Inserting an item into an array differs from replacing an item in an array. In the case of a replacement, an item already exists at the given index position and a simple assignment suffices.

Moreover, the logical size of the array does not change. In the case of an insertion, we must do six things:

1. Check for available space before attempting an insertion; if there is no space, return `false`.

2. Check the validity of the target index and return `false` if it is not >= 0 and <= logical size.

3. Shift the items from the logical end of the array to the target index down by one position.

4. Assign the new item to the cell at the target index.

5. Increment the logical size by one.

6. Return true.

Figure 11-3 shows these steps for the insertion of an item at position 1 in an array of four items.

FIGURE 11-3
Inserting an item into an array

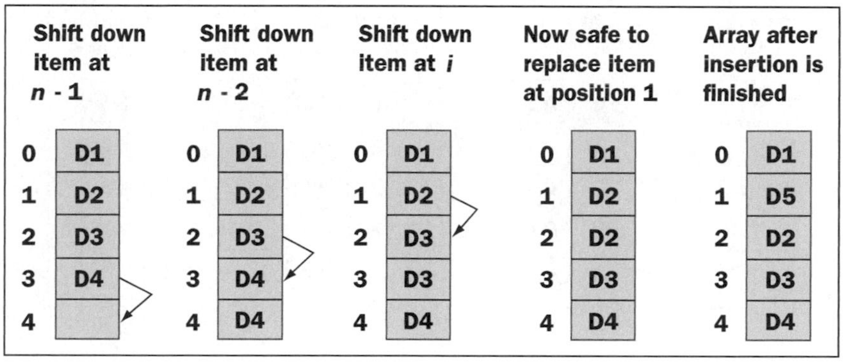

Shift down item at *n* - 1	Shift down item at *n* - 2	Shift down item at *i*	Now safe to replace item at position 1	Array after insertion is finished
0 D1	0 D1	0 D1	0 D1	0 D1
1 D2	1 D2	1 D2	1 D2	1 D5
2 D3	2 D3	2 D3	2 D2	2 D2
3 D4	3 D4	3 D3	3 D3	3 D3
4	4 D4	4 D4	4 D4	4 D4

As you can see, the order in which the items are shifted is critical. If we had started at the target index and copied down from there, we would have lost two items. Thus, we must start at the logical end of the array and work back up to the target index, copying each item to the cell of its successor. Following is the Java code for the insertion operation:

```
// Check for a full array and return false if full
if (logicalSize == array.length)
    return false;

// Check for valid target index and return false if not valid
if (targetIndex < 0 || targetIndex > logicalSize)
    return false;

// Shift items down by one position
for (int i = logicalSize; i > targetIndex; i--)
    array[i] = array[i - 1];

// Add new item, increment logical size, and return true
array[targetIndex] = newItem;
logicalSize++;
return true;
```

Removing an Item from an Array

Removing an item from an array involves the inverse process of inserting an item into the array. Following are the steps in this process:

1. Check the validity of the target index and return `false` if it is not >= 0 and < logical size.

2. Shift the items from the target index to the logical end of the array up by one position.

3. Decrement the logical size by one.

4. Return true.

Figure 11-4 shows these steps for the removal of an item at position 1 in an array of five items.

FIGURE 11-4
Removing an item from an array

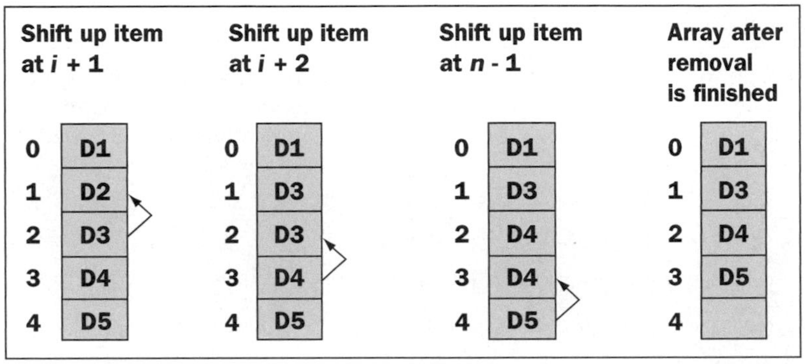

As with insertions, the order in which we shift items is critical. For a removal, we begin at the item following the target position and move toward the logical end of the array, copying each item to the cell of its predecessor. Following is the Java code for the removal operation:

```java
// Check for valid target index and return false if not valid
if (targetIndex < 0 || targetIndex >= logicalSize)
    return false;

// Shift items up by one position
for (int i = targetIndex; i < logicalSize - 1; i++)
    array[i] = array[i + 1];

// Decrement logical size and return true
logicalSize--;
return true;
```

Of course, there are other ways to handle potential errors in these operations, as discussed in earlier chapters. Instead of returning a Boolean value, one can return a string indicating the type of error or `null` indicating success. Alternatively, one can throw an exception for each error and return `void`.

A Tester Program for Array Methods

The operations just discussed are so frequently used that it is a good idea to provide methods for them. Ideally, one implements them as `static` methods in a class that serves a utility function similar to Java's Math class. In the following code, we specify two of these methods in the context of a tester program. We leave their complete development for you to try in Exercise 11.4, Question 2.

A method to insert a new item at a given index position, insertItem, expects the array, its logical size, the target index, and the new item as parameters. insertItem returns true if the operation is successful and false otherwise. This method does not increment the logical size; that responsibility is left to the client, who must check the Boolean value returned to take the appropriate action. A similar method named removeItem can be developed for removals.

Following is a short tester program that uses the method described previously:

```java
// Example 11.4: Test insertions and removals

public class TestInsertAndRemove{

    public static void main(String[] args){

        // Create an initial array with 3 positions
        String[] array = new String[3];
        int logicalSize = 0;
        boolean successful = false;

        // Insert strings at positions 0, 1, 1, and 0
        successful = insertItem(array, logicalSize, 0, "Jack");
        if (successful)
            logicalSize++;

        successful = insertItem(array, logicalSize, 1, "Jill");
        if (successful)
            logicalSize++;

        successful = insertItem(array, logicalSize, 1, "sees");
        if (successful)
            logicalSize++;

        successful = insertItem(array, logicalSize, 0, "Before");
        if (successful)
            logicalSize++;

        // Display new logical size and contents
        System.out.println(logicalSize);
        for (int i = 0; i < logicalSize; i++)
            System.out.print(array[i] + " ");
    }

    // Definitions of array methods go here
    private static boolean insertItem(Object[] array, int logicalSize,
                                      int targetIndex, Object newItem){
        // Exercise
    }

    private static boolean removeItem(Object[] array, int logicalSize,
                                      int targetIndex){
        // Exercise
    }

}
```

Although our methods allow clients to perform insertions and removals, clients must still track the logical size of an array and update it. In addition, there is an upper bound on the number of items a client can insert into an array. We will learn how to overcome these limitations of arrays shortly. But first, we must consider some unfinished business with the use of objects in arrays.

*E*XERCISE 11.4

1. Describe the design strategy for inserting an element at an arbitrary position in an array.

2. Complete the two static methods for insertion and removal of an element at an arbitrary position in an array.

3. Describe what the following code segments do:

   a.

   ```
   if (logicalSize == a.length){
      int[] temp = new int[a.length * 2];
      for (int i = 0; i < a.length; i++)
         temp[i] = a[i];
      a = temp;
   }
   ```

   b.

   ```
   if (a.length >= logicalSize * 4){
      int[] temp = new int[a.length * 2];
      for (int i = 0; i < a.length; i++)
         temp[i] = a[i];
      a = temp;
   }
   ```

11.5 *Working with Arrays of Objects*

The element type of an array can be a primitive type, a reference type (either an abstract or a concrete class), or an interface. The processing of an array of a primitive type, such as array of `int`, is straightforward. Likewise, working with an array of a concrete class, such as `Student`, poses no particular problems. The reason for this is that all of the elements in these arrays, whether integers or students, are of exactly the same type and respond to the same set of operators or messages. When the element type of an array is an interface, an abstract class, or a superclass of one or more other classes, however, the array can actually contain objects of different types, so they might not all respond to a common set of messages. In this section, we deal with the problems that arise with arrays of objects of different types.

Polymorphism, Casting, and `instanceof`

It is quite common to declare and instantiate an array of some interface type, such as the `Shape` interface in Chapter 10. For instance, following is code that reserves 10 cells for shapes:

```
Shape[] shapes = new Shape[10];
```

Now we can store in this array instances of any class that implements `Shape`, such as `Rect`, `Circle`, or `Wheel`, as follows:

```
shapes[0] = new Rect(20, 20, 40, 40);      // Cell 0 refers to a Rect
shapes[1] = new Circle(100, 100, 20);      // Cell 1 refers to a Circle
shapes[2] = new Wheel(200, 200, 20, 6);  // Cell 2 refers to a Wheel
```

As long as we send `Shape` messages to the elements of this array, we can ignore the fact that they are of different concrete classes (that's what polymorphism is all about). For instance, let us now draw all the shapes currently in the array:

```
Pen pen = new StandardPen();
for (int i = 0; i < 3; i++)
    shapes[i].draw(pen);
```

We can also move all the shapes, stretch them, change their colors, or do whatever else is specified in the `Shape` interface quite easily. As soon as we want to do something more specific to a shape, however, such as setting the number of spokes in a wheel, we must resort to some of the tricks mentioned in Chapter 10. Let us assume that we know the position of the wheel object in the array (in our example, it's at position 2). Then, to set its spokes to 5, we perform the following steps:

1. Access the array element with the subscript.

2. Cast the element, which is masquerading as a `Shape`, to a `Wheel`.

3. Send the `setSpokes(5)` message to the result.

   Following is the code:

   ```
   ((Wheel) shapes[2]).setSpokes(5);
   ```

Note the use of parentheses to override the precedence of the method selector, which would otherwise be run before the cast operation. Failure to cast in this code causes a compile-time error.

Now suppose we don't know the position of a wheel in the array of shapes, but we want to set the spokes of each wheel to 5. A loop is a logical choice for this task, but we cannot simply cast each element to a `Wheel` and send it the `setSpokes` message because not all elements are wheels. If we attempt to cast an object to a type that is not its actual type, a `ClassCastException` is thrown. Clearly, in this case, we must first determine that a shape is a wheel before casting, and Java's `instanceof` operator comes to our rescue. Following is a loop that solves the problem:

```
for (int i = 0; i < shapes.length; i++)
    if (shapes[i] instanceof Wheel)
        ((Wheel) shapes[i]).setSpokes(5);
```

Although we have been examining an array of an interface type in this example, the same considerations apply to arrays of abstract classes or of superclasses of one or more other classes. Let us now summarize the use of objects in an array by making two fundamental points:

1. When the element type of an array is a reference type or interface, objects of those types or any subtype (subclass or implementing class) can be directly inserted into the array.

2. After accessing an object in an array, care must be taken to send it the appropriate messages or to cast it down to a type that can receive the appropriate messages.

Arrays of `Object`

The most general type of array is of course an array whose element type is `Object`. This array is the most flexible of any we have seen thus far. Not only can we insert any `Object` into an array of `Object`, but we also can replace any array of `Object` with another array of any reference type (that is, pass one as a parameter or return it as a value of a method). We have already seen examples of general searching and sorting methods that rely on this feature of an array of `Object`. From the implementer's perspective, in the case of a linear search, there is no need to worry about the actual type of the array elements because all objects understand the `equals` message and that is the only message sent to the array elements. In the case of the binary search and the sorting methods, the elements each must be sent the `compareTo` message. Before doing that, the method must cast them to `Comparable` after retrieving them from the array. Therefore, the client must take care to pass an array of comparable objects as a parameter to these methods.

Generally, you should exercise caution after an object is accessed in an array of `Object`. More often than not, casting must occur because `Object` includes so few of the methods that the array element actually supports.

EXERCISE 11.5

1. Assume that the `Student` class used here is as defined in Chapter 9. Describe the errors in the following code segments, or state that they are correct:

   a.

   ```
   Object[] a = new Object[10];
   a[0] = new Student();
   a[1] = "Hi there";
   System.out.println(a[1].indexOf("there"));
   ```

   b.

   ```
   Object[] a = new Object[10];
   a[0] = new Student();
   a[1] = "Hi there";
   System.out.println((String)a[1].indexOf("there"));
   ```

   c.

   ```
   Object[] a = new Object[10];
   a[0] = new Student();
   a[1] = "Hi there";
   System.out.println((String[1]).indexOf("there"));
   ```

   d.

   ```
   Object[] a = new Object[10];
   a[0] = new Student();
   a[1] = "Hi there";
   System.out.println((String[0]).indexOf("there"));
   ```

11.6 The Class java.util.ArrayList

As we have seen, the array is a powerful data structure that has many uses. In earlier sections of this chapter, we developed many complex but useful methods for manipulating arrays. However, arrays are easiest to use when

- We know how many data elements will be added to them, so we don't run out of cells or waste any cells.

- We know they are full.

  When these conditions do not hold, clients must

- Find a way to increase the length of the array when it becomes full or shrink it when many cells become unoccupied.

- Track the array's logical size with a separate variable.

If necessary, we could develop methods that would increase or decrease the length of an array, but they would add complexity to our code and still not relieve clients of the need to maintain a distinct logical size for each array. Fortunately, clients have a better option in these cases. Like most object-oriented languages, Java provides a wide range of classes for maintaining collections of objects. The collection class most like an array is called `ArrayList` and is included in the package `java.util`. In this section, we give an overview of the use of array lists.

What an Array List Is

Like an array, an *array list* is an object that contains a sequence of elements that are ordered by position. Elements in both structures can be accessed and replaced at a given position. However, there are several ways in which an array list is unlike an array:

- The programmer must use methods rather than the subscript operator [ ] to manipulate elements in an array list.

- An array list tracks both its logical size (the number of elements that are currently in it) and its physical size (the number of cells available to store elements).

- When the programmer creates an array list, its logical size is 0. When the programmer inserts elements into an array list, the list automatically updates its logical size and adds cells to accommodate new objects if necessary. The list's logical size is also updated when an element is removed.

- The positions available for access in an array list range from 0 to its logical size minus 1.

Generic Array Lists and Raw Array Lists

Java 5.0 allows the programmer to use *generic array lists*. A generic array list requires the programmer to specify the element type for the list. This must be done when a list variable is declared and when a list is instantiated. The elements inserted into a generic list must have the same type as its element type or be one of its element type's subtypes.

Earlier versions of Java support only raw array lists. A *raw array list* can contain objects of any reference type. Because raw array lists are considered less safe and less convenient to use than generic array lists, we use generic array lists in this book. For details on raw array lists, you can consult Appendix B.

Declaring and Instantiating an Array List

An array list is an object, so it is instantiated like any other object, as in the following example, which creates an array list of strings:

```
import java.util.ArrayList;

ArrayList<String> list = new ArrayList<String>();
```

Note that the programmer specifies no initial physical length, as is done with arrays. An array list has a default physical length, but the programmer has no need to know what it is. Note also the use of the type specifier `<String>` in both the variable declaration and the use of the constructor. The type specifier restricts the elements in this list to be of type `String`.

Using `ArrayList` Methods

The programmer manipulates an array list by sending it messages. There are methods for examining an array list's logical size, testing it for emptiness (it's never full, at least in theory), insertions, removals, examining or replacing elements at given positions, and searching for a given element, among others. Table 11-6 contains descriptions of these commonly used methods. Note that the type `E` mentioned in some methods is a placeholder for the actual element type used when the list is created.

TABLE 11-6
Some commonly used `ArrayList` methods

`ArrayList` METHOD	WHAT IT DOES
`ArrayList<E>()`	Constructor builds an empty array list
`boolean isEmpty()`	Returns true if the list contains no elements and false otherwise
`int size()`	Returns the number of elements currently in the list
`E get(int index)`	Returns the element at index
`E set(int index, E obj)`	Replaces the element at index with `obj` and returns the old element
`void add(int index, E obj)`	Inserts `obj` before the element at index or after the last element if index equals the size of the list
`E remove(int index)`	Removes and returns the element at index
`int indexOf(E obj)`	Returns the index of the first instance of `obj` in the list or −1 if `obj` is not in the list

The methods discussed here represent only a small subset of the methods supported by array lists. For details on the other methods, see Appendix B or consult Sun's documentation.

Let us extend the earlier code segment by loading the array list with several strings and then displaying them in the terminal window:

```
import java.util.ArrayList;

ArrayList<String> list = new ArrayList<String>();
```

```
for (int i = 0; i < 5; i++)              // List contains
   list.add(i, "Item" + (i + 1));        // Item1 Item2 Item3 Item4 Item5

for (int i = 0; i < list.size(); i++)              // Display
   System.out.println(list.get(i));                // Item1
                                                   // Item2
                                                   // Item3
                                                   // Item4
                                                   // Item5


// Or use an enhanced for loop
for (String str : list)                            // Display
   System.out.println(str);                        // Item1
                                                   // Item2
                                                   // Item3
                                                   // Item4
                                                   // Item5
```

The next code segment performs some example searches:

```
System.out.println(list.indexOf("Item3"));   // Displays 2
System.out.println(list.indexOf("Martin"));  // Displays -1
```

Our final code segment removes the first element from the list and displays that element and the list's size after each removal, until the list becomes empty:

```
while (! list.isEmpty()){
   String str = list.remove(0);
   System.out.println(str);
   System.out.println("Size: " + list.size());
}
```

Array Lists and Primitive Types

The array list is a powerful data structure. There is one other restriction on its use, however. Unlike an array, an array list can contain only objects, not primitive types. We explore a way of working around this restriction in the next subsection.

Primitive Types and Wrapper Classes

As mentioned earlier, Java distinguishes between primitive data types (numbers, characters, Booleans) and objects (instances of `String`, `Employee`, `Student`, etc.). Arrays can contain either primitive data values or objects, as in

```
int x;                     // An integer variable
int nums[];                // An array of integers
Student student;           // A Student variable
Student students[];        // An array of Students
```

The elements in an array list must all be objects. Thus, the following attempt to declare and create an array list of int fails with a syntax error:

```
ArrayList list<int> list = new ArrayList<int>();  // Invalid (syntax error)
```

A feature called *wrapper classes* allows us to store primitive data types in array lists. A wrapper class is a class that contains a value of a primitive type. Values of the types boolean, char, int, and double can be stored in objects of the wrapper classes Boolean, Character, Integer, and Double, respectively. The following code segment shows how a wrapper class can be manipulated directly:

```
Integer intObj3 = new Integer(3);              // An Integer object containing 3
Integer intObj4 = new Integer(4);              // An integer object containing 4
int x = intObj3.intValue();                    // Extracts 3 and saves in x
System.out.println(intObj3);                   // Displays 3 using toString()
System.out.println(intObj3.equals(intObj4));       // Displays false
System.out.println(intObj3.compareTo(intObj4));    // Displays a negative
                                                   // number
```

Fortunately, you do not have to bother with these details to use primitive types with array lists. Array lists automatically "box" and "unbox" primitive values when they are used with array list methods. The only requirement is that you use the appropriate wrapper class name as the element type specifier when declaring the array list variable and instantiating the list. The next program example shows some manipulations of a list of integers:

```
// Example 11.5: Test an array list of integers

import java.util.ArrayList;

public class TestArrayList{

    public static void main(String[] args){

        // Create a list of Integers
        ArrayList<Integer> list = new ArrayList<Integer>();

        // Add the ints 1-100 to the list
        for (int i = 1; i <= 100; i++)
            list.add(i);

        // Increment each int in the list
        for (int i = 0; i < list.size(); i++)
            list.set(i, list.get(i) + 1);

        // Display the contents of the list
        for (int i : list)
            System.out.println(i);
    }
}
```

This code works because the methods add and set automatically box an int value into an Integer object, whereas the method get automatically unboxes an Integer object into an int value. Moreover, the enhanced `for` loop at the end of the program also unboxes each `Integer` object into an `int`.

Confusing Arrays and Array Lists

As mentioned earlier, the programmer must send an array list message, whereas the subscript is the only basic array operation. Beginners often confuse the two structures and try to use a subscript with an array list or a method with an array. These two types of errors, both caught by the compiler, are shown in the next code segment:

```
// Create an array containing 3, 4, and 5
int array[] = {3, 4, 5};

// Create a list and add 2, 3, and 4
ArrayList<Integer> list = new ArrayList<Integer>();
list.add(2); list.add(3); list.add(4);

// Syntax errors: use list methods with the array
for (int i = 0; i < array.size(); i++)
   System.out.println(array.get(i));

// Syntax errors: use subscript and length variable with the list
for (int i = 0; i < list.length; i++)
   System.out.println(list[i]);
```

Should I Use Arrays or Array Lists?

Now that we have seen two options for storing sequences of elements, the array and the array list, it's time to consider the reasons why one might prefer one structure to the other.

Both structures allow the programmer to store and access elements by specifying an integer index position. However, the array list is by far the more powerful and easier to use. There are two reasons why this is so:

1. The array list includes many methods for various tasks, such as insertions, removals, and searches. By contrast, an array provides just a subscript operation. The user of an array must implement any higher-level operations by hand.

2. The array list tracks its own logical size and grows or shrinks automatically with the number of elements contained in it. By contrast, an array always has a fixed physical size that's independent of its logical size. This forces the user of an array to keep track of its logical size and to worry about instantiating an array that is large enough to accommodate the data requirements of a program.

These comparisons might lead us to conclude that we should never use an array in a program when an array list is available. However, arrays are still used to implement higher-level data structures, such as matrices and the array list itself.

There are at least two other situations in which an array might be on at least an equal footing with an array list:

1. We know the exact number of data elements to be inserted in advance, and they are all inserted at startup and are never removed. In this case, the array is always full and is fairly easy to process.

2. The operations on the sequence are more specialized than those provided by an array list, or they consist of simple traversals. In these cases, the programmer really only must choose between using the methods `get` and `set` with an array list and using the subscript with an array (or entirely ignoring them in an enhanced `for` loop).

In any case, because programmers have used arrays ever since the first high-level languages were developed, you will likely see arrays in code at one point or another in your programming experience.

EXERCISE 11.6

1. Write a method `sum` that expects an `ArrayList<Integer>` as a parameter. The method returns an `int` representing the sum of the integers in the array list.

2. Do the sort methods developed earlier for arrays of objects work for arrays of `Integer` objects without modification? Justify your answer.

CASE STUDY: Building a Deck of Cards

In this case study, we show how to build resources that are used in an important class of applications – online card games! (*Note*: the authors do not endorse gambling.) We discuss the analysis, design, and implementation of a deck of cards that can be used in various types of card games. The development of programs for the games themselves is left as exercises.

Request

Develop resources for a deck of cards that can be used in online games.

Analysis

You have probably played some card games, such as Rummy, Crazy Eights, and Hearts. Most computer operating systems include one or more card games for entertaining diversion. Common examples are Freecell and Solitaire on Windows systems. Most card games use a deck of cards with the following attributes:

- There are 52 cards in a deck.

- Each card has a suit and a rank.

- There are four suits: Spades, Hearts, Diamonds, and Clubs.

- Each suit has a color: black (Spades and Clubs) or red (Hearts and Diamonds).

- The cards can be ordered from highest to lowest by rank, as follows: King, Queen, Jack, 10, 9,…, 2. An Ace has either the highest or the lowest rank, depending on the game.

- The cards can also be ordered by suit, as follows: Spades, Hearts, Diamonds, Clubs.

- A deck has one card of each rank and each suit, which equals 52 (13 * 4) total cards.

- A card is face up if you can see its suit and rank; otherwise, it is face down.

  Cards and a deck can be manipulated in the following ways:

- Cards can be dealt or transferred from a deck to players.

- A deck can be shuffled, so that the cards can be dealt in random order.

- A card can be turned face up or face down.

- Two cards can be compared for equality, greater than, or less than.

- A card's suit, rank, and color can be examined.

The user interface for this case study consists of several tester programs for the various classes. Modern online card games also typically have flashy graphics that display images of the cards and allow the user to move them around by manipulating a mouse. We defer that aspect to an exercise and for now use a terminal-based interface to develop and illustrate the requirements for our deck of cards.

Classes

The two obvious classes suggested by our discussion of a deck of cards are Deck and Card. A deck contains 0 to 52 cards. It will be convenient to have one other class, called Suit, to represent the suit that each card has. The relationships among these classes are shown in the UML diagram of Figure 11-5.

FIGURE 11-5
The relationships among the classes Deck, Card, and Suit

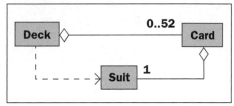

The interfaces of the Deck and Card classes are listed in Tables 11-7 and 11-8. The Card methods require no comment. Because a deck decreases in size as cards are dealt, we include two Deck methods, size() and isEmpty(), to check on the deck's status. There are two methods for dealing cards. deal() returns a single card or null if the deck is empty. deal(anInt) is used to deal a hand of one or more cards all at once. If the size of the deck is greater than or equal to the integer parameter, this method returns an array of that number of cards. Otherwise, the method returns null. The method shuffle does nothing if the deck is not full. The method reset is used to gather the cards back into the deck to make it full.

The following is a short tester program that creates a deck, shuffles it, deals each card, and displays each card's information:

```
// Case Study 11.1: Test a deck

public class TestDeck{

    public static void main(String[] args){
        Deck deck = new Deck();
        deck.shuffle();
        int count = 0;
        while (! deck.isEmpty()){
            count++;
            Card card = deck.deal();
```

```
        System.out.println(count + ": " + card);
      }
    }
  }
```

TABLE 11-7
The interface for the Deck class

DECK METHOD	WHAT IT DOES
Deck()	Constructor; creates a deck of 52 cards, unshuffled
void reset()	Restores the deck to its initial state
void shuffle()	If the deck is full, shuffles it
boolean isEmpty()	Returns true if the deck is empty or false otherwise
int size()	Returns the number of cards in the deck
Card deal()	If the deck is not empty, removes and returns a card; otherwise, returns null
Card[] deal(int n)	If the deck's size is greater than or equal to *n*, removes and returns *n* cards in an array; otherwise, returns null
String toString()	Returns a string representation of the deck

TABLE 11-8
The interface for the Card class

CARD METHOD	WHAT IT DOES
Card(Suit suit, int rank)	Constructor; creates a card with the specified suit and rank
int getRank()	Returns the card's rank
Suit getSuit()	Returns the card's suit
boolean isFaceUp()	Returns true if the card's face is up or false otherwise
boolean isRed()	Returns true if the card's suit color is red or false if it's black
void turn()	If the card is face up, makes it face down; or if it's face down, makes it face up
boolean equals(Object other)	Comparison for equality by rank
int compareTo(Object other)	Comparison for order of rank
String toString()	Returns a string representation of the card

From the client's perspective, Suit objects should be ordered consecutively like integers but named like strings. The strings "Clubs," "Diamonds", "Hearts," and "Spades" happen to have the appropriate natural ordering, so one might wonder why we would bother to define a new class for this purpose. The reason it is better to do so is that suits should be restricted to four distinct values, whereas there are an infinite number of possible string values. Defining a Suit class also gives us an opportunity to introduce an important design technique that we discuss shortly. The interface of the Suit class includes four static constants and the methods compareTo and toString, as listed in Table 11-9.

TABLE 11-9
The interface for the Suit class

SUIT CONSTANT	WHAT IT DOES
static final Suit spade	The Suit value for all spades
static final Suit heart	The Suit value for all hearts
static final Suit diamond	The Suit value for all diamonds
static final Suit club	The Suit value for all clubs
int compareTo(Object other)	The usual behavior; comparison for order: spade > heart > diamond > club
String toString()	Returns a string representation of the suit

Note that there is no constructor in the interface. The only instances of Suit that ever exist are those named by the constants Suit.spade, Suit.heart, Suit.diamond, and Suit.club.

The next code segment is a short tester program that shows how suits are used.

```
// Case Study 11.1: Test the suits

public class TestSuit{

    public static void main(String[] args){

        Suit s = Suit.spade;
        Suit h = Suit.heart;
        Suit d = Suit.diamond;
        Suit c = Suit.club;

        // Display "spades hearts diamonds clubs"
        System.out.println(s + " " + h + " " + d + " " + c);

        System.out.println(s.equals(s));        // Display true
        System.out.println(s.equals(h));        // Display false
        System.out.println(s.compareTo(s));     // Display 0
        System.out.println(s.compareTo(d));     // Display 2
        System.out.println(d.compareTo(s));     // Display -2
    }
}
```

Our final tester program uses suits to build and manipulate some cards:

```
// Case Study 11.1: Test some cards

public class TestCard{

    public static void main(String[] args){
        Card queenSpades = new Card(Suit.spade, 12);
        Card jackClubs = new Card(Suit.club, 11);
        Card twoHearts = new Card(Suit.heart, 2);
        Card twoDiamonds = new Card(Suit.diamond, 2);

        // Display "Queen of spades"
        System.out.println(queenSpades);
            // Display true
            System.out.println(twoDiamonds.equals(twoHearts));
            // Display 1
            System.out.println(queenSpades.compareTo(jackClubs));
    }
}
```

Design and Implementation of Card

The design of the Card class calls for little comment. Note just three points in the implementation that follows. First, Card implements the Comparable interface, allowing cards to be used wherever comparisons are made. Secondly, in the method isRed(), suits are compared for equality using == rather than equals. We can get away with this because there is never more than one instance of each of the four suits. Third and finally, the method turn() flips the card by inverting or logically negating the boolean variable faceUp.

```
// Case Study 11.1: The Card class

public class Card implements Comparable{

    private Suit suit;
    private int rank;
    private boolean faceUp;

    public Card(Suit suit, int rank){
        this.suit = suit;
        this.rank = rank;
        faceUp = false;
    }

    public boolean equals(Object other){
        if (this == other)
            return true;
        else if (! (other instanceof Card))
            return false;
        else{
            Card otherCard = (Card)other;
            return rank == otherCard.rank;
        }
    }
}
```

```
public int compareTo(Object other){
   if (! (other instanceof Card))
      throw new IllegalArgumentException("Parameter must be a Card");
   Card otherCard = (Card)other;
   return rank - otherCard.rank;
}

public int getRank(){
   return rank;
}

public Suit getSuit(){
   return suit;
}

public boolean isFaceUp(){
   return faceUp;
}

public boolean isRed(){
   return suit == Suit.heart || suit == Suit.diamond;
}

public void turn(){
   faceUp = ! faceUp;
}

public String toString(){
   return rankToString() + " of " + suit;
}

private String rankToString(){
   if (rank == 1)
      return "Ace";
   else if (rank == 11)
      return "Jack";
   else if (rank == 12)
      return "Queen";
   else if (rank == 13)
      return "King";
   else
      return "" + rank;
}
}
```

Design and Implementation of Deck

According to the requirements established during analysis, a deck contains from 0 to 52 cards. Thus, an array list of type `card` is an appropriate choice of a data structure to hold the cards. All of the `Deck` methods manage the list of cards for the client. The only method that is complex enough to warrant explicit design is `shuffle()`. A standard way to shuffle real cards is to split the deck and merge the two sets of cards in such a manner that they roughly interleave (the first card of the second half comes after the first card of the first half, and so forth). The development of this algorithm is left as an exercise. Instead, we adopt a simpler method: create a temporary array of 52 positions; remove each card from the list and place it at a random, unoccupied position of the array; and when the list becomes empty, transfer the cards from the array back to the list. Here is the pseudocode for this process:

```
Set array to a new array of 52 cells
While the list is not empty do
   Set card to the last card in the list
   Set index to a random number between 0 and 51
   While array[index] != null
       Set index to a random number between 0 and 51
   Set array[index] to card
For each card in array
   Add the card to the list
```

Note that the nested loop uses random integers to locate an array position that contains null. All of the array's cells are null when the array is instantiated. A null array cell indicates an empty slot in which to insert the next card. Here is a complete listing of the Deck implementation:

```java
// Case Study 11.1: The Deck class

import java.util.*;

public class Deck{

    public static final int MAX_SIZE = 52;

    private ArrayList<Card> cards;

    public Deck(){
        reset();
    }

    public void reset(){
        // Create a new list and add 13 cards from each suit
        cards = new ArrayList<Card>();
        addSuit(Suit.spade);
        addSuit(Suit.heart);
        addSuit(Suit.diamond);
        addSuit(Suit.club);
    }

    // Helper method to add 13 cards from a single suit
    private void addSuit(Suit suit){
        for (int i = 1; i <= 13; i++)
            cards.add(new Card(suit, i));
    }

    public boolean isEmpty(){
      return cards.isEmpty();
    }
```

```java
    public int size(){
        return cards.size();
    }

    public Card deal(){
        if (isEmpty())
            return null;
        else
            return cards.remove(cards.size() - 1);
    }

    public Card[] deal(int number){
        if (number > cards.size())
            return null;
        else{
            Card[] hand = new Card[number];
            for (int i = 0; i < hand.length; i++)
                hand[i] = deal();
            return hand;
        }
    }

    public void shuffle(){
        if (cards.size() < MAX_SIZE)
            return;
        Random gen = new Random();
        // Remove cards from the list and place at random positions
        // in an array
        Card[] array = new Card[MAX_SIZE];
        while (cards.size() > 0){
          Card card = cards.remove(cards.size() - 1);
          int i = gen.nextInt(MAX_SIZE);
          while (array[i] != null)
              i = gen.nextInt(MAX_SIZE);
          array[i] = card;
        }
        // Transfer the shuffled cards back to the list
        for (Card card : array)
            cards.add(card);
    }

    public String toString(){
        String result = "";
        for (Card card : cards)
            result += card + "\n";
        return result;
    }
}
```

Design and Implementation of Suit

The purpose of the Suit class is to provide exactly four distinct instances that represent the suits Spades, Hearts, Diamonds, and Clubs. These objects can be compared for equality and for their relative ordering. As we mentioned earlier, the class's interface includes four static constants for these objects, as well as the methods `compareTo` and `toString`. Equality is determined with the operator `==`.

The design of the class is unusual, in that clients cannot instantiate it. However, four instances are indeed created when the static constants are initialized (at program startup). Each instance has an integer that determines its rank in the ordering of suits and a name that is used for its string representation. A private constructor initializes these variables when the instances are created and assigned to the constants. A listing of the `Suit` class follows.

```java
// Case Study 11.1: A Suit class

public class Suit implements Comparable{

    static public final Suit spade   = new Suit(4, "spades");
    static public final Suit heart   = new Suit(3, "hearts");
    static public final Suit diamond = new Suit(2, "diamonds");
    static public final Suit club    = new Suit(1, "clubs");

    private int order;
    private String name;

    private Suit(int ord, String nm){
        name = nm;
        order = ord;
    }

    public int compareTo(Object other){
        if (! (other instanceof Suit))
            throw new IllegalArgumentException("Parameter must be a Suit");
        Suit otherSuit = (Suit)other;
        return order - otherSuit.order;
    }

    public String toString(){
        return name;
    }
}
```

11.7 Graphics and GUIs: Menus

In this section, we add drop-down menus to our growing repertoire of GUI features. As the number of commands grows, an application's user interface can become increasingly cluttered with a confusing jumble of command buttons. For example, the student test scores application in Section 9.11 already has eight buttons, but many more commands would be typical in a realistic application. Drop-down menus help to economize on a window's real estate by hiding commands under visible labels that expand only when needed.

Extra Challenge

This Graphics and GUIs section gives you the opportunity to explore concepts and programming techniques required to develop modern graphics applications and graphical user interfaces. This material is not required in order to proceed with the other chapters of the book.

Menu Basics

A drop-down menu system consists of a menu bar, a number of menus, and for each menu, several selections. It is also possible to have submenus, but we ignore these for now. It is easy to add a drop-down menu system to an application. For instance, the student test scores program currently has two rows of buttons, one for data access and another for navigation. We would like to add commands for deleting a student and for transferring the database of students to and from a file. The new commands and the data access commands can be placed under three drop-down menus named **File**, **Edit**, and **Data**. The selections under **File** are the standard **New**, **Open**, and **Save**. The selections under **Edit** are **Add**, **Modify**, and **Delete**. The selections under **Data** are **Highest Score** and **Class Average**. The new user interface is shown in Figure 11-6.

FIGURE 11-6
The new user interface for the student test scores program

We create a menu item object for each menu selection (class `JMenuItem`), a menu object for each menu (class `JMenu`), and the menu bar object in which all of the menu objects will appear (class `JMenuBar`). We then add all of the objects to their appropriate containers. The menus and selections are displayed in the order in which they are added in the code. The following code shows a truncated version of the `TestScoresView` class from Section 9.11, which adds the three menus to the application's window:

```
// Example 11.6: TestScoresView class (with menus)

import javax.swing.*;
import java.awt.*;
import java.awt.event.*;

public class TestScoresView extends JFrame{

    // >>>>>>> The model <<<<<<<<

    // Declare the model
    private TestScoresModel model;

    // >>>>>>> The view <<<<<<<<

    // Declare and instantiate the menu items
    private JMenuItem newMI        = new JMenuItem("New");
    private JMenuItem openMI       = new JMenuItem("Open");
    private JMenuItem saveMI       = new JMenuItem("Save");
    private JMenuItem addMI        = new JMenuItem("Add");
    private JMenuItem modifyMI     = new JMenuItem("Modify");
    private JMenuItem deleteMI     = new JMenuItem("Delete");
```

```
private JMenuItem highScoreMI  = new JMenuItem("Highest Score");
private JMenuItem aveScoreMI   = new JMenuItem("Class Average");
// Code for creating the other window objects

// Constructor
public TestScoresView(TestScoresModel m){
    model = m;
    // Organize and install the menu system
    JMenu fileMenu =  new JMenu("File");
    fileMenu.add(newMI);
    fileMenu.add(openMI);
    fileMenu.add(saveMI);
    JMenu editMenu =  new JMenu("Edit");
    editMenu.add(addMI);
    editMenu.add(modifyMI);
    editMenu.add(deleteMI);
    JMenu dataMenu =  new JMenu("Data");
    dataMenu.add(highScoreMI);
    dataMenu.add(aveScoreMI);
    JMenuBar bar = new JMenuBar();
    bar.add(fileMenu);
    bar.add(editMenu);
    bar.add(dataMenu);
    setJMenuBar(bar);
    // Code for installing the other window objects
    // Note: The north panel of buttons has been deleted
    // Attach listeners to buttons and menu items
    addMI.addActionListener(new AddListener());
    previousButton.addActionListener(new PreviousListener());
    // Set window attributes
    setTitle("Student Test Scores");
    setDefaultCloseOperation(JFrame.EXIT_ON_CLOSE);
    pack();
    setVisible(true);
}
// Code for the rest of the class
}
```

Like buttons, menu items emit action events when selected, so the programmer simply attaches action listeners for the appropriate tasks to the menu items. Therefore, the listener classes in the existing code need no modification whatsoever, although new listeners must be defined for the file operations. The completion of the new version is left as an exercise.

Using Menus in a Graphics Application

Menus also play a critical role in graphics applications. For example, the shape manipulation program of Section 10.12 devotes the entire container region of the window to the panel where the shapes are displayed. If we add commands to change the types of shapes, their colors, and so forth, it will be best to hide these under the relevant menus. We now develop a modified version of this program to illustrate the use of menus.

The most recent version of the program draws several circles and rectangles in random colors at startup. The user can then drag these shapes around the window with the mouse. The user should be able to draw new shapes of either type; specify their color, size, and position; and delete a selected shape. We now update the interface by adding the menus and selections described in Table 11-10.

TABLE 11-10
Menu options for the shape-drawing program

MENU/SELECTION	WHAT IT DOES
Shape/Create	Allows the user to draw shapes of the currently selected type and color
Shape/Move	Allows the user to drag shapes around the window
Shape/Delete	Allows the user to delete selected shapes
Type/Circle	Sets the current type of shape to circle
Type/Rectangle	Sets the current type of shape to rectangle
Color/Black	Sets the current drawing color to black
Color/Blue	Sets the current drawing color to blue
Color/Red	Sets the current drawing color to red
Color/Random	Sets the current drawing color to a random color

As we showed in student test scores example, the new menu system can be immediately installed and viewed in the window class. At program startup, no images are displayed. The new user interface is shown in Figure 11-7.

FIGURE 11-7
The new user interface for the shape drawing program

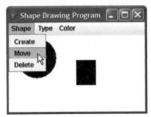
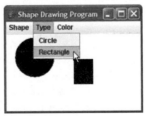
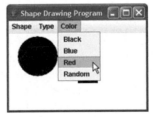

The listeners attached to the menu items respond by sending messages to the panel. These commands have no immediate visible effects. Instead, each command sets an attribute in the panel to a new value. The attributes come into play later, when the user manipulates the mouse in the drawing area. For example, if the user selects **Color/Red**, all shapes created from that time until a new color is selected will be red, and when the user selects **Type/Circle**, all shapes created will be circles until a subsequent selection is made. If the user does not try to draw a shape, however, nothing changes. The **Shape** menu allows the user to choose which basic type of manipulation to perform. When the user selects **Shape/Create**, a new shape does not suddenly pop into view. The user can draw a shape (of the current type and color) by clicking the mouse and dragging it. The coordinates of the initial click determine the upper-left corner of the new shape if it's a rectangle and the center point if it's a circle. The coordinates of the mouse release determine the new shape's width or radius. Movement works as before, by dragging, whereas a deletion takes effect when the mouse clicks on a shape. To change these attributes, the main window class uses three new methods in the panel class listed in Table 11-11.

TABLE 11-11
New ColorPanel Methods

ColorPanel METHOD	WHAT IT DOES
void setManipType(String type)	Sets the type of manipulation to type
void setShapeType (String type)	Sets the type of shape to type
void setColor(Color c)	Sets the color to c

We now structure the application like the student test scores program by using distinct application and view classes. The main method moves from the GUIWindow class to a new class called ShapeApp. main now instantiates GUIWindow and sends it the appropriate messages. GUIWindow now extends JFrame and maintains the menu items and the panel as instance variables. A constructor sets up the menu system and attaches its listeners. The listeners are defined as private inner classes in the usual manner. An abbreviated listing of the GUIWindow class for the new version of the application follows:

```
// Example 11.7: Main view class for shape drawing program
// with menus

import javax.swing.*;
import java.awt.*;
import java.awt.event.*;

public class GUIWindow extends JFrame{

    private JMenuItem createMI = new JMenuItem("Create");
    private JMenuItem moveMI   = new JMenuItem("Move");
    private JMenuItem deleteMI = new JMenuItem("Delete");
    private JMenuItem circleMI = new JMenuItem("Circle");
    private JMenuItem rectMI   = new JMenuItem("Rectangle");
    private JMenuItem blackMI  = new JMenuItem("Black");
    private JMenuItem blueMI   = new JMenuItem("Blue");
    private JMenuItem redMI    = new JMenuItem("Red");
    private JMenuItem randomMI = new JMenuItem("Random");
    private ColorPanel panel   = new ColorPanel(Color.white);

    public GUIWindow(){
        Container pane = getContentPane();
        pane.add(panel);
        JMenu shapeMenu = new JMenu("Shape");
        shapeMenu.add(createMI);
        shapeMenu.add(moveMI);
        shapeMenu.add(deleteMI);
        JMenu typeMenu = new JMenu("Type");
        typeMenu.add(circleMI);
        typeMenu.add(rectMI);
```

```
            JMenu colorMenu = new JMenu("Color");
            colorMenu.add(blackMI);
            colorMenu.add(blueMI);
            colorMenu.add(redMI);
            colorMenu.add(randomMI);
            JMenuBar bar = new JMenuBar();
            bar.add(shapeMenu);
            bar.add(typeMenu);
            bar.add(colorMenu);
            setJMenuBar(bar);
            createMI.addActionListener(new CreateListener());
            moveMI.addActionListener(new MoveListener());
            deleteMI.addActionListener(new DeleteListener());
            circleMI.addActionListener(new CircleListener());
            rectMI.addActionListener(new RectListener());
            redMI.addActionListener(new RedListener());
        }

        private class CreateListener implements ActionListener{
            public void actionPerformed(ActionEvent e){
                panel.setManipType("Create");
            }
        }

        // Other listeners go here (exercise)
    }
```

To the `panel` class we add three new instance variables for the current color, type of shape, and type of user manipulation. The values of these variables at startup are `Color.black`, "Circle," and "Create," respectively.

The actions of the mouse listeners depend on the state of the panel's attributes:

■ `mousePressed` saves the current coordinates like it did in the earlier version. If the manipulation type is "Create," that's all it does. If this value is "Move," the model is asked if the coordinates select a shape. If this value is "Delete," `mousePressed` asks the model to delete the selected shape if one is found.

■ `mouseDragged` simply returns if the manipulation type is "Create" or "Delete." If this value is "Move," `mouseDragged` does what it did in the earlier version.

■ `mouseReleased` completes either a movement or a creation of a shape. The action for movement is not different from the earlier version. When a shape is to be created, however, `mouseReleased` must determine its type, color, size, and position, instantiate it appropriately, and add it to the model.

Here is a complete listing of the `ColorPanel` class:

```
// Example 11.7: displays shapes
// Allows the user to draw shape with a size and position
// Allows the user to drag a shape to another position
// Allows the user to delete a shape
// Uses a distinct data model to maintain the shapes
```

```java
import javax.swing.*;
import java.awt.*;
import java.awt.event.*;              //For the mouse events
import java.util.Random;

public class ColorPanel extends JPanel{

    private ShapeModel database;      // Now just a model
    private Shape selectedShape;      // Used to track selected shape
    private int x, y;                 // Used to track mouse coordinates
    private String manipType;         // Type of user manipulation
    private String shapeType;         // Type of shape to create
    private Color color;              // Color for new shapes

    public ColorPanel(Color backColor){
        setBackground(backColor);
        database = new ShapeModel();  // Now can have any number of shapes
        selectedShape = null;
        manipType = "Create";
        shapeType = "Circle";
        color = Color.black;
        addMouseListener(new PanelListener());
        addMouseMotionListener(new PanelMotionListener());
    }

    public void setManipType(String type){
        manipType = type;
    }

    public void setShapeType(String type){
        shapeType = type;
    }

    public void setColor(Color c){
        color = c;
    }

    public void paintComponent(Graphics g){
        super.paintComponent(g);
        // Draw all the shapes
        database.draw(g);
    }

    private class PanelListener extends MouseAdapter{
        public void mousePressed(MouseEvent e){
            x = e.getX();
            y = e.getY();
            // Do nothing if creating
            if (manipType.equals("Create") ) return;
            //Select a shape if it contains the mouse coordinates
            selectedShape = database.containsPoint(x, y);
            if (manipType.equals("Delete") && selectedShape != null){
                // Delete, deselect, and refresh
```

```java
            database.delete(selectedShape);
            selectedShape = null;
            repaint();
        }
    }

    public void mouseReleased(MouseEvent e){
        int newX = e.getX();
        int newY = e.getY();
        if (manipType.equals("Create")){
            // Use the info to create a shape
            int dx = newX - x;
            int dy = newY - y;
            Shape s;
            if (shapeType.equals("Circle"))
                s = new Circle(x, y, dx, color);
            else
                s = new Rect(x, y, dx, dy, color);
            s.setFilled(true);
            database.add(s);
            repaint();
        }
        x = newX;
        y = newY;
        //Deselect the selected shape
        selectedShape = null;
    }
}

private class PanelMotionListener extends MouseMotionAdapter{
    public void mouseDragged(MouseEvent e){
        // Do nothing if creating or deleting
        if (manipType.equals("Create") || manipType.equals("Delete"))
            return;
        //Compute the distance and move the selected shape
        int newX = e.getX();
        int newY = e.getY();
        int dx = newX - x;
        int dy = newY - y;
        if (selectedShape != null)
            selectedShape.move(dx, dy);
        x = newX;
        y = newY;
        repaint();
    }
}
}
```

SUMMARY

In this chapter, you learned:

- A linear search is a simple search method that works well for small- and medium-sized arrays.

- A binary search is a clever search method that works well for large arrays but assumes that the elements are sorted.

- Comparisons of objects are accomplished by implementing the Comparable interface, which requires the compareTo method.

- Selection sort, bubble sort, and insertion sort are simple sort methods that work well for small- and medium-sized arrays.

- Insertions and removals of elements at arbitrary positions are complex operations that require careful design and implementation.

- One can insert objects of any class into an array of Object. When they are retrieved from the array, however, objects must be cast down to their classes before sending them most messages.

- The limitation of a fixed-size array can be overcome by using Java's ArrayList class. An array list tracks and updates its logical size and provides many useful methods to clients.

- A wrapper class, such as Integer, provides a way of packaging a value of a primitive type, such as int, in an object so that it can be stored in an array of Object or an array list.

VOCABULARY *Review*

Define the following terms:		
Array list	Immutable object	Selection sort
Binary search	Insertion sort	Substring
Bubble sort	Linear search	Wrapper class

REVIEW *Questions*

FILL IN THE BLANK

Complete the following sentences by writing the correct word or words in the blanks provided.

1. A search algorithm that examines each element, starting with the first one, is called a(n) _____ search.

2. A search algorithm that examines the element at the list's midpoint on each pass through the loop is called a(n) _____ search.

3. A sort algorithm that exchanges the smallest element with the first one is called a(n) _____ sort.

4. A sort algorithm that percolates the largest element to the end of a list is called a(n) _____ sort.

5. The method _____, which is required by the _____ interface, is used to compare two objects.

6. After retrieving an object from an array of `Object`, one must be careful to use the _____ operator before sending messages to that object.

7. Java's _____ class supports an array object that tracks its own logical size.

8. Java's _____ classes allow values of primitive types to masquerade as objects.

PROJECTS

PROJECT 11-1

Write a program that uses a scanner to report some statistics about words in an input sentence(see Section 11.1). The outputs should be the number of words in the sentence, the average word length, and the length of the sentence.

PROJECT 11-2

Write a program that inputs 10 integers into an array, sorts the array with a selection sort, and displays its contents before and after the sort.

PROJECT 11-3

Write a program that allows the user to search for a given word in a text file. The two inputs are the file's name and the target word. If the target is not found, the program outputs a message to that effect. Otherwise, the program outputs the number of times that this word occurs in the file and the position where it is first encountered (counting from position 0). The program should ignore case when it compares words.

PROJECT 11-4

The package `java.util` includes an `Arrays` class. This class includes several static methods for searching and sorting arrays, among other things. Browse this class in Sun's documentation to get a sense of its interface and method signatures. Then develop your own class, named `MyArrays`, which includes static methods for the linear search, binary search, and selection sort of arrays of objects. Include a short tester program that exercises the methods of `MyArrays`. (*Note*: `MyArrays` includes only methods, no variables.)

PROJECT 11-5

The following paragraph describes a simplified version of the card game of War. For a more complex version, see Hoyle's *Rules of Games* (New York: Signet Books, 2001).

There are two players in the game of War. During the course of a game, each player will have three piles of cards, named an unplayed pile, a war pile, and a winnings pile, respectively. The game moves forward as cards move from the unplayed piles to the war piles and then to the winnings piles. The game ends when a player's unplayed pile has no more cards. At that point, the player with the largest winnings pile wins the game. Here are the detailed rules for moving cards:

1. Each player is dealt 26 cards to her unplayed pile.

2. Repeat steps 3 through 5 until one or both unplayed piles become empty.

3. Each player plays the topmost card from his unplayed pile by placing it face up on his war pile.

4. If the cards have the same rank, repeat step 2.

5. Otherwise, move both war piles to the winnings pile of the player who has the card of a higher rank at the top of her war pile.

6. The player with the largest winnings pile wins.

Write a terminal-based program that uses the resources developed in the Case Study to play this game. The computer should make all of the moves for both players and display the cards played on each move. You should use the appropriate objects to represent the piles of cards.

PROJECT 11-6

Convert the terminal-based program of Project 11-5 to a GUI program. The main window should contain a labeled text field for each player and a single Play button. The cards are dealt at startup, but play does not start until the user clicks Play. The text fields, initially empty, are updated to display the information on the cards played from each hand after each click on Play. When a game ends, a message dialog box pops up to announce the winner. A Reset button allows the user to start a new game at any time.

PROJECT 11-7

After working on Project 11-6, Jack realizes that the game would be a lot more fun if he displayed realistic images of cards. In this project, modify the `Deck` and `Card` classes so that they are capable of displaying images. Write a short GUI tester program that cycles through a deck of cards and displays their images in a single panel.

Free images for decks of cards can be found at many Web sites. A directory containing some images is available from your instructor.

Each card should have an additional instance variable of type `ImageIcon` to hold its image. A new constructor accepts an image's file name as a parameter. The constructor loads the image from the file and sets the card's image variable. The `Card` class also includes a public method `getImage` that return's a card's image.

The Card class should have an additional instance variable of type ImageIcon to hold its image. A new Card constructor accepts an image's file name as a parameter. The constructor loads the image from the file and sets the card's image variable. The Card class also includes a public method getImage that returns a card's image.

The Deck class should have a new constructor that accepts a directory path name as a parameter. When the constructor enters the loop to create new cards, it uses the pathname to build the appropriate file name of each card's image file. You should adopt a scheme for naming these files that supports this process, such as "s1.gif" for the Ace of Spades' file, and so forth. Resulting file names are then passed to the new Card constructor mentioned earlier.

The tester program creates a new deck at startup. Its window contains a single panel and two buttons, labeled Deal and Reset. Each time that Deal is clicked, a new card is dealt from the deck and the card's image is displayed in the panel. When no more cards are available, a message dialog box pops up and the panel is cleared. Reset clears the panel and creates a new deck of cards at any time. The window's size should be large enough to accommodate a card's image.

The panel is a specialized version of the ColorPanel class used earlier. A new instance variable of type ImageIcon is initially null. A new public method setImage(anImageIcon) sets this variable and repaints the panel. When the panel's image variable is null, paintComponent just calls itself in the superclass, effectively clearing the panel. Otherwise, paintComponent also paints the image.

The window class calls setImage with a card's image when it should be displayed in the panel and calls the same method with null to clear the panel.

PROJECT 11-8

Use Jack's modified resources from Project 11-7 to develop a GUI-based game of War. (*Hint*: Replace the text fields with card panels.)

PROJECT 11-9

Complete the GUI-based student test scores program developed in Section 11.7. Update the data model so that it can hold any number of students.

PROJECT 11-10

Complete the shape-drawing program developed in Section 11.7. Update the data model so that it can hold any number of shapes.

CRITICAL *Thinking*

Jill is trying to decide whether to use an array or an instance of Java's ArrayList class in an application. Explain to her the costs and benefits of using the one data structure or the other.

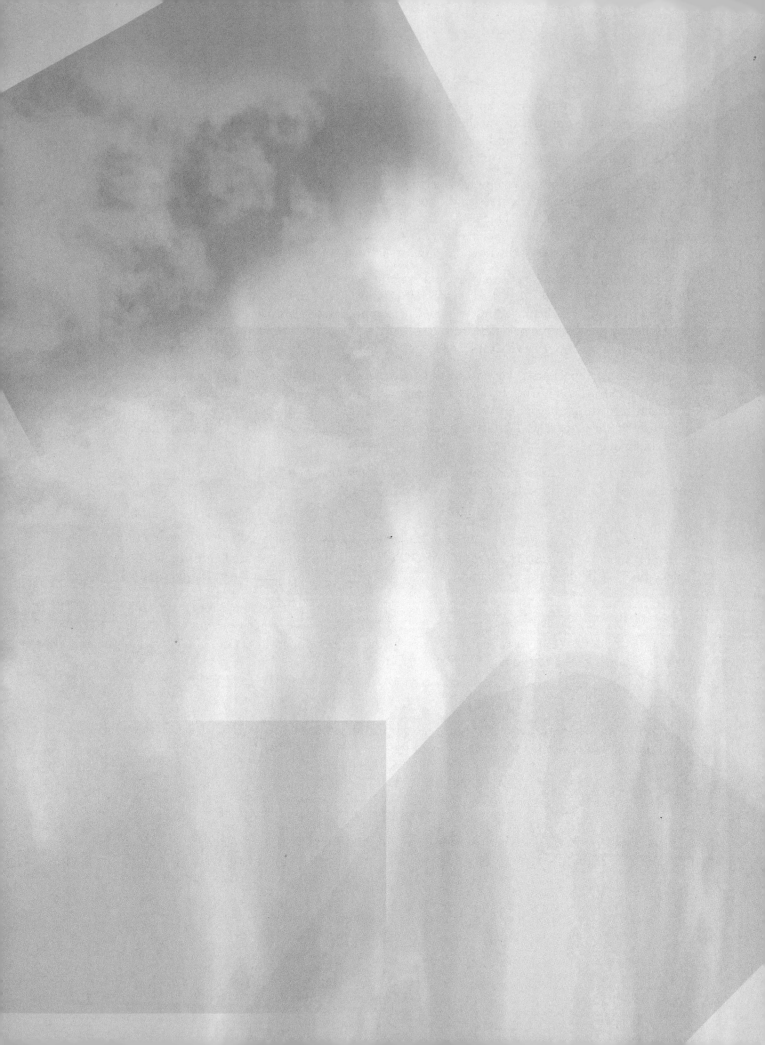

CHAPTER 12

RECURSION, COMPLEXITY, AND SEARCHING AND SORTING

OBJECTIVES

Upon completion of this chapter, you should be able to:

- Design and implement a recursive method to solve a problem.

- Understand the similarities and differences between recursive and iterative solutions of a problem.

- Check and test a recursive method for correctness.

- Understand how a computer executes a recursive method.

- Perform a simple complexity analysis of an algorithm using big-O notation.

- Recognize some typical orders of complexity.

- Understand the behavior of a complex sort algorithm such as the quicksort.

Estimated Time: 4.5 hours

VOCABULARY

Activation record

Big-O notation

Binary search algorithm

Call stack

Complexity analysis

Infinite recursion

Iterative process

Merge sort

Quicksort

Recursive method

Recursive step

Stack

Stack overflow error

Stopping state

Tail-recursive

In this chapter, we continue our discussion of sorting and searching and introduce two new topics: recursion and complexity analysis. These topics are intertwined because searching and sorting can involve recursion and complexity analysis. A recursive algorithm is one that refers to itself by name in a manner that appears to be circular. Everyday algorithms, such as a recipe to bake a cake or instructions to change car oil, are not expressed recursively, but recursive algorithms are common in computer science. Complexity analysis is concerned with determining an algorithm's efficiency—that is, how its runtime and memory usage vary as a function of the quantity of data processed. Consider the searching and sorting algorithms presented in Chapter 11. When we test these algorithms on arrays of 10 to 20 elements, they are blindingly fast, but how fast can we expect them to be when the arrays are 100 times larger? Because painting two houses generally takes twice as long as painting one, we might guess that the same linear relationship between size and speed applies equally to sorting algorithms. We would be quite wrong, however, and in this chapter we learn techniques for analyzing algorithms more accurately. It is left to later computer science courses to study this chapter's topics in greater depth.

12.1 Recursion

When asked to add the integers from 1 to *n*, we usually think of the process iteratively. We start with 1, add 2, then 3, and so forth until we reach *n*, or expressed differently

```
sum(n) = 1 + 2 + 3 + ... + n, where n >= 1
```

Java's looping constructs make implementing the process easy. There is, however, a completely different way to look at the problem, which at first seems very strange:

```
sum(1) = 1
sum(n) = n + sum(n - 1) if n > 1
```

At first glance, expressing `sum(n)` in terms of `sum(n - 1)` seems to yield a circular definition, but closer examination shows that it does not. Consider, for example, what happens when the definition is applied to the problem of calculating `sum(4)`:

```
sum(4) = 4 + sum(3)
       = 4 + 3 + sum(2)
       = 4 + 3 + 2 + sum(1)
       = 4 + 3 + 2 + 1
```

The fact that `sum(1)` is defined to be 1 without making reference to further invocations of `sum` saves the process from going on forever and the definition from being circular. Functions that are defined in terms of themselves in this way are called *recursive*. The following, for example, are two ways to express the definition of factorial, the first iterative and the second recursive:

1. factorial(n) = 1 * 2 * 3 * ... * n, where n >= 1

2. factorial(1) = 1

   factorial(n) = n * factorial(n - 1) if n > 1

In this case, no doubt, the iterative definition is more familiar and thus easier to understand than the recursive one; however, such is not always the case. Consider the definition of Fibonacci numbers first encountered in Chapter 6. The first and second numbers in the Fibonacci sequence are 1. Thereafter, each number is the sum of its two immediate predecessors, as follows:

```
1  1  2  3  5  8  13  21  34  55  89  144  233 ...
```

or

```
fibonacci(1) = 1
fibonacci(2) = 1
fibonacci(n) = fibonacci(n - 1) + fibonacci(n - 2) if n > 2
```

This is a recursive definition, and it is hard to imagine how one could express the definition nonrecursively. Turn back to Chapter 6 to see how difficult it is to write an iterative version of this method.

From these examples, we can see that recursion involves two factors. First, some function `f(n)` is expressed in terms of `f(n - 1)` and perhaps `f(n - 2)` and so on. Second, to prevent the definition from being circular, `f(1)` and perhaps `f(2)` and so on are defined explicitly.

Implementing Recursion

Given a recursive definition of some process, it is usually easy to write a *recursive method* that implements it. A method is said to be recursive if it calls itself. Let us start with a method that computes factorials:

```
int factorial (int n){
//Precondition n >= 1
   if (n == 1)
      return 1;
   else
      return n * factorial (n - 1);
}
```

For comparison, the following is an iterative version of the method. As you can see, it is slightly longer and no easier to understand.

```
int factorial (int n){
   int product = 1;
   for (int i = 2; i <= n; i++)
      product = product * i;
   return product;
}
```

As a second example of recursion, following is a method that calculates Fibonacci numbers:

```
int fibonacci (int n){
   if (n <= 2)
      return 1;
   else
      return fibonacci (n - 1) + fibonacci (n - 2);
}
```

Tracing Recursive Calls

We can better understand recursion if we trace the sequence of recursive calls and returns that occur in a typical situation. Suppose we want to compute the factorial of 4. We call `factorial(4)`, which in turn calls `factorial(3)`, which in turn calls `factorial(2)`, which in turn calls `factorial(1)`, which returns 1 to `factorial(2)`, which returns 2 to `factorial(3)`, which returns 6 to `factorial(4)`, which returns 24, as shown in the following diagram:

```
factorial(4)
        calls factorial(3)
                        calls factorial(2)
                                        calls factorial(1)
                                        which returns 1
                        which returns 2 * 1       which is 2
        which returns 3 * 2     which is 6
which returns 4 * 6       which is 24
```

At first, it seems strange to have all these invocations of the `factorial` method, each in a state of suspended animation, waiting for the completion of the ones further down the line.

When the last invocation completes its work, it returns to its predecessor, which completes its work, and so forth up the line, until eventually the original invocation reactivates and finishes the job. Fortunately, we do not have to repeat this dizzying mental exercise every time we use recursion.

Guidelines for Writing Recursive Methods

Just as we must guard against writing infinite loops, so too we must avoid recursions that never come to an end. First, a recursive method must have a well-defined termination or *stopping state*. For the factorial method, this was expressed in the lines

```
// Preconditon: n >= 1
if (n == 1)
    return 1;
```

Second, the *recursive step*, in which the method calls itself, must eventually lead to the stopping state. For the factorial method, the recursive step was expressed in the lines

```
else
    return n * factorial(n - 1);
```

Because each invocation of the factorial method is passed a smaller value, eventually the stopping state must be reached. Had we accidentally written

```
else
    return n * factorial(n + 1);
```

the method would describe an *infinite recursion*. Eventually, the user would notice and terminate the program, or else the Java interpreter would run out of memory, at which point the program would terminate with a *stack overflow error*.

Following is a subtler example of a malformed recursive method:

```
int badMethod (int n){
    if (n == 1)
        return 1;
    else
        return n * badMethod(n - 2);
}
```

This method works fine if n is odd, but when n is even, the method passes through the stopping state and keeps on going. For instance,

```
badMethod(4)
  calls badMethod(2)
    calls badMethod(0)
      calls badMethod(-2)
        calls badMethod(-4)
          calls... badMethod(-6)
            ...
```

Run-time Support for Recursive Methods

Computers provide the following support at run time for method calls:

- A large storage area known as a *call stack* is created at program startup.

- When a method is called, an *activation record* is added to the top of the call stack.

- The activation record contains, among other things, space for the parameters passed to the method, the method's local variables, and the value returned by the method.

- When a method returns, its activation record is removed from the top of the stack.

To understand how a recursive method uses the call stack, we ignore, for the sake of simplicity, all parts of the activation record except for the parameters and the return value. The method factorial has one of each:

```
int factorial (int n){
   if (n <= 1)
      return 1;
   else
      return n * factorial (n - 1);
}
```

Thus, an activation record for this method requires cells for the following items:

- The value of the parameter n

- The return value of factorial

Suppose we call factorial(4). A trace of the state of the call stack during calls to factorial down to factorial(1) is shown in Figure 12-1.

FIGURE 12-1
Activation records on the call stack during recursive calls to factorial

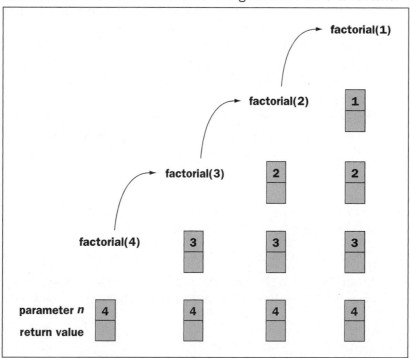

When the recursion unwinds, the return value from each call is multiplied by the parameter n in the record below it, and the top record is removed, as shown in the trace in Figure 12-2.

FIGURE 12-2
Activation records on the call stack during returns from recursive calls to factorial

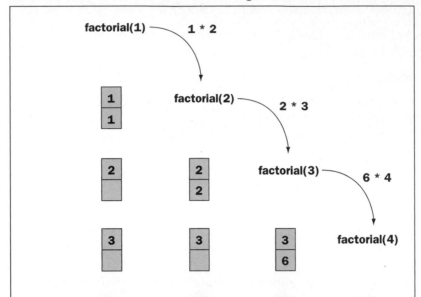

When to Use Recursion

Recursion can always be used in place of iteration, and vice versa. Ignoring the fact that arbitrarily substituting one for the other is pointless and sometimes difficult, the question of which is better to use remains. Recursion involves a method repeatedly calling itself. Executing a method call and the corresponding `return` statement usually takes longer than incrementing and testing a loop control variable. In addition, a method call ties up some memory that is not freed until the method completes its task. Naïve programmers often state these facts as an argument against ever using recursion. However, there are many situations in which recursion provides the clearest, shortest, and most elegant solution to a programming task—as we soon see. As a beginning programmer, you should not be overly concerned about squeezing the last drop of efficiency out of a computer. Instead, you need to master useful programming techniques, and recursion ranks among the best.

We close this section by presenting two well-known and aesthetically pleasing applications of recursion: the Towers of Hanoi and the Eight Queens problem.

Towers of Hanoi

Many centuries ago in the city of Hanoi, the monks in a certain monastery were continually engaged in what now seems a peculiar enterprise. Sixty-four rings of increasing size had been placed on a vertical wooden peg (Figure 12-3). Beside it were two other pegs, and the monks were attempting to move all the rings from the first to the third peg—subject to two constraints:

■ Only one ring could be moved at a time.

■ A ring could be moved to any peg, provided it was not placed on top of a smaller ring.

FIGURE 12-3
The Towers of Hanoi

The monks believed that the world would end and humankind would be freed from suffering when the task was finally completed. The fact that the world is still here today and you are enduring the frustrations of writing computer programs seems to indicate the monks were interrupted in their work. They were, but even if they had stuck with it, they would not finish anytime soon. A little experimentation should convince you that for n rings, $2^n - 1$ separate moves are required. At the rate of one move per second, $2^{64} - 1$ moves take about 600 billion years.

It might be more practical to harness the incredible processing power of modern computers to move virtual rings between virtual pegs. We are willing to start you on your way by presenting a recursive algorithm for printing the required moves. In the spirit of moderation, we suggest that you begin by running the program for small values of n. Figure 12-4 shows the result of running the program with three rings. In the output, the rings are numbered from smallest (1) to largest (3). You might try running the program with different numbers of rings to satisfy yourself that the printed output is correct. The number of lines of output corresponds to the formula given earlier.

FIGURE 12-4
Running the TowersOfHanoi program with three rings

The program uses a recursive method called move. The first time this method is called, it is asked to move all *n* rings from peg 1 to peg 3. The method then proceeds by calling itself to move the top *n* – 1 rings to peg 2, prints a message to move the largest ring from peg 1 to peg 3, and finally calls itself again to move the *n* – 1 rings from peg 2 to peg 3. Following is the code:

```
/* Example 12.1: TowersOfHanoi.java
Print the moves required to move the rings in the Towers of Hanoi problem.
1) Enter the number of rings as input.
2) WARNING: Do not run this program with 64 rings.
*/

import java.util.Scanner;

public class TowersOfHanoi {

    public static void main (String [] args) {
    // Obtain the number of rings from the user.
    // Call the recursive move method to move the rings from peg 1 to peg 3
    // with peg 2 available for intermediate usage.
    //  Preconditions  -- number of rings != 64
    //  Postconditions -- the moves are printed in the terminal window

        Scanner reader = new Scanner(System.in);
        System.out.print("Enter the number of rings: ");
        int numberOfRings = reader.nextInt();
        move (numberOfRings, 1, 3, 2);
    }

    private static void move (int n, int i, int j, int k){
    // Print the moves for n rings going from peg i to peg j
    //  Preconditions  -- none
    //  Postconditions -- the moves have been printed
        if (n > 0){                      //Stopping state is n == 0

            // Move the n-1 smaller rings from peg i to peg k
            move (n - 1, i, k, j);

            // Move the largest ring from peg i to peg j
            System.out.println("Move ring " + n + " from peg " + i + " to " +
                               j);

            // Move the n-1 smaller rings from peg k to peg j
            move (n - 1, k, j, i);

            // n rings have now been moved from peg i to peg j
        }
```

```
    }
}
```

Although you should try this program with different numbers, you should stick with smaller numbers (i.e., <10). Large values of n, even with modern processing speeds, can still take a long time to run and could tie up your computer for some time. Do not attempt to run this program with 64 rings.

Eight Queens Problem

The Eight Queens problem consists of placing eight queens on a chessboard in such a manner that the queens do not threaten each other. A queen can attack any other piece in the same row, column, or diagonal, so there can be at most one queen in each row, column, and diagonal of the board. It is not obvious that there is a solution, but Figure 12-5 shows one.

FIGURE 12-5
A solution of the Eight Queens problem

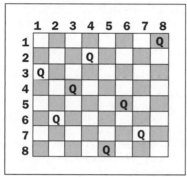

We now present a program that attempts to solve this problem and others of a similar nature. We call it the ManyQueens program, and it attempts to place n queens safely on an n × n board. The program either prints a solution or a message saying that there is none (Figure 12-6).

FIGURE 12-6
Output of the ManyQueens program for boards of size 2, 4, and 8

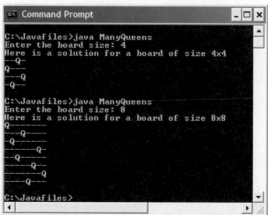

At the heart of the program is a recursive method called canPlaceQueen. Initially, the board is empty, and the first time the method is called, it places a queen at the top of column 1. It then calls itself to place a queen in the first safe square of column 2 and then again to place a queen in the first safe square of column 3 and so forth, until finally it calls itself to place a queen in the first safe square of the last column. If at some step (say, for column 5) the method fails, then it returns and processing resumes in the previous column by looking for the next safe square. If there is one, then the process moves onward to column 5 again or else back to column 3. And so it goes. Either a solution is found or all possibilities are exhausted. The program includes a second method called `attacked`. It determines if a queen placed in row *r*, column *c* is threatened by any queens already present in columns 1 to *c* – 1. Following is the code:

```
/* Example 12.2: ManyQueens.java
Determine the solution to the Many Queens problem for a chessboard
of any size.
1) There is a single input indicating the size of the board.
2) If there is a solution display it, else indicate that there is none.
*/

import java.util.Scanner;

public class ManyQueens {

    public static void main (String [] args) {
    // Process the user's input. Call a recursive function
    // to determine if there is a solution. Print the results.
    //  Preconditions  -- the input is an integer greater
    //                     than or equal to 1
    //  Postconditions -- display a solution or a message stating that there
    //                     is none

        int boardSize;        // The size of the board, for instance, 8 would
                              // indicate an 8x8 board
        boolean[][] board;    // A two-dimensional array representing the board
                              // An entry of false indicates that a square is
                              // unoccupied

        // Initialize the variables
        Scanner reader = new Scanner(System.in);
        System.out.print("Enter the board size: ");
        boardSize = reader.nextInt();
        board = new boolean[boardSize][boardSize];
        for (int row = 0; row < boardSize; row++)
           for (int col = 0; col < boardSize; col++)
              board[row][col] = false;

        // Determine if there is a solution
        if (! canPlaceQueen (0, board))

           // There is no solution
           System.out.println ("Impossible on a board of size " +
                                boardSize + "x" + boardSize);

        else{

           // There is a solution, so print it
           System.out.println ("Here is a solution for a board of size " +
                                boardSize + "x" + boardSize);
           for (int row = 0; row < boardSize; row++){
              for (int col = 0; col < boardSize; col++){
                 if (board[row][col])
                    System.out.print ("Q");
```

```
                else
                    System.out.print ("-");
            }
            System.out.println();
        }


    }
}

private static boolean canPlaceQueen (int col, boolean[][] board){
// Mark as true the first unattacked location in column col that
// permits a solution across the remaining columns.
//  Preconditions  -- 0 <= col < board.length
//  Postconditions -- if an entry in col gets marked true
//                       return true else return false

    for (int row = 0; row < board.length; row++){   // Iterate down the column
        if (! attacked (row, col, board)){            // if square is not under attack
            if (col == board.length -1){              // if this is the last column
                board[row][col] = true;               // end recursion, set square true
                return true;                          // recursive ascent true
             }else{                                    // else
                board[row][col] = true;               // trial solution, set square true
                                                      // if recursive descent succeeds

                if (canPlaceQueen (col + 1, board))
                    return true;                      // recursive ascent true
                else                                  // else
                    board[row][col] = false;          // trial solution didn't work
            }                                         // end if
        }                                             // end if
    }
    return false;                                     // recursive ascent false
 }


 private static boolean attacked (int row, int col, boolean[][] board){
// Determine if the square at location (row, col) is under attack.
// from any queen in columns 0 to col - 1
//  Preconditions  -- 0 <= row, col < board.length
//  Postconditions -- returns true if square under attack else false

// Look for horizontal attack
    int i, j, k;
    for (j = 0; j < col; j++){
        if (board[row][j])
            return true;
    }

    // Look for attack from a descending diagonal
    i = row - 1;
    j = col - 1;
    for (k = 0; k <= Math.min(i, j); k++){
        if (board[i][j])
            return true;
        else{
            i--;
            j--;
        }
    }
```

```
// Look for attack from an ascending diagonal
i = row + 1;
j = col - 1;
for (k = 0; k <= Math.min(board.length - i - 1, j); k++){
    if (board[i][j])
        return true;
    else{
        i++;
        j--;
    }
}

return false;
    }
}
```

EXERCISE 12.1

1. What keeps a recursive definition from being circular?

2. What are the two parts of any recursive method?

3. Why is recursion more expensive than iteration?

4. What are the benefits of using recursion?

5. Consider the following definition of the method raise, which raises a given number to a given exponent:

```
int raise(int base, int expo){
    if (expo == 0)
        return 1;
    else
        return base * raise(base, expo - 1);
}
```

Draw a trace of the complete execution of raise(2, 5).

6. Consider the following method:

```
int whatAMethod(int n){
    if (n == 0)
        return 1;
    else
        return whatAMethod(n);
}
```

What happens during the execution of whatAMethod(3)?

Programming Skills

RECURSION NEED NOT BE EXPENSIVE

We have seen that the use of recursion has two costs: Extra time and extra memory are required to manage recursive function calls. These costs have led some to argue that recursion should never be used in programs. However, as Guy Steele has shown (in "Debunking the 'Expensive Procedure Call' Myth," *Proceedings of the National Conference of the ACM*, 1977), some systems can run recursive algorithms as if they were iterative ones, with no additional overhead. The key condition is to write a special kind of recursive algorithm called a ***tail-recursive*** algorithm. An algorithm is tail-recursive if no work is done in the algorithm after a recursive call. For example, according to this criterion, the factorial method that we presented earlier is not tail-recursive because a multiplication is performed after each recursive call. We can convert this version of the factorial method to a tail-recursive version by performing the multiplication before each recursive call. To do this, we need an additional parameter that passes the accumulated value of the factorial down on each recursive call. In the last call of the method, this value is returned as the result:

```
int tailRecursiveFactorial (int n, int result){
    if (n == 1)
        return result;
    else
        return tailRecursiveFactorial (n - 1, n * result);
}
```

Note that the multiplication is performed before the recursive call of the method—that is, when the parameters are evaluated. On the initial call to the method, the value of `result` should be 1:

```
int factorial (int n){
    return tailRecursiveFactorial (n, 1);
}
```

Steele showed that a smart compiler could translate tail-recursive code in a high-level language to a loop in machine language. The machine code treats the method's parameters as variables associated with a loop and generates an ***iterative process*** rather than a recursive one. Thus, there is no linear growth of method calls, and extra stack memory is not required to run tail-recursive methods on these systems.

The catch is that a programmer must be able to convert a recursive method to a tail-recursive method and find a compiler that generates iterative machine code from tail-recursive methods. Unfortunately, some methods are difficult or impossible to convert to tail-recursive versions, and the needed optimizations are not part of most standard compilers. If you find that your Java compiler supports this optimization, you should try converting some methods to tail-recursive versions and see if they run faster than the original versions.

12.2 Complexity Analysis

There is an important question we should ask about every method we write. What is the effect on the method of increasing the quantity of data processed? Does doubling the amount of data double the method's execution time, triple it, quadruple it, or have no effect? This type of examination is called *complexity analysis*. Let us consider some examples.

Sum Methods

First, consider the sum method presented in Chapter 9. This method processes an array whose size can be varied. To determine the method's execution time, beside each statement we place a symbol (t1, t2, etc.) that indicates the time needed to execute the statement. Because we have no way of knowing what these times really are, we can do no better.

```
int sum (int[] a){
   int result = 0;                        // Assignment: time = t1
   for (int i = 0; i < a.length; i++){    // Overhead for going once around the
                                          // loop: time = t2
      result += a[i];                     // Assignment: time = t3
   }
   return result;                         // Return: time = t4
}
```

Adding these times together and remembering that the method goes around the loop *n* times, where *n* represents the array's size, yields

```
executionTime
   = t1 + n * (t2 + t3) + t4
   = k1 + n * k2              where k1 and k2 are method-dependent constants
   = n * k2                   for large values of n
```

Thus, the execution time is linearly dependent on the array's length, and as the array's length increases, the contribution of k1 becomes negligible. Consequently, we can say with reasonable accuracy that doubling the length of the array doubles the execution time of the method. Computer scientists express this linear relationship between the array's length and execution time using *big-O notation*:

```
executionTime = O(n).
```

Or phrased slightly differently, the execution time is order of *n*. Observe that from the perspective of big-O notation, we make no distinction between a method whose execution time is

```
1000000 + 1000000*n
```

and one whose execution time is

```
n / 1000000
```

although from a practical perspective the difference is enormous.

Complexity analysis can also be applied to recursive methods. Following is a recursive version of the sum method. It, too, is O(n).

```
int sum (int[] a, int i){
    if (i >= a.length)              // Comparison: t1
        return 0;                   // Return: t2
    else
        return a[i] + sum (a, i + 1);  // Call and return: t3
}
```

The method is called initially with i = 0. A single activation of the method takes time

```
t1 + t2        if  i >= a.length
```

and

```
t1 + t3        if  i < a.length.
```

The first case occurs once and the second case occurs the a.length times that the method calls itself recursively. Thus, if n equals a.length, then

```
executionTime
    = t1 + t2 + n * (t1 + t3)
    = k1 + n * k2                   where k1 and k2 are method-dependent constants
    = O(n)
```

Other O(n) Methods

Several of the array processing methods presented in Chapters 9 and 11 are O(n). Following is a linear search method from Chapter 11:

```
int search (int[] a, int searchValue){
    for (int i = 0; i < a.length; i++)   // Loop overhead: t1
        if (a[i] == searchValue)         // Comparison: t2
            return i;                    // Return point 1: t3
    return location;                     // Return point 2: t4
}
```

The analysis of the linear search method is slightly more complex than that of the sum method. Each time through the loop, a comparison is made. If and when a match is found, the method returns from the loop with the search value's index. If we assume that the search is usually made for values present in the array, then on average, we can expect that half the elements in the array be examined before a match is found. Putting all of this together yields

```
executionTime
    = (n / 2) * (t1 + t2) + t3
    = n * k1 + k2                   where k1 and k2 are method-dependent constants.
    = O(n)
```

Now let us look at a method that processes a two-dimensional array:

```
int[] sumRows (int[][] a){
   int[] rowSum = new int[a.length];          // Instantiation: t1
   for (int row = 0; row < a.length; row++){  // Loop overhead: t2
      for (int col = 0; col < a[row].length; col++){  // Loop overhead: t3
         rowSum[row] += a[row][col];          // Assignment: t4
      }
   }
   return rowSum;                             // Return: t5
}
```

Let n represent the total number of elements in the array and r the number of rows. For the sake of simplicity, we assume that each row has the same number of elements, say, c. The execution time can be written as

```
executionTime
    = t1 + r * (t2 + c * (t3 + t4)) + t5
    = (k1 + n * k2) + (n/c) * t2 + n * (t3 + t4) + t5   where r = n/c
    = (k1 + n * k2) + n * (t2 / c + t3 + t4) + t5
    = k2 + n * k3                              where k1, k2, k3, and k4 are constants
    = O(n)
```

Notice that we have replaced `t1` by `(k1 + n * k2)`. This is based on the perhaps unreasonable assumption that the JVM can allocate a block of memory for the array `rowSum` in constant time `(k1)` followed by the time needed to initialize all entries to zero `(n * k2)`.

An $O(n^2)$ Method

Not all array processing methods are $O(n)$, as an examination of the `bubbleSort` method reveals. Let us first analyze a "dumber" version of this method than the one presented in Chapter 11. This one does not track whether or not an exchange was made in the nested loop, so there is no early exit.

```
void bubbleSort(int[] a){
   int k = 0;

   // Make n - 1 passes through array

   while (k < a.length() - 1){            // Loop overhead: t1
      k++;
      for (int j = 0; j < a.length() - k; j++)   // Loop overhead: t2
         if (a[j] > a[j + 1])             // Comparison: t3
            swap(a, j, j + 1);            // Assignments: t4
   }
}
```

The outer loop of the sort method executes $n - 1$ times, where n is the length of the array. Each time the inner loop is activated, it iterates a different number of times. On the first activation it iterates $n - 1$ times, on the second $n - 2$, and so on, until on the last activation it iterates once. Thus, the average number of iterations is $n / 2$. On some iterations, elements $a[i]$ and $a[j]$ are interchanged in time $t4$, and on other iterations they are not. So on the average iteration, let's say time $t5$ is spent doing an interchange. The execution time of the method can now be expressed as

```
executionTime
    = t1 + (n - 1) * (t1 + (n / 2) * (t2 + t3 + t5))
    = t1 + n * t1 - t1 + (n * n / 2) * (t2 + t3 + t4) -
                        (n / 2) * (t2 + t3 + t4)
   = k1 + n * k2 + n * n * k3
 = n * n * k3                    for large values of n
      = O(n²)
```

As discussed in Chapter 11, we can alter this method to track whether or not an exchange was made within the nested loop. If no exchange was made, then the array must be sorted and we can exit the method early. However, because we usually make an exchange on each pass on the average, this trick does not improve the bubble sort's complexity on the average. Nevertheless, it can improve the method's behavior to linear in the best case (a case in which the array is already sorted).

Common Big-O Values

We have already seen several methods that are $O(n)$ and one that is $O(n^2)$. These are just two of the most frequently encountered big-O values. Table 12-1 lists some other common big-O values together with their names.

TABLE 12-1
Names of some common big-O values

BIG-O VALUE	NAME
$O(1)$	Constant
$O(\log n)$	Logarithmic
$O(n)$	Linear
$O(n \log n)$	$n \log n$
$O(n^2)$	Quadratic
$O(n^3)$	Cubic
$O(2^n)$	**Exponential**

As an example of $O(1)$, consider a method that returns the sum of the first and last numbers in an array. This method's execution time is independent of the array's length. In other words, it takes constant time. Later in the chapter, we will see examples of methods that are logarithmic and $n \log n$.

The values in Table 12-1 are listed from "best" to "worst." For example, given two methods that perform the same task, but in different ways, we tend to prefer the one that is O(n) over the one that is O(n^2). This statement requires some elaboration. For instance, suppose that the exact run time of two methods is

```
10,000 + 400n         // method 1
```

and

```
10,000 + n²           // method 2
```

For small values of n, method 2 is faster than method 1; however, and this is the important point, for all values of n larger than a certain threshold, method 1 is faster. The threshold in this example is 400. So if you know ahead of time that n will always be less than 400, you are advised to use method 2, but if n will have a large range of values, method 1 is superior.

By the way, from the perspective of complexity analysis, we do not need to distinguish between base 2 and base 10 logarithms because they differ only by a constant factor:

```
log² n = log¹⁰ n * log² 10
```

To get a feeling for how the common big-O values vary with n, consider Table 12-2. We use base 10 logarithms. This table vividly demonstrates that a method might be useful for small values of n but totally worthless for large values. Clearly, methods that take exponential time have limited value, even if it were possible to run them on the world's most powerful computer for billions of years. Unfortunately, there are many important problems for which even the best algorithms take exponential time. You can achieve lasting fame by being the first person to replace one of these exponential time algorithms with one that takes less than exponential time.

TABLE 12-2
How big-O values vary depending on n

n	1	LOG n	n	n LOG n	n^2	n^3	2^n
10	1	1	10	10	100	1,000	1,024
100	1	2	100	200	10,000	1,000,000	≈ 1.3 e30
1,000	1	3	1,000	3,000	1,000,000	1,000,000,000	≈ 1.1 e301

An O(r^n) Method

We have seen two algorithms for computing Fibonacci numbers, one iterative and the other recursive. The iterative algorithm presented in Chapter 6 is O(n). However, the much simpler recursive algorithm presented earlier in this chapter is O(r^n), where $r \approx 1.62$. While O(r^n) is better than O(2^n), it is still exponential. It is beyond the book's scope to prove that the recursive algorithm is O(r^n). Nonetheless, it is easy to demonstrate that the number of recursive calls increases rapidly with n. For instance, Figure 12-7 shows the calls involved when we use the recursive method to compute the sixth Fibonacci number. To keep the diagram reasonably compact, we write (6) instead of `fibonacci(6)`.

FIGURE 12-7
Calls needed to compute the sixth Fibonacci number recursively

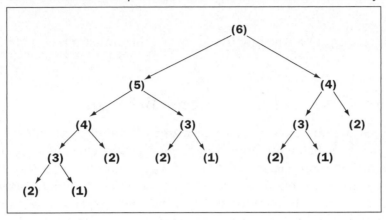

Table 12-3 shows the number of calls as a function of *n*.

TABLE 12-3
Calls needed to compute the *n*th Fibonacci number recursively

n	CALLS NEEDED TO COMPUTE *n*TH FIBONACCI NUMBER
2	1
4	5
8	41
16	1,973
32	4,356,617

The values in Table 12-3 were obtained by running the following program:

```
// Example 12.3: Test fibonacci method

public class Tester{

    private static int count = 0;

    public static void main (String[] args){
        for (int i = 1; i <= 5; i++){
            count = 0;
            int n = (int)Math.pow(2, i);
            int fibn = fibonacci(n);
            System.out.println ("" + n + ":" + count);
        }
    }

    private static int fibonacci (int n){
        count++;
        if (n <= 2)
            return 1;
        else
```

```
            return fibonacci(n - 1) + fibonacci(n - 2);
    }
}
```

Programs such as this are frequently useful for gaining an empirical sense of an algorithm's efficiency.

Best-Case, Worst-Case, and Average-Case Behavior

Many algorithms do not have a single measure of complexity that applies to all cases. Sometimes an algorithm's behavior improves or gets worse when it encounters a particular arrangement of data. For example, the bubble sort algorithm developed in Chapter 11 can terminate as soon as the array becomes sorted. If the input array is already sorted, the bubble sort requires just N comparisons. In many other cases, however, bubble sort requires N2 comparisons. Clearly, a more detailed analysis may be needed to make programmers aware of these special cases.

A thorough analysis of an algorithm's complexity divides its behavior into three types of cases:

1. *Best case*. Under what circumstances does an algorithm do the least amount of work? What is the algorithm's complexity in this best case?

2. *Worst case*. Under what circumstances does an algorithm do the most amount of work? What is the algorithm's complexity in this worst case?

3. *Average case*. Under what circumstances does an algorithm do a typical amount of work? What is the algorithm's complexity in this typical case?

Let's consider three examples of this kind of analysis for summation, linear search, and bubble sort.

Because the summation algorithm must visit each number in the array, no matter how the numbers are ordered, the algorithm is always linear. Therefore, its best-case, worst-case, and average-case behaviors are $O(n)$.

Linear search is a bit different. The algorithm stops and returns a result as soon as it finds the target element. Clearly, in the best case, this element is at the first position. In the worst case, the target is in the last position. Therefore, the algorithm's best-case behavior is $O(1)$ and its worst-case behavior is $O(n)$. To compute the average-case behavior, we add up all of the comparisons that must be made to locate a target in each position and divide by n. This is $(1 + 2 + \ldots + n) / n$, or $n / 2$. Therefore, by approximation, the average-case behavior of linear search is also $O(n)$.

As we saw in Chapter 11, the "smarter" version of bubble sort can terminate as soon as the array becomes sorted. In the best case, this happens when the input array is already sorted. Therefore, bubble sort's best-case behavior is $O(n)$. However, this case is very rare (1 out of $n!$). In the worst case, even this version of bubble sort will have to bubble each element down to its proper position in the array. The algorithm's worst-case behavior is clearly $O(n^2)$. Bubble sort's average-case behavior is closer to $O(n^2)$ than to $O(n)$, although the demonstration of this fact is a bit more involved than it is for linear search.

As we will see, there are algorithms whose best-case and average-case behaviors are similar, but whose behavior degrades to a worst case. Whether you are choosing an algorithm or developing a new one, it is important to be aware of these distinctions.

EXERCISE 12.2

1. Using big-O notation, state the time complexity of the following recursive methods:

   a. `factorial`

   b. `raise` (see Exercise 12.1, Question 5)

2. Recursive methods use stack space. Using big-O notation, state the space complexity of the following recursive methods:

   a. `factorial`

   b. `fibonacci`

3. State the time complexity of the following sort method:

```
void sort(int[] a){
   for (int j = 0; j < a.length - 1; j++){
      int minIndex = j;
      for (int k = j + 1; k < a.length; k++)
         if (a[k] < a[minIndex])
            minIndex = k;
      if (minIndex != j){
         int temp = a[j];
         a[j] = a[minIndex];
         a[minIndex] = temp;
      }
   }
}
```

12.3 Binary Search

Searching is such a common activity that it is important to do it quickly. As mentioned earlier, a linear search starts at the beginning of an array and looks at consecutive elements until either the search value is located or the array's end is encountered. Imagine using this technique to find a number by hand in a list of 10 million entries. It would take an intolerably long time, especially if the elements are strings (recall that all characters in two strings must be compared to ensure equality).

Alternatively, as mentioned in Chapter 11, if we know in advance that the list is in ascending order, we can quickly zero in on the search value or determine that it is absent using the *binary search algorithm*. We shall show that this algorithm is O(log *n*).

We start by looking at the middle of the list. We might be lucky and find the search value immediately. If not, we know whether to continue the search in the first or the second half of the list. Now we reapply the technique repeatedly. At each step, we reduce the search region by a factor of 2. Soon we either must find the search value or narrow the search down to a single element. A list of 1 million entries involves at most 20 steps.

Figure 12-8 is an illustration of the binary search algorithm. We are looking for the number 320. At each step, we highlight the sublist that might still contain 320. Also at each step, all the numbers are invisible except the one in the middle of the sublist, which is the one that we are comparing to 320.

FIGURE 12-8
Binary search algorithm

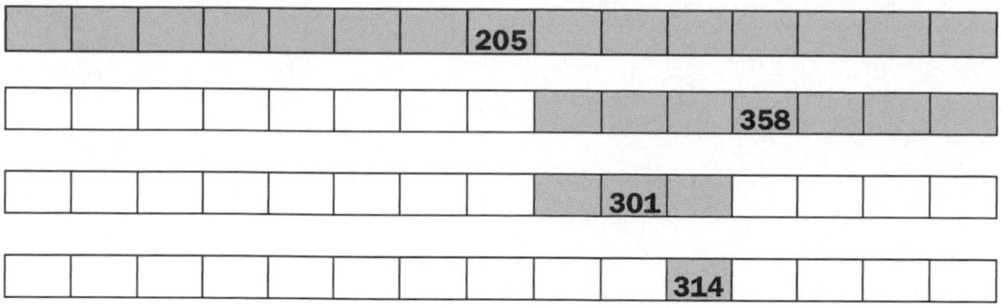

After only four steps, we have determined that 320 is not in the list. Had the search value been 205, 358, 301, or 314, we would have located it in four or fewer steps. The binary search algorithm is guaranteed to search a list of 15 sorted elements in a maximum of four steps. Incidentally, the list with all the numbers visible looks like Figure 12-9.

FIGURE 12-9
The list for the binary search algorithm with all numbers visible

| 15 | 36 | 87 | 95 | 100 | 110 | 194 | 205 | 297 | 301 | 314 | 358 | 451 | 467 | 486 |

Table 12-4 shows the relationship between a list's length and the maximum number of steps needed to search the list. To obtain the numbers in the second column, add 1 to the larger numbers in the first column and take the logarithm base 2. Hence, a method that implements a binary search is $O(\log n)$.

TABLE 12-4
Maximum number of steps needed to binary search lists of various sizes

LENGTH OF LIST	MAXIMUM NUMBER OF STEPS NEEDED
1	1
2 to 3	2
4 to 7	3
8 to 15	4
16 to 31	5
32 to 63	6
64 to 127	7
128 to 255	8
256 to 511	9
512 to 1023	10

TABLE 12-4 Continued

Maximum number of steps needed to binary search lists of various sizes

LENGTH OF LIST	MAXIMUM NUMBER OF STEPS NEEDED
1024 to 2047	11
2^n to $2^{n+1} - 1$	$n + 1$

We now present two versions of the binary search algorithm, one iterative and one recursive, and both $O(\log n)$. We will forgo a formal analysis of the complexity. First, the iterative version, as introduced in Chapter 11:

```
// Iterative binary search of an ascending array
int search (int[] a, int target){
    int left = 0;                          // Establish the initial
    int right = a.length - 1;              // endpoints of the array
    while (left <= right){                 // Loop until the endpoints cross
        int midpoint = (left + right) / 2; // Compute the current midpoint
        if (a[midpoint] == target)         // Target found; return its index
            return midpoint;
        else if (a[midpoint] < target)     // Target to right of midpoint
            left = midpoint + 1;
        else                               // Target to left of midpoint
            right = midpoint - 1;
    }
    return -1;                             // Target not found
}
```

Figure 12-10 illustrates an iterative search for 320 in the list of 15 elements. L, M, and R are abbreviations for `left`, `midpoint`, and `right`. At each step, the figure shows how these variables change. Because 320 is absent from the list, eventually (`left > right`) and the method returns –1.

FIGURE 12-10

Steps in an iterative binary search for the number 320

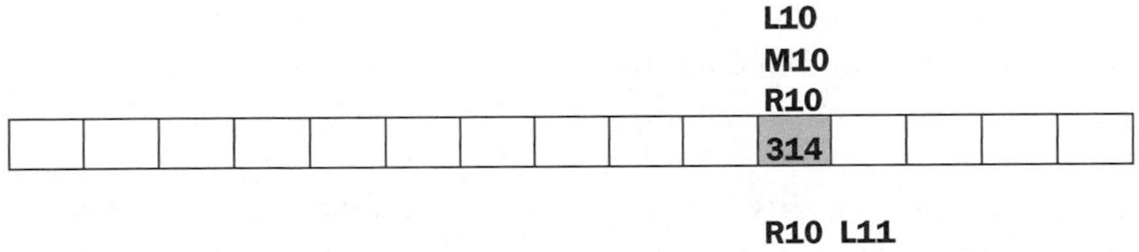

Now for the recursive version of the algorithm:

```
// Recursive binary search of an ascending array
int search (int[] a, int target, int left, int right){
   if (left > right)
      return -1;
   else{
      int midpoint = (left + right) / 2;
      if (a[midpoint] == target)
         return midpoint;
      else if (a[midpoint] < target)
         return search (a, target, midpoint + 1, right);
      else
         return search (a, target, left, midpoint - 1);
   }
}
```

At heart, the two versions are similar, and they use the variables `left`, `midpoint`, and `right` in the same way. Of course, they differ in that one uses a loop and the other uses recursion. We conclude the discussion by showing how the two methods are called:

```
int[] a = {15,36,87,95,100,110,194,205,297,301,314,358,451,467,486};
int x = 320;
int location;

location = search (a, x);                    // Iterative version
location = search (a, x, 0, a.length - 1);   // Recursive version
```

EXERCISE 12.3

1. The efficiency of the method `raise` in Question 5 of Exercise 12.1, can be improved by the following changes: If the exponent is even, then raise the base to the exponent divided by 2 and return the square of this number. Otherwise, the exponent is odd, so `raise` the number as before. Rewrite the method `raise` using this strategy.

2. Draw a trace of the complete execution of `raise(2, 10)` as defined in Question 1 in this exercise.

3. What is the time complexity of `raise` in Question 1?

12.4 Quicksort

The sort algorithms presented in Chapter 11 are $O(n^2)$. There are a number of variations on the algorithms, some of which are marginally faster, but they too are $O(n^2)$. In contrast, there are also several better algorithms that are $O(n \log n)$. *Quicksort* is one of the simplest of these. The general idea behind quicksort is this: Break an array into two parts and then move elements around so that all the larger values are in one end and all the smaller values are in the other. Each of the two parts is then subdivided in the same manner, and so on, until the subparts contain only a single value, at which point the array is sorted. To illustrate the process, suppose an unsorted array, called `a`, looks like Figure 12-11.

FIGURE 12-11
Unsorted array

| 5 | 12 | 3 | 11 | 2 | 7 | 20 | 10 | 8 | 4 | 9 |

Phase 1

1. If the length of the array is less than 2, then it is done.

2. Locate the value in the middle of the array and call it the *pivot*. The pivot is 7 in this example (Figure 12-12).

FIGURE 12-12
Step 2 of quicksort

| 5 | 12 | 3 | 11 | 2 | <u>7</u> | 20 | 10 | 8 | 4 | 9 |

3. Tag the elements at the left and right ends of the array as i and j, respectively (Figure 12-13).

FIGURE 12-13
Step 3 of quicksort

| 5 | 12 | 3 | 11 | 2 | <u>7</u> | 20 | 10 | 8 | 4 | 9 |
| i | | | | | | | | | | j |

4. While a[i] < pivot value, increment i.
   While a[j] > pivot value, decrement j (Figure 12-14).

FIGURE 12-14
Step 4 of quicksort

| 5 | 12 | 3 | 11 | 2 | <u>7</u> | 20 | 10 | 8 | 4 | 9 |
| | i | | | | | | | | j | |

5. If i > j then
       end the phase
   else
       interchange a[i] and a[j] (Figure 12-15).

FIGURE 12-15
Step 5 of quicksort

| 5 | 4 | 3 | 11 | 2 | <u>7</u> | 20 | 10 | 8 | 12 | 9 |
| | i | | | | | | | | j | |

6. Increment i and decrement j.
   If i > j then end the phase (Figure 12-16).

FIGURE 12-16
Step 6 of quicksort

5	4	3	11	2	<u>7</u>	20	10	8	12	9
		i					j			

7. Repeat Step 4, that is,
   While a[i] < pivot value, increment i
   While a[j] > pivot value, decrement j (Figure 12-17).

FIGURE 12-17
Step 7 of quicksort

5	4	3	11	2	<u>7</u>	20	10	8	12	9
			i		j					

8. Repeat Step 5, that is,
   If i > j then
     end the phase
   else
     interchange a[i] and a[j] (Figure 12-18).

FIGURE 12-18
Step 8 of quicksort

5	4	3	<u>7</u>	2	11	20	10	8	12	9
			i		j					

9. Repeat Step 6, that is,
   Increment i and decrement j.
   If i > j then end the phase (Figure 12-19).

FIGURE 12-19
Step 9 of quicksort

5	4	3	<u>7</u>	2	11	20	10	8	12	9
				ij						

10. Repeat Step 4, that is,
    While a[i] < pivot value, increment i
    While a[j] > pivot value, decrement j (Figure 12-20).

FIGURE 12-20
Step 10 of quicksort

5	4	3	_7_	2	11	20	10	8	12	9
			j	i						

11. Repeat Step 5, that is,
    If `i > j` then
        end the phase
    else
        interchange `a[i]` and `a[j]`.

12. This ends the phase. Split the array into the two subarrays `a[0..j]` and `a[i..10]`. For clarity, the left subarray is shaded (Figure 12-21). Notice that all the elements in the left subarray are less than or equal to the pivot, and those in the right are greater than or equal to the pivot.

FIGURE 12-21
Step 12 of quicksort

5	4	3	7	2	11	20	10	8	12	9

Phase 2 and Onward

Reapply the process to the left and right subarrays, and then divide each subarray in two, and so on, until the subarrays have lengths of at most 1.

Complexity Analysis

We now present an informal analysis of the quicksort's complexity. During phase 1, `i` and `j` moved toward each other. At each move, either an array element is compared to the pivot or an interchange takes place. As soon as `i` and `j` pass each other, the process stops. Thus, the amount of work during phase 1 is proportional to n, the array's length.

The amount of work in phase 2 is proportional to the left subarray's length plus the right subarray's length, which together yield n. And when these subarrays are divided, there are four pieces whose combined length is n, so the combined work is proportional to n yet again. At successive phases, the array is divided into more pieces, but the total work remains proportional to n.

To complete the analysis, we need to determine how many times the arrays are subdivided. We make the optimistic assumption that each time the dividing line turns out to be as close to the center as possible. In practice, this is not usually the case. We already know from our discussion of the binary search algorithm that when we divide an array in half repeatedly, we arrive at a single element in about $\log_2 n$ steps. Thus, the algorithm is O($n \log n$) in the best case. In the worst case, the algorithm is O(n^2).

Implementation

The quicksort algorithm can be coded using either an iterative or a recursive approach. The iterative approach also requires a data structure called a *stack*. Because we have described it recursively, we might as well implement it that way too.

```
void quickSort (int[] a, int left, int right){

    if (left >= right) return;

    int i = left;
    int j = right;
    int pivotValue = a[(left + right) / 2];
    while (i < j){
        while (a[i] < pivotValue) i++;
        while (pivotValue < a[j]) j--;
        if (i <= j){
            int temp = a[i];
            a[i] = a[j];
            a[j] = temp;
            i++;
            j--;
        }
    }
    quickSort (a, left, j);
    quickSort (a, i, right);
}
```

EXERCISE 12.4

1. Describe the strategy of quicksort and explain why it can reduce the time complexity of sorting from $O(n^2)$ to $O(n \log n)$.

2. Why is quicksort not $O(n \log n)$ in all cases? Describe the worst-case situation for quicksort.

3. Describe three strategies for selecting a pivot value in quicksort.

4. Jack has a bright idea: When the length of a subarray in quicksort is less than a certain number, say, 50 elements, run an insertion sort to process that subarray. Explain why this is a bright idea.

12.5 Merge Sort

Another algorithm called *merge sort* employs a recursive, divide-and-conquer strategy to break the $O(n^2)$ barrier. Here is an outline of the algorithm:

- Compute the middle position of an array and recursively sort its left and right subarrays (divide and conquer).

- Merge the two sorted subarrays back into a single sorted array.

- Stop the process when subarrays can no longer be subdivided.

This top-level design strategy can be implemented as three Java methods:

- `mergeSort`—the public method called by clients

- `mergeSortHelper`—a private helper method that hides the extra parameter required by recursive calls

- `merge`—a private method that implements the merging process

The merging process uses an extra array, which we call `copyBuffer`. To avoid the overhead of allocating and deallocating the `copyBuffer` each time `merge` is called, the buffer is allocated once in `mergeSort` and subsequently passed to `mergeSortHelper` and `merge`. Each time `mergeSortHelper` is called, it needs to know the bounds of the subarray with which it is working. These bounds are provided by two parameters, low and high. Here is the code for `mergeSort`:

```java
void mergeSort(int[] a){
    // a           array being sorted
    // copyBuffer  temp space needed during merge

    int[] copyBuffer = new int[a.length];
    mergeSortHelper(a, copyBuffer, 0, a.length - 1);
}
```

After checking that it has been passed a subarray of at least two items, `mergeSortHelper` computes the midpoint of the subarray, recursively sorts the portions below and above the midpoint, and calls `merge` to merge the results. Here is the code for `mergeSortHelper`:

```java
void mergeSortHelper(int[] a, int[] copyBuffer,
                     int low, int high){
    // a           array being sorted
    // copyBuffer  temp space needed during merge
    // low, high   bounds of subarray
    // middle      midpoint of subarray

    if (low < high){
        int middle = (low + high) / 2;
        mergeSortHelper(a, copyBuffer, low, middle);
        mergeSortHelper(a, copyBuffer, middle + 1, high);
        merge(a, copyBuffer, low, middle, high);
    }
}
```

Figure 12-22 shows the subarrays generated during recursive calls to `mergeSortHelper`, starting from an array of eight items. Note that in this example the subarrays are evenly subdivided at each stage and there are 2^{k-1} subarrays to be merged at stage k. Had the length of the initial array not been a power of two, then an exactly even subdivision would not have been achieved at each stage and the last stage would not have contained a full complement of subarrays.

FIGURE 12-22
Subarrays generated during calls of `mergeSort`

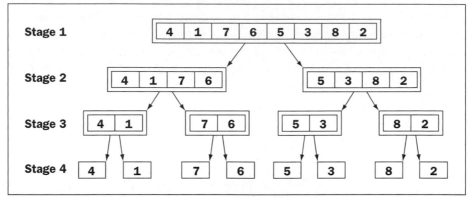

Figure 12-23 traces the process of merging the subarrays generated in the previous figure.

FIGURE 12-23
Merging the subarrays generated during a merge sort

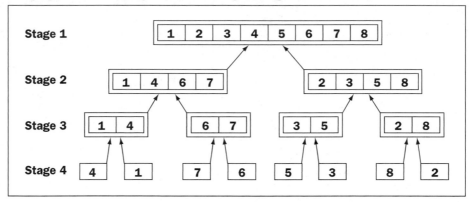

Finally, here is the code for the `merge` method:

```
 1 void merge(int[] a, int[] copyBuffer,
 2            int low, int middle, int high){
 3    // a            array that is being sorted
 4    // copyBuffer   temp space needed during the merge process
 5    // low          beginning of first sorted subarray
 6    // middle       end of first sorted subarray
 7    // middle + 1   beginning of second sorted subarray
 8    // high         end of second sorted subarray
 9
10    // Initialize i1 and i2 to the first items in each subarray
11    int i1 = low, i2 = middle + 1;
12
```

```
13    // Interleave items from the subarrays into the copyBuffer in such a
14    // way that order is maintained.
15    for (int i = low; i <= high; i++){
16       if (i1 > middle)
17          copyBuffer[i] = a[i2++];    // First subarray exhausted
18       else if (i2 > high)
19          copyBuffer[i] = a[i1++];    // Second subarray exhausted
20       else if (a[i1] < a[i2])
21          copyBuffer[i] = a[i1++];    // Item in first subarray is less
22       else
23          copyBuffer[i] = a[i2++];    // Item in second subarray is less
24    }
25
26    for (int i = low; i <= high; i++) // Copy sorted items back into
27       a[i] = copyBuffer[i];          // proper position in a
28 }
```

The `merge` method combines two sorted subarrays into a larger sorted subarray. The first subarray lies between `low` and `middle` and the second between `middle + 1` and `high`. The process consists of three steps:

1. Set up index pointers to the first items in each subarray (line 11). These are at positions `low` and `middle + 1`.

2. Starting with the first item in each subarray, repeatedly compare items. Copy the smaller item from its subarray to the copy buffer and advance to the next item in the subarray. Repeat until all items have been copied from both subarrays. If the end of one subarray is reached before the other's, finish by copying the remaining items from the other subarray (lines 15–24).

3. Copy the portion of `copyBuffer` between `low` and `high` back to the corresponding positions in the array a (lines 26–27).

Complexity Analysis for Merge Sort

The run time of the `merge` method is dominated by the two for statements, each of which loop (`high - low + 1`) times. Consequently, the method's run time is O (`high - low`), and all the merges at a single stage take O(n) time. Because merge sort splits subarrays as evenly as possible at each stage, the number of stages is O(log n), and the maximum run time for merge sort is O($n \log n$) in all cases.

Merge sort has two space requirements that depend on the array's size. First, O(log n)space is required on the call stack to support recursive calls. Second, O(n) space is used by the copy buffer.

Improving Merge Sort

Merge sort can be improved in three ways. First, the `merge` method can be modified so that the first for statement makes a single comparison on each iteration (see the exercises). Second, there exists a complex process that allows one to merge two subarrays without using a copy buffer and without changing the order of the method. Third, subarrays below a certain size can be sorted using an alternative approach.

Case Study: Comparing Sort Algorithms

For the benefit of those who are unconvinced by mathematical analysis, we now develop a program that compares the speed of our two sort algorithms.

Request

Write a program that allows the user to compare sort algorithms.

Analysis

The program compares bubble sort and quicksort. Because quicksort runs much more quickly than bubble sort, we do not run both sorts on the same array. Instead, we run quicksort on an array that is 100 times longer than the array used with bubble sort. Also, because we have already compared these algorithms by counting their operations, we record run times and compare these instead. The proposed interface is shown in Figure 12-24.

FIGURE 12-24
How run time varies with array length for bubble sort on the left and quicksort on the right

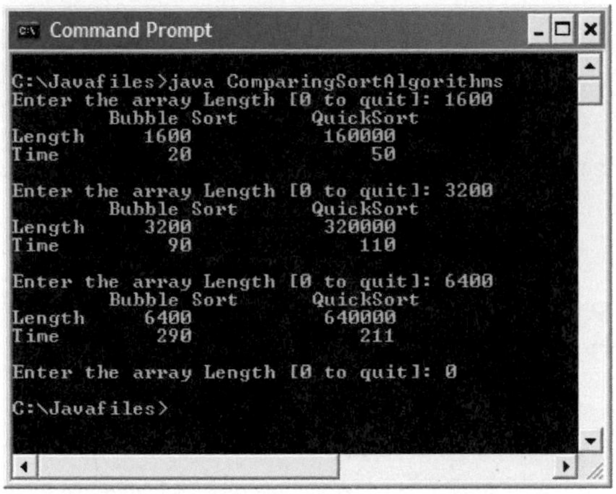

The user enters the size of the array of integers. The program then performs these actions:

1. Loads two arrays with randomly generated integers ranging from 0 to 100,000. One array is of the size specified by the user, and the other array is 100 times that size.

2. Runs the bubble sort algorithm on the smaller array and the quicksort algorithm on the larger array, and records the running times of each sort in milliseconds.

3. Displays the array sizes and run times for each sort in labeled columns.

Design

The bubble sort and quicksort algorithms have already been presented in this text. There are two other primary tasks to consider:

1. Load an array with randomly generated numbers.

2. Obtain the run time of a sort.

We accomplish the first task by using an instance of the `Random` class to generate the integer assigned to each cell in an array.

We accomplish the second task by using Java's `Date` class, as defined in the package `java.util`. When the program creates a new instance of `Date`, this object contains the current date down to the nearest millisecond, on the computer's clock. Thus, one can record the date at the beginning and end of any process by creating two `Date` objects, as follows:

```
Date d1 = new Date();   // Record the date at the start of a process.
<run any process>
Date d2 = new Date();   // Record the date at the end of a process.
```

To obtain the elapsed time between these two dates, one can use the `Date` instance method `getTime()`. This method returns the number of milliseconds from January 1, 1970, 00:00:00 GMT until the given date. Thus, the elapsed time in milliseconds for the example process can be computed as follows:

```
long elapsedTime = d2.getTime() - d1.getTime();
```

Implementation

To obtain the neatly formatted output shown in Figure 12-24, it is convenient to use the `printf` method as explained in Chapter 7. Following is the code:

```
// 12.1 Case Study: Compare two sort algorithms

import java.util.*;

public class ComparingSortAlgorithms {

    public static void main(String[] args){
        Random gen = new Random();
        Scanner reader = new Scanner(System.in);
        while(true){
            System.out.print("Enter the array Length [0 to quit]: ");
            int arrayLength = reader.nextInt();
            if (arrayLength <= 0)
                break;
            // Instantiate two arrays,
            // one of this length and the other a 100 times longer.
            int[] a1 = new int[arrayLength];
            int[] a2 = new int[arrayLength * 100];

            // Initialize the first array
            for (int i = 0; i < a1.length; i++)
                a1[i] = gen.nextInt(100001);
            // Random numbers between 0 and 100,000

            // Initialize the second array
            for (int i = 0; i < a2.length; i++)
                a2[i] = gen.nextInt(100001);

            // Time bubble sort
            Date d1 = new Date();
```

```
      bubbleSort (a1);
      Date d2 = new Date();
      long elapsedTime1 = d2.getTime() - d1.getTime();

      // Time quicksort
      d1 = new Date();
      quickSort (a2, 0, a2.length - 1);
      d2 = new Date();
      long elapsedTime2 = (d2.getTime() - d1.getTime());

      // Display results in pretty format
      System.out.printf("        %12s %14s%n", "Bubble Sort",
                        "QuickSort");
      System.out.printf("Length %8d %16d%n",   arrayLength,  arrayLength
                        * 100);
      System.out.printf("Time    %8d %16d%n%n", elapsedTime1,
  elapsedTime2);
   }
 }

 private static void bubbleSort (int[] a){
    for (int i = 0; i < a.length - 1; i++){
       for (int j = i + 1; j < a.length; j++){
          if (a[i] > a[j]){
             int temp = a[i];
             a[i] = a[j];
             a[j] = temp;
          }
       }
    }
 }

 private static void quickSort (int[] a, int left, int right){
    if (left >= right) return;
    int i = left;
    int j = right;
    int pivotValue = a[(left + right)/2];   // Pivot is at midpoint
    while (i < j){
       while (a[i] < pivotValue) i++;
       while (pivotValue < a[j]) j—;
       if (i <= j){
          int temp = a[i];
          a[i] = a[j];
          a[j] = temp;
          i++;
          j--;
       }
    }
    quickSort (a, left, j);
    quickSort (a, i, right);
 }
}
```

12.6 Graphics and GUIs: Drawing Recursive Patterns

Recursive patterns have played an important role in modern mathematics, art, and the study of nature. In this section, we show how to generate and visualize some recursive patterns that are present in fractals and abstract art. But first we introduce another GUI control, the slider, which is used in our examples.

Extra Challenge

This Graphics and GUIs section gives you the opportunity to explore concepts and programming techniques required to develop modern graphics applications and graphical user interfaces. This material is not required in order to proceed with the other chapters of the book.

Sliders

A slider is a GUI control that allows the user to select a value within a range of values. The slider tool appears as a knob that can be dragged from one value to another along a bar. The bar of values can be oriented vertically or horizontally. The slider is usually labeled with ticks that indicate the positions of discrete values (see Figure 12-25). Alternatively, the user can move the knob in either direction along the bar by pressing the keyboard's left or right cursor key.

FIGURE 12-25
A slider control

The following code segment creates a slider with a horizontal alignment, a range of values from 0 to 500, and an initially selected value of 250. It then sets the major tick spacing to 50 and makes the ticks visible.

```
JSlider slider = new JSlider(SwingConstants.HORIZONTAL, 0, 500, 250);
slider.setMajorTickSpacing(50);
slider.setPaintTicks(true);
```

A slider also responds to the messages `getValue` and `setValue`, which examine and reset its current value, respectively.

When a user moves a slider's knob, the slider emits an event of type `ChangeEvent`. This event can be detected by a listener object that implements the method `stateChanged`. This method is specified in the `ChangeListener` interface. These resources are included in the package `javax.swing.event`. (Until now, all other events and listener resources have come from the package `java.awt.event`.) As usual, the programmer defines a listener class, instantiates it, and attaches this instance to the slider with the method `addChangeListener`.

Armed with this knowledge of sliders, let's modify the temperature conversion program of Section 7.6. In that version of the program, the user enters a Fahrenheit or Celsius value in the appropriate text field and clicks the appropriate button to convert from one type of measure to the other. In the new version, the user manipulates a slider along the Fahrenheit scale and simply observes the appropriate outputs in the two fields. The new user interface is shown in Figure 12-26.

FIGURE 12-26
User interface for the temperature conversion program

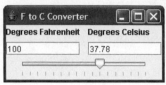

Following is the code for the revised view class, with explanatory comments. Note that Fahrenheit values are now integers and Celsius values are displayed with two figures of precision.

```java
// Example 12.4: Revised temperature conversion program
// that uses a slider to change degrees Fahrenheit and degrees Celsius

import javax.swing.*;
import java.awt.*;
import javax.swing.event.*;

public class GUIWindow extends JFrame{

    // >>>>>>> The model <<<<<<<

    // Declare and intantiate the thermometer
    private Thermometer thermo = new Thermometer();

    // >>>>>>> The view <<<<<<<

    // Declare and instantiate the window objects.
    private JLabel fahrLabel        = new JLabel("Degrees Fahrenheit");
    private JLabel celsiusLabel     = new JLabel("Degrees Celsius");
    private JTextField fahrField    = new JTextField("32.0");
    private JTextField celsiusField = new JTextField("0.0");
    // Create a slider with horizontal orientation, minimum value of -400,
    // maximum value of 400, and initially selected value of 32
    private JSlider slider = new JSlider(SwingConstants.HORIZONTAL, -400,
                                         400, 32);

    // Constructor
    public GUIWindow(){
        // Set up panels to organize widgets and
        // add them to the window
        JPanel dataPanel = new JPanel(new GridLayout(2, 2, 12, 6));
        dataPanel.add(fahrLabel);
        dataPanel.add(celsiusLabel);
        dataPanel.add(fahrField);
        dataPanel.add(celsiusField);
        // Single input control now is a slider
        slider.setMajorTickSpacing(50);
        slider.setPaintTicks(true);
        JPanel sliderPanel = new JPanel();
        sliderPanel.add(slider);
        Container container = getContentPane();
```

```
        container.add(dataPanel, BorderLayout.CENTER);
        container.add(sliderPanel, BorderLayout.SOUTH);
        // Attach a listener to the slider
        slider.addChangeListener(new SliderListener());
    }

    // >>>>>>> The controller <<<<<<<

    // Single listener responds to slider movement
    private class SliderListener implements ChangeListener{
        public void stateChanged(ChangeEvent e){
            int fahr = slider.getValue();                // Obtain slider's value
            fahrField.setText("" + fahr);                // Output Fahrenheit value
            thermo.setFahrenheit(fahr);                  // Reset thermometer
            double celsius = thermo.getCelsius();        // Obtain Celsius value
            String str = String.format("%.2f", celsius); // Format to 2 places
            celsiusField.setText(str);                   // Output Celsius value
        }
    }
}
```

Recursive Patterns in Abstract Art

Abstract art is a style of painting and sculpture that originated and flourished in Europe and the United States in the mid-20th century. One of its primary features was the use of lines, shapes, and colors to form patterns that made no attempt to represent objects in the physical world. These patterns perhaps expressed an idea, a feeling, or an emotion, but that was left to the viewer's interpretation.

The artist Piet Mondrian (1872–1944) developed a style of abstract painting that exhibited simple recursive patterns. For example, an "idealized" pattern from one of his paintings might look like that shown in Figure 12-27.

FIGURE 12-27

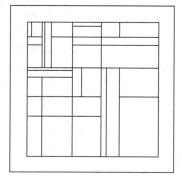

To generate such a pattern with a computer, an algorithm would begin by drawing a rectangle and then repeatedly draw two unequal subdivisions, as shown in Figure 12-28.

FIGURE 12-28
Generating Mondrian-like patterns

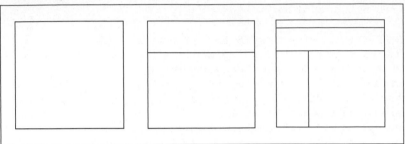

As you can see, the algorithm continues this process of subdivision for a number of levels, until an "aesthetically right moment" is reached. In this version, the algorithm appears to divide the current rectangle into portions representing one-third and two-thirds of its area, and it appears to alternate the subdivisions randomly between the horizontal and vertical axes.

Let's develop a simpler version of this algorithm that divides a rectangle along its vertical axis only. The algorithm starts with a given level and the coordinates of a rectangle's upper-left and lower-right corner points. If the level is greater than 0, the rectangle is drawn and the algorithm is run recursively twice to draw the subdivisions. The first recursive call receives the coordinates of one-third of the rectangle to the left and the second call receives the coordinates of the two-thirds of the rectangle to the right. Both calls receive a level that's one less than the current one. Eventually the level becomes 0 and the algorithm just returns. Here is a pseudocode for this algorithm:

```
mondrian(Graphics g, int x1, int y1, int x2, int y2, int level)
    if (level > 0)
        g.drawRect(x1, y1, x2 - x1, y2 - y1)
        mondrian(g, x1, y1, (x2 - x1) / 3 + x1, y2, level - 1)
        mondrian(g, (x2 - x1) / 3 + x1, y1, x2, y2, level - 1)
```

We now develop a graphics program that allows the user to display Mondrian-like patterns of different levels of detail. The user interface consists of a window with a drawing area and a slider (See Figure 12-29).

FIGURE 12-29
User interface for the Mondrian painting program

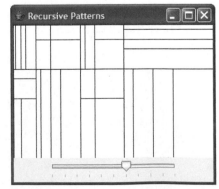

The slider allows the user to select levels from 0 to 10. Level 1 produces a simple rectangle at the bounds of the panel, level 2 subdivides the single rectangle, level 3 divides these results, and so on. Here is the code for the main graphics window class:

```java
// Example 12.5: Main window for drawing recursive patterns

import javax.swing.*;
import java.awt.*;
import javax.swing.event.*;

public class GUIWindow extends JFrame{

    // Create a slider with horizontal orientation, minimum value of 0,
    // maximum value of 10, and initially selected value of 0
    private JSlider slider = new JSlider(SwingConstants. HORIZONTAL,
                                         0, 10, 0);
    private ColorPanel panel = new ColorPanel(Color.white);
    // Track the current value of the slider for state changes
    private int level = 0;

    public GUIWindow(){
        // Add ticks to the slider and show them
        slider.setMajorTickSpacing(1);
        slider.setPaintTicks(true);
        JPanel sliderPanel = new JPanel();
        sliderPanel.add(slider);
        Container container = getContentPane();
        container.add(panel, BorderLayout.CENTER);
        container.add(sliderPanel, BorderLayout.SOUTH);
        // Attach a listener to the slider
        slider.addChangeListener(new SliderListener());
    }

    // >>>>>>> The controller <<<<<<<<

    private class SliderListener implements ChangeListener{
        public void stateChanged(ChangeEvent e){
            int value = slider.getValue();        // Obtain slider's value
            if (value != level){                  // Check for change in value
                level = value;                    // Reset level if changed
                panel.setLevel(level);            // Draw a new picture
            }
        }
    }
}
```

Note that the GUIWindow class maintains an extra instance variable named level. This variable tracks the current value of the slider. The reason we need this extra variable is that a slider can emit change events even if its value doesn't change. We don't want to set the panel's level and draw a new picture each time a change event occurs but only when the change event results in a change of the slider's value. The method stateChanged handles this restriction by examining and updating level if the slider's value has changed since the last event.

The ColorPanel class implements our recursive algorithm to draw the rectangles and also uses a random number to choose whether to subdivide them along the horizontal or vertical axis.

Further refinements, including the addition of color, are left as exercises. Here is the code for ColorPanel:

```java
// Example 12.5: Panel to draw Mondrian-like paintings

import javax.swing.*;
import java.awt.*;
import java.util.Random;

public class ColorPanel extends JPanel{

    private int level;
    private Random gen;

    public ColorPanel(Color backColor){
        setBackground(backColor);
        setPreferredSize(new Dimension(300, 200));
        level = 0;
        gen = new Random();
    }

    public void setLevel(int newLevel){
        level = newLevel;
        repaint();
    }

    public void paintComponent (Graphics g){
        super.paintComponent(g);
        mondrian(g, 0, 0, getWidth(), getHeight(), level);
    }

    private void mondrian(Graphics g, int x1, int y1, int x2, int y2,
                          int level){
        if (level > 0){
            g.drawRect(x1, y1, x2 - x1, y2 - y1);
            int vertical = gen.nextInt(2) // Decide whether to split vertically
            if (vertical == 0){            // or horizontally.
                mondrian(g, x1, y1, (x2 - x1) / 3 + x1, y2, level - 1);
                mondrian(g, (x2 - x1) / 3 + x1, y1, x2, y2, level - 1);
            }
            else{
                mondrian(g, x1, y1, x2, (y2 - y1) / 3 + y1, level - 1);
                mondrian(g, x1, (y2 - y1) / 3 + y1, x2, y2, level - 1);

            }
        }
    }
}
```

Recursive Patterns in Fractals

Fractals are highly repetitive or recursive patterns. A *fractal object* appears geometric, yet it cannot be described with ordinary Euclidean geometry. Strangely, a fractal curve is not one-dimensional, and a fractal surface is not two-dimensional. Instead, every fractal shape has its own fractal dimension.

An ordinary curve has a precise finite length between any two points. By contrast, a fractal curve has an indefinite length between any two points. The apparent length depends on the level of detail considered. As we zoom in on a segment of a fractal curve, we can see more and more details, and its length appears greater and greater. Consider a coastline. Seen from a distance, it has many wiggles but a discernible length. Now put a piece of the coastline under magnification. It has many similar wiggles, and the discernible length increases. Self-similarity under magnification is the defining characteristic of fractals and is seen in the shapes of mountains, the branching patterns of tree limbs, and many other natural objects.

One example of a fractal curve is a *c-curve*. Figure 12-30 shows c-curves of the first seven degrees. The level-0 c-curve is a simple line segment. The level-1 c-curve replaces the level-0 c-curve with two smaller level-0 c-curves meeting at right angles. The level-2 c-curve does the same thing for each of the two line segments in the level-1 c-curve. This pattern of subdivision can continue indefinitely.

FIGURE 12-30
The first seven degrees of the c-curve

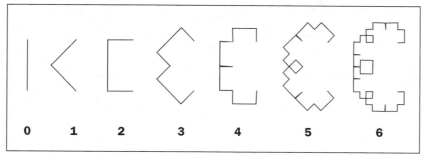

Let's develop an algorithm to draw an *n*-level c-curve. The algorithm receives a graphics object, the current level, and the endpoints of a line segment as parameters. At level 0, the algorithm draws a simple line segment. A level *n* c-curve consists of two level *n* − 1 c-curves constructed as follows:

- Let xm be (x1 + x2 + y1 − y2) / 2.

- Let ym be (x2 + y1 + y2 − x1) / 2.

- The first level *n* − 1 c-curve uses the line segment $(x1, y1)$, (xm, ym), and level *n* − 1, so we recur with these parameters.

- The second level *n* − 1 c-curve uses the line segment (xm, ym), $(x2, y2)$, and level *n* − 1, so we recur with these parameters.

In effect, as we showed in Figure 12-30, we replace each line segment by two shorter ones that meet at right angles. Here is the pseudocode for the algorithm:

```
cCurve (Graphics g, int x1, int y1, int x2, int y2, int level)
   if (level == 0)
        g.drawLine (x1, y1, x2, y2)
   else
      set xm to (x1 + x2 + y1 - y2) / 2
      set ym to (x2 + y1 + y2 - x1) / 2
      cCurve (g, x1, y1, xm, ym, level - 1)
      cCurve (g, xm, ym, x2, y2, level - 1)
```

The user interface of a program to draw c-curves, as shown in Figure 12-31, is the same one used in the abstract art drawing program. The user adjusts the level by dragging or clicking on the slider. The initial window displays a c-curve of level 0. The endpoints of this line segment are (150, 50) and (150, 150). This line segment is a good starting point for higher-degree curves, all of which fit nicely within the initial window boundaries.

FIGURE 12-31
User interface for the c-curve program

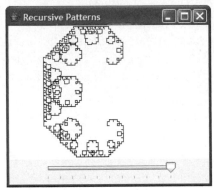

The following code shows the implementation of the class `ColorPanel` for drawing c-curves:

```java
// Example 12.6: Panel to draw c-curves

import javax.swing.*;
import java.awt.*;
import java.util.Random;

public class ColorPanel extends JPanel{

    private int level;

    public ColorPanel(Color backColor){
        setBackground(backColor);
        setPreferredSize(new Dimension(300, 200));
        level = 0;
    }

    public void setLevel(int newLevel){
        level = newLevel;
        repaint();
    }

    public void paintComponent (Graphics g){
        super.paintComponent(g);
        cCurve(g, 150, 50, 150, 150, level);
    }

    private void cCurve (Graphics g, int x1, int y1, int x2, int y2,
                        int level){
        if (level == 0)
            g.drawLine (x1, y1, x2, y2);
```

```
    else{
        int xm = (x1 + x2 + y1 - y2) / 2;
        int ym = (x2 + y1 + y2 - x1) / 2;
        cCurve (g, x1, y1, xm, ym, level - 1);
        cCurve (g, xm, ym, x2, y2, level - 1);
    }
    }
}
```

*E*XERCISE 12.6

1. List how many calls of the cCurve method are produced when the initial level is 2, 4, and 8, and give an estimate of the complexity of the algorithm using big-O notation.

2. The mondrian method always places the smaller rectangle at the top or the left of a subdivision. Explain how you would modify the method so that it will place the smaller rectangle randomly.

Design, Testing, and Debugging Hints

■ When designing a recursive method, be sure that

1. The method has a well-defined stopping state.

2. The method has a recursive step that changes the size of the data, so that the stopping state will eventually be reached.

■ Recursive methods can be easier to write correctly than the equivalent iterative methods.

■ More efficient code is usually more complex than less efficient code. Thus, it may be harder to write more efficient code correctly than less efficient code. Before trying to make your code more efficient, you should demonstrate through analysis that the proposed improvement is really significant (for example, you will get O(n log n) behavior rather than O(n^2) behavior).

SUMMARY

I n this chapter, you learned:

■ A recursive method is a method that calls itself to solve a problem.

■ Recursive solutions have one or more base cases or termination conditions that return a simple value or void. They also have one or more recursive steps that receive a smaller instance of the problem as a parameter.

■ Some recursive methods also combine the results of earlier calls to produce a complete solution.

■ The run-time behavior of an algorithm can be expressed in terms of big-O notation. This notation shows approximately how the work of the algorithm grows as a function of its problem size.

■ There are different orders of complexity, such as constant, linear, quadratic, and exponential.

■ Through complexity analysis and clever design, the order of complexity of an algorithm can be reduced to produce a much more efficient algorithm.

■ The quicksort is a sort algorithm that uses recursion and can perform much more efficiently than selection sort, bubble sort, or insertion sort.

VOCABULARY *Review*

Define the following terms:

Activation record	Infinite recursion	Recursive step
Big-O notation	Iterative process	Stack
Binary search algorithm	Merge sort	Stack overflow error
Call stack	Quicksort	Stopping state
Complexity analysis	Recursive method	Tail-recursive

REVIEW *Questions*

FILL IN THE BLANK

Complete the following sentences by writing the correct word or words in the blanks provided.

1. The _____ of a recursive algorithm is the part in which a problem is solved directly, without further recursion.

2. The _____ of a recursive algorithm is the part in which the problem is reduced in size.

3. The memory of a computer is formatted into a large _____ to support recursive method calls.

4. The memory for each recursive method call is organized in a group of cells called a(n) _____.

5. The type of error in a recursive algorithm that causes it to run forever is called a(n) _____.

6. When a recursive method does not stop, a(n) _____ error occurs at run time.

7. The linear, quadratic, and logarithmic orders of complexity are expressed as _____, _____, and _____ using big-O notation.

8. The bubble sort algorithm has a run-time complexity of _____ in the best case and _____ in the worst case.

9. The quicksort algorithm has a run-time complexity of _____ in the best case and _____ in the worst case.

PROJECTS

Some of the projects ask you to implement a method and test it in a `Tester` program. Be sure that the method is defined as a `static` method; otherwise, you will get a syntax error.

PROJECT 12-1

Use a `Tester` program to implement and test a recursive method to compute the greatest common divisor (gcd) of two integers. The recursive definition of `gcd` is

```
gcd(a, b) = b, when a = 0
gcd(a, b) = gcd(b, a % b), when a > 0
```

PROJECT 12-2

Write a recursive method that returns a string with the characters in reverse order and test the method with a `Tester` program. The string and the index position should be parameters. If the position is less than the string's length, recurse with the rest of the string after this position and return the result of appending the character at this position to the result. Otherwise, return the empty string.

PROJECT 12-3

Design, implement, and test a recursive method that expects a positive integer parameter and returns a string representing that integer with commas in the appropriate places. The method might be called as follows:

```
String formattedInt = insertCommas(1000000);  // Returns "1,000,000"
```

(*Hint*: Recurse by repeated division and build the string by concatenating after each recursive call.)

PROJECT 12-4

The phrase "*n* choose *k*" is used to refer to the number of ways in which we can choose *k* objects from a set of *n* objects, where $n >= k >= 0$. For example, 52 choose 13 would express the number of possible hands that could be dealt in the game of bridge. Write a program that takes the values of *n* and *k* as inputs and displays as output the value *n* choose *k*. Your program should define a recursive method, `nChooseK(n, k)`, that calculates and returns the result. (*Hint*: We can partition the selections of *k* objects from *n* objects as the groups of *k* objects that come from $n - 1$ objects and the groups of *k* objects that include the *n*th object in addition to the groups of $k - 1$ objects chosen from among $n - 1$ objects.) If you test the program with $n = 52$ and $k = 13$, you should be prepared to wait quite a while for the solution!

PROJECT 12-5

Modify the case study of this chapter so that it counts comparison and exchange operations in both sort algorithms and displays these statistics as well. Run the program with two array sizes and make a prediction on the number of comparisons, exchanges, and run times for a third size.

PROJECT 12-6

Write a tester program to help assess the efficiency of the Towers of Hanoi program. This program should be similar to the one developed for the Fibonacci method.

PROJECT 12-7

Write a tester program to help assess the efficiency of the Many Queens program. This program should be similar to the one developed for the Fibonacci method.

PROJECT 12-8

Modify the program that draws Mondrian-like paintings so that it fills each rectangle with a randomly generated color.

CRITICAL *Thinking*

Jill is trying to decide whether to use a recursive algorithm or an iterative algorithm to solve a problem. Explain to her the costs and benefits of using one method or the other.

ARRAYS, RECURSION, AND COMPLEXITY

REVIEW Questions

TRUE/FALSE

Circle T if the statement is true or F if it is false.

T F 1. In Java, an array is an ordered collection of methods.

T F 2. Because arrays are objects, two variables can refer to the same array.

T F 3. The length of a Java array is fixed at compile time.

T F 4. One responsibility of the view portion of a program is to instantiate and arrange window objects.

T F 5. Static variables are associated with a class, not with its instances.

T F 6. Subclasses can see both public and private names declared in their parent classes.

T F 7. If you need to use the cast operator, remember that you never cast down, only cast up.

T F 8. A linear search runs more efficiently than a binary search.

T F 9. Sorting methods generally cannot perform in better than $O(n^2)$ run time.

T F 10. Loops are always preferable to recursive methods for solving problems.

FILL IN THE BLANK

Complete the following sentences by writing the correct word or words in the blanks provided.

1. A(n) _____ is a collection of similar items or elements that are ordered by position.

2. An item's position within an array is called its _____ or _____.

3. Two arrays in which the corresponding elements are related are called _____ arrays.

4. The number of elements currently stored and used within an array is called its _____ size.

5. Classes that are never instantiated are called _____.

6. Java organizes classes in a(n) _____.

7. The `toString` message, which is understood by every object, no matter which class it belongs to, is a good example of _____.

501

8. A search method that repeatedly visits the midpoint of an array is called a(n) _____ search.

9. A sorting method that repeatedly moves elements around a pivot element is called a(n) _____ .

10. Recursive methods have two parts, the _____ and the _____ .

WRITTEN QUESTIONS

Write a brief answer to each of the following questions.

1. Write statements for the following items that declare array variables and assign the appropriate array objects to them.
   A. `intNumbers`, an array of 5 integers

   B. `realNumbers`, an array of 100 real numbers

   C. `bools`, an array of 10 Booleans

   D. `words`, an array of 20 strings

2. Write a `for` loop that initializes an array of 10 integers to the first 10 positive integers.

3. Repeat question 2, but use an initializer list.

4. There are several ways in which methods in a subclass can be related to methods in its superclass. Describe at least two of these.

5. Explain why one would use `static` variables and `static` methods.

PROJECTS

PROJECT 1

Write a program that takes 10 floating-point numbers as inputs. The program then displays the average of the numbers followed by all of the numbers that are greater than the average. As part of your design, write a method that takes an array of doubles as a parameter and returns the average of the data in the array.

PROJECT 2

Write a program to keep statistics for a basketball team consisting of 12 players. Statistics for each player should include shots attempted, shots made, and shooting percentage; free throws attempted, free throws made, and free throw percentage; offensive rebounds and defensive rebounds; assists; turnovers; and total points. Place these data in parallel arrays. Appropriate team totals should be listed as part of the output.

PROJECT 3

Modify the program of Project 2 so that it uses a two-dimensional array instead of the parallel arrays for the statistics.

PROJECT 4

A summation method returns the sum of the numbers from a lower bound to an upper bound. Write a static recursive method for summations and run it with a `tester` program that displays the values of the parameters on each call and the returned value on each call.

PROJECT 5

Write a `static` method that builds a sorted array list from a randomly ordered array list. The method should throw an exception if the parameter's elements are not `Comparable` objects. Test the method in a `tester` program.

CRITICAL *Thinking*

A bank provides several kinds of accounts, among them checking accounts and saving accounts. Design a simple banking system data model that represents these accounts. Be sure to make use of abstract classes, inheritance, polymorphism, and encapsulation. The result of your work should be a set of class summary boxes for the data model of the banking system.

APPENDIX A

Java Resources

Java Documentation and the J2SE

Sun Microsystems maintains an excellent Web site where programmers can find complete documentation for the Java API (Application Programming Interface) and download a free J2SE (Java 2 Standard Edition). The following sections discuss some of the items that you can access on the Web. *Note*: The terms *SDK* (Software Development Kit), *JDK* (Java Development Kit), and *JRE* (Java Runtime Environment) may also appear on Sun's Web site. *J2SE* is an umbrella term that encompasses all of these terms. The term *JRE* (Java Runtime Environment) refers to the JVM (Java Virtual Machine), a small plug-in that can be downloaded just to run Java programs or to update your Web browser. To develop Java programs, you should download the full SDK or JDK that contains both the Java compiler and the JRE.

Sun's Top-Level Java Page (http://www.sun.com/)

This page contains news about events in the Java world and links to documentation, Java-related products, program examples, and free downloads of J2SE.

Products and API (http://java.sun.com/products/)

This page allows you to select the version of J2SE that matches your computer and to begin the download process. You also can download the documentation if you do not want to access it on the Web.

Package Index (http://java.sun.com/j2se/1.5.0/docs/api/)

This page has links to all of the packages in J2SE 1.5.0.

We suggest that you bookmark all of these links and use the last one on a daily basis. You might even bookmark the links to the most commonly used packages, such as `java.lang`, `java.util`, and `javax.swing`. When you visit a package, you can browse all of the classes in that package. When you visit a class, you can browse all of the variables and methods defined in that class. There are numerous cross-references to superclasses and related classes in a given package. You also can download the J2SE documentation for quicker browsing on your hard drive.

Be sure to select J2SE 1.5. Various features of Java, such as the `Scanner` class, the enhanced `for` loop, and generic collections, are not supported in version 1.4 and earlier. Note that at the time of this writing, the most current version of J2SE was J2SE 1.5_05. After downloading, you install the J2SE on your computer by running the installation program. You should print the Readme file for further reference. If you are working on a PC with Windows XP, the installation will leave two J2SE system directories in the c:\Program Files\Java directory.

Using the DOS Command Prompt and Other IDEs

Before you use the J2SE, make sure that your Java source program (`.java`) files are in the current directory (this can be any directory on your computer). You can define more than one class in a source file, but the usual procedure is to have one source file for each class. Each source file should begin with the same name as the class that it contains and should end with `.java`. Remember that Java class names and filenames are case sensitive. If you want to run an applet, the appropriate HTML file also should be in this directory.

Most commercial and free IDEs automatically locate the J2SE system files on your computer. If you use the DOS command prompt to compile and run Java programs, run the following command at the beginning of each working session:

path=c:\Program Files\Java\jdk1.5.0_04\bin

This command allows Windows XP to locate the `javac`, `java`, `javadoc`, and `appletviewer` commands in the system directory.

Using the Basic J2SE Tools

You can then do the following at the system command prompt:

■ *Compile a program.* The basic syntax is `javac <filename>`, where `<filename>` is a Java source filename (ending in `.java`). Java locates and compiles all of the files required by your program. Any syntax error messages are displayed in the command window, and a byte code (`.class`) file is generated for each class defined in your program. The command `javac *.java` is a quick way to compile a program that consists of several source files.

■ *Run an application.* The basic syntax is `java <filename>`, where `<filename>` is the name of the class that defines the main method of your program. Note that the `.class` extension must be omitted. Run-time error messages are displayed in the command window.

■ *Run an applet.* The basic syntax is `appletviewer <filename>`, where `<filename>` is the name of an HTML file that links to your applet.

APPENDIX B

Java Language Elements

This appendix covers some extra features of Java that are useful. We make no attempt to provide a complete description of Java. For a full reference, consult the documentation at Sun's Web site.

Reserved Words

The words shown in bold are not discussed in this book. For a discussion of them, see the references on Sun's Web site.

abstract	do	if	**operator**	switch
boolean	double	implements	**outer**	**synchronized**
break	else	import	package	this
byte	extends	**inner**	private	throw
case	final	instanceof	protected	throws
catch	**finally**	int	public	**transient**
char	float	interface	**rest**	try
class	for	long	return	**var**
const	**future**	**native**	short	void
continue	**generic**	new	static	**volatile**
default	**goto**	null	super	while

Data Types

Java supports two data types: primitive types and reference types. Primitive types represent numbers, characters, and Boolean values. The numeric data types are listed in Table B-1.

TABLE B-1
Java's primitive data types

TYPE	STORAGE REQUIREMENTS	RANGE
byte	1 byte	−128 to 127
short	2 bytes	−32,768 to 32,767
int	4 bytes	−2,147,483,648 to 2,147,483,647
long	8 bytes	−9,223,372,036,854,775,808L to 9,223,372,036,854,775,807L
float	4 bytes	−3.40282347E+38F to 3.40282347E+38F
double	8 bytes	−1.79769313486231570E+308 to 1.79769313486231570E+308

Type char represents the Unicode character set, consisting of 65,536 values. These values include those of the traditional ASCII set and other international characters. A table listing the ASCII character set appears in Appendix D.

Character literals are enclosed in single quotation marks (for example, 'a'). Table B-2 lists some commonly used escape sequences for nonprinting characters.

TABLE B-2
Some escape sequences

ESCAPE SEQUENCE	MEANING
\b	backspace
\t	tab
\n	newline
\"	double quotation mark
\'	single quotation mark
\\	backslash

The type boolean represents the Boolean values true and false. boolean is the type of all expressions that serve as conditions of if statements and loops.

Reference types represent objects, such as strings, arrays, other built-in Java objects, and user-defined objects.

Casting Numeric Types

The numeric types from least to most inclusive are

```
byte  short  int  long  float  double
```

The cast operator converts a more inclusive type to a less inclusive one. The form of the operator is

```
(<less inclusive type name>) <more inclusive value>
```

For instance, following is a sequence of assignment statements in which we begin with a double, cast to an int, and finally cast to a char:

```
double d;
int i;
char c;

d = 65.57;
i = (int) d;              // i contains 65, due to truncation.
c = (char) i;             // c contains 'A'.
writer.println(c);        // Displays 'A'.
```

As we notice in this example, the cast operation can destroy information. In general, the fractional part of a double or float is thrown away when cast to byte, short, int, or long. In addition, if the number being cast is outside the range of the target type, unexpected values can result. Thus,

```
(int)8.88e+009    becomes    290065408
```

The cast operator also can be used within expressions. Normally, when an operator involves mixed data types, the less inclusive type is automatically converted to the more inclusive before the operation is performed. For instance

```
2 / 1.5             becomes    2.0 / 1.5
2 + 1.5             becomes    2.0 + 1.5
aByte  / aLong      becomes    aLong   / aLong
aFloat - anInt      becomes    aFloat  - aFloat
aFloat % aDouble    becomes    aDouble % aDouble
```

We could present other examples in a similar vein. Sometimes, though, we want to override this automatic conversion and, for instance, to treat

```
aFloat / anInt    as    anInt / anInt
```

This can be achieved by using the cast operation again, as illustrated next:

```
(int)aFloat * anInt            becomes    anInt * anInt
aByte       / (byte)aLong      becomes    aByte / aByte
aFloat      + (float)aDouble   becomes    aFloat + aFloat
```

In these expressions, the unary cast operator has higher precedence than the binary arithmetic operators.

Type-Safe Enumerations

Occasionally a program uses a variable that has a special range of values. In many cases where there are only two possible values, the variable can be a Boolean, with the values true or false. For example, a window is either visible or not, and the variable visible is of type boolean, where true means on and false means off.

```
boolean visible = false;    // Visibility is initially off
```

For a variable that has a finite range of more than two values, the programmer can define named integer constants, such as MARRIED, SINGLE, and DIVORCED, for the values. However, because the variable maritalStatus is of type int, *any* integer besides the named constants can be assigned to it, thus opening the door to semantic errors.

```
final int MARRIED = 0;
final int SINGLE = 1;
final int DIVORCED = 2;

int maritalStatus = SINGLE;    // Initially we're all single
maritalStatus = MARRIED;       // Get married
maritalStatus = 15;            // Error: meaning not defined in the domain
```

Java 5.0 includes a data type known as a *type-safe enumeration* to solve this problem. An enumeration is a named type that has one or more named values. The type allows no other values. For example, the enumerated type MartitalStatus with the values MARRIED, SINGLE, and DIVORCED is defined and used in the following code segment:

```
// Define the new type
public enum MaritalStatus = {MARRIED, SINGLE, DIVORCED}

// Declare and manipulate a variable
private MaritalStatus myStatus = SINGLE;
myStatus = MARRIED;
myStatus = 15;                           // Syntax error: incompatible type
System.out.println(myStatus);            // Displays "MARRIED"
```

If a new type is defined as public within a class, the type name and its values can be accessed by programmers by using the usual selector notation. If the previous code segment is nested in the class TaxReturn, then a programmer can run code such as the following:

```
// Declare and initialize a MartialStatus variable
TaxReturn.MaritalStatus myStatus = TaxReturn.MaritalStatus.MARRIED;
```

Control Statements

Compound Statement

A compound statement consists of a list of zero or more declarations and statements enclosed within braces, {}. A semicolon must terminate each statement, except for the compound statement itself. Following is the form:

```
{
    <declaration or statement-1>
    .
    .
    <declaration or statement-n>
}
```

do-while Statement

do-while statements have the following form:

```
do
    <statement>
while (<boolean expression>)
```

SWITCH Statement

The switch statement handles a selection among cases, where each case is a constant of a primitive type. Following is an example:

```
switch (ch){
    case 'a':
    case 'A': doSomething1();
```

```
            break;
    case 'b':
    case 'B': doSomething2();
            break;
    case 'c': doSomething3();
            break;
    default:  doSomething4();
}
```

The break statements are optional in this example, but they are required if the case lists are to be considered mutually exclusive. The default statement is also optional but highly recommended.

Math Class Methods

The Math class includes many static methods that allow clients to perform trigonometric functions and so forth. For example, the code

```
System.out.println(Math.sqrt(2));
```

outputs the square root of 2. Table B-3 lists most of these methods.

TABLE B-3
Math class methods

Math Class METHOD	DESCRIPTION
double abs(double a)	Returns the absolute value of a double value; Similar methods exist for float, int, and long.
double acos(double a)	Returns the arc cosine of an angle, in the range of 0.0 through pi
double asin(double a)	Returns the arc sine of an angle, in the range of –pi/2 through pi/2
double atan(double a)	Converts rectangular coordinates (b, a) to polar (r, theta)
double atan2(double a, double b)	Converts rectangular coordinates (b, a) to polar (r, theta)
double ceil(double a)	Returns the smallest (closest to negative infinity) double value that is not less than the argument and is equal to a mathematical integer
double cos(double a)	Returns the trigonometric cosine of an angle
double exp(double a)	Returns the exponential number e (i.e., 2.718...) raised to the power of a double value
double floor(double a)	Returns the largest (closest to positive infinity) double value that is not greater than the argument and is equal to a mathematical integer
double log(double a)	Returns the natural logarithm (base e) of a double value
double max(double a, double b)	Returns the greater of two double values; Similar methods exist for float, int, and long.

TABLE B-3 Continued
Math class methods

Math Class METHOD	DESCRIPTION
`double min(double a, double b)`	Returns the smaller of two double values; Similar methods exist for `float`, `int`, and `long`.
`double pow(double a, double b)`	Returns the value of the first argument raised to the power of the second argument
`double random()`	Returns a `double` value with a positive sign, greater than or equal to 0.0 and less than 1.0
`double rint(double a)`	Returns the double value that is closest in value to a and is equal to a mathematical integer
`long round(double a)`	Returns the closest `long` to the argument
`double sin(double a)`	Returns the trigonometric sine of an angle
`double sqrt(double a)`	Returns the correctly rounded positive square root of a `double` value
`double tan(double a)`	Returns the trigonometric tangent of an angle
`double toDegrees(double angrad)`	Converts an angle measured in radians to the equivalent angle measured in degrees
`double toRadians(double angdeg)`	Converts an angle measured in degrees to the equivalent angle measured in radians

The Character and Integer Classes

The `Character` and `Integer` classes allow `char` and `int` values to masquerade as objects when included in collections. These classes also include several static methods that are useful in processing numeric data. For example, `Character` methods exist for converting between single digits and the numbers they represent, and `Integer` methods exist for the conversion of strings of digits to numbers. Tables B-4 and B-5 list some of these methods.

TABLE B-4
Some `Character` class methods

Character METHOD	DESCRIPTION
`int digit(char ch, int radix)`	Returns the numeric value of the character `ch` in the specified radix
`char forDigit(int digit, int radix)`	Determines the character representation for a specific digit in the specified radix
`int getNumericValue(char ch)`	Returns the Unicode numeric value of the character as a nonnegative integer
`boolean isDigit(char ch)`	Determines if the specified character is a digit
`boolean isLetter(char ch)`	Determines if the specified character is a letter
`boolean isLowerCase(char ch)`	Determines if the specified character is a lowercase character
`boolean isUpperCase(char ch)`	Determines if the specified character is an uppercase character
`boolean isWhiteSpace(char ch)`	Determines if the specified character is white space according to Java
`char toLowerCase(char ch)`	The given character is mapped to its lowercase equivalent; if the character has no lowercase equivalent, the character itself is returned.
`char toUpperCase(char ch)`	Converts the character argument to uppercase

TABLE B-5
Some `Integer` class methods

Integer METHOD	DESCRIPTION
`int parseInt(String s)`	Parses the string argument as a signed decimal integer
`int parseInt(String s, int radix)`	Parses the string argument as a signed integer in the radix specified by the second argument
`String toString(int i)`	Returns a new `string` object representing the specified integer
`String toString(int i, int radix)`	Creates a string representation of the first argument in the radix specified by the second argument
`Integer valueOf(String s)`	Returns a new `Integer` object initialized to the value of the specified `String`
`Integer valueOf(String s, int radix)`	Returns a new `Integer` object initialized to the value of the specified `String`

The Class `java.util.Arrays`

Common operations on arrays include searching, sorting, comparing two arrays for equality, and filling an array's cells with a default value. The class `java.util.Arrays` includes many static methods that perform these functions. Most of them are overloaded for arrays of different element types, including all the primitive types and the class `Object`. Table B-6 lists one example of each type of operation; we refer the reader to Sun's documentation for descriptions of the others.

TABLE B-6
Some `Arrays` methods

Arrays METHOD	DESCRIPTION
`static int binarySearch(int[]a, int key)`	Searches the array `a` for the integer `key` using the binary search algorithm
`static Boolean equals(int[] a, int[] a2)`	Returns true if the two specified arrays of `ints` are *equal* to one another
`static void fill(int[] a, int val)`	Assigns the specified `int` value to each element of the specified array of `ints`
`static void sort(int[] a)`	Sorts the specified array of `ints` into ascending numerical order

The Class `java.util.ArrayList`

The package `java.util` includes several list classes, each of which implements the `List` interface. The class `ArrayList` provides the basic behavior of an array (including random access of elements) but also allows clients to add or remove elements. An array list tracks the number of elements currently available and also allows the client to set an initial capacity or trim the capacity to the number of elements. Table B-7 describes the `ArrayList` methods. Note that this is the "raw" version of `ArrayList`, which accepts any objects as elements.

TABLE B-7
The `ArrayList` methods

ArrayList METHOD	DESCRIPTION
`ArrayList()`	Constructs an empty list
`ArrayList(Collection c)`	Constructs a list containing the elements of the specified collection, in the order they are returned by the collection's iterator
`ArrayList(int initialCapacity)`	Constructs an empty list with the specified initial capacity
`void add(int index,` `        Object element)`	Inserts the specified element at the specified position in this list
`boolean add(Object o)`	Appends the specified element to the end of this list
`boolean addAll(Collection c)`	Appends all of the elements in the specified `Collection` to the end of this list, in the order that they are returned by the specified `Collection's Iterator`

TABLE B-7 Continued
The ArrayList methods

ArrayList METHOD	DESCRIPTION
boolean addAll(int index, Collection c)	Inserts all of the elements in the specified Collection into this list, starting at the specified position
void clear()	Removes all of the elements from this list
Object clone()	Returns a shallow copy of this ArrayList instance
boolean contains(Object elem)	Returns true if this list contains the specified element
void ensureCapacity(int minCapacity)	Increases the capacity of this ArrayList instance, if necessary, to ensure that it can hold at least the number of elements specified by the minimum capacity argument
Object get(int index)	Returns the element at the specified position in this list
int indexOf(Object elem)	Searches for the first occurence of the given argument, testing for equality using the equals method
boolean isEmpty()	Tests if this list has no elements
int lastIndexOf(Object elem)	Returns the index of the last occurrence of the specified object in this list
Object remove(int index)	Removes the element at the specified position in this list
protected void removeRange(int fromIndex, int toIndex)	Removes from this list all of the elements whose index is between fromIndex, inclusive and toIndex, exclusive
Object set(int index, Object element)	Replaces the element at the specified position in this list with the specified element
int size()	Returns the number of elements in this list
Object[] toArray()	Returns an array containing all of the elements in this list in the correct order
Object[] toArray(Object[] a)	Returns an array containing all of the elements in this list in the correct order
void trimToSize()	Trims the capacity of this ArrayList instance to be the list's current size

Three-Dimensional Arrays

Java does not limit the number of dimensions for arrays. Following is the declaration and initialization of a three-dimensional array:

```
int[][][] threeD = {{{ 1, 2, 3}, { 4, 5, 6}},
                     {{ 7, 8, 9}, {10,11,12}},
                     {{13,14,15}, {16,17,18}}};
```

The array's elements fill a box whose dimensions are 3 by 2 by 3. To refer to an element, we indicate its position in the box, remembering as usual to start counting at 0. Thus, element 8 is at position (1,0,1) and is referred to as follows:

```
threeD[1][0][1]
```

Operator Precedence

Table C-1 shows the operator precedence. The operators shown in bold are not discussed in this book. For a discussion of them, see the references on Sun's Web site.

TABLE C-1
Operator precedence

OPERATOR	FUNCTION	ASSOCIATION
()	Parentheses	Left to right
[]	Array subscript	
.	Object member selection	
++	Increment	Right to left
--	Decrement	
+	Unary plus	
-	Unary minus	
!	Boolean negation	
~	**Bitwise negation**	
(*type*)	Type cast	
*	Multiplication	Left to right
/	Division	
%	Modulus	
+	Addition or concatenation	Left to right
-	Subtraction	
<<	**Bitwise shift left**	**Left to right**
>>	**Bitwise shift right**	
>>>	**Bitwise shift right, sign extension**	

TABLE C-1 Continued
Operator precedence

OPERATOR	FUNCTION	ASSOCIATION
<	Less than	Left to right
<=	Less than or equal to	
>	Greater than	
>=	Greater than or equal to	
instanceOf	Class membership	
==	Equal to	Left to right
!=	Not equal to	
&	**Boolean AND (complete)**	**Left to right**
&	**Bitwise AND**	
^	**Boolean exclusive OR**	**Left to right**
^	**Bitwise exclusive OR**	
I	**Boolean OR (complete)**	**Left to right**
I	**Bitwise OR**	
&&	Boolean AND (partial)	Left to right
II	Boolean OR (partial)	Left to right
?:	**Ternary conditional**	**Right to left**
=	Assign	Right to left
+=	Add and assign	
-=	Subtract and assign	
*=	Multiply and assign	
/=	Divide and assign	
%=	Modulo and assign	
<<=	**Shift left and assign**	
>>=	**Shift right, sign extension, and assign**	
>>>=	**Shift right, no sign extension, and assign**	
&=	**Boolean or bitwise AND and assign**	
I=	**Boolean or bitwise OR and assign**	
^=	**Boolean or bitwise exclusive OR and assign**	

APPENDIX D

ASCII Character Set

Table D-1 shows the ordering of the ASCII character set. The digits in the left column represent the leftmost digits of the ASCII code, and the digits in the top row are the rightmost digits. Thus, the ASCII code of the character R at row 8, column 2, is 82. The printable characters range from ASCII 33 to ASCII 126. The values from ASCII 0 to ASCII 32 and ASCII 127 are associated with white-space characters, such as the horizontal tab (HT), or nonprinting control characters, such as the escape key (ESC).

TABLE D-1
Ordering of the ASCII character set

	0	1	2	3	4	5	6	7	8	9
0	NUL	SOH	STX	ETX	EOT	ENQ	ACK	BEL	BS	HT
1	LF	VT	FF	CR	SO	SI	DLE	DC1	DC2	DC3
2	DC4	NAK	SYN	ETB	CAN	EM	SUB	ESC	FS	GS
3	RS	US	SP	!	"	#	$	%	&	`
4	(	)	*	+	,	-	.	/	0	1
5	2	3	4	5	6	7	8	9	:	;
6	<	=	>	?	@	A	B	C	D	E
7	F	G	H	I	J	K	L	M	N	O
8	P	Q	R	S	T	U	V	W	X	Y
9	Z	[	\	]	^	_	'	a	b	c
10	d	e	f	g	h	i	j	k	l	m
11	n	o	p	q	r	s	t	u	v	w
12	x	y	z	{			}	~	DEL		

APPENDIX E

Number Systems

When we make change at the store, we use the decimal (base 10) number system. The digits in this system are the characters 0 through 9. Computers represent all information in the binary (base 2) system. The digits in this system are just the characters 0 and 1. Because binary numbers can be very long strings of 1s and 0s, programmers also use the octal (base 8) and hexadecimal (base 16) number systems, usually for low-level programming in assembly language. The octal digits range from 0 to 7, and the hexadecimal digits include the decimal digits and the letters A through F. These letters represent the numbers 10 through 15, respectively.

To identify the system being used, one can attach the base as a subscript to the number. For example, the following numbers represent the quantity 414 in the binary, octal, decimal, and hexadecimal systems:

```
414 in binary notation         110011110₂
414 in octal notation          636₈
414 in decimal notation        414₁₀
414 in hexadecimal notation    19E₁₆
```

Note that as the size of the base grows, either the number of digits or the digit in the largest position might be smaller.

Each number system uses positional notation to represent a number. The digit at each position in a number has a positional value. The positional value of a digit is determined by raising the base of the system to the power specified by the position. For an n-digit number, the positions (and exponents) are numbered 0 through $n - 1$, starting with the rightmost digit and moving to the left. For example, as Figure E-1 illustrates, the positional values of a three-digit decimal number are 100 (10^2), 10 (10^1), and 1 (10^0), moving from left to right in the number. The positional values of a three-digit binary number are 4 (2^2), 2 (2^1), and 1 (2^0).

FIGURE E-1
Positional values of base 10 and base 2 numbers

base 10				base 2			
positional values	100	10	1	positional values	4	2	1
positions		2	1	0	positions	2	1	0

The quantity represented by a number in any system is determined by multiplying each digit (as a decimal number) by its positional value and adding the results. The following examples show how this is done for numbers in several systems:

414 base 10 =

$4 * 10^2 + 1 * 10^1 + 4 * 10^0 =$

$4 * 100 + 1 * 10 + 4 * 1 =$

400   + 10   + 4 = 414

110011110 base 2 =

$1 * 2^8 + 1 * 2^7 + 0 * 2^6 + 0 * 2^5 + 1 * 2^4 + 1 * 2^3 + 1 * 2^2 + 1 * 2^1 + 0 * 2^0 =$

$1 * 256 + 1 * 128 + 0 * 64 + 0 * 32 + 1 * 16 + 1 * 8 + 1 * 4 + 1 * 2 + 0 * 1 =$

256   + 128   + 0   + 0   + 16   + 8   + 4   + 2   + 0 = 414

636 base 8 =

$6 * 8^2 + 3 * 8^1 + 6 * 8^0 =$

$6 * 64 + 3 * 8 + 6 * 1 =$

384   + 24   + 6 = 414

19E base 16 =

$1 * 16^2 + 9 * 16^1 + E * 16^0 =$

$1 * 256 + 9 * 16 + 14 * 1$

256   + 144   + 14 = 414

Each of these examples appears to convert from the number in the given base to the corresponding decimal number. To convert a decimal number to a number in a given base, we use division and remainder rather than multiplication and addition. The process works as follows:

1. Find the largest power of the given base that divides into the decimal number.
2. The quotient becomes the digit at that power's position in the new number.
3. Repeat steps 1 and 2 with the remainder until the remainder is less than the number.

4. If the last remainder is greater than 0, the remainder becomes the last digit in the new number.

5. If you must skip a power of the base when performing step 3, then put a 0 in that power's position in the new number.

To illustrate, let us convert the decimal number 327 to the equivalent binary number.

The highest power of 2 by which 327 is divisible is 256 or 2^8. Thus, we'll have a nine-digit binary number, with 1 in position 8:

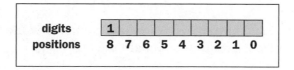

The remainder of the first division is 71. The highest power of 2 by which 71 is divisible is 64 (2^6). Thus, we have skipped 128 (2^7), so we write 0 in position 7 and 1 in position 6:

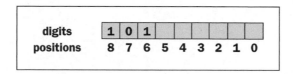

The remainder of the second division is 7. Thus, as you can see, we skip 3 more powers of 2 (32, 16, and 8) on the next division in order to use 4. So, we place 0s at positions 5, 4, and 3, and 1 at position 2 in the new number:

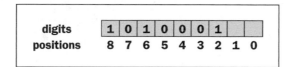

The remainder of the third division is 3. This is divisible by the next power of 2, which is 2, so we put 1 at position 1 in the new number. The remainder of the last division, 1, goes in position 0:

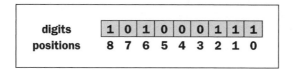

One reason that programmers prefer to use octal or hexadecimal notation instead of binary notation is that octal and hexadecimal are more expressive (one can say more with less). Another reason is that it is very easy to convert an octal number or a hexadecimal number to the corresponding binary number. To convert octal to binary, you assume that each digit in the octal number represents three digits in the corresponding binary number. You then start with the rightmost octal digit and write down the corresponding binary digits, padding these to the left with 0s to the count of 3, if necessary. You proceed in this manner until all of the octal digits have been con-verted. The following examples show such conversions:

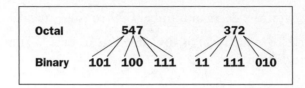

The conversion of hexadecimal numbers to binary numbers works in a similar way, except that each hexadecimal digit translates to four binary digits.

APPENDIX F

Java Exception Handling

Java divides run-time errors into two broad categories: errors and exceptions. Errors are serious run-time problems that usually should not be handled by the programmer. For example, if a method gets stuck in an infinite recursion, Java will throw a StackOverflowError. Java defines a separate class for each type of error. You can browse through these in Sun's Web site, as described in Appendix A, starting with the class Error in the package java.lang.

Exceptions come in two varieties: those that Java requires the programmer to handle, such as IOException, and those that the programmer may or may not handle, such as ArithmeticException and ArrayIndexOutOfBoundsException. To explore Java's Exception class hierarchy on Sun's Web site, select the desired package in the package index and scroll to the bottom of the page. Most of the exception classes are defined in java.lang, but several important ones also are defined in java.io and java.util.

The following code segments show how you might handle exceptions in the cases of division and array subscripting:

```java
// Catch an attempt to divide by zero

try{
   quotient = dividend / divisor;
   System.out.println("Successful division");
}
catch (ArithmeticException e){
   System.out.println("Error1: " + e.toString());
}
```

```java
// Catch an attempt to use an array index that is out of range

try{
   a[x] = 0;
   System.out.println("Successful subscripting");
}
catch (ArrayIndexOutOfBoundsException e){
   System.out.println("Error2: " + e.toString());
}
```

When Java detects an error and throws an exception, control is immediately transferred from the offending instruction in the try statement to the catch statement. Thus, the output of the first message would be skipped if an exception occurs in either of the preceding code segments. If the try statement completes successfully, the catch statement is not executed.

A `try` statement can be followed by more than one `catch` statement. For example, the following code segment combines the exception handling of the previous two segments:

```
// Catch an attempt to divide by zero and to use an array index
// that is out of bounds

try{
   quotient = dividend / divisor;
   System.out.println("Successful division");
   a[x] = quotient;
   System.out.println("Successful subscripting");
 }
catch (ArithmeticException e){
   System.out.println("Error1: " + e.toString());
}
catch (ArrayIndexOutOfBoundsException e){
   System.out.println("Error2: " + e.toString());
}
```

The same two exceptions are possible in this example, but Java will get to throw only one of them. When this occurs, control shifts to the first `catch` statement following the `try` statement. If the class of the exception thrown is the same as or is a subclass of the class of that `catch` statement's parameter, then the code for the `catch` statement executes. Otherwise, Java compares the exception thrown to the parameter of the next `catch` statement and so on.

It is possible (and often desirable) to define new kinds of exceptions that can be thrown by methods in user-defined classes. The complete rules for doing this are beyond the scope of this book but can be found on Sun's Web site.

APPENDIX G

Java Packages and jar *Files*

Using and Developing Packages

A Java package is a name that stands for a set of related classes. For example, the package java.io stands for all of the Java file stream classes. Exceptions and interfaces also can be parts of a package.

The package java.lang contains many commonly used classes, such as Math and String. This package is implicitly imported into every Java program file, so no import statement is required. To use any other package, such as java.io, in a program file, the programmer must explicitly import the package with an import statement.

Programs can import all of the classes in a given package, using the form:

```
import <package name>.*;
```

It is also possible to import selected classes from a given package and omit others. For example, the following line imports just the ArrayList class from the java.util package and omits the others:

```
import java.util.ArrayList;
```

This statement has the effect of making the ArrayList class visible to the program file, but leaves the rest of the classes in the java.util package invisible.

Occasionally, a program uses classes that have the same name but are defined in different packages. For example, the List class in java.awt implements a scrolling list box (similar to javax.swing.JList), whereas the List interface in java.util specifies operations for Java's list collections. To avoid ambiguity in these programs, you must prefix the class name with its package wherever the class name is used. Following is an example:

```
import java.util.*;
import java.awt.*;

  .
  .

   // Instantiate a scrolling list box to display the data
   java.awt.List listView = new java.awt.List();

  .
  .

   // Instantiate an array list to contain the data
   java.util.List<String> listModel = new ArrayList<String>();
```

To define and compile a package, perform the following steps:

1. Create three directories on your disk. Name the first directory `testbed` and the second directory `sources`. The third directory should have the name of the package you are defining, such as `mypackage`. The `sources` and `mypackage` directories should be contained as subdirectories in the `testbed` directory.

2. Place a tester program (say, `Tester.java`) for your package in the `testbed` directory.

3. Open a DOS window and move to the `mypackage` directory.

4. Place the Java source files (`.java` extension) for your package in the `mypackage` directory. Each source file in the package should have the line:

```
package mypackage;
```

   at the beginning of the file.

5. Compile the Java files using the DOS command `javac *.java`. If all goes well, the byte code files (`.class` extension) should be in the `mypackage` directory.

6. Move up to the `testbed` directory and compile the tester program.

7. Run the tester program using the DOS command `java Tester`. If all goes well, your package is ready for release. Before distributing your package, move the source (`.java`) files to the `sources` directory. A package should have just `.class` files.

Go back to Step 5 each time you need to modify a source file in the package.

Using and Developing `jar` Files

A `jar` file contains a collection of Java byte codes and possibly other resources, such as images. `jar` files provide a convenient way to distribute libraries of program code and standalone Java applications. Because they are compressed, `jar` files can also significantly reduce the file size of program code.

All of the Java applications developed in this book consist of one or more byte code files. To run an application, you open a command prompt window and run the `java` command with the byte code file that contains the program's `main` method. Alternatively, if a program's byte codes are bundled in an executable `jar` file, you can launch the program just by double-clicking on the `jar` file's icon.

To create an executable `jar` file, you must perform the following steps:

1. Open a text editor and create a text file named `manifest.tmp`. This file should contain a line of code that specifies the name of the class that contains the `main` method of your Java application. For example, if your main class is named `MyApplication`, the line of code in the file should be:

```
Main-Class: MyApplication
```

   Save the file in the directory that contains your byte code files.

2. At the command prompt run the `jar` command with the tags `cfm`, the name of the `jar` file, name of the manifest file, and the names of the byte code files as command line arguments. For example, the following command will generate an executable `jar` file named `MyApplication.jar` from all of the byte code files in the current directory, using the manifest file `manifest.tmp`:

```
jar cfm MyApplication.jar manifest.tmp *.class
```

3. Test the resulting `jar` file by launching it.

A program library usually consists of one for more Java packages. You can use a library by placing the directories that contain the packages in your current working directory. However, this necessitates moving these directories every time you change to another working directory. A far better way to use (and distribute) a program library is to bundle its packages in a `jar` file. The `jar` file can then be placed in Java's system directory, where it is accessible from any working directory or from most commercial and free IDEs.

To create a `jar` file for a program library, you must perform the following steps:

1. Place the package directory for the library in your current working directory. If there is more than one package in the library, they should already be organized in a hierarchy of subdirectories or as several directories at the same level. Note that the directories should contain just byte code files (files with a `.class` extension).

2. At the command prompt run the `jar` command with the tag `cvf`, the name of the `jar` file, and the top-level package directory name. For example, if the package name is `TurtleGraphics`, you would run the command line:

```
jar cvf TurtleGraphics.jar TurtleGraphics
```

3. To test the resulting `jar` file, copy it to the appropriate places in Java's system directory. On a PC running Windows XP, these two directories are:

```
c:\Program Files\Java\jdk1.5.0_05\jre\lib\ext
c:\Program Files\Java\jre1.5.0_05\lib\ext
```

On a Macintosh, this directory is `Macintosh Hard Drive/Library/Java/Extensions`. Compile and run a Java program that uses the library, after making sure that the library does not exist in the program's current working directory.

APPENDIX H

Files

Data stored in variables is temporary, existing for the lifetime of an application at most. Data that must last longer is saved in files on secondary storage devices, such as magnetic disks, optical disks (CDs and DVDs), and magnetic tapes. When needed again later, the data is read from the files back into variables. Dealing directly with directory structures and file layouts on disk is a complex process, so operating systems provide a layer of software to hide the messy details. In addition, Java has built a hierarchy of classes on top of this layer to give it an object-oriented interface. When working with files, a program deals with these Java classes, which in turn manage the actual transfer of data between memory and secondary storage.

Java supports two types of file access: sequential and random. If we imagine a file as a long sequence of contiguous bytes, then *random access* allows a program to retrieve a byte or group of bytes from anywhere in a file. *Sequential access* forces a program to retrieve bytes sequentially starting from the beginning of a file. Thus, to retrieve the 100th byte, a program must first retrieve the preceding 99. The text files processed in examples in this book are sequential access files.

At the lowest level, Java views the data in files as a stream of bytes. A stream of bytes from which data is read is called an *input stream*, and a stream of bytes to which data is written is called an *output stream*. Java provides classes for connecting to and manipulating data in a stream. The classes are defined in the package `java.io` and are organized in a large complex hierarchy. The classes `Scanner` (from `java.util`) and `PrintWriter` (from `java.io`) are used for text file input/output (I/O) and insulate the programmer from the details of Java's file streams. However, processing other types of files requires the knowledge of several other types of file streams, to which we now turn.

The Classes `FileInputStream`, and `FileOutputStream`

The basic classes for file I/O at the byte level are `FileInputStream` and `FileOutputStream`. When the programmer creates a `Scanner` to read from a text file, the scanner is instantiated as follows:

```
Scanner reader = new Scanner(new File(filename));
```

The scanner in turn wraps a `FileInputStream` around the `File` object as follows:

```
FileInputStream stream = new FileInputStream(aFile);
```

The scanner can then read bytes from this stream and use them to construct whatever tokens (`strings`, `ints`, `doubles`) the client requests.

Likewise, when a `PrintWriter` is created with an output file name, using the notation `new PrintWriter(new File(filename))`, the `PrintWriter` creates a `FileOutputStream` as follows:

```
FileOutputStream stream = new FileOutputStream(aFile);
```

The print writer can then write bytes from its output data to this stream.

The details of opening these streams are hidden from programmers who process text files with a `Scanner` and a `PrintWriter`. However, similar operations must be performed when programmers process other types of files. For convenience, both `FileInputStream` and `FileOutputStream` have a second constructor that accepts a file name as a parameter and wraps a `File` object around it.

Binary Files, Data Input Streams, and Data Output Streams

When the `print` and `println` methods write a number to a `PrintWriter`, they transform the number to its humanly readable character string representations. If the number needs to be read later by another program, the `Scanner` method `nextInt` or `nextDouble` first reads the string representing the number from the text file and then converts it back to the appropriate numeric data type.

Some applications simply need to store data in files without any need to represent it in human readable form. Java provides support for this type of application in the form of *binary file I/O*. A primitive type or string written to a `DataOutputStream` is represented in binary format that may not be humanly readable but can be read back into a program using a `DataInputStream`. Table H-1 lists several useful methods in these two classes.

TABLE H-1
Methods in the classes `DataInputStream` and `DataOutputStream`

METHOD	WHAT IT DOES
`char readChar()`	Reads a `char` from a `DataInputStream`
`double readDouble()`	Reads a `double` from a `DataInputStream`
`int readInt()`	Reads an `int` from a `DataInputStream`
`String readUTF()`	Reads a `String` from a `DataInputStream`
`void writeChar (char ch)`	Writes a `char` to a `DataOutputStream`
`void writeDouble (double d)`	Writes a `double` to a `DataOutputStream`
`void writeInt (int i)`	Writes an `int` to a `DataOutputStream`
`void writeUTF (String s)`	Writes a `String` to a `DataOutputStream`

A program reading from a data input stream must know the order and types of data expected at each moment. To illustrate, we present a sample program that

- Generates a user-specified number of random integers (the number is entered as a parameter in the command line)

- Writes these integers to a data output stream

- Reads them back in from a data input stream

- Outputs the integers to the terminal window

```
/* Example H1: TestDataStreams.java
1) Write randomly generated integers to a data output stream. A command
line parameter specifies the number of integers to generate.
2) Read them back in using a data input stream and display them in
   the terminal window.
*/

import java.io.*;
import java.util.Random;

public class TestDataStreams{

    public static void main (String[] args){
```

```java
// Obtain the number of ints from the command line parameters.
int number = Integer.parseInt(args[0]);

// Generate random ints and write them to a data output stream.
Random gen = new Random();
try{
   FileOutputStream foStream = new FileOutputStream("ints.dat");
   DataOutputStream doStream = new DataOutputStream(foStream);
   int i;
   for (i = 0; i < number; i++)
      doStream.writeInt(gen.nextInt(number + 1));
   doStream.close();
}catch(IOException e){
   System.err.println("Error during output: " + e.toString());
}

// Read the ints from a data input stream and display them in
// a terminal window.
try{
   FileInputStream fiStream = new FileInputStream("ints.dat");
   DataInputStream diStream = new DataInputStream(fiStream);
   while (true){
      int i = diStream.readInt();
      System.out.println(i);
   }
}catch(EOFException e){
    System.out.println("\nAll done.");
}catch(IOException e){

    System.err.println("Error in input" + e.toString());
   }
  }
}
```

A data input stream is processed within an exception-driven loop. Using the expression `while (true)`, the loop continues until an `EOFException` occurs. This exception is not viewed as an error but rather as a good reason to exit the loop. The `catch` statement in this example prints a reassuring message.

Now that we have seen two different ways to handle file input and output, it is natural to ask when to use each one. Here are two rules of thumb:

1. It is appropriate to use a print writer for output and a scanner for input when the file must be viewed or created with a text editor or when the order and types of data are unknown.

2. It is appropriate to use a data input stream for input and a data output stream for output when the file need not be viewed or created with a text editor and when the order and types of data are known.

Serialization and Object Streams

Until now we have focused on reading and writing primitive data types and strings. Java also provides methods for reading and writing complete objects. This makes it easy to save a program's state before closing it and to restore the state when the program is run again. Objects that are saved between executions of a program are said to be *persistent*, and the process of writing them to and reading them from a file is called *serialization*. To use serialization, a programmer must do two things:

1. Make classes `serializable`. (We will explain how this is done momentarily.)

2. Write objects using an `ObjectOutputStream` and read them later using an `ObjectInputStream`.

For example, consider the version of the student test scores program presented in Chapter 10. This program was written using a model/view pattern in which the model encapsulates the program's data requirements and the view manages the user interface. The data model in turn consists of the two classes Student and TestScoresModel. To serialize these classes, we import the package java.io and add the qualifier implements Serializable to each class's definition. The changes are commented in the following code:

```java
import java.io.*;        // Change here

public class TestScoresModel implements Serializable{  // Change here

   // Instance variables
   private Student[] students = new Student[10];
   private int        indexSelectedStudent;
   private int        studentCount;

   . . .

}




import java.io.*;        // Change here

public class Student implements Serializable{          // Change here

   // Instance variables
   private String name;
   private int[] tests = new int[3];

   . . .

}
```

The view class for the program maintains a reference to an object called model that is of type TestScoresModel. Saving and restoring the program's data involves nothing more than serializing this single object, which we do in the methods saveModel and loadModel. These methods are activated when the user selects the corresponding options from the menu.

```java
import java.io.*;
. . .

public class TestScoresView{
   . . .

   private TestScoresModel model;
   . . .

   public TestScoresView(TestScoresModel tm){
      model = tm;
   . . .
   }


   // Controller code


   . . .

   private void saveModel(){
      String outputFileName;
      . . . use a terminal prompt or file dialog to ask the user for the name
            of the output file
      try{
         FileOutputStream foStream = new FileOutputStream(outputFileName);
         ObjectOutputStream ooStream = new ObjectOutputStream(foStream);
         ooStream.writeObject(model);
         foStream.flush();
         foStream.close();
      }catch (IOException e){
         System.out.println("Error during output: " + e.toString());
      }
   }

   private void loadModel(){
      String inputFileName;
      . . . use a terminal prompt or file dialog to ask the user for the name
            of the input file
      try{
         FileInputStream fiStream = new FileInputStream(inputFileName);
         ObjectInputStream oiStream = new ObjectInputStream(fiStream);
         model = (TestScoresModel) oiStream.readObject();
         fiStream.close();
      }catch (Exception e){
         System.out.println("Error during input: " + e.toString());
      }
   }

   . . .
}
```

In this code, the method `writeObject` outputs the model object to the object output stream, which in turn triggers automatic serialization of the array of students and each individual student in the array. Likewise, the method `readObject` inputs the model object and all its constituent parts from the object input stream. Note that

- The method `readObject` returns an `Object`, which is cast to a `StudentTestScoresModel` before it is stored in the variable.

- The methods `readObject` and `writeObject` can throw several different types of exceptions. To catch all of these in a single `catch` clause, we use the generic `Exception` object as a parameter.

The methods `readObject` and `writeObject` can be used with objects of any type, such as strings, arrays, or user-defined objects. When reading an object, the programmer must be aware of its type and its position in the input stream and must cast and store it in the appropriate type of variable. As you can see, object streams and serialization are powerful and convenient tools for managing persistence.

Random Access Files

The types of files thus far discussed are sequential access files. Their data is accessed by reading or writing one value after another, starting with the value at the beginning of the file. By contrast, a random access file allows the programmer to read or write a datum at an arbitrary position in the file. The programmer specifies a position in the file with a special *seek* operation and then reads or writes a datum at that position. Thus, a random access file has the logical behavior of an array and supports much faster access than a sequential access file. The catch, however, is that the programmer must be able to specify the position of a datum in terms of the number of bytes between it and the beginning of the file. To do that, the programmer must also know the type of each datum and the number of bytes required to store it. We give an example of how this is done for a file of integers shortly.

The class `RandomAccessFile` supports random access file processing in Java. The most convenient constructor expects a file name and a *mode* as parameters. The modes "rw" and "r" specify read/write and read-only access, respectively. We use "rw" for output files and "r" for input files in our example.

Like the data I/O streams discussed earlier, `RandomAccessFile` includes several type-specific methods for input and output. For example, `readInt()` reads the four bytes at the current position in the file and returns the integer represented in those bytes. Conversely, `writeInt(anInt)` converts its parameter to four bytes and writes these to the current position in the file.

Before each input or output operation, the method seek(aLong) must be called to locate the position of the datum in the file. The position of the first datum is always 0. The position of the second datum is equal to the byte length of the first datum plus 0. In general, the position of the ith datum after the first one is equal to the position of the datum at position $i - 1$ plus that datum's byte length. The byte lengths of the various primitive types are listed in Table B-1. If we are dealing with a file of a single type of data, such as integers, then calculating the position of each datum can be reduced to a simple expression such as i * 4. The position of a datum is usually called its *offset*, to indicate the number of bytes between it and the beginning position in the file.

Other useful RandomAccessFile methods include length(), which returns the length of the file in bytes, and getFilePointer(), which returns the offset of the current position in bytes.

Our program example tests random access files by doing three things:

1. Create a random access file and save three integers from an array to this file.

2. Open the file for input and read the data at each position in sequence. Each datum and its position are displayed.

3. Open the file for input and read the integer at the file's middle position. The number of integers, the datum, and its position are displayed.

Here is the code:

```java
// Example H2: Test random access files

import java.io.*;

public class TestRandomFile{

    private int[] testArray = {23, 46, 67};

    public static void main(String[] args){
        TestRandomFile app = new TestRandomFile();
    }

    public TestRandomFile(){
        arrayToFile(testArray);
        sequentialTraverse();
        testInput();
    }
```

```java
// Write the numbers from the array to the file
public void arrayToFile(int[] array){
   try{
      RandomAccessFile output = new RandomAccessFile("test", "rw");
      for (int i = 0; i < array.length; i++){
         output.seek(i * 4);
         output.writeInt(array[i]);
      }
      output.close();
   }catch(Exception e){}
}

// Read the number at the midpoint of the file
public void testInput(){
   try{
      RandomAccessFile input = new RandomAccessFile("test", "r");
      int numberOfInts = (int)(input.length() / 4);
      // Get number of ints
      int midpoint = numberOfInts / 2 * 4;
      // Get position of middle int
      input.seek(midpoint);
      // Move directly to midpoint
      int item = input.readInt();
      // read the int
      System.out.println("Number of ints = " + numberOfInts);
      System.out.println("Midpoint       = " + midpoint);
      System.out.println("Middle int     = " + item);
      input.close();
   }catch(Exception e){}
}

// Sequential traversal using indices
void sequentialTraverse(){
   try{
      RandomAccessFile input = new RandomAccessFile("test", "r");
      long numberOfItems = input.length() / 4;
      for (long i = 0; i <= numberOfItems; i++){
         input.seek(i * 4);
         System.out.println(i + ": " + input.readInt());
      }
      input.close();
   }catch(Exception e){}
}
}
```

More detailed information on random access files can be found in Sun's documentation.

File Dialog Boxes

Throughout this book, filenames have been hard-coded into the programs or have been entered from the keyboard. Problems can arise if the specified file does not exist or if the user cannot remember a file's name. These problems are minimized if a file dialog box is used. The user can then browse through the computer's directory structure to find a desired filename or can back out by canceling the dialog box. Figure H-1 shows typical input file and output file dialog boxes as supported by Swing's JFileChooser class. Table H-2 lists important JFileChooser methods.

FIGURE H-1
Typical file dialog boxes

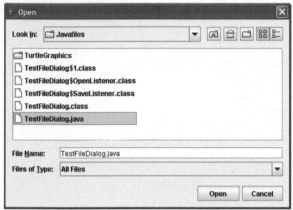 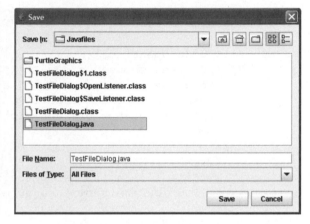

TABLE H-2
Important JFileChooser methods

METHOD	WHAT IT DOES
JFileChooser()	Constructor that creates a file dialog box that is attached to the user's home directory
JFileChooser(String directoryPathName)	Constructor that creates a file dialog box that is attached to the specified directory
int showOpenDialog(JFrame parent)	Opens a file dialog box for an input file and returns the JFileChooser constant APPROVE_OPTION if the user has selected a file or the constant or CANCEL_OPTION if the user has canceled
int showSaveDialog(JFrame parent)	Opens a file dialog box for an output file and returns the JFileChooser constant APPROVE_OPTION if the user has selected a file or the constant or CANCEL_OPTION if the user has canceled
File getSelectedFile()	Returns the selected file

The following program displays file dialog boxes for input and output files. After the dialog boxes close, the code displays the filename if the user did not cancel the dialog box; otherwise, the code displays a message saying the dialog box was canceled. At instantiation, the dialog box is attached to the directory c:\Javafiles (on a PC). The program is entirely GUI-based, using a standard File menu with Open and Save options.

```java
// Example H3: Testing file dialog boxes

import javax.swing.*;
import java.awt.event.*;
import java.io.*;

public class TestFileDialog extends JFrame{

    private void openFile(){
        JFileChooser chooser = new JFileChooser("c:\\Javafiles");
        int result = chooser.showOpenDialog(this);
        if (result == JFileChooser.CANCEL_OPTION)
           JOptionPane.showMessageDialog(this,
                                          "The dialog was cancelled.");
        else
           try{
              File file = chooser.getSelectedFile();
              JOptionPane.showMessageDialog(this, "File name: " +
                                             file.getName());
           }catch(Exception e){
              JOptionPane.showMessageDialog(this,
                                             "Error opening input file " +
                                             e.toString());
           }
    }

    private void saveFile(){
        JFileChooser chooser = new JFileChooser("c:\\Javafiles");
        int result = chooser.showSaveDialog(this);
        if (result == JFileChooser.CANCEL_OPTION)
           JOptionPane.showMessageDialog(this,
                                          "The dialog was cancelled.");
        else
           try{
              File file = chooser.getSelectedFile();
              JOptionPane.showMessageDialog(this,"File name: " +
                                             file.getName());
           }catch(Exception e){
              JOptionPane.showMessageDialog(this,
                                             "Error opening input file " +
                                             e.toString());
           }
    }
```

```java
    private class OpenListener implements ActionListener{
        public void actionPerformed(ActionEvent e){
            openFile();
        }
    }

    private class SaveListener implements ActionListener{
        public void actionPerformed(ActionEvent e){
            saveFile();
        }
    }

    public TestFileDialog(){
        JMenu menu = new JMenu("File");
        JMenuItem openMI = new JMenuItem("Open");
        JMenuItem saveMI = new JMenuItem("Save");
        menu.add(openMI);
        menu.add(saveMI);
        JMenuBar bar = new JMenuBar();
        bar.add(menu);
        setJMenuBar(bar);
        openMI.addActionListener(new OpenListener());
        saveMI.addActionListener(new SaveListener());
    }

    public static void main(String[] args){
        TestFileDialog theGUI = new TestFileDialog();
        theGUI.setSize(100, 100);
        theGUI.setDefaultCloseOperation(JFrame.EXIT_ON_CLOSE);
        theGUI.setVisible(true);
    }
}
```

The TurtleGraphics Package

This appendix provides a quick reference to an open-source package that supports turtle graphics. This package is called `TurtleGraphics`. Methods that are part of `AWT` and `Swing` are so noted. For more details, byte code, source code, a tutorial, and a related package, `BreezySwing`, that uses only Swing components, see the Web site at http://www.wlu.edu/~lambertk/hsjava/.

Programs that use `TurtleGraphics` should import the package as follows:

```
import TurtleGraphics.*;
```

The package provides classes and methods for manipulating a pen in a graphics window. The pen or turtle is an invisible device, initially positioned at the center of a sketchpad. This center point, also called home, is at the origin of a Cartesian coordinate system. The programmer draws images with the pen by sending it messages. There are several types of pens, as listed in Table I-1. All implement the `Pen` interface, as described in the following section.

TABLE I-1
The `Pen` classes

Pen CLASS	FEATURES
StandardPen	Draws with a straight line in the pen's current color
BackwardPen	Moves in the opposite direction of a standard pen
RainbowPen	Draws with a straight line in randomly generated colors
WigglePen	Draws with a wiggly line in the pen's current color
WiggleRainbowPen	Draws with a wiggly line in randomly generated colors

The Pen Interface

The `Pen` interface specifies the methods that all of the types of pens support. A pen is initially positioned at the home position (the origin or center of the sketchpad), faces due north, and is placed down on the sketchpad's surface. A non-rainbow pen's default color is blue. When placed down and moved, the pen draws; when picked up and moved, the pen simply moves without drawing. Following are the methods:

void home()

Action: The pen jumps to the center of the graphics window without drawing and points north.

Example: `pen.home();`

void setDirection(double degrees)

Action: The pen points in the indicated direction. Due east corresponds to 0 degrees, north to 90 degrees, west to 180 degrees, and south to 270 degrees. Because there are 360 degrees in a circle, setting the direction to 400 would be equivalent to 400 – 360 or 40 and setting it to –30 would be equivalent to 360 – 30 or 330.

Example: `pen.setDirection(90);` `// Make the pen point due north`

void turn(double degrees)

Action: The pen adds the indicated degrees to its current direction. Positive degrees correspond to turning counterclockwise. The degrees can be an integer or floating-point number.

Example: `pen.turn(-45);` `// Rotate the pen 45 degrees clockwise`

void down()

Action: The pen lowers itself to the drawing surface.

Example: `pen.down();`

void up()

Action: The pen raises itself from the drawing surface.

Example: `pen.up();`

void move(double distance)

Action: The pen moves the specified distance in the current direction. The distance can be an integer or floating-point number and is measured in pixels (picture elements). The size of a pixel depends on the monitor's resolution. For instance, when we say that a monitor's resolution is 800 by 600, we mean that the monitor is 800 pixels wide and 600 pixels high.

Example: `pen.move(100);`

void move(double x, double y)

Action: The pen moves to the position (x, y).

Example: `pen.move(50, 50);`

void drawString(String string)

Action: The string is drawn at the pen's position.

Example: `pen.drawString("Here is the turtle!");`

void setColor(Color color)

Action: The pen's color is set to the specified color.

Example: `pen.setColor(Color.red);`

void setWidth(int width)

Action: The pen's width is set to the specified width.

Example: `pen.setWidth(8);`

Pens, Sketchpads, and Sketchpad Windows

Three classes cooperate to implement a turtle graphics program. They are one of the pen classes mentioned earlier, the SketchPad class, and the SketchPadWindow class. SketchPadWindow, a subclass of JFrame, provides the application window for turtle graphics. SketchPad, a subclass of JPanel, provides the drawing area within a sketchpad window. Associated with each sketchpad is a pen. Thus, the programmer can manipulate several pens in a single sketchpad window by creating several sketchpads and adding them to the window. In the remaining sections of this appendix, we describe three ways to create turtle graphics applications using these classes.

Method 1: Create Just a Pen

The simplest way to create a turtle graphics program is to instantiate a pen and start sending it messages. The framework automatically associates a pen with a sketchpad, places this panel in a window that is 150 pixels by 150 pixels, and opens the window. Following is an example code segment:

```
import TurtleGraphics.*;

public class TestTurtleGraphics{
   public static void main(String [] args) {
      Pen pen = new StandardPen();
      pen.move(100, 100);
   }
}
```

The constructors for WigglePen and WiggleRainbowPen require the user to specify the number of wiggles and a wiggle angle as parameters. The following code creates a WigglePen with 10 wiggles and a wiggle angle of 45:

```
Pen pen = new WigglePen(10, 45);
```

The user can manipulate a sketchpad window like any other window. Any images that the pen has drawn will automatically be refreshed. Note, however, that the programmer has no control over the window and there is only a single drawing area with one pen.

Method 2: Create a Sketchpad Window with a Pen

To give the programmer control over a pen's window, you can create it before associating it with a pen. The process consists of two steps:

1. Instantiate a SketchPadWindow. Its width and height can be passed as optional parameters, or you get a default size of 150 by 150.

2. Instantiate a pen with the SketchPadWindow as a parameter. The window is opened at this point.

Following is an example code segment:

```
import TurtleGraphics.*;

public class TestTurtleGraphics{
    public static void main(String [] args) {
        SketchPadWindow win = new SketchPadWindow(400, 400);
        Pen pen = new StandardPen(win);
        pen.move(100, 100);
    }
}
```

Method 3: Create a Sketchpad and a Pen

To give the programmer control over a pen's sketchpad or drawing area; to work with multiple drawing areas and pens in a single window; or to associate a sketchpad with any application window, an applet, or a dialog box; you can create a sketchpad before associating it with a pen. The process consists of three steps:

1. Instantiate a SketchPad.

2. Instantiate a pen with the SketchPad as a parameter.

3. Add the SketchPad to the window. You can use the add method if you are implementing an application, dialog box, or applet with JFrame, JDialog, or JApplet. Alternatively, you can instantiate a SketchPadWindow with the SketchPad as a parameter.

The following code segment shows the first option of Step 3. The program creates two sketchpads, sets their background colors, associates them with different types of pens, adds them to an application window, and draws similar images in them.

```
import TurtleGraphics.*;
import javax.swing.*;
import java.awt.*;

public class TestTurtleGraphics extends JFrame{

    private SketchPad leftPad, rightPad;
    private Pen leftPen, rightPen;

    public TestTurtleGraphics(){
        leftPad = new SketchPad();
        rightPad = new SketchPad();
        leftPad.setBackground(Color.pink);
        rightPad.setBackground(Color.yellow);
        leftPen = new StandardPen(leftPad);
        rightPen = new WigglePen(rightPad, 10, 45);
        Container container = getContentPane();
        container.setLayout(new GridLayout(1,2));
        container.add(BorderLayout.WEST, leftPad);
        container.add(BorderLayout.EAST, rightPad);
    }
```

```java
    public static void main(String [] args) {
        TestTurtleGraphics theGUI = new TestTurtleGraphics();
        theGUI.setSize(200, 200);
        theGUI.setDefaultCloseOperation(JFrame.EXIT_ON_CLOSE);
        theGUI.setVisible(true);
        theGUI.leftPen.move(100, 100);
        theGUI.rightPen.move(100, 100);
    }
}
```

APPENDIX J

AP Correlations

This textbook covers all of the required features of Java for the AP A exam, as well as other features potentially relevant to the first course in programming but not tested. Table J-1 provides a reference to these features in the book.

TABLE J-1
AP exam features covered in this text

TESTED IN A EXAM	POTENTIALLY RELEVANT TO CS1 COURSE BUT NOT TESTED
`int, double, boolean` (p. 60, 112, 203)	`short, long, byte, char, float` (p. B-1)
+, -, *, /, %, ++, — (p. 64, 106)	
=, +=, -=, *=, /=, %= (p. 106)	
==, !=, <, <=, >, >= (p. 114)	
&&, ‖, ! and short-circuit evaluation (p. 202, 205)	
`(int), (double)` (p. 67)	Other numeric casts such as `(char)` or `(float)` (p. B-3)
String concatenation (p. 68)	
Escape sequences \" \\ \n inside strings (p. 69)	Other escape sequences (\' \t \unnnn) (p. B-2)
`System.out.print, System.out.println` (p. 44)	System.in, Stream input/output, GUI input/output, parsing input, formatted output (p. 252–258)
	`public static void main(String args)` (p. 355)
1-dimensional arrays, 2-dimensional rectangular arrays (p. 305, 318)	arrays with 3 or more dimensions, ragged arrays (p. B-10)
`if, if/else, while, for, enhanced for, return` (p. 113, 116, 120, 321)	`do/while, switch, break` (p. B-4)
Modify existing classes (p. 155)	Design classes (p. 367–380)

TABLE J-1 Continued
AP exam features covered in this text

TESTED IN A EXAM	POTENTIALLY RELEVANT TO CS1 COURSE BUT NOT TESTED
public classes, private instance variables, public or private methods or constants (p. 163)	protected or package visibility (p. 369)
final local variables, static final class variables (p. 355)	final instance variables, methods or classes (p. 352)
static methods (p. 352)	static non-final variables (p. 352)
null, this, super (p. 161, 167, 370)	super.method(args), this.var, this.method(args), this(args) (p. 370)
Constructors and initialization of static variables (p. 352)	default initialization of instance variables, initialization blocks (p. 313)
Understand inheritance hierarchies, modifying subclass implementations and implementations of interfaces (p. 367)	Design an implement subclasses (p. 367)
Understand the concepts of abstract classes and interfaces (p. 372)	Design and implement abstract classes and interfaces (p. 372)
Understand equals, == and != comparison of objects (p. 405)	Comparable.compareTo, clone, implementation of equals (p. 406, 414–416)
Conversion to supertypes and (Subtype) casts (p. 371)	instanceof (p. 427)
Procedural decomposition	
	Inner classes (p. 190)
Package concept, import x.y.Z; (p. 73)	import x.y.z, defining packages, class path (p. G-1)
Exception concept, common exceptions, throwing standard unchecked exceptions (p. 182, 385)	
String, Math, Random, Object, ArrayList (generic version) (p. 68, 107, 108, 405, 430)	

GLOSSARY

A

absolute path name A string that specifies the location of a resource, such as an HTML file, on a Web server.

abstract Simplified or partial, hiding detail.

abstract class A class that defines attributes and methods for subclasses but is never instantiated.

abstract data type (ADT) A class of objects, a defined set of properties of those objects, and a set of operations for processing the objects.

abstract method A method that is specified but not implemented in an abstract class. The subclasses must implement this method.

Abstract Windowing Toolkit (AWT) A Java package that contains the definitions of classes used to set up graphical user interfaces.

abstraction simplified view of a task or data structure that ignores complex detail.

accessor A method used to examine an attribute of an object without changing it.

accumulator A variable used for the purpose of summing successive values of some other variable.

activation record An area of computer memory that keeps track of a method call's parameters, local values, return value, and the caller's return address. See also **runtime stack**.

actual parameter A variable or expression contained in a method call and passed to that method. See also **formal parameter**.

adapter class A Java class that allows another class to implement an interface class without implementing all of its methods. See also **interface**.

address An integer value that the computer can use to reference a location. Often called address of a memory location.

aggregation A common relationship between two classes in which an object of one class contains an object of the other class. Also called the has-a relationship.

algorithm A finite sequence of effective statements that, when applied to a problem, will solve it.

alias A situation in which two or more names in a program can refer to the same memory location. An alias can cause subtle side effects.

analysis The phase of the software life cycle in which the programmer describes what the program will do.

applet A Java program that can be downloaded and run on a Web browser.

application software Programs that allow human users to accomplish specialized tasks, such as word processing or database management.

argument A value or expression passed in a method call.

arithmetic expression A sequence of operands and operators that computes a value.

arithmetic/logic unit (ALU) The part of the central processing unit that performs arithmetic operations and evaluates expressions.

arithmetic overflow A situation that arises when the computer's memory cannot represent the number resulting from an arithmetic operation.

array A data structure whose elements are accessed by means of index positions.

array index The relative position of the components of an array.

array list A class that represents a linear sequence of zero or more elements and supports many types of operations, including constant-time access by index position.

ASCII character set   The American Standard Code for Information Interchange ordering for a character set (See Appendix D).

assembly language   A computer language that allows the programmer to express operations and memory addresses with mnemonic symbols.

assertion   Special comments used with `if` statements and loops that state what you expect to happen and when certain conditions will hold.

assignment operator   The symbol =, which is used to store a value in a variable.

assignment statement   A method of putting values into memory locations.

association   A pair of items consisting of a key and a value.

associative link   A means of recognizing and accessing items in a network structure, such as the World Wide Web.

attribute   A property that a computational object models, such as the balance in a bank account.

B

behavior   The set of actions that a class of objects supports.

big-O notation   A formal notation used to express the amount of work done by an algorithm or the amount of memory used by an algorithm.

binary digit   A digit, either 0 or 1, in the binary number system. Program instructions are stored in memory using a sequence of binary digits. See also **bit**.

binary search   The process of examining a middle value of a sorted array to see which half contains the value in question and halving until the value is located.

binary search algorithm   A method of searching a collection of items with a natural ordering that allows the search to discard ½ of the elements on each pass.

bit   A binary digit.

bitmap   A data structure used to represent the values and positions of points on a computer screen or image.

block   An area of program text, enclosed in Java by the symbols {}, that contains statements and data declarations.

Boolean expression   An expression whose value is either true or false. See also **compound Boolean expression** and **simple Boolean expression**.

border layout   A Java layout class that allows the programmer to place window objects in five areas (north, south, west, east, and center) of a window. Border layout is the default layout for Java applications.

bottom-up implementation   A method of coding a program that starts with lower-level modules and a test driver module.

boundary condition   A value at which two equivalence classes meet.

boxing   The process whereby the Java Virtual Machine automatically wraps values of primitive types in objects so they can be stored in collections.

bubble sort   A sorting algorithm that swaps consecutive elements that are out of order to bubble the elements to the top or bottom on each pass.

buffer   A block of memory into which data are placed for transmission to a program, usually with file or string processing.

button object   A window object that allows the user to select an action by clicking a mouse.

byte   A sequence of bits used to encode a character in memory. See also **word**.

byte code   The kind of object code generated by a Java compiler and interpreted by a Java virtual machine. Byte code is platform independent.

C

call   Any reference to a method by an executable statement. Also referred to as **invoke**.

call stack   The trace of method calls that appears when Java throws an exception during program execution.

cancellation error   A condition in which data are lost because of differences in the precision of the operands.

cast   An operator that is used to convert a value of one type to a value of a different type (e.g., `double` to `int`).

c-curve   A fractal shape that resembles the letter C.

central processing unit (CPU) A major hardware component that consists of the arithmetic/logic unit and the control unit.

character set The list of characters available for data and program statements.

class A description of the attributes and behavior of a set of computational objects.

class constant A constant that is visible to all instances of a class and, if public, is accessed by specifying the class name. For example, `Math.PI` is a class constant.

class diagram A graphical notation that describes the relationships among the classes in a software system.

class (static) method A method that is invoked when a message is sent to a class. For example, `Math.sqrt` is a class method. See also **message**.

class (static) variable A variable that is visible to all instances of a class and, if public, is accessed by specifying the class name.

client A computational object that receives a service from another computational object.

client/server relationship A means of describing the organization of computing resources in which one resource provides a service to another resource.

coding The process of writing executable statements that are part of a program to solve a problem. See also **implementation**.

cohesive method A method designed to accomplish a single task.

combinatorial explosion A multiplicative growth.

comments Nonexecutable statements used to make a program more readable.

compatible type Expressions that have the same base type. A formal parameter and an actual parameter must be of compatible type, and the operands of an assignment statement must be of compatible type.

compilation error An error detected when the program is being compiled. See also **design error**, **runtime error**, and **syntax error**.

compiler A computer program that automatically converts instructions in a high-level language to machine language.

complete code coverage A set of tests in which every line in a program is executed at least once.

complexity analysis The process of deriving a formula that expresses the rate of growth of work or memory as a function of the size of the data or problem that it solves. See also **big-O notation**.

component An object that supports the display of an image, such as a button, menu item, or window, in a graphical user interface.

compound assignment An assignment operation that performs a designated operation, such as addition, before storing the result in a variable.

compound Boolean expression Refers to the complete expression when logical connectives and negation are used to generate Boolean values. See also **Boolean expression** and **simple Boolean expression**.

compound statement A statement that uses the symbols { and } to group several statements and data declarations as a unit. See also **block**.

concatenation An operation in which the contents of one data structure are placed after the contents of another data structure.

concrete class A class that can be instantiated. See also **abstract class**.

conditional statement See **selection statement**.

conjunction The connection of two Boolean expressions using the logical operator && (AND), returning false if at least one of the expressions is false or true if they are both true.

constant A symbol whose value cannot be changed.

constructor A method that is run when an object is instantiated, usually to initialize that object's instance variables.

contained class A class that is used to define a data object within another class.

container A Java class that allows the programmer to group window objects for placement in a window.

control statement A statement that controls the flow of the execution of program statements.

control structure A structure that controls the flow of execution of program statements.

control unit The part of the central processing unit that controls the operation of the rest of the computer.

coordinate system A grid that allows a programmer to specify positions of points in a plane or of pixels on a computer screen.

counter A variable used to count the number of times some process is completed.

count-controlled loop A loop that stops when a counter variable reaches a specified limit.

D

data The particular characters that are used to represent information in a form suitable for storage, processing, and communication.

data flow diagram A graphical depiction of the communication between program components that share data.

data input stream A Java class that supports the input of data from a binary file.

data output stream A Java class that supports the output of data to a binary file.

data type A formal description of the set of values that a variable can have.

data validation The process of examining data prior to its use in a program.

debugging The process of eliminating errors, or "bugs," from a program.

decrement To decrease the value of a variable.

default constructor A method that Java provides for creating objects of a class. The programmer can override this method to do extra things.

definition list An HTML structure that allows an author to display a keyed list on a Web page.

dependency A common relationship between two classes in which an object of one class uses an object of another class to accomplish a goal.

design The phase of the software life cycle in which the programmer describes how the program will accomplish its tasks.

design error An error such that a program runs, but unexpected results are produced. Also referred to as a logic error. See also **compilation error**, **runtime error**, and **syntax error**.

dialog A type of window that pops up to display information or receive it from the user.

DOS development environment A set of software tools that allows you to edit, compile, run, and debug programs using the DOS operating system.

double A Java data type used to represent numbers with a decimal point (e.g., a real number or a floating-point number).

do-while loop A post-test loop examining a Boolean expression after causing a statement to be executed. See also `for` **loop, loops,** and `while` **loop**.

driver A method used to test other methods.

E

element A value that is stored in an array.

empty statement A semicolon used to indicate that no action is to be taken. Also referred to as a **null statement.**

encapsulation The process of hiding and restricting access to the implementation details of a data structure.

end-of-file marker A special marker inserted by the machine to indicate the end of the data file.

end-of-line character A special character ('\n') used to indicate the end of a line of characters in a string or a file stream.

enhanced `for` loop A special type of `for` loop that traverses an array or array list from beginning to end, binding a local variable to each element in the array or list.

enumeration A user-defined type that consists of a set of symbols.

entry-controlled loop See **pretest loop**.

equivalence class All the sets of test data that exercise a program in the same manner.

error See **compilation error, design error, logic error, runtime error,** and **syntax error.**

event An occurrence, such as a button click or a mouse motion, that can be detected and processed by a program.

event-driven loop A process, usually hidden in the operating system, that waits for an event, notifies a program that an event has occurred, and returns to wait for more events.

exception An abnormal state or error that occurs during runtime and is signaled by the operating system.

exception-driven loop The use of exceptions to implement a normal loop, usually for file input.

execute To carry out the instructions of a program.

exit-controlled loop See **post-test loop**.

explicit type conversion The use of an operation by a programmer to convert the type of a data object.

exponential form See **floating-point**.

extended `if` statement Nested selection in which additional `if-else` statements are used in the `else` option. See also **nested `if` statement**.

external image An image displayed when the user selects a link on a Web page.

extreme condition Data at the limits of validity.

F

Fibonacci numbers A series of numbers generated by taking the sum of the previous two numbers in the series. The series begins with the numbers 1 and 2.

field width The number of columns used for the output of text. See also **formatting**.

file A data structure that resides on a secondary storage medium.

file input stream A Java class used to connect a program to a file for input.

file output stream A Java class used to connect a program to a file for output.

final method A method that cannot be implemented by a subclass.

fixed-point A method of writing real numbers in which the decimal is placed where it belongs in the number. See also **floating-point**.

floating-point A method for writing numbers in scientific notation to accommodate numbers that may have very large or very small values. See also **fixed-point**.

flow layout A Java layout class that allows the user to place window objects in wrap-around rows in a window. Flow layout is the default layout for applets.

flowchart A diagram that displays the flow of control of a program. See also **control structure**.

flushing The process of clearing an output buffer before closing an output file stream.

font The kind of typeface used for text, such as Courier and Times Roman.

for loop A structured loop consisting of an initializer expression, a termination expression, an update expression, and a statement.

forgetful bitmap problem A problem that occurs when an image is lost when the user resizes or minimizes a window.

formal parameter A name, introduced in a method definition, that is replaced by an actual parameter when the method is called.

formal specification The set of preconditions and postconditions of a method.

formatting Designating the desired field width when displaying text. See also **field width**.

fractal geometry A theory of shapes that are reflected in various phenomena, such as coastlines, water flow, and price fluctuations.

fractal object A type of mathematical object that maintains self-sameness when viewed at greater levels of detail.

frame A Java class that defines the window for an application. See also **application software**.

G

garbage collection The automatic process of reclaiming memory when the data of a program no longer need it.

generic array list A type of array list that allows the programmer to declare the element type that is expected when the list is created.

global identifier A name that can be used by all of the methods of a class.

global variable See **global identifier**.

graphical user interface (GUI) A means of communication between human beings and computers that uses a pointing device for input and a bitmapped screen for output. The bitmap displays images of windows and window objects such as buttons, text fields, and pull-down menus. The user interacts with the interface by using the mouse to directly manipulate the window objects. See also **window object**.

graphics context In Java, an object associated with a component where the images for that component are drawn.

grid layout A Java layout class that allows the user to place window objects in a two-dimensional grid in the window.

H

hacking The use of clever techniques to write a program, often for the purpose of gaining access to protected resources on networks.

hardware The computing machine and its support devices.

has-a relationship A relationship between two classes in which one class contains an instance of the other class.

helper method A method used within the implementation of a class but not used by clients of that class.

high-level language Any programming language that uses words and symbols to make it relatively easy to read and write a program. See also **assembly language** and **machine language.**

hyperlinks An item in a hypertext document that allows the user to navigate to another document.

hypermedia A data structure that allows the user to access different kinds of information (text, images, sound, video, applications) by traversing links.

hypertext A data structure that allows the user to access different chunks of text by traversing links.

hypertext markup language (HTML) A programming language that allows the user to create pages for the World Wide Web.

I

identifiers Words that must be created according to a well-defined set of rules but can have any meaning subject to these rules.

identity The property of an object that it is the same thing at different points in time, even though the values of its attributes might change.

if-else statement A selection statement that allows a program to perform alternative actions based on a condition.

immutable object An object whose internal data or state cannot be changed.

implementation The phase of the software life cycle in which the program is coded in a programming language.

increment The process of increasing a number by 1.

index See **array index.**

infinite loop A loop in which the controlling condition is not changed in such a manner to allow the loop to terminate.

infinite recursion The state of a running program that occurs when a recursive method cannot reach a stopping state.

information hiding A condition in which the user of a module does not know the details of how it is implemented, and the implementer of a module does not know the details of how it is used.

inheritance The process by which a subclass can reuse attributes and behavior defined in a superclass. See also **subclass** and **superclass.**

initializer list A means of expressing a set of data that can be assigned to the cells of an array in one statement.

inline image An image that is loaded when the user accesses a Web page.

input Data obtained by a program during its execution.

input assertion A precondition for a loop.

input device A device that provides information to the computer. Typical input devices are a mouse, keyboard, disk drive, microphone, and network port. See also **I/O device** and **output device.**

input stream A data object that allows a program to input data from a file or the keyboard.

insertion sort A sorting algorithm that locates an insertion point and takes advantage of partial orderings in an array.

instance A computational object bearing the attributes and behavior specified by a class.

instance method A method that is called when a message is sent to an instance of a class. See also **message.**

instance variable Storage for data in an instance of a class.

instantiation The process of creating a new object or instance of a class.

integer arithmetic operations Operations allowed on data of type int. These include the operations of addition, subtraction, multiplication, division, and modulus to produce integer answers.

integer overflow A condition in which an integer value is too large to be stored in the computer's memory.

integrated development environment (IDE) A set of software tools that allows you to edit, compile, run, and debug programs within one user interface.

interface A formal statement of how communication occurs between the user of a module (class or method) and its implementer.

Interface A Java file that simply specifies the methods to be implemented by another class. A class that implements several interfaces can thus adopt the behavior of several classes.

invariant expression An assertion that is true before the loop and after each iteration of the loop.

invoke See **call**.

I/O device Any device that allows information to be transmitted to or from a computer. See also **input device** and **output device**.

is-a **relationship** A relationship between two classes in which one class is a subclass of the other class.

iteration See **loops**.

iterative process A running program that executes a loop.

J

Java virtual machine (JVM) A program that interprets Java byte codes and executes them.

just-in-time compilation (JIT) A feature of some Java virtual machines that first translates byte codes to the machine's code before executing them.

justification The process of aligning text to the left, the center, or the right within a given number of columns.

K

key An item that is associated with a value and is used to locate this value in a collection.

keyed list A data structure that allows the programmer to access items by using key values.

keywords See **reserved words**.

L

label object A window object that displays text, usually to describe the roles of other window objects.

library A collection of methods and data organized to perform a set of related tasks. See also **class** and **package**.

lifetime The time during which a data object or method call exists.

linear An increase of work or memory in direct proportion to the size of a problem.

linear search See **sequential search**.

listener A Java class that detects and responds to events.

literal An element of a language that evaluates to itself, such as 34 or "hi there."

loader A system software tool that places program instructions and data into the appropriate memory locations before program start-up.

local identifier A name whose value is visible only within a method or a nested block.

local variable See **local identifier**.

logarithmic An increase of work in proportion to the number of times that the problem size can be divided by 2.

logic error See **design error**.

logical operator Either of the logical connective operators && (and), || (or), or ! (negation).

logical size The number of data items actually available in a data structure at a given time. See also **physical size**.

logical structure The organization of the components in a data structure, independent of their organization in computer memory.

long A Java data type used to represent large integers.

loop A type of statement that repeatedly executes a set of statements.

loop invariant An assertion that expresses a relationship between variables that remains constant throughout all iterations of the loop.

loop variant An assertion whose truth changes between the first and final execution of the loop.

loop verification The process of guaranteeing that a loop performs its intended task.

loops Program statements that cause a process to be repeated. See also do-while **loop**, for **loop**, and while **loop**.

low-level language See **assembly language**.

M

machine language The language used directly by the computer in all its calculations and processing.

main (primary) memory The high-speed internal memory of a computer, also referred to as random access memory (RAM). See also **memory** and **secondary memory**.

main unit A computer's main unit contains the central processing unit (CPU) and the main (primary) memory; it is hooked to one or more **input devices** and one or more **output devices**.

mainframe Large computers typically used by major companies and universities. See also **microcomputer** and **minicomputer**.

mantissa/exponent notation A notation used to express floating-point numbers.

markup tag A syntactic form in the hypertext markup language used to create different elements displayed on a Web page.

mathematical induction A method of proving that parts of programs are correct by reasoning from a base case and an induction hypothesis to a general conclusion.

matrix A two-dimensional array that provides range checking and can be resized.

megabyte Shorthand for 1 million bytes.

memex A hypothetical machine proposed by Vannevar Bush that would allow users to store and retrieve information via associative links.

memory The ordered sequence of storage cells that can be accessed by address. Instructions and variables of an executing program are temporarily held here. See also **main memory** and **secondary memory**.

memory location A storage cell that can be accessed by address. See also **memory**.

menu-driven program A program that allows the user to repeatedly select a command from a list of command options.

menu item A window object that displays as an option on a pull-down menu or pop-up menu.

merge The process of combining lists. Typically refers to files or arrays.

merge sort An $n\log n$ sort algorithm that uses a divide-and-conquer strategy.

message A symbol used by a client to ask an object to perform a service. See also **method**.

message box A window object used to display text to a user, allowing the user to close the box by pressing a button.

method A chunk of code that can be treated as a unit and invoked by name. A method is called when a message is sent to an object. See also **class method** and **instance method**.

method heading The portion of a method implementation containing the function's name, parameter declarations, and return type.

microcomputer A computer capable of fitting on a laptop or desktop, generally used by one person at a time. See also **mainframe** and **minicomputer**.

minicomputer A small version of a mainframe computer. It is usually used by several people at once. See also **mainframe** and **microcomputer**.

mixed-mode Expressions containing data of different types; the values of these expressions will be of either type, depending on the rules for evaluating them.

modal A state in which the computer user cannot exit without explicitly signaling the computer, usually with an "Accept" or "Cancel" option.

model/view/controller pattern A design plan in which the roles and responsibilities of the system are cleanly divided among data management (model), user interface display (view), and user event handling (controller) tasks.

modem A device that connects a computer to a telephone system to transmit data.

module An independent unit that is part of a larger development. Can be a method or a class (set of methods and related data).

module specifications In the case of a method, a description of data received, information returned, and task performed by a module. In the case of a class, a description of the attributes and behavior.

multidimensional array An array whose elements are accessed by specifying more than one index.

mutator A method used to change the value of an attribute of an object.

mutually comparable A property of two items such that they can be related by less than, greater than, or equal to.

N

negation The use of the logical operator ! (not) with a Boolean expression, returning true if the expression is false, and false if the expression is true.

nested if statement A selection statement used within another selection statement. See also **extended if statement**.

nested loop A loop as one of the statements in the body of another loop.

nested selection Any combination of selection statements within selection statements. See also **selection statement**.

network A collection of resources that are linked together for communication.

null statement See **empty statement**.

null value A special value that indicates that no object can be accessed.

O

object A collection of data and operations, in which the data can be accessed and modified only by means of the operations.

object code See **object program**.

object-oriented programming The construction of software systems that use objects.

object program The machine code version of the source program.

off-by-one error Usually seen with loops, this error shows up as a result that is one less or one greater than the expected value.

offset The quantity added to the base address of an array to locate the address of an array cell.

one-dimensional array An array in which each data item is accessed by specifying a single index.

one-way list A list that supports navigation in one direction only.

operating system A large program that allows the user to communicate with the hardware and performs various management tasks.

option panes Window objects that provide standard services, such as prompting for input values, yes/no queries, and message boxes.

ordinal data type A data type ordered in some association with the integers; each integer is the ordinal of an associated value of the data type.

origin The point (0,0) in a coordinate system.

output Information that is produced by a program.

output assertion A postcondition for a loop.

output device A device that allows you to see the results of a program. Typically, it is a monitor, printer, speaker, or network port. See also **input device** and **I/O device**.

output stream A data object that allows a program to output data to a file or the terminal screen.

overflow In arithmetic operations, a value may be too large for the computer's memory location. A meaningless value may be assigned or an error message may result. See also **underflow**.

overloading The process of using the same operator symbol or identifier to refer to many different functions. See also **polymorphism**.

overriding The process of re-implementing a method already implemented in a superclass.

P

package A group of related classes in a named directory.

panel A window object whose purpose is to contain other window objects.

parallel arrays Arrays of the same length but with different component data types.

parameter See **argument**.

parameter list A list of parameters. An actual parameter list is contained in a method call. A formal parameter list is contained in a method heading.

parent   The immediate superclass of a class.

parent   A given node's predecessor in a tree.

peripheral memory   See **memory** and **secondary memory**.

persistence   The property of a data model that allows it to survive various runs of an application. See also **serialization**.

physical size   The number of memory units available for storing data items in a data structure. See also **logical size**.

pivot   A data item around which an array is subdivided during the quicksort.

pixel   A picture element or dot of color used to display images on a computer screen.

polymorphism   The property of one operator symbol or method identifier having many meanings. See also **overloading**.

portable   Able to be transferred to different applications or computers without changes.

Postcondition   A statement of what is true after a certain action is taken.

post-test loop   A loop in which the control condition is tested after the loop is executed. A do-while loop is a post-test loop. Also referred to as an **exit-controlled loop**.

precondition   A statement of what is true before a certain action is taken.

pretest condition   A condition that controls whether or not the body of the loop is executed before going through the loop.

pretest loop   A loop in which the control condition is tested before the loop is executed. A while **loop** is a pretest loop. Also referred to as an **entrance-controlled loop**.

primary memory   See **main memory** and **memory**.

priming input statement   An input statement that must be executed before a loop control condition is tested.

primitive data type   A data type such as char, int, double, or boolean whose values are stored directly in variables of that type. Primitive data types are always passed by value when they are parameters in Java and copied during assignment statements.

private inner class   A class that is defined as a helper class within another class.

private method   A method that is accessible only within the scope of a class definition.

private variable   A variable that is accessible only within the scope of a class definition.

procedural decomposition   A design strategy whereby complex tasks are split into simpler subtasks that are implemented with methods or procedures.

procedural programming   A style of programming that decomposes a program into a set of methods or procedures. See also **procedural decomposition**.

program   A set of instructions that tells the machine (the hardware) what to do.

program proof   An analysis of a program that attempts to verify the correctness of program results.

program walk-through   The process of carefully following, using pencil and paper, steps the computer uses to solve the problem given in a program. It is also referred to as a **trace**.

programming language   Formal language that computer scientists use to give instructions to the computer.

protected variable   A variable that is accessible only within the scope of a class definition, within the class definition of a subclass, or within the class's package.

prototype   A trimmed-down version of a class or software system that still functions and allows the programmer to study its essential features.

pseudocode   A stylized half-English, half-code language written in English but suggesting Java code.

public method   A method that is accessible to any program component that uses the class.

public variable   A variable that is accessible to any program component that uses the class.

pull-down menu   A window object that allows the user to pull down and select from a list of menu items. See also **menu item**.

Q

quadratic   An increase of work or memory in proportion to the square of the size of the problem.

quality assurance   The ongoing process of making sure that a software product is developed to the highest standards possible subject to the ever-present constraints of time and money.

query-controlled input A style of taking multiple user inputs and asking the user if she wants to continue after each one.

queue A data structure that allows the programmer to insert items only at one end and remove them from the other end.

quicksort A sorting technique that moves elements around a pivot and recursively sorts the elements to the left and the right of the pivot.

R

ragged array A two-dimensional array in which each row may have a different length.

random access data structure A data structure in which the time to access a data item does not depend on its position in the structure.

range-bound error The situation that occurs when an attempt is made to use an array index value that is less than 0 or greater than or equal to the size of the array.

rear The end of a queue to which elements are added.

recursion The process of a subprogram calling itself. A clearly defined stopping state must exist. Any recursive subprogram can be rewritten using **iteration**.

recursive method A method that calls itself.

recursive step A step in the recursive process that solves a similar problem of smaller size and eventually leads to a termination of the process.

recursive subprogram See **recursion**.

reference type A data type such as array, `String`, or any other Java class, whose instances are not stored directly in variables of that type. References or pointers to these objects are stored instead. References to objects are passed when they are parameters in Java, and only the references, not the objects, are copied during assignment statements.

refreshable image An image that is redisplayed when the user resizes or minimizes a window.

relational operator An operator used for comparison of data items of the same type.

relative path name A string that specifies the location of a resource without mentioning the Web server.

Repetition See **loops**.

representational error A condition in which the precision of data is reduced because of the order in which operations are performed.

reserved words Words that have predefined meanings that cannot be changed. A list of reserved words for Java is in Appendix B.

return type The type of value returned by a method.

robust The state in which a program is protected against most possible crashes from bad data and unexpected values.

round-off error A condition in which a portion of a real number is lost because of the way it is stored in the computer's memory.

runtime error An error detected when, after compilation is completed, an error message results instead of the correct output. See also **compilation error, design error, exception,** and **syntax error.**

runtime stack An area of computer memory reserved for local variables and parameters of method calls.

S

scope of identifier The largest block in which the identifier is available.

screen coordinate system A coordinate system used by most programming languages in which the origin is in the upper-left corner of the screen, window, or panel, and the y values increase toward the bottom of the drawing area.

secondary memory An auxiliary device for memory, usually a disk or magnetic tape. See also **main memory** and **memory.**

selection The process by which a method or a variable of an instance or a class is accessed.

selection sort A sorting algorithm that sorts the components of an array in either ascending or descending order. This process puts the smallest or largest element in the top position and repeats the process on the remaining array components. See also **quicksort.**

selection statement A control statement that selects some particular logical path based on the value of an expression. Also referred to as a **conditional statement.**

self-documenting code Code that is written using descriptive identifiers.

semantics The rules for interpreting the meaning of a program in a language.

sentinel value A special value that indicates the end of a set of data or of a process.

sequential access A situation in which access to a data item depends on its position in the data structure.

sequential search The process of searching a list by examining the first component and then examining successive components in the order in which they occur. Also referred to as a **linear search**.

serialization A mechanism that maintains the persistence of objects in a data model. See also **persistence**.

server A computational object that provides a service to another computational object.

set An unordered collection of unique items.

short A Java data type used to represent small integers.

short-circuit evaluation The process by which a compound Boolean expression halts evaluation and returns the value of the first subexpression that evaluates to true, in the case of ||, or false, in the case of &&.

side effect A change in a variable that is the result of some action taken in a program, usually from within a method.

simple Boolean expression An expression in which two numbers or variable values are compared using a single relational operator. See also **Boolean expression** and **compound Boolean expression**.

software Programs that make the machine (the hardware) do something, such as word processing, database management, or games.

software development life cycle (SDLC) The process of development, maintenance, and demise of a software system. Phases include analysis, design, coding, testing/verification, maintenance, and obsolescence.

software engineering The process of developing and maintaining large software systems.

software reuse The process of building and maintaining software systems out of existing software components.

source code The program text as viewed by the human who creates or reads it, prior to compilation.

source program A program written by a programmer.

stack A data structure that inserts elements at one end and removes them from the same end.

stack overflow error A situation that occurs when the computer runs out of memory to allocate for its call stack. This situation usually arises during an infinite recursion.

stand-alone program A Java program that runs directly on a computer without the aid of a Web browser.

state The set of all the values of the variables of a program at any point during its execution.

statement An individual instruction in a program.

statement block (synonym compound statement) A form by which a sequence of statements and data declarations can be treated as a unit.

stepwise refinement The process of repeatedly subdividing tasks into subtasks until each subtask is easily accomplished. See also **structured programming** and **top-down implementation**.

stopping state The well-defined termination of a recursive process.

stream A channel in which data are passed from sender to receiver.

string An abbreviated name for a string literal.

string literal One or more characters, enclosed in double quotation marks, used as a constant in a program.

structure chart A graphical method of indicating the relationship between modules when designing the solution to a problem.

structured programming Programming that parallels a solution to a problem achieved by top-down implementation. See also **stepwise refinement** and **top-down implementation**.

stub programming The process of using incomplete functions to test data transmission among the functions.

subclass A class that inherits attributes and behavior from another class.

subscript See **array index**.

substring A string that represents a segment of another string.

Superclass The class from which a subclass inherits attributes and behavior. See also **inheritance** and **subclass**.

Swing Toolkit A set of Java classes used to create programs with graphical user interfaces.

syntax The rules for constructing well-formed programs in a language.

syntax error An error in spelling, punctuation, or placement of certain key symbols in a program. See also **compilation error, design error,** and **runtime error**.

system software The programs that allow users to write and execute other programs, including operating systems such as Windows and MacOS.

T

tail-recursive The property that a recursive algorithm has of performing no work after each recursive step. See also **recursion**.

task-controlled loop A type of loop that terminates when it is finished performing some task.

terminal I/O interface A user interface that allows the user to enter input from a keyboard and view output as text in a window.

text field object A window object in which the user can view or enter a single line of text.

text files Files that contain characters and are readable and writable by text editors.

token An individual word or symbol.

top-down implementation A method for coding by which the programmer starts with a top-level task and implements subtasks. Each subtask is then subdivided into smaller subtasks. This process is repeated until each remaining subtask is easily coded. See also **stepwise refinement** and **structured programming**.

trace See **program walk-through**.

truth table A means of listing all of the possible values of a Boolean expression.

turtle graphics A set of methods that manipulate a pen in a graphics window.

two-dimensional array An array in which each data item is accessed by specifying a pair of indices.

type See **data type**.

type promotion The process of converting a less inclusive data type, such as `int`, to a more inclusive data type, such as `double`.

U

Ubiquitous computing A situation in which computational resources are accessible to people no matter where they are.

unboxing The process whereby the Java Virtual Machine automatically unwraps values of primitive types from objects when they are retrieved from collections.

underflow A value that is too small to be represented by a computer; it is automatically replaced by its negation. See also **overflow**.

unicode A character set that uses 16 bits to represent over 65,000 possible characters. These include the ASCII character set as well as symbols and ideograms in many international languages. See also **ASCII character set**.

Unified Modeling Language (UML) A graphical notation for describing a software system in various phases of development.

uniform resource locator (URL) The address of a page on the World Wide Web.

user-defined class A new data type introduced and defined by the programmer.

user-defined method A new function introduced and defined by the programmer.

user-friendly Describes an interactive program with clear, easy-to-follow messages for the user.

V

variable A memory location, referenced by an identifier, whose value can be changed during execution of a program.

vector A one-dimensional array that supports resizing, insertions, and removals.

virtual machine A software tool that behaves like a high-level computer.

virus A program that can enter a computer and perhaps destroy information.

visibility modifier A symbol (`public`, `protected`, or `private`) that specifies the kind of access that clients have to a server's data and methods.

void method A method that returns no value.

W

waterfall model A series of steps in which a software system trickles down from analysis to design to implementation. See also **software development life cycle**.

while loop A pretest loop that examines a Boolean expression before causing a statement to be executed.

window A rectangular area of a computer screen that can contain window objects. Windows typically can be resized, minimized, maximized, zoomed, or closed. See also **frame**.

window object A computational object that displays an image, such as a button or a text field, in a window and supports interaction with the user.

word A unit of memory consisting of one or more bytes. Words can be addressed.

wrapper class A class designed to contain a primitive data type so that the primitive type can behave like a reference type. See also **primitive data type** and **reference type**.

INDEX